ENGLISH LAW

BY

KENNETH SMITH

M.Sc.(Econ.), B.Com., Ph.D., A.C.C.S., F.S.S.

of Lincoln's Inn, Barrister-at-Law
Late Head of the Department of Commerce and Management
Mid-Essex Technical College and School of Art

AND

DENIS J. KEENAN

LL.B.(Hons.), F.C.I.S., D.M.A.

of the Middle Temple, Barrister-at-Law
Formerly Head of Department of Business Studies and Law
Mid-Essex Technical College and School of Art
Visiting Lecturer, City of London Polytechnic

FOURTH EDITION BY DENIS J. KEENAN

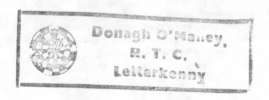
PITMAN PUBLISHING

Fourth Edition 1973
Reprinted 1974
Reprinted 1975

SIR ISAAC PITMAN AND SONS LTD
Pitman House, Parker Street, Kingsway, London WC2B 5PB
Pitman House, 158 Bouverie Street, Carlton, Victoria 3053, Australia
P.O. Box 46038, Banda Street, Nairobi, Kenya
THE CARSWELL COMPANY LTD., TORONTO

Paperback Edition: 0 273 31743 1

Text set in 10/11 pt. Monotype Baskerville, printed by letterpress,
and bound in Great Britain at The Pitman Press, Bath
L.1013:44

PREFACE TO FOURTH EDITION

ENGLISH Law continues to develop rapidly and I have tried in this edition to keep pace with that development even though the book has in consequence increased yet again in length. There are three main approaches to this problem as follows—

1. To retain the subject areas formerly covered but to cut down the content of each.

2. To reduce the number of subject areas covered and retain a reasonable depth of treatment in each.

3. To retain the subject areas formerly covered and the level of treatment, relying on the teacher to make an appropriate selection from the available material.

In my view the approach outlined in paragraph 3 above is to be preferred. In the last analysis, a student's understanding of the subject and the benefit which he derives from it in his subsequent career depends upon the ability of his teacher to decide on the basis of his information with regard to the related studies in a course, of which law is often only a part, which topics ought to be covered and in what depth.

I believe it is wrong for the author of a general work of this kind to reach definitive conclusions as to the academic needs of the generality of students following business studies and other courses. In doing so, he is tending to impose his views upon those whose task it is to teach the subject. This I would not wish to do. Obviously the commercial viability of a book has to be taken into account, but I have been fortunate in my publishers who have never adopted a wholly rigid attitude in this matter. This explains at least in part the success which the book has achieved.

The matter of the suitability of the book for a particular course is also something which I am glad to leave to the teacher concerned and in the case of external examinations, which are fortunately reducing in number, to the examining body involved. It is my hope that both those who teach and those who examine will continue to find the book useful.

The ever-increasing volume of case law has led in this edition to a different approach to certain of the summaries of cases. Where a recent case illustrates only the application of existing law to a new fact situation, the summary of that case has been reduced in size and given the same main number as the leading case, being distinguished from it by the addition of the letters 'a', 'b', 'c' and so on.

I have tried my best to ensure that the book is free from error, but it is unlikely that I have entirely succeeded. In this connection, I would like to say how much I value the comments of teachers, students and reviewers who have been kind enough to draw my attention to mistakes in previous editions.

D.J.K.

May 1972

PREFACE TO FIRST EDITION

THIS book has been written primarily for students preparing for examinations in Elements of English Law or General Principles of English Law in professional and similar examinations. It covers the following syllabuses (among others)—

Chartered Institute of Secretaries
Corporation of Secretaries
Institute of Bankers
Diploma in Municipal Administration
Diploma in Government Administration
Institute of Chartered Accountants in England and Wales
Chartered Insurance Institute
Institute of Export.

It is particularly suitable for students preparing for Ordinary and Higher National Certificates and Diplomas in Business Studies, and it covers both papers of the subject General Principles of English Law set at "A" Level by the Associated Examining Board.

A distinctive feature of the book is the printing of extended summaries of 345 cases, which are segregated in an appendix, numbered consecutively, and referred to in the text by name and number.

The advantages claimed for this treatment and for the greater emphasis on case law are—

1. The segregation of the cases makes for less interruption in the text which is thus rendered more readable.

2. Nevertheless the reader is made aware that the principles of law he is reading have their origin in case law, and that reference to the cases will elucidate their precise scope and significance.

3. The text can be read independently of the cases; this is recommended to beginners who are advised first to read quickly through the whole.

4. The cases can be studied intensively, independently of the text.

5. Examination students who are revising will find that the reading of the text, which contains the names of the cases, will act as a check on their ability to recall the facts of the cases which illustrate the principles enunciated. If they cannot recall the facts of the cases, they have an easy numerical reference.

6. Some cases illustrate several points of law, and a numerical reference enables them to be referred to in several parts of the book without recourse to cumbersome foot-notes and cross-references. This saving enables fuller summaries to be given, containing the relevant

facts, the essential points of the judgment, and, in appropriate cases, the gist of dissenting judgments.

7. The section on Contract is particularly full, since many students of this subject will follow it by a study of Mercantile Law in their Final Examinations.

It is believed that this book will be a boon to busy lecturers in Technical Colleges. The inclusion of cases will save time in dictating or preparing duplicated material. Those who are responsible for teaching law as one subject among several will find it helpful to have an up-to-date and comprehensive set of the main cases needed by their students, keyed specifically to the text containing the principles which the cases illustrate.

A short treatment of criminal law and an adequate treatment of the criminal courts are included, since some examining bodies require this, and in any case we feel that students of the civil aspects of the English legal system should not be ignorant of its criminal aspects.

Our experience as lecturers in a technical college leads us to believe that this book will fill a need felt by those who find that the existing books, whatever their merits, are either too sketchy or too academic for the average professional student. Nevertheless we also believe that, although the book has been written with a particular type of student in mind, it will be found to be of interest to the general reader, and that it will provide useful introductory reading for students who contemplate a legal career, or who propose to study law at a university.

February 1963
K.S.
D.J.K.

CONTENTS

CHAPTER I

THE DEVELOPMENT OF ENGLISH LAW

BEFORE the Norman Conquest in 1066 England was divided into several kingdoms and all laws were *local*, being administered by the Lords of the Manor in the manorial courts, and by the County Sheriffs, often sitting with the Earl and the Bishop, in the courts of the Shires and Hundreds. They administered the law in their respective areas and decided the cases which came before them on the basis of local custom. Many of these customary rules of law were the same or similar in all parts of the country, but there were some differences. For instance, primogeniture, the right of the eldest son to inherit the whole of his father's land where there was no will, applied almost universally throughout England; but in Kent there existed a system of land-holding called gavelkind tenure whereby all the sons inherited equally; while in Nottingham and Bristol, under the custom of Borough-English, the property passed to the youngest son. These customs were finally abolished by the Administration of Estates Act, 1925.

THE COMMON LAW

The administrative ability of the Normans began the process destined to lead to a unified system of law which was nevertheless evolutionary in its development. The Normans were not concerned to change English customary law entirely by imposing Norman law on England. Indeed, many charters of William I giving English boroughs the right to hold courts stated that the laws dispensed in these courts should be laws of Edward the Confessor, which meant that English customary law was to be applied.

The Normans did, however, strive to make the law of England uniform and the chief means by which this was achieved was the introduction of the General Eyre whereby representatives of the King were sent from Westminster on a tour of the Shires for the purpose of checking on the local administration. During the period of their visit they would sit in the local court and hear cases, and gradually they came to have a judicial rather than an administrative function. The judges for the General Eyre were selected from the Court of Common Pleas which normally sat at Westminster but which closed down while the judges were on circuit.

The General Eyre disappeared in the reign of Richard II (1377-99), but a system of circuit judges from the King's Bench took its place, the first circuit commission being granted in the reign of Edward III (1327-77). By selecting the best customary rulings and applying these outside their county of origin, the circuit judges gradually moulded the numerous local customary laws into one uniform law "common" to the whole kingdom. Thus, customs originally local ultimately applied throughout the whole of the realm. However, many new rules were created and applied by the royal judges as they went on circuit and these were added to local customary law to make one uniform body of law called "common law". Even so, there was no absolute unification even as late as 1389, and in a case in the Common Pleas in that year, a custom of Selby in Yorkshire was admitted to show that a husband was not in that area liable for his wife's trading debts, though the common law elsewhere regarded him as liable.

The circuit judges from King's Bench derived their authority from the following Royal Commissions—

COMMISSION OF ASSIZE FOR CIVIL ACTIONS. Although civil actions were normally heard in Westminster, it was often more convenient to settle matters on circuit, particularly when local witnesses had to be called. Judges would try such actions at *Nisi Prius* (that is *unless* they had been heard at Westminster *before* their visit). The convenience of a trial at Nisi Prius was that the witnesses could be heard on circuit and the decision of the jury taken on matters of fact. Matters of law involved in the action were later argued back at Westminster.

COMMISSION OF OYER AND TERMINER. This commission, which dates from 1329, directed the judges to "hear and determine" all complaints of grave crime within the jurisdiction of the circuit.

GENERAL GAOL DELIVERY. This commission, which dates from 1299, gave the judges power to clear the local gaols and try all prisoners within the jurisdiction of the circuit.

The circuit judges were also made Justices of the Peace so as to increase their jurisdiction, and the granting of these commissions marks the real beginning of the assize system.

This system, which has lasted for many years, was brought to an end by the Courts Act 1971, Sect. 1 (2) of which provides that all courts of assize are abolished and commissions to hold any court of assize shall not be issued. (See p. 39.)

Many of the itinerant justices were clerics, initially perhaps because they could read and write. However, it seems likely that the real reason for appointing them to livings in the church was to provide them with an income, a practice followed with other servants of the Crown, the church being rich and the King often poor. In general they had no priestly duties. From the middle of the thirteenth century the number of lay judges gradually increased.

When not on circuit the justices sat in the Royal Courts at Westminster, and it was probably at Westminster that they discussed the differences in the customary law on the various circuits, selecting the best rulings and applying them both at Westminster and on circuit.

The Royal Courts of Westminster developed out of the *Curia Regis* (or King's Council) which was originally a body of noblemen advising the King. The Court of Exchequer was the first court to emerge from the *Curia Regis* and dealt initially with disputes connected with royal revenues; later it dealt with many common law actions not necessarily connected with revenue. The Court of Common Pleas was set up in the time of Henry II to hear disputes between the King's subjects. The Court of King's Bench was the last to emerge from the *Curia Regis* and initially was closely associated with the King himself. This association enabled the Court of King's Bench to exercise a supervisory jurisdiction over the other courts by the use of prerogative writs (now orders). (See pp. 52–54.)

The system was held together by the doctrine of *stare decisis*, or standing by previous decisions. Thus when a judge decided a new problem in a case brought before him, this became a new rule of law and was followed by subsequent judges. In later times this practice crystallised into the form which is known as the binding force of judicial precedent, and the judges felt bound to follow previous decisions instead of merely looking to them for guidance. By these means the common law earned the status of a system. Indeed it was possible for Bracton, Dean of Exeter and a Justice Itinerant of Henry III, to write the first exposition of the common law before the end of the thirteenth century—*A Treatise on the Laws and Customs of England*. There was also an earlier treatise by Ranulph de Glanvill in 1187, but this was not so comprehensive as the work of Bracton.

To sum up, the common law is a judge-made system of law, originating in ancient customs, which were clarified, extended and universalised by the judges, although that part of the common law which concerned the ownership of land was derived mainly from the system of feudal tenures introduced from Europe after the Norman Conquest. It is perhaps also worth noting that the term "common law" is used in four distinct senses, i.e. as opposed to (*a*) local law; (*b*) Equity; (*c*) statute law; and (*d*) any foreign system of law.

EQUITY

To understand the beginnings of Equity it is necessary first to look in outline at the system of common law writs. Writs were issued by the clerks in the Chancellor's office, the Chancellor being in those days a clergyman of high rank who was also the King's Chaplain and Head of Parliament. In order to bring an action in one of the King's courts, the aggrieved party had to obtain from the Chancery a writ for which he had to pay. A writ was a sealed letter issued in the name of the King, and it ordered some person, Lord of the Manor or Sheriff of the County or the defendant, to do whatever the writ specified.

The old common law writs began with a statement of the plaintiff's claim, which was largely in common form, and was prepared in the Royal Chancery and not by the plaintiff's advisers as is the statement of claim today. Any writ which was novel, because the plaintiff or his advisers had tried to draft it to suit the plaintiff's case, might be abated, i.e., thrown out by the court. Thus, writs could only be issued in a limited number of cases, and if the complaint could not be fitted within the four corners of one of the existing writs, no action could be brought. Moreover, writs were expensive, and their very cost might deprive a party of justice.

However, a practice grew up under which the clerks in Chancery framed new writs even though the complaint was not quite covered by an existing writ, thus extending the law by extending the scope of the writ system. This appeared to Parliament to be a usurpation of its powers as the supreme lawgiver. Further, it took much work away from the local courts, diminishing the income of the local barons who persuaded Parliament to pass a statute called the Provisions of Oxford in 1258, forbidding in effect the practice of creating new writs to fit new cases. This proved so inconvenient that an attempt to remedy the situation was made by the Statute of Westminster II in 1285 which empowered the clerks in Chancery to issue new writs *in consimili casu*, (in similar cases), thus adapting existing writs to fit new circumstances. The common law began to expand again, but it was still by no means certain that a writ would be forthcoming to fit a particular case, because the clerks in Chancery used the Statute with caution at first.

Other difficulties arose over the procedure in the common law courts, because even the most trivial error in a writ would avoid the action. If X complained of the trespass of Y's mare, and in his writ by error described the mare as a stallion, this was fatal. Some common law actions were tried by a system called "wager of law," and the plaintiff might fail on what was really a good claim if a defendant could bring more, or more powerful, people to say that the claim was false than the plaintiff could muster to support it.

In common law actions the defendant could plead certain standard defences known as *essoins* which would greatly delay the plaintiff's claim. For example, the defendant might say that he was cut off by floods or a broken bridge, or that he was off on a Crusade. He might also plead the defence of sickness which could delay the action for a year and a day. In early times these defences were verified by sending four knights to see the defendant, but at a later stage there was no verification and the defences were used merely to delay what were often good claims.

The common law was also defective in the matter of remedies. The only remedy the common law had to offer for a civil wrong inflicted on a plaintiff was damages, i.e. a payment of money, which is not in all cases an adequate compensation. The common law could not compel a person to perform his obligations or cease to carry on a wrong, though it is not true to say that the common law was entirely devoid of equitable principles, and even in early times there were signs of some equitable development; but generally the rigidity of the forms of action tended to stifle justice.

Furthermore, the common law did not recognise trusts (see pp. 338–359) and there was no way of compelling the trustee to carry out his obligations under the trust. Thus if S conveyed property to T on trust for B, T could treat the property as his own and the common law would ignore the claims of B. Many people, therefore, unable to gain access to the King's courts, either because they could not obtain a writ, or because the writ was defective when they got it, or because they were caught in some procedural difficulty, or could not obtain an appropriate remedy, began to address their complaints to the King in Council. For a time the Council itself considered such petitions, and where a petition was addressed to the King in person, he referred it to the Council for trial. Later the Council delegated this function to the Chancellor, and eventually petitions were addressed to the Chancellor alone.

The Chancellor appears to have been chosen because he was already involved in legal matters. His clerks were engaged in the issue of common law writs and so it was convenient to delegate this new function to him. His jurisdiction had nothing to do with his supposed position of Keeper of the King's Conscience, i.e. the person to whom the King confessed his sins. In fact a compilation of the King's Confessors reveals that not one of them was Chancellor, though it is true that the early Chancellors were clerics.

The Chancellor began to judge such cases in the light of conscience and fair dealing. He was not bound by the remedies of the common law and began to devise remedies of his own. For example, the Chancellor could compel a person to perform his obligations by issuing a decree of *specific performance* or could stop him from carrying on a wrong by the issue of an *injunction*. The Chancellor also recognised interests in property which were unknown to the common law, in particular the concept of the *use*, which later became the *trust*, under which persons might be made the legal owners of property for the use or benefit of another or others. As we have seen, the common law did not recognise the interests of the beneficiaries under a trust, but allowed the legal owner to deal with the property as if no other interests existed. Equity, however, enforced the beneficial interests. In order to bring persons before him the Chancellor issued a form of summons, called a *subpoena*. Equity was thus not cramped by anything analogous to the writ system. Eventually as new Chancellors took over, and Vice-Chancellors were appointed to cope with the increasing volume of work, uncertainty crept into the system, conflicting decisions abounded, and it was said that "Equity varies with the Chancellor's foot."

At this stage in its development Equity began to follow the practice of *stare decisis* which had proved so powerful a force in unifying the diverse systems of local custom under the common law. This was precipitated by the Reformation and by the appointment in 1530 of Sir Thomas More as Chancellor. More was a common lawyer and not a cleric. From then on non-clerical Chancellors were drawn from the ranks of the common lawyers and naturally followed the system of precedent which they had seen used in the common law courts. Lord Ellesmere (1596–1617) began to apply the same principles in all cases of the same type, and later, under Lord Nottingham (1673–1682), Lord Hardwicke (1736–1756) and Lord Eldon (1801–1827), Equity developed in scope and certainty.

Relationship of Law and Equity. Although Law and Equity eventually operated alongside each other with mutual tolerance, there was a period of conflict between them. This arose out of the practice of the Court of Chancery which issued "common injunctions" forbidding a person on pain of imprisonment from bringing an action in the common law courts, or forbidding the enforcement of a common law judgment if such a judgment had been obtained.

Thus, if X by some unconscionable conduct, such as undue influence, had obtained an agreement with Y, whereby Y was to sell X certain land at much below its real value, then, if Y refused to convey the land, X would have his remedy in damages at common law despite his unconscionable conduct. However, if Y appealed to the Chancellor, the latter might issue a common injunction which would prevent X from bringing his action at common law unless he wished to suffer punishment for defiance of the Chancellor's injunction. Similarly, if X had already obtained a judgment at common law, the Chancellor would prevent its enforcement by ordering X, on pain of imprisonment, not to execute judgment on Y's property.

However, the common law courts retaliated by waiting for the Chancellor to imprison the common law litigant for defiance of the injunction, and then the common law would release him by the process of *habeas corpus*.

This period of rivalry culminated in the *Earl of Oxford's* case in 1615,[1] when it was decided that where common law and equity were in conflict Equity should prevail. Thereafter the two systems settled down and carved out separate and complementary jurisdictions. Equity filled in the gaps left by the common law, and became a system of case law governed by the binding force of precedent. By the same token, it lost much of its earlier freedom and elasticity. It is certainly no longer a court of conscience.

Many reforms were still to come. Equitable and legal remedies had to be sought in different courts, but this in due course was rectified by the Judicature Acts, 1873–1875, which brought about an amalgamation of the English Courts. Since then both common law and equitable remedies have been available to a litigant under the same action and in the same court.

LEGISLATION

In early times there were few statutes and the bulk of law was case law, though legislation in one form or another dates from A.D. 600. The earliest Norman legislation was by means of Royal Charter, but the first great outburst of legislation came in the reign of Henry II (1154–1189). This legislation was called by various names: there were Assizes, Constitutions, and Provisions, as well as Charters. Legislation at this time was generally made by the King in Council, but sometimes by a kind of Parliament which consisted in the main of a meeting of nobles and clergy summoned from the shires.

In the fourteenth century parliamentary legislation became more general. Parliament at first requested or prayed the King to legislate, but later it presented a bill in its own wording. The Tudor period saw the development of modern procedure, in particular the practice of giving three readings to a bill; and this was also the age of the *Preamble*, which was a kind of preface to the enactment, describing often at great length the reasons for passing it and generally justifying the measure.

From the Tudor period onwards Parliament became more and more independent and the practice of law making by statute increased. Nevertheless statutes did not become an important source of law until the last two centuries, and even now, although the bulk of legislation is large, statutes form a comparatively small part of the law as a whole. The basis of our law remains the common law, and if all the statutes were repealed we should still have a legal system, even if it were inadequate; whereas our statutes alone would not provide a system of law but merely a set of disjointed rules.

Parliament's increasing incursions into economic and social affairs increased the need for statutes. Some aspects of law are so complicated or so novel that they can only be laid down in this form; they would not be likely to come into existence through the submission of cases in court. A statute is the ultimate source of law, and, even if a statute is in conflict with the common law or equity, the statute must prevail. It is such an important source that it has been said—"A statute can do anything except change man to woman," although in a purely legal sense even this could be achieved. No court or other body can question the validity of an Act of Parliament. (*Cheney* v. *Conn*, 1968.)[2]

Statute law can be used to abolish common law rules which have outlived their usefulness, or to amend the common law to cope with the changing circumstances and values of society. Once enacted, statutes, even if obsolete, do not cease to have the force of law, but common sense usually prevents most obsolete laws from being invoked. In addition, statutes which are no longer of practical utility are repealed from time to time by Statute Law Repeal Acts. Nevertheless, a statute stands as law until it is specifically repealed by Parliament. (*Prince of Hanover* v. *Attorney General*, 1956.)[3]

An Act of Parliament is absolutely binding on everyone within the sphere of its jurisdiction, but all Acts of Parliament can be repealed by the same or subsequent Parliaments; and this is the only exception to the rule of the absolute sovereignty of Parliament—it cannot bind itself or its successors. (*Vauxhall Estates Ltd.* v. *Liverpool Corporation*, 1932.)[4]

DELEGATED LEGISLATION

Many modern statutes require much detailed work to implement and operate them, and such details are not normally contained in the statute itself, but are filled in from some other source. For example, much of our Social Security legislation gives only the general provisions of a complex scheme of social benefits, and an immense number of detailed regulations have had to be made by civil servants in the name of, and under the authority of, the appropriate Minister. These regulations, when made in the approved manner, are just as much law as the parent statute itself. This form of law is known as delegated or subordinate legislation.

CUSTOM

In early times custom was taken by the judges and turned into the common law of England, and it is still possible, even today, to argue the existence of a custom before the courts (*Beckett* v. *Lyons*, 1967),[5] though its operation is usually restricted to a particular area, or to a particular trade or profession. Such customs may be local, general or conventional.

1. **Local Custom.** Such a custom may be raised to the level of law in a particular area. To be recognised by the courts as having the force of law, a local custom must fulfil the following requirements—

IMMEMORIAL EXISTENCE. It must have existed at the commencement of legal memory—"from the time when the memory of man runneth not to the contrary" (Blackstone). Actually the limit of legal memory is arbitrarily fixed at A.D. 1189, and existence from this date will be readily presumed. In fact, proof of existence within living memory will shift the burden of proof on to the person who asserts that the custom did not exist in 1189. (*Simpson* v. *Wells*, 1872.)[6]

The 1189 rule appeared in the sixteenth century and seems to have been applied because customary rights were becoming too easy to establish. In particular, too much land was being transferred from Lords of the Manor to their tenants under supposed customary rights.

CONTINUITY. The claim to enforce the customary right must have been continuous, and the right to exercise it must not have been interrupted. This does not mean that the right must have been continuously exercised, so long as the claim to enforce it has not been abandoned or positively disputed. (*Mercer* v. *Denne*, 1904.)[7]

CERTAINTY. The area of the application of the custom must be certain, and the subject matter and the persons benefited by the custom must be capable of precise identification.

USER MUST BE *nec vi, nec clam, nec precario.* This means without force, stealth or permission. In particular it must be noted that, where the so-called custom has been exercised by permission or licence, it will be impossible to establish it as a custom. (*Mills* v. *Colchester Corporation*, 1867.)[8]

USER MUST BE REASONABLE. The courts are not anxious to establish a custom which is manifestly unreasonable. (*Bryant* v. *Foot*, 1868.)[9]

THE CUSTOM MUST HAVE OBLIGATORY FORCE. People must feel bound to observe it. Thus, while it is a custom of sorts to wear black at a funeral, it is unlikely to become law, because people do not feel bound to observe it.

CONSISTENCY. A custom can only be admitted as law if it is consistent with other customs, and is not contrary to statute or to a rule of common law.

LOCALITY. It would be difficult for people in Cumberland to set up customary rights in Kent. If they have such rights, they must be part of the common law and not based on local custom.

2. General Custom or Usage. Such customs are to be found mainly in mercantile transactions. The cases show a certain amount of conflict, and it is not certain whether it is still possible to incorporate new mercantile customs into the common law. *Goodwin* v. *Robarts* (1875)[10] suggests that it is possible; *Crouch* v. *Credit Foncier of England* (1873)[11] suggests that it is not. The test which the courts apply in establishing general custom is universality of observance rather than immemorial antiquity.

3. Conventional Custom. Such customary rulings are never raised to the level of the common law, but may affect the rights of parties to a contract who, because they are members of a certain trade or profession, find that certain customary usages have been incorporated into their contract. Here again the test is universality of observance rather than immemorial existence. Such usages are found in the customs of the Stock Exchange and the rules relating to the Sale of Goods and to Bills of Exchange, although most of the latter have been incorporated in the Sale of Goods Act, 1893, and the Bills of Exchange Act, 1882. Generally both parties must belong to the same trade or profession before the application of a custom will be implied.

As an instrument for the development of English law, custom has almost ceased to exist, since the stringent requirements set out above limit its efficacy as a law-creating force.

THE LAW MERCHANT

Mercantile Law, or *Lex Mercatoria*, is based upon mercantile customs and usages. The Middle Ages saw the development of foreign trade, and this led to trading disputes with which the common law of England could not cope, since it was at that time mainly concerned with land and rights over land. The merchants, therefore, began to decide disputes for themselves according to the trade customs of their own countries. Much of this law came from the Mediterranean area and from Western Europe, and contained elements of Roman law. The traders acted as judges in courts held in fairs and markets; these courts became known as Courts of Pie Powder (*pieds poudrés*), after the dusty feet of the traders who used them.

There were also Courts of the Staple. Edward III (1327–77) gave foreign merchants the right to trade in certain English towns known as Staple towns. These towns were required to hold courts to decide the trading disputes of the merchants, and here again the customs of foreign merchants were used, since the common law was deficient in commercial rulings. Moreover, even if the common law did provide a remedy, its slow, complicated, and hazardous procedure compared ill with the quick decisions obtainable in mercantile courts.

When the Court of Admiralty developed, it took over much of the work of the merchants' courts, but from the seventeenth century onwards the common law courts began to acquire the commercial work, and many rules of the Law Merchant were incorporated into the common law, Lord Mansfield and Lord Holt playing a great part in this development, in particular by recognising the main mercantile customs in the common law courts without requiring proof of them on every occasion. Perhaps the most important mercantile custom recognised was that a bill of exchange was negotiable. In this way the custom of merchants relating to negotiable instruments and the sale of goods became part of the common law, and later, by codification, of statute law in the Bills of Exchange Act, 1882, and the Sale of Goods Act, 1893.

CANON LAW

Before the Norman Conquest the then existing courts heard all suits, both lay and ecclesiastical, and the Bishop and the Earl sat as joint judges. These joint courts were disliked by the Papacy because of the quarrels which took place between the lay and ecclesiastical members of the various tribunals. Prior to his conquest of England, William I had promised to set up separate ecclesiastical courts in this country, in return for the Pope's blessing of his proposed campaign. After the Conquest, William carried out his promise and removed suits "which belong to the government of souls" from lay to ecclesiastical courts, and thus began the separation of the two.

The ecclesiastical courts dealt not only with offences against doctrine and morality, but also with secular matters, e.g. matrimonial causes, legitimacy, and testamentary succession. Many of their rules were derived from Roman Law, and were inherited by the civil courts, to which the jurisdiction was transferred in 1857.

England was divided into the provinces of Canterbury and York, each having an Archbishop or Metropolitan at its head. Each province was divided into dioceses under the Bishop or Ordinary, and each diocese had a diocesan or consistory court, presided over by a chancellor as the Bishop's representative.

From the consistory courts, appeal lay to the Provincial Courts, i.e. in the Province of Canterbury to the Court of Arches, presided over by the Dean of Arches; and in the Province of York to the Court of Chancery, presided over by the Official Principal. Appeal lay from the Provincial Courts to the Pope of Rome until this was abolished by the Statute of Appeals, 1532. Thereafter appeals lay for a short time to the Crown in Chancery, but were soon transferred to the Court of Delegates—an *ad hoc* court of three judges and three Doctors of Civil Law. In 1833 the Judicial Committee Act transferred appeals to the Judicial Committee of the Privy Council, to which appeal still lies in those matters over which the ecclesiastical courts retain jurisdiction.

The Matrimonial Causes Act, 1857, transferred matrimonial causes to a new civil court called the Divorce Court. The Court of Probate Act, 1857, transferred suits concerning wills to a new court called the Probate Court. The Judicature Act, 1873, incorporated the Probate and Divorce Courts into a newly created Supreme Court of Judicature as part of the Probate, Divorce and Admiralty Division, which under Sec. 1 of the Administration of Justice Act, 1970, becomes the Family Division (see p. 38), and the legal principles evolved over the centuries were expressly incorporated in the laws of England.

The present position is that the Church Courts remain to deal with disciplinary and moral offences committed by the Clergy and certain of the Laity, e.g. parish clerks and churchwardens, of the Church of England, and certain other matters, e.g. permission to remove church spires or to alter church premises.

The court of first instance is that of the diocesan chancellor, who must be a member of the Church of England and is usually a practising barrister. Appeal lies from him to the Court of Arches in the province of Canterbury, and to the Chancery Court of York in the northern province. On matters concerning conduct, there is a further appeal to the Judicial Committee of the Privy Council and on other matters there may be an appeal to the Court of Ecclesiastical Cases Reserved. The church courts are not courts of common law and the prerogative orders (see p. 52)—which operate as a valuable check on the abuse of power by other courts and tribunals—do not apply to them.

LEGAL TREATISES

One last source remains to be considered, namely legal treatises. Throughout the centuries great English jurists have written books, some in the nature of legal text-books, which have helped to shape the law and inform the legal profession.

We have already mentioned *Bracton* whose *Treatise on the Laws and Customs of England* was written in the thirteenth century and was probably based on the decisions of Martin de Pateshull, who was Archdeacon of Norfolk, Dean of St. Pauls and an Itinerant Justice from 1217 to 1229, and on those of William de Raleigh who was the Rector of Bratton Fleming in Devon and an Itinerant Justice from 1228 to 1250.

Another early work was *Littleton's Tenures* which was used for 300 years as a standard text-book on land law. Littleton was made a

Judge of Common Pleas in 1466 and died in 1481. Most of his writing was concerned with the law of real property.

Another writer of note was *Sir John Fortescue* whose best-known work is entitled: "*In praise of the Laws of England.*" It was written between 1470 and 1471 while Fortescue was exiled in France because of his association with the Lancastrian party. Fortescue was Chief Justice of King's Bench in 1442 to 1461.

Coke's is a celebrated name and his *Institutes* covered many aspects of law. For example, his First Institute, published in 1628, was concerned with land law. His Second Institute, published in 1642, was concerned with the principal statutes. The Third Institute, published in 1644, dealt with Criminal Law, while the Fourth Institute, also published in 1644, was concerned with the Jurisdiction and History of the Courts, this work containing bitter attacks on the Court of Chancery. During his lifetime Coke occupied the offices of Recorder of London, Solicitor-General, Speaker of the House of Commons, Attorney-General, and finally Chief Justice of Common Pleas.

Sir Matthew Hale, another well-known writer, was made Judge of Common Pleas in 1654 and later became Chief Justice of King's Bench in 1671. His three main works were: *Jurisdiction of the Lords House*, *History of Pleas of the Crown*, and *History of the Common Law*.

Sir William Blackstone published his *Commentaries* in 1765. These are concerned with various aspects of law and are based on his lectures at Oxford. He was a Judge of the Common Pleas and was also the first Professor of English Law to be appointed in any English University.

In addition to older treatises such as those mentioned above, the works of modern writers, sufficiently eminent in the profession, are sometimes quoted when novel points of law are being argued in the Courts. (*Boys* v. *Blenkinsopp*, 1968.)[12]

CHAPTER II

THE COURTS OF LAW

BEFORE attempting a general survey of the English system of courts, we must first look at the Supreme Court of Judicature, established by the Judicature Acts, 1873–75, which came into force on 1st November, 1875. It consists of the High Court of Justice and the Court of Appeal and under Sect. 1 of the Courts Act, 1971, the new Crown Court also forms part of the Supreme Court. Prior to the Judicature Acts there had been a considerable number of courts. There were three common law courts—the Court of Queen's Bench, the Court of Common Pleas, and the Court of Exchequer, having jurisdictions which differed in some respects and overlapped in others. There was the Court of Chancery, established in the fourteenth century and concerned with administering Equity. There was the High Court of Admiralty, which administered Admiralty law, and the Court of Probate and the Divorce Court. Appeals were to the Court of Exchequer Chamber or to the Court of Appeal in Chancery. Appeals from Colonial, Admiralty and Ecclesiastical Courts were to the Judicial Committee of the Privy Council. In particular, since the courts of common law and the courts of Equity had evolved separately, injustice often resulted from the separate administration of the two systems. For example, in *Knight* v. *Marquis of Waterford* (1844), 11 Cl. & Fin. 653, the appellant was told by the House of Lords, after 14 years of litigation, that he had a good case but must begin his action again in a common law court.

THE SUPREME COURT OF JUDICATURE (I)

It was to rationalise the jurisdiction of these numerous and over-lapping courts that the Supreme Court of Judicature was established. Under the Judicature Acts the High Court of Justice was divided into five divisions: Queen's Bench Division, Common Pleas Division, Exchequer Division, Chancery Division, and Probate Divorce and Admiralty Division, the number being reduced to three by an Order in Council in 1881, when the Common Pleas and Exchequer Divisions were merged into the Queen's Bench Division. The Court of Appeal was given jurisdiction over appeals which formerly lay to the Court of Exchequer Chamber and the Court of Appeal in Chancery.

All actions can be brought before the High Court, and it is not necessary, as it was before the Judicature Acts, to bring common law actions in common law courts, and matters involving equity in the Court of Chancery. All remedies available can now be obtained in a single court. However, for convenience, certain matters are assigned to each division. The Judicature Acts provide that in case of conflict between

SYSTEM OF COURTS EXERCISING CIVIL JURISDICTION

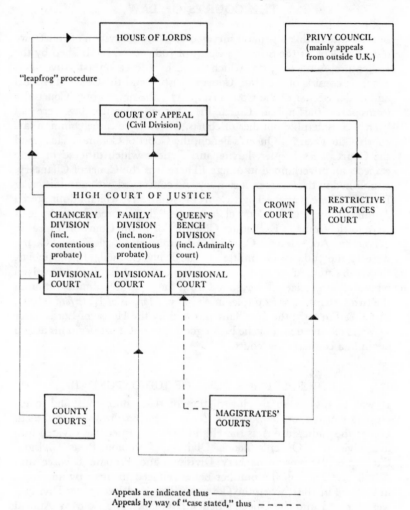

Appeals are indicated thus ——————

Appeals by way of "case stated," thus — — — — —

N.B. This diagram assumes full implementation of the Administration of Justice Act, 1970, and the Courts Act 1971.

SYSTEM OF COURTS EXERCISING CRIMINAL JURISDICTION

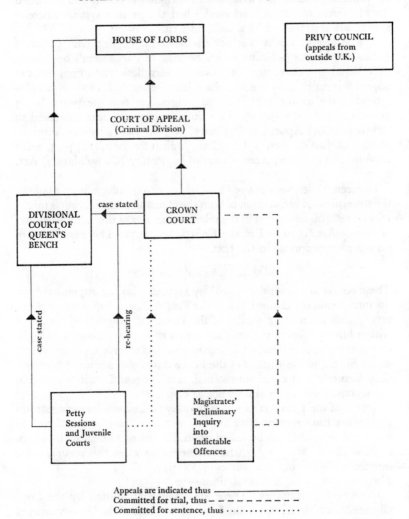

Appeals are indicated thus ——————
Committed for trial, thus — — — — — — — — —
Committed for sentence, thus · · · · · · · · · · · · · · · ·

N.B. This diagram assumes full implementation of the Administration of Justice Act, 1970, and the Courts Act 1971.

Common Law and Equity, Equity shall prevail; but it should be noted that the Acts fused the tribunals, not Law and Equity. The two systems are still separate and distinct; equitable remedies are still discretionary and are not available as of right. The Acts also abolished the old forms of action, and established the present system whereby actions are commenced by a uniform writ.

The House of Lords was not included in the Supreme Court of Judicature by the Judicature Acts because of Parliament's opposition to its hereditary character. However, its jurisdiction as a final court of appeal was restored by the Appellate Jurisdiction Act, 1876, which also provided the House with trained judges, i.e. two life peers, being persons with legal training. This number has now been increased to eleven Lords of Appeal in Ordinary, or Law Lords by the Administration of Justice Act, 1968. The Judicature Acts, 1873–75, were consolidated in the Supreme Court of Judicature (Consolidation) Act, 1925.

In recent times, very many far-reaching changes have been made in the structure and jurisdiction of both the civil and criminal courts by the various reforms contained in the relevant sections of the Administration of Justice Act, 1970 and in the Courts Act, 1971. These sections are set out as appropriate in the text.

MAGISTRATES' COURTS

These courts are generally staffed by laymen who are appointed by a document called a Commission of the Peace. There is no legal or property qualification but a Justice of the Peace (or Magistrate) must live within fifteen miles of the area for which he is commissioned. Magistrates, other than Stipendiaries, are unpaid but receive expenses which, under Sect. 4 of the Justices of the Peace Act, 1968, are more generous than formerly and cover subsistence, travelling and various financial losses consequent upon attendance at court.

Sect. 2 of the 1968 Act provides that lay and stipendiary magistrates shall retire from regular duty at 70 though they can be transferred to the supplemental list to be called upon if required to deal with certain types of cases. Magistrates who were over 70 when this section came into force will be retired in stages up to 1973.

Magistrates may be of several kinds—

County Magistrates. These are laymen appointed by the Lord Chancellor on the advice of the Lord Lieutenant of the County assisted by an advisory committee. They have jurisdiction throughout the county, except in certain boroughs which have a separate commission of the peace.

Borough Magistrates. These are laymen appointed by the Lord Chancellor on the advice of a local advisory committee. They have jurisdiction within the area of the borough only.

Stipendiary Magistrates. These are full-time salaried magistrates appointed to certain large boroughs, e.g. Birmingham and Leeds, which apply for such appointment. They are appointed by the Queen on the recommendation of the Lord Chancellor, and must be solicitors or barristers of at least seven years' standing.

METROPOLITAN STIPENDIARY MAGISTRATES. These are the counterpart in London of the Stipendiary magistrates in the provinces and are appointed in the same way.

EX-OFFICIO MAGISTRATES. Persons could become magistrates by holding another office, e.g. mayor. Sect. 1 of the Justices of the Peace Act, 1968, abolished this concept except for High Court Judges and in the City of London where the Lord Mayor and aldermen continue to be City Magistrates. Mayors of other boroughs may, however, exercise the functions of justices on the supplemental list.

Although the main jurisdiction of magistrates is in respect of cases arising within the county or borough for which they are appointed. Sect. 28 of the Criminal Justice Act, 1967, provides that magistrates may now hear *any summary charge* wherever committed in respect of a defendant appearing before them on any other charge.

Each bench of lay magistrates has a salaried clerk, who is usually employed whole time. He assists the magistrates on questions of procedure and law, and is responsible for the administration of the court.

The Justices of the Peace Act, 1968, has provided means by which the status and powers of the clerk can be improved in the future. Under Sect. 5. rules may be made delegating to the clerk or a qualified assistant the functions of a single justice. This could include pre-trial work such as committals and the issue of warrants. Sect. 5 also deals with the power of the clerk to advise the magistrates. It declares that the functions of the clerk include giving to the magistrates *at their request* advice regarding law, practice or procedure on any matter arising in connection with the discharge of their functions, including questions arising after the magistrates have retired to consider a verdict. Furthermore, the clerk may at any time and *whether requested or not* bring to the attention of the magistrates any matter of law, practice or procedure that is or may be involved. The magistrates are not bound to follow this advice but most responsible magistrates would. It is also worth noting that the Magistrates' Courts (Forms) Rules of 1968 empower Justices' Clerks to sign certain forms which previously could only be signed by a justice. In addition it was held in *Simms* v. *Moore*, [1970] 3 All E.R. 1, that where at a summary trial the prosecutor is not legally represented the clerk can, subject to a number of safeguards, examine the witnesses for the prosecution.

Most clerks now are, and in due course all will be, professionally qualified. A qualified clerk must be a barrister or solicitor of not less than five years' standing. Clerks are appointed by the Magistrates' Courts Committee for the county or for a borough which has a separate commission for the peace. Magistrates' Courts Committees in counties and county boroughs carry out a general supervision of the administration of magistrates' courts, and recommend to the Lord Chancellor any alteration thought desirable in the division of such courts. The committees also arrange for instruction to be given to newly appointed magistrates.

Before discussing the powers of magistrates in regard to criminal prosecutions, it is necessary to classify criminal offences for procedural purposes.

SUMMARY OFFENCES. Summary offences may be divided into two classes—

(i) *Offences triable by magistrates only.* In these cases it is not possible for the accused to opt for trial by jury, and the matter can be dealt with only by magistrates and never by anyone else. Examples of such offences are drunkenness, and some offences under Road Traffic legislation such as exceeding the speed limit.

(ii) *Summary offences triable by jury.* In those cases where upon conviction for a summary offence the magistrates can impose a sentence of *more than three months'* imprisonment without the option of a fine, the accused has a right to a jury trial on indictment. The court has a duty to inform the accused of this right before he pleads to the charge, and if he claims a jury trial, the magistrates become examining magistrates. Examples of such offences are cruelty to children and dangerous driving.

INDICTABLE OFFENCES. An indictment is a formal written accusation of crime which is read out to the jury before the trial. Indictable offences may be divided into two classes—

(i) *Crimes triable on indictment only.* In general the most serious criminal offences are triable only in this way. They include treason, murder, manslaughter, perjury, conspiracy, bigamy, rape, robbery and burglary.

(ii) *Indictable offences triable summarily.* The Magistrates' Courts Act, 1952, (Sched. 1), and the Criminal Justice Administration Act, 1962, (Sched. 3), provide that certain indictable offences are triable summarily. The category includes all offences under the Theft Act, 1968 (except robbery, aggravated burglary, blackmail, assault with intent to rob, handling stolen goods from an offence committed abroad and certain ordinary burglaries); unlawful wounding and other indictable assaults under the Offences Against the Person Act, 1861; most offences of damage to property under the Criminal Damage Act, 1971, and certain offences of forgery under the Forgery Act, 1913.

The magistrates can decide to try the charge themselves at any time during the hearing, but usually the decision is made at the outset at the suggestion of the prosecution. The question of summary trial really depends upon how serious the particular offence is. Where a person is tried summarily for an indictable offence, he can be sent to the Crown Court for sentence if the magistrates feel that he should in the circumstances receive greater punishment than they can give.

OFFENCES WHICH ARE BOTH INDICTABLE AND SUMMARY. Statute may place an offence in the above category, and where this is so the procedure is as follows.

The prosecution may apply for a summary trial before any evidence is called. If no such application is made the magistrates will treat the offence as indictable and act as examining magistrates. If, on the application of the prosecution, the magistrates decide to treat the offence as a summary offence, the accused will usually be able to claim trial on indictment if he wishes, because most of these hybrid offences are punishable with more than three months' imprisonment. If the accused asks for trial on indictment, the magistrates become examining magistrates again. If an offence is to be tried summarily the procedure is, therefore, that the prosecution must apply, the magistrates must agree, and the accused must consent.

However, the magistrates do have power to try the offence summarily without the application of the prosecution if the accused consents. Further, if the magistrates have decided to treat the offence as a summary offence, they may still, before the conclusion of the evidence for the prosecution, decide that the offence should be tried on indictment, and carry on proceedings as examining magistrates. A common example of a hybrid offence of this nature is being drunk in charge of a motor car.

Functions of Magistrates. The general procedures of magistrates are governed by the Magistrates' Courts Act, 1952, and the Criminal Justice Act, 1967, and trial in a magistrates' court is without a jury.

With regard to crimes the magistrates have two functions—

1. **Preliminary Investigation into Indictable Offences.** Here the magistrates are investigating a case which will have to go for trial to a higher court. The accused is charged before a magistrates' court, and a preliminary investigation is held in that court to see if the prosecution can make out a *prima facie* case against the accused; if not, then the charge is dismissed, although this does not operate as an acquittal, and the accused could be charged again with the same offence at a later date. If the prosecution do make out a case against the accused, he is committed (i.e. sent) for trial in the Crown Court where he will be tried on the indictment. The Courts Act, 1971 abolished quarter sessions and assizes, and provision is now made for committal to the Crown Court. For the purposes of preliminary investigation, only one magistrate need be present. However, if more than one is sitting, the decision to commit or not to commit is a *majority* one and need not be unanimous. Where the justices are equally divided on the question of committal a rehearing must be ordered before a bench uneven in number so that a decision is ensured.

Committal proceedings must be *open to the public* unless—

(i) the court is of the opinion that the ends of justice would not not be served by sitting in public, in which case the whole or part of the proceedings may be *in camera*; or

(ii) statute requires that the particular committal be heard *in camera*, e.g. a prosecution under the Official Secrets Acts.

In general the only evidence given at committal proceedings is by the prosecution, the accused merely reserving his defence for the actual trial. In the past when full reporting of committal proceedings was allowed, the accused could be prejudiced because by the time his trial occurred the general public, including probably the jury, had read only one side of the case and might have reached the conclusion that the accused was guilty. Now under Sect. 3 of the Criminal Justice Act, 1967, newspaper, television and radio reports of committal proceedings are restricted to the following matters—

(*a*) the name of the court and the names of the justices;

(*b*) the names, addresses, ages and occupations of the prosecutor, defendants and witnesses,

(*c*) the offences under consideration,

(*d*) the names of the advocates,

(*e*) the decision of the court;

(*f*) where a committal is ordered, the charges involved;

(*g*) the name of the higher court to which the committal is ordered;

(*h*) in the case of an adjournment the date and place to which the hearing is adjourned;

(*i*) any order as to bail and whether or not legal aid was granted.

However, if a defendant or one of a number of co-defendants applies to the court for unrestricted reports the court must so order. The order applies to the totality of the committal proceedings unless they are severed as between defendants, so that full reports can be made of the evidence against all of the defendants whether they have agreed or not. (*R.* v. *Russell ex parte Beaverbrook Newspapers*, [1968] 3 All E.R. 695.) Furthermore there is no restriction on reporting if the magistrates decide not to commit for trial. After the trial of the defendant (or the last if there is more than one defendant) reporters can mention in detail matters raised in committal proceedings.

Finally, where a preliminary hearing changes into a summary trial reporters can report fully the committal proceedings which took place before the summary trial.

There are now three types of committal for trial—

(*a*) *A committal procedure under the Criminal Justice Act*, 1967, *in which the evidence consists of written statements.* Before such a committal is made the magistrates must be satisfied that—

(i) all the evidence for both prosecution and defence consists of written statements;

(ii) the defendant is represented by a solicitor or barrister;

(iii) there is no submission by the defendant that the statements disclose insufficient evidence for committal.

If the court is satisfied that the above three matters have been complied with it may commit for trial without reading out or even considering the contents of the statements.

(*b*) *Old procedure.* Here the defendant need not be legally represented. The prosecution will call its witnesses and the defendant or his advocate may cross-examine them. The evidence of each witness must be written down or typed and signed by the witness after it has been read over to him. This is a deposition, and, if the magistrates decide to commit, will be sent to the court of trial with the other papers relevant to the case

(*c*) *Hybrid procedure.* This procedure follows closely upon that in (*b*), above, except that written statements by witnesses are accepted even though such witnesses are not present. However, the magistrates can insist on the personal attendance of a witness even though they are in possession of a written statement from him.

Place and time of trial. Under Sect. 7(1) of the Courts Act, 1971, a magistrates' court committing a person for trial on indictment to the Crown Court will have to specify the Crown Court centre at which he is to be tried and in selecting that centre must have regard to—

(*a*) the convenience of the defence, the prosecution and the witnesses;

(*b*) the expediting of the trial;

(*c*) any directions regarding the distribution of Crown Court business given by the Lord Chief Justice or by an officer of the Crown Court with the concurrence of the Lord Chancellor under Sect. 4(5) of the Act.

Under Sect. 7(2) of the Act, the Crown Court may alter the place of any trial on indictment by varying the decision of the magistrates or a previous decision on the matter made by the Crown Court. Under Sect. 7(3) the defendant or the prosecutor, if dissatisfied with the place of trial as fixed by the magistrates or by the Crown Court, may apply to the Crown Court to vary the place of trial. The Crown Court may deal with the application as it sees fit. An application under Sect. 7(3) must be heard in open Court by a High Court judge.

The above provisions are designed to bring an accused person to trial as quickly as possible. However, the prosecutor and the accused and his advisers must be given time in which to prepare the case properly. Accordingly, Sect. 7(4) provides for the laying down under Crown Court Rules of minimum and maximum periods from the date of committal when the trial shall commence. These minimum periods cannot be *shortened* without the consent of the accused and the prosecutor or *lengthened* without an order of the Crown Court.

Bail. Where a person has been arrested by the police (or by a private citizen who has handed him over to police custody) the police may release him on bail and *must* do so if he cannot be brought before a magistrates' court within twenty-four hours of being charged with an offence. If the police refuse to grant bail an accused person may ask for it when he is brought before the magistrates. The magistrates have a discretion whether to grant bail or not though if the offence charged is treason or murder it cannot be given. An appeal against refusal to grant bail or against the amount of bail required, lies to a High Court judge. Sect. 18 of the Criminal Justice Act, 1967, which is designed to reduce the number of accused persons remanded in custody before trial, imposes some restrictions on the magistrates' discretion to refuse bail. The section states that a magistrates' court *must* grant bail to an adult accused where he is charged—

(*a*) with a summary offence which is punishable with not more than six months' imprisonment; or

(*b*) with a hybrid or indictable offence which is triable summarily and it is intended to proceed to summary trial.

However, even in these circumstances the magistrates are not bound to grant bail if the accused has, for example, previously been sentenced to imprisonment; has no fixed abode; is charged with an offence involving an assault or threat of violence or having an offensive weapon; or it appears that unless detained he is likely to commit another offence.

A person who is given bail is required to sign a recognisance which is an undertaking to surrender for trial in due course or forfeit a sum of money set out in the recognisance. One or more sureties may be required as well. The amounts of money set out in a recognisance may vary considerably, though the Bill of Rights 1688 provides that they shall not be 'excessive'. Conditions may be attached to bail such as reporting to a police station at stated intervals.

Alibi. The abuse of "sprung" or late alibis had been so widespread in criminal trials that Sect. 11 of the Criminal Justice Act, 1967, provides that, in general, notice of alibi must be given in advance of a trial on indictment. This is not required in summary trials because of the ease with which the prosecution can ask for an adjournment where the defendant "springs" an alibi on the prosecution at the last moment.

The following warning (or one similar to it) must be given during the course of committal proceedings—

> You will be committed for trial by jury, but I must warn you that at that trial you may not be permitted to give evidence of an alibi or to call witnesses in support of an alibi unless you have earlier given particulars of the alibi and of the witnessess. You may give those particulars now to this court or any time in the next seven days to the solicitor for the prosecution, who is . . . (name and address of solicitor).

Although this warning need not be given if it seems unnecessary having regard to the nature of the offence charged, it should as a general rule be given where there is any doubt, because the Act provides that failure to give it will allow the defendant to introduce a last-minute alibi at his trial.

Where an unrepresented defendant does not appear to understand what is meant by "alibi," the word must be explained to him.

There is a discretion in the trial judge to allow alibi evidence to be heard even though particulars of it were not given within seven days provided the prosecution has been given time to investigate the alibi before the trial started. (*R.* v. *Sullivan*, [1970] 2 All E.R. 681.)

2. Summary Trial of Petty Offences and Other Offences Triable Summarily. The magistrates can actually determine such offences, and do not merely investigate the prosecutor's case. In order that the magistrates may exercise their full powers in a summary trail, there must be two or more magistrates, with a maximum of seven, sitting in open court, in a place marked out as the petty sessional court house.

When sitting in the *petty sessional court house*, the maximum penalty which they may impose for any one offence is in most cases six months' imprisonment, unless the accused is convicted of two or more indictable offences which have been dealt with summarily, in which event the aggregate of the terms so imposed must not exceed twelve months. The maximum fine for any one offence may now be as much as £400. There are certain offences under Customs and Excise legislation for which the magistrates may impose a sentence on summary conviction of twelve months. In addition, under Sect. 11(2) of the Criminal Justice Act, 1948, a magistrates' court, when placing an offender on probation or discharging him conditionally or absolutely, may order him to pay damages for injury to his victim up to a maximum of £100. Under the Criminal Damage Act, 1971, the magistrates can order a person convicted of damaging property to pay compensation up to £400.

Suspended Prison Sentences. Sects. 39–42 of the Criminal Justice Act, 1967, introduced the concept of suspended sentences. The Act (as amended by the Criminal Justice Bill, 1972) provides that any court which passes a sentence of imprisonment for a term of not more than two years *may* order the sentence as a suspended sentence and announce the *operational period*, i.e. the length of the term of suspension. The maximum operational period is two years and the minimum one year.

Under the 1967 Act a court wishing to sentence for six months or less *had* to order a suspended sentence except in certain cases, e.g. offences involving assault. Under the 1972 Bill there is no case where a court *must* suspend a sentence. Such sentences are now merely a way of dealing with offenders alternative to a short term of imprisonment. However, if the magistrates send an adult first offender to prison they must state and record their reasons.

Where a suspended sentence is ordered the defendant does not go to prison unless during the operational period he is convicted for a further offence punishable by imprisonment. Since the magistrates can, in general, impose a maximum penalty of six months' imprisonment they were especially likely to be subject to those provisions of the Criminal Justice Act, 1967, which related to suspended prison sentences, though the provisions, as we have seen, apply to courts generally.

The suspended sentence has not proved such a valuable device as was hoped. Its major drawbacks have been as follows—

(*a*) The mandatory suspension provisions rendered the magistrates courts, in particular, powerless to give prison sentences in many cases where such a sentence could have a salutary deterrent effect upon an offender.

(*b*) Suspended sentences tended to replace other forms of non-custodial penalties such as probation. This had an unfortunate effect on criminal reform since there was no supervision of persons on suspended sentence nor could there be in the absence of a substantial expansion of the probation service.

The Criminal Justice Bill, 1972 gives power to impose a *suspended sentence with supervision* where a court gives a sentence of more than six months, the supervision to be by probation officers. The Bill also provides two useful miscellaneous powers. Firstly, a court can defer sentencing for six months to see how an offender behaves after conviction. Secondly, it may disqualify from driving *all* those involved (not only the driver) where a vehicle has been used to facilitate an offence punishable by at least two years' imprisonment.

CHILDREN AND YOUNG PERSONS. The magistrates also have a part to play in regard to children and young persons *whose behaviour or circumstances* require some form of official action. For this purpose the magistrates sit as a *juvenile court*. This court must sit in a different building or room from that in which other courts are held, or else must sit on a different day. The magistrates involved are drawn from a special panel and must be under 65 years of age. It is usual for a woman magistrate(s) to be present on these occasions.

Part I of the Children and Young Persons Act, 1969, introduces a number of major changes in the operation and powers of the juvenile court. The Act is based upon the White Paper, *Children in Trouble* (Cmnd. 3601), published in 1968, and must be seen against the background of criticism which there has been over the years with regard to the way in which young offenders have been dealt with. Although the philosophy in cases involving children and young persons has for many years been that the court must have regard to the *welfare of the child*, this philosophy has had to be implemented, as far as possible, by a form of criminal trial in a juvenile court with all the social stigma which that involves.

Care proceedings. To avoid this stigma, Sect. 1 of the Act introduces to the juvenile court a new form of *civil* proceedings called "care proceedings." These proceedings are available for all persons under seventeen who, although they have not committed an offence, are in need of care, protection or control. Under Sect. 4, care proceedings also entirely replace criminal proceedings against children under fourteen who have committed offences (except in homicide cases) and, under Sect. 5, are to be a preferred alternative to criminal proceedings against young persons between fourteen and seventeen who have committed offences.

The primary choice open to the court in care proceedings will be between a *supervision order* by which the child or young person will be placed under the supervision of a probation officer, local authority, or other person, and a *care order* by which the juvenile will be removed from his home environment and committed to the care of the local authority for residential treatment. There are other alternatives which may be used, i.e. binding over, compensation and hospital orders.

Criminal proceedings against young persons. Although care proceedings are favoured by the Act, it is still possible to bring criminal proceedings against young persons in certain types of cases. Details of these are left to the Home Secretary to prescribe by regulation but it is likely that criminal proceedings will be permitted where—

(i) the offence is homicide or some other serious offence;

(ii) the offence is of a type causing much public concern;

(iii) the young person appears not to be in need of sustained support or treatment but the nature of the offence and his home circumstances suggest that a court appearance and a simple deterrent, e.g. a fine, would be appropriate;

(iv) the offence is a traffic offence with possible disqualification or endorsement;

(v) the offence was committed in company with some other person(s), whether over or under seventeen, who is to be prosecuted.

When criminal proceedings are brought against a young person the trial will be before a juvenile court in nearly all cases, though trial in a superior court will occur in the case of homicide and some other grave offences, and where joint trial with adult members of, say, a gang is desirable.

The area of choice as to sentence in criminal proceedings will be restricted. Approved schools are abolished and attendance and detention centres will be gradually wound-up. The power to send juveniles to Borstal will disappear when the minimum age for Borstal training has been raised to seventeen. The probation order will be supplanted by the supervision order so that eventually the juvenile courts will be left with the following powers in criminal proceedings—supervision orders; care orders which involve secure accommodation in a local authority establishment; fines; binding over; compensation; disqualification from driving and endorsement of licences; hospital and guardianship orders under the Mental Health Act, 1959.

CIVIL JURISDICTION. The magistrates also have a civil jurisdiction, e.g. the making of affiliation orders and authorising the recovery of small debts. Their main civil jurisdiction is concerned with domestic proceedings, and applications for matrimonial relief such as separation and maintenance orders may be made to the magistrates. They also deal with questions concerning the custody and adoption of children, and the giving of permission for persons under eighteen to marry when they cannot obtain their parents' consent. Domestic proceedings are normally heard in closed court, and appeal lies to a Divisional Court of the Family Division of the High Court.

Apart from the matters outlined above, a justice can exercise certain other powers such as issuing a summons or a warrant for arrest, and justices also have functions such as licensing premises, and the enforcement of rates.

APPEALS. An accused person who had been convicted and sentenced by the magistrates for a summary offence could appeal to quarter sessions. On the abolition of. quarter sessions, appeal is now to the Crown Court (Sect. 8 and Sch. 1, Courts Act, 1971). Appeal from the magistrates lies at the instance of the accused only. The appeal may be against conviction or sentence on questions of law or fact and no permission is required. The appeal takes the form of a re-hearing and fresh evidence is admissible on both sides, though no jury is present. The powers of the new Crown Court in respect of appeals from magistrates are to be as follows—

(*a*) the Crown Court may correct any error or mistake in the order or judgment containing the decision which is the subject of the appeal (Courts Act, 1971, Sect. 9(1));

(*b*) at the end of hearing an appeal against part or the whole of a decision the Crown Court may, under Sect. 9(2) of the Courts Act, 1971—

(i) confirm, reverse or vary the decision appealed against, or
(ii) remit the matter with an opinion thereon to the magistrates whose decision is appealed against, or
(iii) make such other order in the matter as the court thinks just, and by that order exercise any power which the magistrates might have exercised.

(*c*) under Sect. 9(3) if the appeal is against a conviction or a sentence, the Crown Court has power to award any punishment whether more or less severe than that awarded by the magistrates' court whose decision is appealed against provided that the punishment is one which the magistrates themselves might have awarded but no more.

It should be noted that an appeal from the Crown Court to the Divisional Court of Queen's Bench lies by way of case stated at the instance of either side. A case may only be stated on a question of law, and to facilitate the appeal the Crown Court is then required to state the reasons for its findings in writing. Alternatively either side may appeal direct from the magistrates to a Divisional Court by way of case stated on a point of law. If the accused pleads guilty before the magistrates, he cannot appeal to the Crown Court against conviction, but can appeal to a Divisional Court on a point of law.

Since the Administration of Justice Act, 1960, cases originating in the magistrates' courts can now reach the House of Lords. Appeal lies to the House of Lords if the Divisional Court or the House of Lords gives leave, so long as the Divisional Court certifies that the case involves a question of law of general public importance which ought to be considered by the House of Lords.

FORMER COURTS OF QUARTER SESSIONS AND THE CROWN COURT

These were County Quarter Sessions or Borough Quarter Sessions, both having similar jurisdiction. Sect. 3 or the Courts Act, 1971, abolished these courts and replaced them by a single Crown Court able to sit anywhere in England and Wales. In the case of County Quarter Sessions the judges were the county magistrates, of whom at least two had normally to be present to constitute a court. However, Sect. 4 of the Criminal Justice Administration Act, 1962, provided that where, at a County Quarter Sessions other than for London, a legally qualified chairman was the only magistrate available, he could, if delay would otherwise be involved, proceed to try a case alone. The Lord Chancellor could appoint a legally qualified chairman, who was either a solicitor or a barrister of at least ten years' standing, or might be one of the Law Officers, a Recorder, or a High Court Judge. The Criminal Justice Administration Act, 1962, Sect. 5, provided that no Chairman of County Quarter Sessions could be elected unless he was a legally qualified chairman. Borough Quarter Sessions were held by a Recorder, who was the sole judge of the court, and Recorders were appointed from barristers of at least five years' standing. As the name suggests, quarter sessions were held quarterly, or, by adjournment, more often.

The jurisdiction of the former Courts of Quarter Sessions which related to the trial of indictable offences and appeals from magistrates courts has, under Sect. 8 of the Courts Act, 1971, been transferred to the new Crown Court.

(i) *Trial of indictable offences.* The jurisdiction of quarter sessions with regard to the trial of indictable offences was to some extent limited so that, e.g. offences for which a person might be sentenced to life imprisonment could not be tried there. The Crown Court has power to try *all* indictable offences so that its jurisdiction is more extensive than that of the quarter sessions. There are, however, provisions under which certain cases which are not appropriate for trial in a Crown Court by a Circuit Judge or Recorder but are reserved for trial in that Court by a High Court Judge. All offences have now been divided for the purposes of trial into four classes—*Class* 1. To be tried by a High Court Judge: (1) any offences for which a person may be sentenced to death, (2) misprision of treason and treason felony, (3) murder, (4) genocide, (5) an offence under Sect. 1 of the Official Secrets Act, 1911, (6) incitement, attempt or conspiracy to commit any of the above offences. *Class* 2. To be tried by a High Court Judge unless a particular case is released by or on the authority of a presiding judge (see p. 69): (1) manslaughter, (2) infanticide, (3) child destruction, (4) abortion, (5) rape, (6) sexual intercourse (including incest) with a girl under 13, (7) sedition, (8) an offence under Sect. 1 of the Geneva Conventions Act, 1957, (9) mutiny, (10) piracy, (11) incitement, attempt or conspiracy to commit any of the above offences. *Class* 3. All indictable offences other than those in Classes 1, 2, and 4 (below). These offences will normally be listed for trial by a High Court Judge unless the listing officer decides after consulting with a presiding judge that the case should be listed for trial by a circuit judge or recorder. A case in classes normally tried by a High Court Judge may be listed for a circuit judge or recorder where, for example, the circumstances of the offence are not of unusual gravity. *Class* 4. May be tried by a High Court Judge but will normally be listed for trial by a Circuit Judge or Recorder: (1) all offences which may, in appropriate circumstances, be tried either on indictment or summarily. They include—(*a*) indictable offences which may be tried summarily under Sect. 19 of and Sched. I to the Magistrates' Courts Act, 1952; (*b*) offences which are both indictable and summary under Sect. 18 of the Magistrates' Courts Act, 1952; (*c*) offences punishable on summary conviction with more than three months' imprisonment where the accused may claim to be tried on indictment under Sect. 25 of the Magistrates' Courts Act, 1952, (2) conspiracy to commit any of the above offences, (3) the following offences: (*a*) causing death by dangerous driving; (*b*) wounding or causing grievous bodily harm with intent; (*c*) certain burglaries in dwellings; (*d*) robbery or assault with intent to rob; (*e*) certain offences under the Forgery Act, 1913; (*f*) incitement, attempt or conspiracy to commit any of the above offences; (*g*) conspiracy to commit an offence which is in no circumstances triable on indictment or an act which is not an offence, (4) any offence in Class 3 if included in Class 4 in accordance with directions, which may be either general or particular, given by a presiding judge or on his authority. It should be noted that in all cases trial is by jury.

(ii) *Appeals from the magistrates' courts.* These are now heard in the Crown Court. So far as appeals from juvenile courts are concerned, these will be heard by a Juvenile Appeals Court comprised of a Circuit Judge and two magistrates drawn from the juvenile court panel.

MAGISTRATES' COURTS IN GREATER LONDON

The above outline of the organisation of magistrates' courts is modified on the area of Greater London. The Administration of Justice Act, 1964, was passed to achieve this, and was necessary in view of the establishment of the new administrative area, known as Greater London, by the London Government Act, 1963. Sect. 2 of the Administration of Justice Act, 1964, provides for the division of Greater London into five areas, each having its own commission of the peace and deemed for judicial purposes to be a county. The areas are as follows—

(1) Middlesex—which is substantially the old county of Middlesex;

(2) Inner London—which is the former county of London;

(3) Three new areas, which did not previously exist as separate counties, called North East London, South East London and South West London.

Sect. 3 of the Act gives power to alter the boundaries of these areas by means of an Order in Council.

MAGISTRATES' COURTS. The Administration of Justice Act, 1964, in Sects. 9–17, deals only with the area known as Inner London, and integrates the work of the stipendiary magistrates with the work of the lay justices in the area.

Formerly, summary jurisdiction in the London area was dealt with almost exclusively by stipendiary magistrates, though licensing and juvenile work were carried out by lay justices. Sect. 9 provides that, in the case of Inner London, the jurisdiction of the lay justices is to be completely co-extensive with that of the stipendiary magistrates in that area. Sect. 10 raises the number of stipendiaries from thirty-five to forty.

The Act goes on to provide for the division of work in Inner London between lay and stipendiary magistrates. Sect. 12 provides that the lay justices are to continue to exercise exclusive jurisdiction in juvenile courts, but whereas formerly the Home Secretary nominated the juvenile panel and its chairman, this is now to be done by the Lord Chancellor.

Where the magistrates are trying a person for any offence in their own commission area, they may also try him for an offence committed in any other commission area. (Sect. 28, Criminal Justice Act, 1967.)

The Administration of Justice Act, 1964, left unaltered the system of magistrates' courts in the 677 acres at the centre of London known as the City. In that area, the Lord Mayor and Aldermen were *ex-officio* the only City magistrates and traced their jurisdiction back to before Magna Carta. As we have seen, the Justices of the Peace Act, 1968, set out to largely abolish *ex-officio* magistrates but opposition to this provision was made in Parliament in respect of the City. Eventually the following compromise was reached—

(a) Sec. 1(2) of the Act of 1968 provides for "a commission of the peace to be issued for the City as a county of itself." This allows lay justices to be appointed to share the bench with the Lord Mayor and the twenty-five aldermen to dispense summary justice in the magistrates' courts at Guildhall and the Mansion House.

(*b*) Sch. 2 provides that there shall be no distinction between magistrates sitting *ex-officio* or under the Commission and that, subject to the ordinary retirement age, the Lord Mayor shall be chairman of the bench —elsewhere chairmen are elected by the magistrates. Up to eight aldermen who are former mayors are deputy chairmen in addition to deputy chairmen elected in the ordinary way.

QUARTER SESSIONS. It should be noted that quarter sessions in London is abolished by the Courts Act, 1971, and replaced by the Crown Court system.

THE COUNTY COURT

The Magistrates' Courts deal with most of the less serious criminal matters in this country. At something like the same level, but dealing exclusively with civil cases, is the County Court. County Courts were created by the County Courts Act, 1846, to operate as the chief lower courts for the trial of civil disputes, and a large number of cases are heard in these courts annually. The County Court is presided over by a judge appointed by the Crown on the advice of the Lord Chancellor from barristers of at least seven years' standing. Under the Courts Act, 1971, Sects. 16 and 20, all existing county court judges become Circuit judges of the Crown Court and in future county court judges will be called Circuit judges. Thus they will play an increasing role in the administration of criminal justice in the new High Court and Crown Court centres (see p. 36). In addition, the Courts Act, 1971 provides that every judge of the Court of Appeal and of the High Court and every Recorder may sit as a judge in a County Court if he consents and the Lord Chancellor thinks that it is desirable. The judge usually sits alone, though there is provision for a trial by a jury of eight persons in some cases, e.g. where fraud is alleged. Appeal lies direct to the Court of Appeal (Civil Division). There are over four hundred courts in existence and under the Administration of Justice Act, 1968, an Act of Parliament is no longer necessary to increase the maximum number of judges. Subject to the approval of both Houses, the Lord Chancellor has power to do so by order. This power has been exercised a number of times, the last occasion being in 1970 when the number of County Court judges was increased to 125. One judge may have a circuit of several courts, though in busy areas there may be more than one judge to a court. The judge is assisted by a Registrar who is appointed by the Lord Chancellor from solicitors of at least seven years' standing. The Registrar acts as Clerk of the Court, and has had since 1970 power to try certain cases where the amount involved does not exceed £75 and no objection is raised by any of the parties. If the parties agree, his jurisdiction extends to any action or matter within the general jurisdiction of the court.

Regarding the jurisdiction of the court, there are limitations as to place, and as to the nature and amount of the claim. The general rule is that the plaintiff must bring his action in the court of the district where the defendant dwells or carries on business. Where land is involved, the action is generally brought in the court of the district in which the land is situated. An action for an injunction or a declaratory judgment which states the legal position of the parties cannot be commenced in or transferred to the County Court unless money in the form of damages is a major and essential part of the claim (*Thompson* v. *White*, [1970] 3 All E.R. 678). Thus, if X sues Y for trespass to X's land and Y says that the land belongs to him, a County Court could give a declaratory judgment as to the ownership of the land because this would be an essential part of X's claim for damages. The court could not, however, make a declaration in the absence of a claim for damages.

The general jurisdiction of County Courts and procedure therein are governed by the County Courts Act, 1959 (as amended in particular by the Administration of Justice Act, 1969), and the County Court Rules. The latter are in the form of delegated legislation and are set out in an annual volume known as the County Court Practice. In general terms, the extent of the jurisdiction is as follows—

(i) *Actions founded on contract and tort* with a limit of £750 unless the parties agree to waive the limit. For certain torts (i.e. libel and slander) the court has no jurisdiction unless both parties agree.

(ii) *Equity matters*, e.g. mortages and trusts where the amount involved does not exceed £5,000, unless the parties agree to waive the limit.

(iii) *Actions concerning title to land, and actions for recovery of possession of land*, where the rateable value of the land does not exceed £400. There is unlimited jurisdiction in cases within the Rent Acts or by agreement between the parties.

(iv) *Bankruptcies*. Here there is unlimited jurisdiction, but not all county courts have bankruptcy jurisdiction. (Bankruptcy Act, 1914.) Bankruptcy cases in the Metropolitan Area are heard in the Bankruptcy Court of the High Court.

(v) *Company winding up*, where the paid-up share capital of the company is below £10,000, if the court has a bankruptcy jurisdiction.

(vi) *Probate proceedings*, where the value of the deceased's estate is estimated to be under £1,000.

(vii) *Admiralty matters*. Some County Courts in coastal areas have Admiralty jurisdiction which is limited to £1,000 except in salvage cases where the limit is £3,500. The parties may by agreement waive these limits.

(viii) *Matrimonial Causes*. The Matrimonial Causes Act, 1967, confers jurisdiction on County Courts in certain matrimonial proceedings.

A County Court designated by the Lord Chancellor as a "divorce county court" shall have jurisdiction in certain matters relating to any undefended matrimonial cause, but may *try* such a cause only if further designated as a court of trial (Sect. 1(1)). Every matrimonial cause shall be commenced in a divorce county court, though under rules of court defended cases *will* be transferred to the High Court and even undefended cases *may* be so transferred (Sect. 1(3)). There is also provision for the transfer from the High Court to a divorce county court of a matrimonial cause which becomes undefended (Sect. 1(4)).

Divorce county courts may make orders for ancillary relief and the protection of children and may deal with wilful neglect to maintain and the variation of maintenance agreements (Sect. 2). They may also hear applications made before presentation of the petition which relate to arrangements made between parties (Sect. 3). The jurisdiction of divorce county courts may be exercised in the principal probate registry (Sect. 4). The Lord Chancellor may assign particular county court judges to matrimonial proceedings (Sect. 5).

(ix) *Miscellaneous matters.* The County Court derives an important part of its jurisdiction from social legislation, e.g. adoption of children, guardianship of infants, legitimacy, race relations, and the enforcement of legislation concerning landlord and tenant.

Although in many matters the County Court has concurrent jurisdiction with the High Court, there are certain matters over which the County Courts have *exclusive* jurisdiction so that actions concerning them cannot be commenced in the High Court, e.g. Hire Purchase, Rent Restriction and under the Administration of Justice Act, 1970, actions for the recovery of land situated outside Greater London or the County Palatine of Lancaster where the rateable value does not exceed £400. In addition, the Act of 1970 gives the County Court alone the power to order attachment of earnings for ordinary civil debt.

Cases may also be remitted from the High Court to the County Court for determination. Thus, if a person serves a High Court writ to commence an action for breach of contract, the value of which is £750 or less, in the High Court, then, in the preliminary stages of the case, the plaintiff may be required to proceed in the County Court. If he refuses he may, even if he wins his case in the High Court, receive only County Court costs from the defendant and not the higher actual costs which he has incurred by going to the High Court. Conversely, potentially difficult actions may be transferred from the County Court to the High Court. In general terms, if a claim exceeds £150 it is open to the defendant to give notice of objection to a county court hearing and if the judge considers that an important question of law or fact may arise he will order transfer of the action to the High Court.

Appeal from a decision of a county court judge lies direct to the Court of Appeal (Civil Division) on a point of *law* and, provided in general terms that at least £200 is in dispute, appeal also lies on a question of *fact*.

THE SUPREME COURT OF JUDICATURE (II)

The Courts Act, 1971, gives effect, with some modifications, to the report of the Royal Commission on Assizes and Quarter Sessions (or Beeching

Commission) (Cmnd. 4153). Under Sect. 1 of the Courts Act, 1971, the Supreme Court will consist of the Court of Appeal and the High Court together with the Crown Court which was established by the Act. Thus, Courts of Assize and Quarter Sessions are replaced by a single Crown Court able to sit anywhere in England and Wales, as is the High Court for the trial of civil cases (Sects. 1(2) and 3).

THE NEW CROWN COURT

Sect. 4(1) of the Act establishes the Crown Court for England and Wales and states that this court shall be a superior court of record. It deals in the main with criminal work though all the domestic, betting and gaming, and the licensing jurisdiction of Quarter Sessions is transferred to the Crown Court (Sect. 8 and Sched. 1).

Judges of the Crown Court

Sect. 4(2) provides that the jurisdiction and powers of the Crown Court may be exercised by any judge of the High Court or any Circuit judge or Recorder. In certain circumstances magistrates are required to sit with the judge or Recorder (see below). The persons mentioned above are, when exercising the jurisdiction and powers of the Crown Court, to be known as Crown Court judges. Under Sect. 4(3) any judge of the Court of Appeal may, on the request of the Lord Chancellor sit and act as a judge of the Crown Court and when so sitting shall have the powers of a judge of the High Court and in general be so regarded. Except in those cases where magistrates are required to sit (see below), all proceedings in the Crown Court shall be heard and disposed of before one judge.

Magistrates as judges of the Crown Court. The magistrates, who as we have seen took part in the working of Quarter Sessions, still retain a role in the Crown Court. When the Crown Court is hearing an appeal from a magistrates' court or a case in which the magistrates have committed an accused person to the Crown Court for sentence, the Crown Court shall consist of a judge of the High Court or a Circuit judge or a Recorder who shall sit with not less than two or more than four magistrates (Sect. 5(1)). The number of magistrates sitting on an appeal or committal for sentence together with their qualifications are laid down in the Crown Court rules and different provisions may be made for different types of cases and different places of sitting (Sect. 5(2)).

Apart from appeals and committals for sentence, magistrates can be brought into the Crown Court on other occasions where it is felt that a particular type of hearing would benefit from the presence of lay magistrates. The cases or classes of cases suitable for allocation to a Crown Court comprising magistrates, including trials on indictment, shall be determined in accordance with directions given by or on behalf of the Lord Chief Justice with the concurrence of the Lord Chancellor (Sect. 5(3) and (4)). Under Crown Court rules a judge of the High Court, Circuit judge or Recorder may take over or continue with an appeal or committal or other proceedings, at which magistrates are required to be present, without sufficient or any magistrates present in fact (Sect. 5(6)). No decision made in the absence of magistrates or a sufficient number of them shall be questioned subsequently unless the objection regarding the absence of magistrates was taken by or on behalf of a party to the proceedings not later than the time when proceedings commenced or when the numbers present ceased to be as prescribed (Sect. 5(7)). When a judge of the High Court, Circuit judge or Recorder sits with magistrates he shall preside and the decision of the Crown Court may be by a majority. If the members of the court are equally divided the High Court or Circuit judge or Recorder shall have a second or casting vote (Sect. 5(8)). A magistrate shall not be disqualified from acting as a judge of the Crown Court merely because the proceedings are not at a place within the area for which he was appointed or are not related to that area in any way (Sect. 5(9)). The above provisions will involve the magistrates in more work since some Crown Court trials may last for a longer period of time than is usual in cases coming before the magistrates at present.

Appointment of Circuit Judges. The Queen may from time-to-time appoint, on the recommendation of the Lord Chancellor, Circuit judges to serve in the Crown Court for certain levels of criminal work and *county courts* for civil work and to carry out such other judicial work as may be conferred on them by Act of Parliament (Sect. 16(1) and (4)). The maximum number of Circuit judges is to be determined from time to time by the Lord Chancellor with the agreement of the Minister for the Civil Service (Sect. 16(2)). No person shall be appointed a Circuit judge unless he is a barrister of at least ten years' standing or a Recorder who has held that office for at least five years (Sect. 16(3)). Since a solicitor of ten years' standing may be appointed as a part-time Recorder, he could after five years in post become eligible for full-time membership of the Circuit bench (see p. 35). Under Sect. 16(5) and Sched. 2 (Part I) of the Act holders of certain continuing judicial offices become Circuit judges. These are the Vice-Chancellor of the County Palatine of Lancaster, the Recorder of the City of London and the Common Serjeant. Holders of certain other judicial offices *which are abolished* by the Act also become Circuit judges. These are the Official Referee of the Supreme Court, the Recorders of Liverpool and Manchester, additional judges of the Central Criminal Court, assistant judges of the Mayors and City of London Court, *County Court judges* (see p. 30), and whole-time Chairmen and Deputy Chairmen of the former courts of Quarter Sessions for Greater London, Cheshire, Durham, Kent and Lancashire. A Circuit judge *retires* at the end of the completed year of service in which he attains the age of seventy-two (Sect. 17(1)), though where the Lord Chancellor thinks it desirable he may authorise the continuance in office of a Circuit judge up to the age of seventy-five. A Circuit judge may be *removed* from office by the Lord Chancellor on the ground of inability or misbehaviour (Sect. 17(4)). A Circuit judge is disqualified for membership of the House of Commons (Sect. 17(5), and cannot practise as a lawyer while he holds office as a Circuit judge (Sect. 17(6)). The salaries, allowances and pensions of Circuit judges are dealt with in Sects. 18 and 19 of the Courts Act, 1971.

Appointment of Recorders. Under Sect. 21 of the Courts Act, 1971, the Queen may, on the recommendation of the Lord Chancellor, appoint qualified persons called Recorders to act as part-time judges of the Crown Court and to carry out such other judicial functions as may be given to them by statute. In order to be qualified for appointment as a Recorder a person must be a barrister or solicitor of at least ten years' standing, and the appointment must state the period of time for which the Recorder is to act. This period may be extended by the Lord Chancellor with the agreement of the Recorder concerned, but the initial term or any extension of it cannot continue after the end of the completed year of service in which the Recorder reaches the age of seventy-two. The Lord Chancellor may terminate the appointment of a Recorder on the ground of inability or misbehaviour or failure to comply with the terms of his appointment as where he does not make himself available to act at the times and places specified in the appointment.

Circuit Judges or Recorders Sitting as High Court Judges. Under Sect. 23 of the Courts Act, 1971, a Circuit judge or Recorder may be required by the Lord Chancellor to sit as a judge of the High Court for the hearing of such case or cases or at such place and for such time as may be specified by or on behalf of the Lord Chancellor. While acting in this capacity, a Circuit judge or Recorder has all the powers of a High Court judge. On the expiration of the period specified by the Lord Chancellor the person concerned reverts to the powers and functions of a Circuit judge or Recorder as the case may be. He may, however, attend at the High Court to give judgment or to deal with any ancillary matter relating to any case which he heard when sitting as a High Court judge. On these occasions he has once again the powers of a High Court judge.

Temporary High Court and Circuit Judges. Under Sect. 24 of the Courts Act, 1971, the Lord Chancellor may appoint suitably qualified persons to act as temporary High Court or Circuit judges during such period or on such occasions as the Lord Chancellor thinks fit. This power could be used to relieve pressure on the permanent judges of the High Court and Crown Court and to prevent undue delay in bringing cases to trial on occasions when the court concerned has a heavy case-load. In general terms, the persons qualified for appointment are barristers of at least ten years' standing and persons who have held a judicial office.

Location of Sittings and Business of the High Court. Under Sect. 2 of the Courts Act, 1971, sittings of the High Court may be held and any other business of the High Court may be conducted at any place in England and Wales. The places at which the High Court sits—other than at the Royal Courts of Justice in London—are to be determined by the Lord Chancellor.

Location of sittings and business of the Crown Court. Under Sect. 4(4) of the Courts Act, 1971, any Crown Court business may be conducted at any place in England or Wales. Sittings of the Crown Court at any place may be continuous or intermittent or occasional, and cases may be adjourned from one centre to another at any time.

Under Sect. 4(5) the cases or classes of cases to be dealt with by a judge of the High Court or a Circuit judge or Recorder and all other matters relating to the distribution of Crown Court business are to be determined by or on behalf of the Lord Chief Justice with the agreement of the Lord Chancellor (see p. 27). When the Crown Court sits in the City of London it is to be known as the Central Criminal Court and the Lord Mayor of the City and any Aldermen of the City may sit as judges of the Central Criminal Court *with* any judge of the High Court or any Circuit judge or Recorder. This is a departure from the general rule laid down in Sect. 4(4) of the Courts Act, 1971, which states that normally all proceedings in the Crown Court shall be heard and disposed of before a single judge.

High Court and Crown Court Centres. The Lord Chancellor announced in parliament on 26th January, 1971, his intentions with regard to the places which would become regular High Court and Crown Court centres replacing Assizes and Quarter Sessions. Places described in the following list as first-tier centres deal with both civil (High Court) and criminal (Crown Court) cases and will be visited by both High Court and Circuit judges. Second-tier centres deal with criminal cases only and will be visited by both High Court and Circuit judges. Third-tier centres deal with criminal cases only and will be visited only by Circuit judges.

Midland and Oxford Circuit: First-tier—Birmingham, Lincoln, Nottingham, Stafford, Warwick. *Second-tier*—Leicester, Northampton, Oxford, Shrewsbury, Worcester. *Third-tier*—Coventry, Derby, Dudley, Grimsby, Hereford, Huntingdon, Stoke-on-Trent, Walsall, Warley, West Bromwich, Wolverhampton. Peterborough will replace Huntingdon, as a third-tier centre, as soon as suitable court accommodation can be provided there.

North Eastern Circuit: First-tier—Leeds, Newcastle upon Tyne, Sheffield, York. *Second-tier*—Durham, Teeside. *Third-tier*—Beverley, Bradford, Doncaster, Huddersfield, Kingston upon Hull, Wakefield. Beverley will cease to be a third-tier centre as soon as additional court accommodation can be made available at Kingston upon Hull.

Northern Circuit: First-tier—Carlisle, Liverpool, Manchester, Preston. *Third-tier*—Barrow-in-Furness, Birkenhead, Burnley, Kendal, Lancaster.

South Eastern Circuit: First-tier—Greater London, Norwich. *Second-tier*—Chelmsford, Ipswich, Lewes, Maidstone, Reading, St. Albans. *Third-tier*—Aylesbury, Bedford, Brighton, Bury St. Edmunds, Cambridge, Canterbury, Chichester, Guildford, Kings Lynn, Southend.

Wales and Chester Circuit: First-tier—Caernarvon, Cardiff, Chester, Mold, Swansea. *Second-tier*—Carmarthen, Newport, Welshpool. *Third-tier*—Dolgellau, Haverfordwest, Knutsford, Merthyr Tydfil.

Western Circuit: First-tier—Bodmin, Bristol, Exeter, Winchester. *Second-tier*—Dorchester, Gloucester, Plymouth. *Third-tier*—Barnstaple, Bournemouth, Poole, Devizes, Newport (I.O.W.), Portsmouth, Salisbury, Southampton, Swindon, Taunton.

It appears that a High Court or Circuit judge may exceptionally visit a town which is not a regular court centre to meet the convenience of witnesses and others who live in a remote area.

Jurisdiction of High Court and Crown Court Centres. These centres take over the criminal and civil jurisdiction of the former Assize Courts and Quarter Sessions.

Trial of Indictable Offences. *All* proceedings on indictment will have to be brought before the Crown Court. Prior to the 1971 Act, Assize Courts tried serious indictable crimes such as treason, murder, manslaughter, or offences punishable by imprisonment for life, while Quarter Sessions dealt with other indictable crimes of a less serious or less difficult nature. Under the Courts Acts, 1971, jurisdiction of these two courts is now exercised in a High Court and Crown Court centre and the nature of the offence or civil claim will have relevance only in regard to the judge who tries it, i.e. a High Court Judge, or Circuit Judge or a Recorder. (See p. 28.)

Appeals from the Magistrates' Courts. As we have seen the Crown Court now takes over the appeals jurisdiction of the former courts of Quarter Sessions.

Civil Jurisdiction. The civil jurisdiction is the same as that of the High Court but in practice only Queen's Bench cases, such as disputes in contract and tort, and matrimonial causes will be heard.

Appeals from High Court and Crown Centres are as follows—

(*a*) in respect of civil cases heard by the High Court in these centres in exercising the former civil jurisdiction of Assizes—to the Court of Appeal (Civil Division);

(*b*) in respect of criminal cases heard by the Crown Court in these centres in exercising the former criminal jurisdiction of Assizes—to the Court of Appeal (Criminal Division);

(*c*) in respect of criminal cases heard by the Crown Court in these centres in exercising the former criminal jurisdiction of Quarter Sessions—to the Court of Appeal (Criminal Division) or by way of case stated to a divisional court of Queen's Bench.

THE HIGH COURT

Under Sect. 1(1) of the Administration of Justice Act, 1968, the High Court is staffed by a maximum of seventy judges known as puisne judges (pronounced "puny"). Under Sect. 1(2) of the 1968 Act the number of puisne judges may be increased by order in Council. Appointment is by the Queen on the advice of the Lord Chancellor and the qualification is being a barrister of at least ten years' standing. They hold office "during good behaviour" and their salaries are secured on the national revenues and are not voted by Parliament. They can only be removed on the petition of both Houses of Parliament, a procedure which has not been resorted to for centuries. Puisne judges once held office for life, but under the Judicial Pensions Act, 1959, new appointees after 1959 retire at seventy-five years of age, and judges who already held office in 1959 may, if they choose, retire under the new provisions. Allocation to the various divisions is by the Lord Chancellor. They are referred to orally as, e.g., "Mr. Justice Snooks," and in writing as "Snooks, J." Under Sect. 1 of the Courts Act, 1971, the High Court may sit anywhere in England and Wales.

THE QUEEN'S BENCH DIVISION has the largest staff, some forty puisne judges. The court is presided over by the Lord Chief Justice. In addition to the civil cases heard in the Strand, the judges of the Queen's Bench Division also helped to staff the Assize Courts (and now the High Court and Crown Court centres) on the various circuits into which England and Wales were divided. The judges of the Queen's Bench Division also sit in the Court of Appeal (Criminal Division), the Divisional Court of Queen's Bench, the Courts Martial Appeal Court, and are required to hear cases in the Central Criminal Court which becomes a Crown Court. The court has jurisdiction over every type of common law civil action. In fact it may be said that, if the writ can be served, the High Court has power to hear the case; though the High Court cannot usurp the jurisdiction of the Court of Appeal or the House of Lords. In particular, contract and tort actions are tried by the judges of this division. Under Sect. 1 of the Administration of Justice Act, 1970, Admiralty business is now assigned to a separate court called the Admiralty Court within the Queen's Bench Division.

THE CHANCERY DIVISION has some ten puisne judges and is presided over by the Lord Chancellor. However, he is nominal head only and does not try cases. Under Sect. 5 of the Administration of Justice Act, 1970, a Vice-Chancellor has been appointed to perform organisational and administrative functions as deputy to the Lord Chancellor. The Division deals with those matters formerly assigned to courts of equity, e.g. partnerships, mortages, trusts, companies, some revenue and bankruptcy matters, rectification of deeds and documents and the administration of the estates of deceased persons. Under Sect. 1 of the Administration of Justice Act, 1970, business in these areas which concerns family property and children is assigned to the new Family Division, and the Chancery Division acquires probate business except non-contentious probate which remains with the Family Division.

THE FAMILY DIVISION (formerly Probate, Divorce and Admiralty) has some seventeen puisne judges and is presided over by the President of the Division. The business which it does is apparent from its name; it deals with all High Court business which concerns marriage, family property and children, including adoption and wardship.

A High Court judge may be required by the Lord Chancellor to sit in any division of the High Court or to sit in the Court of Appeal (either division).

DIVISIONAL COURTS

The Divisional Court of Queen's Bench has a twofold jurisdiction.

(i) *An appellate jurisdiction.* The Court hears appeals on points of law, on cases stated by the Magistrates, and the Crown Court.

(ii) *A supervisory jurisdiction.* The divisional court exercises the power of the High Court to discipline inferior courts—which will include the Crown Court—and to put right their mistakes by means of the orders of *mandamus, certiorari* and *prohibition* (see p. 52). It can also deal with writs of *habeas corpus*, and election petitions.

The appellate and supervisory jurisdiction of the court may be exercised by two or more judges sitting without a jury. The Chancery Division and the Family Division also have divisional courts constituted of two or more judges sitting without a jury. So, for example, the Divisional Court of the Family Division hears appeals from the magistrates' courts in matrimonial cases, and the Divisional Court of the Chancery Division hears appeals on bankruptcy cases from County Courts, outside London, the Bankruptcy Court of the Chancery Division hearing bankruptcy appeals from London.

CROWN COURTS OF LIVERPOOL AND MANCHESTER

The Crown Courts of Liverpool and Manchester were set up by the Criminal Justice Administration Act, 1956. Before the 1971 Act they did the work of Quarter Sessions and Assizes in the area of Liverpool and Manchester. The work was shared by a full-time judge in each court, who was called a Recorder, and High Court Judge who heard the civil cases at Assizes. The two courts were always in session. Appeal on the criminal side was to the Court of Appeal (Criminal Division), and on the civil side to the Court of Appeal (Civil Division). Under the Courts Act, 1971, these courts are now absorbed into the structure of High Court and Crown Court centres (see p. 36).

ASSIZES

Prior to the 1971 Act, these courts sat for the purpose of trying criminal cases by virtue of commissions of oyer and terminer and general gaol delivery. The judge sat with a jury, and the court might try any indictable offence. An Assize court had no appellate jurisdiction. The judges were usually judges of the Queen's Bench Division and the P.D.A. Division, though eminent members of the Bar and county court judges were also appointed Commissioners of Assize. The civil jurisdiction was the same as that of the High Court, but in practice only Queen's Bench and divorce cases were heard. It was largely a matter of convenience whether a case was heard in London or on circuit. Appeals lay to the Court of Appeal (Criminal Division) or Court of

Appeal (Civil Division) as the case might be. Under the Courts Act, 1971, these courts are now absorbed into the structure of High Court and Crown Court Centres (see p. 36).

As a transitional measure the Administration of Justice Act, 1970, implemented a recommendation of the Beeching Commission to enable the holding of Assizes to be dispensed with wholly or for a particular sort of business in places where the visit of a judge and his retinue was not justified by the volume of business awaiting trial. If there was a small amount it might be transferred to some other Assize court. A further implementation of the report of the Beeching Commission is the appointment of Circuit Administrators and Presiding judges (see p. 68).

THE CENTRAL CRIMINAL COURT

This court was established by the Central Criminal Court Act, 1824. The Administration of Justice Act, 1964, repealed the provisions of that Act but largely re-enacted them in its First Schedule. The Central Criminal Court, commonly called the "Old Bailey," was formerly the assize court for London and Middlesex, and parts of Essex, Kent and Surrey, but was given jurisdiction over the whole of Greater London which led to a considerable increase in its work. Under Sect. 8 of the Administration of Justice Act, 1970, the Central Criminal Court is enabled to sit at any place in Greater London and not only within the area of the City. The judges of the court are: The Lord Mayor and Aldermen of the City of London, the Lord Chancellor, judges of the Queen's Bench Division, the Recorder of London, the Common Serjeant and the judges of the City of London Court. In practice the Recorder, the Common Serjeant and a judge of the City of London Court hear all the cases except the more serious ones, which are heard by a judge of the Queen's Bench Division. Each judge forms a separate court, and appeal lies to the Court of Appeal (Criminal Division). The Central Criminal Court was also the court of Quarter Sessions for the City of London. This court now becomes a Crown Court under the Courts Act, 1971, though it retains its name as the Central Criminal Court and its special judges (see p. 36).

THE COMMERCIAL COURT

Sect. 3 of the Administration of Justice Act, 1970, constitutes, as part of the Queen's Bench Division, a Commercial Court for the trial of causes of a commercial nature, e.g. insurance matters. The Act merely gives formal independence to the Commercial Court. Commercial litigation has since 1895 been dealt with in the Queen's Bench Division on a simplified procedure and before a specialist judge, the intention being to overcome the reluctance of commercial men, who prefer the privacy of arbitration, to resort to the machinery of the courts. Two specific steps were proposed in the Administration of Justice Bill to attract such customers: first a power was to be taken to allow the court to sit in private and to receive evidence which would not normally be admissible in an ordinary court, and secondly High Court judges were to be allowed to sit as arbitrators. The first of these proposals was rejected by the House of Commons at the Report Stage but the second was passed into law and Sect. 4 of the 1970 Act enables the judges of the Commercial Court to take arbitrations. They must, however, ask the Lord Chief Justice to approve their availability from judicial business. Thus, although in theory the Court has no wider power than other courts of the Queen's Bench Division, there is, in practice, a general discretion for departures in procedure and admission of evidence where the parties consent or where the interests of justice demand it or where it is necessary to expedite business. The power to hold hearings in private is restricted but Sect. 12 of the Administration of Justice Act, 1960, gives a power which could be used if, for example, trade secrets were involved. Commercial cases may be tried by a judge alone, or by a judge and a jury. It was once a special jury in that it consisted of persons who had knowledge of commercial matters. An ordinary jury would now be used since Sect. 40 of the Courts Act, 1971, abolishes special juries. All actions in the Commercial Court are tried in the City of London.

THE COMPANIES' COURT

This is really a court of the Chancery Division where company matters are tried before a single judge whose special concern is with company work. The work of the court is divided into company liquidation proceedings, and other company matters.

THE BANKRUPTCY COURT

The bulk of the bankruptcy work of the Chancery Division is performed by Registrars in Bankruptcy who deal with cases arising in the London area, provincial bankruptcies being dealt with by the local county court.

THE RESTRICTIVE PRACTICES COURT

This is a superior court of record set up by the Restrictive Trade Practices Act, 1956. The Act, which is further discussed in the chapter on the law of contract, is designed to prevent manufacturers entering into agreements which restrict free competition and tend to fix prices. The court investigates agreements which may be of this nature to see whether they are contrary to the public interest. The court has power to enforce its ruling by injunction, but in practice business men do not try to implement an agreement which the court has not sanctioned. The court also deals with the question of resale price maintenance agreements under the Resale Prices Act, 1964. (See page 188.) It consists of the following judges—one of whom is appointed by the Lord Chancellor to be President of the Court—three puisne judges of the High Court; one judge of the Court of Session of Scotland; one judge of the Supreme Court of Northern Ireland. The judges, who are nominated by the Lord Chancellor, are assisted by up to ten laymen appointed by the Queen on the recommendation of the Lord Chancellor, being persons with experience in industry and commerce. The court may sit in divisions, each division being constituted by one judge and two laymen. The judges decide matters of law but matters of fact are decided by a majority of the members of the court.

THE COURT OF APPEAL (CIVIL DIVISION)

The work of the court is carried out by the Master of the Rolls (at present Lord Denning) and up to fourteen Lords Justices of Appeal. These appointments are made by the Queen on the advice of the Prime Minister and the qualification is fifteen years' standing as a barrister or having been a puisne judge. Generally, a Lord Justice of Appeal has been a puisne judge for some years. They are referred to orally as, e.g. "Lord Justice Snooks" and in writing as "Snooks, L.J." Also included in the civil division are the Lord Chancellor, any ex-Lord Chancellor or Lord of Appeal willing to Act, the Lord Chief Justice and the President of the Family Division. The Lord Chancellor may also request judges of the High Court to sit in order to make up a quorum. The Court sits in divisions, the quorum for which is three. It is possible for a Lord Justice of Appeal to sit alone at first instance and they also may sit in the new Crown Court.

There is a right of appeal on law or fact from any division of the High Court; from a County Court; and from interlocutory orders of Judges in Chambers and Masters in Chambers on matters which have arisen before trial. The court may uphold or reverse the decision of the lower court, or substitute another judgment. It may order a new trial in a proper case.

COURT OF APPEAL (CRIMINAL DIVISION)

The Criminal Appeal Act, 1966 (see now Criminal Appeal Act, 1968), abolished the Court of Criminal Appeal and transferred its jurisdiction to the Court of Appeal. Sect. 1 provides that the Court of Appeal shall consist of two divisions, (a) the civil division which exercises the jurisdiction formerly exercised by the Court of Appeal, and (b) the criminal division.

The work of the criminal division is done by the Lord Chief Justice, the Lords Justices of Appeal and, under Sect. 9 of the Administration of Justice Act, 1970, any judge of the High Court asked to sit by the Lord Chief Justice.

Three of these usually sit to hear a case but sometimes a "full" court of five or more (always an uneven number) will sit if the case is a difficult one. Under Sect. 9 of the Administration of Justice Act, 1970, a court consisting of two judges may exercise certain of the powers of the court, e.g. rehearing applications for bail refused by a single judge. Decision is by a majority and the Criminal Division delivers only one judgment "except where the judge presiding over the court states that, in his opinion, the question is one of law on which it is convenient that separate judgments should be pronounced" (Sect. 2(4)). It was felt that to give separate judgments regularly, as in civil appeals, would lead to uncertainty in the criminal law. The court hears appeals from both the Central Criminal Court and the newly constituted Crown Courts. Appeal lies: (*a*) without leave on any ground involving a question of law; (*b*) by leave of the Court of Appeal, or more rarely on the certificate of the judge of the lower court, on any ground; (*c*) by leave of the Court of Appeal against sentence, unless such sentence is fixed by law, e.g. murder. The court may dismiss the appeal, or allow it and quash the conviction. In addition, the Home Secretary may refer a case to the Court of Appeal (Criminal Division) so that, for example, a sentence might be reviewed. Furthermore, the Attorney-General may under the Criminal Justice Bill, 1972, refer for an opinion a point of law arising from a charge which resulted in an acquittal. (See p. 69.)

The court has power to award a *venire de novo*, i.e. to order a new trial, where the original trial is a nullity. Thus, in *R.* v. *Ishmael*, [1970] Crim. L.R. 399, the accused had been sentenced to life imprisonment having pleaded guilty at his trial to an offence under Sect. 3 of the Malicious Damage Act, 1861 (which was punishable by life imprisonment), thinking that he was charged with an offence under Sect. 7 of the same Act (which was punishable with a maximum of fourteen years' imprisonment). The Court of Appeal decided that he must be tried again.

The Court also has power to order a new trial under the Criminal Appeal Act, 1968. However, this power to order a new trial can only be used in cases where there is fresh and credible evidence and the court considers that it is in the interests of justice to receive it even though it was available and admissible at the trial.

If the court orders a new trial, the appellant can only be retried for the offence for which he was convicted, or any other offence for which he could have been convicted at the original trial. Thus, in a trial for murder the jury may bring in a verdict of manslaughter, and the appellant, if convicted of murder at the original trial, might be retried for manslaughter. He may also be retried for any offence which was charged on the original indictment in respect of which the jury were not required to bring in a verdict. If, on a retrial, the appellant is again convicted, the court which convicts him may pass any sentence authorised by law not being a sentence of greater severity than was passed at the first trial. The Act makes similar provisions for retrial by court-martial.

The Court of Criminal Appeal could vary sentence and might even increase sentence where the appeal was against sentence, thus tending to discourage frivolous appeals.

However, the Criminal Appeal Act, 1968, provides that in no circumstances shall the Court of Appeal be able to impose a sentence on an appellant which is of greater severity, taken as a whole, than that passed at the trial. The Act further provides that the time during which an appellant is in custody pending the determination of his appeal shall, subject to any direction which the Court of Appeal may give to the contrary, be reckoned as part of the term of his sentence. There is no power to give this direction where leave to appeal is granted by the Court of Appeal or the trial judge, but where the appellant renews his application to the full court after it has been rejected by a single judge of the Court of Appeal he is at risk of losing time, though if the court does order that a period of custody shall not count as sentence it must give reasons, e.g. that the appeal is frivolous.

The Criminal Appeal Act, 1968, enables rules of court to be made to provide for the recording of criminal trials on indictment by "mechanical means or otherwise" in addition to the traditional shorthand note. Tape recorders could presumably be used under this provision. The Act further provides that the Court of Appeal must allow an appeal, *inter alia,* if they think the verdict of the jury should be set aside on the ground that under all the circumstances of the case it is unsafe and unsatisfactory, or if they think that there was a material irregularity in the course of the trial.

This is an important provision because the broad picture that had emerged from appeals in the old Court of Criminal Appeal was that the judge's direction, evidence and procedures, and the occasional point of law had received the main attention and not so much the general "merits" of the case. Now the Court of Appeal (Criminal Division) is directed under Sect. 2 of the Criminal Appeal Act, 1968, to allow appeals on decisions by juries which are unsafe or unsatisfactory even though the trial was conducted in a technically correct manner.

Appeal from the Court of Appeal lies to the House of Lords in its judicial capacity under the provisions of the Criminal Appeal Act, 1968, but—

(i) the Court of Appeal must certify that a point of law of general importance is involved; *and*

(ii) either the Court of Appeal or the House of Lords must grant leave to appeal.

If the above conditions are satisfied either the prosecution or the person convicted may appeal to the House of Lords.

THE HOUSE OF LORDS

The House of Lords is not part of the Supreme Court of Judicature and relies for its jurisdiction as a final court of appeal upon the Appellate Jurisdiction Act, 1876 (see p. 16). The court is constituted by the Lord Chancellor and the eleven Lords of Appeal in Ordinary, together with other peers holding or having held high judicial office. The Lords of Appeal in Ordinary (or "Law Lords") are life peers and each of them is appointed by the Queen on the Prime Minister's advice from barristers of at least fifteen years' standing or from puisne judges who have held office for at least two years. Most appointments are made from among the Lords Justices of Appeal who can normally meet the above requirements.

Appeals can be heard during prorogation of Parliament, and, in certain circumstances, during the dissolution of Parliament. The decision is that of the majority, though each member of the court normally delivers a separate judgment. In civil matters the court hears appeals from the Court of Appeal (Civil Division) in England, from the Court of Session in Scotland, and from the Supreme Court of Northern Ireland. There can be no appeal unless the lower court or the Lords gives leave. On the criminal side the House of Lords hears appeals from the Court of Appeal (Criminal Division) and from the Divisional Court of Queen's Bench, but the lower court must certify that a point of law of general public importance is involved, and either the lower court or the House of Lords must give leave.

Each case must be heard by at least three of the following: (i) the Lord Chancellor; (ii) the Law Lords; and (iii) such peers as hold or have held high judicial office, e.g. the present Lord Chief Justice or a former Lord Chancellor. Since the House of Lords has jurisdiction to hear civil appeals from Scotland and Northern Ireland, one or two of the Law Lords are usually former judges or advocates of the Scottish Court of Session and a law lord may be appointed from Northern Ireland. The persons so appointed are not restricted to hearing appeals from Scotland or Northern Ireland. The Lord Chancellor presides if he is present—which he rarely is these days, as his parliamentary functions take an increasing amount of his time. By convention, peers who are not qualified for appointment as law lords do not sit so that the judicial functions of the House of Lords are, in practice, carried out by a very small section of it.

Sects. 12-16 of the Administration of Justice Act, 1969, provide for appeals from the High Court or a Divisional Court *in civil proceedings* to go direct to the House of Lords. All parties must consent and the proposed appeal must raise a question(s) of law of general public importance involving either the construction of a statute or a statutory instrument or an issue on which the court of trial is bound by a previous decision of the Court of Appeal or the House of Lords. The trial judge (or a Divisional Court) must certify that the appeal is one in which the "leapfrog" procedure would be appropriate and application for leave to appeal must then be made to the House of Lords. The pleadings, judgment and certificate are sent to the House of Lords for consideration by a committee of three. If the Lords allow the application there is no appeal to the Court of Appeal but the House of Lords may then hear the full appeal. The period for appeal to the Court of Appeal is suspended during the time in which the committee of three is considering the application so that if it is refused the appellant may seek to appeal to the Court of Appeal. This "leapfrogging" procedure is most likely to be used in revenue appeals, and patent matters where construction of statutes is very often involved.

THE JUDICIAL COMMITTEE OF THE PRIVY COUNCIL

The Privy Council is a lineal descendant of the ancient King's Council, and was originally a sort of cabinet advising the Crown. The Judicial Committee, which is not part of the Supreme Court, is a final court of appeal in civil and criminal matters from the courts of some Commonwealth and Colonial territories, but the changes which have taken place in the Commonwealth have restricted the number of cases coming before it, many Commonwealth countries preferring to hear appeals within their own judicial systems. However, some aspects of this jurisdiction survive. The court is still the final court of appeal from the Channel Islands, the Isle of Man, Protectorates and Trust Territories. There is strictly speaking no right of appeal, but it is customary to petition the Crown for leave to appeal. It is also the final court of appeal from English ecclesiastical courts, and here it is assisted by the Archbishops of Canterbury and York who, as assessors, advise on ecclesiastical matters. In wartime it hears appeals from the Admiralty Court on matters concerning prize. The Judicial Committee is comprised of the Lord Chancellor, the Lords of Appeal in Ordinary, and all Privy Councillors who have held high judicial office in the United Kingdom, together with Commonwealth judges who have been appointed members of the Privy Council. It does not actually decide cases, but advises the Crown which implements the advice by an Order in Council. This advice used to be unanimous, but since March, 1966, dissenting members of the Privy Council who were present at the hearing of the appeal may express their dissent, giving reasons therefor. The Court is not bound by its own previous decisions.

CORONERS' COURTS

These courts are perhaps the oldest English courts still in existence. Their chief function is to inquire into cases of sudden death, or death by violence, or death in suspicious circumstances. They also inquire into deaths in prison and deaths by hanging—which is still a possible punishment, for example, for the crime of treason. The procedure is that of an inquest or inquiry; it is not a trial. The object is to find out the identity of the deceased, the cause of his death, and where the death took place. In cases such as suspected murder or death in prison, the coroner must summon a jury of from seven to eleven persons, and he may accept the verdict of the majority so long as there are not more than two dissentients. The coroner can require a post-mortem, and the attendance of medical and other witnesses who may be examined on oath. If the court finds that a death was the result of murder, manslaughter or infanticide, this does not operate to convict the person said to be responsible, but the coroner is then under a duty to issue a warrant for the arrest of the person concerned who may later be committed for trial in the usual way. Coroner's inquests into unlawful homicide do not take place until the Director of Public Prosecutions or the Prosecuting Solicitor's Department of the police authority has seen the papers and decided not to proceed with a prosecution. Nevertheless, the inquest may reveal further evidence leading to arrest on a coroner's warrant followed by prosecution.

Coroners are appointed by the county council for the county or by the borough council for a borough having a separate commission of the peace. They are barristers, solicitors or medical practitioners having five years' standing in their profession. The appointment is generally part-time and a coroner can be dismissed for inability or misbehaviour.

The coroner also retains jurisdiction in treasure trove. Treasure trove is money, coin, manufactured gold, silver plate or bullion deliberately hidden in the earth or other private place, the owner being unknown. Such property belongs to the Crown. The coroner is concerned to establish whether or not the property was deliberately hidden because, if it was not, but merely lost, the finder, not the Crown, acquires a good title to it, except as against the true owner. However, if the finder makes prompt report of his discovery of treasure trove, the present practice of the Crown is to restore the article to him, or, if it is required for a museum, to pay him its value.

ADMINISTRATIVE JUSTICE

One of the most significant legal developments of this century is the considerable increase in what is called administrative justice. This has arisen from the great extension in the functions of government which has taken place, particularly in the last twenty years. For example, the government pays pensions to various classes of persons, it pays sickness benefit and industrial injuries benefit, family allowances and the like. In order to further schemes of social welfare, it is often necessary for a public body to acquire land by compulsory purchase, and it has also been necessary to establish a system of controlling the rents of dwellings, so that the free operation of the laws of supply and demand might be restricted.

Obviously disputes arise between individuals and the State. A person may claim a benefit which the State suggests he is not entitled to, and landowners are often aggrieved by the compulsory purchase of their land and the compensation offered for it. The settlement of such disputes might have been given over to the ordinary courts of law, but instead, increasing use has been made of an administrative court of one kind or another.

Lord Denning, in *Freedom under the Law*, has said of these tribunals—

> They are a separate set of courts dealing with a separate set of rights and duties. Just as in the old days there were ecclesiastical courts dealing with matrimonial cases and the administration of estates and just as there was the Chancellor dealing with the enforcement and administration of trusts so in our day there are the new tribunals dealing with the rights and duties between man and the State.

It should not be assumed, however, that all administrative tribunals are concerned with disputes between man and the State. Some deal with disputes between individuals. The Rent Assessment Committees set up under rent control legislation are an example of a situation in which the Government has provided a specialised court to deal with certain disputes between landlord and tenant rather than give the particular jurisdiction to the ordinary courts of law.

Furthermore, administrative justice is not always meted out in an independent tribunal. For example, in the field of housing and town and country planning there is in general no right to appeal from a decision of the Government or local authority to an independent tribunal. Instead there is an opportunity to put a case against the decision to a public local enquiry conducted by an inspector—usually an official of the appropriate Ministry. The inspector reports to the Minister, whose decision is final.

In addition, there are some cases in which no machinery is provided for appeal to a tribunal or a local enquiry. For example, there is no appeal against withdrawal of a passport by the Foreign Office.

1. Administrative Tribunals. The *social security tribunals* may be included under this heading. Regarding family allowances and national insurance, claims are first made to a local insurance officer. There is an appeal from his decision to a local Appeal Tribunal, consisting of a lawyer and two laymen. If the tribunal allows the appeal the local insurance officer may appeal to the Chief National Insurance Commissioner, as may the claimant if the tribunal does not allow the appeal. Where the ground of appeal involves a question of law of special difficulty, the Chief Commissioner may refer it to a panel of three Commissioners, and where there are difficult questions of fact the Chief Commissioner may appoint an assessor to assist him. Decisions of the Chief Commissioner are final. The Chief Commissioner and Commissioners are appointed by the Crown from among barristers and solicitors of not less than ten years' standing. Certain questions are decided by the Minister, e.g. whether the contribution for any benefit are satisfied, and the class of insured persons in which a person is to be placed. Regarding industrial injuries, a claim is first made to a local insurance officer, and appeal lies to a Local Appeal Tribunal consisting of a lawyer and two laymen, together with medical men as assessors on occasion. Final appeal is to the Chief Commissioner. Where claims for industrial injuries are mainly of a medical character, the question is decided by a Local Medical Board, with appeal to a Medical Appeal Tribunal. Certain questions are decided by the Minister, e.g. whether a person is in insurable employment, and there is an appeal in this case to the High Court. If a patient is aggrieved about the standard of medical care provided by the professional members of the health service, he can complain to a Service Committee of the Local Executive Council, which reports and recommends action to the full Council. There is an appeal to the Minister. If the Executive Council recommends that the practitioner be removed from the service, there is an appeal to the National Health Service Tribunal; and if the practitioner is dissatisfied, the Minister may hold an inquiry into the case. There are also Industrial Tribunals which were set up to deal, among other things, with disputes arising under the Contracts of Employment Act, 1963, and the Redundancy Payments Act, 1965. *The Special Commissioners of Income Tax* are a group of civil servants who hear appeals against income tax assessments.

Another important tribunal is the *Lands Tribunal* which deals with disputes arising over the valuation and compensation payable on compulsory acquisition of land by public authorities under a variety of statutes, together with appeals from local valuation courts on the value of property for rating purposes. The tribunal has a President, who is either a person who has held high judicial office or a barrister of at least seven years' standing, and other members, who must be solicitors or barristers of like standing, or persons experienced in the valuation of land. The jurisdiction of the tribunal may be exercised by any one or more of its members. Procedure is governed by rules made by the Lord Chancellor, and these are published by Statutory Instrument. The tribunal ordinarily sits in public and travels round the country, and there is a right of audience and legal representation. The decisions of the tribunal are written and reasoned, and appeal lies to the Court of Appeal on points of law. Either party can require the tribunal to state a case for consideration by the Court of Appeal. Legal aid, and by implication legal representation, is available in respect of proceedings in the Lands Tribunal. There are also *Rent Tribunals* set up to assess rents for certain types of *furnished* dwellings, though the County Courts administer the Rent Restriction Acts which govern the rents of *unfurnished* accommodation.

2. **Administrative Enquiries.** As we have seen in some areas of administrative action, e.g. housing and town and country planning, there is in general no right of appeal from the initial decision of the Government or a local authority to an independent tribunal. The relevant Acts of Parliament normally provide for an opportunity to put a case against the decision at a public enquiry conducted before an inspector who is normally a Ministry official. The inspector makes a report to the Ministry concerned and the final decision is made by the Minister himself or a senior civil servant on his behalf. Sometimes the inspector makes the final decision.

As a method of deciding disputes, administrative tribunals and enquiries have advantages. For example, the tribunals and enquiries generally specialise in a particular field, and can thus acquire a detailed knowledge of disputes in that field. The procedure of tribunals is simple and informal, and it is often suggested that this puts those appearing before them at ease so that they are better able to present their case. Certainly administrative justice is cheaper, and, as there are in general no court fees and costs, appellants may take full advantage of the rights of appeal given. Generally speaking, administrative tribunals and enquiries give quick decisions, and appellants are not subjected to the delays which are sometimes met with in ordinary courts of law. Tribunals and enquiries are usually local by nature; they are therefore able to acquaint themselves with local conditions, and can carry out inspections of property and sites where this would assist them in their decision.

The disadvantages attaching to the use of administrative tribunals and enquiries lie in the lack of publicity which attaches to their findings. Until recently reports of ministerial inspectors before whom the parties had appeared were not made public. In some cases, the party whose dispute is being heard does not appear in person before the court, and the public are sometimes excluded from the hearing. Even when the tribunal or enquiry publishes its decision, it does not always give a reasoned judgment, so that it may be impossible to ascertain why it decided as it did. There is the possibility of political interference, since the members of tribunals and inspectors are often appointed by the Minister or are employed by the government; and since one party in a dispute is generally a governmental authority, there may be bias, though there is no evidence that this exists. Often there is no appeal from a tribunal or a Minister after an enquiry but a reason must be given for rejecting an Inspector's finding of facts. (*Coleen Propts Ltd.* v. *Min. of Hsg & L. Govt.*, [1971] 1 All E.R. 1049.)

Some of these difficulties have been overcome by the Tribunals and Inquiries Acts, 1958 and 1966. The 1958 Act was passed to put into effect certain of the recommendations of the Franks Committee on Administrative Tribunals which reported in 1957. The Act sets up a Council of Tribunals, the function of which is to keep under consideration the personnel and working of the tribunals set out in the Act, and to report to the Lord Chancellor on any other matters relevant to administrative tribunals which he may refer to them. The Lord Chancellor nominates the members of the Council, and the dismissal of a member of a tribunal must be approved by him, thus giving the members of the various tribunals increased independence. A right of appeal to the High Court is given on points of law in many cases, even if an existing statute prevents or limits the right, and there are no restrictions whatever on the supervisory jurisdiction of the High Court by means of the prerogative orders, where these are appropriate. An attempt has also been made to institute public hearings, legal representation, and reasoned decisions, and the reports of inspectors who have conducted enquiries are to be made available. The 1966 Act extends the provisions of the 1958 Act by giving the Council on Tribunals wider powers over local enquiries. These Acts, now consolidated in the Tribunals and Inquiries Act, 1971, may answer the criticisms made of tribunals and enquiries if their provisions are fully utilised. Unfortunately, Governments have often set up new tribunals without proper consultation with the Council to see whether an existing tribunal might take on the work. This has resulted in a proliferation of tribunals with a bewildering multiplicity of separate jurisdictions.

DOMESTIC TRIBUNALS

Another area in which persons or groups of persons or other public agencies exercise judicial or quasi-judicial functions over others is to be found in the system of domestic tribunals. These are, in general, disciplinary committees concerned with the regulation of certain professions and trades, some having been set up by statute and others merely by contract between members and the association concerned. Examples of tribunals regulating professions are the General Medical Council, Architects' Registration Council, The Law Society, the General Nursing Council, and the Inns of Court. Discipline over barristers was exercised for many years by the Inns of Court. The Masters of the Bench could disbar a member altogether or suspend him from practice for a time where he had been guilty of misconduct. In 1966 the benchers of the Inns passed a resolution transferring their disciplinary powers to a Senate of the four Inns of Court. The Disciplinary Committee of the Law Society hears complaints against solicitors and has power to strike them off the roll or suspend and fine them. Appeal from the Senate lies to a committee of judges appointed by the Lord Chancellor. Appeal from a decision of the Disciplinary Committee is to a divisional court of the Queen's Bench Division and thence to the Court of Appeal. There are also certain trade organisations which are corporate bodies set up under statute. They represent the producers and distributors of particular commodities, and they control the production and sale of those commodities mainly by fixing prices. They are able to enforce their instructions by levying fines on members or excluding them from the scheme, and are mainly concerned with agriculture. Each Board has a Disciplplinary Committee which has a chairman who is generally a lawyer. The parties are normally entitled to an oral hearing in public, and the Committee may subpoena witnesses and take evidence on oath. One of the most important Boards is the Milk Marketing Board.

The supervisory jurisdiction of the High Court is exercisable over these tribunals by means of remedies similar to those available against administrative tribunals (see below).

JUDICIAL CONTROL OVER INFERIOR COURTS
AND TRIBUNALS

We must now consider what *control* the ordinary courts of law have over administrative action as expressed in the decisions of tribunals and inquiries and what *methods* are used to exercise that control. Before considering these methods of control it should be noted that the Law Commission has produced a Working Paper on Remedies in Administrative Law (No. 40) which favours the substitution of a single "application of review" for injunctions, declaratory judgments and the highly technical prerogative orders which are currently the main means by which decisions of administrative tribunals can be questioned.

Where, as in the case of the Lands Tribunal, the Act of Parliament setting up or controlling the tribunal gives a right of appeal to the ordinary courts of law, the courts are entitled to re-hear the whole case and are not limited to a consideration of the reasons given by the tribunal for its decision. The court can consider the whole matter afresh, and can substitute a new decision for that of the tribunal.

Prerogative Orders. Where no right of appeal is given it may be possible to challenge the decision of an inferior court or tribunal, including those of the new Crown Court (Sect. 10, Courts Act, 1971), by having recourse to the supervisory jurisdiction of the High Court.

This jurisdiction is exercised by the Queen's Bench Division of the High Court by means of the prerogative orders known as *certiorari, prohibition*, and *mandamus*. These orders, which are not available as of right but at the discretion of the court (*R. v. Aston University Senate, ex parte Roffey*, 1969[16b]), were formerly prerogative writs, which a subject might obtain by petitioning the Crown. The Crown's prerogative extended to the granting of these writs in cases thought to be deserving, and the writ was effective to control inferior courts and to correct their mistakes. The Sovereign has no such power today, the control being exercised by the Queen's Bench Division, the former writs being now called orders. (Administration of Justice (Miscellaneous Provisions) Act, 1938.) Before a person can invoke the supervisory jurisdiction of the High Court, he must in general have exhausted all other remedies and rights of appeal.

Certiorari lies to have the record of the proceedings of an inferior court removed into the High Court for review on certain limited grounds set out below. It is not an appeal as to the general merits of the case. The High Court may quash the decision, if it is bad. What is an inferior court for this purpose is a difficult matter for the High Court to decide. Certainly the order of *certiorari* (and *prohibition*) applies only in relation to a body which has a duty to act judicially. *Certiorari* has been held to lie against the Patents Appeal Tribunal, a legal aid committee, a local valuation court, rent tribunals, and the decision of a Minister in a planning matter. The grounds on which *certiorari* lies are as follows—

WANT OR EXCESS OF JURISDICTION. This exists where the inferior court has adjudicated on a matter which it had no power to decide, i.e. where it is acting beyond its powers (*ultra vires*). (*R. v. London County Council, ex parte Entertainments Protection Association*, 1931.)[13]

DENIAL OF NATURAL JUSTICE. The principle is that although an administrative tribunal should not be required to conform to judicial standards, but should be free to work out its own procedures, nevertheless it must, if it is exercising judicial functions, observe the rules of natural justice, i.e. there must be no bias and both sides should be heard. A mere general interest will not constitute bias (such as that of a Minister or local authority in a planning enquiry); there must be some direct connection with the subject matter. (*R. v. Deal Justices, ex parte Curling*, 1881.)[14] A pecuniary interest, however slight, will disqualify (*Dimes v. Grand Junction Canal*, 1852);[15] as also will a personal bias, e.g. where a judge is a relative of a party, or is personally hostile to a party because of events happening before or during the trial. Both sides should be heard, but there is no inherent right to an oral hearing; written evidence may be acceptable. The right to be heard (*audi alteram partem*) implies that *notice* of the hearing or other method of stating one's case must be given together with notice of the case which is to be met. The courts have, on occasions, been more inclined to read into statutory provisions under which a person might be deprived of a right of property or of an office or membership of a professional or social body, a right to be heard in his own defence. The law is, however, not entirely clear and it is difficult to generalise from the decisions made (*R.* v. *Metropolitan Police Commissioners, ex parte Parker*, 1953;[16] *Ridge* v. *Baldwin*, 1964;[16a] *R.* v. *Aston University Senate, ex parte Roffey*, 1969[16b]). The law relating to the right to cross-examine witnesses is also in a somewhat confused state. In *Ceylon University* v. *Fernando*, [1960] 1 All E.R. 631, the Judicial Committee of the Privy Council held that the rules of natural justice did not require that a party should have the right to cross-examine. However, Diplock, L.J., in *Wednesbury Corporation* v. *Ministry of Housing and Local Government* (No. 2), [1965] 3 All E.R. 571, said that a reasonable opportunity to cross-examine was required at an enquiry.

With regard to legal representation, two recent cases—*Pett* v. *The Greyhound Racing Association Ltd.*, 1968,[17] and *Enderby Town Football Club Ltd.* v. *The Football Association Ltd.*, 1971[18]—have laid down some general principles. These principles appear to be as follows—

(*a*) there is no inherent right to legal representation, though if the case involves difficult points of law legal representation should be allowed. A rule forbidding legal representation absolutely and in any circumstances is probably invalid;

(*b*) cases involving difficult points of law should not in general be decided by domestic tribunals. The parties should ask the ordinary courts for a declaratory judgment setting out their rights. The ordinary courts are better-equipped to deal with cases of legal difficulty and to follow the arguments of lawyers.

It is not certain in the present state of the law whether failure to comply with the rules of natural justice makes the decision of a tribunal void or voidable. In *R.* v. *University of Oxford, ex parte Bolchover* (1970), *The Times*, 7th October, and *Glynn* v. *University of Keele* (1970), *The Times*, 18th December, the Court took the view that its decision was voidable and that it had, therefore, a discretion whether to upset it or not. This involves the Court in a decision as to the merits of the course of action taken by the tribunal, which is a matter of opinion not law. The better view is that denial of natural justice should always render the tribunal's decision void, which was the position taken in *Ridge* v. *Baldwin*, 1964.[16a]

ERROR OF LAW ON THE FACE OF THE RECORD

Certiorari lies to quash a decision the record of which discloses an error of law. According to Lord Denning in *R.* v. *Northumberland Compensation*

Appeal Tribunal ex parte Shaw, [1952] 1 All E.R. 122, the record consists of "the document which initiates the proceedings, the pleadings (if any), and the adjudication, but not the evidence or the reasons unless the tribunal chooses to incorporate them." As we have seen, the Tribunals and Inquiries Act, 1971, requires reasoned decisions in cases coming before tribunals and inquiries so that there should now normally be a record giving reasons which will assist the High Court in exercising its supervisory jurisdiction. In addition, if a reasoned decision is required by the 1971 Act the order of *mandamus* lies to compel the tribunal or inquiry to give one.

Certiorari does not lie where the decision is executive or administrative, even in respect of acts which have some analogy to the judicial. (*R.* v. *Metropolitan Police Commissioners, ex parte Parker*, 1953.)[16] Applications for *certiorari* and *prohibition* are often brought together, e.g. to quash a decision already made by a tribunal, and to prevent it from continuing to exceed or abuse its jurisdiction.

Prohibition lies to prevent an inferior tribunal from exceeding its jurisdiction, or infringing the rules of natural justice. It is governed by similar principles to *certiorari*, except that is does not lie when once a final decision has been given (*certiorari* is then the appropriate order). The object of prohibition is to prevent an inferior tribunal from hearing and deciding a matter which is beyond its jurisdiction. Prohibition and *certiorari* are available against the Crown but not against private persons or bodies, e.g. committees of clubs.

The Order of Mandamus may be issued to any person or body (not necessarily an inferior court, since it might be issued to a local authority). It commands him or them to carry out some public duty. It might be used to compel an administrative tribunal to hear an appeal which it is refusing to hear, or to compel a local authority to carry out a duty lying upon it, e.g. to produce its accounts for inspection by a ratepayer. (*R.* v. *Bedwellty U.D.C.*, [1943] 1 K.B. 333.) *Mandamus* lies to compel the exercise of a duty and of a discretionary power, though in the case of the latter not in a particular way. It is not available against the Crown itself; but it may issue against Ministers or other Crown servants to enforce a personal statutory duty. Thus in *Padfield* v. *Minister of Agriculture, Fisheries and Food*, [1968] 1 All E.R. 694, the House of Lords decided that an order of *mandamus* should issue to the Minister of Agriculture requiring him to refer a complaint by milk producers against the working of a Milk Marketing Board scheme to a committee of investigation in the exercise of a discretionary power conferred on him by Sect. 19 of the Agricultural Marketing Act, 1958.

Habeas corpus. It has been mentioned that *prohibition, mandamus* and *certiorari* were once prerogative writs and that they are now referred to as prerogative orders. It is convenient to mention here one important prerogative writ which remains—that of *habeas corpus*. The writ is designed to provide a person, who is kept in confinement without legal justification, with a means of obtaining his release. If he can show a *prima facie* case that he might be unlawfully detained, he would usually apply to a Divisional Court of the Queen's Bench Division, but application may be made to any judge of the High Court during vacation time. The person detained applies, through counsel, for the writ to be issued, the facts alleging unlawful detention being set out on an affidavit supporting the application. It was once thought that application could be made successively to every judge of the High Court, and, except in a criminal matter, by way of appeal to the Court of Appeal and the House of Lords; but, in *Re Hastings*, [1959] 3 All E.R. 221, it was held that there was no such right.

The position has been clarified by the Administration of Justice Act, 1960. Under the provisions of the Act it appears that, where the application is in respect of a criminal cause or matter, or is in respect of a detainee under the Mental Health Act, 1959, Part 5, a single judge may order release, and there is no appeal whatever from his decision. A single judge cannot refuse an order for release, but must refer the matter to a Divisional Court of Queen's Bench which has power to refuse such an order. In respect of civil applications, e.g. detention of a wife by her husband, or detention of a child in a home or like institution against its parents' wishes, application may be made to a single judge or to a Divisional Court of Queen's Bench; but a single judge still has power to grant or refuse release. It is still possible to appeal in both civil and criminal matters against release and refusal to release, except in the circumstances outlined above. In criminal cases, appeal lies from the Divisional Court of Queen's Bench to the House of Lords; and in civil cases, appeal lies from a judge or the Divisional Court to the Court of Appeal (Civil Division), and thence to the House of Lords, with leave of the Court of Appeal (Civil Division) or the House of Lords.

Where a civil or criminal application for *habeas corpus* has been made, no further application shall be made in respect of the same person, unless there is fresh evidence. The right given by the Habeas Corpus Act, 1679, to apply for *habeas corpus* to the Lord Chancellor is repealed.

Injunction and Declaratory Judgment. The High Court can also exercise control over the decisions of inferior tribunals by granting, at its discretion, an injunction to prevent, for example, the implementation of a decision made by an inferior tribunal which does not observe the rules of natural justice. The remedy is not available against the Crown. Defiance of an injunction amounts to contempt of court. A *declaratory judgment* may be asked for by a person aggrieved by the decision of an inferior tribunal so that the High Court can state the legal position of the parties. Defiance of a declaratory judgment is not a contempt of court but the parties usually observe it. It is particularly useful in respect of complaints against the Crown.

The Parliamentary Commissioner. A further check on abuse of power by government departments was created by the appointment of the Parliamentary Commissioner (or "Ombudsman") under the provisions of the Parliamentary Commissioner Act, 1967. The Commissioner is appointed by the Crown and has the same security of tenure as a judge of the Supreme Court. He is also a member of the Council on Tribunals. His function is to investigate complaints relating to the exercise of administrative functions. However, investigation is made only at the request of a Member of Parliament and a citizen who wishes to have a complaint investigated must first bring it to the notice of an M.P.

Unfortunately, the jurisdiction of the Ombudsman is limited and does not include, for example, local government and the police. Furthermore he is in many cases limited to a consideration of the *administrative procedures* followed and is powerless to act if the correct procedure has been followed even though the decision is bad. Nevertheless, in the period April, 1967, to May, 1970, 3,110 complaints were referred to him, most of them involving Government departments in constant contact with the public. Over £100,000 has been paid out by Government departments in financial remedies to claimants since the office of Parliamentary Commissioner was established in April, 1967, and proposals have recently been made to extend the ombudsman system to local government and the National Health Service.

Under the Act of 1967 the Parliamentary Commissioner is given discretion whether to investigate a complaint or not. In consequence, the order of *mandamus* will not issue to him since he has no duty to hear a complaint (*re Fletcher's Application*, [1970] 2 All E.R. 527).

LABOUR COURTS

A system of labour courts is established by the Industrial Relations Act, 1971. These courts are intended to have an exclusive jurisdiction in civil cases arising from industrial disputes. Individual claims in respect of, for example, redundancy or unfair dismissal will normally be dealt with by Industrial Tribunals consisting of a lawyer, a trade unionist and an employer, and assisted if necessary by Conciliation Officers of the Department of Employment. If, however, the case is expected to be long or complex or contains important issues it may be transferred from an Industrial Tribunal to the National Industrial Relations Court. The N.I.R.C. consists of a President and other members of the higher judiciary in England and Scotland, and "lay" members with relevant industrial relations experience. It is able to sit in more than one division and in various parts of the country. It deals with collective issues such as legally enforceable collective agreements and sometimes with cases involving individuals as outlined above. The Commission on Industrial Relations, the Chairman and members of which are appointed by the Secretary of State, is available to the N.I.R.C. as a kind of investigating agent in deciding matters such as union recognition in respect of negotiations with an employer. In addition, the Industrial Arbitration Board consisting of a lawyer, as chairman, with a lay panel is available to receive references authorised by the N.I.R.C. Appeal from Industrial Tribunals is to the N.I.R.C. and thence to the Court of Appeal and the House of Lords.

The Registrar of Trade Unions and Employers' Associations also has certain powers in relation to union rules and their observance and appeal from him is to the N.I.R.C.

JURIES IN CRIMINAL AND CIVIL CASES

Persons between the ages of twenty-one and sixty may be called for jury service, provided that they own freehold property of an annual value of £10, or leaseholds, for not less than twenty-one years, of an annual value of £20; or if they are householders, residing in property of an annual value of £30 in the Metropolitan district, and £20 elsewhere. Responsibility for summoning jurors has been distributed between sheriffs and clerks of the peace. Under the Courts Act, 1971, Sect. 3, it becomes the responsibility of the Lord Chancellor, though no doubt the courts administration at each centre will act as summoning officer. The jury list is based on the Parliamentary Electoral Roll. Certain persons are exempt from jury service, e.g. peers, Members of Parliament, clergymen, barristers, solicitors and their managing clerks, medical practitioners, and members of H.M. Forces. In addition, certain persons such as those who hold judicial office, officers of the Court, members of the legal profession and police officers may claim exemption for a further ten years *after* ceasing to hold such office or employment. (Criminal Justice Act, 1967, Sect. 16.) Furthermore, certain persons such as aliens, persons attainted of treason, persons of unsound mind and persons who are deaf or blind are disqualified. In addition, Sect. 34 of the Courts Act, 1971, makes a change by providing that a person summoned for jury service may be excused for good reasons whether he is in one of the special classes outlined above or not. Sect. 37 of the same Act now provides for exemptions to be granted administratively for previous jury service. Before, only the trial judge could grant exemption. By Sect. 14 of the Criminal Justice Act, 1967, persons who have been sentenced to imprisonment for life or to a term of five years of more and persons who have within the preceding ten years been sentenced to a term of three months imprisonment or more are also disqualified. However, Sect. 15 of the Criminal Justice Act, 1967, provides that the verdict of a jury in criminal and other proceedings is not void *by reason only* that a member of the jury is disqualified from serving on the jury in those proceedings. Jurors are paid travelling and subsistence allowances and are compensated for loss of earnings and other expenses.

Criminal Jury. There were two juries in criminal cases; the grand jury considered the bill of indictment and, if satisfied that a *prima facie* case had been made out against the accused, certified it as a "true bill." The jury which tried the accused was known as the petty jury. The grand jury was abolished by the Criminal Justice Act, 1948. A preliminary hearing before a magistrate now takes the place of the hearing before the grand jury. All indictable offences are triable before a petty jury, though some may be tried summarily by the magistrates if the accused consents. In certain offences punishable on summary conviction by the magistrates, the accused may claim to be tried by jury before the recently constituted Crown Court set up under the Courts Act, 1971. There is no jury trial in the case of petty offences. In fact, the majority of indictable offences are tried summarily; even where the accused is sent for trial by jury, he often pleads guilty so that only a small percentage of indictable offences are so tried.

Certain advantages are claimed for jury trial in criminal matters. Some take the view that the verdict of a jury is more acceptable to the public than the verdict of a judge, and certainly the jury system gives ordinary persons a part to play in the administration of justice. It is perhaps better that laymen and women should decide matters of fact and the credibility of witnesses. The jury system also tends to clarify the law, in that the judge has to explain the important points arising at the trial in clear and simple terms, in order that the jury may arrive at a reasonable verdict. On the other hand, juries may be too easily swayed by experienced counsel and the method of selection sometimes produces a jury which is not as competent as it might be in weighing the evidence and following the arguments presented. It has been suggested that trial by (say) three judges would be better, particularly where difficult issues are involved.

Majority Verdicts. The Criminal Justice Act, 1967, introduced majority verdicts of juries in criminal proceedings. Sect. 13 provides that the verdict of a jury in criminal proceedings need not be unanimous if—

 (*a*) in a case where there are not less than *eleven* jurors, *ten* of them agree on the verdict; and
 (*b*) in a case where there are *ten* jurors, *nine* of them agree on the verdict.

A court must not accept a majority verdict of guilty unless the foreman of the jury has stated in open court the number of jurors who respectively agreed to and dissented from the verdict. No such statement is required if the verdict is one of not guilty so that it will not be known that a verdict of not guilty was by a majority. Furthermore, a court must not accept a majority verdict unless it appears to the court that the jury have had not less than two hours for deliberation or such longer period as the court thinks reasonable, having regard to the nature and complexity of the case. Nevertheless, the judge must encourage the jury in the first instance to try to arrive at a unanimous decision. He cannot accept a majority verdict after less than two hours' deliberation and if the jury is not unanimous after two hours he should send them back, at least once more, to try to reach unanimity. If they still cannot he should send them back to see if they can reach a decision by the necessary majority, having directed them on the law relating to majority verdicts. When the jury returns to the Court room the judge will ask whether the required majority has agreed on a verdict. If they have, the verdict is accepted *provided*, according to a Practice Direction made on 11th May,

1970, that at least two hours *and ten minutes* have elapsed between the time at which the last juror left the jury box to go to the jury room and the time when the judge asked whether the jury had reached a verdict by the required majority. Before the judge asks whether the jury has reached a majority verdict the senior officer of the court present must announce the deliberation time which the jury has had. The extra ten minutes was added in order to reduce the number of appeals made to the Court of Appeal on the ground that majority verdicts had been accepted although the deliberation time had been less than two hours, as for example, where the jury had returned to put a question to the Court during the deliberation period. The majority provision is probably the most controversial one in the whole of the Criminal Justice Act because the principle of the unanimous decision was an old and much respected feature of English law. The main reason for the change was the growing problem of deliberate corruption or intimidation of jurors to secure an aquittal. The majority of ten to two was chosen because it was felt that it would be difficult to find more than one or two who were susceptible to bribery or intimidation, particularly in view of the provisions of Sect. 14 which excludes those with criminal records from jury service.

Alternative Verdicts. The common law as re-stated by Sect. 6(3) and (4) of the Criminal Law Act, 1967, provides for alternative verdicts, which means that a jury can convict an accused of an offence other than the one with which he is charged. Although the wording of Sect. 6 appears wider than the common law rule, subsequent cases seem to indicate that a jury cannot convict of an offence different in *character* from the offence charged. The power is limited to a conviction for an offence involving *the same criminal act* but with a lesser degree of aggravation, e.g. of common assault on a charge of unlawful wounding.

The number of jurors will normally be twelve, unless the number has been reduced in accordance with Sect. 1 of the Criminal Justice Act, 1965. The section provides for the continuation of criminal trials where a juror dies or is discharged by the court whether through illness or any other reason. If the number of members of the jury is not reduced below nine, the trial may proceed and a verdict may be given accordingly. However, on a trial for murder or for any offence punishable with death, e.g. treason, this rule only applies if assent in writing is given by or on behalf of both the prosecution and the accused, or each of the accused if there are more than one. Moreover, the court has discretion in any criminal trial to discharge the jury if it sees fit to do so when its numbers are depleted. If a trial has continued under the Act of 1965 with nine jurors, Sect. 13 of the Act of 1967 does not apply and the verdict must be unanimous.

Civil Jury. The Administration of Justice (Miscellaneous Provisions) Act, 1933, gives the court discretion with regard to juries in civil cases, though a jury must be empanelled at the request of the defendant where fraud is alleged, or at the request of either party in cases of libel, slander, malicious prosecution, and false imprisonment. If the trial is likely to involve long and detailed examination of documents or accounts, or scientific evidence, the court has the discretion to refuse a jury trial even in these cases. The percentage of jury trials in civil actions is very small.

Juries are not used in Admiralty cases but there is power to summon a jury in the Chancery Division. This power is, in practice, neglected. Juries are sometimes applied for in defended divorce petitions, and where a will is contested.

A civil jury consists of twelve persons, though the parties may, in a particular case, agree to proceed with less. There is a right to ask for a jury of eight persons in a county court, where the case is an appropriate one. These rights are rarely exercised. In addition, a coroner must summon a jury of seven to eleven persons in some cases and may accept the verdict of the majority if the dissentients are not more than two. Where there is no jury, the judge determines the facts as well as the law.

Apart from a coroner's jury a civil jury had formerly to be unanimous. However, under the Courts Act, 1971, Sect. 39, the verdict of a jury in civil proceedings in the High Court need not be unanimous if—

(*a*) where there are not less than eleven jurors ten of them agree on the verdict; and

(*b*) where there are ten jurors nine of them agree on the verdict.

The verdict of a complete jury of eight persons in a county court need not be unanimous if seven of them agree on the verdict. The two hours deliberation necessary for a jury before a majority verdict is permissible is not required for a civil jury. It is enough if it appears to the court that the jury had such period of time for deliberation as the court thinks reasonable having regard to the nature and complexity of the case. Majority verdicts by consent of the parties continues to be possible in civil cases *with the consent of both of the parties*.

Reform. Radical reforms of the present system of jury service are now under consideration. These reforms are based upon the recommendations of the Committee on Jury Service which sat between 1963 and 1965 under the chairmanship of Lord Morris. The reforms are designed to change the composition of the average jury which, as Lord Devlin once said, is "predominantly male, middle-aged, middle-minded and middle-class."

The reforms would allow all citizens who are qualified to vote in parliamentary elections to serve on a jury as long as they were not younger than 18 or older than 65. They would have to have lived continuously in the United Kingdom for five years, the period commencing before the age of 16, and be able to read, write and understand English. The latter provision would prevent immigrants who might understand little or no English from being called upon, together with other jurymen, to determine the guilt or otherwise of an accused. Under the existing property provisions this can happen.

THE LEGAL PROFESSION

The legal profession in England has two branches. There are barristers and solicitors. Each profession has developed independently, and each has its own controlling body. No person may practise in both capacities at the same time.

Barristers. Barristers conduct cases in court, and generally draft the pleadings which outline the manner in which the case is to be conducted. They also give opinions on difficult legal problems. Barristers have an exclusive right to be heard in the House of Lords, the Judicial Committee of the Privy Council, the Court of Appeal, the three divisions of the High Court. They have a concurrent right with solicitors to appear in the Crown Court including the Central Criminal Court (but see p. 63) and also in county courts and in magistrates' courts.

Call to the English Bar is the prerogative of the four Inns of Court—Lincoln's Inn, Gray's Inn, the Inner Temple and the Middle Temple. A candidate must apply to become a student at one of the Inns and it is then necessary for him to keep law terms by dining in hall the requisite number of times. There are four law terms in a year.

Before call the candidate must pass the Bar examinations, and if he has passed the Bar Final Examination, a student may present himself for call to the Bar after keeping the requisite number of terms. This involves attending at his Inn and dining on a specified number of occasions for three years. The Inns of Court are unincorporated societies governed by Masters of the Bench, who are judges or senior barristers, and Call to the Bar is by the Benchers who could also disbar a barrister for misconduct. In 1966 disciplinary powers were transferred to a Senate of the four Inns of Court and are now exercised by a Disciplinary Committee. Appeal is to a domestic tribunal consisting of the Lord Chancellor and judges of the High Court.

The Council of Legal Education is responsible for the education and examination of students, and holds lectures which are conducted by leading academic and practising lawyers. There is no requirement as to articles but if a barrister intends to practise in England or Wales he will have to become, for a period of twelve months, the pupil of a senior barrister, often referred to as a pupil master, or attend an approved Practical Training Course.

After call, a barrister intending to practise will join a circuit and he will then practise within that circuit though he may take cases on others. At one time, these circuits broadly followed the Assize circuits of England and Wales. Now that the Courts Act, 1971, is in force the link is with the new High Court and Crown Court Centres. In addition, since these new centres will operate as continuous or semi-continuous courts, barristers will tend to practise in one centre only. There will be no Assize Court judges progressing from one town to another and the circuit organisation of barristers will tend to disappear in favour of a stronger local organisation based upon one High Court and Crown Court Centre. There are no partnerships at the Bar, and one barrister cannot employ another, but it is usual for counsel to group together in chambers and employ a clerk who is responsible for the administration of the chambers, fees, appointments and instructions.

Experienced barristers may apply to the Lord Chancellor to "take silk," i.e. to become Queen's Counsel, and the Lord Chancellor recommends suitable applicants to the Queen who makes the appointment. After appointment as Queen's Counsel a barrister will not in general appear without a junior, i.e. another barrister who is not a Q.C., and his practise henceforth tends to be restricted to the more important cases requiring two counsel. The judges are chosen from eminent members of the Bar, who need not be Queen's Counsel.

A barrister will not normally deal directly with a client but must be briefed by a solicitor, and he cannot sue for his fees, though a solicitor who fails to pay over to counsel fees received from a client is liable to disciplinary action. A barrister is not liable to his client for professional negligence in regard to his conduct and management of litigation whether in court or at an earlier stage. However, this immunity may not extend to work of a non-litigious nature, though the matter is not decided. (*Rondel* v. *Worsley*, 1967.)[19]

In matters of etiquette, counsel is under an obligatory duty to conduct his case in a proper manner. He must inform the court of all the relevant statutes and precedents, and, where a legal authority is against his argument, he must not suppress it, though he may attempt to distinguish or criticise it. He must also ensure that his client has a fair hearing. If a prosecuting counsel in a criminal case is aware of facts which support the case for the accused, or lessen the gravity of the offence, he must state them. Counsel may not plead guilty for a client, but may persuade him to do so if it is in the client's interest. The General Council of the Bar is a body elected from members of the profession, and is concerned with general welfare, etiquette and professional conduct, but has no disciplinary powers.

Solicitors. The profession of solicitor is derived from three former branches of the legal profession. The early stages of litigation in the King's Bench and Common Pleas was conducted by *attorneys*; in the Court of Chancery by *solicitors* and in the Ecclesiastical Courts and Admiralty by *proctors*. These three branches fused in 1831 to form the Law Society. Today a solicitor is in some respects a business man who advises his clients on legal, financial and other matters. His work is not all of a legal nature, but most of it requires legal training. Much of the work of a solicitor is concerned with property. He investigates title to land, prepares contracts of sale, conveyances and wills, and often acts as executor and trustee. He also assists promoters in company formation. Some solicitors are commissioners for oaths and any person who is required to sign a document and swear as to the truth of the statements in it may go to a solicitor who is also a commissioner for oaths so that the latter can declare that he has witnessed the taking of the oath. Some documents, particularly those required for use abroad such as dishonoured bills of exchange (see p. 252), must be sworn before a solicitor who is also a "notary public."

The distinction between solicitors and barristers is quite marked in the matter of litigation. The solicitor's function is to prepare the case, ascertain the facts, and arrange for the presence of the necessary witnesses and any documents which may be required. He also conducts any disputes over costs which have been awarded after judgment. Regarding advocacy, a solicitor has a right to be heard in county courts and magistrates' courts. He may also be heard in bankruptcy matters in the High Court and Divisional Court, and in interlocutory proceedings in the House of Lords, the Court of Appeal and the High Court. The Lord Chancellor may under Sect. 12 of the Courts Act, 1971, issue directions regarding the right of audience of solicitors in the Crown Court. Under directions recently made a solicitor may appear in, conduct, defend and address the Court in criminal or civil appeals or committals where he or his partner or employee appeared for the defendant in the magistrates' court. As we have seen, it will also be possible under the Courts Act, 1971, for solicitors to be eligible for appointment to the circuit bench.

A candidate must serve articles for the requisite period of time with a solicitor of at least five years' standing, and must then pass the examinations of The Law Society. He may then apply to The Law Society for admission as a solicitor, and his admission must be approved by the Master of the Rolls, since a solicitor is an officer of the court. He may then practise alone, or as a member of a partnership, though every practising solicitor must take out an annual practising certificate. A number of solicitors are employed in local and central government departments and by commercial firms.

Sect. 82 of the Criminal Justice Act, 1967, gives the Lord Chancellor power to set up a tribunal to hear complaints against barristers and solicitors, and if necessary exclude from acting for legally assisted persons, either permanently or temporarily, any barrister or solicitor against whom a complaint is proved.

Legal Executives. The Institute of Legal Executives which was established in 1963 gives professional status to the unadmitted staff employed in solicitors' offices. Senior unadmitted employees are known as managing clerks and they frequently carry heavy responsibilities in connection with the business of the firm. There are two examinations, the first leads to Associate membership of the Institute and the second, which is of higher standard, leads to Fellowship.

Reform. It has often been suggested that members of the public would be able to obtain cheaper legal services if the two branches of the profession were to merge. This is to some extent true in that only one person would be employed throughout the case doing both the pre-trial work and acting as advocate in court.

However, there are disadvantages involved in an amalgamation some of which are as follows—

(*a*) *Independence.* Since a barrister is not involved to a great extent or at all with the client in pre-trial work, he is better able to treat the case when it gets to court with detachment as regards, for example, the personality and social background of the client. He sees the case as a legal problem requiring solution and this attitude of detachment is regarded by many as necessary if the Court is to reach sound the unemotional decisions.

(*b*) *Availability.* At the present time the services of a barrister who is an expert in a particular branch of law are available to the clients of all solicitors, subject only to the ability to pay. Fusion of the profession would be likely to lead to larger firms of lawyers, some specialising in pre-trial work, and some in advocacy and opinions in special areas. The services of these specialists would unfortunately tend to be available, in the main, to clients of the particular firm and not to others.

(*c*) *Relationship of Bench and Bar.* Since the judiciary is for the most part selected from members of the Bar a special relationship of trust exists between judge and advocate. This can and does result in the speeding up of trials since the judge can accept more readily the method of dealing with the case which the advocates on both sides have agreed upon. This may mean, for example, that certain witnesses are not heard on the ground that the point which their evidence would make is accepted by both sides.

Some fusion of the education and training of the two branches of the profession is likely as a result of the Report of the Committee on Legal Education—the Ormerod Report (Cmnd. 4595). The report recommends that law teaching for the legal profession should be integrated as far as possible, particularly at the early stages of education and training. If the report is accepted, those seeking to qualify as solicitors or barristers will be taught together for a large part of the necessary period of study in either universities or poyltechnics. The report requires acceptance by the Bar Council and the Law Society before it can be implemented.

LEGAL AID AND ADVICE

Criminal Cases. Part IV of the Criminal Justice Act, 1967, consolidates and amends the law relating to legal aid in criminal proceedings which was formerly contained in a number of enactments. This part of the Act of 1967 results from the recommendations of a Departmental Committee under the Chairmanship of Mr. Justice Widgery which was set up in 1964 and reported in 1966.

The most important change is in the financial basis upon which legal aid may be granted. Under the previous system a person who was unable to pay the whole cost of legal representation was granted legal aid free of charge. Now the courts have power to require a legally aided person to make a contribution to the costs according to his means, as is the case in the civil legal aid scheme. Provision is made for the reference of cases to the Supplementary Benefits Commission for inquiry as to means.

The Act of 1967 also introduces more effective arrangements for providing those persons convicted on indictment with legal advice regarding appeals.

The Act covers most criminal proceedings ranging from those in magistrates' courts to appeals to the House of Lords and appeals from courts-martial. However, appeals to the Divisional Court of Queen's Bench and from that Court to the House of Lords are dealt with under the civil legal aid scheme.

The Act also provides that applicants for legal aid may be required to make a payment on account of any contribution which may be ordered at the end of the case.

There is also the custom of "Dock Briefs" under which a prisoner can, for a small fee ($£2.22\frac{1}{2}$p), choose any counsel who is robed and present in Court to defend him. Counsel so chosen is bound to defend the prisoner for that fee.

Civil Cases. The Legal Aid and Advice Acts, 1949, 1960 and 1964, provide for a system of legal aid and advice. The system is administered by The Law Society through area committees consisting of solicitors and barristers. These committees are under the general control of the Lord Chancellor. The scheme is financed by the Treasury through the Legal Aid Fund. There is a means test which the applicant for legal aid must undergo, and this is conducted by the Supplementary Benefits Commission. Eligibility for legal aid depends upon the applicant's disposable income and his capital. An applicant may be required to make some contribution to his own costs and, where his action or defence fails, he may also be required to make a contribution towards his opponent's costs, depending upon what the court thinks it is reasonable for him to pay.

The Legal Aid Committee must be satisfied that the applicant's claim or defence is a reasonable one.

Oral Legal Advice. There is also provision for oral legal advice to be given by solicitors, even though no action is proposed. There are two systems for obtaining such legal advice—

(*a*) The applicant may subject himself to a means test, and if he qualifies for aid, he will pay the solicitor $12\frac{1}{2}$p. as a fee which will entitle him to an interview of up to ninety minutes. The solicitor receives $£1$ per half-hour from the legal aid funds.

(*b*) Under what is called the Voluntary Legal Aid Scheme introduced by the Council of the Law Society a person may ask a solicitor to give him legal advice without submitting to a means test. In this case, the person seeking advice must pay the solicitor a fee of £1 for every thirty minutes of the interview. A solicitor approached under this scheme can refuse to give advice, and is not obliged to give reasons for his refusal.

Reform. There has been much criticism of the present system of legal aid and advice. In the first place it is felt that there is an unmet need for legal assistance, particularly in poor urban areas. Secondly there is disquiet with regard to the erratic way in which legal aid is granted and new litigation, i.e. the Legal Advice and Assistance Bill is now before Parliament. The Bill enables £25 worth of advice to be given to those qualifying without prior consultation. If advice and assistance is likely to cost more than £25 approval from "the appropriate author-ity," i.e. a committee to be set up by regulations, is required. Those eligible to receive free or subsidised advice are persons with a disposable income not exceeding £20 per week and disposable capital not exceed-ing £125. Free advice will be given to those whose disposable income does not exceed £11; others will contribute. The Bill excludes assist-ance to those appearing before tribunals except to negotiate a settlement but includes a "dock brief" system for solicitors in magistrates' courts. An interesting project which already exists is the North Kensington Neighbourhood Law Centres which was opened in 1970. The Centre, which is financed by charities and income from the Legal Aid Fund, is open from 9.30 a.m. to 9.00 p.m. on week-days and until 5.00 p.m. on Saturdays. The Centre sees quite a large number of clients about half of which want legal advice only. The main problems of these clients are criminal matters, landlord and tenant, social security, em-ployment, hire-purchase, family, children and matrimonial disputes and difficulties.

SOME IMPORTANT JUDICIAL OFFICERS

The Lord Chancellor is the Speaker of the House of Lords and the ultimate head of the Judiciary in that he is the chief judge in the coun-try, and controls the administration of the courts of law. He is also the Chairman of the Judicial Committee of the Privy Council. He advises the Crown on the appointment of High Court Judges, and appoints county court Judges without reference to the Crown. He is responsible for the appointment of Justices of the Peace, and advises on the appointment of Recorders, Stipendiary Magistrates and Metropolitan Police Magistrates. He is the custodian of the Great Seal, which represents the signature of the Crown in its corporate capacity, and all writs of summons in the High Court are witnessed in his name. Unlike the Speaker of the House of Commons, he may take part in debates and may vote in all divisions, but has no casting vote. The office is political, and the holder is a Cabinet Minister. His position serves to support the contention that there is no separation of judicial, legislative and executive powers in the British Constitution.

The Attorney-General and the Solicitor-General are known as the Law Officers. The appointments are political and change with the Government. As a rule the Law Officers are not members of the Cabinet.

THE ATTORNEY-GENERAL is appointed by Letters Patent under the Great Seal, and is usually a member of the House of Commons. He represents the Crown in civil matters and prosecutes in important criminal cases. He is the Head of the English Bar, and points of professional etiquette are referred to him. He also advises government departments on legal matters, and advises the court on matters of parliamentary privilege. He can institute litigation on behalf of the public, e.g. to stop a public nuisance and to enforce or regulate public charitable trusts.

THE SOLICITOR-GENERAL is the subordinate of the Attorney-General, and sometimes gives a joint opinion with him when asked by government departments. In spite of his title he is a barrister, and he need not, strictly speaking, be in the House of Commons. His duties are similar to those of the Attorney-General and he is in many ways his deputy. Both Law Officers are precluded from private practice. The Law Officers Act, 1944, provides that any functions authorised or required to be discharged by the Attorney-General may be discharged by the Solicitor-General, if the office of Attorney-General is vacant, or if the Attorney-General is unable to act because of absence or illness, or where the Attorney-General authorises the Solicitor-General to act in any particular matter.

Masters. Many matters arise for decision between the time of issue of the writ and the trial of the action, e.g. what documents must be shown by one side to the other; what time should be allowed for putting in statements of claim and defences; what is the most convenient and proper place for the trial to be held. These will usually be dealt with by a master, but sometimes by a judge.

QUEEN'S BENCH MASTERS are salaried officials of the High Court appointed from among barristers of not less than ten years' standing. They have some judicial functions and deal with matters leading to the trial of cases in the Queen's Bench Division.

CHANCERY MASTERS are salaried officials of the High Court appointed from among solicitors of not less than ten years' standing. They also have certain judicial functions and deal with matters leading to the trial of cases in the Chancery Division.

DISTRICT REGISTRARS. In most important provincial towns there is a District Registry under the supervision of a District Registrar, who performs the same functions as a master in London.

TAXING MASTERS are salaried officials of the Supreme Court concerned with the levying of costs. They fix the amount which one party to an action is directed to pay to the other party by way of costs. They are solicitors of at least ten years' standing, and are appointed by the Lord Chancellor with the agreement of the Treasury.

Treasury Counsel. Treasury Counsel are barristers who have been nominated by the Attorney-General to receive briefs from the Director of Public Prosecutions in respect of prosecutions at the Central Criminal Court.

The Director of Public Prosecutions. The office of Director of Public Prosecutions was created by the Prosecution of Offences Act, 1879. He is appointed by the Home Secretary from among barristers or solicitors of not less than ten years' standing but acts under the superintendence of the Attorney-General. He must prosecute through his own staff or Treasury Counsel in those cases where the offence is punishable by death, in manslaughter, and where a statute requires him to conduct or consent to a prosecution.

He must give advice, either on his own initiative, or when requested to do so, to clerks, to justices, chief officers of police, or other persons concerned in criminal proceedings, and he may intervene at any time in proceedings which have actually begun, and take over the prosecution from either the police or a private prosecutor where the case is of special importance or difficulty. He also acts in cases where the public interest requires a prosecution, and where a private individual fails to prosecute or where there are special difficulties in the way. Unless there is a representative of a government department or a private prosecutor acting, he appears for the Crown on appeals to the Court of Appeal.

The Official Referee. The Official Referee is a salaried official of the High Court appointed from among barristers of not less than ten years' standing. Cases which involve detailed examination of books and documents, e.g. accounts, are referred to him for trial. Under Schedule 2 of the Courts Act, 1971, the Official Referee becomes a Circuit Judge.

The Official Solicitor. The Official Solicitor is an officer of the Supreme Court who acts in litigation to protect the interests of persons suffering under mental disability. He is also concerned to protect the interests of children in adoption matters and those of persons imprisoned for contempt of court.

Circuit Administrators. The Royal Commission on Assizes and Quarter Sessions (Beeching Commission) recommended the appointment of a Circuit administrator in each of the six Circuits into which England and Wales was divided. The posts are open to persons aged from 45 to 55. A legal qualification is not essential, but if the applicant is legally qualified he must be a barrister or solicitor of at least 10 years' standing during which time he or she must have been in practice or had substantial experience in the courts. Their function is to a large extent managerial and they take over from Clerks of Assize, Clerks of the Peace, and other officers of the numerous different courts who previously had to try to provide the public and the legal profession with a court service. There will now be one person at each High Court and Crown Court Centre to whom all involved can turn in respect of administrative problems.

The first task of the Circuit administrators will be to plan the changes in the legal system recommended by the Royal Commission and, insofar as legislation is required, provided for by the Courts Act, 1971. They will also ensure prompt hearings for civil and criminal cases at their centres. All six appointments have been made and Circuit administrators are now based in London, Bristol, Birmingham, Cardiff, Leeds and Manchester. Their function in the new High Court and Crown Court Centres will be to decide whether cases should be heard by High Court Judges or Circuit Judges.

Presiding Judges. Two High Court Judges known as Presiding Judges were assigned to each of the six Circuits in England and Wales. They will take it in turn to spend substantial periods of time in the area and will have general responsibility for the local High Court and Crown Court Centre. They will see to the convenient and efficient distribution of judges in the area, acting on the advice of the Circuit Administrator. There are three Presiding Judges on the South Eastern region, one of whom is the Lord Chief Justice.

CRIMINAL JUSTICE BILL, 1972

The most significant provisions of this Bill which is now before Parliament, are the removal of the mandatory suspension of sentences of six months or less; the revision and widening of the powers of the court to order compensation for injury or loss arising from crime; the provisions of an appeal to the Court of Appeal by the prosecution on a point of law; a new arrangement for suspended sentences with supervision and orders to carry out community work together with day training centres for those on probation and treatment for alcoholics.

CHAPTER III

LAW IN ACTION

THE word "source" has various meanings when applied to law. One may treat the word "source" as referring to the *historical or ultimate origins of law* and trace the *development* of the common law, equity, legislation, delegated legislation, custom, the law merchant, canon law and legal treatises, as we have done in Chap. I. But on the other hand one may treat the word "source" as referring to the *methods by which laws are made or brought into existence*, and consider the current processes of legislation, delegated legislation, judicial precedent and, to a limited extent, custom. In this chapter we shall be concerned with the *methods by which laws are made*, i.e. the *active* or *legal* sources of law.

LEGISLATION

It is common knowledge that much of our law is contained in Acts of Parliament. Parliament consists of two chambers—the House of Commons and the House of Lords. The House of Commons contains 630 members, each of whom represents a geographical area in the country called his constituency. Members of Parliament are elected *en bloc* at general elections. Casual vacancies, occurring through the death or withdrawal of a member, are filled separately at by-elections. The House of Lords, on the other hand, consists in the main of hereditary peers, though under the provisions of the Life Peerages Act, 1958, there has been added a number of distinguished people from various walks of life who hold life peerages, but whose descendants will have no right to a seat when the life peers are dead.

An Act of Parliament begins as a Bill, which is the draft of a proposed Act.

Types of Bills. A Session of Parliament normally lasts for one year commencing in October or November. During that time, a large number of Bills become law most of which are *Government Bills*. The Government is formed by the parliamentary party having a majority of members in the House of Commons, or more rarely by a coalition of two or more parties who between them can command such a majority. The Government is led by a Prime Minister who appoints a variety of other Ministers such as the Chancellor of the Exchequer, the Home Secretary, the Foreign Secretary, and others to manage various departments of State. A small group of these Ministers, called the Cabinet, meets frequently under the chairmanship of the Prime Minister and formulates the policy of the Government, and an important part of this policy consists of presenting Bills to Parliament with a view to their becoming law in due course. Such Bills are usually presented by the Minister of the department concerned with their contents.

The legislative intentions of the Government are given in outline to Parliament at the commencement of each session in the Queen's Speech. This is read by the Queen but is prepared by the Government of the day. Most Government Bills are introduced in the House of Commons, going later to the House of Lords and finally for the Royal Assent. However, some of the less controversial Government Bills are introduced in the House of Lords, going later to the Commons and then for the Royal Assent. Members of either House whether Government supporters or not have a somewhat restricted opportunity to introduce *Private Members' Bills*. Such Bills are not likely to become law unless the Government provides the necessary Parliamentary time for debate. Some, however, survive to become law, for example, the Murder (Abolition of Death Penalty) Act, 1965. A Session of Parliament is brought to an end by prorogation and a Bill which does not complete the necessary stages and receive the Royal Assent in one Session will lapse. It can be introduced in a subsequent Session but must complete all the necessary stages again. Bills also lapse when Parliament is dissolved prior to a General Election.

Bills are also divided into *Public* and *Private* Bills. *Public Bills*, which may be Government or Private Members' Bills, alter the law throughout England and Wales and extend also to Scotland and Northern Ireland unless there is a provision to the contrary. A *Private Bill* does not alter the general law but confers special local powers. These Bills are often promoted by local authorities, i.e. County Councils and County Boroughs and could, for example, involve an extension of boundaries. Enactment of these Bills is by a different Parliamentary procedure.

Enactment of Bills. A Public Bill and a Private Members' Bill follow the same procedure in Parliament. These Bills may be introduced in either House; though a money Bill, which is a public Bill certified by the Speaker as one containing only provisions relating to taxation or loans, must be introduced in the Commons by a Minister and not a Private member. The following procedure relates to a Public or Private Members' Bill introduced in the Commons.

On its introduction the Bill receives a purely formal first reading, at which it is not read at all. This stage is used to tell members that the Bill exists and that they can now get printed copies. Later it is given a second reading, at which point its general merits are debated, but no amendments are proposed to the various clauses it contains.

In 1965 a special procedure was introduced under which the House need not debate the Bill, the second reading being merely formal. This procedure does not apply if twenty members rise to object. Having survived this stage, probably as a result of a division in the House, the Bill passes to the Committee stage. Here details are discussed by a Standing Committee of fifteen to twenty members chosen in proportion to the strength of the parties in the House of Commons. Amendments to the clauses are proposed, and, if not accepted by the Government, are voted on, after which the Bill returns to the House at the Report stage. The Committee mentioned may be a Committee of the Whole House, if the legislation is sufficiently important. At the Report stage the amendments may be debated, and the Bill may in some cases be referred back for further consideration. It is then read for the third time, when only verbal alterations are permissible.

After passing the third reading, the Bill is sent to the House of Lords where it goes through a similar procedure. If the Lords propose amendments, the Bill is returned to the Commons for approval. At one time the House of Lords had the power to reject Bills sent up by the Commons. Now, under the provisions of the Parliament Acts, 1911 and 1949, this power amounts to no more than an ability to delay a Public Bill (other than a money Bill) for a period of one year; a money Bill may be delayed for one month only. The supremacy of the Commons stems from the fact that it is an elected assembly, responsible to its electors and coming periodically at intervals of not more than five years before the public for re-election.

The main difference between the enactment of a *Private Bill* and a *Public Bill* is that the committee stage of a Private Bill is judicial. For example, in the case of a Bill promoted by a local authority seeking to extend its boundaries, the local authority and those who object may brief counsel or appear themselves to state their case. Witnesses may be called and cross-examined. Since this is a somewhat lengthy procedure, some statutes allow ministers to grant special powers to local authorities by what is called a Provisional Order. Such an order does not take effect unless and until it is embodied (usually along with others) in a Provisional Order Confirmation Bill which is passed by Parliament and given the Royal Assent.

When a Bill has passed through both the Commons and the Lords, it is transmitted to the Queen for the Royal Assent, which in practice is given by a committee of three peers, including the Lord Chancellor. The Royal Assent Act, 1967, provides that an Act is duly enacted and becomes law if the Royal Assent is notified to each House of Parliament, sitting separately, by the Speaker of that House or acting Speaker. The former Bill is then referred to as an Act or a Statute, and may be regarded as a *literary* as well as a *legal* source of law. However, an Act may specify a future date for its coming into operation, or it may be brought into operation piecemeal by ministerial order.

It should be noted that, as well as having a title setting out what its objects are, each Act has, under the provisions of the Short Titles Act, 1896, a short title to enable easy reference to be made. Each Act has also an official reference. The Companies Act, 1948, is the short title of an Act whose official reference is 11 & 12 Geo. 6, c. 38, which means that the Companies Act, 1948, was the thirty-eighth statute passed in the eleventh and twelfth years of the reign of George the Sixth.

The Acts of Parliament Numbering and Citation Act, 1962, provides that chapter numbers assigned to Acts of Parliament passed in 1963 and after shall be assigned by reference to the calendar year and not the session in which they are passed. For example, the official reference of the Companies Act, 1967, is 1967, c. 81

The essential differences between statute law and case law are apparent from the definition of a statute. It is—

> an express and formal laying down of a rule or rules of conduct to be observed in the future by the persons to whom the statute is expressly or by implication made applicable.

Thus a statute openly creates new law, whereas a judge would disclaim any attempt to do so. Judges are bound by precedent and merely select existing rules which they apply to new cases. A statute lays down general rules for the guidance of future conduct; a judgment merely applies an existing rule to a particular set of circumstances. A judgment gives reasons and may be argumentative; a statute gives no reasons and is imperative.

Law Reform. It should be noted that a number of official bodies exist to consider and make proposals for *law reform*, and the work of these bodies can have a considerable influence on the development of statute law. The most important of these bodies is the Law Commission, which was set up by the Law Commission Act, 1965. Sect. 1 of the Act establishes the Commission to promote the reform of English Law and deals with the constitution of the Commission. The Lord Chancellor appoints the members of the Commission, on a full-time basis, from among persons holding judicial office, experienced barristers and solicitors and university teachers of law. Sect. 3 states the duty of the Commission to be to keep under review the whole of English law with a view to its systematic development and reform, including the codification of such law, the elimination of anomalies, the repeal of obsolete enactments and generally the simplification and modernisation of the law. The present programme of the Law Commission includes the codification of the law of contract. The Criminal Law Act, 1967, which abolished the distinction between felonies and misdemeanors and certain obsolete crimes, resulted from proposals made by the Commission.

In arriving at its programme the Commission consults with the chairmen of the Criminal Law Revision Committee and the Law Reform Committee, which are bodies set up on a part-time basis by the Home Secretary to consider specific matters of law reform which he may refer to them in the fields of criminal and civil law respectively. The work of the Commission and the Committees may be regarded as a source of law in that it is an *historical source* of the law contained in a statute which implements its proposals. Thus the proposals of the Law Commission may be regarded as an historical source of the Criminal Law Act, 1967.

In connection with reform, it is interesting to note recent proposals by the Statute Law Committee for the publication of a new official edition of the Statute Book. Although the Committee has made no recommendations as to the method of printing, it has been suggested that computer typesetting be used. This would enable the text to be analysed and searched by computer and would assist research into methods of drafting and interpretation.

DELEGATED LEGISLATION

Many Acts of Parliament deal with matters so complex that the Act itself can only lay down a framework of general principles and much of the detail will have to be filled in in other ways. This is generally done by civil servants in the name of and under the authority of the appropriate Minister.

ADVANTAGES. Legislation of this kind is called delegated legislation and it has many advantages—

(a) *Parliament has so much to do and so little time in which to do it* that it is convenient, indeed essential, to delegate to Ministers the power to make detailed rules.

(b) *Parliament is not always in session and its procedure is slow* whereas delegated legislation has the advantage of speed. Rules and orders can be made very rapidly under emergency powers legislation to cope with national emergencies.

(c) *Even if Parliament wished to include within the statute itself a complete system, it cannot foresee what problems may arise* out of a measure which is currently under consideration. It is often necessary, therefore, to give an administrative authority power to deal with future situations, as they arise, by means of delegated legislation.

(d) *Subordinate legislation is less rigid than an Act of Parliament.* If a regulation proves impracticable it can be readily withdrawn; an Act of Parliament can only be repealed by a further Act. Thus subordinate legislation has the advantage of elasticity.

(e) *There are limits on the aptitude of the legislature.* Members of Parliament often lack competence in the purely technical field. Much legislation is technical by nature and is probably best left to the experts in the Departments of State.

DISADVANTAGES. Delegated legislation has, of course, certain disadvantages of which the following are the chief—

(a) *Parliamentary control over new legislation is said to be reduced*; indeed Lord Chief Justice Hewart has called this system "The New Despotism." But there are safeguards since draft statutory instruments are normally laid before Parliament for approval. There is a Select Committee on Statutory Instruments, set up in 1944 as a permanent organ, consisting of eleven members chosen from the House of Commons to scrutinise the Rules and Orders made by the various departments in the exercise of their delegated powers, and in the last analysis Parliament retains the right to take away from a Minister his power to make delegated legislation. Furthermore, under the Statutory Instruments Act, 1946, statutory instruments may be submitted to Parliament and will cease to be operative if either House so resolves within forty days, and in some cases *positive approval* is required by both Houses. However, much depends on the procedure laid down in the parent Act and in many cases this procedure does not require statutory instruments to be laid before Parliament.

(*b*) *It is said that there is too much delegated legislation*, so that it is difficult for everyone to know the law when new regulations are issued so rapidly. This has a particular bearing on the application of the maxim *Ignorantia juris neminem excusat* (ignorance of the law excuses no man). Ignorance of a statutory instrument cannot be pleaded as a defence.

(*c*) *It is said that there is insufficient notice given to the public of delegated legislation.* Although the popular press does give the substance of important new statutes, it does not accord the same treatment to delegated legislation.

In recent times it has become increasingly difficult even for the professional press to comment on new provisions. For example, it is not unknown for a statutory instrument to be published and laid before Parliament only one day before it comes into force.

(*d*) *Further dangers arise from sub-delegation.* In its reports to Parliament the Select Committee on Statutory Instruments has drawn attention to what is called five-tier legislation. On one occasion, referring to the Defence Regulations, the Committee observed that it had sometimes had to take note of a pedigree of five generations—

   (i) The Parent Statute,
  (ii) The Defence Regulations made under the Statute,
 (iii) The Orders made under the Defence Regulations,
 (iv) Directions made under the Orders,
  (v) Licences issued under the Directions.

This, of course, does tend to reduce very seriously the control by Parliament of the making of new laws.

TYPES OF DELEGATED LEGISLATION

It is necessary now to consider the different types of delegated legislation—

1. **Orders in Council.** These are made by the Queen in Council under powers given in an Act of Parliament. The Council is the Privy Council, which is a large body of persons, but for this purpose the Council consists of a few Cabinet Ministers. These orders are usually issued without further reference to Parliament, and are useful in cases of national emergency such as strikes.

2. **Rules and Orders Made by Ministers.** Such Rules must normally be submitted to Parliament either before or after coming into force, and they are made in the Departments of State. By the Statutory Instruments Act, 1946, a new term, "statutory instrument," was made

applicable to any document by which Her Majesty in Council, or a Minister of the Crown, exercises the statutory power to make orders. Thus it gives delegated legislation the uniform name of "statutory instruments."

3. By-Laws of Local Authorities and Other Public Bodies. These are made by County Councils, Borough Councils, District Councils, and so on under powers given to them by Acts of Parliament. All such by-laws require the approval of the appropriate Minister.

4. Rules of Court. These are made by Rule Committees of the Superior Courts and relate to matters of procedure.

JUDICIAL AND OTHER CONTROLS
OVER DELEGATED LEGISLATION

In addition to the Parliamentary safeguard there is a judicial safeguard of limited application. The courts cannot declare an Act of Parliament *ultra vires*, or beyond its powers, but they can and do declare the exercise of delegated powers invalid under the *ultra vires* rule, saying, in effect, that the Minister has in the instrument exceeded the powers given to him by the parent statute. (*Hotel and Catering Industry Training Board* v. *Automobile Proprietary Ltd.*, 1969.)[20] It must be noted, however, that Parliamentary draftsmen sometimes diminish the value of this safeguard by introducing special clauses (called Henry VIII Clauses, after the way in which that Monarch legislated in an arbitrary way by Proclamation). For example, the Rating and Valuation Act, 1925, Sect. 67 (now repeated), provided—

> If any difficulty arises in bringing into operation any of the provisions of this Act, the Minister may by order remove the difficulty or do anything necessary or expedient to bring it into effect.

It would be hard indeed for the court to declare any order made under the above section *ultra vires*, and judicial review is virtually excluded. Further, the Defence Regulations were a wartime measure, but certain powers have been found useful in peacetime, and have been converted into a permanent part of the Statute Book by means of various Supplies and Services Acts. These Acts provide a sweeping code under which almost every aspect of economic life can be controlled, and the number of valid orders which could be made under these provisions is incalculable.

Another safeguard is the public inquiry, and some Acts provide that a public inquiry shall be held before an order is made, if there are objections to the draft order. This inquiry may bring to light any oppressive measures, and it also gives persons affected a chance to state their views before an administrative tribunal.

By-laws can also be controlled by the courts on the ground that they must be *intra vires* and reasonable. (*Denithorne* v. *Davies*, 1967.)[21]

It has already been mentioned that the House of Commons Select

Committee operates as a safeguard against oppressive legislation, and it should be noted that the Committee is particularly concerned with (*a*) those instruments which purport to raise or levy new taxes; (*b*) those which seem to exclude judicial review; (*c*) those in which a Minister seems to have made an unusual use of his powers; (*d*) cases where there has been unjustifiable delay in presenting the draft instrument to the Committee; and (*e*) cases where the statutory instrument requires elucidation because it is vague and uncertain.

CASE LAW OR JUDICIAL PRECEDENT

Case Law provides the bulk of the law of the country. Some case law enunciates the law itself, and some is concerned with the interpretation of statutes. We will examine first the case law which is law in its own right. Case law is built up out of precedents, and a precedent is a previous decision of a court which may, in certain circumstances, be binding on another court in deciding a similar case. This practice of following previous decisions is derived from custom, but it is a practice which is generally observed. As Park, C.J., said in *Mirehouse* v. *Rennell* (1833), 1 Cl. & Fin. 527, "Precedent must be adhered to for the sake of developing the law as a science." Even in early times the itinerant judges adopted the doctrine of *stare decisis*, and this doctrine has been developed in modern times so that it means that a precedent binds, and must be followed in similar cases, subject to the power to distinguish cases in certain circumstances.

The modern doctrine of the binding force of judicial precedent only fully emerged when there was (*a*) good law reporting; and (*b*) a settled judicial hierarchy. By the middle of the nineteenth century law reporting was much more efficient, and the Judicature Acts, 1873–75, created a proper pyramid of authority which was completed when the Appellate Jurisdiction Act, 1876, made the House of Lords the final Court of Appeal. Judicial precedents may be divided into two kinds—

1. Binding Precedents
2. Persuasive Precedents

but before we elucidate the precise meaning of these terms, we have still to ascertain where these precedents are to be found. The answer is in the law reports; and as we have seen the doctrine of judicial precedent depends upon an accurate record being kept of previous decisions.

Law Reports. Bracton was the first person to compile cases (some two thousand of them) in his Notebook which appeared before the Year Books. The latter were gossipy and fragmentary notes of cases, written in Anglo-Norman, and covering a period of two and a half centuries from the reign of Edward I to that of Henry VIII—that is from the thirteenth century to about the middle of the sixteenth. The Year Books are little used by the modern practitioner because of their many inaccuracies, because of the language in which they are written, and because they do not always report the *ratio decidendi* of the case, but they were studied by the law apprentices in the Inns of Court. Access to court records was only allowed to lawyers acting on behalf of the Crown. Hence we get the private reports, one of the first sets being Dyer's Collection, 1513–1582. Like the Year Books, many early private reports are of doubtful quality being inaccurate and gossipy. For example, it was said of Barnardiston who was a King's Bench reporter from 1726 to 1735 "that he was accustomed to slumber over his notebook and the wags in the rear took the opportunity of scribbling nonsense in it." The following are among the most notable and accurate early collections: Plowden's Reports, Coke's Reports, and Burrow's Reports. The last-named runs from 1736–72, and is the first attempt to report in the modern sense of the word, an effort being made to report arguments and judgments. Other good collections are those of Barnewell & Cresswell, and Meeson & Welsby.

Since 1865 law reports have been published under the control of what is now called the Incorporated Council of Law Reporting, which is a joint committee of the Inns of Court, The Law Society, and the Bar Council. They are known simply as the Law Reports, and they have priority in the courts because the judge who heard the case sees and revises the report before publication. Nevertheless private reports still exist, and of these the All-England Reports, published weekly and started in 1936, are the only *general* reports existing in the private sector. These reports are now revised by the judge concerned with the case, though this was not always so and differences do appear between the version of a case in the official reports and that in the unrevised All-England Reports. In addition, there is some judicial editing of the transcript of the trial prior to publication in the reports. This has extended beyond minor textual amendments and in some cases the report states rules of law which were not in fact laid down in the judgment given at the trial. In 1953 the Incorporated Council began to publish reports on a weekly basis and these are known as the Weekly Law Reports. *The Times* newspaper publishes summarised reports of certain cases of importance and interest on the day following the hearing and there are also certain specialised series of reports covering, for example, the fields of taxation and shipping. It is not absolutely essential that a case should have been reported in order that it may be cited as a precedent, and occasionally oral evidence of the decision by a barrister who was in court when the judgment was delivered may be brought.

Decided cases are usually referred to as follows: *Smith* v. *Jones*, 1959. This means that, in a court of first instance, Smith was the plaintiff, Jones the defendant, and that the case was published in the set of reports of 1959, though it may have been heard at the end of 1958. This is called the Short Citation. A longer citation is required if the report is to be referred to, and might read as follows: *Smith* v. *Jones*, [1959] 1 Q.B. 67 at p. 76. The additional information means that the case is to be found in the First Volume of the Reports of the Queen's

Bench Division, the report commencing on page 67, the number 76 being used to indicate the page on which an important statement is to be found. Where the date is cited in square brackets it means that the date is an essential part of the reference, and without the date it is very difficult to find the report in question. For many years now the Incorporated Council's reports have been written up in a certain number of volumes each year. It will be seen that a mere reference to Vol. 1 of the Queen's Bench Division will not be sufficient unless the year is also quoted.

The early reports by the Incorporated Council and other collections did not use the year as a basic item of the citation, but continued to extend the number of volumes regardless of the year. So a case may be cited as follows: *Smith* v. *Jones*, 17 Ch. D. 230. It can be found by referring to Vol. 17 of the Chancery Division reports, and it is not necessary to know the year in which the report was published, though this will be ascertained when the report is referred to. Where the date is not an essential part of the citation, the date is quoted in round brackets. The abbreviations used for the various divisions are: Q.B. for Queen's Bench; Ch. for Chancery; P. for Probate, Divorce and Admiralty; and A.C. for the House of Lords and Privy Council (Appeal Cases). The reports of decisions of the Court of Appeal appear under the reference of the division in which they were first heard.

Precedents. We are now in a position to refer to a decided case but we still have to ascertain where the precedent is to be found, since the whole of the case is reported, and the judge may have said things which are not strictly relevant to the final judgment. We must know what to take as precedent, and what to ignore, so that we can find what is called the *ratio decidendi*. This is the principle on which the case was decided. In this connection it is worth noting the remarks of Sir George Jessel in *Osborne* v. *Rowlett* (1880), 13 Ch. D. 774, that "the only thing in a judge's decision binding as an authority upon a subsequent judge is the principle upon which the case was decided."

The *ratio decidendi* of a decision is ascertained by a subsequent judge before whom the case is cited as an authority. Thus the eventual and accepted *ratio decidendi* of a case may not be the *ratio decidendi* that the judge who decided the case would himself have chosen, but the one which has been approved by subsequent judges. This is inevitable; because a judge, when deciding a case, does not usually distinguish in his remarks between what we have called the *ratio decidendi* and what are called *obiter dicta*. The latter are things said in passing, and they do not have binding force. Such statements of legal principle are, however, of some persuasive power, particularly the *dicta* of cases heard in the House of Lords. The reason why *obiter dicta* are merely persuasive is because the prerogative of judges is not to make the law by formulating it and declaring it (this is for the legislature) but to make the law by applying it to cases coming before them. A judicial decision, unaccompanied by judicial application, is not of binding authority.

A judge does sometimes indicate which of his statements are *obiter dicta*. For example he may say: "If it were necessary to decide the further point, I should be inclined to say that . . . ." What follows is said in passing.

From the foregoing remarks it may therefore be said that the *ratio decidendi* of any given case is an abstraction of the principle from the facts and arguments of the case, and, of course, the higher the level of abstraction, the more circumstances the *ratio decidendi* will fit.

BINDING FORCE. It is now necessary to examine which precedents are binding, and this depends upon the level of the court in which the decision was reached. Starting with the highest authority, the House of Lords, we find that this body was bound by its own former decisions (*London Street Tramways* v. *London County Council*, [1898] A.C. 375), except where the previous decision had been made *per incuriam*, i.e. where an important case or statute was not brought to the attention of the court when the previous decision was made. However, in July, 1966, the House of Lords abolished the rule that their own decisions on points of law were absolutely binding upon themselves. The Lord Chancellor announced the change on behalf of himself and the Lords of Appeal in Ordinary in the following statement—

> Their Lordships regard the use of precedent as an indispensable found-ation upon which to decide what is the law and its application to individual cases. It provides at least some degee of certainty upon which individuals can rely in the conduct of their affairs, as well as a basis for orderly development of legal rules.
>
> Their Lordships nevertheless recognise that too rigid adherence to pre-cedent may lead to injustice in a particular case and also unduly restrict the proper development of the law. They propose therefore to modify their present practice and, while treating former decisions of this House as normally binding, to depart from a previous decision when it appears right to do so.
>
> In this connexion they will bear in mind the danger of disturbing retro-spectively the basis on which contracts, settlements of property and fiscal arrangements have been entered into and also the especial need for certainty as to the criminal law.
>
> This announcement is not intended to affect the use of precedent elsewhere than in this House.

A practice directive issued in March, 1971, by the Appeal Committee of the House of Lords requires lawyers concerned with the preparation of cases of appeal to state clearly in a separate paragraph of the case any intention to invite the House to depart from one of its own decisions.

On the next rung of the hierarchy there is the Court of Appeal (Civil Division), and this court is bound by its own previous decisions, as well as by those of the House of Lords. (*Young* v. *Bristol Aeroplane Co.*, [1944] 2 All E.R. 293.) The Court of Appeal is not bound by its own decisions, if the decision cannot stand with a decision of the House of Lords.

On the criminal side, the Court of Appeal (Criminal Division) is bound by the decisions of the House of Lords and normally by its own decisions and those of the former Court of Criminal Appeal and the earlier Court for Crown Cases Reserved. However, the Criminal Division may deviate from its own previous decisions more easily than the Civil Division because different considerations apply in a criminal appeal where the liberty of the accused it at stake (*R.* v. *Gould,* 1968),[22] and in any case a full court of the Criminal Division can overrule its own previous decisions. A full court generally consists of five judges instead of three as is usual in an ordinary sitting. A decision of the Civil Division is not binding on the Criminal Division and vice versa.

Divisional Courts are, in civil cases, bound by the decisions of the House of Lords, the Court of Appeal (Civil Division) and by their own previous decisions. In criminal cases there is, under the Administration of Justice Act, 1960, an appeal from the Divisional Court of the Queen's Bench Division straight to the House of Lords, and for this reason it is likely that in future the Divisional Court will not be bound by the decisions of the former Court of Criminal Appeal and the new Criminal Division of the Court of Appeal.

At the next lower stage, a High Court judge, although bound by the decisions of the Court of Appeal, the House of Lords and the Divisional Court of the same division, is not bound by the decisions of another High Court judge sitting at first instance. (*Huddersfield Police Authority* v. *Watson,* [1947] 2 All E.R. 193.) Nevertheless such a judge will treat previous decisions as of strong persuasive authority. The present High Court is not bound by the decisions of the old courts of Common Pleas, Queen's Bench or Exchequer.

A judge sitting in a Crown Court, the jurisdiction of which is confined to criminal cases, is bound by decisions made in criminal matters by the House of Lords and Court of Appeal (Criminal Division). A judge sitting in a County Court and exercising a civil jurisdiction is bound by the decisions of the House of Lords, Court of Appeal and the High Court.

The decisions of the Judicial Committee of the Privy Council are not binding, either on the Committee itself or on other English courts save the Ecclesiastical and Prize Courts. Its decisions are technically only of persuasive authority in English law, and this derives from the fact that the Judicial Committee hears appeals from many overseas territories. Thus, when it hears an appeal from Nigeria, it may not apply a rule of law used (say) in a previous appeal from Australia.

Now that Courts Act, 1971, is in force the above rules of precedent have been considered in the light of the fact that Assizes and Quarter Sessions are now replaced by the new Crown Court, which is a superior court of record at the level of the High Court.

Exceptions. Having examined the relationship of the above courts with regard to the doctrine of binding precedent, it should be noted that a court is not always bound to follow a precedent which according to the rules outlined above ought to be binding on it. Thus, when the court in question is invited to follow a binding precedent, it may refuse to do so—

    (i) by *distinguishing* the case now before it from the previous case *on the facts*;

    (ii) by refusing to follow the previous case because its *ratio* is *obscure*;

    (iii) by declaring the previous case to be in *conflict with a fundamental principle of law*, as where, for example, the court in the previous case has not applied the doctrine of privity of contract;

    (iv) by finding the previous decision to be *per incuriam*, i.e., where an important case or statute was not brought to the attention of the court when the previous decision was made;

    (v) by declaring the principle or *ratio* of the previous decision to be *too wide*, and regarding some of it as *obiter* and therefore not binding;

    (vi) because the previous decision is one of several *conflicting decisions* at the same level;

    (vii) because the *previous decision* has been *overruled by statute*.

Cases heard in the county courts and in the magistrates' courts are not generally reported, and do not create binding precedents. It is probable that it would not be desirable to report such cases, for English law already possesses such a large number of reported cases that decisions are sometimes made in which relevant precedents are not cited or considered, and may therefore be *per incuriam*. Moreover decisions on civil matters in assize courts are sometimes criticised, since time does not always allow for full consideration of all the points involved.

SOME PRECEDENTS ARE NOT BINDING BUT HAVE ONLY PERSUASIVE FORCE. These consist of decisions made in lower courts, of *obiter dicta* at all levels and particularly if made in the House of Lords, and also decisions of Irish, Scottish, Dominion, and United States courts, the reason being that these nations also base their law on the common law of England, though some parts of the law of Scotland are derived from Roman Law. Cases coming to the House of Lords from Scotland do not bind English courts. They are only persuasive unless the legal principles involved are the same in both systems of law. The House of Lords normally gives a directive as to the binding nature of such decisions; for example, *Donoghue* v. *Stevenson*, 1932,[354] which is a most important case on the law of negligence, is binding in both jurisdictions, although it was an appeal from the Scottish Court of Session. In the absence of any persuasive authority from the above sources the court may turn to text-books and sometimes to Roman law. The weight which a court will give to persuasive authority may depend upon the standing of the judge whose decision or dictum it was and reserved judgments, i.e. cases in which the court has taken time to consider the judgment, are highly regarded. Undefended cases in which the issues have not been fully argued on both sides do not carry great weight.

One further classification of precedents must be noted. They may be either "declaratory" or "original"—

> A *declaratory precedent* is one which is merely the application of an existing rule of law.
>
> An *original precedent* is one which creates and applies a new rule. Original precedents alone develop the law; declaratory precedents are merely further evidence of it. Thus, if a judge says: "The matter before us is not covered by authority and we must decide it on principle. . . ." an original precedent is indicated.

It often happens that when a case has been decided in (say) the High Court, a decision is taken to appeal to an appellate court, in this case the Court of Appeal. The Court of Appeal will re-examine the case and, if it comes to a different conclusion from the judge in the High Court, it reverses his decision. Reversal, therefore, applies to a decision of an appellate court in the same case. Sometimes, however, the case which comes before the appellate court has been decided by following a previously decided case, the judge having followed precedent. In this case, if the appellate court decides to differ from the decision reached in the lower court, it is said to over-rule the case which formed the basis of the precedent. *Reversal affects the parties*, who are bound by the decision of the appellate court, and it affects precedent because lower courts will in future be bound to follow the decision. *Over-ruling affects precedent*, but does not reach back to affect the parties in the original case, now regarded as wrongly decided. If a judge of the High Court refuses to follow a previous decision on a similar point of law, the case books will contain two decisions by judges of equal authority, and the cases will remain in conflict until the same point of law is taken to an appeal before a higher tribunal whose decision will then resolve the position.

A case is *distinguished* when the court considers that there are points of difference between the case now before it and a previous decision which it is being invited to follow. As Lord Halsbury said in *Quinn* v. *Leathem*, [1901] A.C. 495—

> Every judgment must be read as applicable to the particular facts proved, or assumed to be proved, since the generality of the expressions which may be found there are not intended to be expositions of the whole law but govern and are qualified by the particular facts of the case in which such expressions are found.

This process of narrowing down the implications of the *ratio decidendi* of a previous case by 'distinguishing' is a device often used by a court which does not wish to follow an earlier decision which would otherwise be binding on it.

If a court feels that an earlier case was wrongly decided but cannot overrule it because the *ratio decidendi* of the case now before it does not cover all the matters raised in the earlier case, it may, by way of *obiter dictum*, *disapprove* the earlier case which is then to some extent affected as a precedent.

Advantages and Drawbacks of Case Law

THE SYSTEM OF JUDICIAL PRECEDENT HAS SEVERAL ADVANTAGES. Up to a point it can claim the advantage of certainty, since it is possible to predict the ruling of a court because judicial decisions tend to be consistent. Nevertheless judges have a habit of distinguishing cases on the facts, or of limiting the application of a principle which had formerly been thought to be of wider scope. This means that the claim to certainty has to be taken with reservations. Another claim put forward in favour of case law is its power of flexibility and growth. New decisions are constantly being added as new cases come before the courts. In this way the law tends to keep pace with the times and can adapt itself to changing circumstances. Judicial precedent covers a wealth of detail. There is a case in point for every rule, and there is a practical character to judicial rulings. Legal rules are made only as the need arises, and the law is not made in advance on the basis of theory. When a case arises, a decision is taken and the ruling is usually recorded, so that when a similar case arises again the law will be there to be applied.

CASE LAW HAS CERTAIN DRAWBACKS. Jeremy Bentham criticised the principle of the "law following the event," and applied the epithet "dog's law" to the system. "It is," he says, "the judges that make the common law. Do you know how they make it? Just as a man makes laws for his dog. When your dog does something you want to break him of, you wait till he does it and then beat him. This is the way you make laws for your dog: this is the way the judges make law for you and me."

A further criticism is that *the binding force of precedent limits judicial discretion*. It has been said that judges are engaged in "forging fetters for their own feet." This can be illustrated by the doctrine of common employment, which was laid down by the House of Lords in *Priestley* v. *Fowler* (1837), 3 M. & W. 1. This doctrine said that if an employee was injured by a fellow employee whilst both were acting within the scope of their employment, their employer was not liable vicariously for that negligence. The rule operated in a most unjust fashion during the period of great industrial development, but it continued to bind judges for over a century until it was finally abolished by the Law Reform (Personal Injuries) Act, 1948. All the judges could do in the meantime was to try to limit its scope. Limiting the scope of a decision may lead to the court's making *illogical distinctions*. In order to avoid following precedent, judges and counsel pay attention to differences in cases which are fundamentally similar, in order to uphold the doctrine of precedent and still not feel bound to follow an inconvenient rule. Often these distinctions have real substance, but occasionally they are illogical and serve to complicate the law.

Difficulties of the kind outlined above may not now arise in such an acute form because, as we have seen, the House of Lords is no longer bound by its own decisions, though this tends to detract from the element of certainty.

A final criticism must be noted—that of *bulk and complexity*. The number of reported cases is so large that the law can be ascertained only by searching through a large number of reports. This search has been eased somewhat where case law has been codified by statute in order to produce a rational arrangement. The Bills of Exchange Act, 1882, the Sale of Goods Act, 1893, and the Law of Property Act, 1925, have to a large extent produced order in what might have been called chaos, but case law still tends to develop even around a codifying statute, and its sections soon have to be read in the light of interpretative cases.

INTERPRETATION OF STATUTES

The main body of the law is to be found in statutes, together with the relevant statutory instruments, and in case law as enunciated by judges in the courts. But the judges not only have the duty of declaring the common law, they are also frequently called upon to settle disputes as to the meaning of words or clauses in a statute.

Parliament is the supreme lawgiver, and the judges must follow statutes. Nevertheless there is a considerable amount of case law which gathers round important Acts of Parliament, since the wording sometimes turns out to be obscure. Statutes were at one time drafted by practising lawyers who were experts in the particular branch of law of which the statute was to be a part. Today, however, statutes are drafted by parliamentary counsel to the Treasury, and, although such persons are skilled in the law, statutes may still be obscure and cases continue to come before the courts in which the rights of the parties depend upon the exact meaning of a section of a statute. When such a case comes before a judge, he must decide the meaning of the section in question. Thus even statute law is not free from judicial influence.

The judges have certain recognised *aids to interpretation*, and they will have regard to the following—

1. **Statutory Aids.** Judges may get some guidance from statute law.

(*a*) The Interpretation Act, 1889, which is itself a statute, defines terms commonly used in Acts of Parliament.

(*b*) A complex statute will normally contain an interpretation section, defining the terms used in the particular Act, e.g. Sect. 455 of the Companies Act, 1948, and the judges have recourse to this.

(*c*) Every Act of Parliament used to have what was known as a preamble, which set out at the beginning the general purpose and scope of the Act. The preamble was often quite lengthy and assisted the judge in ascertaining the meaning of the statute. Modern Public Acts do not have this type of preamble, but have instead a long title which is not of so much assistance in interpretation. All Private Acts must have a preamble setting out the objects of the legislation, and this preamble must be proved by the promoters at the Committee stage in the House of Lords. So far as private acts are concerned the preamble may be of considerable assistance.

2. General Rules of Interpretation Evolved by Judges. There are a number of generally recognised rules or canons of interpretation, and some of the more important ones are now given.

(*a*) THE MISCHIEF RULE. This was propounded in *Heydon's* case, (1584), 3 Co. Rep. 7a. Under this rule the judge will look at the Act to see what was its purpose and what mischief in the common law it was designed to prevent. As was said in *Heydon's* case—

> Four things are to be discussed and considered: (i) What was the common law before the making of the Act? (ii) What was the mischief and defect for which the common law did not provide? (iii) What remedy hath Parliament resolved and appointed to cure the disease of the commonwealth? (iv) What is the true reason for the remedy? Judges shall . . . make such construction as shall suppress the mischief and advance the remedy.

Broadly speaking, the rule means that where a statute has been passed to remedy a weakness in the law the interpretation which will correct that weakness is the one to be adopted.
An example of the use of the rule can be seen in *Gardiner* v. *Sevenoaks R.D.C.*, 1950.[23]

(*b*) THE LITERAL RULE. According to this rule, the working of the Act must be construed according to its literal and grammatical meaning whatever the result may be. The same word must normally be construed throughout the Act in the same sense, and in the case of old statutes regard must be had to its contemporary meaning if there has been a change with the passage of time.

The Law Commission, in an instructive and provocative report on the subject of interpretation (Law Com. 21), said of this rule that "to place undue emphasis on the literal meaning of the words of a provision is to assume an unattainable perfection in draftsmanship."

(*c*) THE GOLDEN RULE. This rule is to some extent an exception to the literal rule and under it the words of a statute will as far as possible be construed according to their ordinary plain and natural meaning, unless this leads to an absurd result. (*Prince of Hanover* v. *Attorney-General*, 1956.)[32] It is used by the Courts where a statutory provision is capable of more than one literal meaning or where a study of the statute as a whole reveals that the conclusion reached by applying the literal rules is contrary to the intentions of Parliament.

The classic example is perhaps Sect. 105 of the Law of Property Act, 1925, which provides as follows—

> Where a mortgagee [*the Act is here describing a lender*] sells land to re-
> cover the amount of a loan advanced on the security of the land and the land
> realises more than the balance of the mortgage the balance after sale shall go
> to the person entitled to the mortgaged property.

By applying the Literal Rule to the last six words the purchaser from
the mortgagee would be entitled. Since this would be absurd, the
words have been taken to refer to the mortgagor (or borrower).

(*d*) THE *ejusdem generis* RULE. This is a rule covering things of the
same genus, species or type. Under it, where general words follow
particular words, the general words are construed as being limited to
persons or things within the class outlined by the particular words.
So in a reference to "dogs, cats, and other animals," the last three
words would be limited in their application to animals of the domestic
type, and would not be extended to cover animals such as lions
and tigers. (*Evans* v. *Cross*, 1938,[24] and *Lane* v. *London Electricity
Board*, 1955.)[25]

(*e*) *Expressio unius est exclusio alterius* (the expression of one thing
implies the exclusion of another). Under this rule, where specific
words are used and are not followed by general words, the Act applies
only to the instances mentioned. Where a statute contains an express
statement that certain statutes are repealed, there is a presumption
that other relevant statutes not mentioned are not repealed.

(*f*) *Noscitur a sociis* (the meaning of a word can be gathered from its
context). Under this rule words of doubtful meaning may take colour
and precision from the nature of the words and phrases with which
they are associated. (*Muir* v. *Keay*, 1875.)[26]

3. Other Presumptions. In addition to the major rules of interpretation, there are also several other considerations which the judge
will have in mind. He will concern himself only with the wording of
the Act, and will not go to *Hansard* to look up reports of the debates
during the passage of the Act. Nor will he take notice of the statements
of Ministers, or the recommendations of committees which may have
led to the legislation. An Act of Parliament comes into being as a result
of many recommendations, and is modified in the course of debate, and
it would be impracticable to refer to such miscellaneous sources with
any degree of certainty as to their value. There is here some conflict
with the Mischief Rule, since it might be thought that there is no better
way to ascertain what mischief the Act was designed to prevent than
by reference to the debates. Nevertheless, the Law Commission decided
against the use of Hansard since they doubted the reliability of statements made in Parliamentary debates. However, in *Letang* v. *Cooper*,
1964,[436] Lord Denning, M.R., said—

> It is legitimate to look at the report of a Committee leading to legislation
> to ascertain what was the mischief at which the Act was directed, but the
> judge should not be influenced by the Committee's recommendations.

A statute is presumed not to alter the existing law unless it expressly states that it does. There is also a presumption against the repeal of other statutes and that is why statutes which are repealed are repealed by specific reference.

In *R.* v. *Schildkamp*, [1970] 2 WLR 279, the House of Lords considered, *inter alia*, the extent to which marginal notes and punctuation might be used to clarify the meaning of a particular section or paragraph. In the course of his judgment Lord Reid said "So, if the Authorities are equivocal and one is free to deal with the whole matter, I would not object to taking all these matters into account provided that we realise that they cannot have equal weight with the words of the Act. Punctuation can be of some assistance in construction. A cross-heading ought to indicate the scope of the sections which follow it but there is always a possibility that the scope of one of the sections may have been widened by amendment. But a side-note is a poor guide to the scope of a section for it can do no more than indicate the main subject with which the section deals."

When a statute deprives a person of property, there is a presumption that compensation will be paid. Unless so stated it is presumed that an Act does not interfere with rights over private property. Acts are presumed not to have retrospective effect, and there is a presumption against alteration of the common law. Any Act which presumes to restrict private liberty will be very strictly interpreted, though the strictness may be tempered in times of emergency. It is presumed that an Act does not bind the Crown on the ground that the law, made by the Crown on the advice of the Lords and Commons, is made for subjects and not for the Crown.

It must be noted that the courts do not appear to favour what is known as a Social Policy Rule, or the interpretation of Acts in the direction of the social policy behind them by filling in gaps and omissions. Denning, L.J., in *Magor and St. Mellons R.D.C.* v. *Newport Corporation*, [1951] 2 All E.R. 839, said: "Having discovered the intention of Parliament the judge may achieve it by filling in gaps in the Statute if such appear." On appeal to the House of Lords, Lord Simonds said: "There is no such rule; if a gap is disclosed the remedy lies in an amending Act." However, if and when the Law Commission's recommendations are implemented it is likely that more emphasis will be placed on the importance of interpreting a statute in the light of the general legislative purpose underlying it.

It may seem that in their interpretation of statute law the judges tend to restrict rather than expand the statute, but this is of value in times of social reform, since social reform presupposes a collectivist outlook with a tendency to impose liability without fault, e.g. The Factories Act, 1961, and the various Food and Drugs Acts. It is possible, therefore, that judicial restriction of statute law may be to the advantage of the community. Further, the rules of interpretation tend to some extent to cancel each other. Thus by using one or other of these rules judges can be narrow, reformist, or conservative. In fact Pollock, in his *Essays in Jurisprudence and Ethics*, suggests—

> English judges have often tended to interpret statutes on the theory that Parliament generally changes the law for the worse and that the business of the judges is to keep the mischief of its interference within the narrowest possible bounds.

CHAPTER IV

SOME FUNDAMENTAL LEGAL CONCEPTS

BEFORE entering into a more detailed study of the various branches of substantive law we must first of all examine certain fundamental legal concepts and classifications.

PRIVATE AND PUBLIC LAW

Private law is concerned with the legal relationships of ordinary persons in everyday transactions. It is also concerned with the legal position of corporate bodies and associations of persons the first of which are endowed with a special form of legal personality. Private law includes contract and commercial law, the law of tort, family law, e.g. divorce, adoption and guardianship, trusts and the law of property which involves what rights can exist in property and how it can be transferred.

Public law is concerned with the constitution and functions of the many different kinds of governmental organisations, including local authorities, such as county and borough councils, and their legal relationship with the citizen and each other. These relationships form the subject matter of constitutional and administrative law. Public law is also concerned with crime which involves the state's relationship with and power of control over the individual.

There is also a division into *criminal and civil law*. Criminal law is concerned with legal rules which provide that certain forms of conduct shall attract punishment by the state, e.g. homicide and theft. Civil law embraces the whole of private law and all divisions of public law except criminal law.

In order to understand the various branches of substantive private law which are considered in detail later, it is necessary to be able in particular to distinguish the following—

Contract. A contract is an agreement made between two or more persons which is intended to have legal consequences. Thus, if there is a breach of contract, the parties can go to court and obtain a remedy. We shall see in the appropriate chapter which agreements the courts will enforce, under what conditions they are enforceable, and what remedies are available to injured parties. It should be noted that the parties to a contract enter voluntarily into their obligations; the function of the law is merely to enforce or adjudicate on such agreements.

Tort. A tort on the other hand, is a civil wrong independent of contract. It arises out of a duty imposed by law, and a person who commits a tortious act does not voluntarily undertake the liabilities which the law imposes on him. There are many kinds of tort with a common characteristic; injury of some kind inflicted by one person on another. Nuisance, trespass, slander and libel are well-known civil wrongs. The typical remedy in this branch of the law is an action for damages by the injured party against the person responsible for the injury. Such damages are designed not to punish the wrongdoer but to compensate the injured party.

Crime. A crime is in a different category. It is difficult to define a crime, but it is a public offence against the State, and, while an individual may be injured, the object of a criminal charge is to punish the offender, not to compensate the victim. Criminals are prosecuted, usually by the police, and if found guilty receive the appropriate punishment.

Trusts. A trust arises where one person holds property for the benefit of another. Suppose a man wishes to provide for his children when he dies; he may leave them some of his property on trust, particularly if they are minors i.e. under age 18 years. He will appoint trustees in whom the property will be vested, but they will not benefit from the proceeds, since the income arising from the trust property will have to be devoted to the purposes of the trust; in this case for the benefit of the children, who are called the beneficiaries or the *cestuis que trust* (pronounced "setty que trust"). Trusts may also be set up by living persons. The characteristics of a trust are that the trustees own the property but the *cestuis que trust* get the benefits.

It must not be assumed that all acts fall into these tidy categories. Certain breaches of trust are also criminal offences. Some activities may be both torts and crimes, and an act which is a breach of contract is often a tort. Thus, if a taxi-driver drives dangerously and injures a passenger, he is liable for a breach of contract to his fare, for the tort of negligence, and possibly for the criminal offence of dangerous driving for which he may be punished.

SOME COMMON LEGAL RELATIONSHIPS

The law recognises and defines certain common relationships. The following, in particular, have relevance to the various branches of substantive law dealt with in later chapters.

Agency. It is quite common to find parties having the relationship of principal and agent. Sometimes a person (the principal) wishes to have certain tasks carried out—he may wish to sell a house or buy shares in a company. He therefore employs an estate agent or a stockbroker to carry out his purposes. Sometimes an agent is a specialist who carries out a limited range of duties, e.g. an auctioneer who sells a wardrobe put into an auction. Sometimes he has wider powers, and may even be able to bind the principal in all the ways the principal could bind himself, as where the agent has a power of attorney.

An agent may be specifically appointed as such, but in some cases an agent acquires his status without specific authority being given to him, and such an agent may bind his principal by what is called usual authority. If P appoints A to be the manager of an hotel, A may be able to bind P in a contract although he had no actual authority to make it, for the law is not solely concerned with the actual authority of an agent but regards him as having the usual powers of an agent of his class. It follows that the usual powers of an hotel manager will be relevant in deciding the sort of agreement which A can make on behalf of P. The doctrine of usual authority does not apply where the third party knows that the agent has no authority to make the contract.

An agent's powers may also be extended in an emergency. If A is a carrier of perishable goods for P, he may be able to sell them on behalf of P if the goods are deteriorating and he cannot get P's instructions with regard to disposal. A becomes an agent of necessity for the purpose of sale, though his actual authority is to carry the goods. At common law a wife could in circumstances of necessity pledge her husband's credit for necessaries for herself and the family. This right was removed by Sect. 41 of the Matrimonial Proceedings and Property Act, 1970. Agency may also arise out of conduct resulting from apparent authority. If a husband pays the debts which his wife incurs with a local dressmaker, he may be liable to pay for an expensive article of clothing which she buys without his consent, because the husband has, by his conduct, led the dressmaker to believe that the wife has power to bind her husband in contracts of this nature. This type of agency which is not peculiar to a wife is not affected by the Act of 1970. It is also possible in certain circumstances for a principal to ratify, i.e. adopt, the contracts of his agent, even though the agent had no actual authority when making the contract.

Bailment. A bailment arises when one person (the bailor) hands over his property to the care of another (the bailee). The reasons for such a situation are many. The bailee may have the custody of the property by way of loan or for carriage. The article may be pledged, or left with another to be repaired or altered. Sometimes the bailee has the mere custody of the goods; sometimes he may use the property, as when he "purchases" a radio set under a hire-purchase agreement or borrows a lawn mower. In all cases of bailment, the property or ownership remains with the bailor; the possession with the bailee.

A bailment is an independent legal transaction and need not necessarily originate in a contract. When X hands his goods to Y under a bailment Y has certain duties in regard to the care of the goods even though the bailment is not accompanied by a contract. Thus Y may be held liable for negligent damage to the goods even though he had not been promised any money or other benefit for looking after them. Bailment is considered in more detail on pp. 334–37.

Lien. A lien is a right over the property of another which arises by operation of law and can be independent of any contract. In its simplest form it gives a creditor, such as a shoe repairer, the right to retain possession of debtor's property, in this case his shoes, until he has paid or settled the debt, incurred in this case as a result of repairing the shoes. Lien is considered in more detail of pp. 319–21.

LEGAL PERSONALITY

A person in law is regarded as the subject of certain rights and duties, and generally speaking an adult human being is a legal person and may be referred to as a *natural person*. Alternatively, a legal person may not be a human being; in fact various bodies and associations attach to themselves similar rights and duties as are attached to ordinary human beings, and so become "*juristic persons.*"

Moreover it should be noted that even with regard to human beings the law distinguishes between certain classes, and ascribes to them a *status* which may carry with it a more limited set of rights and duties than are ascribed to the normal male adult. These classes are minors, persons of unsound mind, married women, bankrupts and aliens. At one time many of these classes had severe restrictions placed on their legal capacity, but the tendency has been for these restrictions to be removed, and the significance of belonging to certain of these categories will be more fully examined in connection with each branch of the law in the appropriate place. However, the basic rules applying to the various categories of persons are given below

NATURAL PERSONS

Natural persons are affected by the following legal concepts—

Domicil. The basis of jurisdiction and the law to be applied in many matters coming before English courts, e.g. wills, matrimonial causes and taxation, may depend on the domicil of the parties. A person's domicil is the country which he regards as his permanent home, and thus contains a dual element of actual residence in a country and the intention of remaining there. Where a country has within its national boundaries several jurisdictions, the person's domicil must be determined with reference to a particular jurisdiction, e.g. there is no such thing as a domicil in the United States of America, though a person may be domiciled in a particular State. England, Scotland, Northern Ireland, the Channel Islands, and the Isle of Man are distinct jurisdictions within the British Isles. A person must always have a domicil, and he can only have one domicil at a time. It should be noted that the concepts of domicil and nationality are *mutatis mutandis* applied to corporate bodies.

Domicil of Origin. The domicil of origin of a child is that of its father at the date of the child's birth if the father is alive at that date and is married to the child's mother, i.e., if the child is legitimate. (*Henderson* v. *Henderson*, 1965.)[27] If the child is illegitimate or, though legitimate, the father is not alive when it is born, it takes its domicil of origin from that of its mother at the date of the child's birth. Foundlings take their domicil of origin from the place where they were found.

Dependent Domicil. Infants and married women may have a dependent domicil.

(*a*) INFANTS, I.E. PERSONS UNDER THE AGE OF 21 YEARS. The domicil of a legitimate, legitimated or adopted infant is dependent on, and changes with that of its father or adoptive father, and after the father's death with that of its mother or adoptive mother. However, in the latter case, the mother can, on altering her own domicil, leave the infant's domicil unchanged if this is in its interests. (*Re Beaumont*, 1893.)[28] The domicil of an illegitimate infant depends on, and changes with, that of its mother. So far as English authorities are concerned the domicil of an infant child remains that of his father even though the parents are divorced and the child is in the custody of the mother. This was also the view taken by the Scottish Court of Session in *Shanks* v. *Shanks*, [1965] S.L.T. 330. However, a recent case in Northern Ireland, *Hope* v. *Hope*, [1968] N.I. 1, decides that where the parents of an infant child are divorced and the wife has been given custody of the child by a competent court, that child's domicil is dependent on and changes with that of his mother.

(*b*) MARRIED WOMEN. On her marriage, a woman even though an infant, automatically acquires her husband's domicil, and there-after her domicil is dependent on, and changes with, that of her husband whilst the marriage subsists. Where a marriage has been void *ab initio*, e.g. where one of the parties is under age, the woman, having never acquired the status of a married woman, does not acquire her husband's domicil, unless by living with him in his own country she acquires there a domicil of choice. On divorce, or nullity of a voidable marriage, or on widowhood, a woman retains her former husband's domicil until she acquires a new domicil of choice. It is not certain whether an infant widow retains her deceased husband's domicil or re-acquires her father's domicil.

Domicil of Choice. A person, other than an infant or a married woman, can change his domicil of his own volition. To dò so he must be in the new country, and have a "fixed and settled intention" to abandon his domicil of origin or choice, and to settle instead in the new country.

A person retains his domicil of origin until he acquires a domicil of choice, and since a person must always have a domicil, there can be no abandonment of the domicil of origin unless a domicil of choice is acquired instead. However, having acquired a domicil of choice, a person who abandons it without acquiring a fresh domicil of choice, reverts to his domicil of origin. (*Harrison* v. *Harrison*, 1953.)[29]

The country in which a person resides is on the face of it the country of his domicil. Where it is claimed that a domicil of origin has been changed for one of choice, the onus of proof is on the party claiming that such a change has taken place. Examples of evidence which suggest a change of domicil are oral or written declarations to this effect, letters, the adoption of a new name, an application for naturalisation, the purchase of land, or a grave, or the establishment of a home in the new country.

Reform. The Law Commission in Working Paper No. 28 recommend a change in the law of domicil which would enable a married woman (including a married infant) to acquire her own domicil as if she were single. This change would apply only in respect of matrimonial proceedings and not in other branches of law, e.g. liability for tax. Such a change would enable a married woman to obtain a divorce more quickly in this country even though her husband was domiciled abroad. At the present time if her husband is domiciled abroad her domicil is the same as his and the Court has no jurisdiction to hear the case on this ground, though it can after she has been resident here for twelve months. Under the proposed change a married woman could immediately acquire a domicil here and bring divorce proceedings straight away.

Residence. The residence of a person is important for certain purposes. For example, the jurisdiction of magistrates in matrimonial matters is based on the residence of the parties and not their domicil, as is the right to vote in a particular constituency at an election. Domicil must, therefore, be distinguished from residence.

The term residence imports a certain degree of permanence, and must not be casual or merely undertaken as a traveller. In *Fox* v. *Stirk*, [1970] 3 All E.R. 7, the Court of Appeal decided that two undergraduates were resident at their universities and entitled to have their names on the electoral register for that constituency although their parental homes were elsewhere. Obviously, residence can be changed at any time by moving to a new home. The residence of a wife who is not judicially separated from her husband is *prima facie* that of her husband. Temporary absences abroad while on holiday or on business do not create a gap in the period of residence, which is determined on the facts of the case.

Nationality. The main importance of nationality today is in the realm of public law, since aliens and nationals are treated similarly in most matters of civil law. However, matters such as allegiance, the right to vote at elections and sit in Parliament are governed by the nationality of the person concerned. A person may have a dual or multiple nationality or may be stateless, as where he has been deprived of the nationality of one country without having acquired the nationality of another. British Nationality is now governed by the British Nationality Act, 1948 (as amended), and the 1948 Act creates the status of citizenship. Every person who under the Act is a citizen of the United Kingdom and Her Colonies, or is a citizen of certain other countries, often referred to as "sub-section (3)" countries, e.g. Canada, Australia, New Zealand, India, Pakistan, Ceylon, Ghana, Nigeria and Sierra Leone, among others, has, by virtue of that citizenship, the status of a British subject.

In the United Kingdom there are now three main classes of persons—

(i) Citizens of the United Kingdom and Colonies,

(ii) Citizens of other Commonwealth countries, i.e. Commonwealth citizens, and

(iii) Aliens.

The first two classes constitute British subjects.

Citizenship of the United Kingdom and Her Colonies may be acquired in the following ways—

By Birth. Citizenship is acquired by a person born within the United Kingdom or Colonies, unless his father (not being himself a citizen of the U.K. or Colonies) possesses diplomatic immunity, or unless the birth was in a place then occupied by an enemy, and the father is an enemy alien.

By Descent. Citizenship is acquired by descent by a person whose father is a citizen of the United Kingdom and Colonies, irrespective of the place of birth, but the birth must be registered at a United Kingdom consulate within one year, or, with the permission of the Home Secretary, at any time.

By Registration. A citizen of a sub-section (3) country, or of Eire, who is of full age and capacity, may register as a citizen of the U.K. and Colonies if he can satisfy the Home Secretary that—

(i) he is ordinarily resident in or is in the Crown Service of the U.K., or partly one and partly the other; and
(ii) he has remained so throughout the preceding five years.

The South Africa Act, 1962, provides that from 31st May, 1962, South Africa will be treated as a foreign country, but the right to registration as a citizen of the U.K. and Colonies endured, provided application was made before the end of 1965, or notice of intention to make such application was given within that period, and the application was made within five years of the notice.

A woman (whether or not of full age) who is married to a citizen of the U.K. and Colonies may register, but if she is an alien she must take an oath of allegiance. A woman married to a U.K. citizen after 1st January, 1949, does not thereby acquire citizenship. A person who has been deprived of citizenship of the U.K. and Colonies, or has renounced it, may register if the Home Secretary gives permission. A minor child of a citizen of the U.K. and Colonies may be registered upon application by his parent or guardian. It should be noted that the Immigration Act, 1971, removes the right of registration as a citizen of the U.K. and Colonies formerly possessed by a Commonwealth citizen after he had been here for five years. Registration under the Act of 1971 is at the discretion of the Home Secretary and there is no right of appeal against refusal of citizenship. However, Commonwealth citizens who were resident in the U.K. on 31st July, 1971, will retain their entitlement to registration on completing five years' ordinary residence. (See p. 99.)

By Naturalisation. Citizenship by naturalisation is acquired at the Home Secretary's discretion by an alien of full age (18 years) and capacity who can show, that—

(i) throughout the year preceding his application he has resided in the U.K. or been in the service of the Crown; and
(ii) for four of the seven years immediately preceding such year he has either resided in the U.K. or any colony, or has been in the service of the Crown, and
(iii) he is of good character, and

(iv) he has a sufficient knowledge of the English language, and

(v) he intends, if a certificate is granted, either to reside in the U.K. or any colony, or to enter or continue in Crown service under the U.K. government, or in the service of an international organisation of which the U.K. government is a member.

The wife of a naturalised alien may acquire citizenship by registration.

BY INCORPORATION OF TERRITORY. Sect. 11 of the British Nationality Act, 1948, provides—

> If any territory becomes a part of the United Kingdom and Colonies, His Majesty may, by Order in Council, specify the persons who shall be citizens of the U.K. and Colonies by reason of their connection with that territory: and those persons shall be citizens of the U.K. and Colonies as from a date to be specified in the Order.

The Act provides for loss of United Kingdom citizenship by renunciation and deprivation as follows—

(a) A citizen of the U.K. and Colonies of full age, who is also a citizen of a sub-section (3) country or of Eire or who is a foreign national, can renounce citizenship by declaration. In time of war the Home Secretary may withhold registration of the declaration.

(b) A citizen of the U.K. and Colonies by registration or by naturalisation can be deprived of citizenship, if the Home Secretary is satisfied that registration or naturalisation was obtained by fraud, false representation, or concealment of a material fact.

(c) A naturalised person can be deprived of citizenship if the Home Secretary is satisfied that he has—

(i) shown himself by act or speech to be disloyal or disaffected towards Her Majesty, or

(ii) in time of war traded with the enemy, or

(iii) within five years after becoming naturalised been sentenced in any country to not less than 12 months' imprisonment, or

(iv) continuously resided in a foreign country for seven years, and during that period has neither at any time been in the service of the Crown or of certain international organisations, nor registered annually at a U.K. consulate his intention to retain citizenship.

Under these provisions the Home Secretary must also be satisfied that it is not conducive to the public good that such a person should continue to be a citizen of the U.K. and Colonies.

(d) Where a naturalised person is deprived of citizenship of a sub-section (3) country or of Eire, the Home Secretary may also deprive him of citizenship of the U.K. and Colonies.

Aliens. An alien cannot acquire property in a British ship, save as a member of limited liability company if the company itself is British, nor can he become the master of a British ship. Aliens cannot vote at elections or become members of Parliament. They also require work permits if they wish to take up employment here and may be deported if convicted of certain crimes. Citizens of the Republic of Ireland are not treated as aliens and may vote at elections and become members of Parliament.

Immigration. The Immigration Act, 1971, replaces the Aliens Restriction Act, 1914, the Commonwealth Immigrants Acts, 1962 and 1968, and the Immigration Appeals Act, 1969, with "a single code of permanent legislation on immigration control."

Control of Immigration. The Act provides a single system for control of entry to Britain for Commonwealth citizens and aliens. Commonwealth citizens coming to Britain for work no longer have an automatic right to settle. They will in future require a work permit issued for a specific job in a specific place for a fixed initial period, usually twelve months. The work permit must be obtained by the prospective employer from the Department of Employment before the employee's arrival in Britain. After arrival, employment may be changed only with the approval of the Department, and registration with the police is required. At the end of a year a Commonwealth citizen may apply for an extension of stay in approved employment. After four more years of permitted stay the above conditions are cancelled unless there are grounds for keeping them. Thus, there will be no time limit on his stay and he may change his employment at will. Furthermore, his obligation to register with the police ends. Wives and children of those coming to work will be admitted but must register as the head of the family does. In addition the head of the family must show that he is able to provide accommodation as well as financial support. Commonwealth citizens already *lawfully settled* in the U.K. on 31st July, 1971, are entitled to bring dependents to the U.K. "Settled" means being here without conditions on length of stay in the country.

The U.K., the Irish Republic, the Channel Islands and the Isle of Man remain a common travel area and in consequence Irish citizens will continue to be admitted for employment and other purposes without work permits or other restrictions.

Commonwealth doctors or dentists taking up professional appointments may enter without work permits. This also applies to aliens in the above categories. If these persons do not have pre-arranged appointments they may stay for six months without a permit provided they have a place in the attachment scheme run by the Department of Health and Social Security.

Students may enter as before, i.e. subject to an initial limitation of not more than one year. Extensions are granted in appropriate circumstances, e.g. to continue studies. Visitors and tourists are not affected and Commonwealth and alien girls may enter as "au pair" to learn English. For this purpose they may live for a reasonable time as a member of a resident English-speaking family. Representatives of overseas firms, ministers of religion and certain seasonal workers may enter without work permits or employment vouchers.

Registration. When a Commonwealth or Irish citizen has lived in the United Kingdom for five years (or has worked in Crown service for the same period) he may apply to be registered as a citizen of the United Kingdom and Colonies. His application may be granted if—

(*a*) he is of good character;
(*b*) he has sufficient knowledge of English;
(*c*) he intends to reside in the United Kingdom or a dependent territory.

Unless he is already a citizen of a country in which Her Majesty is also Queen, registration will involve taking an oath of allegiance. Registration is at the discretion of the Home Secretary and there is no appeal against refusal.

Commonwealth citizens who were resident in the U.K. on 31st July, 1971, without any time limit on their stay retain their *right* to registration on completion of five years' ordinary residence. (See p. 96.)

Right of Abode (Patrial). The Act sets out certain categories of people who have a "right of abode" in the U.K. and are free of immigration control. They are persons having direct personal or ancestral connection with the U.K. and are as follows—

(*a*) all persons who are citizens of the U.K. and Colonies by being born here or who become citizens of this country by adoption, registration or naturalisation in the U.K. or who have a parent who was born here or acquired citizenship by adoption, registration or naturalisation;
(*b*) citizens of the United Kingdom and Colonies who have come from overseas and been accepted for permanent residence and since that acceptance have resided here for five years;
(*c*) Commonwealth citizens who have a parent born in the United Kingdom.

Persons in the above category are described by the Act as "patrials". Immigration control for those who, while holding U.K. passports are not patrials, continues. They are required to have special vouchers before they are admitted for settlement, and can also apply for work permits in the same way as Commonwealth citizens.

Right of Appeal. All persons subject to immigration control have a right of appeal against refusal of admission to an independent adjudicator and then to a tribunal. Both the adjudicator and the tribunal are within the scope of the Tribunals and Inquiries Act, 1971. A person who is refused entry on arrival because he has not got a work permit, entry certificate or visa will first have to return to his country and make appeal from there in the same way as he would if he had been refused an entry certificate or visa before departure. He is not allowed to stay here until the appeal is pending because of the difficulties this would cause to the immigration authorities at sea and airports.

Decisions taken by the Home Secretary personally on the ground that entry or continued presence here *is not conducive to the public good* are not subject to appeal. Thus the special appeal procedure for security and political cases which caused criticism in the Dutschke case is abolished.

Deportation. The Act extends to Commonwealth citizens the Home Secretary's power to deport an alien if he considers his presence is not conducive to the public good. There are also powers under which the dependents of a deported person may themselves be deported. Patrials are exempt from deportation so that a Commonwealth citizen or alien may obtain exemption after five years' residence by acquiring citizenship be registration or naturalisation. The Act re-states the main grounds for deportation as follows—

(*a*) conviction of an offence punishable with imprisonment where the court has recommended deportation, and

(*b*) breach of the conditions imposed on a stay in this country.

The Act also creates a new offence of assisting illegal entry and empowers immigration officers to require persons admitted for a limited time to register with the police. Aliens who are here for more than six months are *required* in any case to register with the police.

Race Relations. The law of persons clearly includes legislation relating to race. In this connection two Acts of Parliament are relevant—the Race Relations Acts, 1965 and 1968. The Race Relations Act, 1965, makes provisions to prevent racial discrimination. Sect. 1 makes it unlawful for the proprietor or manager of certain places of public resort listed in the Act to practise discrimination on the ground of colour, race, or ethnic or national origins by refusing or neglecting to afford a person, on any of those grounds, access to the place or the same facilities or services which are offered to others. The places of public resort include public houses, hotels, cafés, cinemas, swimming pools, buses and trains. Tenancies are also included. Sect. 2 constitutes a Race Relations Board which must in turn constitute local conciliation committees to consider complaints concerning contraventions of Sect. 1 and to try to settle differences and ensure that they are not repeated. Where the committees cannot secure a settlement or assurances are not being complied with, they must report the matter to the Board.

Sect. 6 creates the offence of incitement to racial hatred by publishing or distributing written matter, or using words in a public place or at a public meeting, which are threatening, abusive or insulting. The offence is punishable on summary conviction by imprisonment not exceeding six months or a fine not exceeding £200 or both (on indictment 2 years or a fine not exceeding £1,000 or both).

The Race Relations Act, 1968, extends the provisions of the Act of 1965 to cover provision of goods, facilities and services, employment, membership of trade unions, employers' associations, professional bodies, housing and business premises. The 1968 Act retains conciliation through the Race Relations Board but supplements it by providing that if conciliation fails proceedings may be brought in special designated county courts which hear applications for injunctions and try actions for civil damages brought by the Race Relations Board. The County Court judge sits with two assessors. It will be seen, therefore, that apart from Sect. 6 of the 1965 Act, the sanctions of this anti-discrimination legislation are civil and not criminal. (See also Theatres Act, 1968, p. 269.)

The Race Relations Board has taken proceedings in a number of cases. These have been concerned with discrimination in respect of the purchase of property, rented accommodation, including a seaside boarding house which issued a brochure saying it regretted that coloured guests could not be taken, and a complaint relating to an alleged refusal by a publican to serve a group of West Indians. Nevertheless, it was decided in *Ealing London Borough Council* v. *Race Relations Board*, [1972] 1 All E.R. 105, that it was lawful under the Race Relations Act, 1968, for a housing authority to impose a rule to limit applications for housing to British subjects.

Husband and Wife. Although marriage is in essence a form of contract, it has special features in that it alters the status of the parties. Persons under the age of sixteen cannot be married nor can persons who are too closely related. Until recently, the contract of marriage could not be discharged by mutual consent. However, under the Divorce Reform Act, 1969, a divorce decree may be granted where the parties have been separated by consent for a continuous period of at least two years immediately preceding the presentation of a petition for divorce by one of them and the other consents to a decree being granted. (Sect. 2(1)(d).)

In addition, divorce without consent of both parties is possible provided that they have lived apart for a continuous period of at least five years preceding the presentation of the petition. (Sect. 2(1)(e).) This is the most controversial provision of the Act in that it permits an "innocent" party to be divorced against his or her will.

Regarding property, the status of married woman was low during the nineteenth and early twentieth centuries and in particular all the wife's personal property passed to the husband on marriage. However, their emancipation was brought about by a series of statutes culminating in the Law Reform (Married Women and Tortfeasors) Act, 1935, so that today their status is the same as that of a *feme sole* (single woman).

In addition there have been a number of important developments in regard to distribution of matrimonial property on breakdown of marriage. These are beyond the scope of a general book.

The following aspects of the legal position of husband and wife are worthy of note here.

    (i) The husband has a duty to maintain his wife and children and where a husband is destitute his wife must maintain him if her income allows;

    (ii) there is a duty to cohabit;

(iii) husband and wife have special rights with regard to succession on death (see p. 376);

(iv) a wife may, in certain circumstances, have authority to act as her husband's agent.

However, since Sect. 41 of the Matrimonial Proceedings and Property Act, 1970, abolished a wife's agency of necessity there is no form of agency which arises solely from the status of a wife (see p. 92).

Since the Law Reform (Husband and Wife) Act, 1962, husband and wife have been able to sue each other in tort. (See p. 216.)

Parents and Legitimate Children. At common law a child is legitimate only if his parents are lawfully married to each other at the time of his conception or birth or at any intervening time between the two, though, where the marriage is void, e.g. in the case of a bigamous marriage, the child will be legitimate only if at the time of its conception or, if later at the time of celebration of the "marriage", both or either parent reasonably believed that the marriage was valid. (Sect. 2, Legitimacy Act, 1959.)

The duty to maintain a legitimate child is that of the father, though the mother is liable where the father fails to maintain. However, a child is under no legal duty to maintain his parents. A legitimate child has a right to succeed to the property of his father and mother where they die without having made a will (i.e. intestate).

The father retains a basic right to decide matters relating to the child's upbringing, e.g. religion and education, though in a case of dispute the interests of the child and his welfare predominate.

Illegitimate Children. A child which cannot satisfy the tests of legitimacy outlined above is illegitimate. Where the mother is un-married the child must be illegitimate, subject of course to the provisions of Sect. 2 of the Legitimacy Act, 1959, which relate to void marriages (see above). If the mother is married, then a presumption that her husband is the father of the child arises. This is a presumption of ligiti-macy and must be rebutted if illegitimacy is to be established. In the past the standard of proof offered in rebuttal had to be very strong; generally speaking, proof beyond a reasonable doubt. However, Sec. 26 of the Family Law Reform Act, 1969, now provides that the presumption of legitimacy may be rebutted on a balance of probabilities. Three main types of evidence are relevant—

(*a*) *Evidence of Non-access*, which means that the husband could not or did not have sexual intercourse with the wife at the time when the child was conceived, as where he was serving in the Forces overseas.

(*b*) *Blood tests*, which have become more popular in recent times be-cause of improved medical techniques. Such a test can exclude the possibility of a particular man being the father of the child but cannot prove that he is, though it may show that he could be. Part III of the Family Law Reform Act, 1969, contains the following important pro-visions relating to blood tests—

(i) any court can in any civil proceedings in which a person's legitimacy is in question give directions for the use of blood tests (Sect. 20);

(ii) the court cannot order a party to submit to a test, the following consents being necessary—in the case of an adult or of a child who has reached the age of 16, his own consent; in the case of a child under 16, the consent of the person having care and control of him (Sect. 21);

(iii) if a person does not consent, the court can draw such inference as seems proper in the circumstances (Sect. 23(1))—thus refusal may be some evidence against what a party says; if refusal is by a party claiming relief and relying on a presumption of legitimacy, the court may adjourn the case to enable him to comply and if he does not do so within a reasonable time may dismiss the claim (Sect. 23(2)), this could apply to a mother claiming maintenance for a child but refusing to submit herself or the child for a test.

(*c*) *Previous affiliation proceedings.* By Sect. 12 of the Civil Evidence Act, 1968, the fact that a man has been adjudged to be the father of a child in affiliation proceedings in any court in the U.K. is *prima facie* (not conclusive) evidence of his paternity in other civil proceedings. This Section reverses for this purpose the rule in *Hollington* v. *Hewthorn*, [1943] K.B. 587 which provided that the fact that one court had been satisfied as to a particular matter was not admissible in evidence in another trial.

RIGHTS OF THE ILLEGITIMATE CHILD. These are as follows—

(*a*) *Matrimonial proceedings.* The Matrimonial Proceedings and Property Act, 1970, increases the rights of illegitimate children by providing that the court can in matrimonial proceedings make provision for any "child of the family." There is no reference to parentage so that the expression will include any child of either party, including illegitimate children and for example an orphaned child who had been brought up as one of the family. Under the Act, either a husband or wife can be ordered to make periodical payments or pay a lump sum or transfer property for the benefit of a child of the family. Payments cease at eighteen unless the child is receiving instruction at an educational institution or undergoing training for a trade or profession. Sect. 5(3) of the Act does, however, provide that in making an order for payments to a child which is not his the court may take into account how far the husband has accepted responsibility for it and whether acceptance of his responsibility was with the knowledge that the child was not his together with the liability of any other person to maintain the child.

Matrimonial proceedings before magistrates continue to be governed by the Matrimonial Proceedings (Magistrates' Courts) Act, 1960. Under Sect. 16 of that Act, maintenance can be ordered for a "child of the family." The expression has a more restricted meaning, however, and includes illegitimate children only if they are children of both parties or of one party accepted as a member of the family by the other.

(*b*) *Affiliation Orders.* These orders, under which the father of an illegitimate child is required to make payments, are made in favour of the mother but are of indirect benefit to the illegitimate child which is the intention.

(*c*) *Fatal Accidents Acts.* The Fatal Accidents Acts, 1864–1959, give the dependents of a person who is killed as a result of a tort, a right of action against the tortfeasor. (See p. 219.) Dependents include an illegitimate child. (1959 Act, Sect. 1 (2).)

(*d*) *Social Security.* An illegitimate child is eligible for family allowances (Family Allowances Act, 1965, Sect. 17 (5)) and Supplementary benefits.

(*e*) *Succession.* The Family Law Reform Act, 1969, Sect. 14, has given extended rights of succession to an illegitimate child. On the death intestate (without a will) of either of his parents an illegitimate child, or if he is dead his issue, take the same interest as he would have taken had he been legitimate. Furthermore, if an illegitimate person dies intestate both his parents take the same interest as they would have taken had he been legitimate. (See p. 377.). Sect. 15 of the Act of 1969 also provides that a gift in a will or other instrument to a child or other relation includes illegitimate persons (see p. 377). In addition, Sect. 18 of the 1969 Act brings illegitimate dependents within the scope of the Inheritance (Family Provision) Acts, 1938–66. These Acts apply where a deceased person has not made reasonable provision by his will or on intestacy for his dependents (see p. 367).

Legitimation. Legitimation of an illegitimate child by the subsequent marriage of his parents was permitted by the Legitimacy Act, 1926, provided that neither parent was married to another person at the time of birth.

This proviso was removed by the Legitimacy Act, 1959, and now even an "adulterine" may be legitimated. A person may now be therefore—

(i) legitimate, i.e. born in lawful wedlock;
(ii) illegitimate, i.e. not so born and not legitimate; or
(iii) legitimated.

A person who is legitimated acquires most of the rights of a legitimate person from the date of the marriage of his parents. From that time onwards he will be treated as legitimate for all purposes. However, legitimation is not retrospective as regards rights to property arising under wills and other instruments coming into force before legitimation, the legitimated person being treated as illegitimate at that time. In the case of wills and other instruments coming into force on or after 1st January, 1970, his rights as an illegitimate child would of course be improved. (See p. 377.)

Application for a declaration of legitimacy may be made to the High Court or in some circumstances to the County Court, and persons who may be affected, e.g. in matters of succession, may oppose the application. However, the court has power to make a declaration of legitimacy only where the petitioner's own status is in issue and cannot make a declaration as part of other proceedings by another petitioner. *Aldrich* v. *Attorney-General* (1967), 111 S.J. 945.

Adoption. Adoption was not possible in England until the passing of the Adoption of Children Act, 1926. The rules relating to adoption are now governed by the Adoption Act, 1958, and adoption may be effected by order of a magistrates' court, a county court or the High Court, though different procedures are involved. An order will be made if the court is satisfied as to the welfare of the child only if—

(i) the adopter is at least twenty-five years old; or

(ii) the adopter is the father or the mother of the child; or

(iii) the adopter is at least twenty-one years old and related to the child.

It is not usual for an order to be made in favour of a sole male adopter where the child is a female.

Joint adoptions by a husband and wife may be made if—

(*a*) one of them is the parent of the child; or

(*b*) one of them is related to the child and the husband and wife are over twenty-one years of age; or

(*c*) one adopter is over twenty-five years of age and the other is over twenty-one.

An adoption order has the effect of placing the child in the same position as if he were a legitimate child of the adopter.

Parental consent is normally required but the court has power to dispense with this under the Adoption Act, 1958, as follows—

(*a*) where the parent has absconded, neglected or ill-treated the child (Sect. 5(1)(*a*)); and

(*b*) where the parent cannot be found, or is incapable of giving consent or is unreasonably withholding it.

It is illegal to give any person any reward in consideration of the adoption by that person of a child.

Reform. A major criticism of existing adoption law is that it some-times seems to place the personal satisfaction of the parents or adopters above the well-being of the child. This is the view of the Departmental Committee on the Adoption of Children set out in a White Paper entitled "Adoption of Children" published in October, 1970, which suggests a number of changes in the law.

The Adoption Act, 1968, which received the Royal Assent on 26 July, 1968, enables adoptions authorised in other countries to be effective in the United Kingdom.

Minors. The Family Law Reform Act, 1969, Sect. 1(1) reduces the age of majority from twenty-one to eighteen years. This provision operates from 1st January, 1970, and if a person was over eighteen and under twenty-one years on 1st January, 1970, he was deemed to have attained his majority on that date. There is also a provision in the Act which states that a person attains a particular age, i.e. not merely the age of majority, at the first moment of the relevant birthday, though this rule is subject to any contrary provision in any instrument (i.e. a deed) or statute. (Sect. 9.) However, the common law rule that the age is attained at the first moment of the day preceding the birthday is at least repealed.

Sect. 1 (2) provides that the age of eighteen is to be substituted for twenty-one wherever there is a reference to "full age", "infant", "infancy", "minor", "minority" in—

(*a*) any statutory provision made *before or after* 1st January, 1970;

(*b*) any deed, will or other instrument made *on or after* that date.

This subsection draws a distinction between *statutory provisions* and *private dispositions*. In the case of the former the new age of eighteen is substituted. Thus, in the Infants' Relief Act, 1874, references to "infants" will be construed as applying to persons under eighteen years of age. However, in the case of private dispositions such as deeds, wills and settlements the Act does not apply retrospectively. Accordingly, if in a deed made before 1st January, 1970, a person X is to take property "on attaining his majority," he will take it at age twenty-one years. If the deed was made on or after 1st January, 1970, he would take it at eighteen years. The reason for this rule is that where persons in the past have arranged their affairs in reliance on the law as it stood, it would be unjust to interfere.

The law has always regarded minors as being in need of protection, and consequently they enjoy certain immunities and are subject to certain disabilities at law. We have dealt with the legal position of minors with regard to domicil and nationality (see pp. 93–98, and we shall be giving fuller consideration to their position in contract, tort, property, and succession (including the making of wills) in the chapters on those topics which follow. However, certain general matters may be considered at this point.

(i) A minor cannot contract a valid marriage under the age of sixteen years and requires the consent of his parents (or on failure that of a magistrates' court) to marry under eighteen years of age.

(ii) A person under eighteen years cannot vote at elections and must be 21 before he can sit in Parliament or be a member of the council of a local authority.

(iii) With regard to civil litigation, a minor sues through a "next friend", i.e. an adult who is liable for the costs (if any) awarded against the minor in the action, though the minor must indemnify him. A minor defends an action through a "guardian *ad litem*" who is not liable for costs. The minor's father usually acts as "next friend" or "guardian *ad litem*."

In criminal matters the minor himself is the person prosecuted and may defend himself or be represented by a solicitor or counsel.

(iv) For the purposes of criminal liability minors are divided into three classes—

(*a*) *Those under ten years.* It is presumed that minors under ten years of age are incapable of any crime, and the presumption is irrebuttable. (Children and Young Persons Act, 1963.)

(*b*) *Those between ten and fourteen years.* The presumption is that the minor is incapable of forming a guilty intent, but this can be rebutted by proving precocity, i.e. that he is old beyond his years.

(*c*) *Minors of fourteen years and over* are fully liable for crimes, but there are certain differences as to procedure and punishment, e.g. a person who is a minor at the time of the commission of a murder is not sentenced to life imprisonment but is detained during Her Majesty's pleasure under the Children and Young Persons Act, 1933, Sect. 53(1).

The Government intends to raise the minimum age for prosecution to twelve but only when it is satisfied that local authorities have enough care facilities to cope with the change.

In the meantime, children from ten upwards will remain liable for criminal proceedings though from 1st January, 1971, new provisions under the Children and Young Persons Act, 1969 (see p. 24), relating to care proceedings will come into force; care orders will replace approved school orders and fit person orders and the new provisions on supervision and intermediate treatment will come into force. The courts will, however, retain, alongside of these orders, their present powers to order borstal training, to commit to junior detention centres and to order attendance at junior attendance centres. These will continue until the Government is satisfied with the alternative methods of dealing with young offenders.

The following additional matters relating to minors are of interest—

(*a*) A person of sixteen or over can give valid consent to medical treatment and it is not necessary as before to obtain the consent of a parent or guardian. (Family Law Reform Act, 1969 (Sect. 8).)

(*b*) The Tattooing of Minors Act, 1969, makes it an offence for a person other than a duly qualified medical practitioner to tattoo a person under the age of eighteen (£50 on first conviction, £100 subsequently). The person charged with the offence will have a defence if he can show that at the time he had reasonable cause to believe that the person tattooed was eighteen years of age or over.

Persons Suffering from Mental Disorder. We shall be giving fuller consideration to the position of mentally disordered persons in contract, tort and succession in the chapters on those topics which follow. However, the position in criminal law is worth noting at this point and is to some extent governed by the following rules which arise from the case of *R.* v. *M'Naghten* (1843), 10 Cl. & Fin. 200.

(i) Every man is presumed to be sane until the contrary is proved.

(ii) To establish a defence on the ground of insanity, it must be clearly proved that, at the time of the committing of the act, the party accused was labouring under such a defect of reason, from disease of mind (*R.* v. *Kemp*, 1957),[30] as not to know the nature and quality of the acts he was doing; or, if he did know it, that he did not know he was doing what was wrong. It is a question of the party's knowledge of right and wrong in respect of the very act with which he is charged.

(iii) If the accused labours under a partial delusion only, he must be considered in the same situation as to responsibility as if the facts with respect to which the delusion exists were real.

If a man suffering from a delusion supposes another man to be in the act of killing him, and he kills this man, as he supposes, in self-defence, he would be exempt from punishment. If the delusion was that the victim had inflicted a serious injury to his character and fortune, and the accused killed him in revenge for such a supposed injury, he would be liable to punishment.

If the defence of insanity is successful, the verdict is "Not guilty by reason of insanity," and the accused has a right of appeal on the same conditions applicable to criminal appeals generally.

DIMINISHED RESPONSIBILITY. By virtue of Sect. 2 of the Homicide Act, 1957, this defence is now available in respect of a murder charge only. The burden of proof is on the defence, and if the defence is successfully established, it reduces the conviction for murder to one of manslaughter.

The defence must show that the accused "was suffering from such abnormality of mind (whether arising from a condition of arrested or retarded development of mind, or any inherent causes, or induced by disease or injury) as substantially impaired his mental responsibility for his acts and omissions in doing, or being a party to, the killing."

It should be noted that the Mental Health Act of 1959 now gives a comprehensive and more enlightened definition of mental disorder which is as follows—

Mental illness, arrested or incomplete development of mind, psychopathic disorder, and any other disorder or disability of the mind.

The accused's sanity or mental disorder is also relevant—

(*a*) *When he is put up for trial.* Although there may be no doubt that the accused was sane when he did the act with which he is charged, he may be too insane to stand trial or as it is usually put—"unfit to plead." If this is found to be so by a jury, he will be detained during the Queen's pleasure until he recovers. He could then be tried but in practice never is.

(*b*) *On conviction.* Here the accused's mental condition is relevant to punishment. Under the Mental Health Act, 1959, the court can make a variety of hospital and guardianship orders though not in the case of murder.

(*c*) *After sentence*. If the accused is found to be suffering from mental disorder after receiving a sentence of imprisonment he may be transferred to a mental hospital under the Mental Health Act, 1959.

If a person suffering from mental disorder goes through a ceremony of marriage but cannot understand the nature of marriage, i.e. the responsibilities and change of status involved, the marriage will be void.

In connection with mental disorder, it is of interest to note the existence of the Court of Protection which is concerned with proper management of a mental patient's property. The Court operates through receivers who may, in many cases, be close relatives of the patient.

CORPORATIONS AND UNINCORPORATED ASSOCIATIONS

The Joint Stock Company. The enormous increase in industrial activity during the industrial revolution made necessary and inevitable the emergence of the joint stock company and the concept of limited liability. For the first time it was possible for the small investor to contribute to the capital of a business enterprise with the assurance that, in the event of its failure, he could lose no more than the amount he had contributed or agreed to contribute. The principles of "legal entity" and "perpetual succession" apply, whereby the joint stock company is deemed to be a distinct legal person, able to hold property and carry on business in its own name, irrespective of the particular persons who may happen to be the owners of its shares from time to time. (*Salomon* v. *Salomon*, 1897.)[31]

Joint Stock Companies are formed by registration under the Companies Act, 1948, or previous Acts. The current controlling statutes are the Companies Acts, 1948 and 1967. The Acts provide for two types of registered companies: the Public Company and the Private Company. A registered company is fully liable for its debts but the liability of the members may be limited either to the amount unpaid on their shares, i.e. *a company limited by shares*, or to the amount they have agreed to pay if the company is brought to an end (wound up), i.e. *a company limited by guarantee*. Some companies are *unlimited* and the members are fully liable for the unpaid debts of the company.

The Finance Act, 1965, introduced for the purposes of taxation two further classifications of companies, i.e. *Close companies*, which are in general companies under the control of five or fewer persons, and *Associated companies*. The eighteenth schedule of the Act of 1965 provides in effect that company A and company B are to be treated as associated companies if at any time within one year previously company A controlled company B or vice versa, or company A and company B were both under the control of the same persons.

The capital of a public company is usually raised by the public subscribing for its shares, which are issued with varying rights as to dividends, voting powers, and degrees of risk. Shares are freely transferable and are almost invariably quoted on the Stock Exchange.

When making a public issue of shares, the company is under a statutory obligation to publish full particulars of the history, capital structure, loans, profit record, directors, and many other matters calculated to assist the intending shareholder to assess the possibilities of the company. Such a document is called a Prospectus, and the directors are liable to penalties for fraud, misrepresentation or failure to disclose the material information as required by the Fourth Schedule to the Companies Act, 1948.

The minimum number of members is seven, but there is no upper limit. Incorporation is achieved by lodging with the Registrar of Companies at Companies House, 55–71 City Road London, E.C.1, certain documents of which the following are the most important—

(a) *The Memorandum of Association* is a document which defines the constitution of the company, and sets out in the Objects Clause the powers of the company. This clause governs the activities into which the company can legally enter, and it may be said that the Memorandum governs the company's relations with the outside world. In the Memorandum one also finds the company's name; together with a statement that the liability of the members is limited (where this is the case); the situation of its Registered Office, e.g. England (this governs the company's nationality and domicile); the amount of its Authorised Capital; and an Association Clause in which the subscribers ask for incorporation and agree to take at least one share.

(b) *The Articles of Association* contain the regulations governing the relationship between the company and its members, and thus cover the internal or domestic affairs of the company. Such matters as alteration of shareholders' rights, powers of directors, conduct of meetings, and resolutions, are contained in the Articles.

The directors of a public company stand in a position analogous to that of trustees towards the shareholders whose money they control, and many of the provisions of the Companies Acts, 1948 and 1967, are so framed as to ensure the maximum possible degree of disclosure by the directors of information calculated to keep the members acquainted with the affairs of the company.

The Memorandum and Articles of Association are public documents which must be deposited with the Registrar of Companies, and are open to public inspection along with other records relating to charges on the company's property, and copies of important resolutions. Each year the company's Annual Return, giving particulars of share capital, debentures, mortgages and charges, list of members, particulars of directors and secretary, and having attached the company's accounts together with the auditor's report, must be filed with the Registrar. Any person may inspect the Register of Members at the Registered Office of the company.

The private company with a minimum of two members and in general a maximum of fifty is now a firmly established feature of the present-day business world. The private company is barred from going to the general public for subscriptions for its shares and must restrict in some manner the right of share transfer.

Dissolution of a registered company usually takes place by the company being put into liquidation, as a result of the process of winding up.

Other Types of Corporation. Incorporation may also be achieved by a *Royal Charter* granted by the Crown. The procedure is for the organisation desiring incorporation to address a petition to the Privy Council, asking for the grant of a charter and outlining the powers required. If the Privy Council consider that the organisation is an appropriate one, the Crown will be advised to grant a charter. Charter companies were formerly used to further the development of new countries, e.g. the East India Company and the Hudson Bay Company, but now they are usually confined to non-commercial corporations, e.g. the Institute of Chartered Accountants and the Chartered Institute of Secretaries. Municipal and County Boroughs are also incorporated in this way. It is possible for the liability of members to be limited, and a chartered company, sometimes known as a "Common Law Corporation," has the same powers as an individual person in spite of limitations in its charter. However, it is said that the Crown may forfeit the charter if the company pursues *ultra vires* activities, and certainly a member can ask the court to grant an injunction preventing the company from carrying out *ultra vires* activities. (*Jenkin* v. *Pharmaceutical Society*, 1921.)[32]

Companies may be created by special Act of Parliament, and are governed by their special Acts and also by Acts which apply to statutory companies generally, which are known as "Clauses Acts." These Acts together define and limit their activities. The purpose of statutory companies is to promote undertakings of the nature of public utility services, e.g. water supply, where monopolistic powers and compulsory acquisition are essential to proper functioning. The liability of members may be limited. Many of the former statutory public utility companies have now been nationalised by other statutes and are operated on a national basis, e.g. the National Coal Board.

All the forms of incorporation which we have discussed have one feature in common, i.e. they produce corporations aggregate having more than one member. However, English law recognises the concept of the *Corporation Sole*, i.e. a corporation having only one member. A number of such corporations were created by the common lawyers because they were concerned that land did not always have an owner, and that there could be a break, however slight, in ownership. Church lands for example were vested in the vicar of the particular living, and at higher levels in other church dignitaries, such as the bishop of the diocese. When such persons died, the land had no legal owner until a successor was appointed, so the common lawyers created the concept of the corporation sole whereby the office of Vicar or Bishop was a corporation, and the present incumbent the sole member of that corporation. The death of the incumbent had thereafter no effect on the corporation, which never dies, and each successive occupant of the office carries on exactly where his predecessor left off. The Bishop of London is a corporation sole, and the present holder of the office is the sole member of the corporation. The Crown is also a corporation sole.

It does not seem likely that any further corporations sole will be created by the common law, but they may still be created by statute. For example, the Public Trustee Act, 1906, sets up the office of Public Trustee as a corporation sole. The Public Trustee is prepared to act as executor or trustee, when asked to do so, and much property is vested in him from time to time in the above capacities. It would be most inconvenient to transfer this property to the new holder of the office on death or retirement, and so the person who holds the office of Public Trustee is the sole member of a corporation called the Public Trustee, and the property over which he has control is vested in the corporation, and not in the individual who is the holder of the office.

Unincorporated Associations. Many groups of people and institutions exist which carry on their affairs in much the same way as incorporated associations, but which are in fact unincorporated. Examples are cricket clubs, tennis clubs, and societies of like kind. Such associations have no independent legal personality, and their property is treated as the joint property of all the members. The main areas of legal difficulty arising in regard to these associations are as follows—

Liability of members in contract. This rests on the principles of the law of agency. Thus a member who purports to make a contract on behalf of his club is usually personally liable. The other members will only be liable as co-principals if they had authorised the making of the contract. This would be the case, if, for example, the rules of the club so provided. Alternatively, the members may ratify the contract after it is made. However, it appears that no member has authority to make a *purchase on credit (Flemyng* v. *Hector* (1836), 2 M & W 172) unless he is specifically authorised to do so. Membership of a club usually involves payment of an annual subscription and nothing more. Consequently it is expected that everything needed by the club will be paid for from existing funds. If more money is needed a meeting of members should be called so that subscriptions might be raised rather than pledge the credit of the members.

Liability of members in tort. A person is liable if he committed the tort and in addition may be liable vicariously for the tort of his servant (see p. 221). These principles have been applied to clubs in two main types of case, viz.—

(*a*) Where a person has been injured as a result of the dangerous condition of the club premises. The tendency here is to hold all the members liable as "occupiers" and not merely the club's officers or a committee or trustees. (*Campbell* v. *Thompson*, [1953] 1 QB 445.)

(*b*) Where a person has been injured as a result of the negligence of a servant of the club. The tendency here is to find that the servant is employed by the officer or committee or trustees who appoint him. (*Bradley Egg Farm Ltd.* v. *Clifford*, [1943] 2 All E.R. 378.)

Rights of members in the assets of the association. While a club is functioning the individual members have no separate rights in its property. They do, however, acquire realisable rights when the club is dissolved. On dissolution the general rule is that the assets are sold and after liabilities have been discharged any surplus is divided equally among the members (*Brown* v. *Dale* (1879), 8 Ch. D. 78), subject, of course, to any contrary provision in the rules of the club. It should be noted that a club is not dissolved simply because it changes its name and constitution with the express or implied consent of the members. (*Abbatt* v. *Treasury Solicitor*, [1969] 1 W.L.R. 1575.)

Rights of members under the rules. The rules of an unincorporated association constitute a contract between the members of the association and the court will grant an injunction to a member who is denied a right given under the rules, e.g. the right to vote at meetings (*Woodford* v. *Smith*, [1970] 1 All E.R. 1091), or if he is expelled either where there is no power of expulsion under the rules, or if the power exists it has not been exercised properly as where the principles of natural justice have not been observed.

Procedure. If only a few of the members are liable no problems arise since they can all be sued personally. If, however, it is intended to allege that all the members are liable this procedure is impracticable since all would have the right to be individually defended and represented. In this sort of case a representative action is available. Under the Rules of Supreme Court and the County Court rules the plaintiff may ask for a *representative order* to be made against certain members of the association and sue them. If he is successful these members will be liable to pay the damages but may also be entitled to an indemnity from the funds of the association, and in this way the plaintiff is in effect paid from the association's funds. Similarly some members of an unincorporated association can sue for wrongs done to the association by means of the representative order procedure.

Trade Unions were originally regarded as unlawful combinations in restraint of trade and were treated as conspiracies. Eventually, however, they were legally recognised, and could be registered with the Registrar of Friendly Societies. They held property by means of trustees. Nevertheless they were markedly different from other associations in that under the Trade Disputes Act, 1906, Sect. 4, a trade union could not be sued for torts committed by the union or on its behalf. The Act, therefore, clearly protected the union funds against all actions in tort, even those which were not connected with a trade dispute.

However, since a trade union has no separate legal personality in the way that a company has, there existed a possibility of an action against the officials and members as individuals for torts committed by or on behalf of the union by making these persons defendants instead of the union. The Act of 1906 clearly protected officials and members against this representative liability. Nevertheless officials and members of a union, when organising a strike, are quite likely to commit certain torts, such as inducing employees to disregard their contractual obligations to the employer and interfering with the employer's business activities. In this connection the Act of 1906 gave officials and members a more limited protection should they be sued *personally* in respect of such torts. This aspect of the 1906 Act and the effect of the Trade Disputes Act, 1965, and the Industrial Relations Act, 1971, is more fully discussed in the chapter on the law of torts. It will suffice here to say that under the Act of 1971 registered trade unions and other industrial relations organisations, e.g. employer's associations, lose their immunity from actions in tort not connected with an industrial dispute. The immunity given to a trade union, its officials and members in respect of torts connected with an industrial dispute continue to apply in respect of actions brought in the ordinary courts of law. However, in respect of actions brought in the new Labour Courts (see p. 56), the immunity applies only where the union is registered under the Act, though even where the union is registered there is no immunity in relation to what is called unfair industrial action (see page 218). An additional advantage of registration is that the organisation can hold property in its own name.

Contracts made by a trade union are normally enforceable in accordance with the general principles of the law of contract, but under Sect. 4 of the Trade Union Act, 1871, some contracts cannot be enforced, e.g. the union cannot sue a member for non-payment of his subscriptions or for an agreed penalty incurred by him for some infringement of the rules. Similarly a member cannot sue the union in respect of any promise to give him legal aid should the union not be prepared to assist him in action. The section was intended to keep agreements which are of a domestic nature out of the ordinary courts. It did, however, result in collective agreements between unions and employers' associations unenforceable since agreements between unions were covered by Sect. 4. The Industrial Relations Act, 1971, now provides that such agreements may have binding force. A union can be sued for breach of contract in its own name, but, since it is not a *persona at law*, the person or persons liable on the contract will be decided on the general principles applicable to contracts made by unincorporated associations as outlined above.

The Partnership. A partnership is defined in Sect. 1 of the Partnership Act, 1890, as "the relationship which subsists between persons carrying on a business in common with a view of profit." It will be noted that there must be a business; that it must be carried on in common by the members (whether by all of them, or by one or more of them acting for the others, will depend on the agreement subsisting between them); and that there must be the intention to earn profits. An association of persons formed for the purpose (say) of promoting some educational or recreational object to which the whole of the funds of the association shall be devoted, and from which no advantage in the nature of a distribution of a profit shall accrue to the members, is not a partnership.

Participation in the profits of a business may be regarded as *prima facie* evidence of a partnership, but it is not conclusive—the intention of the parties must be examined. Thus, an employee whose remuneration is based on a share of profits, or the widow or child of a deceased partner receiving an annuity in the form of a share of profits, would not legally be deemed to be partners. Neither does the common ownership of property constitute a partnership, nor the lending of money in consideration of an agreement to pay the interest, or to repay the capital, out of profits as they accrue. (But in such a case the lender should take the precaution of having the agreement embodied in writing, signed by all the parties, and setting out clearly the fact that he is not to be considered a partner.)

The question of citation as a partner is of great importance because the existence of a partnership, if such is proved, will involve all parties cited as partners in unlimited liability for the debts of the firm. Partners are agents for the firm, and can bind the other partners in contracts concerning the business of the firm.

Two or more persons can combine to form a partnership, which can be brought into existence in a highly formal or a very casual manner. *No legal formalities are essential*, but it is desirable and usual for the rights and liabilities of the partners to be defined in a formal Deed of Partnership, or at least in a written Partnership Agreement. On the other hand, a mere oral agreement is equally binding, and in extreme cases a relationship of partnership may be inferred from the conduct of the parties. The partners are at liberty to vary the arrangements made between them, and where the conduct of the parties has for a lengthy period been inconsistent with the terms as originally agreed, it will be presumed that they intend that the new arrangements shall be binding on them. The Partnership Act makes provisions as to contribution of capital, division of profits, rights of partners to participate in active management, and so on, but these only apply in so far as they are not varied by agreement between the partners.

Sect. 434 of the Companies Act, 1948, prohibits the formation of a partnership consisting of more than twenty persons for the purpose of carrying on any business for gain. However, certain partnerships of solicitors, accountants and members of stock exchanges were exempted from this prohibition by Sect. 120 of the Companies Act, 1967. Regulations made by the Board of Trade (now Department of Trade and Industry) in 1968 exempt from the prohibition in Sect. 434 of the

Act of 1948 certain partnerships of patent agents and also certain partnerships of surveyors, auctioneers, valuers and estate agents.

There is no limitation on the activities of partners provided these are legal; nor is there any limit to the liability of the individual partners for the debts of the firm, each partner being liable to the full extent of his personal estate for any deficiencies of the partnership. However, provision is made for the introduction of limited partners whose liability is limited to the amount of capital they have introduced, though there must always be at least one general partner who is fully liable for the debts of the firm. Such a partnership must be registered as a limited partnership under the Limited Partnerships Act, 1907.

The partnership was the normal form of business organisation for operations on a fairly large scale before the advent of the joint stock company, but it is now largely restricted to the type of enterprise requiring intimate personal collaboration between the members, or where incorporation is not possible or desirable, as among doctors, solicitors and accountants. However, this type of business organisation has become more popular now that Corporation Tax is payable by companies.

One of the defects of the partnership is its lack of continuity. The death of a partner automatically dissolves the partnership, and the continuing partners must account to his personal representatives for the amount of his interest in the firm. This difficulty may be met to some extent by providing funds out of the proceeds of an insurance policy on the deceased partner's life, or by arranging for the balance of his capital account to be left in the business as a loan, but failing these measures the sudden withdrawal of a large amount of capital may well cause serious dislocation of the business, or even end its operations. The most serious defect of a partnership, however, is the difficulty of providing additional funds for expansion, and this may induce partners to admit new members for the sake of their capital, regardless of their fitness for taking an active part in controlling the business.

A partnership firm is not a persona *at law;* a partnership is an aggregate of its members. In the matter of procedure it is possible for the firm to sue and be sued in its own name, but this does not confer upon it a legal personality as is possessed by a corporation.

THE CROWN

The Crown is the executive head in the United Kingdom and Commonwealth, and government departments and civil servants act on behalf of the Crown.

Until 1947 the Crown was not liable for the tortious acts of its servants, and was liable only to a limited extent in contract, though the actual tortfeasor could be sued and the Crown often stood behind him and paid the damages awarded against him. Actions in contract could only be started by a cumbrous procedure known as a Petition of Right, with the consent of the Crown given on the advice of the Attorney-General.

The rather anomalous position at common law which has been outlined above arose out of the ancient maxim, "The King can do no wrong," which was extended to cover the activities of the Departments of State and their servants. The Crown Proceedings Act, 1947, and the Rules of the Supreme Court (Crown Proceedings) Act, 1947, which were required to support the Act in the matter of procedure, came into force together on 1st January, 1948, to rectify the matter.

The general effect of this legislation is to abolish the rule that the Crown is immune from legal process, and to place the Crown as regards civil proceedings in the same position as a subject. Proceedings by Petition of Right are abolished, and all claims which might before the Act have been enforced by Petition of Right can be brought by ordinary action in accordance with the Act.

The Crown is now liable in contract where a Petition of Right could have been brought before, and also in tort, but the following exceptions should be noted. Regarding contractual claims, there are some limitations upon the rights of the other party, viz.—

(*a*) *Executive necessity.* In *Rederiaktiebolaget Amphitrite* v. *R.*, [1921] 3 K.B. 500, a neutral shipowner's vessel was detained in England although the British Legation in Stockholm had given an undertaking that it would not be. The basis of Rowlatt's, J., decision for the Crown was that the Government cannot by contract hamper its freedom of action in matters which concern the welfare of the State.

This statement has been regarded as much too wide and is probably of very limited application.

(*b*) *Parliamentary funds.* In *Churchward* v. *R.* (1865), 1 Q.B. 173, a contract to carry mail for eleven years was terminated by the Crown in the fourth year. Shee, J., in deciding for the Crown, held that it was a condition precedent of the contract that Parliament would allocate funds and if they chose not to there was no claim. This view came under criticism in subsequent cases and the better view is that the decision is limited to cases where Parliament has *expressly* refused to grant the necessary funds.

(*c*) *Freedom to legislate.* In *Reilly* v. *R.*, [1934] A.C. 176, a barrister who was employed by the Canadian Government had his contract terminated by legislation. The Privy Council found for the Crown on the ground that the Crown cannot by contract restrict its right to legislate.

(*d*) *Contracts of employment.*

(i) *Military personnel.* Military employees cannot successfully claim against the Crown for breach of contract (*Dickson* v. *Combermere* (1863), 3 F. & F. 527) nor can they claim arrears of pay. (*Leaman* v. *R.*, [1920] 3 K.B. 663.)

(ii) *Civil Servants.* Civil servants are dismissible at pleasure (*Shenton* v. *Smith*, [1895] A.C. 229) but can claim arrears of pay. (*Kodroswaren*

v. *A.G. of Ceylon*, [1970] 2 W.L.R. 456.) Furthermore, *dicta* in *Reilly* v. *R.*, [1934] A.C. 176 suggests that an express promise to employ for a definite period, the contract to be determinable only "for cause," e.g. misconduct, overrides the implied term relating to dismissal at pleasure.

Actions in tort will lie against the Crown for the torts of its servants or agents committed in the course of their employment; for breach of duty owed at common law by an employer to his servants; for breach of the duties attaching to the ownership, occupation, possession or control of property; and for breach of statutory duties, e.g. breaches of the duty of fencing dangerous machines under the Factories Act. No proceedings lie in tort against Her Majesty in her private capacity.

The law as to indemnity and contribution under the Law Reform (Married Women and Tortfeasors) Act, 1935, applies to Crown cases, so if the Crown is a joint tortfeasor, it can claim a contribution from fellow wrongdoers, and where the Crown is led into publishing a libel, it may claim an indemnity against the party responsible. The Law Reform (Contributory Negligence) Act, 1945, also applies to Crown cases.

No action lies in tort against the Crown or the individual Crown servant for anything done or omitted to be done in relation to any postal packet or telephone communication, except that an action will lie for damages for loss of a registered inland postal packet, not being a telegram. Such action must be brought within twelve months of the date of posting of the packet. (Law Reform (Limitation of Actions, etc.) Act, 1954.) It should be noted that the Post Office Act, 1969, established the Post Office as a public authority which is not an agent of the Crown and does not enjoy the immunities and privileges of the Crown. Nevertheless, the immunities outlined above still apply being contained in Sections 20 and 21 of the Act of 1969. Both the Crown and any member of the Armed Forces are immune from liability in tort in respect of the death of, or personal injury to another member of the Armed Forces on duty, provided that the death or injury arises out of service which ranks for the purpose of pension.

Actions under the Act may be brought in the High Court or a county court, and the Treasury is required to publish a list of authorised government departments for the purposes of the Act, and of their solicitors. Actions by the Crown will be brought by the authorised department in its own name, or by the Attorney-General. Actions against the Crown are to be brought against the appropriate department, or, where there is doubt as to the department responsible or appropriate, against the Attorney-General.

In any civil proceedings by or against the Crown, the court can make such orders as it can make in proceedings between subjects, except that no injunction or order for specific performance can be granted against the Crown. The court can, in lieu thereof, make an order declaratory of the rights of the parties in the hope that the Crown will abide by it. No order for the recovery of land, or delivery up of property, can be made against the Crown, but the court may instead make an order that the plaintiff is entitled as against the Crown to land or to other property or to possession thereof. No execution or attachment will issue to enforce payment by the Crown of any money or costs. The procedure is for the successful party to apply for a certificate in the prescribed form giving particulars of the order. This is served on the solicitor for the department concerned, which is then required to pay the sum due with interest if any. The above exceptions show that, in spite of the Act, the rights of the subject against the Crown are still somewhat imperfect.

Crown Privilege in Civil Proceedings. Either party to a civil action can, amongst other things, ask the Court to order the other party to produce any relevant documents for inspection. Under Sect. 28 of the Crown Proceedings Act, 1947, this right lies against the Crown though the Crown could refuse to obey the order if production of the document(s) would be injurious to the public interest. It had been felt for some time that Ministers whose departments were involved in civil litigation had abused this right. Undoubtedly, some plaintiffs failed in an action against the Crown because even the judge could not obtain access to documents necessary to support the claim. As a result of a number of cases of this kind, the House of Lords decided in *Conway* v. *Rimmer*, [1968] 1 All E.R. 874 that even though a Minister certifies that production of a particular document would be against the public interest the judge may nevertheless see it and decide whether the Minister's view is correct. If the judge cannot accept the Minister's decision he may overrule him and order disclosure of the document to the party concerned. Thus the decision of the Minister is no longer conclusive though it is unlikely that a judge would order disclosure if there was a danger of real prejudice to the national interest.

CHAPTER V

THE LAW OF CONTRACT

A CONTRACT may be defined as an *agreement*, enforceable by the law, between two or more persons to do or abstain from doing some act or acts their intention being to create *legal relations* and not merely to exchange mutual promises.

The definition can be criticised in that some contracts turn out to be unenforceable and, in addition, not all legally binding agreements are true contracts. For example, a transaction by deed under seal derives its legally binding quality from the special way in which it is made rather than from the operation of the laws of contract. In consequence, transactions under seal are not true contracts at all. Nevertheless, the definition at least emphasises the fact that the basic elements of contracts are (i) an agreement; and (ii) an intention to create legal relations.

THE ESSENTIALS OF A VALID CONTRACT

The essential elements of the formation of a valid and enforceable contract can be summarised under the following headings—

    (i) There must be an offer and acceptance, which is in effect the agreement.

    (ii) There must be an intention to create legal relations.

    (iii) There is a requirement of written formalities in some cases.

    (iv) There must be consideration (unless the agreement is under seal).

    (v) The parties must have capacity to contract.

    (vi) There must be genuineness of consent by the parties to the terms of the contract.

    (vii) The contract must be legal and possible.

In the absence of one or more of these essentials, the contract may be void, voidable, or unenforceable.

CLASSIFICATION OF CONTRACTS

Before proceeding to examine the meaning and significance of the points enumerated above the following distinctions should be noted.

Void, voidable and unenforceable contracts. A *void* contract has no binding effect at all and in reality the expression is a contradiction in terms. However, it has been used by lawyers for a long time in order to describe particular situations in the law of contract and its usage is now a matter of convenience. A *voidable* contract is binding but one party has the right, at his option, to set it aside. An *unenforceable* contract is valid in all respects except that it cannot be enforced in a court of law by one or both of the parties should the other refuse to carry out his obligations under it.

Executed and Executory Contracts. A contract is said to be *executed* when one or both of the parties have done all that the contract requires. A contract is said to be *executory* when the obligations of one or both of the parties remain to be carried out. For example, if A and B agree to exchange A's scooter for B's motor cycle and do it immediately, the *possession* of the goods and the *right* to the goods are transferred *together* and the contract is *executed*. If they agree to exchange the following week the *right* to the goods is transferred but not the *possession* and the contract is *executory*. Thus an *executed* contract conveys a *chose in possession*, while an *executory* contract conveys a *chose in action*.

Speciality and Simple Contracts and Contracts of Record. *Speciality contracts* are also called contracts under seal, or deeds. All the terms of such contracts are reduced to writing and then the contract is signed, sealed and delivered. The signature is usually attested, i.e. witnessed. A deed operates from the date of delivery, though a deed is presumed to have been delivered on the day of the date of the deed, unless this can be rebutted by evidence to the contrary. Delivery may be (*a*) *actual*, where the deed is handed over to the other party, or (*b*) *constructive*, where the party delivering the deed touches the seal with his finger and says: "I deliver this my act and deed!" This is then construed as delivery and the deed becomes operative. In many cases, however, there is no delivery, actual or constructive, and once a deed has been signed by the parties, it will be extremely difficult for either of them to show that the deed was not delivered. (*Per* Danckwerts, J., in *Stromdale and Ball Ltd.* v. *Burden*, [1952] 1 All E.R. 59.)

The general law of contract *requires* a deed in only one case, i.e. a lease of more than three years, which must be under seal if it is to create a legal estate.

Sometimes a deed is delivered subject to a condition, e.g. that it is not effective until the purchase money has been paid; or is delivered now, but is not to become operative until some future time. In these cases, the deed is not operative until the condition is carried out or the stipulated time has elapsed and such a deed has the special name of "escrow." (*Vincent* v. *Premo Enterprises (Voucher Sales) Ltd.*, 1969.)[33]

There are two forms of escrow—

(i) Where the deed is delivered to a third party who delivers to the other party when the condition is fulfilled.

(ii) Where the deed is delivered to the other party directly, but is not operative until the condition is fulfilled.

An escrow is useful where a person is selling property but will be abroad before completion. He may sign and deliver an escrow before leaving the country so that the deal can be completed if the conditions are carried out.

A deed has certain characteristics which serve to distinguish it from a simple contract—

(*a*) *Merger.* If a simple contract is afterwards embodied in a deed made between the same parties, the simple contract merges into, or is swallowed up by the deed, for the deed is the superior document. But if the deed is only intended to cover part of the terms of the previous simple contract, there is no merger of that part of the simple contract not covered by the deed.

(*b*) *Limitation of Actions.* The right of action under a speciality contract is barred unless it is brought within twelve years from the date when the cause of action arises on it, i.e. when the deed could first have been sued upon. Time does not run from the date of making the deed. A similar right of action is barred under a simple contract after only six years. (Limitation Act, 1939.)

(*c*) *Consideration is not essential* to support a deed, though specific performance will not be granted if the promise is gratuitous (see p. 208). Simple contracts must be supported by consideration.

(*d*) *Estoppel.* Statements in a deed tend to be conclusive against the party making them, and although he might be able to prove they were not true, the rule of evidence called "estoppel" will prevent this by excluding the very evidence which would be needed. In modern law, however, a deed does not operate as an estoppel where one of the parties wishes to bring evidence to show fraud, duress, mistake, lack of capacity, illegality, or that the deed is an escrow. In addition, where a deed is rectifiable (see p. 155) the doctrine of estoppel by deed does not bind the parties to it. (*Wilson* v. *Wilson*, 1969.)[34]

Simple contracts form the great majority of contracts, and are sometimes referred to as parol contracts. This class includes all contracts not under seal, and for their enforcement they require consideration. Simple contracts may be made orally or in writing, or they may be inferred from the conduct of the parties; but no simple contract can exist which does not arise from a valid offer and a valid acceptance supported by some consideration. When these elements exist, the contract is valid in the absence of some vitiating element such as lack of capacity of one of the parties, lack of reality of consent, or illegality or impossibility of performance.

A contract of record consists of obligations imposed upon a person by the Crown in its judicial capacity. Examples are a recognisance binding a person over to be of good behaviour and arising from criminal proceedings, or a recognisance to appear as a witness in a case in the Crown Court after giving a deposition before the magistrates. Such contracts are formed by an entry on the Court Records and the signing of a form by the individual concerned. There is no need for the Crown to sue on a recognisance. On failure to observe its terms, an extract of it is copied from the court's record and sent to the clerk of the peace, who directs the sheriff immediately to levy execution of the goods of the person giving the recognisance. There is a sense in which such contracts are not true contracts because of the absence of agreement of the person against whom the judgment is entered.

THE FORMATION OF CONTRACT

In order to decide whether a contract has come into being it is necessary to establish that there has been an *agreement* between the parties. In consequence it must be shown that an *offer* was made by one party (called the offeror) which was *accepted* by the other party (called the offeree) and that *legal relations* were intended.

OFFER AND ACCEPTANCE

A contract is an agreement and comes into existence when one party makes an offer which the other accepts. The person making the offer is called the offeror, and the person to whom it is made is called the offeree. An offer may be express or implied. Suppose X says to Y—"I will sell you this watch for £5," and Y says—"I agree." An express offer and acceptance have been made; X is the offeror and Y the offeree. Alternatively Y may say to X—"I will give you £5 for that watch." If X says—"I agree," then another express offer has been made, but Y is the offeror and X is the offeree. In both cases, the acceptance brings a contract into being. In order to find out what makes the offer and who the acceptance, it is necessary to examine the way in which the contract is negotiated. Often it matters little, if at all; in some cases it is crucial.

Offer. An offer may be made to a specific person or to any member of a group of persons, or to the world at large (*Carlill* v. *Carbolic Smoke Ball Co.*, 1893),[35] though sometimes what looks like an offer may be no more than an invitation to make an offer, or as it is sometimes called an *invitation to treat*. If I expose in my shop widow a coat priced £15, this is not an offer to sell. It is not possible for a person to enter the shop and say: "I accept you offer; here is the £15." It is the would-be buyer who makes the offer when tendering the money. (*Pharmaceutical Society of Great Britain* v. *Boots Cash Chemists Ltd.*, 1953.)[36] If by chance the coat has been wrongly priced, I shall be entitled to say: "I am sorry; the price is £50," and refuse to sell.

The same principles have been applied to prices set out in price lists, catalogues and circulars. (*Spencer* v. *Harding*, 1870,[37] and *Partridge* v. *Crittenden*, 1968.[38]) In other cases, such as automatic vending machines, the position is doubtful, and it has not been decided whether such machines are invitations to treat or represent an implied offer which is accepted when a coin is put into the machine. However, it does seem that if a bus travels along a certain route, there is an *implied offer* on the part of its owners to carry passengers at the published fares for the various stages, and it would appear that when a passenger boards the bus, he makes an *implied acceptance* of the offer, agreeing to be bound by the company's conditions and to pay the appropriate fare. (*Wilkie* v. *London Passenger Transport Board*, [1947] 1 All E.R. 258.) With regard to negotiations for the sale of land, the same principles are again applied with perhaps this difference, that in the case of a sale of land the court is likely to regard a communication as an invitation to treat unless the intention to contract is very clear. (*Harvey* v. *Facey*, 1893,[39] and *Clifton* v. *Palumbo*, 1944.)[40]

Problems relating to contractual offers have risen in the case of *auction sales* but the position is now largely resolved. An advertisement of an auction is not an offer to hold it. (*Harris* v. *Nickerson*, 1873.)[41] At an auction the bid is the offer; the auctioneer's request for bids is merely an invitation to treat. The sale is complete when the hammer falls, and until that time any bid may be withdrawn. (*Payne* v. *Cave* (1789), 3 Term Rep. 148.)

The position when the auction is without reserve is not absolutely certain because it has never been clearly decided whether an advertisement to sell articles by auction without any reserve price constitutes an offer to sell to the highest bidder. If it does constitute such an offer, the article is purchased and the contract is made when the highest bidder is ascertained by the cessation of bids, and there is no need for the auctioneer to accept by fall of the hammer. The matter was considered *obiter* in *Warlow* v. *Harrison* (1859), 1 E & E 309, and it was said that once bidding commences in an auction without reserve, the auctioneer must sell to the highest bidder.

Acceptance. Once the existence of an offer has been proved, the Court must be satisfied that the offeree has accepted the offer, otherwise there is no contract. An agreement may nevertheless be inferred from the conduct of the parties. (*Brogden* v. *Metropolitan Railway*, 1877.)[42]

The person who accepts an offer must be aware that the offer has been made. Thus if B has found A's lost dog and, not having seen an advertisement by A offering a reward for its return, returns it out of goodness of heart, B will not be able to claim the reward. He cannot be held to accept an offer of which he is unaware. However, as long as the acceptor *is aware* of the making of the offer, his motive in accepting it is immaterial. (*Williams* v. *Carwardine*, 1833.)[43]

Conditional Assent. An acceptance must be absolute and unconditional. One form of conditional assent is an acceptance "subject to contract." The law has placed a special significance on these words, and they are always construed as meaning that the parties do not intend to be bound until a formal contract is prepared. (*Winn* v. *Bull*, 1877.)[44] However, if the statement is qualified and the terms of a proposed contract can be identified, the court will enforce it. (*Filby* v. *Hounsell*, 1896.)[45] A potential purchaser can generally recover any deposit paid if he does not continue with a "subject to contract" purchase. (*Chillingworth* v. *Esche*, 1923.)[46] Where the deposit had been paid to an estate agent it was thought that he received it as agent for the vendor so that the latter was liable to return the money even though he had not received it. (*Goding* v. *Frazer*, 1966,[47] and *Burt* v. *Claude Cousins & Co. Ltd.*, 1971,[47a] but see now *Barrington* v. *Lee*, 1971.)[648]

In other cases of conditional assent the attitude of the court is not so predictable, but it would seem that if the court decides that the further agreement of the parties is not a condition precedent to the formation of the contract, but is merely part of the performance of an already binding agreement, the court will enforce the contract. (*Branca* v. *Cobarro*, 1947.)[48] The effect of the use of the words "without prejudice" in letters forming the basis of negotiations between parties to a contract was considered by the court in *Tomlin* v. *Standard Telephone and Cables Ltd.*, 1969.[49] It was decided that the words meant "without prejudice to the position of the writer of it if the terms which he proposed therein were not accepted." If the terms were accepted a binding contract was established.

Contractual Terms. While considering the matter of conditional assent, it is convenient to deal briefly with an additional problem which may face a court in certain of these cases.

A contract will not be enforced unless the parties have expressed themselves with reasonable clarity on the matter of essential terms. A situation may therefore exist in which there is sufficient assent to satisfy the basic requirements of offer and acceptance yet the contract is incomplete (or inchoate) as to certain of its terms.

In such a case it may be possible for the court to complete the contract by reference to a *trade practice* or *course of dealing* between the parties. (*Hillas* v. *Arcos*, 1932.)[50] Sometimes the agreement itself may provide a method of completion. (*Foley* v. *Classique Coaches Ltd.*, 1934.)[51] However, if the court cannot obtain assistance from these sources, it will not usually complete the contract for the parties, and the contract, being *inchoate*, cannot be enforced. (*Scammell* v. *Ouston*, 1941.)[52] However, a covenant in a conveyance that the purchaser should be given "the first option of purchasing . . . at a price to be agreed upon" certain adjoining land imposes an obligation on the vendor at least to offer the land at a price at which he is willing to sell. (*Smith* v. *Morgan*, *The Times*, March 26th, 1971.)

It should be noted that the court may *imply a term* into a contract in order to give "business efficacy" to it. Such an implied term is based upon the presumption that both parties would have agreed to include it in the contract if they had thought about it, and that the term is essential in order to achieve the *clear* intentions of the parties. (*The Moorcock*, 1889.)[53]

Furthermore, it is necessary to distinguish between a term which has yet to be agreed by the parties and a term on which they have agreed but is in the event meaningless or ambiguous. In the first case, no contract exists unless the deficiency can be made good by the methods outlined above. In the second case, it may be possible to ignore the term and enforce the contract without it. (*Nicolene* v. *Simmonds*, 1953.)[54] However, the court cannot ignore a term unless it represents the *final* agreement of the parties. If, as in *Scammell* v. *Ouston*, 1941,[52] the term is still being negotiated the contract will be inchoate and unenforceable. In addition, the term must be *clearly* severable from the rest of the contract, i.e. it must be possible to enforce the contract without it, which was not the case in *Scammell* v. *Ouston*, 1941.[52]

Counter Offer. A counter-offer is a rejection of the original offer and in some cases has the effect of cancelling it. Where the counter-offer *introduces a new term*, the original offer is cancelled (*Hyde* v. *Wrench*, 1840,[55] *Neale* v. *Merrett*, 1930,[55a] and *Northland Airlines Ltd.* v. *Dennis Ferranti Meters Ltd.*, 1970[55b]); but a simple request for information where the offeree merely *tries to induce a new term* may not amount to an actual counter-offer. (*Stevenson* v. *McLean*, 1880.)[56]

Retrospective Acceptance. Acceptance may be retrospective, i.e. the parties may carry out certain acts on the assumption that a contract will eventually be made. When the acceptance is eventually made, it is capable of operating retrospectively, thus giving legal effect to everything that has been done before. That the contract is to operate retrospectively may be provided for by an express term in the contract or may be inferred from conduct. (*Trollope and Colls Ltd.* v. *Atomic Power Construction Ltd.*, 1962.)[57]

Tenders. It is common enough in business for companies wishing to buy goods to invite suppliers to submit tenders giving details of the price for which the goods may be bought. It is essential to understand precisely what is meant by "accepting" a tender, since different legal results are obtained according to the wording of the invitation to tender. If the invitation by its wording implies that the potential buyer *will* require the goods, acceptance of a tender sent in response to such an invitation results in a binding contract under which the buyer undertakes to buy all the goods specified in the tender from the person who has submitted it. On the other hand, if the invitation by its wording suggests that the potential buyer *may* require the goods, acceptance of a tender results in a standing offer by the supplier to supply the goods set out in the tender as and when required by the person accepting it. Each time the buyer orders a quantity, there is a contract confined to that quantity; but if the buyer does not order any of the goods set out in the tender, or a smaller number than the supplier quoted for, there is no breach of contract. Conversely, if the person submitting the tender wishes to revoke his standing offer, he may do so, except in so far as the buyer has already ordered goods under the tender. These must be supplied or the tenderer is in breach of contract. (*Great Northern Railway* v. *Witham*, 1873.)[58]

Methods of Acceptance. An acceptance may be made in various ways. It may be made in writing or orally, but it must in general be communicated and communication must be made by a person authorised to make it. (*Powell* v. *Lee*, 1908.)[59] Silence cannot amount to acceptance, except perhaps in the case of prior consent by the offeree. Thus if P says to Q: "If I do not hear from you before noon tomorrow, I shall assume you accept my offer," he will find he is unable, at least without Q's consent, to bind Q in this way, and Q need take no action at all. (*Felthouse* v. *Bindley*, 1862.)[60] This rule of the common law goes some way towards preventing inertia selling, though protection is now given by the Unsolicited Goods and Services Act, 1971.

However, there are some cases in which the offeror is deemed to have waived communication of the acceptance. This most often occurs in the case of *unilateral contracts* such as promise to pay money in return for some act to be carried out by the offeree. Performance of the act operates as an acceptance, and no communication is required. (*Carlill* v. *Carbolic Smoke Ball Co.*, 1893.)[35]

The offeror may stipulate a method of acceptance (*Eliason* v. *Henshaw*, 1819),[61] and where this is done it would seen that, if the offeror makes it clear that one method only will suffice, then there is no contract unless the offeree accepts by the method prescribed. Nevertheless, in such a case the offeror could waive his right to have the acceptance communicated in a given way and agree to the substituted method. If the offeror has stipulated a method of acceptance *but does not make it clear that only one method will suffice*, then a quicker or equally expeditious method will be effective, since there is no prejudice to the offeror if he learns that the offer has been accepted sooner than, or at the same time as he would have known had the offeree used the prescribed method. (*Manchester Diocesan Council for Education* v. *Commercial and General Investments Ltd.*, 1969.)[62] Certainly an offer by telegram is good evidence of the offeror's desire for a quick reply so that a reply by letter would probably be ineffective.

If the offeror has not stipulated a method of acceptance, the offeree may choose his own method, though where acceptance is by word of mouth it is not enough that it be spoken, it must actually be heard by the offeror. In this connection an interesting development occurs with the use of the telephone and teleprinter. Since these are methods of instantaneous communication, it is held that the contract is not complete unless the apparent communication takes place. (*Entores Ltd.* v. *Miles Far East Corporation*, 1955.)[63]

Use of Post. The general rule is that acceptance must be communicated to the offeror and that the contract is made *when* and *where* the acceptance is received by the offeror. (*Entores Ltd.* v. *Miles Far East Corporation*, 1955.)[63]

However, if the Post is the proper method of communication between the parties then acceptance is deemed complete immediately the letter of acceptance is posted, even if it is delayed or is lost or destroyed in the post so that it never reaches the offeror. (*Household Fire Insurance Co.* v. *Grant*, 1879.)[64] Nevertheless, the letter of acceptance must be properly addressed and properly posted (*Re London and Northern Bank, ex parte Jones*, 1900),[65] and the court must be satisfied that it was within the contemplation of the parties that the post might be used as a method of communicating acceptance. It is not certain whether the exchange of contracts for the sale of land falls within the post rule and whether posting or delivery is the vital time. However, where the sale is governed by the Law Society's Conditions posting is regarded as the time of exchange. Where there is a misdirection of the letter containing the offer, then the offer is made when it actually reaches the offeree, and not when it would have reached him in the ordinary course of post. (*Adams* v. *Lindsell*, 1818.)[66] In contrast with the rule regarding acceptance by post, a letter of revocation is not effective until it actually reaches the offeree, whereas a letter of acceptance is effective when it is posted. (*Byrne* v. *Van Tienhoven*, 1880.)[67] A telegram is effective as an acceptance when it is handed in at the post office.

The better view is that, in English law, an acceptance cannot be recalled once it has been posted even though it has not reached the offeror. Thus, if X posted a letter accepting Y's offer to sell goods, X could not withdraw the acceptance by telephoning Y and asking him to ignore the letter of acceptance when it arrived, and Y could hold X bound by the contract if he wished to do so. This is obvious, the rules being what they are, since otherwise Y would be bound when the letter was posted, and X would be reserving the right to withdraw his acceptance during the transit of the letter even though Y was still bound. However, by Scots law the affect of an acceptance can be altered after posting. (*Dunmore (Countess)* v. *Alexander*, 1839.)[68]

There is some controversy as to whether agreement can result from *cross-offers*. For example, suppose X by letter offers to sell his scooter to Y for £50, and Y, by means of a second letter, which crosses X's letter in the post, offers to buy X's scooter for £50. Can there be a contract? The matter was discussed by an English court in *Tinn* v. *Hoffman* (1873), 29 L.T. 271, and the court's conclusion was that no contract could arise. However, the matter is still at large and it is possible to hold the view that a contract would come into being where it appears that the parties have intended to create a legally binding agreement on the same footing.

Revocation of offer. The general rule is that *an offer may be revoked at any time before the acceptance*, though sometimes there is what is known as an option attached to the offer, and time is given in which to make the decision whether to accept or not. If the offeror agrees to give seven days, then the offeree may accept the offer at any time within seven days, or he need not accept at all. However, the offeror need not keep the offer open for seven days but can revoke it, unless the offeree has given some consideration for the option. The option is really a separate contract to allow time to decide whether to accept the original offer or not. It was thought at one time that, where the option to buy property was not supported by consideration, the offer could be revoked by its sale to another, but in modern law it is necessary for the offeror to communicate the revocation to the offeree either himself, or by means of some reliable person. (*Stevenson* v. *McLean*, 1880.)[56]

Revocation, to be effective, must be communicated to the offeree before he has accepted the offer. The word "communication" merely implies that the revocation must have come to the knowledge of the offeree. (*Byrne* v. *Van Tienhoven*, 1880.)[67] Communication may be made directly by the offeror or may reach the offeree through some other reliable source. Suppose X offers to sell a car to Y and gives Y a few days to think the matter over without actually giving him a valid option. If, before Y has accepted, X sells the car to Z and Y hears from P that X has in fact sold the car, it will be of no avail for Y to purport to accept and try to enforce the contract against X. (*Dickenson* v. *Dodds*, 1876.)[69]

Where the offer consists of a promise in return for an act, as where a reward is offered for the return of lost property, the offer, although made to the whole world, can be revoked as any other offer can. It is thought to be enough that the same publicity be given to the revocation as was given to the offer, even though the revocation may not be seen by all the persons who saw the offer.

A more difficult problem arises when an offer which requires a certain act to be carried out is revoked after some person has begun to perform the act but before he has completed it. If, for example, X offers £1,000 to anyone who can successfully swim the Channel, and Y, deciding he will try to obtain the money, starts his swim from Dover, can X revoke his offer when Y is half-way across the Channel? The better view is that he cannot on the grounds that an offer of the kind made by X is two offers in one, namely (i) to pay £1,000 to a successful swimmer and (ii) something in the nature of an option to hold the offer open for a reasonable time once performance has been embarked upon, so that the person trying to complete the task has a reasonable time in which to do so.

Lapse of Time. If a time for acceptance has been stipulated, then the offer lapses when the time has expired. If no time has been stipulated, then the acceptance must be within a reasonable time. What is reasonable is determined by the court from the circumstances of the case. (*Ramsgate Victoria Hotel Co.* v. *Montefiore*, 1866,[70] *Manchester Diocesan Council for Education* v. *Commercial and General Investments Ltd.*, 1969.[62]) Where the offer is made by telegram, it is likely to lapse very quickly.

Conditional Offers. An offer may terminate on the happening of a given event if it is made subject to a condition that it will do so, e.g. that the offer is to terminate if the goods offered for sale are damaged before acceptance. Such a condition may be made expressly, but may also be implied from the circumstances. (*Financings Ltd*, v. *Stimson*, 1962.)[71]

Effect of Death of a Party. The effect of death would appear to vary according to the type of contract in question, whether the death is that of the offeror or offeree, and whether death takes place before or after acceptance.

(*a*) DEATH OF OFFEROR BEFORE ACCEPTANCE. It would seem that if the contract envisaged by the offer is not one involving the personality of the offeror, the death of the offeror will not, until notified to the offeree, prevent acceptance. (*Bradbury* v. *Morgan*, 1862.)[72] If the contract envisaged by the offer does involve a personal relationship, such as an offer to act as agent, then the death of the offeror prevents acceptance.

(*b*) DEATH OF OFFEREE BEFORE ACCEPTANCE. Once the offeree is dead, there is no offer which can be accepted. His executors cannot, therefore, accept the offer in his stead. The offer being made to a' living person can only be accepted by that person and assumes his continued existence. The rule would seem to apply *whether the proposed contract involves a personality relationship or not.* (*Re Cheshire Banking Co., Duff's Executors' Case*, 1886.)[73]

(*c*) DEATH OF PARTIES AFTER ACCEPTANCE. Death after acceptance has normally no effect unless the contract is for personal services, when the liability under the contract ceases. Thus, if X sells his car to Y and before the car is delivered X dies, it would be possible for Y to sue X's personal representatives for breach of contract if they were to refuse to deliver the car. But if X agrees to play the piano at a concert and dies two days before the performance, one could hardly expect his personal representatives to play the piano in his stead.

INTENTION TO CREATE LEGAL RELATIONS

The law will not necessarily recognise the existence of a contract simply because of the presence of mutual promises. Some agreements are not intended to be the subject of legal actions, and if the parties expressly declare, or clearly indicate in their agreement, that they do not intend to assume contractual obligations, then the law accepts and implements their intention. There are many promises made which are of such a nature that no reasonable person could imagine that there was any intention to create legal relations. If P invites Q to dinner, he does not also invite an action for damages if he fails to keep the appointment.

In deciding the question of intention the courts use an objective, not a subjective test, and what the parties had in mind is not conclusive. The court considers what inferences reasonable people would draw from the words or conduct of the parties. If reasonable people would assume that there was no intention to create a binding agreement, the courts will not enforce it.

The subject can be considered under two headings—

(i) Cases where the parties have not expressly denied their intention to create legal relations.

(*a*) *Advertisements.* It is a commonplace in business to advertise goods by making extravagant claims as to their efficacy, often supported by promises or guarantees of a vague character if the goods do not live up to expectations. The construction placed by the courts on such statements depends on the circumstances, but where a company deposits money in the bank against possible claims, then the court is likely to hold that legal relations were contemplated. (*Carlill* v. *Carbolic Smoke Ball Co.*, 1893.)[35] But not all advertisements are treated as serious offers, and advertising "puffs" are often treated as mere sales talk; otherwise the courts would be perpetually passing judgment on the merits or demerits of a host of products.

(*b*) *Family Agreements.* Many of these cannot be imagined to be the subject of litigation, but some may be. The question is basically one of construction, and the court looks at the words and the surrounding circumstances. With regard to agreements between husband and wife, it is difficult to draw precise conclusions from the decided cases. However, it seems that the courts will not enforce these agreements where—

(i) the husband and wife were living together when the agreement was made—on the ground perhaps that in the view of the court it would be unseemly and distressing to use legal proceedings for settling marital differences (*Balfour* v. *Balfour*, 1919,[74] and *Spellman* v. *Spellman*, 1961[75]; however, where husband and wife were not living together in amity when the agreement was made the court may enforce it. (*Merritt* v. *Merritt*, 1969);[76]

(ii) the words used by the parties were uncertain—on the ground perhaps that uncertainty in deciding upon important terms of the agreement leads to the conclusion that there was no intention to create legal relations (*Gould* v. *Gould*, 1969).[77]

An agreement between husband and wife is much more likely to be enforced if it is clear and unequivocal. This might be achieved if the parties made an agreement supported by a simple note or memorandum setting out the terms and preferably prepared by a solicitor.

It should be noted that agreements of a non–domestic nature made between husband and wife may be enforceable, e.g. a husband may be his wife's tenant.

In family agreements other than those between husband and wife, the court may reach the conclusion that legal relations can be inferred and the injured party may be given a remedy. (*Simpkins* v. *Pays*, 1955.)[78] This is particularly true where one of the parties has altered his position to his detriment in reliance on the promises of the other (*Parker* v. *Clark*, 1960),[79] though uncertainty as to terms normally leads to the conclusion that there was no contractual intent. (*Jones* v. *Padavatton*, 1969.)[80]

(iii) *Other cases.* In other situations whether there is an intention to create legal relations must be deduced by the court from the circumstances of the case. (*Buckpitt* v. *Oates*, 1968.)[81] However, in the case of clubs and societies, many of the relationships which exist and promises which are made are enforceable only as moral obligations. Thus, if a man competes for a prize in a golf competition and is the winner, he may not be able to sue for the prize he has won if it is not otherwise forthcoming.

(ii) **Cases where the parties expressly deny any intention to create legal relations.** Some types of agreement, which would normally be the subject of a contract, are expressly taken outside the scope of the law by the parties' agreeing to rely on each other's honour. (*Jones* v. *Vernon's Pools Ltd.*, 1938.)[82] In such cases there is a standardised agreement and the advantage of excluding legal action appears to be predominantly in favour of one of the parties, although it is difficult to see how pools could run if they had the prospect of weekly legal actions from disgruntled investors. It has been pleaded, but without success, that standardised agreements which exclude the possibility of legal redress are against public policy, and clearly if such procedures become widespread Parliament may have to intervene. There is no such objection where business men reach agreements at arm's length, and if the parties expressly declare or clearly indicate that they do not wish to assume contractual obligations, then the law accepts and implements their decision. (*Rose and Frank Co.* v. *Crompton and Brothers Ltd.*, 1925.)[83]

FORMALITIES

We have already discussed the main differences between contracts under seal and simple or "parol" contracts. In most cases, it does not matter which of the various forms of simple contract is used and a contract made orally or by conduct will usually be just as effective as a written one. Exceptionally, however, written formalities are required.

Contracts which must be in Writing. The following simple contracts are required by statute to be in writing otherwise they are *void*—

(a) bills of exchange and promissory notes (see p. 295);
(b) hire purchase contracts;
(c) contracts of marine insurance;
(d) acknowledgments of statute-barred debts (see p. 201).

Contracts which must be Evidenced in Writing. In two cases writing, though not essential to the formation of a contract, is needed for evidential purposes, and in its absence the courts will not enforce the agreement. These two special cases are—

(i) contracts of guarantee, and
(ii) contracts for the sale or other disposition of land or any interest in land.

The Statute of Frauds, 1677, originally set out six classes of contracts which required this evidential writing. The provision concerning land was embodied in Sect. 40 of the Law of Property Act, 1925, as part of the consolidation of the law of property. The provision regarding guarantees remained after the Statute of Frauds was largely repealed by the Law Reform (Enforcement of Contracts) Act, 1954.

Even in these cases the writing need not be in the form of a contract, but may be the exchange of letters or other memoranda; and where one party has partly performed his side of the contract, the courts may dispense with the need for written evidence. Further, the absence of a memorandum must be specially pleaded by the party seeking to rely on its absence, otherwise the court will hear oral evidence to prove the contract.

These rules apply to contracts of guarantee but they do not apply to contracts of indemnity. It is necessary, therefore, to distinguish between these two. In a contract of indemnity, the person giving the indemnity makes himself primarily liable by using such words as, "I will see that you are paid." In a contract of guarantee, the guarantor expects the person he has guaranteed to carry out his obligations, and the substance of the wording would be, "If he does not pay you, I will." An indemnity does not require writing because it did not come within the Statute of Frauds; a guarantee requires a memorandum. (*Mountstephen* v. *Lakeman*, 1871.)[84]

In this connection it should be noted that it is an essential feature of a guarantee that the person giving it is totally unconnected with the contract he guarantees except by reason of his promise to pay the debt. Thus, a *del credere* agent who for an extra commission promises to make good losses incurred by his principal in respect of the unpaid debts of third parties introduced by the agent, gives an indemnity and not a guarantee because his undertaking to reimburse his principal is part of a wider transaction, i.e., agency.

Difficulties have arisen in the application of the provisions concerning land in cases dealing with the sale of crops. A distinction must be made between *fructus naturales* (natural products of the soil, or the products of things which do not have to be sown each year) and *fructus industriales* (crops produced annually by man). Thus, an agreement to sell growing timber or grass must be evidenced in writing, but an agreement to sell growing potatoes need not be. (*Parker* v. *Staniland* (1809), 11 East, 362.) However, if the *fructus naturales* are to be cut at once by either party and therefore *no further benefit is to be derived from the soil* the contract is regarded as one for the sale of goods and no memorandum is required. (*Marshall* v. *Green* (1875), 1 C.P.D., 35.)

THE MEMORANDUM. The memorandum in writing, to satisfy the courts in the two cases where it is now required, need not be made when the contract is made, but must exist before the action is brought. There are four requirements—

(i) *It must contain the names or a sufficient description of the parties.* It must state which is the buyer and which is the seller, and it is not sufficient to call the seller the vendor, since the court wishes to ascertain the owner and not the person who purports to sell. It is sufficient if they are described so as to be capable of identification, even if this involves the giving of some oral evidence (*Carr* v. *Lynch*, 1900)[85] and the fact that one of the parties is misnamed will not prevent the contract being enforced if he can be identified by reference to characteristics other than his name. (*F. Goldsmith (Sicklesmere) Ltd.* v. *Baxter*, 1969.)[86]

(ii) *The subject matter of the contract must be described so that it can be identified, and all the material terms of the contract must be stated.* However, the subject matter may be sufficiently described without going into great detail, e.g. a memorandum recording the sale of "24 acres of land at Totmanslow," was held sufficient on proof that the seller had no other land there .(*Plant* v. *Bourne* [1897], 2 Ch. 281.) The absence of a material term may be fatal to the memorandum, though not if it is beneficial to one party and the other party agrees to carry it out or the party to benefit agrees to waive it. (*Hawkins* v. *Price*, 1947,[87] and *Scott* v. *Bradley*, 1971.)[87a]

(iii) *The consideration must appear*, except in contracts of guarantee. In the latter case Sect. 3 of the Mercantile Law Amendment Act, 1856, dispenses with the necessity for setting out the consideration, but it must exist. The consideration for a guarantee is usually the extension of credit. It follows that the guarantee must be given before the credit was extended, otherwise it is for past consideration, and is unenforceable unless made under seal.

(iv) *The memorandum must contain the signature of the party to be charged or his agent properly authorised to sign*. This means in effect that there may be cases where one party has a sufficient memorandum to found an action, whereas the other may lack the necessary signature. The rule is made less rigid by a somewhat free interpretation of the word signature, and it may take any form so long as it was intended to be a signature. (*Caton* v. *Caton*, 1867.)[88] It may be printed, typed, or stamped, and mere initials or an identifying mark will suffice. It need not be at the end of the document, but may be in the middle or at the beginning. In the case of an auction sale, the auctioneer or his clerk signs for both buyer and seller.

The rigidity of these rules is further mitigated by the fact that the memorandum need not be a single document, but may consist of a number of connected documents. Oral evidence will be admitted to connect them if (*a*) one refers to the other; or (*b*) the documents are *orima facie* connected, since in the latter case proof of connection is not entirely oral. (*Pearce* v. *Gardner*, 1897,[89] and *Timmins* v. *Moreland Street Property Ltd.*, 1958.)[90] In addition, a memorandum is not defective merely because it contains the words "subject to contract" provided that there is evidence to show that the parties have waived the provision. (*Griffiths* v. *Young*, 1970.)[91]

In the absence of a memorandum the contract is not void at common law but is unenforceable, although it may sometimes be relied upon as a defence. Thus, if X orally agrees to let Y dig for gravel on X's land, Y would not commit a trespass if he entered on the land to dig. If, however, X asks him to leave and Y refuses, then he may become a trespasser in spite of the contract, since it was at best a licence which has now been withdrawn. It follows that if the contract is not void, money paid or property transferred under it cannot be recovered, unless there is a total lack of consideration. (*Monnickendam* v. *Leanse*, 1923.)[92]

Although the common law requires a written memorandum, there may still be equitable remedies, and equity will grant specific performance in suitable cases where the plaintiff has partly performed his agreement. This remedy is particularly appropriate in contracts for the sale or other disposition of land. The basis of this equitable jurisdiction probably stems from the maxim: "Equity will not allow a statute to be used as an engine of fraud."

The following conditions must exist before the doctrine can operate—

(a) *The contract must be one of which specific performance will be granted.*
Specific performance is a discretionary remedy and it follows that; "He
who comes to Equity must come with clean hands." It will not be
granted where the court thinks damages are an adequate remedy, and
never in the case of contracts with minors. This seems to confine the
remedy to contracts concerning land, because Equity will not specifically enforce a guarantee.

(b) *Relationship of the act of part performance to the alleged contract.* In
Chaproniere v. Lambert, [1917] 2 Ch. 356, Washington, L.J., laid down in
the Court of Appeal the doctrine that the acts of part performance relied
on must be not only referable to a contract such as that alleged but
referable to no other, and this rule was applied in some subsequent
cases. (*Rawlinson v. Ames*, 1925,[93] and *Broughton v. Snook*, 1938.)[94] However, strict adherence to this doctrine could produce hardship and in
some circumstances run contrary to the overriding principle that a
Court of Equity will not allow a statute to be used as an engine of fraud.
(*Daniels v. Trefusis*, 1914.)[95]

Accordingly, in *Kingswood Estate Co. Ltd. v. Anderson*, [1962] 3 All
E.R. 593, the Court of Appeal refused to follow *Chaproniere v. Lambert*
and stated that the plaintiff's part performance need not be unequivo-
cally or exclusively referable to the contract alleged. It was sufficient
if it proved the existence of some contract and was consistent with the
plaintiff's claim. This principle was applied by Stamp, J., in *Wakeham
v. Mackenzie*, 1968.[96]

However, acts of part performance may presumably still be ineffective
if they are explainable on grounds other than the existence of a contract. (*Maddison v. Alderson*, 1883.)[97]

(c) *There must be adequate oral evidence of the terms of the contract, and the
act of part performance must be the act of the plaintiff.* A mere payment of
money is not by itself a sufficient act of part performance for this purpose,
because money has no exclusive nature; such a payment raises no equity
except the right to recover the money. Occupation of property is usually
considered a sufficient act of part performance.

The Moneylenders Act, 1927. Under Sect. 6 of the Moneylenders Act,
1927, no contract for the repayment by a borrower of money lent by a
moneylender (as defined in Sect. 6), and no security given by the
borrower, is enforceable unless a memorandum is drawn up in accordance with this section. The memorandum must contain all the terms
of the contract, and in particular must state the amount of the loan,
the rate of interest, and the date on which the loan was made. (*Congresbury Motors Ltd. v. Anglo-Belge Finance Co. Ltd.*, 1969.)[98]

It differs from the Statute of Frauds as follows—

(a) These provisions only operate against the lender.

(b) The memorandum must be signed by the borrower personally;
it need not be signed by the lender.

(*c*) The memorandum must be signed or the security (if any) given, before the money is actually lent and a copy must be sent to the borrower within seven days of making the contract.

(*d*) The memorandum must be drawn up expressly to record the transaction.

(*e*) Securities and guarantees are unenforceable.

A point of similarity between this statute and the Statute of Frauds is that money actually paid under oral contracts is in all cases irrecoverable, as the contracts are only unenforceable, not void, and title to the money has passed.

CONSIDERATION

Consideration, which is essential to the formation of any contract not made under seal, was defined in *Currie* v. *Misa*, (1875), L.R. 10 Ex 153 as—

> Some right, interest, profit or benefit accruing to one party, or some forbearance, detriment, loss or responsibility given, suffered or undertaken by the other.

The payment of money is a common form of consideration.

Consideration may be *executory*, where the parties exchange promises to perform acts in the future, e.g. C promises to deliver goods to D and D promises to pay for the goods; or it may be *executed*, where one party promises to do something in return for the act of another, rather than for the mere promise of future performance of an act. Here the performance of the act is required before there is any liability on the promise. Where X offers a reward for the return of his lost dog, X is buying the act of the finder, and will not be liable until the dog is found and returned.

The definition in *Currie* v. *Misa* suggests that consideration always refers to the type called executed consideration, since it talks of "benefit" and "detriment," whereas in modern law executory contracts are enforceable. Perhaps the definition given by Sir Frederick Pollock is to be preferred—

> An act or forbearance of one party, *or the promise thereof*, is the price for which *the promise* of the other is bought, and the promise thus given for value is enforceable.

This definition which was adopted by the House of Lords in *Dunlop* v. *Selfridge*, 1915,[99] fits executory contracts.

There are a number of general rules governing consideration—

(*a*) *Simple contracts must be supported by consideration.* This has a long history, and we can note only the following points.

Towards the end of the eighteenth century, Lord Mansfield attacked the doctrine of consideration in two ways. In *Pillans* v. *Van Mierop* (1765), 3 Burr. 1663, he said that where a contract was reduced to writing no consideration was necessary, thus reducing consideration to an aspect of evidence. It may be that this is why consideration is not necessary in a deed, for a deed is good evidence, being written and sealed, and entered into with due solemnity. In France and Scotland, gratuitous promises are enforced, but the court normally requires some good evidence, and often asks for writing. However, Lord Mansfield's attempt to dispense with consideration was short-lived, and his ruling was rejected in *Rann* v. *Hughes* (1778), 7 Term Rep. 350 n. Lord Mansfield also desired the recognition of pre-existing moral obligations as consideration, e.g. a promise to pay a statute-barred debt, or a promise after attaining majority to pay a debt contracted during infancy, but this view was finally rejected in *Eastwood* v. *Kenyon* (1840), 11 Ad. & El. 438. Some of these matters are now dealt with by statute, e.g. a written acknowledgment of a statute-barred debt is binding, even though not supported by consideration. (Limitation Act, 1939, Sect. 23.) Nevertheless, a promise to pay a debt incurred during infancy is not enforceable. (Infants' Relief Act, 1874, Sect. 2.)

(*b*) *Consideration need not be adequate, but must have some value, however slight.* The courts do not exist to repair bad bargains, and though consideration must be present, the parties themselves must attend to its value. (*Haigh* v. *Brooks*, 1839.)[100] But the value must be of an economic character, and mere natural affection of itself is not enough. (*White* v. *Bluett*, 1853.)[101] Nevertheless, acts or omissions even of a trivial nature may be sufficient to support a contract. (*Chappell* v. *Nestle*, 1960.)[102] A self-seeking act in itself may not suffice, and in the case of *Carlill* v. *Catholic Smoke Ball Co.*, 1893,[35] the consideration was provided not by using the smoke ball to cure influenza, but by the unpleasant method of its use. A gift promised conditionally may be binding, if the performance of the condition causes the promisee trouble or inconvenience, e.g. "I will give you my old car if you will tow it away." So too may a gift of property with onerous obligations attached to it, e.g. a promise to give away a lease would be binding, if the donee promised to perform the covenants to repair and pay rent. A promise to give away shares which were partly paid up would be good, if the donee promised to pay the outstanding calls.

The concept of *bailment* gives rise to problems because a person may be held liable for negligent damage to or loss of goods in his care, although he received no money or other consideration for looking after them. (*Coggs* v. *Bernard*, 1703,[103] and *Gilchrist Watt and Sanderson Pty.* v. *York Products Pty.*, 1970.)[103a] However, confusion can best be avoided by regarding bailment as an independent transaction, which has characteristics of contract and tort but is neither. It seems that when X hands his goods to Y under a bailment Y has certain duties in regard to the care of the goods, whether the bailment is accompanied by a contract or not.

However, where the consideration embodied in a deal is woefully inadequate, it may raise a suspicion of fraud, duress or undue influence on the part of the person gaining the advantage.

(*c*) *Consideration must be sufficient.* Sufficiency of consideration is not the same thing as adequacy of consideration. The concept of sufficiency arises in the course of deciding whether the acts in question *amount to consideration at all.* This situation arises where the consideration offered by the promisor is an act which he is already bound to carry out. Thus, the discharge of a *public duty* imposed by law is not consideration. (*Collins* v. *Godefroy*, 1831);[104] nor is the performance of a *contractual duty* already owed to the defendant (*Vanbergen* v. *St. Edmund's Properties Ltd.*, 1933;[105] *Stilk* v. *Myrick*, 1809).[106] However, where the contractual duty is not precisely coincident with the public duty but is in excess of it, performance of the contractual duty may provide consideration (*Ward* v. *Byham*, 1956)[107] and the actual performance of an outstanding contractual obligation may be sufficient to support a promise of a further payment by a third party. (*Shadwell* v. *Shadwell*, 1860.)[108]

(*d*) *Consideration must be legal.* An illegal consideration makes the whole contract invalid.

(*e*) *Consideration must not be past.* Sometimes the act which one party to a contract puts forward as consideration was performed before any promise of reward was made by the other. Where this is so, the act in question may be regarded as *past consideration* and will not support a contractual claim. This somewhat technical rule seems to be based on the idea that the act of one party to an alleged contract can only be regarded as consideration if it was carried out in response to some promise of the other. Where this is not so, the act is regarded as gratuitous, being carried out before any promise of reward was made. (*Roscorla* v. *Thomas*, 1842,[109] and *Re McArdle*, 1951.)[110]

However, there are exceptions to this rule—

(i) Where services are rendered at the express or implied request of the promisor in circumstances which raise an implication of a promise to pay. (*Re Casey's Patents, Stewart* v. *Casey*, 1892.)[111] This exception is not entirely a genuine one since the promisor is assumed to have given an implied undertaking to pay at the time of the request, his subsequent promise being regarded as deciding merely *the actual amount to be paid.* In this situation the act, which follows the request but precedes the settling of the reward, is more in the nature of *executed consideration* which, as we have seen, will support a contract.

(ii) Where a debt is barred by the Limitation Act, 1939, since this can be revived by a subsequent acknowledgement in writing. Such an acknowledgement is effective if it indicates that a debt is due even if it does not state the amount. (*Dungate* v. *Dungate* 1965.)[112] Again, this exception is not wholly genuine since the Limitation Act, 1939, does not provide that past consideration will support the subsequent acknowledgement of debt. The Act simply states that *no consideration of any kind* need be sought.

(iii) Sect. 27 of the Bills of Exchange Act, 1882, provides that past consideration will support a bill of exchange. This genuine exception was probably based on a pre-existing commercial custom.

(*f*) *Consideration must move from the promisee*, i.e. the person to whom the promise is made must give some consideration for it. This arises from the doctrine of privity of contract.

Privity of Contract. This means that in general third parties cannot sue for the carrying out of promises made by the parties to a contract. (*Tweddle* v. *Atkinson*, 1861,[113] *Dunlop* v. *Selfridge*, 1915,[99] *Dunlop* v. *New Garage and Motor Co. Ltd.*, 1915.)[114]

However, there are cases in which a person is allowed to sue upon a contract to which he is not a party—

(*a*) A principal, even if undisclosed, may sue on a contract made by an agent. This exception is perhaps more apparent than real, because in fact the principal is the contracting party who has merely acted through the instrumentality of the agent.

(*b*) Attempts have been made to modify the rule of privity by invoking the equitable doctrine of the constructive trust. Thus, if A and B agree to confer a benefit on C, it may be possible to regard B as a constructive trustee for C of the benefit of the contract. C would then have an action against B if the latter had received the benefit and would not pass it on to C, or against A. However, if A were sued, B would be joined in the action. The application of this principle has always been uncertain and limited, and the courts to not seem eager to extend it. However, one aspect of this equitable doctrine has been established in the commercial world, and was recognised by the House of Lords in *Les Affréteurs Réunis Société Anonyme* v. *Walford*, 1919.[115]

(*c*) In other cases, where a fund is created in the hands of one of the contracting parties in favour of a third party, it may be possible to give the latter a remedy in quasi-contract on the grounds that to allow the contacting party to keep the fund would be to allow unjust enrichment. (*Shamia* v. *Joory*, 1958.)[116]

(*d*) The assignee of a debt or chose in action may, if the assignment is a legal assignment, sue the original debtor. (See p. 293.)

(*e*) The holder for value of a bill of exchange can sue prior parties and the acceptor. (See p. 298.)

(*f*) Under the Restrictive Trade Practices Act, 1956, Sect. 25, the supplier of goods is given a statutory case of action, so that he may enforce against a person not a party to the contract of sale a condition as to re-sale price. However, the re-sale price agreement must have been approved under the provisions of the Resale Prices Act, 1964, otherwise there can be no enforcement of it. (See p. 187.)

(*g*) Certain other exceptions are to be found in statute, e.g. Sect. 11 of the Married Women's Property Act, 1882, provides that if a man insures his life for the benefit of his wife and/or children, or a woman insures her life for the benefit of her husband and/or children, a trust is created in favour of the objects of the policy, and the policy moneys are not liable for the deceased's debts, other than estate duty. (Finance Act, 1968.)

(*h*) The position in land law is that benefits and liabilities attached to or imposed on land may in certain circumstances follow the land into the hands of other owners. (*Smith and Snipes Hall Farm* v. *River Douglas Catchment Board*, 1949,[117] and *Tulk* v. *Moxhay*, 1848.)[118]

(*i*) Bankers' Commercial Credits also present problems in the field of privity. It is common commercial practice for an exporter, E, to ask the buyer of the goods, B, to open, with his banker, a credit in favour of E, the credit to remain irrevocable for a specified time. B agrees with his banker that the credit should be opened and, in return, promises to repay the banker, and usually gives him a lien over the shipping documents. The banker will also require a commission for his services. B's banker then notifies E that a credit has been opened in his favour, and E can draw upon it on presentation of the shipping documents.

However, if B's banker refuses to pay E on presentation of the documents, E could sue B on the original contract of sale, but would be unable to sue B's banker if the rule of privity were applied. The credit arises out of an agreement between B and his banker, and E is a stranger to it. It is unfortunate that this convenient commercial practice should be of questionable legal validity and it is to be hoped that if an exporter had to sue the buyer's banker on a commercial credit the court would allow the action as an exception to the rule of privity on the grounds that a commercial practice in favour of third party rights exists.

(*j*) Attempts have also been made to modify the rule of privity by an *appropriate interpretation of Section* 56(1) *of the Law of Property Act*, 1925.

The subsection provides that "a person may take an immediate or other interest in land or other property, or the benefit of any condition, right of entry, covenant or agreement over or respecting land or other property, although he may not be named as a party to the conveyance or other instrument."

Section 205(1) of the 1925 Act provides that "unless the context otherwise requires, the following expressions have the meanings hereby assigned to them . . . (xx) 'property' includes any thing in action and any interest in real or personal property."

Section 56(1) certainly applies to provisions in covenants concerning land. Thus, if X derives his title to real property under a conveyance of, say, 1970, he can enforce a restrictive covenant regarding the use of the land made in an earlier conveyance between other parties. However, some judges, including Lord Denning, have been of the opinion that the word "property" in Section 56(1) should be interpreted as covering all things in action, even contractual rights in a contract not concerned with land. This interpretation would open the door to claims formerly barred by the rule of privity, and would do away with the rule in *Tweddle* v. *Atkinson*, 1861,[113] and similar cases.

The matter came before the House of Lords in *Beswick* v. *Beswick*, 1967,[119] and their Lordships could not accept the wider interpretation of Section 56(1) advocated by Lord Denning and others in previous cases, but regarded the subsection as being limited to cases concerning real property.

Before leaving the subject of privity, it is perhaps worth noting that the fact that an insurance company has agreed to indemnify one of the contracting parties does not rule out the existence of a contract between those parties. (*Charnock* v. *Liverpool Corporation*, 1968.)[120]

Accord and Satisfaction. Where X has performed his part of a contract, but Y has not, X may release Y from his obligations under the contract, but only if the release is under seal or if X receives valuable consideration for forgoing his rights. Such an agreement, where there is the necessary consideration, is called *accord and satisfaction*. The accord is the agreement by which the obligation is discharged; the satisfaction is the consideration which makes the agreement operative.

The doctrine may be illustrated by the following example. Payment of a smaller sum of money is not satisfaction of an agreement to pay a larger sum, even though the creditor agrees to take it in full discharge. If Y owes X £100, and X agrees to take £75, X can subsequently sue Y for the balance of £25 since there is no consideration for his forgiveness. There is accord but no satisfaction. The rule is an ancient one and an early example of it is to be found in the judgment of Brian, C.J., in *Pinnel's* Case (1602), 5 Co. Rep. 117a, Pinnel sued Cole in Debt for £8 10s. which was due on a bond on 11th November, 1600. Cole's defence was that, at Pinnel's request, he had paid him £5 2s. 6d. on 1st October, and that Pinnel had accepted this payment in full satisfaction of the original debt. Although the court found for Pinnel on a technical point of pleading, it was said that—

(*a*) Payment of a lesser sum on the due day in satisfaction of a greater sum cannot be any satisfaction for the whole; but that

(*b*) Payment of a smaller sum at the creditor's request before the due day is good consideration for a promise to forgo the balance, for it is a benefit to the creditor to be paid before he was entitled to payment, and a corresponding detriment to the debtor to pay early.

The first branch of the rule in *Pinnel's* case was much criticised, but was approved by the House of Lords in *Foakes* v. *Beer*, 1884,[121] and the doctrine then hardened because of the system of binding precedent.

However, the practical effect of the rule is considerably reduced by the following—

(i) Where there is a dispute as to the sum owed, if the creditor accepts less than he thinks is owed to him, the debt will be discharged.

(ii) Where the creditor agrees to take something different in kind, e.g. a chattel, the debt is discharged by *substituted performance*. A cheque for a smaller sum *no longer* constitutes substituted performance except perhaps where the creditor has asked for payment by cheque. (*D. & C. Builders Ltd.* v. *Rees*, 1965.)[122]

(iii) The payment of a smaller sum before the larger is due gives the debtor a good discharge. This is the second branch of the rule in *Pinnel's* case.

(iv) If a debtor makes an arrangement with his creditors to compound his debts, e.g. by paying them 85p in the £, he is satisfying a debt for a larger sum by the payment of a smaller sum. Nevertheless, it is a good discharge, the consideration being the agreement by the creditors with each other and with the debtors not to insist on their full rights. (*Good* v. *Cheeseman*, 1831.)[123]

(v) Payment of a smaller sum by a third party operates as a good discharge. (*Welby* v. *Drake*, 1825.)[124]

(vi) Forbearance to sue may be valuable consideration. It is important that there should be some evidence that the debtor requested the forbearance, either expressly or by implication (*Combe* v. *Combe*, 1951),[125] and, if a person forbears to sue on a claim which is clearly invalid, and the plaintiff knows this to be so, there is no consideration. Thus a promise by a bookmaker not to sue his client for the amount of lost bets is no consideration for a promise made in return by the client, but a promise to abandon a claim that is doubtful is sufficient consideration, for the claim may turn out to be good. (*Haigh* v. *Brooks*, 1839.)[100]

(vii) The equitable rule of *promissory estoppel*, derived from the judgment of Lord Cairns in *Hughes* v. *Metropolitan Railway* (1877), 2 App. Cas. 439, and again enunciated in the *High Trees* case[126] may apply. When a promise is made which is intended to create legal relations, which is likely to be acted upon, and which is acted upon by the person to whom it is made, the law does not give a cause of action if the promise is broken, but it will require the promise to be honoured to the extent of refusing the promissor the right to act inconsistently with it, even though the promise is not supported by consideration. Thus, if a landlord agrees to remit a portion of the rent of a property, and the tenant pays the reduced rent for a certain period, the landlord will not be able to claim as arrears the rent which he has voluntarily remitted, since the tenant may have altered his position in reliance upon the remission of rent. (*Central London Property Trust Ltd.* v. *High Trees House Ltd.*, 1947.)[126]

The doctrine of equitable or promissory estoppel seems most often to operate when the terms of one contract are modified or varied by a later promise. However, in *Durham Fancy Goods Ltd.* v. *Michael Jackson (Fancy Goods) Ltd.*, 1968,[127] Donaldson, J., was of the opinion that a pre-existing contractual relationship (assumed by Lord Cairns in *Hughes* v. *Metropolitan Railway* (1877), 2 App. Cas. 439) was not essential "provided that there is a pre-existing *legal* relationship which could in certain circumstances give rise to liabilities and penalties."

Nevertheless, the doctrine cannot be used by a plaintiff who alleges that a simple contract has been formed without consideration. As Birkett, L.J., said in *Combe* v *Combe*, 1951,[125] "The principle must be used as a shield not a sword." The doctrine which gives a defence against a claim and is not sufficient to found an action may be summed up in the words of Lord Cohen in *Tool Metal Manufacturing Co. Ltd.* v. *Tungsten Electric Co. Ltd.*, [1955] 2 All E.R. 657.

> It is not thought right that a man who has indicated that he is not going to insist on his strict legal rights as a result of which the other party has altered his position should be able at a minute's notice to insist upon his rights however inconvenient it may be to the other party.

The doctrine was further considered in *Ajayi* v. *Briscoe*, 1964,[128] where it was held that the promisor may resile from the promise to discharge the promisee until the promisee has acted in reliance on it and has altered his position. Further, it was held in *D. & C. Builders* v. *Rees*, 1966,[122] that if the promisee has extorted the promise, as in that case by threatening a breach of contract, the promise will not bind the promisor and the original contract will apply.

CAPACITY TO CONTRACT

Adult citizens have full capacity to enter into any kind of contract, but certain groups of persons, and corporations or unincorporated groups, have certain disabilities in this connection.

Aliens. They normally have full capacity to contract, but they cannot acquire property in a British ship (Merchant Shipping Act, 1894, Sect. 1), save as a member of a limited liability company if the company itself is British. However, contracts with *enemy aliens* during the period of hostilities are illegal and void. The term "enemy alien" includes not only aliens, but British subjects voluntarily resident or carrying on business in the enemy's country or in a country occupied or controlled by the enemy. The test is not nationality, but the place where the person resides or carries on business.

An enemy alien who is in England during the period of hostilities *may be sued* in the English courts but he cannot himself *bring an action* in those courts. (*Porter* v. *Freudenberg*, [1951] 1 K.B. 857.) However, an enemy alien present in England by licence of the Crown, as where he is registered under relevant legislation such as the Aliens Restriction Acts, may sue and be sued in the English courts and may make valid contracts even during hostilities.

Contracts made during peace with persons who later become enemy aliens by reason of outbreak of war and which require continuous business relations or are prejudicial to this country, e.g. armaments contracts, are treated as follows—

(*a*) *The contract gives no rights after the outbreak of war.* It is thus cut short and enforcement of the contract will relate only the part which was *executed* before the war, the *executory* rights and duties being cancelled. Thus, if A and B enter into a contract under which A charters a ship from B for ten years, then if after two years B becomes an enemy alien, the contract will be cut in effect to two years and the parties released from all obligations arising under the charter after the outbreak of war. This is so even though hostilities may cease before the eight years remaining under the charter have elapsed.

(*b*) *The rights and duties outstanding in respect of performance before the outbreak of war are not destroyed though they cannot be enforced until hostilities cease.* Thus a debt due under a contract before the outbreak of war would survive the hostilities and be enforceable on the return of peace. (*Arab Bank Ltd.* v. *Barclays Bank*, [1954] A.C. 495.) Where the contract does not involve commercial intercourse with the enemy alien or prejudice to this country, the rights and duties are merely suspended and not destroyed. Thus, in a separation agreement made between husband and wife before the outbreak of hostilities the husband would be liable after the war to pay to the wife sums falling due by way of maintenance during the period of hostilities even though the wife became an enemy alien for that period. (*Bevan* v. *Bevan*, [1955] 2 Q.B. 227.)

Foreign sovereigns and diplomats are in a privileged position, since they cannot be sued at civil law or prosecuted in this country unless they submit to the jurisdiction of our courts. (*Mighell* v. *Sultan of Johore*, 1894.)[129]

The law relating to the privileges and immunities of diplomatic representatives in the United Kingdom is now laid down by the Diplomatic Privileges Act, 1964.

The Act gives effect to most of the provisions of the Vienna Convention on Diplomatic Relations, 1961, and replaces the Diplomatic Privileges Act, 1708. The Act divides the members of a diplomatic mission into three classes—

(*a*) Members of the diplomatic staff who have full personal immunity, civil and criminal, with three exceptions;

(i) a real action relating to private immovable property situated in the territory of the receiving State, unless the diplomatic agent holds it on behalf of the sending State for the purposes of the mission;

(ii) an action relating to succession in which the diplomatic agent is involved as an executor, administrator, heir or legatee as a private person and not on behalf of the sending State;

(iii) an action relating to any professional or commercial activity exercised by the diplomatic agent in the receiving State outside his official functions.

(*b*) Members of the administrative and technical staff, who enjoy full immunity for official acts, but who are liable civilly, though not criminally, for acts performed outside the course of their duties.

(*c*) Members of the service staff, who enjoy immunity for official acts, but are liable civilly and criminally for acts performed outside the course of their duties.

It follows from the above provisions of the Act that the courts will, for the first time, have power to determine whether an act committed by a member of a diplomatic mission was performed in the course of his duties.

Privileges and immunities may be withdrawn by Her Majesty by Order in Council from any State granting fewer privileges and immunities to British missions. The certificate of the Foreign Secretary is conclusive as to the entitlement of a person to any privilege or immunity, though as we have seen, the courts have the power to decide whether the act was performed in the course of his duties.

The privileges and immunities set out in the Diplomatic Privileges Act, 1964, are extended to the following persons among others—

(i) The chief representatives of the Republic of Ireland and Commonwealth countries, e.g. High Commissioners, their staffs, families and servants (Diplomatic Immunities (Commonwealth Countries and Republic of Ireland) Act, 1952).

(ii) Persons concerned with International Organisations of appropriate status, immunity being derived from the International Organisations Act, 1968. Such organisations are defined from time to time by Orders in Council made in pursuance of the Act, and include such bodies as the United Nations Organisation and the International Court of Justice.

Immunity is not normally conferred on persons of quasi-diplomatic character, such as consular officials, but an exception may be made where the diplomatic and consular functions are carried out by the same person. However, some immunities, e.g. in respect of rates and taxes, are given to consular officers by orders made under the Consular Relations Act, 1968, and Diplomatic Privileges Act, 1971.

Diplomatic privilege may be waived, though in the case of an ambassador or other head of a mission, waiver must be with the consent of his Sovereign. In other cases waiver must be by the head of the mission.

Minors. The Family Law Reform Act, 1969, Sect. 1(1) reduces the age of majority from 21 to 18 years. This provision operates from 1st January, 1970, and if a person is over 18 and under 21 years on 1st January, 1970, he is deemed to have attained his majority on that date. There is also a provision in the Act which states that a person attains a particular age, i.e. not merely the age of majority, at the first moment of the relevant birthday, though this rule is subject to any contrary provision in any instrument (i.e. a deed) or statute. (Sect. 9.) However, the common law rule that the age is attained at the first moment of the day preceding the birthday is at least repealed.

Sect. 1(2) provides that the age of 18 is to be substituted for 21 wherever there is a reference to "full age," "infant," "infancy," "minor," "minority" in—

(a) any statutory provision made *before or after* 1st January, 1970;
(b) any deed, will or other instrument made *on or after* that date.

This subsection draws a distinction between *statutory provisions* and *private dispositions*. In the case of the former the new age of 18 is substituted. Thus, in the Infants' Relief Act, 1874, references to "infants" will be construed as applying to persons under 18 years of age. However, in the case of private dispositions such as deeds, wills and settlements the Act does not apply retrospectively. Accordingly, if in a deed made before 1st January, 1970, a person X is to take property "on attaining his majority", he will take at age 21 years. If the deed was made on or after 1st January, 1970, he would take at 18 years. The reason for this rule is that where persons in the past have arranged their affairs in reliance on the law as it stood, it would be unjust to interfere.

With regard to procedure, a minor sues through a "next friend," i.e. an adult who is liable for the costs (if any) awarded against the minor in the action, though the minor must indemnify him. A minor defends an action through a "guardian *ad litem*," who is not liable for costs.

A minor's contracts may be void, valid, voidable or unenforceable

Void Contracts Include the Following—

    (*a*) *Those under the Infants' Relief Act, 1874, Sect. 1—*

        (i) Contracts for the repayment of money lent or to be lent. (*Coutts & Co.* v. *Browne-Lecky*, 1947.)[130]

        (ii) Contracts for goods supplied, or to be supplied, other than necessaries.

        (iii) All accounts stated with minors, e.g. I.O.U.'s, and other statements of indebtedness.

    (*b*) *Those under the Betting and Loans (Infants) Act, 1892.* This Act renders void any agreement made by a person after he comes of age to pay a loan contracted during minority.

A minor cannot be held liable on a bill of exchange (e.g. a cheque) even though given in payment of a debt incurred for necessaries supplied and delivered. (Bills of Exchange Act, 1882, Sect. 22.) So far as the actual supplier is concerned there would be an action in quasi-contract on the consideration, i.e. for a reasonable price, not necessarily the contract price, but third parties, to whom the bill had been negotiated, would have no claim whatever on the minor.

It appears that despite the use of the words "absolutely void" in Sect. 1 of the Infants' Relief Act, 1874, a minor can sue on the void contract, except as against another minor, because an adult party cannot use the other's minority as a defence to an action. Furthermore, it will be seen that the minor cannot recover money paid or goods transferred under a void contract unless there has been total failure of consideration. In addition, the minor seems to obtain property in the goods and can give a good title to third parties. However, in some cases the courts have held contracts within Sect. 1 to be without any legal effect. (*Coutts & Co.* v. *Browne-Lecky*, 1947;[130] *R.* v. *Wilson*, 1879.)[131]

Valid Contracts are of Two Types—

(*a*) *Executed contracts for necessaries.* These are defined in the Sale of Goods Act, 1893, Sect. 2, as "goods suitable to the condition in life of the infant and to his actual requirements at the time of sale and delivery."

If the goods are deemed necessaries, the minor may be compelled to pay a reasonable price which is not necessarily the contract price. The minor is not liable if the goods, though necessaries, have not been delivered. This illustrates that a minor's liability for necessaries is only quasi-contractual.

The general test of necessaries is that of utility, and in this connection the minor's condition of life, together with the supply of such goods which he already has, becomes relevant. (*Nash* v. *Inman*, 1908.)[132] Thus food, clothes, lodging and the like are obviously necessary; but educational books, medical attention, burial of the minor's wife or children, and legal advice, and in some cases even articles of apparent luxury are classed as necessaries. (*Elkington* v. *Amery*, 1936.)[133] Necessaries for a married minor's family are judged by the same standards as necessaries for himself. These considerations apply not merely to the purchase of goods but also to necessary services. Thus a contract to hire a car may be a necessary contract for a minor salesman.

(*b*) *Contracts for the minor's benefit.* A minor may make valid contracts if they are for his benefit, but these have generally been contracts of apprenticeship, contracts of service, contracts for education, or something analogous thereto. (*Roberts* v. *Gray*, 1913.)[134] However, the concept of the beneficial contract may not be so restricted. (*Chaplin* v. *Leslie Frewin* (*Publishers*), 1965.)[135] Nevertheless, a contract which is in general for the minor's benefit will not be enforced if its terms are onerous, although the court will look at the whole contract not merely at isolated terms, and will arrive at its decision on the total effect of the agreement. (*De Francesco* v. *Barnum*, 1890,[136] and *Clements* v. *L. and N. W. Railway Co.*, 1894.)[137] Trading contracts of minors are not enforceable, no matter how beneficial they may be to the minor's trade or business. (*Mercantile Union Guarantee Corporation Ltd.* v. *Ball*, 1937.)[138]

Voidable Contracts. These are usually contracts by which the minor acquires an interest of a permanent nature in the subject matter of the contract, e.g. a lease of premises, a partnership contract, or the holding of shares in a company. Such contracts bind the minor unless he takes active steps to avoid them either during his minority (*Steinberg* v. *Scala*, 1923),[139] or within a reasonable time thereafter. (*Davies* v. *Beynon-Harris*, 1931,[140] and *Goode* v. *Harrison*, 1821.)[141]

Contracts within the Infants' Relief Act, 1874, Sect. 2. This section is concerned with the effect of the minor's ratification after full age of a contract made during minority and with fresh promises made by the minor after reaching full age in respect of transactions which took place during minority.

Before the effect of Sect. 2 can be appreciated it is necessary to look at the common law position before the Act of 1874 was passed. The common law classified contracts as follows—

(i) *Contracts for necessaries*, where the seller had a quasi-contractual claim and there could be no ratification after full age.

(ii) *Contracts of a continuing nature*, e.g. leases and partnerships. Such contracts were voidable during infancy or within a reasonable time thereafter, so that the minor could and still can ratify a contract of this nature.

(iii) *Loans*. These were void at common law and there could be no ratification by the minor after age, but a fresh promise plus new consideration, e.g. a fresh advance, might bind the minor.

(iv) *Contracts of a beneficial nature*. These were and are still binding on the minor.

All other contracts made by minors were voidable at common law, and consequently were capable of ratification after full age. The most important contracts in this residuary class were (*a*) the minor's contract of engagement, which was capable of ratification after full age; and (*b*) debts incurred under contracts for non-necessary goods, which debts could also be ratified after full age.

Sect. 2 provides—

No action shall be brought whereby to charge any person upon any promise made after full age to pay any debt contracted during infancy or upon any ratification made after full age of any promise or contract made during infancy whether there shall or shall not be any new consideration for such promise or ratification after full age.

The effect of this section is as follows—

(i) It prevents ratification of contracts of engagement and debts for non-necessaries (*Coxhead* v. *Mullis*, 1878);[142] but

(ii) A fresh promise binds in the case of engagements (*Northcote* v. *Doughty*, 1879)[143] but not in the case of a debt even if the fresh promise after age is supported by new consideration.

Sect. 2 of the Infants' Relief Act, 1874, was not entirely effective in the case of loans. It rendered certain promises unenforceable against the minor but, although the promise to repay the loan was unenforceable, the lender could sell any security the minor had used to secure the loan, because here he was pursuing a real remedy against the security and was not suing the minor on his promise.

The Betting and Loans (Infants) Act, 1892, was therefore passed rendering loans as distinct from debts void, so that any security taken is also void, and the lender can neither enforce the minor's promise, nor proceed against any security the minor may have given to secure the loan.

It is noteworthy that, since a minor's contracts cannot in general be enforced against him, Equity will not grant him the remedy of specific performance. He may, however, sue at common law for damages, since common law, unlike Equity, does not require mutuality of remedies.

When a minor has paid money under a void or voidable contract, although he can repudiate the contract and disclaim all future liability, he cannot recover money paid unless he can prove a total failure of consideration, i.e. that he has received no benefit at all under the contract. It would seem that the court is reluctant to find that no benefit has been received (*Pearce* v. *Brain*, 1929,[144] and *Steinberg* v. *Scala*, 1923),[139] though if there has been no consideration at all the minor will be able to recover his money. (*Corpe* v. *Overton*, 1833.)[145]

While the Infants' Relief Act, 1874, states that contracts for goods other than necessaries are absolutely void, yet the minor can give a good title to a third party who acquires goods which have been bought by the minor, provided the third party takes *bona fide* and for value. (*Stocks* v. *Wilson*, 1913.)[146] The tradesman who sold the goods to the minor cannot recover them from the third party; whether he can recover money paid to the minor for the goods is doubtful. (*Stocks* v. *Wilson*, 1913,[146] and *Leslie* (*R*) *Ltd.* v. *Sheill*, 1914.)[147]

Where a minor has committed a fraud, e.g. overstated his age, then the equitable doctrine of restitution of the goods is available to the tradesman, assuming the goods are non-necessaries and that no action for a reasonable price is available. The remedy of restitution exists so long as the minor still has the goods in his possession and they can be identified. It is well established that a tradesman cannot sue the minor on the tort of deceit, as this would amount to using the law of torts to circumvent the Infants' Relief Act (*Leslie* v. *Sheill*, 1914),[147] though, apart from circumstances such as this, a minor is fully liable in tort. (*Burnard* v. *Haggis*, 1863.)[148]

The doctrine of estoppel, which is a rule of evidence rather than a rule of law, means that a person is sometimes prevented from denying in court the truth of a statement which he has made where another person has relied on that statement to his detriment. This doctrine might have prevented a fraudulent minor from proving his real age when defending an action for the price of goods delivered to him, but the court is so concerned that the 1874 Act should not be circumvented that this doctrine has been held not to apply to a minor so as to prevent him from setting up his real age as a defence.

Married Women. Married women used to be under certain disabilities in regard to the making of contracts and the holding of property, but since the Law Reform (Married Women and Tortfeasors) Act, 1935, and the Married Women (Restraint upon Anticipation) Act, 1949, a married woman has had the same contractual capacity as an unmarried woman (*feme sole*) or a man. Although a husband is not in general liable for his wife's contracts, a wife may, in certain circumstances, bind her husband in contract under the law of agency, though she can no longer be an agent of necessity in respect of domestic transactions. (See pp. 91–92.)

Corporations. Corporations are another special case of capacity to contract. A corporation aggregate may be a body incorporated by Royal Charter, a corporation formed by a special Act of Parliament, or a company registered under the Companies Act, 1948, or previous Acts.

The contractual capacity of a corporation is limited—

(a) *By natural impossibility*, which arises from the fact that it is an *artificial* and not a *natural* person. Thus it can only make contracts through an agent and in consequence cannot fulfil contractual obligations of a *personal nature*. It is obviously impossible for a corporation to marry and it cannot act as a solicitor, doctor or accountant, nor can it act as the treasurer of a friendly society. (*Re West of England and South Wales District Bank* (1879), 11 Ch. D. 768.)

(b) *By legal impossibility*, since corporations are subject to what is called the *ultra vires* rule, which limits what they can legally do. A corporation can only act within its powers, and actions outside this scope are called *ultra vires*, or beyond its powers.

Charter corporations may contract as an ordinary person can, and even though the Charter may impose limitations on the corporation's contractual capacity, any contracts which it makes beyond those limitations are nevertheless good. (*Baroness Wenlock* v. *River Dee Co.* (1887), 36 Ch. D. 674.) The Crown may in such a case forfeit the Charter, or a member of the corporation may ask the court to restrain the corporation by injunction from doing acts which are *ultra vires*. (*Jenkin* v. *Pharmaceutical Society*, 1921.)[32]

Statutory corporations have powers contained in the statute setting them up, and these powers are sometimes increased by subsequent statutes or by delegated legislation. Any acts beyond these powers are *ultra vires* and void.

Registered companies possess powers determined by the Objects Clause of their Memorandum of Association, and an act in excess of the powers given in this Memorandum is *ultra vires* and void. (*Ashbury Railway Carriage and Iron Co.* v. *Riche*, 1875,[149] and *Re Jon Beauforte*, 1953.)[150] Corporations may carry out acts "fairly incidental" to the specified objects (*Deuchar* v. *Gas, Light and Coke Co.*, 1925)[151] though whether an activity was fairly incidental has hitherto been a matter for the court to decide. However, the rule has been so uncertain in its operation that it has become customary for legal draftsmen to draft objects clauses which are extremely wide in scope and, in addition, include a provision that each specified object or power should be considered separate and distinct and in no way ancilliary to, or dependent upon, any other object (*Cotman* v. *Brougham*, 1918).[152] In this way, the severe limitations placed on a company's business by the *ultra vires* rule have been mitigated, provided that each paragraph of the objects clause can genuinely be regarded as separate and distinct. (*Re Introductions Ltd*, 1969.)[153] However, in a recent case the Court of Appeal made a decision which may, in effect, allow the directors of a company to usurp the courts in deciding what is reasonably incidental to the company's stated objects, and furthermore allow them, through ignorance or mistaken intention, to bind the company to an activity which cannot conveniently be combined with the existing objects, and is therefore *ultra vires*. (*Bell Houses Ltd. v. City Wall Properties Ltd.*, 1966.)[154]

At common law contracts made by corporations had to be under seal. The requirement of sealing would have been extremely onerous but for the exceptions allowed, e.g. contracts of trifling importance or daily necessity were not required to bear the company's seal.

The above rules have been amended by statute. The Companies Act, 1948, provides in Sect. 32 that a registered company need not contract under seal except where an ordinary person would have to do so, and the Corporate Bodies' Contracts Act, 1960, extends this privilege to all companies, no matter how formed, in respect of contracts made after 29th July, 1960.

Unincorporated Bodies. In addition to corporations there are certain types of unincorporated bodies, such as tennis clubs and other societies. These bodies contract through agents, and the persons authorising these agents are personally liable, since the association has no separate existence in law, being only an agregate of its members, though the rules of the Supreme Court allow unincorporated groups of persons to sue or to be sued collectively. The liability of the members in contract has already been considered (see p. 112).

Persons Suffering from Mental Disorder. Contracts made by a person of unsound mind are valid, but if the other party knew that he was contracting with a person who, by reason of the unsoundness of his mind, *could not understand the nature of the contract*, then the contract is voidable at the option of the insane party. The person of unsound mind must prove (*a*) the unsoundness of mind at the time of the contract, and (*b*) that the other party knew of it. (*Imperial Loan Co. v. Stone*, [1892] 1 Q.B. 599.)

A person of unsound mind can make a valid contract during a lucid interval, even though the other party knew that he was insane at times. Further, a contract made during insanity can be ratified during a lucid interval.

There seems to be no reason why persons suffering from some forms of mental disorder should not make valid contracts for non-necessary goods and services even where the other party knows of the disorder. Provided the person concerned understands the *nature* of the transaction a contract resulting from it could be binding. For example, a person who suffers under an insane delusion that he is Napoleon may nevertheless understand the nature of a commercial transaction such as the purchase of a watch. Where this is so he may be bound by a contract to buy the watch even though the seller knew of the delusion. (*Birkin* v.

Wing (1890), 63 L.T. 80.) Nevertheless, it is likely that the court would regard the contract as voidable if there was evidence to show that the person suffering from the delusion had been overreached as where the price asked for the watch was extortionate.

The above rules of law relating to persons of unsound mind must now be read in the light of the provisions of the Mental Health Act, 1959. This Act, which came into operation fully on 1st November, 1960, introduced a completely new code and system for the care, treatment, and detention, of persons suffering from mental disorder. "Mental disorder" is now a statutory term embracing all forms of unsoundness of mind and in particular a person of unsound mind whose property is subject to the control of the Court under Part VIII of the Act cannot personally make a valid contract. However, persons of unsound mind whose property is not subject to the control of the court are governed in contractual matters by the common law rules given above.

Drunkards. Similar rules apply to contracts made by drunkards. The contract is voidable at the option of the party who was drunk at the time it was made, if he can show (i) that he was drunk, and (ii) that the other party knew this. (*Gore* v. *Gibson* (1845), 14 L.J. Ex. 151.) A contract made by a person when drunk can be ratified by him when he is sober. (*Matthews* v. *Baxter* (1873), L.R. 8 Ex. 132.) Both insane and drunken persons have a quasi-contractual liability to pay a reasonable price for necessaries supplied to them. (Sale of Goods Act, 1893, Sect. 2.)

REALITY OF CONSENT

A contract which is regular in all other respects may still fail because there is no real consent to it by one or both of the parties. There is no *consensus ad idem* or meeting of the minds. Consent may be rendered unreal by mistake, fraud, misrepresentation, duress and undue influence.

MISTAKE

Mistake rarely affects the validity of a contract, but mistake which has this effect is called an operative mistake, and must be one of fact and not of law. (*Sharp Bros.* and *Knight* v. *Chant*, 1917.)[155] An operative mistake renders the contract void.

The concept of mistake has a somewhat technical meaning, and what would be considered a mistake by the layman will not always amount to an operative mistake. For example, errors of judgment are not operative mistakes. So if A buys an article thinking it is worth £100 when in fact it is worth only £50, the contract is good and A must bear the loss if there has been no misrepresentation by the seller. A mistake by one party as to his power to perform the contract is not an operative mistake. Where X agrees to build a house by 1st July, and finds he cannot complete the job before 1st September, he will be liable to an action for damages.

OPERATIVE MISTAKE. Operative mistakes may be classified into the following categories—

(1) Mistake as to the nature of the contract itself.

(2) Unilateral mistake, i.e. a mistake made by one party only.

(3) Bilateral mistake, i.e. where both parties make a mistake, and subdivided into (a) Common Mistake; (b) Mutual Mistake.

These categories are helpful, but students find considerable difficulty in distinguishing between common and mutual mistake because the words are frequently confused, or used synonymously, even in law reports. This can be illustrated in the case of *Solle* v. *Butcher*.[156] Bucknill, L.J., in the course of his judgment is reported in the *All England Reports*, [1949] 2 All E.R. at page 1116 as saying: "In my opinion, therefore, there was a *mutual* mistake of fact on a matter of fundamental importance."

In the *Law Reports*, [1950] 1 K.B. at page 686 this is rendered as: "In my opinion, therefore, there was a *common* mistake of fact on a matter of fundamental importance."

In *Cooper* v. *Phibbs* (1867),[157] L.R. 2 H.L. at page 170, Lord Westbury says: ". . . but if the parties contract under a *mutual* mistake and misapprehension as to their relative and respective rights, the result is, that that agreement is liable to be set aside as having proceeded upon as a *common* mistake.

We therefore propose to use words more self-identifying than common or mutual in order to assist the reader to understand and remember the categories. Common mistake occurs where *both* parties have made the *same* mistake and will be called, alternatively, *identical bilateral* mistake. Mutual mistake occurs where *both* parties make a *different* mistake and will be called *non-identical bilateral* mistake. These will then be clearly differentiated between themselves and contrasted with *unilateral* mistake.

1. Mistake as to the Nature of the Contract Itself. If a person signs a contract in the mistaken belief that he is signing a document of a different nature, there will be a mistake which avoids the contract. (*Foster* v. *Mackinnon*, 1869.)[158] He will be able to plead *non est factum.* The plea of mistake is available in such circumstances unless the document happens to be a negotiable instrument which has been taken by an innocent third party for value. In such a case the person signing under a mistake is liable to the third party unless he can show that he was not negligent in so doing. In the case of other contracts, the person signing was not liable even if he had been negligent. (*Carlisle and Cumberland Banking Co.* v. *Bragg*, 1911.)[159] This view of the state of the law came under considerable criticism in *Gallie* v. *Lee*, 1968,[160] and when the case came to the House of Lords under the name of *Saunders* v. *Anglia Building Society*, 1970,[160a] *Bragg's* case was overruled.

2. Unilateral Mistake. Unilateral mistake occurs when one of the parties to a contract is mistaken as to some fundamental fact concerning the contract and *the other party knows or ought to know this.* (*Legal and General Assurance Society Ltd.* v. *General Metal Agencies Ltd.*, 1969.)[161] This latter requirement is important because if Y does not know that X is mistaken, the contract is good. (*Higgins* v. *Northampton Corporation*, 1927.)[162]

EFFECT OF UNILATERAL MISTAKE AT COMMON LAW. The cases are mainly concerned with mistake by one part as to the *identity* of the other party. Thus, a contract may be void if X makes a contract with Y, thinking that Y is another person, Z, and if Y knows that X is under that misapprehension. Proof of Y's knowledge is essential, but since in most cases Y is a fraudulent person, the point does not present great difficulties. (*Cundy* v. *Lindsey*, 1878.)[163]

It is also essential that there should exist in the mind of the party who has been misled some other person (or entity) with whom the contract could have been made, as in *Cundy* v. *Lindsay*, 1878.[163] If Jones contracts with Brown by leading Brown to believe that he (Jones) is Green, the contract *will not be void* for mistake if Brown has never heard before of either Jones or Green. It *may be voidable* for fraud but the difference may vitally effect the interests of third parties. (*King's Norton Metal Co. Ltd.* v. *Edridge, Merrett & Co. Ltd.*, 1897.)[164] However, even where there are two entities, the court may still find, *on the facts of the case*, that the contract is not void for mistake. (*Phillips* v. *Brooks*, 1919,[165] *Ingram* v. *Little*, 1961[166] and *Lewis* v. *Averay*, 1971.)[649]

EFFECT OF UNILATERAL MISTAKE IN EQUITY. Equity follows the law and regards a contract affected by unilateral mistake as void, and will rescind it or refuse specific performance of it. (*Webster* v. *Cecil*, 1861.)[167]

3. Bilateral Mistake. A bilateral mistake arises when both parties to a contract are mistaken. They may have made a *common* or *identical* mistake; or a *mutual* or *non-identical* mistake.

(*A*) *COMMON OR IDENTICAL MISTAKE.* This occurs when the two parties have reached agreement but both have made an identical mistake as to some fundamental fact concerning the contract. Suppose, for example, that X sells a particular drawing to Y for £5,000 and all the usual elements of agreement are present including offer and acceptance and consideration, and the agreement concerns an identified article. Nevertheless, if both X and Y think that the drawing is by Rembrandt, when it is in fact only a copy worth £25, then the agreement is rendered imperfect by the *identical* or *common* mistake.

EFFECT OF IDENTICAL BILATERAL MISTAKE AT COMMON LAW. At common law a mistake of the kind outlined above has no effect on the contract, and the parties would be bound in the absence of fraud or misrepresentation. There are only two cases in which the common law appears to regard an *identical bilateral* mistake as a vitiating element, and even these cases are probably examples of precedent impossibility rather than mistake. The two categories of case are—

(*a*) *Cases of Res Extincta*

(i) *Identical bilateral mistake as to the existence of the thing contracted for.* If X agrees to sell his car to Y, and unknown to them both the car had at the time of the sale been destroyed by fire, then the contract will be void because X has innocently undertaken an obligation which he cannot possibly fulfil. (*Couturier* v. *Hastie*, 1856.)[168] There are, however, cases in which the court may assume from the circumstances that the seller is warranting the existence of the goods. (*McRae* v. *Commonwealth Disposals Commission*, 1951.)[169]

If the goods are lost after the sale takes place then the contract is good, and the loss lies with the buyer if the property in the goods has passed to him; if not, the loss lies with the seller. The goods must also be specific or ascertained, otherwise the property will not normally pass, and the seller must supply similar goods or be liable in breach of contract.

(ii) *Identical bilateral mistake as to the existence of a state of affairs forming the basis of the contract.* If A and B, believing themselves to be married, enter into a separation agreement and later learn that they are not validly married, the agreement is void.

(b) *Cases of Res Sua.* These occur where a person makes a contract to buy something which already belongs to him. Such a contract is void. (*Cochrane* v. *Willis*, 1865.)[170]

Apart from cases of *res extincta* and *res sua* the common law does not seem to recognise an *identical* bilateral mistake as having any effect on a contract. (*Bell* v. *Lever Bros. Ltd.*, 1932,[171] and *Leaf* v. *International Galleries*, 1950.)[172]

EFFECT OF IDENTICAL BILATERAL MISTAKE IN EQUITY. The position in Equity is as follows—

(a) *Cases of Res Extincta and Res Sua.* Equity treats these in the same way as the common law, regarding the agreement as void. Consequently Equity will not grant specific performance of such an agreement (*Jones* v. *Clifford*, 1876)[173] but will rescind it. (*Cooper* v. *Phibbs*, 1867.)[157]

(b) *Other Cases.* Equity will apparently regard an agreement affected by *identical* bilateral mistake as *voidable*, even though the case is not one of *res extincta* or *res sua*. (*Solle* v. *Butcher*, 1950,[156] and *Magee* v. *Pennine Insurance Co. Ltd.*, 1969.)[174] This remedy is a discretionary one and the party seeking it may be put on terms. (*Solle* v. *Butcher*, 1950.[156] *Grist* v. *Bailey*, 1966.)[175]

(c) *Rectification.* Equity has power to rectify agreements affected by *identical bilateral* or common mistake.

If the parties are agreed on the terms of their contract, but by mistake write them down incorrectly, the court may order equitable rectification of the contract. In order to obtain rectification it must be proved—

(i) that there was complete agreement on all the terms of the contract or at least some outward expression of agreement between the parties *on the term in question*. (*Joscelyne* v. *Nissen*, 1969.)[176]

(ii) that the agreement continued unchanged until it was reduced into writing (for if the parties disputed the terms of the agreement, then the written contract will be taken to represent their final agreement); and

(iii) that the writing does not express what the parties had agreed. (*Rose* v. *Pim*, 1953.)[177]

The power of the court to rectify agreements is generally confined to identical bilateral and not to unilateral mistake. (*Higgins (W.) Ltd.* v. *Northampton Corporation*, 1927.)[162] In the case of unilateral mistake, rectification will only be granted in cases of fraud or misrepresentation. Rectification is not a remedy when the parties to a contract have always been at cross purposes.

(*B*) *MUTUAL OR NON-IDENTICAL MISTAKE.* This occurs where the parties are both mistaken as to a fundamental fact concerning the contract but each party has made a *different* mistake. Thus if X offers to sell Car A, and Y agrees to buy thinking X means Car B, there is a bilateral mistake which is *non-identical*. This may prevent a contract coming into being between the parties because of *defective offer and acceptance*, and may result from the negligence of a third party. (*Henkel* v. *Pape*, 1870.)[178] It will be remembered that in the previous category the mistake was bilateral but both parties had made an *identical* mistake.

EFFECT OF NON-IDENTICAL BILATERAL MISTAKE AT COMMON LAW. The contract is not necessarily void because the court will try to find the "sense of the promise," i.e. the sort of bargain which the reasonable man looking at the dealings of the parties would have thought had been made.

In many cases of *non-identical mistake* the court has been able to ascertain the "sense of the promise" and has decided that an enforceable contract has been made *on the terms understood by one of the parties*. (*Wood* v. *Scarth*, 1858.)[179] If the circumstances are such that the court cannot find the "sense of the promise," then the contract is void not so much because of mistake as because of uncertainty. (*Raffles* v. *Wichelhaus*, 1864,[180] and *Scriven Brothers & Co.* v. *Hindley & Co.*, 1913.)[181]

EFFECT OF NON-IDENTICAL BILATERAL MISTAKE IN EQUITY. Equity also tries to find the "sense of the promise," thus following the law in this respect. (*Tamplin* v. *James*, 1880.)[182] However, equitable remedies are discretionary, and even where the "sense of the promise" can be ascertained, Equity will not necessarily insist on performance, particularly if this would cause hardship to the defendant. (*Wood* v. *Scarth*, 1858.)[179]

MISREPRESENTATION

Representation—meaning of. A representation is an inducement only and its effect is generally to lead the other party merely to make the contract. A representation must be a statement of some *specific existing* and *verifiable* fact or *past event* and in consequence the following are excluded.

(*a*) *Statements of law.*

(*b*) *Statements as to future conduct or intention.* In some cases, however, a statement of intention may, in effect, be a representation of existing fact. (*Edgington* v. *Fitzmaurice*, 1885.)[183]

(*c*) *Statements of opinion.* However, if it can be shown that the person making the statement had no such opinion, it may be considered in law to be a misstatement of existing fact. (*Smith* v. *Land and House Property Co.*, 1884.)[184]

(*d*) *Mere "puffing," as in advertising or sales talk.* Not all statements amount to representations. Some of them are obviously of the nature of sales talk and cannot be relied upon. If a salesman says: "This polish is as good as Snook's Polish," this is a mere statement of opinion. If he says: "This is the finest polish in the world," this is mere sales talk. However, if he says: "This polish has as much wax in it as Snook's Wax Polish," he is making a statement of specific verifiable fact. The first two of these statements have no effect on the contract whether true or untrue; the third if untrue will amount to a misrepresentation.

(*e*) *Silence.* Silence or non-disclosure by one or both of the parties does not normally affect the contract. However, it may do so—

(i) *where the statement is a half-truth*—if the statement made is true but *partial* so that a false impression is created it may be regarded as an actionable misrepresentation (*Curtis* v. *Chemical Cleaning and Dyeing Co.*, 1951);[185]

(ii) *where the statement was true when made but became false before the contract was concluded*—where a statement is made in the course of negotiating a contract and that statement, though true when it was made, becomes false because of a change in circumstances, there is a duty on the party making the statement to disclose the change, otherwise the contract may be rescinded (*With* v. *O'Flanagan*, 1936);[186]

(iii) *where the contract is uberrimae fidei* (of utmost good faith) such as a contract of insurance (see p. 170);

(iv) *where there is a fiduciary or confidential relationship between the parties*—the equitable doctrine of *constructive fraud* may be applied whenever the relationship between the parties to a contract is such that one of them has a special influence over the other.

In such a case, the person having the special influence cannot hold the other to the contract unless he can satisfy the court that it was advantageous to the other and that there was full disclosure of all material facts. A situation of special influence occurs for example in family relationships such as parent and child (see p. 171), but the doctrine of constructive fraud may be applied—

Whenever two persons stand in such a relation that, while it continues, confidence is necessarily reposed by one, and the influence which naturally grows out of that confidence is possessed by the other, and this confidence is abused, or the influence is exerted to obtain an advantage at the expense of the confiding party, the person so availing himself of his position will not be permitted to retain the advantage, although the transaction could not have been impeached if no such confidential relation had existed.

Per Lord Chelmsford in *Tate v. Williamson*, 1866.[187]

Inducement—meaning of. In order to operate as an inducement the representation must—

(*a*) be made with the intention that it should be acted upon by the person misled (*Peek* v. *Gurney*, 1873,[188] and *Gross* v. *Lewis Hillman Ltd.*, 1969);[189]

(*b*) induce the contract so that the person making the claim to have been misled must not have relied on his own skill and judgment (*Redgrave* v. *Hurd*, 1881);[190]

(*c*) be material in the sense that it affected the plaintiff's judgment (*Smith* v. *Chadwick* 1884);[191]

(*d*) be known to the plaintiff. (*Horsfall* v. *Thomas*, 1863.)[192]

Types of Actionable Misrepresentation. A *purely innocent misrepresentation* is a false statement made by a person *who had reasonable grounds* to believe that the statement was true not only when he made it but also at the time the contract was entered into.

A *negligent misrepresentation* is a false statement by a person *who had no reasonable grounds* for believing the statement to be true. A *fraudulent misrepresentation* is a false representation of a material fact made knowing it to be false, or believing it to be false, or recklessly, not caring whether it be true or false. (*Derry* v. *Peek*, 1889.)[193]

In addition, under the law of agency, where an agent represents himself as having authority he does not possess, the third party may sue the agent for breach of warranty of authority if he suffers loss by not obtaining a contract with the principal, the action being based on quasi-contract. (See p. 210.)

Furthermore, under Sect. 43 of the Companies Act, 1948, company promoters and directors are liable for negligent misstatements in prospectuses though they have certain defences (see p. 162). It should also be noted that the House of Lords has ruled in *Hedley Byrne* v. *Heller and Partners*[194] that where there is a sufficient "special relationship" between the maker of the statement and the person who is to rely on it, the former owes the latter a duty of reasonable care in making the statement and may be liable in damages to the recipient if the statement contains false information given negligently rather than intentionally.

REMEDIES

There are the following possible remedies for misrepresentation—

(*a*) Rescission of the contract is a possible remedy in all cases of misrepresentation whether fraudulent, negligent or purely innocent.

(*b*) The refusal of the injured party to perform his part of the contract if he has not already done so. He can then raise the misrepresentation as a defence to an action for specific performance or damages.

(*c*) An action for damages in the case of fraud. In this case the plaintiff sues not on the contract but on the tort of deceit.

The object of damages in fraud is to compensate the plaintiff for all the loss he has incurred as a result of the fraudulent inducement (*Doyle* v. *Olby* (*Ironmongers*) *Ltd.*, 1969)[195] although it has not been finally decided whether an award of exemplary damages may be made. (*Mafo* v. *Adams*, 1970.)[196]

(*d*) Where the misrepresentation is negligent the person making the false statement is liable in damages and the onus of proving that the statement was not made negligently, but that there were reasonable grounds for believing it to be true, is on the maker of the statement (or representor). (Misrepresentation Act, 1967, Sect. 2(1).) (*Gosling* v. *Anderson*, 1972.)[650]

(*e*) A purely innocent misrepresentation may be remedied by an award of damages but these cannot be claimed as such. The person seeking relief must ask for rescission of the contract and the court may, in its discretion, award damages instead. (Misrepresentation Act, 1967, Sect. 2(2).)

Rescission. Rescission dates from the time when the party misled notifies his repudiation of the contract to the other party, or does any other act indicating repudiation. (*Car & Universal Finance Co.* v. *Caldwell*, 1963.)[197] A contract induced by fraud or misrepresentation (innocent or negligent) is voidable at the option of the party misled, but the injured party may lose the right of rescission.

(i) *If the injured party affirms the contract, he cannot rescind.* He will affirm the contract if, with full knowledge of the misrepresentation, he *expressly* affirms it by stating that he intends to go on with it, or if he does some act from which an implied intention may properly be deduced. (*Long* v. *Lloyd*, 1958.)[198]

Lapse of time, or delay in asking for the remedy, is evidence of affirmation and can defeat an action for rescission. This is sometimes known as the doctrine of *laches*, and it is based on the maxim: "Delay defeats equities." (*Leaf* v. *International Galleries*, 1950.)[172] Lapse of time has no effect on rescission where fraud is alleged as long as the action is brought within six years of the time when the fraud was, or with reasonable diligence could have been, discovered. (Limitation Act, 1939, Sect. 26.)

(ii) *Rescission is impossible if the parties cannot be restored to their original positions.* (*Clarke* v. *Dickson*, 1858.)[199]

(iii) *It cannot be obtained where third party rights have accrued.* Rescission of a contract to take shares in a company cannot be obtained if the company has gone into liquidation because creditor's rights are paramount. Further, if X obtains goods from Y by fraud and pawns them with Z, Y cannot rescind the contract on learning of the fraud in order to recover the goods from Z. (*Phillips* v. *Brooks Ltd.*, 1919,[165] and *Gross* v. *Lewis Hillman Ltd.*, 1969,[18 9]and *Lewis* v. *Averay*, 1971.)[649]

(iv) There were two further rules which had a serious effect on the remedy—

(*a*) Where a representation had been sufficiently important to be incorporated in the contract, the party to whom it was made could not claim rescission of the contract in equity but had to pursue the common law remedies for breach of a term. These remedies depended upon the status of the term. If a condition was broken the aggrieved party could repudiate the contract, but for breach of warranty the only remedy was a claim for damages

Now the equitable right of rescission is preserved even where the representation has been incorporated in the contract. (Misrepresentation Act, 1967, Sect. 1(a).) Although the Section says "Where . . . the misrepresentation has become a *term* of the contract," it is not thought that there is a right to rescind for breach of warranty but only for a representation *incorporated in* the contract. If this is so, the availability of a remedy as drastic as rescission for a misrepresentation of minor importance when mere damages are available for a more serious breach of warranty is anomalous. Possibly, if the court is asked to rescind a contract for misrepresentation of minor importance, it will exercise its discretion under Sect. 2(2) of the 1967 Act to award damages in lieu of rescission.

(*b*) Where the contract had been performed, rescission could not be obtained if the misrepresentation was non-fraudulent. (*Seddon* v. *North Eastern Salt Co. Ltd.*, 1905,[200] and *Angel* v. *Jay*, 1911.)[201] Now a person is not prevented from asking for rescission merely because the contract has been performed. *Misrepresentation Act*, 1967, *Sect.* 1(*b*).

Certain problems are raised by the provisions of this section which are illustrated by the following example. A buys a drawing from B having been told by B, in innocence, that it is by Constable though it is in fact a fake. This assertion is then written in the subsequent contract as a condition of sale. If A wishes to reject the goods, he must do so within a reasonable time otherwise conditions become warranties for the purposes of remedies and A will have only an action for damages for the breach of condition. However, it seems that under Sect. 1(b) of the 1967 Act, A may ask for rescission for the purely innocent misrepresentation made by B. It would seem illogical to allow a person to rescind for purely innocent misrepresentation when his right to reject for breach of condition is barred. The problem may be solved by treating performance of the contract as *evidence* of the plaintiff's intention to treat the contract as subsisting, leaving him with an action for damages for the misrepresentation.

Damages for Non-Fraudulent Misrepresentation. Damages are obtainable for non-fraudulent misrepresentation in the following cases—

(1) *Purely Innocent Misrepresentation*

(*a*) Section 2 (2) of the *Misrepresentation Act*, 1967, provides that—

Where a person has entered into a contract after a misrepresentation has been made to him otherwise than fraudulently, and he would be *entitled*, by reason of the misrepresentation, to rescind the contract, then, if it is claimed, in any proceedings arising out of the contract, that the contract *ought to be* or has been rescinded, the court or arbitrator may declare the contract subsisting and award damages in lieu of rescission, if of opinion that it would be equitable to do so, having regard to the nature of the misrepresentation and the loss that would be caused by it if the contract were upheld, as well as to the loss that rescission would cause to the other party.

This subsection seems to be designed to give the court discretion to treat a contract as subsisting and award damages to the injured party in those cases where the misrepresentation is of a minor nature. However, damages cannot be awarded unless the party seeking them would have been *entitled* to rescind. Presumably, therefore, if a bar to rescission exists, e.g. delay, then damages cannot be awarded either. However, the subsection also uses the words "ought to be . . . rescinded" and this may give the court a discretion to award damages even when a bar to rescission exists. For example, A sells a car to B, innocently representing that it is a 1948 model whereas it is a 1939 model. Six months later B discovers this fact and asks for rescission. Presumably, B is not *entitled* to rescind on grounds of delay, but whether he can obtain damages or not will depend upon which of the two constructions outlined above is adopted by the court.

(*b*) *Agency*. Where an agent in good faith represents himself as having authority he does not possess, the third party may sue the agent for breach of warranty of authority if he suffers loss by not obtaining a contract with the principal, the action being based on quasi-contract.

(2) *Negligent Misrepresentation*

(*a*) Section 2 (1) of the *Misrepresentation Act*, 1967, provides that—

Where a person has entered into a contract after a misrepresentation has been made to him by another party thereto and as a result thereof he has suffered loss, then, if the person making the misrepresentation would be liable to damages in respect thereof had the misrepresentation been made fraudulently, that person shall be so liable notwithstanding that the misrepresentation was not made fraudulently, unless he proves that he had reasonable ground to believe and did believe up to the time the contract was made that the facts represented were true.

Presumably, the representor must have reasonable grounds for believing the statement to be true when he made it and right up to the time the contract was made. Thus, if a person makes a representation honestly and reasonably believing it to be true, and before contract receives additional information, which makes his belief unreasonable, he may be liable for negligent misrepresentation if he does nothing to correct his statement.

(*b*) Under Sect. 43 of the *Companies Act*, 1948, where the directors publish a prospectus containing false statements made innocently, the directors will have to pay what is called compensation unless—

(i) the directors had reasonable grounds for believing the statement to be true;

(ii) the statements were made on the authority of an expert who was thought to be competent; or

(iii) the statements were a copy of an official document.

(*c*) *Negligence at Common Law.* Where the parties concerned were not in a pre-contractual relationship when the statement was made Section 2(1) of the Misrepresentation Act, 1967, will not apply. However, an action for damages for negligence will lie in tort provided the false statement is made negligently and a special relationship exists between the parties. (*Hedley Byrne & Co. Ltd.* v. *Heller and Partners Ltd.*, 1963.)[194] (See p. 256.)

(3) *Misrepresentation may Raise an Estoppel.* If a person has relied on a misstatement and has altered his previous position because of it, he may be able to base an action for damages on estoppel. (*Henderson* v. *Williams*, 1895.)[202]

It is also possible to recover a monetary indemnity for some losses caused by misrepresentation. This remedy can be asked for along with rescission where the court decides it will not award damages. Sect. 2(2) of the Misrepresentation Act, 1967, gives the court power to award damages instead of rescission but it cannot award both. Thus, if the court decides to grant rescission it is limited in its monetary award to that amount of loss for which Equity would give an indemnity. (*Whittington* v. *Seale-Hayne*, 1900.)[203]

Criminal Penalties. In addition to the civil law remedies set out above the Trade Descriptions Act, 1968, makes it a criminal offence for a person to falsely or misleadingly describe goods.

TERMS OF THE CONTRACT

Up to this point, we have been considering the principles relating to *the formation of a contract* by outlining the rules governing offer and acceptance, intention to create legal relations, consideration, capacity, and genuineness of consent. In consequence we have seen that failure to satisfy the requirements of the law in these areas can prevent *the formation of a valid contract*.

However, even where it is clear that a valid contract has been made it is still necessary to decide precisely what it is the parties have undertaken to do in order to be able to say whether each has performed, or not performed, his part of the agreement.

EXPRESS TERMS

The Statements of the Parties. In order to decide upon the *express terms* of the contract, it is necessary to find out what was said or written by the parties.

Where the contract is wholly oral this is a matter of fact to be decided by the court from the evidence presented to it and may give rise to problems where the evidence is conflicting and difficult to substantiate.

In the case of a written contract it is usually obvious what the parties have written down though there may be problems of interpretation arising, for example, from ambiguity, which the court may have to resolve. In addition it should be noted that where the terms of a contract have been written down the court may refuse to allow oral evidence to be admitted if it has the effect of adding to, varying or contradicting the written agreement. This rule is, however, subject to the following exceptions—

(*a*) *Oral Evidence may be Admitted to Prove a Trade Custom or Usage.* This will usually have the effect of adding a term or terms to the agreement.

(*b*) *Oral Evidence may be Admitted to Show that the Contract has not yet Become Effective.* This is not truly an exception since the contract is not varied, added to or contradicted. (*Pym* v. *Campbell*, 1856.)[204]

(*c*) *Oral Evidence may be Admitted where the Court is of the Opinion that the Written Document Contains Part only of the Agreement.* This device is quite frequently used by the courts and represents a major exception to the rule relating to the admission of oral evidence. (*Quickmaid Rental Services* v. *Reece*, 1970.)[205]

Representation and Terms. Having ascertained what the parties said or wrote it is necessary to decide whether the statements are representations or terms. Representations are statements which merely induce a contract whereas terms are part of the contract itself and make up its contents. The distinction is, of course, less important than it was since before the Misrepresentation Act, 1967, there was often no remedy for a misrepresentation which was not fraudulent and in such a case the plaintiff's only hope of obtaining a remedy was to convince the court that the defendant's statement was not a mere inducement but a term of the contract of which the defendant was in breach. As we have seen, the Misrepresentation Act, 1967, has broadened the scope of the remedies available for non-fraudulent misrepresentation.

Certain tests may be applied in order to decide whether a statement is a representation or a term of the contract—

(i) The court is always concerned to implement the *intentions of the parties* as they appear from statements made by them. Where, in a written contract, the parties have by their words indicated that a particular provision is to be considered as a term of the contract, then the court will normally follow that intention. Where the statement is an oral one, the court will decide the question by trying to ascertain the intentions of the parties and may come to the conclusion that the circumstances suggest that the statement was intended to be a term.

(ii) A statement is not likely to be a term if the person making the statement asks the other party to check or verify it, e.g. "The car is sound, but I should get an engineer's report on it."

(iii) A statement is likely to be a term if it is made with the intention of preventing the other party from finding any defects, and succeeds in doing this, e.g. "The horse is sound; you need not look him over."

(iv) If the statement is such that the aggrieved party would not have made the contract without it, then the statement will be a term of the contract. (*Bannerman* v. *White*, 1861.)[206]

(v) A statement made during *preliminary negotiations* tends to be pre-contractual. Where the interval between the making of the statement and the making of the contract is distinct, then the statement is almost certain to be a representation. However, the interval is not always so well marked, and in such cases there is difficulty in deciding whether the statement is a representation or a term.

If the statement was oral and the contract was afterwards reduced to writing then the terms of the contract tend to be contained in the writing, and all oral statements tend to be pre-contractual.

(vi) Where one of the parties has *special knowledge or skill* with regard to the subject-matter of the contract, then such a party can more easily give warranties to the other, and will find it difficult to convince the court that warranties have been given to him. (*Oscar Chess Ltd.* v. *Williams*, 1957.)[207]

The case of *D'Mello* v. *Loughborough College of Technology*, 1970,[208] is a good example of the difficulties which may face a court in deciding whether or not preliminary dealings are part of a contract.

Collateral Contracts. The courts have sometimes resorted to the concept of the "collateral contract" or "collateral warranty" in order to provide a remedy of damages for what was, in effect, non-fraudulent misrepresentation.

The concept proved useful where an important statement made by the defendant could not, under the rules outlined above, be regarded as a term of the basic contract but might be construed as a separate and parallel contractual obligation for breach of which damages could be awarded.

The concept has been used in two sorts of case—

(*a*) *Cases where only Two Parties are Involved.* Suppose that X is leasing a house to Y and the terms of the lease are written up in a document, but that Y is induced to sign the lease by an innocent misstatement by X that the drains are sound. If the court had treated this sort of statement as a mere innocent misrepresentation then Y would most probably have been left without a remedy, since, before the Misrepresentation Act, 1967, he could not have recovered damages in respect of the statement, and it was also likely that for one reason or another he had lost his right to rescind. Therefore, to provide a remedy in appropriate cases, the court would sometimes regard innocent misstatements as collateral contracts or warranties and award damages for their breach. (*De Lassalle* v. *Guildford*, 1901.)[209]

Now that damages may be awarded for innocent misrepresentation under Sect. 2(2) of the Misrepresentation Act, 1967, and that the right to rescind is not lost by mere performance of the contract under Sect. 1(b) of the same Act, the concept of the collateral contract may have become redundant where the only persons involved are the two parties to the contract. In the case of negligent misstatements, the court might, before the Misrepresentation Act, 1967, have had to resort to the concept of the collateral contract because although *Hedley Byrne* v. *Heller and Partners*, 1963,[194] had established a potential action for damages in respect of negligent misstatements resulting in monetary loss, the boundaries of the action were not, and still are not, clear.

However, the Misrepresentation Act, 1967, Sect. 2(1) gives the court power to award damages for negligent misrepresentation and it should no longer be necessary to resort to the concept of the collateral contract or warranty in the case of negligent misrepresentation.

(b) *Cases in which Three Parties are Involved.* The concept of the collateral contract or warranty has also been used in cases where the representation upon which the plaintiff claims has been made to him by a stranger to the main contract.

Suppose that X, a representative of A Brand paint, calls on Y, a householder, to try to sell him some paint. In the course of conversation X makes a statement that the paint will last for five years and Y is impressed but does not buy any paint from X. However, the next day when contracting with a decorator, D, for the painting of his house, Y insists that D uses A Brand paint for the job. D buys the paint from the manufacturer, receiving no undertakings as to its lasting qualities, and uses it to paint Y's house. Twelve months later the paint is peeling badly and Y wishes to sue the firm. However, since X's misstatement did not induce a contract between Y and the paint manufacturer, there should, strictly speaking, be no action in contract against the manufacturer. Nevertheless, the court might use the concept of the collateral contract to give Y damages against the manufacturer. (*Shanklin Pier Ltd.* v. *Detel Products Ltd.*, 1951.)[210]

Since, in this three-party situation, there is still no contract between the plaintiff and the third party, the provisions of the Misrepresentation Act, 1967, will not help, but the decision in *Hedley Byrne & Co. Ltd.* v. *Heller and Partners Ltd.*, 1963,[194] may provide persons in the position of Y with an action for damages in pure tort, provided the statement is made negligently and the special relationship aspect of the decision is satisfied.

Conditions and Warranties. Not all of the obligations created by a contract are of equal importance and this is recognised by the law which has applied a special terminology to contractual terms in order to distinguish the vital or fundamental obligations from the less vital, the expression *condition* being applied to the former and the expression *warranty* to the latter.

A *condition* is a vital term which goes to the root of the contract. It is an obligation which goes directly to the substance of the contract, or is so essential to its very nature that its non-performance may be considered by the other party as a substantial failure to perform the contract at all.

A *warranty*, on the other hand, is subsidiary to the main purpose, and there is no right in the injured party to repudiate the contract; there is only an action for damages. A warranty has been variously defined, but it may be said to be an obligation which, though it must be performed, is not so vital that a failure to perform it goes to the substance of the contract.

Whether a stipulation is a condition or a warranty is a question of the intention of the parties, and this is deduced from the circumstances of the case. Furthermore, the words used by the parties, while not conclusive will often be followed. They may have called a particular term a condition or a warranty, or even have used less specific terms whose intention is clear. In some cases where the parties state the effect of a breach, it becomes clear whether a condition or warranty was intended. (*Harling* v. *Eddy*, 1951.)[211] If there is no such indication, the court may address itself to the commercial importance of the term. (*Behn* v. *Burness*, 1863.)[212] An interesting contrast is provided in *Poussard* v. *Spiers and Pond*, 1876,[213] and *Bettini* v. *Gye*, 1876.[214] Where there is a breach of condition, the injured party may elect either to repudiate the contract or claim damages. For a breach of warranty the only remedy is an action for damages.

Exception, Exemption or Exclusion Clauses. The parties may insert terms into their contract excluding or limiting liability in certain contingencies. Such terms are permissible and effective provided they are *communicated* to the other party. However, in the absence of fraud or misrepresentation, a person is not excused if he does not read a written contract. So if a contract contains exemption clauses, and the person concerned does not bother to read the document which manifestly purports to set out those terms, he will be bound by them in spite of his ignorance. There are circumstances in which the person accepting the offer is not aware of the conditions attaching to it, but is nevertheless bound by them. The situation often occurs where a ticket or other document, containing the terms of the contract or an indication as to where they may be found, is delivered to the acceptor but it not read by him.

In such cases, it is essential that the ticket or other document should be an integral part of the contract and not, for example, a mere receipt evidencing payment. (*Chapelton* v. *Barry U.D.C.*, 1940.)[215] If it is such a document, much depends upon whether it was signed by the acceptor or not. Where an unsigned document sets out the terms of the contract, or says where they may have found, then the acceptor may have constructive notice of the terms and conditions, so long as the ticket or other document adequately draws the attention of a reasonable person to the existence of such terms and conditions. (*Thompson* v. *L.M.S. Railway*, 1930,[216] and *Richardson Steamship Co. Ltd.* v. *Rowntree*, 1894.)[217] Where the document is signed by the acceptor, it will be difficult for him to avoid the terms and conditions (*L'Estrange* v. *Graucob Ltd.*, 1934),[218] though it may be possible for him to do so if he is misled as to the effect of the document. (*Curtis* v. *Chemical Cleaning and Dyeing Co.*, 1951,[185] and *Mendelssohn* v. *Normand Ltd.*, 1969.)[185(a)]

Any conditions attaching to the offer must be notified at the time the offer is made, since a belated notice is valueless. (*Olley* v. *Marlborough Court Ltd.*, 1949,[219] and *Thornton* v. *Shoe Lane Parking Ltd.*, 1971.)[219a] It is true that where a ticket is used to communicate conditions, the notice may often be belated, but it seems that, in this sort of case, the law assumes that members of the public must realise that certain conditions will be attached to such contracts. In any case, they have a right to assume that the conditions when ascertained will be reasonable, and the court would presumably strike out an unreasonable clause which had been communicated solely by constructive notice. Moreover, a person cannot take advantage of an exemption clause in a contract to which he was not a party. (*Adler* v. *Dickson*, 1955.)[220]

In the absence of any contractual document, the principle of constructive notice implicit in the "ticket cases" has no application, and previous dealings between the parties are relevant only if they prove knowledge of the terms, actual or constructive, and also prove assent to them. (*McCutcheon* v. *David MacBrayne Ltd.*, 1964.)[221] Any ambiguities in an exclusion clause are construed against the party who inserted the clause. (*Akerib* v. *Booth*, 1961.)[222]

Effect of Misrepresentation Act, 1967. Section 3 of the Act provides as follows—

If any agreement (whether made before or after the commencement of this Act) contains a provision which would exclude or restrict—

(*a*) any liability to which a party to a contract may be subject by reason of any misrepresentation made by him before the contract was made; or

(*b*) any remedy available to another party to the contract by reason of such a misrepresentation;

that provision shall be of no effect except to the extent (if any) that, in any proceedings arising out of the contract, the court or arbitrator may allow reliance on it as being fair and reasonable in the circumstances of the case.

The section, although attacking exclusion clauses designed to exclude liability for misrepresentation, appears to allow a person to exclude his liability for breaches of conditions and warranties. Furthermore, the Court is given a discretion and may allow an exceptions clause to take effect in appropriate circumstances.

The Doctrine of Fundamental Breach. This doctrine was usually invoked when a plaintiff sought a remedy on a contract which contained exemption clauses which had been adequately communicated. It amounted to saying that where a person had committed a fundamental breach of his contract he could not rely on exemption clauses introduced into the contract for his benefit. (*Karsales (Harrow) Ltd.* v. *Wallis*, 1956,[223] and *Alexander* v. *Railway Executive*, 1951.)[224]

It also appeared that the person who alleged fundamental breach bore the burden of proving that this was so. (*Hunt* and *Winterbotham (West of England) Ltd.* v. *B.R.S. (Parcels) Ltd.*, 1962.)[225]

There has always been difficulty over the meaning of a fundamental breach and attempts have been made to distinguish it from a condition (or repudiatory breach) so that an exemption clause excluding liability for breach of condition would be ineffective to exclude liability for fundamental breach, but as a result of *Suisse Atlantique Société D'Armament Maritime S.A.* v. *N.V. Rotterdamsche Kolen Centrale*, 1966,[226] known as the *Suisse Case*), and *Harbutt's Plasticine Ltd.* v. *Wayne Tank and Pump Co. Ltd.*, 1970,[227] the position appears to be as follows—

(1) There is no breach of contract more fundamental than a breach of condition. In the *Suisse Case*[226] the House of Lords defined a fundamental breach as a breach by one party entitling the other to treat the contract as terminated. This definition equates fundamental breach with repudiatory breach of condition.

(2) The effect of a breach of condition on an exclusion clause would appear to be as follows—

(*a*) If on breach of condition the innocent party *elects* to repudiate and bring the contract to an end the clause falls with the contract and does not exclude liability for the breach of condition. (*Suisse Case*.)[226] But the breach must amount to a *totally different mode of performance* before this rule and those following apply. (*Suisse Case*[226] and *Kenyon, Son & Craven Ltd.* v. *Baxter Hoare, Ltd.*, 1971.)[651]

(*b*) The position is the same where the defendant's breach of condition brings the contract to an end *automatically* without the innocent party being in a position to *elect* (*per* Lord Denning in *Harbutt's Case*).[227]

(*c*) If a breach of condition is established but the innocent party with knowledge of the breach proceeds to treat the contract as continuing and then sues for damages, the exclusion clause may survive and be raised as a defence. Whether it will be effective to exclude or modify the defendant's liability will depend upon the relevant rules of construction of contracts (*per* Lord Denning in *Harbutt's Case*).[227] These are as follows—

(i) under the *contra preferentem rule* exclusion clauses are read strictly against those wishing to rely on them (*Alexander* v. *Railway Executive*, 1951;[224] *Akerib* v. *Booth*, 1961);[222]

(ii) a court will either strike out or modify an exemption clause which is repugnant to the *main purpose* of the contract (*Pollock & Co.* v. *Macrae*, 1922),[228] the application of this rule would be an alternative way of arriving at the decision in *Karsales (Harrow) Ltd.* v *Wallis*, 1956;[223]

(iii) exemption clauses only protect a party when he is acting within *the four corners of the contract*, deviation from the contract is usually regarded as a fundamental breach (*Thomas National Transport (Melbourne) Pty. Ltd. & Pay* v. *May and Baker (Australia) Pty. Ltd.*, 1966,[229] and *Mendelssohn* v. *Normand Ltd.*, 1969);[185a]

(iv) in addition the courts may reject, as a matter of construction, even the widest exemption clause if it " . . . would lead to an absurdity, or because it would defeat the main object of the contract or perhaps for other reasons. And where some limit must be read into a clause, it is generally reasonable to draw the line at fundamental breaches." (*Per* Lord Denning in *Harbutt's Case*.)[227]

This general rule of construction that normally an exception or exclusion clause or similar provision in a contract should be construed as not applying to a situation created by a fundamental breach of contract was approved by the House of Lords in the *Suisse Case*[226] and applied by the Court of Appeal in *Farnworth Finance Facilities* v. *Attryde*, 1970.[227a]

(*d*) In order to determine whether a breach is fundamental or not the court may look with hindsight at its *results* and not merely at its *quality* (per Lord Denning in *Harbutt's Case*).[227]

IMPLIED TERMS

In addition to the *express* terms inserted by the parties a contract may contain and be subject to *implied* terms. Such terms are derived from custom or statute. Furthermore, a term may be implied by the court where it is necessary in order to achieve the result which the parties obviously intended the contract to have.

Customary Implied Terms. A contract may be subject to customary terms not specifically mentioned by the parties. (*Hutton* v. *Warren*, 1836.)[230] However, customary terms will not be implied if the express terms of the contract reveal that the parties had a contrary intention.

Statutory Implied Terms. In a contract for the sale of goods or hire-purchase the Sale of Goods Act, 1893, or the Hire Purchase Act, 1965, settles the matter of implied terms unless the relevant provisions have been specifically excluded. Certain implied terms under the Hire Purchase Act, 1965, cannot be excluded. The terms implied by these Acts relate to fitness for the purpose and quality.

Judicial Implied Terms. The court may imply a term into a contract whenever it is necessary to do so in order that the express terms decided upon by the parties shall have the effect which was presumably intended by them. This is often expressed as the giving of "business efficacy" to the contract, the judge regarding himself as doing merely what the parties themselves would have done in order to cover the situation if they had addressed themselves to it. The operation of the doctrine is illustrated by *The Moorcock*, 1889,[53] and *Lister* v. *Romford Ice and Cold Storage Co. Ltd.*, 1957.[231]

CONTRACTS UBERRIMAE FIDEI

A contract *uberrimae fidei* is a contract of the utmost good faith. There is generally no obligation on a contracting party to enlighten the other party even where he knows or suspects there is a misapprehension. For example, X offers to sell a watch to Y, and Y, thinking it is a gold watch, offers £30 for it. X, knowing the watch is not gold, accepts Y's offer without enlightening him. The contract is binding provided X made no representation in the matter. The essential maxim in such cases is *caveat emptor!* (Let the buyer beware!) This rather harsh rule is modified in certain circumstances, e.g. in the case of sales by dealers, the Sale of Goods Act, 1893, imports into all contracts for the sale of goods certain implied conditions and warranties, unless the parties exclude them.

There are certain contracts in which disclosure of material facts is required by law. They are called contracts *uberrimae fidei* or contracts of the utmost good faith. Here silence can amount to misrepresentation, in the sense that non-disclosure of some material fact by one of the parties to the contract will give rise to a remedy in the injured party. The following contracts are of this type—

(i) *Contracts of Insurance.* There is a duty on the person insured to disclose to the insurer all facts which might affect the premium. Failure to do so renders the contract voidable at the option of the insurer.

(ii) *Contracts to Take Shares in a Company under a Prospectus.* There is a duty on the company or its promoters to disclose the various matters set out in the Fourth Schedule to the Companies Act, 1948. Failure to do so may render those responsible liable in damages, and give the injured party the right to rescind his contract as against the company.

(iii) *Family Arrangements.* In contracts and dealings between members of a family, each member must disclose all material facts within his knowledge.

(iv) *Contracts for the Sale of Land.* The vendor is under a duty to disclose all defects in his title if they are known to him, and also the extent of any restrictive covenants affecting the land.

(v) *Suretyship and Partnership Contracts.* There is a duty on partners to disclose all matters within their knowledge which affect or may affect the business. Similarly there is some duty of disclosure between a creditor and the person who guarantees the debt due from the principal debtor.

Probably, contracts of insurance are the only true contracts *uberrimae fidei*. The others are analogous thereto, but are based more on the equitable concept of fiduciary relationship. The question of disclosure in the case of company prospectuses is, of course, statutory, the courts having consistently refused to declare that a contract to take shares from a company was of the class *uberrimae fidei*, though a rather higher duty of disclosure was placed on company promoters and directors. A contract of service does not give rise to duties of disclosure. (*Bell* v. *Lever Bros. Ltd.*, 1932.)[171]

DURESS AND UNDUE INFLUENCE

Contracts and gifts effected by duress or undue influence are voidable at the option of the party coerced or influenced. *Duress* is limited to actual violence or threats of violence to the person, or imprisonment or the threat of criminal proceedings to the person coerced or those near and dear to him. (*Cumming* v. *Ince*, 1847.)[232] Threats to property are not enough.

The doctrine of *undue influence* was developed by Equity. Where no special relationship exists between the parties, the party seeking to avoid the contract must prove that he was subject to influences which excluded free consent (*Williams* v. *Bayley*, 1866.)[233] But where a confidential or *fiduciary* relationship exists between the parties, the party in whom the confidence was reposed must show that undue influence was not used; i.e. that the contract was the act of a free and independent mind. It is desirable, though not essential, that independent advice should have been given.

There are several confidential relationships known to the law, viz. parent and child, solicitor and client, trustee and *cestui que trust* (or beneficiary), guardian and ward; but there is no presumption of such relationship between husband and wife. The fiduciary relationship between parent and child continues until the child is emancipated, which is usually, but not necessarily, on reaching eighteen or on getting married. (*Lancashire Loans Ltd.* v. *Black*, 1934.)[234]

It should be noted, however, that there may be a presumption of undue influence even though the relationship between the parties is not in the established categories outlined above. *In re Craig dec'd*, [1970] 2 W.L.R. 1221, Ungoed Thomas, J., held that a presumption of undue influence arose on proof—

(*a*) of a gift so substantial or of such a nature that it could not on the face of it be accounted for on the grounds of the ordinary motives on which ordinary men acted; and

(*b*) of a relationship of trust and confidence such that the recipient of the gift was in a position to exercise undue influence over the person making it. (*Hodgson* v. *Marks*, 1970.)[235]

A claim to set aside a contract for undue influence must be made within a reasonable time after the contract was made or the influence ceased to have effect. Delay in claiming relief may bar the claim since delay is possible evidence of affirmation. (*Allcard* v. *Skinner*, 1887.)[236]

A contract procured by under influence cannot be avoided by rescission after affirmation, express or implied, nor against persons who acquire rights for value without notice of the facts; but it may be avoided against third parties for value who had notice of the undue influence, and also against volunteers (i.e. persons who have given no consideration) even though they were unaware of the facts.

ILLEGAL CONTRACTS

When the word "illegal" is used of a contract, it does not mean that a criminal offence is necessarily involved. It does mean, however, that the courts will not enforce the contract because it is in some way injurious to society.

According to the decision in *Goodinson* v. *Goodinson*, 1954,[237] illegal contracts can be divided into two classes.

(i) Illegal contracts strictly so called because although not necessarily criminal they involve a degree of moral wrong; and

(ii) Illegal contracts traditionally so called by the courts but which do not involve a degree of moral wrong.

Illegal Contracts Strictly so Called

CONTRACTS WHICH INVOLVE THE COMMISSION OF A CRIME OR CIVIL WRONG. Obviously, contracts to commit crimes are rarely brought before the courts for enforcement, but such cases have occurred. (*Dann* v. *Curzon*, 1911.)[238] The following are examples of agreements to commit a civil wrong—

(i) Agreements to procure a breach of contract, e.g. where X contracts with Y that Y will break his contract with Z; the agreement between X and Y is illegal.

(ii) Agreements between a principal debtor and the creditor which are prejudicial to the surety, e.g. in the case of a fidelity bond for an officer of a company; the contract is avoided by a material change in the duties of the office, if the change increases the risk of misconduct in the officer.

(iii) Contracts under which agents take double or secret commissions, since the interest and duty of the agent are then in conflict.

CONTRACTS PROHIBITED BY STATUTE

(*a*) *Contracts which Incidentally Infringe the Provisions of a Statute.* A contract may be restricted or controlled by the provisions of a statute, but it does not follow that every contract which infringes the statutory provisions will necessarily be void. It seems that—

(i) The contract will be void if it appears from the wording of the statute that the legislature intended the statute to preserve public order, to maintain or improve public safety, or to protect the public, and the contract tends to endanger this objective. (*Anderson* v. *Daniel*, 1924,[239] and *Shaw* v. *Groom*, 1970.)[240]

(ii) The contract will be valid if it appears that the statutory provision was imposed for some administrative purpose only, and one which is not directly connected with the making of the contract itself. (*Smith* v. *Mawhood*, 1845.)[241]

   (*b*) *Cases where a Statute definitely Prohibits a Certain Type of Contract.* Two of the more important examples of these are (i) Contracts infringing the Restrictive Trade Practices Act, 1956 (these will be dealt with along with contracts in restraint of trade), and (ii) Gaming and Wagering Contracts.

   Wagering contracts are defined by Hawkins, J., in *Carlill* v. *Carbolic Smoke Ball Co. Ltd.*, 1892,[35] as those "by which two persons professing to hold opposite views touching the issue of a future uncertain event mutually agree that dependent upon the determination of that event one shall win from the other and that other shall pay or hand over to him a sum of money or other stake; neither of the contracting parties having any other interest in that contract than the sum or stake he will so win or lose, there being no other real consideration for the making of such contract by either of the parties."

   For a wager to exist it must be possible for one party to win and one party to lose, and there must be two persons or two groups opposed to each other. Thus, where X, Y and Z each put £5 into a fund to be given to the party whose selected horse wins a given race, there is no wager. A contract is not a wager if the person to whom the money is promised on the occurrence of the event has an interest in the non-occurrence of that event, e.g. where a man pays a premium to insure his house against destruction by fire. Such an interest is call an *insurable interest*. To insure someone else's property would be a wager.

   In order to ascertain whether a contract is or is not a wager in doubtful cases, the court will go to the substance of the contract and will not concern itself solely with external appearances. So what looks like a contract of sale may in fact be a wager. (*Brogden* v. *Marriott*, 1836,[242] and *Rourke* v. *Short*, 1856.)[243]

   Gaming means the playing of a game of chance for winnings in money or money's worth. A gaming contract is not necessarily a wager since there may be more than two parties to it. In general such transactions are lawful if all the players have an equal chance of winning. A bet on the outcome of a game is, of course, a wager.

   IMMORAL CONTRACTS. These may be considered under two headings—

   (*a*) *Sexual Immorality.* It seems that the court has no general power to declare transactions immoral but is restricted to contracts involving sexual immorality. Agreements for illicit cohabitation are therefore void. But the rule applies only to a contract in which men and women agree to live in sin in the future. A contract in which a man promises to pay a woman money in return for past cohabitation is not illegal because it does not necessarily encourage future immorality between the parties. Such a contract will, however, be unenforceable unless made under seal, because it is for a past consideration. Contracts the purpose of which is *prima facie* good will be unenforceable if they are knowingly made to further an immoral purpose. (*Pearce* v. *Brooks*, 1866.)[244]

(*b*) *Immoral Publications.* No enforceable contract can arise out of a blasphemous, seditious or indecent publication. Here again, the courts do not seem to have a general power to declare publications immoral. It would seem that, unless the publication is one which infringes the present rules of the criminal law and is punishable as a crime, the civil courts have no power to declare a contract made in connection with the publication illegal.

CONTRACTS CONTRARY TO PUBLIC POLICY. Such contracts do not necessarily involve the commission of a legal wrong, but are disapproved of by the law because—

(i) they tend to be prejudicial to the State in its relations with other States; or

(ii) they affect adversely the internal relations of the State, i.e. good rules and government and the proper administration of justice; or

(iii) they are in derogation of marriage; or

(iv) they involve unreasonable and excessive interference with the lawful activities and duties of individual citizens.

It was at one time thought that the judiciary had wide powers of discretion in the matter of creating new categories of public policy, but this view is now unacceptable. In *Fender* v. *Mildmay*, [1938], A.C.1 the House of Lords declared against the extension of the heads of public policy at least by the judiciary. There is a suggestion in the case that the categories of public policy are closed, and it is thought to be difficult and unusual for the judiciary to discover a new one.

The major categories of Public Policy are—

(*a*) *Contracts Affecting the State in External Relations*

(i) Trading contracts with the enemy. At common law all contracts made with a person (regardless of nationality) living in enemy territory in time of war are illegal, unless made with licence of the Crown. During the war of 1914–18, and the more recent one of 1939–45, common law on the subject was reinforced by emergency legislation.

(ii) Contracts to carry out acts which are illegal by the law of a foreign and friendly country. Examples of such contracts are found in *Foster* v. *Driscoll*, 1929,[245] and *Regazzoni* v. *K. C. Sethia*, 1958.[246]

(*b*) *Contracts Prejudicial to the Administration of Justice*

(i) Contracts stifling a prosecution for a criminal offence, and contracts tending to defeat the bankruptcy laws. (*John* v. *Mendoza*, 1939.)[247]

(ii) Collusive divorce occurs where the parties to a marriage make an agreement which concerns the commencement of a suit for divorce, or provides for its conduct, e.g. an agreement to commit adultery to provide grounds for a petition.

(iii) Contracts of champerty and maintenance were considered illegal as tending to upset the proper administration of justice. A person who encouraged another to bring a civil action committed the tort and crime of maintenance. If he agreed to take a share in the proceeds of the action he was guilty of the further offence of champerty. The Criminal Law Act, 1967, in Sections 13 and 14, abolishes champerty and maintenance as crimes and as torts, but contracts involving these former offences are by Sect. 14 unenforceable.

(c) *Contracts Tending to Corruption in Public Life*, e.g. the sale of public offices, the assignment of the salaries of public officials, or contracts to procure titles. (*Parkinson* v. *College of Ambulance*, 1925.)[248]

(d) *Contracts to Defraud the Revenue*, whether national or local (*Napier* v. *National Business Agency Ltd.*, 1951;[249] *Alexander* v. *Rayson*, 1936.)[250]

Illegal contracts strictly so called may be illegal as formed, that is, agreements which cannot be lawfully performed, such as an agreement to commit a crime. Thus in *Dann* v. *Curzon*, 1911,[238] the contract was illegal as formed.

Such a contract is void and neither party can claim any right or redress under it, for the maxim is *ex turpi causa non oritur actio* (no right of action arises from a base cause). Thus in *Napier* v. *National Business Agency Ltd.*, 1957,[249] the servant could not recover arrears of salary. Money paid or property transferred under the contract are not usually recoverable for in *pari delicto potior est condito defendentis* (or *possidentis*) (where both parties are equally in the wrong, the position of the defendant (or possessor) is the stronger). Thus in *Parkinson* v. *College of Ambulance*, 1925,[248] the plaintiff was unable to recover money paid under an illegal contract to procure a title.

However, recovery is possible in the following situations—

(i) Where ownership has not been transferred under the contract, the plaintiff may be able to recover his property without pleading the illegal contract. Thus if A leases property to B for 5 years and A knows that B intends to use the property as a brothel, then A cannot recover rent or require any covenant to be performed without pleading the illegal lease. However, at the end of the term A can bring an action for the return of his property as *owner* and not as a landlord under an illegal lease. However, if the action is to redress a wrong which, although in a sense connected with the contract, can really be considered independent of it, the law will allow the action. (*Edler* v. *Auerbach*, 1950.)[251] It is this basic principle which allows a party to an illegal transaction to recover property transferred under it if he can do so without relying on the illegal contract as by proving his ownership of the goods. (*Bowmakers Ltd.* v. *Barnet Instruments Ltd.*, 1944.)[252]

The rule is restricted to the recovery of property other than money for there cannot be a bailment of money, and when a person hands over money he hands over the entire title. To recover he must proceed on the contract and if it is illegal there can be no recovery.

(ii) The plaintiff will recover in spite of a defence of illegality unless the defendant can show that the plaintiff had *knowledge* of the illegality and *actively participated* in it. (*Fielding and Platt Ltd.* v. *Najjar*, 1969.)[253] However, where the parties have both participated in the illegal transaction but are not in *pari delicto* (equal wrong) the less guilty party may be allowed to recover. However, in order to rebut the presumption of equal guilt it must be shown that the defendant was guilty of fraud or oppression, or abused a fiduciary position. (*Atkinson* v. *Denby*, 1862;[254] *Hughes* v. *Liverpool Victoria Friendly Society*, 1916.)[255]

In the case of statutory illegality, it may be that the object of the statute is to protect a class of persons and the plaintiff is within that class. If so, the plaintiff may be able to recover money or property transferred under the contract, for he is not deemed to be in *pari delicto* (*Kiriri Cotton Co. Ltd.* v. *Dawani*, 1960.)[256]

(iii) Where the illegal purpose has not been fully performed because of the plaintiff's repentance, he may be allowed to recover. Problems have arisen in deciding what constitutes full performance and it would seem that a person may repent after *partial* performance (*Taylor* v. *Bowers*, 1876),[257] but not after *substantial* performance (*Kearley* v. *Thomson*, 1890.)[258] However, in spite of the two cases mentioned, the better view is that the plaintiff must also show that his repentance is *voluntary*, and not that he has merely been thwarted in an illegal scheme. (*Bigos* v. *Bousted*, 1951.)[259]

It should be noted that collateral transactions *between the same parties* are void. (*Fisher* v. *Bridges*, 1854.)[260] Where *a third party* enters into a collateral contract with one or both of the parties to the original transaction his rights will depend upon whether he knew or not that the original transaction was illegal. (*Southern Industrial Trust* v. *Brooke House Motors*, 1968.)[261]

In all actions brought in England the contract is subject to English rules of public policy even though the proper law of the contract is not English law. (*Kaufman* v. *Gerson*, 1904.)[262]

Illegal as performed, means that the contract is in respect of a *prima faci* innocent transaction but one party performs part of the agreement in an illegal manner. (*Cowan* v. *Milbourn*, 1867.)[263]

Where the contract is of this type the guilty party cannot sue on the contract for damages (*Cowan* v. *Milbourn*, 1867),[263] nor can he recover property delivered to the other party under the contract. (*Berg* v. *Sadler and Moore*, 1937.)[264] However, the position of the innocent party is strong, for he can:

(i) Sue on a *quantum meruit* (as much as he has earned) (see p. 207) for work done (*Clay* v. *Yates*, 1856),[265] or *quantum valebant* (as much as they are worth) for goods supplied;

(ii) sue on a separate promise, if one was given, that the work would be legally performed (*Strongman* v. *Sincock*, 1955);[266]

(iii) recover money paid or property transferred, because he is not in *pari delicto*;

(iv) recover damages for breach of contract (*Marles* v. *Trant (Philip) & Sons Ltd.*, 1954).[267]

Illegal Contracts Traditionally so Called

Some writers do not apply the word "illegal" to the following contracts because they do not regard it as appropriate. Instead they refer to the contracts as "void at common law on grounds of public policy."

CONTRACTS TO OUST THE JURISDICTION OF THE COURTS. A contract which has the effect of taking away the right of one or both of the parties to bring an action before a court of law is illegal. (*Re Davstone Estates Ltd.*, 1969.)[268] This rule does not render illegal contracts where the parties do not intend to create legal relationships (see pp. 130). In such cases, the parties *do not intend to be bound by the contract at all*. If, however, the contract is to be binding, then the parties cannot exclude it from the jurisdiction of the courts.

Many commercial contracts contain an arbitration clause, the usual object being to provide a cheaper or more convenient remedy than a court action. An arbitration clause in a contract is not illegal if the effect of it is that the parties are to go to arbitration *first* before going to court. An arbitration clause which denies the parties access to the courts completely is invalid.

CONTRACTS IN DEROGATION OF MARRIAGE. A contract in absolute restraint of marriage (i.e. one in which a person promises not to marry at all) is void. Partial restraints, if reasonable, are valid, e.g. a contract not to marry a person of certain religious faith. Marriage brokage contracts (i.e. contracts to introduce men and women with a view to their subsequent marriage) are also void.

Contracts by persons already married to marry a third party are void as being in derogation of marriage and also because they tend to immorality. Thus, if X, a married man, promises to marry Y, a spinster, the contract cannot be enforced by X; nor in damages by Y if she was aware of X's marital state. Agreements between spouses for future separation are void if made before marriage or during cohabitation. Separation agreements are valid where they set out the rights of persons already separated, or are part of a reconciliation agreement.

CONTRACTS IN RESTRAINT OF TRADE. These are so important that they will receive separate treatment. (See p. 178.)

CONTRACTS RESTRAINING THE LIBERTY OF THE INDIVIDUAL ARE ILLEGAL (*Horwood* v. *Millar's Timber and Trading Co. Ltd.*, 1917),[269] though such restrictions may be valid for certain purposes. (*Denny's Trustee* v. *Denny*, 1919.)[270] Contracts which seek to stifle comment on public affairs are void either under this heading or as in restraint of trade. (*Neville* v. *Dominion of Canada News Co. Ltd.*, 1915.)[271]

EFFECT OF ILLEGALITY WHERE CONTRACT IS TRADITIONALLY CALLED ILLEGAL. Such contracts are void only in so far as they conflict with the rules of public policy. (*Wallis* v. *Day*, 1837.)[272] Money paid and property transferred is recoverable. (*Hermann* v. *Charlesworth*, 1905.)[273] The doctrine of severance applies so that where the contract is legal in part only, it may be possible to obtain the assistance of the court in enforcing the good part of the agreement. It was held in *Goodinson* v. *Goodinson*, 1954,[237] that—

(*a*) there can be no severance of contracts which are illegal in the strict sense;

(*b*) there may be severance where the contract is illegal only in the traditional sense.

If the illegal part is a substantial part of the contract as a whole, severance may prove impossible; but if the illegal part is subsidiary, the legal part may be enforced. Thus, a servant, who has entered into a contract of service which contains a restraint which is too wide can recover his wage or salary because the restraint is subsidiary, the substantial purpose of the contract being to obtain the services of the employee.

The court will not add to a contract or in any way redraft it, but will merely strike out the offending words. What is left must make sense without further additions, otherwise the court will not sever the illegal part in order to enforce the good part. It should be noted that, even where severance is possible, the court is not bound to sever, and the court will not sever a contract unless the provisions left leave the contract substantially what it was before. Severance will not be allowed if it alters the nature of the contract. (*Kenyon* v. *Darwin Cotton Manufacturing Co.*, 1936.)[274]

CONTRACTS IN RESTRAINT OF TRADE

Restraints of trade may appear in ordinary contracts, leases and mortgages. In *Nordenfelt* v. *Maxim Nordenfelt Guns and Ammunition Co.*, 1894,[275] the House of Lords laid down that all restraint of trade are void unless reasonable in the interests of the parties and the public. Later in *Morris* v. *Saxelby* (1916),[276] the House decided that, to be reasonable between the parties, the restraint must be no wider than required to protect the covenantee's interests; mere competition not being an interest entitled to such protection.

However, special considerations seem to apply to transactions concerning land such as leases and mortgages. Thus, a landlord being fully entitled to the property at the end of the lease (i.e. the reversion) or on forfeiture, can protect the amenities or structure of the property by restraints on the tenant's trade. Similarly, a mortgagee (the lender) may impose restraint on the trade of the mortgagor (the borrower) as in the case of a public house, where the brewery, having lent money to the publican by mortgage, can insert a covenant binding the publican to sell no other beer but that of the lending brewery. Furthermore, when a landlord conveys his land or a part of it, he may reserve a proprietary right as to the use to be made of the land by the owner. (*Foley* v. *Classique Coaches Ltd.*, 1934.)[51] However, in *Esso Petroleum Co. Ltd.* v. *Harper's Garage (Stourport) Ltd.*, 1967,[277] and *Cleveland Petroleum Co. Ltd.* v. *Dartstone*, 1969,[277a] it was decided that the rules against unreasonable restraints of trade can apply, even where restraint is confined to a particular piece of land and is in a mortgage or a lease. However, a covenant not to *let* premises for a particular purpose cannot be enlarged into a covenant not to *permit* the premises to be *used* for that purpose. *Rother* v. *Colchester Corporation*, 1969.)[278] Contracts in restraint of trade may be divided into five classes—

(*a*) agreements between the buyer and seller of a business;

(*b*) agreements between employer and employee;

(*c*) agreements between partners;

(*d*) agreements between manufacturers, and between manufacturers and retailers, with regard to price maintenance and restrictive practices generally;

(*e*) regulation of the conduct of members by professional associations.

1. Agreements between the Buyer and Seller of a Business. The restraining clauses which commonly appear in contracts made between the buyer and seller of a business are usually intended to protect a proprietary interest such as the sale of the goodwill of a business, or to protect trade secrets and special processes.

In these cases the court has to reconcile two conflicting principles, i.e. to uphold and honour business agreements freely entered into whilst at the same time recognising that restraints of trade create monopolies and that the public interest requires a man to be free to use his business talents or professional skill as he wishes. Accordingly, a restraint in a contract between the buyer and seller of a business will be enforced only if it is: (*a*) no wider than is reasonably necessary to protect the party in whose interest it is imposed; (*b*) reasonable with reference to the party against whom it is made; and (*c*) reasonable with reference to the public as a whole.

What is reasonable depends very much on the circumstances. A world-wide restraint not to compete in the manufacture of certain goods for a period of twenty-five years has been held valid, whereas an agreement as part of the same contract not to compete in any way was held to be unreasonable and void. This shows that if the whole contract is unreasonable it cannot be enforced; but if certain clauses are reasonable, and are so arranged that they can be severed, the court will enforce the reasonable clauses. (*Nordenfelt* v. *Maxim Nordenfelt Guns and Ammunition Co.*, 1894.)[275]

2. Agreements between Employer and Employee. The restraining clauses which appear in contracts of service usually consist of agreements under which an employee covenants with his employer that on the termination of his contract he will not enter a rival firm or start a competing business. It is not unusual to find that, where a person is to be engaged on work of a confidential or secret nature, or where his employment brings him into personal contact with his employer's customers and business associates, his contract of employment includes a clause limiting his future activities in that particular field. However, it should be noted that since in a contract of service the parties are not on an equal bargaining footing, master and servant restraints are construed more strictly than business restraints, though in some cases the standard applied may be that between buyer and seller of a business. (*George Silverman Ltd.* v. *Silverman*, 1969.)[279]

Whether a restraint in a contract of service will be regarded as valid and enforceable must always depend upon the circumstances of each case, and no hard and fast rules can be laid down. However, a number of principles have emerged from decided cases and they are as follows.

The Purpose of the Restraint. The restraint must seek to protect the genuine trade interests of the party enforcing it, and not be an attempt to control the movements of employees, unless there is an underlying need for protection of a legally recognised interest. A classical statement of the law in this respect was made by Lord Parker of Waddington in *Morris* v. *Saxelby*, 1916,[276] where he said.

> I cannot find any case in which a covenant against competition by a servant or apprentice has, as such, ever been upheld by the court. Wherever such covenants have been upheld it has been on the grounds, not that the servant or apprentice would, by reason of his employment or training, obtain the skill and knowledge necessary to equip him as a possible competitor in the trade, but that he might obtain such personal knowledge of, and influence over, the customers of his employer, or such acquaintance with his employer's trade secrets as would enable him, if competition were allowed, to take advantage of his employer's trade connections or utilise information confidentially obtained.

Thus in *Attwood* v. *Lamont*, 1920,[280] a covenant, which, in effect, restrained competition was held unenforceable.

Consideration. Consideration is necessary to support a contract in restraint of trade, even though the agreement is under seal. This factor will not normally present a problem in the case of a contract of service, because it is difficult to imagine such a contract existing without consideration, as the whole purpose of such agreements, from the employee's point of view, is remuneration.

The Status of the Employee. In considering whether a person ought to be restricted in his future business activities, it is generally necessary to have regard to the position in which he was employed. It was suggested in *Morris* v. *Saxelby*, 1916,[276] that apart from trade secrets, the master cannot restrict servants merely because they have contact with customers; they must also have some influence over them. Thus, it would be difficult to show the necessity to restrain the future activities of an office boy, but where the person restrained was in a managerial or other influential position, this difficulty would probably not arise. Thus in *M. & S.*

Drapers v. *Reynolds*, [1956] 3 All E.R. 814, the Court of Appeal would not allow a restraint in respect of a person employed to canvass customers and solicit orders, because although it was limited as to time, there was no limit as to area. However, the Court of Appeal recognised that there could be reasons why a restraint unlimited as to area might be upheld. It depended on the kind of employee who was to be subject to the restraint. In *Gilford Motor Co. Ltd.* v. *Horne*, [1933] Ch. 935, where the employee was the managing director of a firm of car dealers, it was held that his position required that he be restrained from acting against the interests of his employer, though no area was specified.

The Duration of the Restraint. The duration of the restraint must be reasonable and may be long or short depending upon the minimum period required for it to be effective, though in exceptional cases a restraint unlimited in time has been allowed. (*Fitch* v. *Dewes*, 1921.)[281] Where it is sought to establish a long restraint, the burden of proving its reasonableness will be a heavy one and will rest upon the party who seeks to enforce it, i.e. the master.

The Area of the Restraint. This must be considered in the light of all the circumstances, and it may be necessary to allow a world-wide restraint in order to protect the genuine trade interests of the plaintiff. (*Nordenfelt* v. *Maxim-Nordenfelt Guns & Ammunition Co.*, 1894.)[275] However, much depends on the influence over customers and clients which the servant may have acquired, and in *S. W. Strange Ltd.* v. *Mann* [1965], 1 All E.R. 1069, Stamp, J., drew a distinction between a credit business and a cash business. In a cash business the names of customers are known only to the employees and are not recorded in the books of the firm. For this reason the employees in a cash business are more likely to have influence over the customers of the firm and the court may be more sympathetic towards a wider restraint in respect of them, provided it does not exceed the area of the employer's trade. Nevertheless, in *Empire Meat Co. Ltd.* v. *Patrick*, [1939] 2 All E.R. 85 a restraint concerning a retail butcher's business which was unlimited in time was held to be invalid because the area within which the employee agreed not to carry on or be employed in the business of butcher, although it was only five miles from the place where the employer carried on business, was too wide in view of the limited area of the employer's trade.

Covenants against Solicitation. In cases where it is felt that an area restraint not to enter a similar employment is inappropriate, it may be possible to use a covenant against *solicitation* of persons with whom the employer does business, though it may be necessary to restrict the restraint to persons with whom the servant has *actually dealt*. No problem of area arises in this type of covenant though its duration must be reasonable. (*G. W. Plowman & Son Ltd.* v. *Ash*, 1964[282]; *Home Counties Dairies Ltd.* v. *Skilton*, 1970,[282a] and *Gledhow Autoparts Ltd.* v. *Delaney*, 1965.)[283]

In order to enforce a covenant in restraint of solicitation it is normally necessary to show that the business has recurring customers. (*Scorer* v. *Seymour Jones*, 1966.)[284]

Established Customs. It is permissible for a party to attempt to establish the validity of a covenant by giving evidence that similar covenants are usually undertaken in employments of the same kind.

The Duty of Fidelity. It is also possible to prevent an employee from using trade secrets or business connections without any specific contract in restraint of trade. Certain activities by employees are regarded by the law as breaches of the duty of faithful service which an employee owes to his employer. Breaches of the duty of fidelity will sometimes be prevented by the court so a person who retains secret processes in his memory can be restrained from using them to his employer's disadvantage (*Printers & Finishers Ltd.* v. *Holloway*, 1964),[285] and a servant who copies names and addresses of his employer's customers for use after leaving his employment, can be restrained from using the lists without any express restriction in his contract. (*Robb* v. *Green*, 1895.)[286] Reliance on the duty of fidelity is to some extent unsatisfactory, because the master has usually no method of discovering whether a servant copied lists of customers, or if he has done so, what use has been made of it.

In connection with the duty of fidelity it should be noted that it does not matter who initiates the infidelity and, although in most cases the employee approaches the customers, the rule still applies even where the customers approach the employee. (*Sanders* v. *Parry*, 1967.)[287]

Furthermore, skilled men with access to their employers' secrets may not be able to work for a rival firm even in their spare time. (*Hivac Ltd.* v. *Park Royal Scientific Instruments Ltd.*, 1946.)[288]

Area Covenants. In the protection of trade secrets as distinct from trade connections, employers have relied on area covenants and the implied duty of fidelity.

Area *covenants* must be aimed at the protection of true trade secrets and must not be concerned to prevent the employee's use of his general skill and his knowledge of his employers' general organisation and business methods. The duration of the restraint must be reasonable and in this connection it seems that a longer restraint is possible where a trade is static than in cases where there is rapid development as, for example, in the plastics industry. The area must be reasonable and the restraint must be restricted to the sphere of activity in which the employee has been engaged. (*Commercial Plastics Ltd.* v. *Vincent*, 1965.)[289]

The operation of the implied duty of fidelity in connection with trade secrets is illustrated by *Printers & Finishers Ltd.* v. *Holloway*, 1964.[285]

Generally. It should be noted that the principles outlined above still apply if the restraint is contained in a contract between two employers with respect to their employees. (*Kores Manufacturing Ltd.* v. *Kolok Manufacturing Co. Ltd.*, 1959.)[290]

It must also be remembered that a covenant in restraint of trade is merely part of a larger contract of employment, so that if the master unjustifiably terminates the contract, as by wrongfully dismissing his servant, or the servant is, in the circumstances, justified in terminating his employment, the restraint will be enforceable. (*General Billposting Co.* v. *Atkinson*, 1909.)[291]

Furthermore, an employer cannot enforce a covenant restraining his employee from entering a particular field of business activity on the ground that the employer *may* at a *later date* wish to set up business in that field. (*Bromley* v. *Smith*, 1909.)[292] It should also be noted that a restraint may be applied even where an employee forms a limited company to carry on a business in defiance of a restraint. Corporate status cannot generally be used for such a purpose.

In addition, where entry into a pension scheme is a term of a contract of service, a term in the scheme that the pension is to be forfeited if the employee works for a competitor is void as an unreasonable restraint of trade. (*Bull* v. *Pitney-Bowes*, 1966.)[293]

Finally, a servant is under no implied obligation not to disclose information concerning his employer's misconduct if it ought in the public interest to be disclosed to a person having a proper interest to receive it. (*Initial Services* v. *Putterill*, 1967.)[351]

3. **Agreements between Partners.** Clauses restricting an outgoing or retiring partner from practising within a defined area are frequently found in partnership agreements between professional men. Such clauses will not be enforceable if they are wider than is reasonably necessary for the protection of the practice. However, protection *against competition* as such is to some extent allowed and this distinguishes professional practice restraint from master and servant restraint, though the test of reasonableness still applies. (*Lyne-Pirkis* v. *Jones*, 1969.)[294]

4. **Agreements between Manufacturers, and between Manufacturers and Retailers with regard to Restrictive Practices Generally.** This branch of the law is now largely regulated by statute, i.e. the Restrictive Trade Practices Act, 1956. Nevertheless it is necessary to consider the common law position because not all restrictive agreements are necessarily covered by the Act and, in cases where the Act does not apply, the common law on the topic may be invoked. For example, the restrictive agreement which was at the root of *Kores Manufacturing Co. Ltd.* v. *Kolok Manufacturing Co. Ltd.*, 1959,[290] was not covered by the Act and was decided on common law principles.

At common law an agreement between a group of manufacturers or persons engaged in a particular industry, regulating the conditions of that industry and the price of its products, is binding although it is in restraint of trade, provided that it does not impose a restraint which is unreasonable in the interests of the parties themselves, or one which is disadvantageous to the public. As far as the parties themselves are concerned the court usually regards them as the best judges of their own interests and is loth to interfere. The court will, however, interfere on behalf of the public, though once it has been decided that a contract in restraint of trade is reasonable as between the parties, then the burden of showing that it is unreasonable in the public interest is a heavy one. The burden could be discharged by showing that the agreement created a monopoly calculated to enhance prices to an unreasonable extent, though the courts did not support free and unrestrained competition. The attitude of the common law may be found in the remarks of Lord Haldane in *North Western Salt Co. Ltd.* v. *Electrolytic Alkali Co. Ltd.*, [1914] A.C. 461.

> An ill-regulated supply and unremunerative prices may in point of fact be disadvantageous to the public. Such a state of affairs may, if not controlled, drive manufacturers out of business or lower wages, and so cause labour disturbance and unemployment. It must always be a question of circumstances whether a combination of manufacturers in a particular trade is an evil from the public point of view.

5. **Regulation of the Conduct of Members by Professional Associations.** A resolution by a professional association regulating the conduct of its members will be void if it is in unreasonable restraint of trade. (*Pharmaceutical Society of Great Britain* v. *Dickson*, 1968.)[295]

THE RESTRICTIVE TRADE PRACTICES ACTS, 1956 & 1968

This legislation was introduced because of the failure of the courts to accept responsibility as guardian of the public interest. The main provisions of the act are as follows—

1. **Registration and Investigation of Restrictive Agreements.** The rules and procedure for registration are set out in Sects. 1 and 6–19 of Part I of the Act. Sect. 1 creates the post of Registrar of Restrictive Practices and states that he shall be in charge of a public register in which all restrictive agreements are to be registered, though provision is made for some agreements to be kept in a secret section of the Register. (Sect. 11(3).)

Sect. 6 is concerned with the important though difficult task of defining the types of restrictive agreements to which the Act applies. Broadly speaking, all agreements between two or more people are registrable if they lead to a restriction in—

(a) the prices to be charged, quoted or paid for goods;
(b) the terms or conditions of supply of goods;
(c) the quantities or descriptions of goods to be produced;
(d) the process of manufacture to be applied to any goods; or
(e) the classes of buyers and sellers.

Sect. 6(3) defines "*agreement*" in rather loose terms as including "any agreement or arrangement, whether or not it is intended to be enforceable . . . by legal proceedings," and "*restriction*" as including "any negative obligation, whether express or implied and whether absolute or not". It was hoped that this wide definition would bring most trade association agreements within the scope of the Act.

In this connection the case of *Re Electrical Installations at Exeter Hospital Agreement*, [1970] 1 W.L.R. 1391, is of interest. The Restrictive Practices Court decided that an agreement between contractors to delay submitting tenders until they had a meeting to discuss each others tenders was a restrictive trading agreement requiring registration under Sect. 6 of the 1956 Act.

Sect. 7 provides for various exceptions to the general rule of registration. These exceptions relate, for example, to trade union agreements, patent and some trademark restrictions, export agreements and information agreements.

Failure to require registration of agreements for the exchange of information leads to a major loophole in the registration provisions in relation to open price agreements. Under such an agreement each of the firms involved notifies a central agency, such as a trade association, of the prices it is charging for its goods, a full list of such prices being made available to all the members of the trade association. Since there is no restriction of any kind but merely an exchange of information, the agreement did not come within the scope of the 1956 Act. Nevertheless, it will be seen that such agreements provided ample scope for price leadership, collusion and even coercion.

Although Sect. 14 gives the Registrar certain powers to enable him to obtain information regarding restrictive agreements, these can only be used if "he has reasonable cause to believe" that they exist. Furthermore, the Act did not provide for the setting up of an organisation and staff to discover unregistered agreements. In consequence, the Registrar has had to rely largely on the co-operation of businessmen in providing details of restrictive agreements and fortunately this co-operation has been forthcoming. Nevertheless, some unregistered but registrable agreements have been discovered as a result of investigation by the Registrar.

Sect. 12 of the 1956 Act gives a power to remove agreements "of no substantial economic significance" from the register. This provision shows the economic character of the legislation, which is not concerned merely with restrictive agreements generally but mainly with those which are of substantial economic importance.

Agreements remaining on the register may have to be justified as being in the public interest by the firms concerned before a specially formed tribunal consisting of High Court Judges and laymen with experience in business, and entitled the Restrictive Practices Court.

Possible grounds for justification are set out in the Act and are as follows—

(a) to protect the public from danger or injury;
(b) that "other benefits" would suffer by removal;
(c) to counteract similar practices abroad;
(d) to apply "countervailing power" against a monopoly or monopsony;
(e) maintenance of employment in a concentrated area;
(f) maintenance of export trade;
(g) maintenance of another restrictive agreement already approved.

The jurisdiction of the court is invoked by the Registrar, and ability to prove justification for a restrictive agreement on one or other of the above grounds would not of itself give sufficient grounds for approval. The court would consider whether the public interest was being harmed, taking all the circumstances into account. It is obvious from the agreements reviewed to date that the court is not taking a lenient attitude towards restrictive practices, and most of the agreements put forward have been rejected by the court. The court has power to issue injunctions if its rulings are not carried out, but in most cases the firms concerned do not attempt to operate the agreement if it has been rejected by the court.

However, in *Re Galvanized Tank Manufacturers' Association's Agreement*, [1965] 1 W.L.R. 1074 the court imposed fines amounting to £102,000 on eight members of the Association for contempt of court in breaking their undertakings to the court that they would not enforce or give effect to the restrictions in a price-fixing agreement which the court had declared to be contrary to the public interest six years before.

The 1956 Act is not entirely effective to protect the public from restrictive practices in trade for the following reasons—

(i) Business men are not prevented from exchanging information about prices without an actual agreement. (See now Sect. 5 of 1968 Act.) Nor are they prevented from following the prices of a member of their branch of trade whom they acknowledge as a price leader.

(ii) The fact that the law will not allow different companies to agree to trade in a restrictive manner has probably led some of them to merge in order to trade restrictively.

The Restrictive Trade Practices Act, 1968, came into force on 25th November, 1968. It is intended to amend Part I of the Restrictive Trade Practices Act, 1956, and to make further provision as to agreements conflicting with Free Trade agreements.

Under Sect. 1 the Department of Trade and Industry may exempt from registration for a specific period under the 1956 Act, any agreement which it considers necessary to promote the carrying out of a project or scheme of national importance and the aim of which is to promote efficiency in a trade or industry.

Sect. 2 gives certain government departments power to exempt from registration agreements relating exclusively to prices, and designed to prevent or restrict price increases or to secure reductions in prices.

Sect. 4 extends the scope of existing provisions to allow exemption from registration of agreements relating to standards of design, quality or dimension.

Sect. 5 gives the Department power to bring certain classes of agreements for exchange of information within Part I of the Act of 1956. This power has now been exercised by the Restrictive Trade Practices (Information Agreements) Order, 1969 (S.I. 1969/1842). Under the

Order, Part I of the act of 1956 is applied to information agreements which provide for the furnishing of information about prices and the terms and conditions of sale of goods or the application of any manufacturing process to goods. However, by Part I of the Schedule to the Order certain categories of information agreements are exempted from registration and judicial investigation, e.g. agreements relating to exports.

The principal change under Sect. 6 is that particulars of new restrictive agreements must be given to the Registrar before the restrictions take effect or before the expiration of three months from the making of the agreement, whichever is the earlier. Sect. 6 also provides that agreements which were in existence before the commencement of the 1968 Act but had not been registered had to be registered within three months of the commencement of the Act. During this amnesty period about a hundred such agreements were disclosed.

Sect. 7 proposes that any restrictive agreement which is not registered is, for that reason, void and it is unlawful to enforce it or carry it out.

Sect. 10 provides that parties to restrictive agreements should have a new defence in proceedings before the Restrictive Practices Court, *viz.* that a restriction does not directly or indirectly restrict or discourage competition to any material degree.

This defence was in issue in *Brekkes Ltd.* v. *Cattel, The Times,* 12th November, 1970. A ruling by the Birmingham Fish Association that fish landed at Hull should be transported by only one company was held to be an unlawful interference with the Hull fish merchants' trade. Pennycuick, V.-C., granted an interim injunction to prevent operation of the rule although it had been submitted to the Restrictive Practices Court under Sect. 10 of the 1968 Act. The injunction was granted on the basis that the defence would not apply and that the Restrictive Practices Court would declare the rule void.

2. Resale Price Conditions. The 1956 Act made collective determination of prices and the enforcement of penalties for breach by means of stop lists or less-favourable terms illegal unless sanctioned, although Sect. 25 allowed individual suppliers to enforce resale price maintenance agreements even against a person not a party to the first sale, providing prior notice of the conditions had been given.

The purpose of Sect. 25 was to allow a manufacturer to bring a cut-price retailer before an ordinary court of law, which was not possible before 1956 unless the retailer had bought the goods direct from the manufacturer. Consequently manufacturers, not having access to the ordinary courts of law, often brought the retailer before a secret and possibly unjust trade association tribunal which might put the retailer quite unreasonably on a stop list so that he was denied supplies.

The section still exists, but before a manufacturer can have recourse to it to enforce resale price condition, the agreement imposing the minimum resale price must comply with the Resale Prices Act, 1964.

THE RESALE PRICES ACT, 1964

The enforcement of resale price conditions is now governed by the Resale Prices Act, 1964.

1. Terms and Conditions in Contracts. Any term or condition of a contract for the sale of goods by a supplier to a dealer, i.e. a wholesaler or retailer, or any agreement between a supplier and a dealer, shall be void so far as it purports to establish or provide for the establishment of minimum prices to be charged on the resale of goods in the United Kingdom, whether the goods are patented or not. (Sect. 1(1).)

It is unlawful for suppliers to include such a term or condition in their contracts, or to require an undertaking as to resale price as a condition of supplying goods to a dealer, or to send to dealers notification of minimum resale prices. However, suppliers or trade associations or their agents are not precluded from notifying dealers or otherwise publishing prices at which it would be *appropriate* to sell the goods. (Sect. 1(4).)

A contract of sale or other agreement containing a term regarding resale price maintenance is not wholly void, but remains enforceable except for the term relating to the resale price. (Sect. 1(3).)

In the case of *patented goods*, where the proprietor of the patent has granted a licence to another person to make the patented article provided he does not sell below a certain price, the terms of the licence are not affected by Sect. 1(1) and remain enforceable; similarly where a patent has been assigned subject to a provision regarding the resale price of the patented article. Thus the proprietor of the patent can sue the licensee or the assignee for infringing a provision relating to the resale price of the article. (Sect. 1(2).)

2. Withholding Supplies from Dealers. Sect. 2(1) provides that it shall be unlawful for any supplier to withhold supplies of any goods, or procure another supplier to withhold goods from a dealer seeking to obtain them for resale in the United Kingdom on the grounds that the dealer—

(i) has in the United Kingdom sold or advertised below resale price goods obtained either directly or indirectly from that supplier, or has supplied goods either directly or indirectly to a third party who has done so; or

(ii) is likely, if the goods are supplied to him, to sell them in the United Kingdom at a price below that price, or supply them directly or indirectly to a third party who would be likely to do so.

For the purposes of the 1964 Act a supplier of goods is to be treated as withholding supplies from the dealer—

(*a*) If he refuses or fails to supply those goods to the order of the dealer;

(*b*) If he refuses to supply those goods to the dealer except at prices or on terms or conditions as to credit, discount or other matters, which are significantly less favourable than those at or on which he normally supplies those goods to other dealers carrying on business in similar circumstances; or

(c) If, although he contracts to supply the goods to the dealer, he treats him in a manner significantly less favourable than that in which he normally treats other such dealers in respect of times or methods of delivery or other matters arising in the execution of the contracts. (Sect. 2(3).)

If, of course, the supplier has other reasons for withholding supplies, as where the dealer owes him money, then the supplier will not be treated as withholding supplies of goods for the purposes of the Act. (Sect. 2(4).) In *Oxford Printing Ltd.* v. *Letraset Ltd.*, [1970] 2 All E.R. 815, when Letraset were sued by the plaintiffs for an injunction to prevent withholding of supplies, it was held by Plowman, J., that the defendants had a good defence when they showed that their reason for withholding supplies was that the plaintiffs were, in addition to cutting the price, also using the defendants' products to promote the sales of the goods o a rival firm. The injunction was refused.

3. **Loss Leaders**. A supplier may withhold supplies from a dealer, or procure other suppliers to do so, if within the previous twelve months the dealer, or any other dealer supplied by him, has been using the goods withheld or similar goods as loss leaders. (Sect. 3(1).)

Goods are used as *loss leaders* when they are sold cheaply in order to attract to the establishment customers likely to purchase other goods, or merely to advertise the business of the dealer. (Sect. 3(2).)

The provisions of the above subsection do not apply where—

(i) The goods are sold by the dealer as part of a *genuine* seasonal or clearance sale;

(ii) The consent of the manufacturer has been obtained; or

(iii) The consent of the supplier has been obtained where the goods were made to the design of the supplier, or where they are made to his order and bear his trade mark.

4. **Remedies for Breach of Restrictions**. No criminal proceedings shall arise out of any contravention of the Act. (Sect. 4(1).) However, any person who is affected by a contravention of the Act may bring a civil action against the supplier for damages or an injunction. The provisions of the Act are also enforceable by the Crown by injunction. (Sect. 4(2) and (3).)

Where the dealer to the knowledge of the supplier has within six months prior to the withholding of the goods sold goods below resale price, and the supplier was, down to the time of withholding the goods, doing business with the dealer or supplying goods of similar description to other dealers, there is a presumption that the supplier is unlawfully withholding supplies. (Sect. 4(4).) The presumption does not apply if the restrictions placed on the dealer by the supplier consist only of time or method of payment for the goods. (Sect. 4(4).)

5. Power of Court to make Exemption Orders. The Restrictive Practices Court may, on a reference made by the Registrar of Restrictive Trading Agreements, order that goods of any class specified in the order shall be *exempted goods* for the purposes of the Act. Particulars of such goods must be entered in the Register kept for this purpose. (Sect. 5(1).)

Sect. 5(2) lays down the *circumstances under which an exemption order may be made*. The Restrictive Practices Court may make an order directing that goods shall be exempted goods if it appears to the court that unless a system of maintained minimum resale prices is allowed, then—

(*a*) The quality of the goods available for sale, or the varieties of the goods so available, would be substantially reduced to the detriment of the public as consumers or users of such goods; *or*

(*b*) The number of establishments in which the goods are sold by retail would be substantially reduced to the detriment of the public as consumers or users; *or*

(*c*) The prices at which the goods are sold by retail would in general and in the long run be increased to the detriment of the public as consumers and users; *or*

(*d*) The goods would be sold by retail under conditions likely to cause danger to health in consequence of their misuse by the public as consumers or users; *or*

(*e*) Any necessary services actually provided in connection with or after the sale of goods by retail would cease to be provided or would be substantially reduced.

In re Medicaments Reference (No. 2), [1970] 1 W.L.R. 1339 the Restrictive Practices Court held, on an application by the Association of the British Pharmaceutical Industry, that drugs were exempt under Sect. 5(2) of the 1964 Act. Although when medicines were prescribed under the Health Service they were not "sold" within the meaning of Sect. 5(2), they were nevertheless available for sale. In addition, without resale price maintenance, distributors would emerge who would only stock fast-moving drugs. Furthermore, as the majority of chemists made only small profits and would be likely to make less if supermarkets could undercut them, a declaration that drugs be exempted should be made.

6. Registration of Goods for Exemption. Sect. 6(2) provides that any supplier who supplies goods under arrangements for maintaining minimum prices on resale, or any trade association whose members consist of or include such suppliers, may give notice to the Registrar claiming registration in respect of the goods. This notice had to be given within three months of the section coming into force, i.e. three months from 16th August, 1964.

The Registrar has a duty to prepare, compile and maintain a Register of goods in respect of which notices are given to him under Sect. 6. He must also make reference to the court under Sect. 5 in respect of all goods of which particulars are for the time being entered in the Register.

On receipt of a notice under Sect. 6(2) the Registrar must enter on the Register particulars of the goods and of the person giving notice and also particulars of the minimum resale price arrangements. Once such a notice is entered on the Register, the resale price arrangements may continue until the court makes or refuses to make an order under Sect. 5 in respect of the goods registered. (Sect. 6(3).)

The Registrar is required by Sect. 6(4) to *publish the following* lists from time to time—

(i) *A list of the classes of goods which are entered on the Register.* In any legal proceedings resulting from a resale price maintenance agreement the fact that the goods are included in a list published by the Registrar shall be *conclusive evidence* that they are goods of which particulars are entered on the Register. Where goods are not included in the list it shall be *prima facie* evidence that they are not goods of which particulars are so entered.

(ii) *Lists of the classes of goods in respect of which the court has made or refused to make or has discharged orders under the Act.*

The above lists may be combined and the Registrar may combine or divide the goods into such classes as appear to him to be appropriate (Sect. 6(6).)

7. **Late Application to and Review of Decisions by the Court**. If a supplier has not given notice to the Registrar under Sect. 6(1) within the time laid down in that subsection, the court may at any time thereafter make an order exempting or refusing to exempt the goods. (Sect. 7(1).)

The court is also given power under Sect. 7(2) to review its previous decisions, and upon application being made to the court for review, the court may—

(*a*) discharge any order previously made by the court directing that the goods of any class shall be exempted goods;

(*b*) make an order exempting goods where an order was previously refused or has been discharged.

Application under Sect. 7(1) or (2) may be made by the Registrar, by any supplier of goods of the class in question, or by any trade association whose members consist of or include suppliers of such goods. (Sect. 7(3).)

No application to the court can be made under Sect. 7(1) or (2) unless the court gives leave. (Sect. 7(4).) *Leave will not be granted unless—*

(i) in the case of an application to exempt goods under Sect. 7(1) there is *prima facie* evidence of facts suggesting that the goods ought to be exempted; and

(ii) in the case of an application to review a previous decision under Sect. 7(2) there is *prima facie* evidence of material changes in the relevant circumstances since the last decision of the court in respect of the goods in question.

Some suppliers and trade associations applied to the Restrictive Practices Court under the Restrictive Trade Practices Act, 1956, and were successful in establishing a resale price maintenance agreement. It would not be fair to ask such suppliers and associations to apply under the 1964 Act and prove their case all over again, so Sect. 13 of the Resale Prices Act, 1964, provides that such approved schemes are to continue in force and are not affected by the Act.

In re Chocolate and Sugar Confectionery Reference, 1967,[296] was the first case to be contested under the Resale Prices Act and is illustrative of the attitude of the Restrictive Practices Court to what is, in effect, a general ban on resale price maintenance.

OTHER RELEVANT STATUTES

Before leaving the topic of restrictive practices, it is worth noting the broad provisions of two other important statutes as follows—

(a) *The Monopolies and Restrictive Practices Act*, 1948. This Act makes provision for inquiry into mischief resulting from monopoly or restriction. It set up the Monopolies Commission with power to obtain information. The Department of Trade and Industry may refer cases involving monopoly situations to the Commission. A monopoly is defined as control of one-third of the sales in a market and the basis of investigation is the public interest. Under this Act the Commission could make recommendations only and had no sanctions. In addition there were a wide range of exempted activities, notably professional and other bodies.

(b) *Monopolies and Mergers Act*, 1965. This Act extends the range of the 1948 Act. In particular it gives the Monopolies Commission power to investigate the supply of services. The Department of Trade and Industry is empowered to make orders enforcing the anti-monopoly recommendations of the Commission. Mergers, involving monopolies of more than £5m can be referred to the Commission by the Department for Trade and Industry for recommendations as to the likely effect on the public interest.

DISCHARGE OF A CONTRACT

A contract is discharged when the obligation created by it ceases to be binding on the promisor, who is then no longer under a duty to perform his part of the agreement. Discharge may take place in various ways.

1. Discharge by Agreement. A contract is made by agreement; and it is also possible to end it by a subsequent agreement if there is new consideration for the discharge, or if it is under seal. Where the contract is executory, i.e. a promise for a promise, and there has been no performance, the mutual release of the parties provides the consideration and is called bilateral discharge. But where the contract is executed, i.e. where it has been performed or partly performed by one party, then the party to be released must provide consideration, unless the **agree-ment** to abandon the contract is under seal. In other words, there must be *accord and satisfaction*, the agreement to discharge being the accord and the new consideration being the satisfaction. This method of discharge is called unilateral discharge. Where the discharge by agreement takes the form of the substitution of a new contract, the substitution is called a novation.

Sometimes a contract makes provision for its own discharge. It may make the completion of the contract subject to the fulfilment of a condition precedent or warranty. Thus, if I say I will buy your car if you fit new tyres to it, I shall incur no liability unless the tyres are so fitted. Similarly a contract to purchase land subject to planning permission being obtained can be rescinded if planning permission is refused. (*Hargreaves Transport Ltd.* v. *Lynch*, [1969] 1 All E.R. 455.)

A contract may provide that it shall be discharged by a *condition subsequent*, i.e. upon the occurrence of a certain subsequent event. An example of this is found in pre-incorporation contracts which company promoters make on behalf of a company in process of formation. The law does not allow them to act as agents for the company which, until incorporation, is a non-existent principal. Further, the company is not allowed to ratify the contract after incorporation, but must enter into a new contract or novation if it is to become liable. The promoters are, therefore, likely to incur personal liability. In order to avoid this, promoters' contracts may provide that they shall be discharged if the company is not incorporated at all, or within a reasonable time, or if the company when formed does not accept the contract by novation.

Contracts of employment usually provide for their own discharge in this way but it should be noted that the Contracts of Employment Act, 1963 (as amended by Sect. 19 of the Industrial Relations Act, 1971), provides for certain minimum periods of notice to be given by and to employees whose contracts are terminable by notice. These periods are as follows—

Period of employee's continuous service	Minimum notice	
	by employer	by employee
13 weeks–2 years	1 week	1 week
2 years–5 years	2 weeks	1 week
5 years–10 years	4 weeks	1 week
10 years–15 years	6 weeks	1 week
more than 15 years	8 weeks	1 week

Longer periods of notice can, of course, be provided for expressly in particular contracts.

With regard to the form of discharge, a contract which is made in writing may be rescinded or varied by an oral agreement. A contract under seal may be rescinded or varied by a simple contract. However, while a contract required by statute to be evidenced in writing can be rescinded, i.e. totally discharged, by an oral agreement, if an oral attempt is made to vary it, the contract can be enforced in its original form, the oral variation being disregarded.

It is also possible to discharge a contract by release. At any time before a contract is due to be performed, or after a breach of contract has taken place, a release of the obligations under the contract may be granted by deed. Such a deed dissolves the contract and is binding, whether or not it is based on consideration. No new contract is made; the old obligations are simply released.

2. **Discharged by Performance**. A contract may be discharged by performance, the discharge taking place when both parties have performed the obligations which the contract places upon them. The general rule is that the manner of performance must comply exactly with the terms of the contract (*Moore & Co.* v. *Landauer & Co.*, 1921)[297] and the strict application of this rule would mean that all contracts would be entire so that no payment could be obtained for partial performance. The law assumes a contract between X and Y to be entire when it appears on construction of the contract that X has undertaken his obligations on the express or implied condition that he will not be obliged to perform those obligations unless Y completes or is willing to complete his obligations fully and exactly. (*Cutter* v. *Powell*, 1795.)[298]

However, there are *certain exceptions* to the rule of precise performance—

(i) *Where the Contract is Divisible.* Although there is a presumption in favour of entire contracts, the court may sometimes find that a contract is a divisible one, a usual instance being the contract between landlord and tenant. This means that the tenant cannot refuse to pay the rent even though the landlord is not carrying out the covenants of the lease, e.g. a covenant to repair. The tenant can sue the landlord for breach of covenant but must continue to pay.

(ii) *Where a Partial Performance has been Accepted.* Where one of the parties to the contract has only partially carried out his obligations under the contract but the other party appears from his conduct to have accepted the benefit of the partial performance, the court may infer a promise to pay for the benefit received, and allow an action on a *quantum meruit* to the party who has partly performed the contract. If, for example, S agrees to deliver 3 dozen bottles of brandy to B and delivers 2 dozen bottles only, then B may exercise his right to reject the whole consignment. But if he has accepted delivery of the 2 dozen bottles he must pay a reasonable price for the bottles retained, and S's *quantum meruit* will normally be the agreed contract price per bottle.

However, the mere conferring of a benefit on one party by another is not enough; there must be evidence of the acceptance of that benefit by the party upon whom it was conferred. (*Sumpter* v. *Hedges*, 1898.)[299]

(iii) *Where Performance is Prevented by One Party.* Here the party who cannot further perform his part of the contract may bring an action on a *quantum meruit* against the party in default for the value of work done up to the time when further performance was prevented. (*De Barnardy* v. *Harding,* 1853.)[300]

(iv) *Where there has been Substantial Performance.* The doctrine of substantial performance is based on the notion that precise performance of every term of the contract by one party is not required in order to make the other party liable to some extent on it. If the court, as a matter of construction, decides that there has been substantial performance, the plaintiff may recover for work done under the contract, though the defendant can, of course, counter-claim for any defects in performance. (*Hoenig* v. *Isaacs,* 1952.)[301]

In this connection it should be noted that where a contractor is employed under the Royal Institution of British Architects' standard form of contract, an architect's final certificate that the work has been carried out properly is conclusive evidence in any proceedings. (*Hosier & Dickinson* v. *P. & M. Kaye,* [1972] I All E.R.121.

In construing a contract to see whether a particular term must be fully performed or whether substantial performance is enough, the court must refer to the difference between conditions and warranties. A condition must be wholly performed, whereas substantial performance of a warranty is enough. (*Poussard* v. *Spiers & Pond,* 1876,[213] and *Bettini* v. *Gye,* 1876.)[214]

A contract may provide for optional methods of performance. (*Narbeth* v. *James. The Lady Tahilla,* 1967.)[302]

The time for performance may in some cases be *of the essence of the contract* and in others it may not. At common law, where the parties have fixed a time for performance, time is the essence of the contract, even though the parties have not expressly said so in the contract. The rule may be applied even where performance is earlier than the contract specifies. (*Bowes* v. *Shand,* 1877.)[303]

However, Equity took a different view, and where the plaintiff was asking for an equitable remedy, e.g. for specific performance of a contract to sell land, the failure of either the vendor or the purchaser to complete exactly to time did not prevent a claim for specific performance so long as no injustice was done to either party. *Time was of the essence even in Equity:* (*a*) where the parties had stipulated a time for performance in the contract and had in addition indicated that this time was in the nature of a condition; (*b*) where time was not originally of the essence but had been made so by the aggrieved party giving notice to this effect (*Rickards (Charles) Ltd.* v, *Oppenheim,* 1950);[304] or (*c*) where from the circumstances of the case it appeared that the contract should be performed at the agreed time.

The sale of a reversionary interest would come into this last category. Suppose property is left by will to X for life with remainder to Y, then

if Y sells his remainder, as he may do, it is obvious that the contract of
sale should be completed at the agreed date, for delay will mean that
the life tenant T is growing older and the value of the reversion is therefore increasing. Similarly in the sale of a business, Equity will generally
take the view that the contract should be completed on time so that
uncertainties regarding a change of owner should not be so prolonged
as to affect adversely the goodwill of the business. Further, it was held
in *Hare* v. *Nichol*, [1966] 1 All E.R. 285, that time is the essence of the
contract where the property concerned is shares of a highly speculative
nature. In addition, there is a presumption that time is of the essence
of all mercantile contracts unless the circumstances show otherwise.
(*Elmdore Ltd.* v. *Keech*, 1969.)[305]

Where the contract is capable of specific performance, the equitable
rule still applies, even though the plaintiff may in fact be asking for
damages. In other cases, the common law rule that time is of the essence
of the contract prevails. (Sect. 41, Law of Property Act, 1925.)

With regard to the manner of performance, the question of what is good
tender arises. *Tender is an offer of performance which complies with the terms
of the contract.* If goods are tendered by the seller and refused by the
buyer, the seller is freed from liability, given that the goods are in accordance with the contract as to quantity and quality. A tender of money
which is refused does not discharge the tenderer, but if he pays the
money into court without delay he will have a good defence to an action
brought against him, and the debt will not bear interest. In a tender of
money, the exact amount must be tendered without request for change.
In England and Wales the notes of the Bank of England are legal tender.
From 15th February, 1971, the decimal bronze coins became legal
tender for amounts up to 20p. Silver or cupro-nickel coins up to and
including the 10p piece are legal tender for amounts up to £5. The 50p
coin is legal tender up to £10. The old 10s note ceased to be legal tender
after 20th November, 1970. The old penny and the old threepenny
piece were withdrawn on 31st August, 1971. Tender by cheque or other
negotiable instrument is not good tender unless the creditor does not
object; and the debt is discharged when the instrument is honoured,
not when it is received. If the instrument is dishonoured, the creditor
may sue for his money under either the contract or on the instrument.
The tender must be unconditional, and must comply with the terms of
the contract as to time, place and mode of performance. A payment of
the amount due under a contract is a discharge, but the payment of a
smaller sum is no discharge unless made earlier than it is due or by a
third party.

It is customary to give *receipts* on payment, but a recept is only *prima
facie* and not conclusive evidence of payment. A payment may be proved
by parol in cases where a receipt is lost or no receipt is given. At common
law there is no right to demand a receipt, but under the Stamp Act,
1891, a receipt of £2 and upwards had to be stamped with a twopenny
stamp, and if the creditor for such an amount refused to give a receipt

when asked or did not stamp a receipt, he was liable to a penalty of £10. There were certain exceptions to this rule, e.g. a receipt for the payment of wages need not be stamped.

The Finance Act, 1970, abolished the old 2d. duty on bills of exchange and receipts as from 1st February, 1971.

If money is sent by post it is not good payment if the letter is lost in the post unless the creditor requested payment in this way. Even a request to pay through the post does not absolve the debtor from paying in a reasonable manner and according to business practice, e.g. by registered cash. Where there is such a request, payment is established by proof of posting, even though the letter is lost in transit, and delay in the post excuses late payment.

It is important to consider the *rules governing appropriation of payments*. Certain debts are barred by the Limitation Act, and money which has been owed for six years under simple contracts or twelve years under specialty contracts, without acknowledgment, may not be recoverable by an action in the courts. Where a debtor owes several debts to the same creditor and makes a payment which does not cover them all, there are rules governing how the money should be appropriated—

(*a*) The debtor can appropriate the payment expressly or by implication. If he owes two debts, one of £50 and one of £25, and sends a cheque for £25, there is an implied appropriation to the second debt.

(*b*) If there is no appropriation by the debtor, the creditor can appropriate the payment to any of the debts at any time, even to a statute-barred debt, since such a debt has not been extinguished; only the right of action in court has been lost.

(*c*) Where there is what is called a current account, appropriation follows the rule in *Clayton's* case (1816), 1 Mer. 572. Bank current accounts provide a good example of accounts to which this rule applies. *Clayton's* case says that, in the absence of contrary intention, the money first paid in is to be regarded as the money which is first withdrawn. (*Deeley* v. *Lloyds Bank Ltd.*, 1912.)[306]

3. **Discharge by Breach.** A breach does not of itself discharge a contract, but it may in some circumstances give the innocent party the right to treat it as discharged if he so wishes.

There are several forms of breach of contract—

(*a*) Failure to perform the contract is the most usual form, as where a seller fails to deliver goods by the appointed time, or where they are not up to standard as to quality or quantity.

(*b*) Express repudiation arises where one party states that he will not perform his part of the contract. (*Hochster* v. *De La Tour*, 1853.)[307]

(*c*) Some action by one party may make performance impossible, as where A agrees to marry B in June but in fact marries C in April. (*Omnium D'Entreprises* v. *Sutherland*, 1919.)[308]

Any breach which takes place before the time for performance has arrived is called an anticipatory breach.

The remedies where a contract has been discharged by breach are an action for damages if any have been suffered, or, if the parties have stipulated the damages to be payable on breach, an action for that sum which is called liquidated damages. Not every breach entitles the innocent party to treat the contract as discharged. It must be shown that the breach affects a vital part of the contract, i.e. that it is a breach of condition rather than a breach of warranty, or that the other party has no intention of performing his part of the contract. In the case of anticipatory breach, the innocent party may treat the contract as discharged at once and sue for damages, though the Court may have regard to whether the contract could have been carried out by the plaintiff at the time scheduled for performance. (*The Mihalis Angelos*, 1969.)[309] Alternatively he may ignore the breach and wait until the time for performance arrives. It may be dangerous to wait since the contract may later become impossible for performance, so providing the party who was in breach with a good defence to an action. (*Avery* v. *Bowden*, 1855.)[310]

Where one party to a contract wrongfully repudiates it and the other party refuses to accept the repudiation, it seems that the contract survives and the rights of the innocent party are preserved. He may, if it is within his power, perform his part of the contract and recover on that basis, for there is no duty on him to vary the contract at the request of the other party so as to deprive himself of its benefit. (*White and Carter (Councils) Ltd.* v. *McGregor*, 1961.)[311]

It should also be noted that where a person is entitled to repudiate his liability under a contract by reason of the other party's breach his delay in so doing will not operate against him unless other parties are prejudiced or the delay is so long as to indicate to the court that he has accepted liability. (*Allen* v. *Robles* (*Compagnie Parisienne de Garantie, Third Party*), 1969.)[312]

4. Discharge by Subsequent Impossibility (or Frustration).

If an agreement is impossible of performance from the outset, it is no contract; but sometimes it is possible to enter into a contract which subsequently becomes impossible to carry out in full or in part. The view of the early common law judges was that such eventualities should be provided for in the contract, and if this was not done the party liable for the performance of an impossible undertaking would be obliged to pay damages to the other party for such non-performance.

This rule was gradually modified and made less rigorous, but even now the courts are not anxious to give remedies for eventualities which could have been foreseen, e.g. if a strike prevents performance this could have been provided for in the contract. (*Davis Contractors Ltd.* v. *Fareham U.D.C.*, 1956.)[313]

The present doctrine is that if performance was possible when the contract was made, subsequent impossibility may discharge it in the following cases—

(*a*) If the impossibility is due to changes in law or operation of law, the contract is discharged. (*Re Shipton, Anderson & Co. and Harrison Brothers' Arbitration,* 1915.)[314]

(*b*) If the contract is for personal services, it becomes discharged by the death or incapacity of the person who has to perform it. Temporary illness will not in most cases discharge a contract (*Storey* v. *Fulham Steel Works,* 1907,[315] but if the illness goes right to the root of the contract, it will (*Poussard* v. *Spiers and Pond,* 1876.)[213]

(*c*) If the performance depends upon the existence of a certain thing, or a state of affairs which ceases to exist, the contract is discharged. (*Taylor* v. *Caldwell,* 1863,[316] and *Krell* v. *Henry,* 1903.)[317] But it must be shown that the contract will be substantially affected by the new circumstances. (*Herne Bay Steam Boat Co.* v. *Hutton,* 1903.)[318]

(*d*) A contract is also discharged when its commercial purpose is frustrated, often because its completion would be so delayed as to make the performance, when it occurred, of little or no value. (*Joseph Constantine Steamship Line Ltd.* v. *Imperial Smelting Corporation Ltd.,* 1942,[319] and *Jackson* v. *Union Marine Insurance Co. Ltd.,* 1874.)[320]

The doctrine will not apply—

(i) where the parties have made express provision for the event which has occurred. In such a case, the provisions inserted into the contract by the parties will apply;

(ii) where the frustrating event is self-induced (*Maritime National Fish Ltd.* v. *Ocean Trawlers Ltd.,* 1935);[321]

(iii) probably to a lease, because a lease creates an estate not a mere contract. The same rule may also apply to an agreement for a lease and a contract for the sale of land. (*Cricklewood Property and Investment Trust Ltd.* v. *Leightons Investment Trust Ltd.,* 1945;[322] *Hillingdon Estates Co.* v. *Stonefield Estates Ltd.,* 1952.)[323]

An important modern statute has laid down the conditions which will govern the rights and duties of the parties when certain contracts are frustrated. This measure is the Law Reform (Frustrated Contracts) Act, 1943. Before this Act it was the law that when subsequence impossibility discharged a contract, it did not discharge it *ab initio* (from the beginning), but only from the time when the event making the contract impossible of performance actually occurred. Thus any loss lay where it fell. Money not due at the time could not be claimed. Money due and not paid could be claimed. Money paid under the contract before it became impossible could not be recovered. (*Chandler* v. *Webster,* 1904.)[324] However, money paid was recoverable if there was a total failure of consideration. (*The Fibrosa Case,* 1943.)[325]

The statute has amended the common law and provides what shall happen if the contract becomes discharged by frustration—

(i) All money paid before discharge is recoverable.
(ii) Money which was payable ceases to be payable.

(iii) The court will allow the parties to recover sums of money paid out on expenses incurred in connection with the contract, or to retain such sums from money already received under the contract.

(iv) It is also possible to recover, on a *quantum meruit*, a reasonable sum of money as compensation where one of the parties has carried out acts of part performance before frustration, i.e. where one party has received a benefit under the contract other than a money payment.

The Act does not apply to contracts for the carriage of goods by sea or to contracts of insurance. If X insures against sickness on 1st January, and dies on 1st February, his executors cannot recover eleven-twelfths of the premium paid, even though the contract is now impossible of performance.

The Act also excepts from its provisions certain *sales* of *specific* goods which have *perished*, the effect of which is, broadly speaking, as follows—

(*a*) *The goods must be Specific and Not Unascertained.* Sect. 62 of the Sale of Goods Act, 1893, states that specific goods are goods identified and agreed upon at the time the contract of sale is made. Thus a contract to sell "my 1969 Morris Minor" is a contract to sell specific goods, whereas a contract to sell "one of my two cars" would be a contract for the sale of unascertained goods since it is not certain which of the two cars will be sold.

(*b*) *The Goods Must have Perished.* Goods are regarded as having perished—

(i) where they have been physically destroyed, say by fire; or

(ii) where although they physically exist they are so damaged that they cannot reasonably be regarded as the goods actually purchased, e.g. apples contaminated by sewage.

(*b*) *The Contract Must be a Sale and Not an Agreement to Sell.* A *contract of sale* is one in which the property (normally ownership) in the goods is transferred to the buyer at the time when the contract is made. In an *agreement to sell*, ownership is transferred to the buyer at a future date after the making of the contract. It should be noted that in English Law the transfer of ownership does not depend upon *delivery* of the goods. Where the goods are specific and in the absence of any contrary intention, the property in the goods passes to the buyer when he accepts the seller's offer, even though the seller physically retains the goods.

The application of these concepts may be illustrated by the following examples—

1. If A offers to sell the only car he has, which is at his home, to B for £100 and B accepts the offer, the contract will be for the sale of specific goods and ownership (and normally risk) will pass to B when he accepts A's offer regardless of actual delivery of the vehicle. Ordinarily A will deliver the car to B and all will be well; but let us suppose that the car is destroyed by fire before delivery, so that A cannot perform the con-

tract. In such circumstances the legal position would appear to be as follows—

(*a*) If the car was destroyed *before* B accepted A's offer the contract is rendered *void* by Sect. 6 of the Sale of Goods Act, 1893. Thus A need not pay damages for non-performance nor is B obliged to pay for the car. Furthermore, if B had made a payment to A it could be recovered.

(*b*) If the car was destroyed *after* B accepted A's offer B would have become owner of the car and would have to pay A £100 for it even though the car could never be delivered.

(*c*) If in the course of selling the car to A it was agreed that ownership should not pass for one week, then if the car was destroyed before the week had elapsed the position would be a follows—

(i) A would have to bear the loss of the car; and

(ii) the contract would be avoided by Sect. 7 of the Sale of Goods Act, 1893, so that A would not be liable in damages for failure to perform the contract—B would not be required to pay for it and could recover any money paid to A.

2. If the goods were *unascertained*, as where A sold to B "one of my two cars," then if one or both of the cars were destroyed before ascertainment the Act of 1943 would apply and the rules laid down therein would come into force, though B could of course accept the remaining car if he wished. B would probably not be compelled to accept the remaining car unless perhaps it was in all respects the same as the one destroyed. This is unlikely in the case of a car but might apply where the goods were, say, sugar or wheat.

3. If the goods were *specific* but had not *perished* as where A's only car was requisitioned by the Crown in an emergency, then the Act of 1943 and the rules thereunder would also apply.

Before leaving the topic of frustration, it should be noted that the Act of 1943 does not apply to contracts governed by foreign law.

5. Discharge by Lapse of Time. Contracts entered into for a specified time are discharged when that period of time has elapsed. In other cases time is of no effect as regards discharge, but lapse of time may render contracts unenforceable in a court of law.

The Limitation Act, 1939, provides that actions on simple contracts are barred after six years from the date upon which the plaintiff could first have brought his action. Actions on speciality contracts are barred after twelve years from the cause of action. The Act does not truly discharge a contract, it merely makes it unenforceable in a court of law. It can, therefore, be made actionable again by a subsequent payment of money not appropriated by the debtor, or by the debtor, or his duly authorised agent, making a written acknowledgment of the debt to the creditor or his agent. Such an acknowledgment need not have been written for the purpose and is effective if it indicates that a debt is due even if it does not state the amount. (*Dungate* v. *Dungate*, 1965.)[112] Thus, a statement of liabilities to "sundry creditors" in a company balance sheet was held to be enough. *Jones* v. *Bellgrove Properties Ltd.*, [1949] 2 K.B. 700. A person cannot, however, be forced to acknowledge a statute barred debt. (*Lovell* v. *Lovell*, 1970.)[350]

Where the plaintiff is a minor or person of unsound mind, the period of limitation does not run against him until his contractual disability ends, i.e. at eighteen (or twenty-one if the cause of action arose before 1st January, 1970 (Family Law Reform Act, 1969, Sch. 3)) or on becoming sane. But once time has started to run, any subsequent incapacity will not stop it running. The defendant's fraud may also prevent his pleading the Statutes of Limitation. (*Lynn* v. *Bamber*, 1930.)[326]

6. **Discharge by Operation of Law.** This may occur in certain cases—

(*a*) MERGER. A simple contract is swallowed up, or merged into, a subsequent deed covering the same subject matter, and in such circumstances an action lies only on the deed. Similarly a judgment, which is a contract of record, merges the contract debt on which the action was brought, so that all future actions are based on the judgment.

(*b*) MATERIAL ALTERATION. An alteration of a material part of a deed or written contract, made by one party intentionally and without the consent of the other party, will discharge the contract. The alteration must alter the legal effect of the contract, and the mere alteration of a misdescription of one of the parties, or the insertion of the true date, will not operate as a discharge.

(*c*) DEATH. Death will discharge a contract for personal services. Other contractual rights and liabilities survive for the benefit, or otherwise, of the estate.

(*d*) BANKRUPTCY. A right of action for breach of contract possessed by a debtor, which relates to his property and which if brought will increase his assets, will pass to his trustee in bankruptcy, e.g. a contract with a third party to deliver goods or to pay money to the debtor. The right to sue for injury to the debtor's character or reputation does not pass to the trustee, even though it arises from a breach of a contract. (*Wilson* v. *United Counties Bank*, 1920.)[327]

With regard to contracts for personal services, it depends upon the date of the breach whether the debtor's right to sue remains with him or passes to his trustee. If the breach occurs before the commencement of the bankruptcy, the right of action passes to the trustee; if it occurs after this date, the debtor may sue, but the trustee may intervene and deduct from the sum recovered such sums as are not required for the reasonable maintenance of the bankrupt and his family. A trustee cannot force the debtor to carry out contracts involving personal service by him.

REMEDIES FOR BREACH OF CONTRACT

When there is a breach of contract the following remedies may be available—

(i) A right of action for damages at common law (the most common remedy).

(ii) A right of action on a *quantum meruit*.

(iii) A right to sue for specific performance or for an injunction.

(iv) A right to ask for rescission of the contract.

(v) A refusal of any further performance by the injured party.

It will be convenient to consider also, in this section, those cases where similar remedies are available in non-contractual actions, e.g. tort.

1. **Damages.** Damages are the common law remedy consisting of a payment of money and are intended as compensation for the plaintiff's loss and not as punishment for the defendant. The aim is to put the injured party in the same financial position as he would have been if the contract had been performed according to its terms. (*B. Sunley & Co. Ltd.* v. *Cunard White Star Ltd.*, 1940.)[328] Expenses incurred prior to the date of contract may be recovered if they were within the contemplation of the parties as a likely result of the breach. In *Anglia Television Ltd.* v. *Reed*, [1971] 3 All E.R. 690, A Ltd. engaged R to act in a film having previously spent £2,750 in employing a director and designer. R repudiated the contract and A Ltd. recovered £2,750 from him. On rare occasions punitive damages were awarded, i.e. damages in excess of the actual loss, and these might be appropriate in cases of breach of promise of marriage, particularly if there had been a seduction. Under the Law Reform (Miscellaneous Provisions) Act, 1970, Sect. 1, engagements to marry are not enforceable at law. Compensation for pregnancy where this has occurred must now be pursued in affiliation proceedings in a Magistrates' Court. Generally, however, the aim of damages is one of simple compensation for actual loss, though much depends upon the nature of the property forming the subject matter of the claim. (*Harbutt's Plasticine* v. *Wayne Tank & Pump Co. Ltd.*, 1970.)[227] Difficulty in assessing damages is not necessarily a bar to a claim. (*Chaplin* v. *Hicks*, 1911.)[329]

The plaintiff's liability to taxation is taken into account. (*Beach* v. *Reed Corrugated Cases Ltd.*, 1956.)[330]

Apart from the question of assessment, the question of *remoteness of damage* arises. The consequence of a breach of contract may be far-reaching, and the law must draw the line somewhere and say that damages incurred beyond a certain limit are too remote to be recovered. Damages in contract must therefore be proximate. The modern law regarding remoteness of damage in contract is founded upon the case of *Hadley* v. *Baxendale*, 1854.[331] The case is authority for the statement that damages in contract will be too remote to be recovered unless they are such that the defendant, as a reasonable man, would have foreseen them as likely to result, according to the usual course of things or because of special facts made known to him. Where damages do not arise naturally from the breach, they may be recovered only if the defendant was made aware of the possibility of such damage (*Horne* v. *Midland Railway Co.*,

1873),[332] though notice of possible loss can be constructive as well as actual. (*Pinnock Bross.* v. *Lewis and Peat Ltd.*, 1923.)[333]

Regarding changes in the relative value of currencies, these are irrelevant in assessing damages and in the payments of debts if—

(i) they occur *after* the date on which damages are assessed or the debt became due—thus a revaluation of sterling after a case has been decided and the judge has awarded damages, or after the date on which a debt should have been paid, must be ignored and the defendant will pay at the rate of exchange prevailing when the award of damages was made or the debt became due;

(ii) they occur *on or before* the date on which damages were assessed or the debt became due *unless* the loss caused by revaluation can be shown to have been within the assumed contemplation of the parties or the contract expressly provides for variations in price if prevailing rates of exchange vary; otherwise the court will not increase the sterling value of the damages or the debt in order to give the plaintiff the same amount of money under the new rate of exchange as he would have received under the old. (*Aruna Mills* v. *Dhanrajmal Gobindram*, [1958] 1 All E.R. 113, and *The Teh Hu*, [1969] 3 All E.R. 1200.)

It must be understood that, when a breach occurs, the party suffering from the breach must do all he can to reduce his loss, and he cannot recover damages which have resulted from his failure to do so. If a person cancels a hotel booking, the hotel proprietor must try to relet the rooms. If a seller refuses to deliver goods, the buyer must attempt to obtain supplies elsewhere. In the latter case, where there is an available market, the damages might amount to no more than the difference between the contract price and the market price on the day appointed for delivery, together with incidental expenses. These principles can be seen in the context of contract in *Charter* v. *Sullivan*, 1957,[334] and *Thompson (W.L.) Ltd.* v. *Robinson (Gunmakers) Ltd.*, 1955.[335] Mitigation is also relevant in tort. (*Luker* v. *Chapman*, 1970.)[336]

It is possible to classify damages under a number of headings, and this classification applies to both contract and tort.

(*a*) ORDINARY DAMAGES. These are damages assessed by the court for losses arising naturally from the breach of contract; and in tort for losses which cannot be positively proved or ascertained, and depend upon the court's view of the nature of the plaintiff's injury. For example, the court may have to decide what to award for the loss of an eye, there being no scale of payments; and this is so whether the action be in tort or for breach of contract.

(*b*) SPECIAL DAMAGES. These are awarded in tort for losses which can be positively proved or ascertained, e.g. damage to clothing; garage bills, where a vehicle has been damaged; doctor's fees; and so on. However, where it is difficult to determine the exact proportions of a claim for special damages, e.g. loss of profit not supported by accurate figures the court must do its best to arrive at a fair valuation. (*Dixons Ltd.* v. *J. L. Cooper Ltd.* (1970), 114 S.J. 319.) In contract, the term covers losses which do not arise naturally from the breach, so that they will not be recoverable unless within the contemplation of the parties as described above.

(*c*) EXEMPLARY AND AGGRAVATED DAMAGES. The usual object of damages both in contract and tort is to compensate the plaintiff for loss which he has incurred arising from the defendant's conduct. The object of *exemplary damages* is to punish the defendant, and to deter him and others from similar conduct in the future. Thus, it was at one time thought that, if the court had arrived at a sum of money which would sufficiently compensate the plaintiff, it could award a further sum, not as compensation for the plaintiff, but as a punishment to the defendant, the exemplary damages being in the nature of a fine. An award of exemplary damages had always confused the functions of the civil and criminal law, and it would appear that since the judgment of Lord Devlin in *Rookes* v. *Barnard*, [1964] 1 All E.R. 367, an award of exemplary damages should only be made in certain special cases. (See below.)

Aggravated damages, on the other hand, can be awarded (generally only in tort) where the defendant's conduct is such that the plaintiff requires more than the usual amount of damages to *compensate him* for the unpleasant method in which the tort was committed against him. However, an award of aggravated damages is still *compensatory*.

The state of the law after *Rookes* v. *Barnard*, [1964] 1 All E.R. 367, may perhaps be illustrated by taking a hypothetical case. Suppose a tenant T is evicted from his flat by the landlord L before T's term has expired, and that in order to evict T the landlord uses excessive violence. The court may decide that in an ordinary case of trespass and assault T would be adequately compensated by an award of damages of (say) £500. However, if the court considers that L used particularly violent and unpleasant methods to achieve this eviction, it may award a further sum (say) £100 as aggravated damages because, on the facts of the case, this is necessary to compensate T. It would appear that the court cannot now go on and make a further award to T in order to punish and deter L.

Exemplary or punitive damages were sometimes awarded in contract for breach of promise of marriage, particularly where a female plaintiff had allowed the defendant to have sexual intercourse with her on the promise of marriage. This action is now abolished by the Law Reform (Miscellaneous Provisions) Act, 1970, Sect. 1 and examples of exemplary damages would seem in the main to be confined to actions in tort. As a result of Lord Devlin's judgment in *Rookes* v. *Barnard*, [1964] 1 All E.R. 367 exemplary damages can be awarded only—

(i) *Where there is arbitrary or unconstitutional action by servants of the State*, e.g. an unreasonable false imprisonment or detention by State authorities.

(ii) *Where the defendant's conduct has been calculated by him to make a profit for himself which may well exceed the compensation payable to the plaintiff.* Thus a newspaper may decide that the increased sales of the paper containing a libel will more than compensate for any damages which may have to be paid to the person libelled. In such a case exemplary damages may be awarded to the plaintiff, though the intention to profit must be proved. It is not enough that the newspaper has been sold and some profit necessarily made.

(iii) *Where exemplary damages are expressly authorised by statute.*

It is perhaps worth noting that having apparently restricted the number of situations in which exemplary damages might be awarded, Lord Devlin said at one point in his judgment (see *Rookes* v. *Barnard*, [1964] 1 All E.R. 367 at p. 411): "Exemplary damages can properly be awarded whenever it is necessary to teach a wrongdoer that tort does not pay." The ramifications of this statement were considered in regard to the tort of deceit in *Mafo* v. *Adams*, 1969.[196] In addition, the House of Lords in *Cassells & Co. Ltd.* v. *Broome* [1972] 1 All E.R. 801 were of the opinion that *Rookes* v. *Barnard*[520] was properly decided in this respect and that the pre-1964 common law no longer applied.

(d) NOMINAL DAMAGES. Sometimes a small sum (say £2) is awarded where the plaintiff proves a breach of contract, or the infringement of a right, but has suffered no actual loss.

(e) CONTEMPTUOUS DAMAGES. A farthing was sometimes awarded to mark the court's disapproval of the plaintiff's conduct in bringing the action. Such damages have been awarded to male plaintiffs in breach of promise of marriage actions, and where the plaintiff has sued for defamation of character in spite of the fact that he has engaged in defamatory activities against the defendant. Since farthings are no longer legal tender, the new decimal halfpenny will be used in future.

(f) LIQUIDATED DAMAGES. These are damages agreed upon by the parties to the contract, and only a breach of contract need be proved; no proof of loss is required. Damages in tort are not liquidated.

(g) UNLIQUIDATED DAMAGES. Where no damages are fixed by the contract it is left to the court to decide their amount. In such a case the plaintiff must produce evidence of the loss he has suffered, as is normal in the case of tort.

Liquidated damages must appear to be a genuine pre-estimate of loss, not a *penalty* inserted to make it an ill bargain for the defendant not to carry out his part of the contract. The court will not enforce a penalty, but will award damages on normal principles. It will be seen, therefore, that the term "penalty clause" is a misnomer in that a clause which is truly penal will not be enforced. Nevertheless, this terminology is often used in commercial contracts but such a clause is unenforceable unless it defines a method of calculating liquidated damages.

Certain tests are applied in order to decide whether or not the provision is a penalty. Obviously extravagant sums are generally in the nature of penalties. Where the contractual obligation lying on the defendant is to pay money, then any provision in the contract which requires the payment of a larger sum on default of payment is a penalty, because the damage can be accurately assessed. Where the sum provided for in the contract is payable on the occurrence of any one of several events, it is probably a penalty; for it is unlikely that each event can produce the same loss (*Ford Motor Co. (England) Ltd.* v. *Armstrong*, 1915),[337] though this rule is not always applied. (*Dunlop* v. *New Garage and Motor Co. Ltd.*, 1915.)[114] If a sum is agreed by the parties as liquidated damages, it will be enforced as agreed, even though the actual loss is greater or smaller. (*Cellulose Acetate Silk Co. Ltd.* v. *Widnes Foundry Ltd.*, 1933.)[338]

2. **Quantum meruit.** This remedy means that the plaintiff will be awarded as much as is earned or deserved. In the event of a breach of contract, the injured party may have a claim other than the one for damages. He may have carried out the work or performed services and for such he may be entitled to claim on a *quantum meruit*. He will be awarded what the court thinks the work or services are worth. This action is quite distinct from an action for breach of contract and is in the nature of restitution for work done. The remedy can be used contractually or quasi-contractually, and, although the topic cannot be treated fully, examples of the use of the remedy are given below—

(*a*) CONTRACTUALLY. Here it may be used to recover a reasonable price or remuneration where there is a contract for the supply of goods or services, but the contract does not fix any precise sum to be paid. It may also be used where the original contract has been replaced by a new one, and a payment is required under the new agreement, e.g. X orders 20 bottles of brandy from Y at a certain price, and Y sends 18 bottles of brandy and 2 bottles of whisky. X is not, of course, bound to take delivery, but if he does he must pay a reasonable price for the whisky on a *quantum meruit*.

(*b*) QUASI-CONTRACTUALLY. Here the remedy may be used to recover a sum of money for work done under a contract discharged by the defendant's breach. This is really an alternative to a claim for damages for breach of contract, but it does enable the court to award whatever it thinks the plaintiff has earned by his work, and this may be greater than the contract price. The remedy is also available when a contract is void, since for breach of a void contract no damages can be awarded (*Craven-Ellis* v. *Canons Ltd.*, 1936);[339] and sometimes where the contract is frustrated. (*Davis Contractors Ltd.* v. *Fareham U.D.C.*, 1956.)[313] The remedy is also available where there never was a contract. However, where A continues to pay B an agreed fee in respect of certain work and later B agrees to do further work, without a further fee being mentioned, B cannot claim payment in respect of the further work on a *quantum meruit* while the original contract subsists and has not been discharged. (*Gilbert and Partners* v. *Knight*, 1968.)[340]

3. **Specific Performance and Injunction.** These are equitable remedies and are not available by right, as is the case with damages, but

at the discretion of the court. Formerly these remedies would have had to be sought in the courts of Equity, but since the Judicature Acts, 1873–75, these remedies, as well as damages, are available in any court.

A degree of *specific performance* is an order of the court, and constitutes an express instruction to a party to a contract to perform the actual obligation which he undertook under its terms. It is often granted in contracts connected with land, and under the Companies Act, 1948, a contract to take debentures in a company can be specifically enforced, though normally a specific performance of a loan would not be granted. In the case of contracts for the sale of goods, specific performance is not usually given, unless the goods are unique and cannot be purchased easily in the market, or where their value is difficult to assess.

An *injunction* is an order of the court whereby an individual is required to refrain from the further doing of the act complained of. It may be used to prevent many wrongful acts, e.g. torts, but in the context of contract the remedy will be granted to enforce a negative stipulation in a contract in a case where damages would not be an adequate remedy. Its application may be extended to contracts where there is no actual negative stipulation but where one may be *inferred*. (*Metropolitan Electric Supply Co.* v. *Ginder*, 1901.)[341] In a proper case an injunction may be used as an indirect method of enforcing a contract for personal services, but in that case a *clear* negative stipulation is required. (*Whitwood Chemical Co.* v. *Hardman*, 1891,[342] and *Warner Bros. Pictures Incorporated* v. *Nelson*, 1937,[343] but see now *Hill* v. *Parsons*, 1971.)[652]

Injunctions may be (*a*) Interlocutory, (*b*) Perpetual, (*c*) Prohibitory, (*d*) Mandatory. An *interlocutory injunction* is granted before the hearing of the action, the plaintiff undertaking to be responsible for any damage caused to the defendant if in the subsequent action the plaintiff does not succeed. There is a form of interlocutory injunction called *quia timet* (because he fears). This may be granted, though rarely, even though the injury has not taken place but is merely threatened. A *perpetual injunction* is granted after a trial, and when the point at issue has been finally determined. A *prohibitory injunction* orders that a certain act shall not be done; a *mandatory injunction* orders that a certain positive act shall be done, e.g. an order to pull down a wall erected in breach of covenant.

Since specific performance is an equitable remedy, it will be granted only when certain conditions apply—

(i) CONSIDERATION MUST EXIST, since "Equity will not assist a volunteer."

(ii) THE COURT MUST BE ABLE TO SUPERVISE THE PERFORMANCE. Specific performance will not be granted if constant supervision is necessary to ensure that the defendant complies with the decree. (*Ryan* v. *Mutual Tontine Westminster Chambers Association*, 1893.)[344]

(iii) IT MUST BE JUST AND EQUITABLE THAT THE REMEDY BE GRANTED. If the court considers that damages are an adequate remedy, it will not grant an equitable one.

(iv) BOTH PARTIES MUST BE ABLE TO OBTAIN THE REMEDY. The courts will not grant equitable remedies to an infant because his contracts cannot be enforced against him, and Equity requires equality or mutuality.

(v) THE PLAINTIFF MUST SHOW THAT HE WAS IN A POSITION TO CARRY OUT HIS PART OF THE BARGAIN AT THE TIME FIXED FOR PERFORMANCE.

(vi) THE PLAINTIFF'S OWN CONDUCT IN THE MATTER MUST BE ABOVE REPROACH: for it is said that "He who comes into Equity must come with clean hands."

A contract for personal services will not be specifically enforced because—

(*a*) it would be undesirable to force persons to work together if they did not wish to do so; and

(*b*) it would be impossible to ensure that the contract was properly carried out unless the defendant were under the constant supervision of the court.

However, as we have seen, the court may *encourage* but not *compel* performance of a contract of personal service by means of an injunction. (*Whitwood Chemical Co.* v. *Hardman*, 1891,[342] and *Warner Bros. Pictures Incorporated* v. *Nelson*, 1937.)[343] If the effect of an injunction would be to *compel* performance it will not be granted. (*Page One Records Ltd.* v. *Britton*, 1967,[345] but see now *Hill* v. *Parsons*, 1971.)[652]

Defiance of the court's order granting an equitable remedy constitutes contempt of court, which is punishable by fine or imprisonment. The court's order is, therefore, likely to be obeyed. Some equitable remedies must be asked for within a given time by statute, but otherwise they must be asked for within a reasonable time, since "Delay defeats Equities." What is a reasonable time is determined by the court from the circumstances.

4. Rescission This is a further equitable remedy for breach of contract. The rule is the same when the remedy is used for breach as it is when it is used for misrepresentation. If the contract cannot be completely rescinded, it cannot be rescinded at all; it must be possible to restore the *status quo*. All part payments must be returned on rescission and cannot be retained as security against future damages, but there are circumstances where part payment is regarded as a guarantee for the due performance of the payer's obligations, and, if this is so, it will be forfeited if he does not go on with the contract, although Equity will sometimes grant relief against forfeiture of deposits.

5. Refusal of Further Performance. If the person suffering from the breach desires merely to be quit of his obligations under the contract, he may refuse any further performance on his own part and set up the breach as a defence if the party who has committed the breach attempts to enforce the contract against him. Even so, he may, if he wishes, reinforce his position by bringing an action for rescission.

The Recovery of Interest. The rules governing the recovery of interest are as follows—

(*a*) It is payable where the parties have so agreed in the contract.

(*b*) The dealings between the parties may show that an agreement to pay interest may be implied.

(*c*) Overdue bills of exchange and promissory notes bear interest.

(*d*) Under the Law Reform (Miscellaneous Provisions) Act, 1934, the court may *at its discretion* allow interest at such a rate as it thinks fit on all claims for debt or special damages from the date when the claim arose to judgment.

It should be noted, however, that under Sect. 22 of the Administration of Justice Act, 1969, as from 1st January, 1970, judges are *directed* in personal injury cases to award interest on damages, though the rate of interest, the portion of the judgment on which it is to be calculated, and the particular period during which interest is to be paid, is left to the discretion of the court.

QUASI-CONTRACTUAL RIGHTS AND REMEDIES

Before moving on to the law of tort, it is necessary to consider an area of law referred to as quasi-contract. Quasi-contract is based on the idea that a person should not obtain a benefit or an unjust enrichment as against another merely because there is no obligation in contract or another established branch of law which will operate to make him account for it. The Law may in these circumstances provide a remedy by implying *a fictitious promise* to account for the benefit or enrichment. This promise can then form the basis of an action in quasi-contract. The main areas in which quasi-contractual remedies have been used are as follows—

Actions for Money Paid. Where A has a secondary and B has a primary *legal liability* to a third person and A has paid over money which B was in the ultimate liable to pay, an action will lie in quasi-contract to enable A to recover from B. (*Brook's Wharf and Bull Wharf Ltd.* v. *Goodman Bros.*, 1936.)[346]

It is essential to the claim that B should have been under a *common and legal obligation* to pay. (*Metropolitan Police District Receiver* v. *Croydon Corporation*, 1957.)[347]

Actions for Money Had and Received. An action for money had and received by the defendant to the use of the plaintiff lies in the following circumstances—

(*a*) *Total Failure of Consideration.* The plaintiff must prove that there has been a *total* and not a *partial* failure of consideration. A partial failure of consideration may result in an action for damages. A *total* failure will result in recovery of all that was paid. A common reason for total failure of consideration arises where A, who has no title, sells goods to B and B has to give up the goods to the true owner. (*Rowland* v. *Divall*, 1923.)[348]

In addition the action is based on *failure* of consideration not its *absence*. Thus, money paid by way of a gift cannot be recovered in quasi-contract.

(*b*) *Mistake of Fact*. Where there is a fundamental and material mistake of fact which results in a payment of money, there may be an action in quasi-contract to recover the sums so paid either in whole or in part according to the effect of the mistake. (*Cox* v. *Prentice*, 1815.)[349]

(*c*) *Mistake of Law*. Money paid as a result of a mistake of law cannot generally be recovered since ignorance of the law is no excuse. However, as we have seen, it is not easy to distinguish a mistake of law from a mistake of fact, and legislation relating to rents and security of tenure has produced some interesting cases showing the different results obtainable according to the category into which the mistake is put. (*Sharp Bros. and Knight* v. *Chant*, 1917,[155] *Solle* v. *Butcher*, 1950,[156] and *Grist* v. *Bailey*, 1966.)[175] It appears that a mistake as to a person's legal rights can be construed, at least in equity, as a mistake of fact thus giving rise to a remedy. (*Cooper* v. *Phibbs*, 1867.)[157]

There may be another ground for recovering money paid in circumstances of mistake of law, e.g. as in the case of an oppressed party to an illegal contract not *in pari delicto* with the other. Where this is so, the plaintiff will not be prevented from succeeding simply because he has made a mistake of law. (*Kiriri Cotton Co.* v. *Dawani*, 1960.)[256]

(*d*) *Duress and Extortion*. Money paid under threats of physical violence or undue influence, i.e. moral duress, is not paid voluntarily and may be recovered in quasi-contract.

(*e*) *Money Received from a Third Person*. An application of this aspect of quasi-contract is to be found in insurance. If an insurance company pays out a sum of money to A (the insured) in respect of loss or damage to himself or his property and A later recovers additional money in respect of the loss from another, e.g. the person causing the loss, the insurance company may sue A in quasi-contract to recover the sums received from the third person. (*Darrell* v. *Tibbitts* (1880), 5 Q.B.D. 560.)

In addition, where A has received money from B with instructions to pay it to C, then C may sue A in quasi-contract if A refuses to pay the money over. (*Shamia* v. *Joory*, 1958.)[116]

(*f*) *Waiver of Tort*. If A steals B's car which is valued at £500 and sells it to a dealer C for £550, then B may sue A or C for the tort of conversion but can if he wishes waive his right to sue in tort and recover the money in quasi-contract. The action in quasi-contract has some advantages over the action in tort, e.g. A may prove in a winding-up or bankruptcy for the sum of £550 which he cannot do if his claim is in tort and has not reached judgment.

Claims on a Quantum Meruit. Where a plaintiff has done work for the defendant but no specific sum is owing, the plaintiff can recover a reasonable sum of money on a *quantum meruit*. This aspect of quasi-contract is dealt with on page 207.

Accounts Stated. If A gives B an I.O.U. for £10, the I.O.U. operates as an admission of the debt and gives a separate cause of action in quasi-contract. An I.O.U. is not conclusive and A may prove the debt is void for want of consideration or illegal or that he gave the I.O.U. under circumstances of mistake. Nevertheless, A has the burden of proving these matters and, if he cannot, B will succeed on the I.O.U.

Furthermore, if A (a debtor) and B (a creditor) have an account recording a number of transactions and agree to strike a balance at an agreed figure, this operates as an account stated and B can sue in quasi-contract for the amount. This is a separate source of action and would enable B to recover even in respect of debts which were formerly statute barred.

CHAPTER VI

THE LAW OF TORTS

It is difficult to give a satisfactory definition of a tort. According to Professor Winfield "tortious liability arises from a duty primarily fixed by law: this duty is towards persons generally and its breach is redressible by an action for unliquidated damages."

THE NATURE OF A TORT

It is a matter of dispute whether there is a law of tort or a law of torts: there are two schools of thought. One maintains that there is a law of tort, i.e. that all harm is actionable in the absence of just cause or excuse. If there were merely a law of specific torts, then no new torts could be created by the courts and the categories of tortious liability would be closed. It is urged that under the flexibility of case law new torts have come into being, and in no case has an action been refused simply because it was novel. This is called the *general principle of liability theory*. The other, and probably the better view, is that there is a law of torts—that there are only specific torts and unless the damage suffered can be brought under a known or recognised head of liability, there is no remedy. This view is supported by modern cases where an attempt has been made, unsuccessfully, to establish a purported tort of eviction (*Perera* v. *Vandiyar*, 1953),[352] and a tort of perjury. (*Hargreaves* v. *Bretherton*, 1958,[353] and *Roy* v. *Prior*, 1969.)[353a] Thus the courts have refused to create new torts even when given the opportunity.

In addition, there is a danger in modern society of a serious invasion of privacy resulting from the increasing availability and use of electronic and other devices as a means of surreptitious surveillance and the accumulation of personal information about individuals in data banks, computers and credit registers. Apart from the law of defamation which protects against the publication of falsehoods and the law of trespass which protects against infringement of property rights, the law of tort does not appear to be capable of extending to a remedy for invasion of privacy as such and legislation has been recommended.

Hence we may conclude that there is no general principle of liability in tort. Nevertheless, if judges have not created new torts, they have applied old cases to new situations. This has resulted in an extension of the old torts and there is a tendency to expand the area of liability, particularly in the field of negligence. (See p. 256.) If this continues, the law may reach a stage approximating to a general liability for wrongful acts, for, as Lord Macmillan said in *Donoghue* v. *Stevenson*, 1932,[354] "the categories of negligence are never closed."

DAMAGE AND LIABILITY

The law distinguishes between two concepts—1. *Damnum*, which means the damage suffered, and 2. *Injuria*, which is an injury having legal consequences. Sometimes, but not always, these two go together. For instance, if I negligently drive a car and injure a person, he suffers *damnum* (the hurt) and *injuria* (because he has a right of action to be compensated). There are, however, cases of 1. *Damnum sine injuria* (damage suffered without the violation of a legal right), and 2. *Injuria sine damno* (the violation of a legal right without damage).

The mere fact that a person has suffered damage does not entitle him to maintain an action in tort. Before an action can succeed, the harm suffered must be caused by an act which is a violation of a right which the law vests in the plaintiff or injured party. (*Best* v. *Samuel Fox & Co. Ltd*, 1952.)[355] Damage suffered in the absence of the violation of such legal right is known as *damnum sine injuria*. Furthermore a person who suffers *damnum* cannot receive compensation on the basis of *injuria* suffered by another. (*Electrochrome Ltd.* v. *Welsh Plastics Ltd.*, 1968.)[356]

The fact that the defendant acts with malice, i.e. with the intention of injuring his neighbour, does not give rise to a cause of action unless a legal right of the plaintiff is infringed. (*Bradford Corporation* v. *Pickles*, 1895,[357] and *Langbrook Properties* v. *Surrey County Council*, 1969.)[357a] On the other hand, whenever there is an invasion of a legal right, the person in whom the right is vested may bring an action and recover damages (though these may be nominal) or, what may be more important, obtain an injunction, although he has suffered no actual harm. For example, an action will lie for an unlawful entry on the land of another (trespass) although no actual damage is done. Furthermore, in *Ashby* v. *White* (1703), 2 Ld. Raym. 938, it was held that an elector had a right of action when his vote was wrongly rejected by the returning officer although the candidate for whom he tried to vote was elected. This is known as *injuria sine damno*.

It is important to be clear on the mental element or the question of malice in tort. The law of torts is concerned more with the effects of injurious conduct than the motives which inspired it. Hence, just as a bad intention will not necessarily make the infliction of damage actionable (*Bradford Corporation* v. *Pickles*, 1895),[357] so an innocent intention is usually no defence. (*Wilkinson* v. *Downton*, 1897.)[358] However, there are circumstances in which malice is important. The publication of a libel is in law presumed to be malicious, and where a person puts in motion the criminal law against another, this is actionable if malice is shown to be present and is known as the tort of malicious prosecution. Furthermore the question of malice may be raised when certain *defences* are pleaded. Thus in the law of defamation the defences of qualified privilege and fair comment are allowed only where the defendant has not been malicious.

PARTIES IN THE LAW OF TORT

It is now necessary to consider certain categories of persons whose capacity in connection with tortious acts is limited.

Minors. A minor can sue in tort as a plaintiff in the ordinary way except that, as in contract, he must sue through an adult as next friend. He cannot compromise his action except by leave of the court, unlike an adult, who does not require such permission. In this connection it is interesting to note that English law provides no authority on the question whether a child can claim damages for injuries sustained in his mother's womb (*in utero*) through another's alleged negligence. In *Dulieu* v. *White & Sons*, 1901,[359] the injury to the unborn child was regarded as aggravating the damages awarded to the mother and not as a separate head of claim. In addition, the "Thalidomide" cases were settled before judgment and therefore provide no assistance.

A minor is liable as defendant for all his torts except in a limited number of instances. Where the tort alleged requires a mental ingredient, the age of the minor (in cases of extreme infancy) may show an inability to form the necessary intent. In cases of negligence, a very young child cannot be expected to show the same standard of care as an older person. Nor can a minor be made liable on contracts which do not bind him by the device of suing him in tort. (*Jennings* v. *Rundall*, 1799.)[360] However, if the act complained of is associated with a contract but is independent of it, then the minor can be made liable. (*Burnard* v. *Haggis*, 1863.)[148]

A minor is not liable on the tort of deceit where he has by a fraudulent misrepresentation induced another party to contract with him and where there would otherwise be no contract, as in a loan of money. But where a minor obtains an advantage by falsely stating himself to be of full age, Equity requires him to restore his ill-gotten gains, but not if to do so would be to enforce a contract against the infant. "Restitution ends where repayment begins." This maxim means that, if there is no possibility of restoring the very thing obtained by fraud, the minor cannot be made liable to pay an equivalent sum, since this would amount to enforcing a void contract. (*Leslie* v. *Sheill*, 1914.)[147]

A minor is liable on the tort of detinue or conversion if he hires goods and fails to return them. (*Ballett* v. *Mingay*, 1943.)[361]

Basically children are, therefore, liable for their own torts, but a father may be liable vicariously, if the relationship of master and servant exists between him and the child or if there is the relationship of principal and agent. Simply as a father he is not liable unless the injury is caused by his negligent control of the child (*Donaldson* v. *McNiven*, 1952),[362] and even where he is so liable, it is really for his own tort, i.e. negligence in looking after the child. (*Bebee* v. *Sales*, 1916.)[363] Such a liability may extend to other persons (not being parents) who have control of children, e.g. teachers and education authorities, and, if such persons or authorities act negligently, they

8

may be held responsible for the harm caused by children under their care or control. Nevertheless, the basis of the action is negligent control or supervision. (*Carmarthenshire C.C.* v. *Lewis*, 1955,[364] and *Butt* v. *Cambridgeshire and Isle of Ely County Council*, 1969.)[364a]

Persons Suffering from Mental Disorder. In criminal law a person of unsound mind has considerable exemption from criminal liability, but these rules have never been applied to civil injuries. This is understandable if it is borne in mind that the aim of the law of torts is to compensate the injured party, not to punish the offender. In the light of this, any exemptions accorded to a person of unsound mind should be narrow, and he should be liable unless his state of mind prevents his having the necessary intent (when a mental ingredient is part of the tort) and in extreme cases where no voluntary act is possible. (*Morriss* v. *Marsden*, 1952.)[365]

Husband and Wife. The rule used to be that a married woman was liable for her torts only to the extent of her separate property and that beyond this the husband was fully liable. Since the Law Reform (Married Women and Tortfeasors) Act, 1935, the wife is fully liable for her torts and the husband as such is no longer held responsible, unless, as in the case of a minor, there is a relationship of master and servant or principal and agent.

The old common law rule whereby one spouse could not sue the other in tort has now been altered. The Law Reform (Husband and Wife) Act, 1962, provides that each of the parties to a marriage shall have the like right of action in tort against the other as if they were not married, but where the action is brought by one of the parties to the marriage against the other during the subsistence of the marriage, the court may stay the action if it appears—

(*a*) that no substantial benefit would accrue to either party from the continuation of the proceedings; or

(*b*) that the question or questions in issue could more conveniently be disposed of on an application made under Sect. 17 of the Married Women's Property Act, 1882. (This provides for the determination of questions between husband and wife regarding title to or possession of property by a summary procedure.)

It should also be noted that a husband has a right of action against a person who by a tortious act deprives him of the society and services of his wife, i.e. loss of consortium. A wife has no such right in respect of loss of consortium. (*Best* v. *Samuel Fox & Co. Ltd.*, 1952.)[355]

The Crown and its Servants. Prior to 1947 the Crown had considerable immunity in the law of tort and contract stemming from the common law maxim: "The King can do no wrong." We have already seen that, by the Crown Proceedings Act, 1947, the Crown is, in general, now liable in the same way as a subject.

The Crown is not liable for torts committed by the police nor is the local authority which appoints and pays them. However, the Police

Act, 1964, Sect 48 (1), provides that the chief officer of police for any police area is liable for the torts of police officers, e.g. wrongful arrest. The Act also provides that any damages and costs awarded against the chief officer shall be payable out of police funds.

Judicial Immunity. A judge has absolute immunity for acts in his judicial capacity, and this probably applies to justices of the peace when acting within their jurisdiction. (*Law* v. *Llewellyn*, 1906.)[366] Counsel and witnesses have immunity in respect of all matters relating to the cases in which they are concerned. This is mainly of importance in connection with possible actions for slander.

Foreign Sovereigns and Ambassadorial Staffs. This heading includes all the categories of persons already enumerated in the chapter on Contract as having diplomatic immunity, and their liability is outlined on pp. 144–5. However, it should be noted that if persons with immunity remain after finishing their duties, they may become liable even if the tort was committed before. They may, of course, voluntarily submit to the jurisdiction of our courts, since immunity is from suit and not from liability. (*Dickinson* v. *Del Solar*, 1929.)[367]

Aliens. Enemy aliens, including British subjects who voluntarily reside or carry on business in an enemy state, cannot bring an action in tort, although they themselves can be sued. Other aliens have neither disability nor immunity.

Corporations. A corporation can, as a plaintiff, sue for all torts committed against it. Obviously certain torts, such as assault, cannot by their nature be committed against corporations, but a corporation can maintain an action for injury to its business. (*D and L Caterers Ltd.* v. *D'Anjou*, 1945.)[368] In cases where the corporation is the defendant we must consider separately tortious acts which are *intra vires* (within its powers) and *ultra vires* (outside its powers).

(*a*) *Intra vires Activities.* Where a servant or agent of the corporation commits a tort while acting in the course of his employment in an *intra vires* activity, then the corporation is liable. Although it has been said that any tort committed on behalf of a corporation must be *ultra vires* (since Parliament does not authorise corporations to commit torts) this view is fallacious, since a corporation can have legal liability without legal capacity. A corporation is liable under the principles of master and servant or principal and agent for the torts of its servants or agents committed on *intra vires* activities.

(*b*) *Ultra vires Activities.* Here we have to distinguish between express and non-express authority. A corporation will not be liable if a servant engages in an *ultra vires* activity without express authority. Thus, if a corporation has not got authority and has not given it, you cannot infer it. (*Poulton* v. *L. & S.W. Railway*, 1867.)[369] On the other hand, where a tortious action is *ultra vires* but has been expressly authorised, the courts have taken the view that the *ultra vires* doctrine is irrelevant, and the corporation is liable for it. (*Campbell* v. *Paddington Borough Council*, 1911.)[370]

Trade Unions. The Industrial Relations Act, 1971, retains the former immunity of trade unions in respect of actions in the new Labour Courts (see p. 56) arising out of an industrial dispute provided the union concerned is registered. Officials and members of a trade union continue to be immune from actions for conspiracy and interference with contract provided they are *authorised officials* acting in a situation of industrial dispute and the union is registered. There is no immunity, however, in respect of unfair industrial action.

Joint Tortfeasors. Formerly there was no right of contribution between joint tortfeasors, but under the Law Reform (Married Women and Joint Tortfeasors) Act, 1935, it is laid down that, if one joint tortfeasor is sued and pays damages, he can claim a contribution from fellow wrongdoers. Thus, if damage is caused by two or more persons *jointly*, e.g. master and servant (*Lister* v. *Romford Ice and Cold Storage Co.*, 1957),[231] or *severally*, but at the same time, as where the negligent driving of A *and* B causes injury to C, one tortfeasor has a right of contribution against the other or others. However, there can be no contribution where the person claiming it is liable to *indemnify* the person from whom it is claimed. The amount of the contribution is settled by the court on the basis of the responsibility of each party for the injury and may be the full amount of the damages originally awarded against the person claiming the contribution.

In connection with the right of contribution the Law Reform (Husband and Wife) Act, 1962, has an important effect. Where a spouse A is injured by the joint negligence of the other spouse B and of a third party C, e.g. in a car accident, if C is sued by A, he can now claim a contribution from the negligent spouse B, since B is now a person liable for the purposes of the Act of 1935.

Executors and Administrators. The common law maxim was *actio personalis moritur cum persona* (a personal action dies with the person). Consequently at common law an executor could only sue for torts to property, and not for torts against the person of the deceased. Now by the Law Reform (Miscellaneous Provisions) Act, 1934, all causes of action subsisting at the time of a person's death survive for or against his estate. Nevertheless, there is one exception where there can be no action after death. This is in the case of defamation unless there is damage to the deceased's property.

Under the Proceedings Against Estates Act, 1970, all actions against the personal representatives of a deceased person, whether founded in contract or tort, are now subject to the normal three-year or six-year limitation period.

Damages recoverable in an action by the representatives of the deceased shall not include exemplary damages, and the damages are calculated without reference to any loss or gain to the estate caused by the death, (e.g. benefits under insurance policies), although funeral expenses can be awarded. Damages are recoverable in respect of loss of expectation of life though the sums awarded are not large because of the difficulty of assessment. In *Benham* v. *Gambling*, [1941] A.C. 157, the House of Lords held that the amount recoverable is not to be affected by the wealth of the deceased, nor his prospects of future earnings, nor his views as to his future happiness, but by the happiness he might in fact enjoy. Their Lordships awarded £200 in this case, but in more recent cases the court has taken into account the fall in the value of money and awards of up to £500 have been made.

As we have seen by the Law Reform (Miscellaneous Provisions) Act, 1934, all causes of action subsisting at the time of a person's death survive for the benefit of his *estate*. However, under the provisions of the Fatal Accidents Acts, 1846 to 1959, the person whose wrongful act caused the death may have an *additional* liability to certain relatives of the deceased who have suffered financial loss because of the death, though damages recoverable under the Fatal Accidents Acts will be reduced by any sums awarded to the deceased's estate under the Act of 1934 if the estate devolves on the dependants either under a will or on intestacy.

The following persons are entitled to claim under the Fatal Accidents Acts; husband, wife, children, grandchildren, parents, grandparents, brothers, sisters, aunts and uncles and their issue; the relationship may be traced through step relatives, adoption or illegitimacy, and relatives by marriage have the same rights as the deceased's own relatives. However, in *Harrison* v. *London and North Western Railway Co.* (1885), C. & E. 540, it was *held* that a husband living apart from his wife had no claim under the Acts. Similarly in *Stimpson* v. *Wood* (1888), 57 L.J.Q.B. 484, it was *held* that a woman separated from, and not maintained by, her husband could not recover under the Acts in respect of his death. However, it is submitted that she could have made a claim if she was being maintained by him or was taking legal action to obtain maintenance. It was decided in *Burns* v. *Edman*, [1970] 1 All E.R. 886, that if a man who has lived on the proceeds of crime is killed by the negligence of the defendant, his widow and children who he has supported cannot claim damages under the Fatal Accidents Acts. It would be contrary to public policy to award compensation for the loss of an income dishonestly acquired. The cost of the funeral was, however, recoverable.

In the *George and Richard* (1871), 24 L.T. 717, it was decided that a child *en ventre sa mère* could claim.

A single action must be brought on behalf of all the eligible dependants and the total damages apportioned according to their dependancy. The action may be brought by the personal representatives of the deceased, but if there are none, or if they fail to bring the action within six months from the death, the dependants may bring it. The action is barred if it is not brought within three years of the death which is the subject of the claim.

It should be noted that the infliction of death is not, in itself, a tort against the person killed and relatives who have suffered financial loss have no right of action unless the deceased would have had one had he merely been injured. Furthermore, if the deceased was guilty of contributory negligence the damages awarded to dependants will be reduced according to the degree to which the deceased was at fault.

To sustain an action under the Acts, the plaintiff must show reasonable probability of pecuniary loss by reason of the death, a mere possibility is not enough, and damages are not recoverable for mental suffering or loss of companionship, for if this were so young children, persons of unsound mind and posthumous children would be excluded. Funeral and mourning expenses are recoverable, though expenses in connection with monuments are not.

The probability of pecuniary loss is a matter for the plaintiff to prove, and the court to decide as a matter of fact. However, it should be noted that the object of the Fatal Accidents Acts is to provide *maintenance* for relatives who have been deprived of maintenance by the death. Therefore, if the relative seeking to claim is already adequately provided for from some other source, he will not be able to claim under these provisions. Damages awarded are not, however, to be reduced on account of any insurance money, National Insurance or Friendly Society or Trade Union benefit, pension, or gratuity accruing to a relative, even though the pecuniary loss is thereby reduced.

In *Franklin* v. *South East Railway* (1858), 3 H. & N. 211, an old infirm father was *held* entitled to damages on his son's death since the son assisted his father with the latter's work. Probable earnings may be taken into account and in *Duckworth* v. *Johnson* (1859), 29 L.J. Ex. 25, the father of a boy of fourteen years who had earned fourteen shillings per week was awarded damages when the boy was killed, although he was unemployed at the time. Further, in *Taff Vale Railway Co.* v. *Jenkins*, [1913] A.C. 1, damages were recovered in respect of a girl who at her death was merely an apprentice dressmaker. Damages may include the cost of replacing services normally rendered free by a deceased relative, and in *Berry* v. *Humm*, [1915] 1 K.B. 627, it was *held* that a husband might claim in respect of his deceased wife where he was compelled to employ a housekeeper consequent upon his wife's death.

With regard to inflation, the House of Lords decided in *Mallett* v. *McNonagle*, [1969] 2 All E.R. 178, that in assessing damages under the Fatal Accidents Acts the only practical course to adopt was to leave out of account the risk of further inflation and the high interest rates which reflect the fear of it and capital appreciation of property and equities which are a consequence of it.

Partners. Principals and Agents Generally. Partners are liable for the torts of other partners committed in the ordinary course of business. A principal is liable for the torts of his agent committed within the scope of his authority, whether by prior authority or subsequent ratification.

VICARIOUS LIABILITY

While the person who is actually responsible for the commission of a tort is always liable, sometimes another person may be liable although he has not actually committed it. In such a case both are liable as joint tortfeasors. This is the doctrine of vicarious liability, and the greatest area of this type of liability is that of master and servant. A master is liable for the torts of his servant committed in the course of his employment, and so wide is the risk that it is commonly insured against. Under the Employers' Liability (Compulsory Insurance) Act, 1969, an employer *must* insure himself in respect of vicarious liability for injuries caused by his employees to their colleagues. Insurance is not compulsory in respect of injuries to persons other than employees.

Who is a servant? According to Salmond on Torts, a servant may be defined as "any person employed by another to do work for him on the terms that he, the servant, is to be subject to the control and direction of his employer in respect of the manner in which his work is to be done." This definition was approved by the court in *Hewitt* v. *Bonvin*, [1940] 1 K.B. 188. In most cases the relationship is established by the existence of a *contract of service*, which may be express or implied and is usually evidenced by such matters as, for example, the power to appoint, the power of dismissal, the method of payment, the stamping of insurance cards, the deduction of tax under P.A.Y.E., and membership of pension schemes (if any).

However, in deciding whether the relationship of master and servant exists, the courts have not restricted themselves to cases in which there is an ordinary contract of service but have often stated that the right of *control* is the ultimate test. In *Performing Right Society Ltd.* v. *Mitchel and Booker (Palais de Danse) Ltd.*, [1924] 1 K.B. 762 at p. 767, McCardie, J., said—

> The nature of the task undertaken, the freedom of action given, the magnitude of the contract amount, the manner in which it is paid, the powers of dismissal, and the circumstances under which payment of the reward may be withheld, all these bear on the solution of the question. But it seems clear that a more guiding test must be secured . . . It seems . . . reasonably clear that the final test, if there be a final test, and certainly the test to be generally applied, lies in the nature and degree of detailed control over the person alleged to be a servant. This circumstance is, of course, one only of several to be considered but it is usually of vital importance.

The learned judge then went on to decide that the defendants, who employed a dance band under a written contract for one year, were liable for breaches of copyright, which occurred when members of the band played a piece of music without the consent of the holder of the copyright, because the agreement gave the defendants "the right of continuous, dominant and detailed control on every point, including the nature of the music to be played."

The existence of the control test means that where a master (X) lends out his servant (Y) to another employer (Z), then Z may be

liable for the wrongs of Y even though there is no contract of service
between Y and Z, though such liability is rare.

A master also owes certain duties to his servants, e.g. to provide
proper plant, equipment and premises, and this is a further reason for
deciding whether Z has become the master by virtue of the control test.
(*Garrard* v. *Southey*, 1952.)[371] There is a presumption that control remains
with X and the onus is upon him to prove that control has passed to
Z. The burden is a heavy one and the temporary employer will not
often become liable as master. (*Mersey Docks and Harbour Board* v. *Coggins
and Griffiths (Liverpool) Ltd.*, 1947.)[372] Nevertheless, transfer of control
may be more readily inferred where a man is lent on his own without
equipment (*Garrard* v. *Southey*, 1952),[371] or where he is unskilled.

Transfer of control is often a convenient method of making the temporary employer liable to, and for, the servant and does not affect the
contract of service. A contract of service is a highly personal one and
it cannot be transferred from one employer to another without the
consent of the servant. However, where there is a contract for hire of
plant and the loan of a servant to operate it, the contract of hiring
may provide that the hirer shall indemnify the owners for claims
arising in connection with the operation of the plant by the servant.
(*Wright* v. *Tyne Improvement Commissioners*, 1968.)[373]

The control test was an appropriate one in the days when a master
could be expected to be superior to his servant in knowledge, skill and
experience. However, in modern times it is unreal to say that all
employers of skilled labour can tell employees *how* to do their work.
Accordingly the test has been modified in recent cases, the court tending to look for the power to control in incidental or collateral matters,
e.g. hours of work and place of work. The existence of this sort of
control enables the court to decide whether a person is part of the
organisation of another, and it might be called a "when and where"
test. (*Cassidy* v. *Minister of Health*, 1951.)[374]

The control test also gives rise to difficulties in the case of the employees of companies. Subordinate employees are controlled by
superior servants and some control is obviously present if the management is regarded as "the company." However, when one considers
the position of directors and top management it is difficult to see how
the company, being inanimate, can exercise control. In the case of
"one-man" companies, where the managing director is also virtually
the sole shareholder, the reality of the situation is that the servant
controls the company and not vice versa. Nevertheless, directors of
companies, even "one-man" companies, are regarded as servants,
presumably because the usual incidents of a contract of service are
present and despite the absence of genuine control. (*Lee* v. *Lee's Air
Farming Ltd.*, 1961.)[375]

Although control is the ultimate test in establishing the relationship
of master and servant, it is also necessary to deal briefly with other
circumstances which may be taken as evidence of the existence of the

relationship. In *Short* v. *J. W. Henderson Ltd.* (1946), 62 T.L.R. 427, Lord Thankerton regarded the power to select or appoint, the power to dismiss, and the payment of wages, as relevant in establishing the existence, or otherwise, of a contract of service.

THE POWER TO SELECT OR APPOINT. The absence of a power to select or appoint may prevent the relationship of master and servant arising. Thus, in *Roe* v. *Minister of Health*, 1954,[498] Denning, L.J., as he then was, made it clear that a hospital authority is not liable for the negligence of a doctor or surgeon who is *selected* and *employed* by the patient himself. The master need not make the appointment himself, and an appointee may be a servant even though the master *delegated* the power of selection to another servant, or even an independent contractor, such as a firm of management consultants, or was *required by law to accept* the servant, e.g. Ministers of State often have power to appoint members of statutory bodies who become the servants of those bodies.

THE POWER TO DISMISS. An express power of dismissal is strong evidence that the contract is one of service. Many public bodies have a restricted power of dismissal in the sense that rights of appeal are often provided for, but such rights do not prevent a contract of service from arising, nor does the fact that these authorities cannot dismiss certain of their servants without the approval of the Crown or a Minister.

PAYMENT OF WAGES OR SALARY. A contract of service must be supported by consideration which usually consists of a promise to pay wages, or a salary. Where the amount of remuneration or the rate of pay is not fixed in advance, this suggests that the contract is not one of service, but is for services. The master usually pays his servants directly, but in *Pauley* v. *Kenaldo Ltd.*, [1953] 1 All E.R. 226, at p. 226, Birkett, L.J., said, ". . . a person may be none the less a servant by reason of the fact that his remuneration consists solely of tips."

A servant may be employed on terms that his remuneration is to consist wholly or partly of commission which the master pays directly, the commission being a method of assessment of the amount of the remuneration.

Salaries are paid to people who are certainly not servants, e.g. Members of Parliament, whereas payment of wages generally indicates a contract of service. However, little, if anything, turns on the distinction between wages and salaries, and we may conclude that the terms used to describe the way in which a person is paid have little bearing on the relationship between himself and the person who pays him.

In addition to the above indications of a contract of service the following matters have also been regarded as relevant in deciding difficult cases of relationship.

DELEGATION. In the normal contract of service the servant performs the work himself, and *power to delegate performance of the whole contract* to another is some indication that there is no contract of service.

However, the fact that delegation is forbidden does not show *conclusively* that the contract is one of service, for agreements with independent contractors may forbid delegation.

EXCLUSIVE SERVICE. The fact that an employer can demand the *exclusive services of another* is a material factor leading to the inference of a contract of service and in some cases it has been the deciding factor. However, in the absence of an express contractual provision a master cannot usually require the exclusive services of his servant, and cannot complain if the servant works for someone else in his spare time, though *Hivac Ltd.* v. *Park Royal Scientific Instruments Ltd.*, 1946,[288] is an exceptional case. This being so, a servant and independent contractor are usually both able to work for more than one person, and the exclusive service test may not help in deciding difficult cases of relationship. However, it is true to say that the typical servant works for one person, and the typical independent contractor works for many.

PLACE OF WORK. If the services are always rendered on the *employer's premises* this is some evidence of the existence of a contract of service, though it is not conclusive. Similarly, the fact that a person works at his home or other premises is some evidence of a contract for services.

It may also be a material factor whether the services are rendered by a person having a *recognised trade or profession*, e.g. a surveyor, or a consulting engineer, which he is exercising in a business because such persons tend to be independent contractors rather than servants, and persons not exercising a particular calling may more easily be regarded as the servants of those who employ them.

PLANT AND EQUIPMENT. *Provision of large-scale plant and equipment* by the employer is an indication of the existence of a contract of service and a person who supplies his own large-scale plant and equipment is often an independent contractor. However, provision of minor equipment, such as tools, carries little weight as a test of relationship, for many servants provide their own tools.

OBLIGATION TO WORK. A contract of service and one for services usually *impose an obligation to do the work concerned* and an *obligation to work* is not helpful in the matter of relationships. However, persons such as salesmen, who are paid entirely by commission, and who are not obliged to work at all are probably not working under a contract of service.

HOURS OF WORK AND HOLIDAYS. The right to control the *hours of work and the taking of holidays* is also regarded as evidence of the existence of a contract of service. Further an independent contractor is usually engaged for a specific job, whereas a servant is usually employed for an indefinite time.

SERVANTS AND INDEPENDENT CONTRACTORS. A servant is a person whose work is at least *integrated* into the master's business organisation, whereas an independent contractor merely *works for* the business but is *not integrated* into it. Thus, firms of builders, architects, and estate agents are usually regarded as independent contractors, while factory and office workers are usually regarded as servants.

A servant works under a contract of service, whereas an independent contractor's contract is said to be one "for services" under which he is to carry out a particular task or tasks. Although he may be sued for breach of contract if he fails to carry out his contract properly, the purchaser of his services has no other control over the manner of his work.

Nature of Vicarious Liability. The doctrine seems at first sight unfair because it runs contrary to two major principles of liability in tort, viz.—

> (*a*) that a person should be liable only for loss or damage caused by his *own acts or omissions*; and
>
> (*b*) that a person should only be liable where he was at *fault*.

The doctrine of vicarious liability is a convenient one in the sense that masters are, generally speaking, wealthier than their servants and are better able to pay damages, though the doctrine is often justified on the grounds that a master *controls* his servant. However, it should be noted that control is not in itself a ground for imposing vicarious liability, e.g. parents are not vicariously liable for the torts of their children. It is also said that vicarious liability is just because the master profits from the servant's work and should therefore bear losses caused by the servant's torts. Again, the master *chooses* his servant and there are those who say that if he chooses a careless servant he ought to compensate the victims of the careless servant's torts. Further, master and servant are often identified in the sense that the act of the servant is regarded as the act of his master and this theory that a master and his servant are part of a *group* in much the same way as other associations of persons, e.g. companies, is expressed in the often quoted maxim *qui facit per alium facit per se* (he who does a thing through another does it himself). However, in practice the master does not really suffer loss because he commonly insures against the possibility of vicarious liability and usually the cost of this insurance is put on to the goods or services which he sells. This has the effect of spreading the loss over a large section of the community in much the same way as welfare state benefits.

In order to establish vicarious liability it is necessary to show that the relationship between the defendant and the wrongdoer is that of master and servant, and that when the servant committed the wrong he was in the *course of his employment*. It is sometimes difficult to decide whether a particular act was done during the course of employment, but the following matters are relevant.

ACTS PERSONAL TO THE SERVANT. Some acts done by a servant while at work are so personal to him that they cannot be regarded as being within the scope of employment. Servants do not generally have authority to use violence against third parties, and the use of such violence will usually be beyond the scope of employment, and the master will not be liable. Thus in *Warren* v. *Henlys Ltd.*, [1948] 2 All E.R. 935, the employer of a petrol pump attendant was held not liable for the latter's assault on a customer committed as a result of an argument over payment for petrol. However, where such authority exists, e.g. in the case of door-keepers at dance halls, the master will be liable if the servant ejects a troublemaker but uses excessive force.

IMPROPER PERFORMANCE OF ACTS WITHIN SCOPE OF EMPLOYMENT. The master may be liable where the tort committed by the servant is not a personal or independent act but is merely an improper way of performing an act which is within the scope of employment. (*Century Insurance Co.* v. *Northern Ireland Road Transport Board*, 1942.)[376]

The tortious acts for which a master may be liable must arise out of the servant's employment, but the master may be liable in such circumstances even if the act is one which he has expressly forbidden his servant to do, since the courts will not allow the master to evade his responsibilities by secret instructions to his servants. (*Limpus* v. *London General Omnibus Co.*, 1862.)[377] The point has arisen in cases in which servants have given lifts to third parties in the master's vehicle. In *Twine* v. *Bean's Express Ltd.*, [1946] 1 All E.R. 202, a driver employed by the defendants gave a lift to a third person who was killed by reason of the servant's negligent driving. Instructions that servants were not to give lifts were displayed in the van. The court held that the employers were not liable because in giving a lift to a third person the driver went *beyond the scope of his employment* and that the *passenger was a trespasser*. Therefore, by analogy with trespass to land, it could be said that the defendants owed no duty to a trespasser unless they knew he was there and even then their duty would only have been not to injure him wilfully or recklessly. In *Conway* v. *Geo. Wimpey & Co.*, [1951] 1 All E.R. 363, the facts were similar although lifts were frequently given but this was unknown to the employers, and again they were not liable, the same line of argument being followed. The reasoning in these cases has been subjected to criticism because it is difficult to regard the plaintiff as a trespasser when the servant has invited him into the vehicle and in both of the cases the servant did inflict the injury on the passenger while in the course of his employment because in driving the vehicle he was doing what he was employed to do.

It is clear that the servant in such cases has a duty of care towards the passenger, but in *Twine* and *Conway* the court seems also to have regarded the master as having a similar duty of care. This has led to unreal arguments regarding scope of employment and a sounder solution to the problem may be found by regarding the servant, but not the master, as having a duty of care towards the passenger. This would avoid straining the concept of scope of employment, for it can then be said that the breach of the duty of care arises out of the employment, but the duty does not. This would make the servant liable but not the master, and the servant could be regarded as having imposed a duty of care upon himself, but not his master, by giving the lift to a third person. It is thought also that, since the master's instructions in the two cases were not secret but displayed, the master should have had the defence of *volenti non fit injuria* even if it was decided that he owed a duty of care, which it is suggested he does not. However, where the passenger is a fellow servant riding in the vehicle with the consent of the driver and a superior servant, the master will be liable, because it seems from the decision in *Young* v. *Edward Box & Co. Ltd.*, [1951] 1 T.L.R. 789, to be within the ostensible authority of a superior servant, and possibly of the driver, to sanction lifts for fellow employees but not strangers.

The position where a company provides a vehicle for employees to come and go from work was considered in *Vandyke* v. *Fender*, 1970,[378] and in *Nottingham* v. *Aldridge*, 1971,[378a] the Court was concerned with a situation in which the employee was using his father's vehicle to transport himself and a fellow-worker for which he was paid a mileage allowance for himself and his passenger.

EMERGENCIES. Where the servant takes emergency measures with the intention of benefiting his master in cases where the latter's property appears to be in danger, the master will tend to be liable even though the acts of the servant are excessive. Thus in *Poland* v. *John Parr & Sons*, [1927] 1 K.B. 236, a boy was injured by a carter who knocked the boy off the back of his cart to protect his master's property from theft. It was held that the carter's action was within his implied authority and his masters were liable. If, however, the servant's act is not merely *excessive* but *outrageous* as in, *Warren* v. *Henlys Ltd.*, [1948] 2 All E.R. 935, the master will not be liable.

SERVANT MIXING MASTER'S BUSINESS WITH HIS OWN. The cases under this heading have arisen largely out of the use of motor vehicles, and since it is clear that there can be no vicarious liability if the servant's wrong is not the result of his carrying out his contract of service, the master will not be liable if he lends his vehicle to his servant entirely for the servant's own purpose. (*Britt* v. *Galmoye*, 1928.)[379]

However, a more difficult situation arises where the activity is basically an authorised one but the servant deviates from it in order to execute some business of his own. The mere fact of deviation will not prevent the master being liable and this was made clear in the judgment of Cockburn, C.J., in *Storey* v. *Ashton* (1869), L.R. 4 Q.B. 476, when he said—

> I am very far from saying that, if the servant when going on his master's business took a somewhat longer road, that, owing to this deviation he would cease to be in the employment of the master so as to divest the latter of all liability; in such cases it is a question of degree as to how far the deviation could be considered a separate journey. Such a consideration is not applicable to the present case, because here the carman started on an entirely new and independent journey which had nothing to do with his employment.

However, if the journey is unauthorised the servant does not render his master liable merely by performing some small act for his master's benefit during the course of it. Thus in *Rayner* v. *Mitchell* (1877), 2 C.P.D. 257, a brewer's vanman, without permission, took a van from his master's stables for personal reasons, namely to deliver a coffin to a relative's house. On the way back he picked up some empty beer barrels and then was involved in an accident injuring the plaintiff. It was held that the brewer was not liable.

SERVANT USING HIS OWN PROPERTY ON MASTER'S BUSINESS. The mere fact that a servant is using his own property in carrying out his master's business will not prevent the master from being liable for torts arising out of the use of the servant's property. The decided cases are largely concerned with methods of travel, and in *McKean* v. *Rayner Bros. Ltd.* (*Nottingham*), [1942] 2 All E.R. 650, a servant who was told to deliver a message by using the firm's lorry was held to be in the course of his employment when he performed the task by driving his own car, contrary to his instructions. However, if the servant's act is unreasonable, as where a servant who is authorised to travel by car charters an aeroplane and flies it himself, then the act will be unauthorised and the master will not be liable if the servant, or a third party, is injured.

EFFECT OF CONTRACTUAL EXCEPTIONS CLAUSES. Cases may arise in which the master has attempted to exempt himself for the wrongs of his servant by means of an exemption clause in a contract with a third person who is injured. Such clauses will be effective to exempt the master from liability if they are properly communicated to the third person. However, they will not protect the servant against his personal liability because he has not usually given any consideration to the third person and is not in privity of contract with him. (*Adler* v. *Dickson*, 1955.)[220]

FRAUDULENT AND CRIMINAL ACTS. In early law the courts would not accept the principle of vicarious liability in fraud but gradually the concept was extended, first to cases in which the servant's fraud was committed for his master's benefit, and later even to cases where the fraud was committed by the servant entirely for his own ends. (*Lloyd* v. *Grace, Smith & Co.*, [1912] A.C. 716.)

A more difficult situation arises where the servant makes a representation which he believes to be true but which the master knows to be false. Suppose the master, a landowner, knows that the drains of one of his farm cottages are faulty but has not told his servant, and the servant, in the course of his employment, represents to a potential purchaser that the drains are sound, believing this to be true. It might be thought that, in this sort of situation, the untrue statement of the servant could be added to the knowledge of the master so as to make the master liable in deceit, but in *Armstrong* v. *Strain*, 1952,[380] the Court of Appeal rejected this idea and stated, in effect, that a master would not be liable in deceit unless it could be established that he kept his servant in ignorance of the truth in the *expectation* and *hope* that he would make some false statement in connection with the transaction.

However, it is almost certain that on the facts of *Armstrong* v. *Strain*,[380] liability in damages for negligence would now be imposed on the master because English Law now recognises that there may be liability for negligent misstatements (*Hedley Byrne & Co. Ltd.*, v. *Heller & Partners Ltd.*, 1964),[194] and the Misrepresentation Act, 1967, also provides for the payment of damages for negligent misstatements which induce a contract. It is probable that for the purpose of both jurisdictions, negligence could be inferred from the fact that a servant makes a statement in the course of his employment which another servant or the master knows is untrue. (*Gosling* v. *Anderson*, 1972.)[650]

Criminal conduct on the part of a servant may be regarded as being in the course of his employment so that the master will be liable at civil law for any loss or damage caused to a third person by the servant's criminal act. (*Morris* v. *C. W. Martin and Sons Ltd.*, 1966.)[381]

CASUAL DELEGATION. If Y lends his car to X for X's own purposes, then Y is not liable, even if in a general way X is his servant. (*Britt* v. *Galmoye*, 1928.)[377] Nevertheless, if Y has a purpose and X also has a purpose, and X is driving a car of Y's partly for his own and partly for Y's purposes, then Y would apparently be liable if X committed a tort. (*Ormrod* v. *Crossville Motor Services*, 1953,[382] *Morgans* v. *Launchbury*, 1972,[382a] and *Rambarran* v. *Gurrucharran*, 1970.[382b]) This is known as a case of casual delegation of authority. In these cases of casual delegation, the courts are guided by the doctrine of the *de facto* servant, and by using this doctrine they have extended the vicarious liability of the master into the area of principal and agent. In fact the person actually committing the wrong is often called the agent. The result is to extend the area of operation of the doctrine of vicarious liability since it is easier to find the relationship of principal and agent than it is to establish the relationship of master and servant.

However, the question of service or agency is ultimately a question of fact and the particular circumstances of a case will govern the decision. There will, of course, be no vicarious liability in the owner where he did not consent to the taking of the vehicle. (*Klein* v. *Calnori*, 1971.)[383]

LIABILITY FOR TORTS OF INDEPENDENT CONTRACTORS

An independent contractor is by definition a person whose methods and modes of work are not controlled by the person who employs him, and this being so it would be unfair to give an employer general liability for the torts of such a contractor. However, there are circumstances in which a person may be liable for the torts of an independent contractor employed by him and these are as follows—

(a) *Where the employer authorises or ratifies the torts of the contractor.* If, for example, an employer authorises, or afterwards, with knowledge, approves the conduct of an independent contractor in tipping the employer's industrial waste material on another's land, both the employer and the contractor will be liable in trespass as joint tort-feasors.

(b) *Where the employer is negligent himself*, as where he selects an independent contractor without taking care to see that he is competent to do the work required, or gives a competent contractor imperfect instructions or information.

(c) *Where liability for the tort is strict, so that responsibilty cannot be delegated.* Thus, an employer is liable for injuries to workmen resulting from failure to securely fence dangerous machinery. This duty is laid down by the Factories Act, 1961, and it is no defence that the employer has delegated the task of fencing to an independent contractor who has failed to do the job properly. Moreover, liability under the rule in *Rylands* v. *Fletcher*, 1868 (see pp. 270–71), cannot be avoided by employing an independent contractor. It seems also that liability is strict where there is interference with an easement of support. Thus in *Bower* v. *Peate*, 1876,[384] the employer was held liable where he asked an independent contractor to pull down his house and excavate foundations for a new one and the contractor failed to support the house next door so that it was damaged.

(d) Finally there is a miscellaneous group of cases in which an employer has been held liable for the torts of an independent contractor and the principle which seems to run through them all is that the work which the employer has instructed the independent contractor to undertake is extra hazardous. Thus, work on the highway is attended with some risk if due precautions are not taken. However, work near the highway is not for that reason alone regarded as extra hazardous. (*Salsbury* v. *Woodland*, 1969.)[385] In *Pickard* v. *Smith* (1861), 10 C.B., N.S. 470, the defendant who was the tenant of a refreshment room at a railway station was held liable when a coal merchant's servant left the coal cellar flap open while delivering coal to the defendant and a passenger on railway premises fell into the cellar and was injured. Again in *Honeywill & Stein Ltd.* v. *Larkin Bros. Ltd.*, [1934] 1 K.B. 191, the plaintiffs had received permission from the theatre owner to take photographs in a theatre on which the plaintiffs had recently done work. A firm of photographers was employed by the plaintiffs and in order to take indoor photographs had, in those days, to use magnesium flares with the result that the theatre curtains caught fire and much damage was caused. The plaintiffs paid for the damage, and sued the photographers for an indemnity to which the court said they were entitled. It also emerged that the plaintiffs would have been liable if they had been sued by the theatre owner.

Where an employer is held liable to a third person for the torts of an independent contractor he will, in most cases, be able to claim an indemnity from the contractor. It should also be noted that an employer is not liable for what are called the *collateral* wrongs of his contractor, but only for wrongs which necessarily arise in the course of the contractor's employment. Thus, if A employs B, an independent contractor, to do some excavation work on his land, A will be liable if, say, his neighbour's greenhouse is damaged by the excavations but A will not be liable for loss caused by B's servants making off with the plants. (*Padbury* v. *Holliday*, 1912.)[386]

The matter of the liability of an employer for the torts of an independent contractor is one which is likely to become more important in the future. The heavy cost of employing servants since the imposition of Selective Employment Tax has led to labour being presented, particularly in the building trade, in the form of gangs of men who are very often independent contractors so far as the builder is concerned. If this practice continues it may well produce a number of cases in which the liability of an employer for independent contractors is in question and the law may well be clarified and liability extended. However, Government measures such as the halving of S.E.T. and the abolition of other tax advantages in this form of contracting may end the practice.

GENERAL DEFENCES

Some torts have special defences which can be raised in a particular action, but there are certain general defences which can be raised in any action in tort if they seem to be appropriate—

1. **Volenti non fit injuria.** (To one who is willing no harm is done.) This is alternatively called the doctrine of the assumption of risk. There are two main aspects of this defence—

(*a*) Deliberate harm.
(*b*) Accidental harm.

In the first case the plaintiff's assent may prevent his complaining of some deliberate conduct of the defendant which would normally be actionable. If A takes part in a game of Rugby football, he must be presumed to accept the rough tactics which are a characteristic and *normal* part of the game, and any damage caused would not give rise to an action, although if the same tactics were employed in the street, an action could be sustained. Similarly, although to stick a knife into a person would normally be actionable, if a surgeon does it with the consent of the patient it is not so.

The plaintiff may impliedly consent to run the risk of accidental harm being inflicted upon him. Thus one of the normal risks incidental to watching an ice-hockey match is that the puck may strike and injure you (*Murray* v. *Harringay Arena Ltd.*, 1951)[387] or in attendance at a motor race, cars may run off the track for various reasons, injuring spectators. (*Hall* v. *Brooklands Auto Racing Club*, 1933.)[388] These are normal hazards and the maxim *volenti non fit injuria* would apply. In addition, the plaintiff may be *expressly* put on notice that he undertakes a particular activity at his own risk. (*Bennett* v. *Tugwell*, 1971.)[389] It is a question of fact and not of law whether a plaintiff voluntarily incurs the risk, and the burden of proof is on the defendant. Furthermore, a plea of *volenti* is open to a defendant against a plaintiff who is a minor. (*Buckpitt*

v. *Oates*, 1968,[81] and *Geier* v. *Kujawa*, 1970.)[390] If a person's assent to harm being inflicted upon him is purely contractual, it can only operate within the limits allowed by the law of contract; the doctrine of privity of contract applies. (*Adler* v. *Dickson*, 1955.)[220]

It does not follow that because a person has knowledge of a potential danger he assents to it. (*Baker* v. *James*, 1921.)[391] Knowledge is not assent; it is merely evidence of assent. (*Dann* v. *Hamilton*, 1939.)[392] This principle is most often exemplified in the master and servant cases and in the rescue cases, and has restricted the application of the defence.

Where the danger is inherent in the job, as in the case of a test pilot, the maxim applies; but where the danger is not inherent, then the defence will rarely succeed. (*Smith* v. *Baker*, 1891.)[393] In instances where an employee expressly assumes a risk, and is even paid extra for doing so, the harm resulting will hardly ever be laid at the door of the master, unless there is evidence that the master was negligent and created a risk which was not normally present even in a job inherently dangerous. Nevertheless the doctrine of *volenti non fit injuria* cannot be pleaded by an employer in an action for damages based on breach of a statutory duty, e.g. to fence machinery under the Factories Act, 1961. The reason is that the object of the statute, to protect workmen, cannot be defeated by a private agreement between master and servant.

However, where an employee is in breach of a statutory duty and the employer is not, then if the party injured by the breach of statutory duty seeks to make the employer vicariously liable for the tort of the employee, the employer can plead the defence if the circumstances are appropriate. (*I.C.I. Ltd.* v. *Shatwell*, 1964.)[394]

A different situation arises in what are known as the *rescue cases*. In these the plaintiff is injured while intervening to save life or property put in danger by the defendant's negligence. If the intervention is a reasonable thing to do for the saving of life or property, then this does not constitute the assumption of risk, nor does the defence of contributory negligence apply (*Haynes* v. *Harwood*, 1935,[395] and *Baker* v. *Hopkins*, 1959);[396] but if it is not reasonable then the defences of *volenti* and contributory negligence could apply. (*Cutler* v. *United Dairies*, 1933.)[397] A person may take greater risks in protecting or rescuing life than in the mere protection of property. (*Hyett* v. *G.W. Railway*, 1948.)[398] We reach the conclusion, therefore, that the operation of the maxim *volenti non fit injuria* is excluded when a man of ordinary courage would feel bound to intervene. It is worthy of note, however, that even where knowledge of a risk does not bar the claim, it may reduce damages under the doctrine of contributory negligence. However, the rescuer may recover even though no duty was owed to the person rescued. (*Videan* v. *B.T.C.*, 1963.)[399]

Finally, it is important to remember that the question whether the plaintiff has assented to the possibility of harm being inflicted upon him does not arise until it has been shown that the defendant has committed a tort against the plaintiff. If the harm is not tortious the defence is irrelevant. (*Wooldridge* v. *Summer*, 1962,[400] and *Wilks* v. *Cheltenham Home Guard Motor Cycle and Light Car Club*, 1971.)[400a]

2. Inevitable Accident. The mere fact that the damage caused is accidental cannot itself be a defence if there is a duty to avert the particular consequences, but there are occasions where the defence of inevitable accident can be raised. Such an accident would be one which was not avoidable by any precautions a reasonable man could have been expected to take. (*Stanley* v. *Powell*, 1891.)[401] Thus where a horse, which was drawing a carriage, bolted unexpectedly without any apparent cause and caused damage in spite of every effort to control it, the defence was successfully raised. It should be noted, however, that most so-called accidents have a cause, and this defence is of comparatively rare occurrence.

3. Act of God. This is something which occurs in the course of nature, which was beyond human foresight, and against which human prudence could not have been expected to provide. It is something in the course of nature so unexpected in its consequences that the damage caused must be regarded as too remote to form a basis for legal liability. (*Nichols* v. *Marsland*, 1876.)[402]

4. Necessity. This defence is put forward when damage has been intentionally caused, either to prevent a greater evil or in defence of the realm. Such damage is justifiable if the act was reasonable. (*Cresswell* v. *Sirl*, 1948.)[403] Thus where a whole area is threatened by fire, the destruction of property not yet alight with a view to stopping the spread of the flames would be damage intentionally done but reasonable in the circumstances. (*Cope* v. *Sharpe*, 1912.)[404] However, duress does not appear to be a defence and in *Gilbert* v. *Stone* (1647), Aleyn 35, the defendant was held liable for trespass although he entered the plaintiff's house only because twelve armed men had threatened to kill him if he did not do so.

5. Mistake. It is normally no defence in tort to say that the wrongful act was done by mistake. Even if the consequences of an act were not fully appreciated, everyone is presumed to intend the probable consequences of his acts. A mistake of law is no excuse, and this is usually true of a mistake of fact, unless it is reasonable in the circumstances, e.g. in a case of wrongful arrest. (*Beckwith* v. *Philby*, 1827.)[405]

6. Intention. It is a defence to an action in tort that the defendant neither intended to injure the plaintiff nor could have avoided doing so by the use of reasonable care. (*National Coal Board* v. *Evans*, 1951.)[406]

7. Act of State. Sometimes the state finds it necessary to protect persons from actions in court when they have caused damage whilst carrying out their duties. (*Buron* v. *Denman*, 1848.)[407] This defence cannot be raised in respect of damage done anywhere to British subjects (*Nissan* v. *Att. Gen.*, 1969)[408] or where the court holds that damage has been done to a friendly alien. (*Johnstone* v. *Pedlar*, 1921.)[409]

8. Statutory Authority. The acts of public authorities, e.g. County Councils, are often carried out under the provisions of a statute. This statutory authority to act may give the public authority concerned a good defence if an action in tort arises as a result. However, much depends upon the wording of the relevant statute. *Statutory authority may be absolute* in which case the public authority concerned has a *duty* to act. Alternatively, *statutory authority may be conditional*, in which case the public authority concerned has the *power* to act but is not bound to do so.

If the authority given is *absolute*, then the body concerned is not liable for damage resulting from the exercise of that authority provided it has acted reasonably and there is no alternative way of performing the act. (*Vaughan* v. *Taff Vale Railway*, 1860.)[410]

On the other hand, if the authority given is *conditional*, the body concerned may carry out the relevant act only if there is no interference with the rights of others. (*Penny* v. *Wimbledon, U.D.C.*, 1899.)[411]

Whether statutory authority is *absolute* or *conditional* is a matter of construction of the statute concerned, though statutory powers are usually conferred in *conditional* or permissive form. The basic rules of construction in these cases appear to be as follows—

(i) Is the authorised act of such public importance as to over-ride private interests?

(ii) If it is not, statutory powers are probably conferred subject to common law rights.

In addition, the matter of statutory compensation may be relevant. If the statute provides for compensation for loss resulting from an authorised act there may be no other claim even though the maximum compensation allowed by the statute is less than the actual loss. (*Marriage* v. *East Norfolk River Catchment Board*, 1950.)[412] On the other hand, if there is no provision for compensation in the statute there is a presumption that private rights remain and that an action in respect of any infringement of these rights may be brought.

It should be noted that the above principles also apply where the act done is authorised by delegated legislation.

9. Private Defence. Where a person commits a tort in defence of himself or his property, he will not be liable provided the act done in such defence is reasonable or proportionate to the harm threatened. The defence extends to acts in defence of the members of one's family and probably to acts in defence of persons generally.

REMEDIES

The remedies available to a person who has suffered injury or loss by reason of the tort of another are *damages*, the granting of an *injunction*, and in some cases an order for *specific restitution* of land or chattels of which the plaintiff has been dispossessed.

Damages. As we have seen in the chapter on the law of contract damages may be nominal, contemptuous, punitive (or exemplary), aggravated or compensatory (which includes special damages).

Usually the damages awarded are *compensatory* and the underlying principle is that of *restitutio in integrum*, i.e. the damages awarded are designed to put the plaintiff in the position he would have been in if he had not suffered the wrong.

In the case of *personal injuries*, e.g. loss of a limb, damages obviously cannot restore the plaintiff to his previous position and, in order to establish some uniformity in damages awarded for personal injuries the Court of Appeal ruled in *Ward* v. *James*, [1965] 1 All E.R. 563, that juries should not normally be used in trials concerning personal injuries. Damages for personal injuries may be awarded under the following heads—

    (i) pain and suffering;
    (ii) loss of enjoyment of life, or of amenity;
    (iii) loss of expectation of life;
    (iv) loss of earnings, both actual and prospective.

The House of Lords decided in *British Transport Commission* v. *Gourley*, [1955] 3 All E.R. 796, that the fact that the plaintiff would have paid tax on his earnings must be taken into account so as to reduce the damages awarded. Furthermore under the Law Reform (Personal Injuries) Act, 1948, Sect. 2, one-half of the value of any National Insurance benefit received by the plaintiff must be deducted, though if the plaintiff did not know that he had a right to a particular form of national insurance benefit, e.g. disablement benefit, and had not acted unreasonably in failing to claim it, the sum which he might have received will not be deducted from the damages awarded. (*Eley* v. *Bradford*, *The Times*, 5th May, 1971.) Sums received from other forms of insurance are not taken into account, nor is a disability or state retirement pension. (*Parry* v. *Cleaver*, 1969,[413] and *Hewson* v. *Downes*, 1969.)[414]

REMOTENESS OF DAMAGE. The consequences of a defendant's wrongful act or omission may be endless. Even so a plaintiff who has established that the defendant's wrong caused his loss may be unable to recover damages because his loss is not sufficiently connected with the defendant's wrong to make the latter liable. In other words, the loss is too remote a consequence to be recoverable. The principles which determined at what point damage became too remote used to be as follows—

(*a*) REGARDING CULPABILITY OR RESPONSIBILITY FOR THE HARM. All that the law required was that the reasonable man would have foreseen that his act would have caused the plaintiff *some* harm.

(*b*) REGARDING LIABILITY TO COMPENSATE THE PLAINTIFF. Given that the dependant would, as a reasonable man, have foreseen some harm as likely to result from his act, he became liable for all the direct consequences of the act even though such consequences could not possibly have been foreseen.

This test can be seen in operation in *Smith* v. *London and South Western Railway*, 1870,[415] and in *Re Polemis and Furness Withy & Co.*, 1921.[416]

This method of establishing liability was rather hard on the defendant because he was often made liable for damage which he could not possibly have foreseen, and certain inroads into the doctrine were made (*Liesbosch* v. *Edison*, 1933),[417] though the general principles of *Re Polemis*[416] were never over-ruled. However, the decision of the Judicial Committee of the Privy Council in *Overseas Tankship (U.K.) Ltd.* v. *Morts Dock and Engineering Co. Ltd.*, 1961[418] (generally referred to as *The Wagon Mound*), lays down a new test for remoteness of damage in tort which is as follows—

(*a*) REGARDING CULPABILITY OR RESPONSIBILITY FOR THE HARM. The test is still an objective test rather than a subjective one, because the law substitutes for the defendant a hypothetical reasonable man, and then proceeds to make the defendant only responsible for the damage which the reasonable man would have foreseen as a likely consequence of his act.

(*b*) REGARDING LIABILITY TO COMPENSATE THE PLAINTIFF. The law now requires the defendant to compensate the plaintiff only for the foreseeable result of his act. The defendant is no longer liable for all the direct consequences of his act, but only for those which, as a reasonable man, he should have foreseen. However, it appears from more recent decisions that the *precise* nature of the injury suffered need not be foreseeable: it is enough if the injury was of a *kind* that was foreseeable even though the form it took was unusual. (*Hughes* v. *Lord Advocate*, 1963,[419] *Bradford* v. *Robinson Rentals*, 1967,[419a] and *Weiland* v. *Cyril Lord Carpets Ltd.*, 1969.)[419b] Nevertheless difficulties still exist in regard to the application of the principles laid down in *Hughes*[419] and *Bradford*[419a]. These difficulties are illustrated by the decisions reached in *Doughty* v. *Turner Manufacturing Co. Ltd.*, 1964,[420] and *Tremain* v. *Pike*, 1969.[421]

Certain problems were raised by the decision in *The Wagon Mound*.

(1) Being a decision of the Judicial Committee of the Privy Council, it was not binding on English courts but was persuasive only. The decision in *Re Polemis* was made by the Court of Appeal which is bound by its own decisions, and ought therefore to have followed the decision in *Re Polemis* in future similar cases, rather than the decision in *The Wagon Mound*. However, it did seem likely that the House of Lords would over-rule *Re Polemis* if a similar case came before it, and the Court of Appeal would, it was thought, be reluctant to make an award of damages under *Re Polemis* knowing that almost certainly the House of Lords would reverse the decision on appeal. It was thought also that the Court of Appeal might refuse to follow its own previous decision in *Re Polemis* on the grounds that the House of Lords had on a number of occasions suggested that *Re Polemis* was wrongly decided without actually over-ruling it.

The Court of Appeal in *Doughty* v. *Turner Manufacturing Co. Ltd.*, 1964,[420] and the House of Lords in *Hughes* v. *Lord Advocate*, 1963,[419] treated the decision in the *Wagon Mound* as a correct statement of the law, subject in *Hughes'* case to an additional principle that the precise chain of circumstances need not be envisaged if the consequence turns out to be within the general sphere of contemplation and not of an entirely different kind which no one can anticipate.

(2) It remains to be seen how far the *Wagon Mound* has affected what is generally called "the unusual plaintiff" rule. For example, if X strikes Y a puny blow which might be expected merely to bruise him, but in fact Y has a thin skull and dies from the blow, the law has regarded X as liable for Y's death. The same rule has been applied where the plaintiff is a haemophilic, i.e. a person with a constitutional tendency to severe bleeding. This rule squares with *Re Polemis* but cannot be reconciled with the decision in *The Wagon Mound*. However, it is likely that the "unusual plaintiff" rule will survive the decision in the *Wagon Mound* and be regarded as an exception to it. (*Smith* v. *Leech Braine & Co. Ltd.*, 1962.)[422]

The test of remoteness of damage in tort as laid down in *The Wagon Mound* relies upon the foreseeability of a reasonable man both in respect of culpability and liability to compensate. It is therefore much the same as the test laid down in *Hadley* v. *Baxendale*, 1854,[331] which is used to decide questions of remoteness in contract. (See p. 203.) This can be regarded as an improvement in the law. Claims for injuries are often actionable as breaches of contract and as torts. It can only be confusing for the court to apply two tests in deciding liability for the same act.

Finally, it is perhaps worth noting that *damage which is intended* is never too remote and in this connection there is an inference that a man intends the natural consequences of his acts.

NOVUS ACTUS INTERVENIENS. (A new act intervening.) A loss may be too remote a consequence to be recoverable if the chain of causation is broken by an extraneous act. The scope of this concept is as follows—

(*a*) When the act of a third person intervenes between the original act or omission and the damage, the original act or omission is still the direct cause of the damage if the act of the third person might have been expected in the circumstances. (*Scott* v. *Shepherd*, 1773.)[423] There is a duty to guard against a *novus actus interveniens*. (*Davies* v. *Liverpool Corporation*, 1949.)[424]

(*b*) If the act of the third person is such as would not be anticipated by a reasonable man, the chain of causation is broken, and the third party's act and not the initial act or omission will be treated as the cause of the damage. (*Cobb* v. *Great Western Rly.*, 1894.)[425]

(*c*) The *novus actus* may be the act of the plaintiff and in these cases liability will turn on the precise facts. (*Sayers* v. *Harlow U.D.C.*,

1958,[426] and *McKew* v. *Holland and Hannan,* and *Cubitts (Scotland) Ltd.,* 1969.)[426a]

(*d*) In order to establish the liability of the intervenor, it is essential to show that he appreciated the consequences of his action. (*Philco Radio Corporation* v. *Spurling,* 1949.) [427]

NERVOUS SHOCK. Damages for illness brought on by nervous shock are not necessarily too remote and may be recoverable where—

(*a*) The defendant *intended* the shock (*Wilkinson* v. *Downton,* 1897);[358]

(*b*) the shock was caused by the plaintiff's *reasonable fear* for his *own safety* (*Dulieu* v. *White,* 1901),[359] or *for the safety of other persons* (*Hambrook* v. *Stokes,* 1925);[428]

(*c*) it is foreseeable that a normal person would suffer shock *by seeing or hearing the accident* (*Owens* v. *Liverpool Corporation* 1939,[429] and *Hinz* v. *Berry,* 1970),[429a] or *its after effects* (*Chadwick* v. *British Railways Board,* 1967).[430]

However, damages will not be recoverable unless—

(*a*) the defendant *owed a duty of care* to the plaintiff (*Bourhill* v. *Young,* 1943);[431]

(*b*) the shock was caused by *actually witnessing or hearing the accident* and not by *the account of others after the event* (*Hambrook* v. *Stokes,* 1925).[428]

The above rules have been developed because of the following problems inherent in actions for nervous shock—

(*a*) the difficulty of proving the degree of suffering involved and the possibility of fraudulent claims; thus, only where a known physical or mental condition is manifest are damages awarded;

(*b*) the difficulty which might arise if the number of possible claims, e.g. from relatives not present at the accident, was not limited; thus, the rule of foreseeability requires that the person claiming should at least have seen or heard the accident or witnessed its aftermath.

DAMAGES AFTER SUCCESSIVE ACCIDENTS. Difficult legal problems arise when different tortfeasors *successively* injure the same plaintiff. In *Baker* v. *Willoughby,* 1969,[432] the House of Lords held that a tortfeasor's liability is unaffected by a later event which causes the same or greater damage to the plaintiff. A defendant who injures a plaintiff *who has already* been injured will be liable only insofar as his tortious act increases or exacerbates the pre-existing injury. (*Performance Cars Ltd.* v. *Abraham,* 1961,[433] and *Cutler* v. *Vauxhall Motors Ltd.,* 1970.[433a]

Injunction. An injunction may be granted to prevent the commission, continuance or repetition of an injury, and there is a form of interlocutory injunction called *quia timet* (because he fears) which may be granted, though rarely, even though the injury has not taken place but is merely threatened. As we have seen, injunctions are discretionary remedies and cannot be obtained as of right. Furthermore, an injunction will not be granted where damages would be an adequate remedy. However, it is no defence to say that it will be costly to comply with the injunction.

Other Remedies. The court may order *specific restitution* of land or goods where the plaintiff has been deprived of possession and a plaintiff may be given an order for an *account* of profits received as a result of a wrongful act. Thus where a company or other business organisation carries on business under a name calculated to deceive the public by confusion with the name of an existing concern, it commits the tort of *passing off* and can be restrained by injunction from doing so. In addition, the existing concern may be given an order for an *account* of profits received by the offending concern as a result of the deception.

CESSATION OF LIABILITY

Liability in tort may be terminated by *death* (see p. 218), and also by *judgment, waiver, accord, satisfaction* and *lapse of time*.

Judgment. Successive actions cannot be brought by the same person on the same facts and if a competent court gives a final judgment in respect of a right of action that right of action is *merged* into the judgment. However, there are certain exceptional cases, for example, where two separate rights have been infringed. Thus in *Brunsden* v. *Humphrey* (1884), 14 Q.B.D. 141, the Court of Appeal held that a cab driver who had brought a successful action for damage to his cab caused by the defendant's negligence was able to bring a further action for personal injuries.

Waiver. The same conduct by the defendant may sometimes represent two separate and distinct torts or causes of action. If the plaintiff obtains judgment and satisfaction by electing to sue on tort A rather than tort B he cannot later sue in respect of tort B. However, the mere bringing of the action will not operate as an election: there must be judgment and satisfaction. (*United Australia Ltd.* v. *Barclays Bank Ltd.*, 1941.)[434] Furthermore *adoption* of the transaction giving rise to the tort operates as a waiver. (*Verschures Creameries Ltd.* v. *Hull and Netherlands S.S. Co. Ltd.*, 1921.)[435]

Accord and Satisfaction. A person may surrender a right of action in tort by deed or an agreement for consideration.

Lapse of Time. Under the provisions of the Limitation Act, 1939, Sect. 2, the general period of limitation in tort is six years from the date on which the *cause of action accrued*, i.e. the date on which the plaintiff could first have brought his action. Where the action is in respect of personal injuries, including trespass to the person (*Letang* v. *Cooper*, 1964),[436] the limitation is three years from the date on which the cause of action accrued. (Law Reform (Limitation of Actions, etc.) Act, 1954, Sect. 1 (1).)

Where the tort is actionable without proof of damage, as in the case of trespass, time usually begins to run when the tort is committed, even if the aggrieved party is ignorant of the fact of its commission, provided that there is no fraudulent concealment of the tort by the defendant. However, if the tort is actionable only on proof of damage, as in the case of negligence, time begins to run under the Limitation Act, 1939, from the date on which the damage is caused. This rule created hardship where the plaintiff had suffered personal injuries. For example, if X had been run down by Y's negligent driving, and unknown to X the injuries inflicted on him at the time of the accident caused him to go blind (say) four years after the accident, then X's cause of action in respect of his blindness was barred before he knew it existed. The Limitation Act, 1963 (as amended by the Law Reform (Miscellaneous Provisions) Act, 1971) now provides that an action may be brought even though the three-year period has elapsed if—

(*a*) the material facts relating to the cause of action were at all times outside the knowledge of the plaintiff until a date falling outside the three-year limitation period, or a date not earlier than twelve months before the end of that period; *and*

(*b*) the action is commenced within three years of the plaintiff's becoming aware of the material facts relating to the cause of action; *and*

(*c*) the leave of the court is obtained either before or after the commencement of the action.

An action under the 1963 Act (as amended) may be brought by dependents or on behalf of the estate of a deceased person.

Thus actions may be brought within three years of the date of death or of the date on which the personal representatives or dependents, as the case may be, acquired a knowledge of the relevant facts.

If the tort is of a continuing nature, as in the case of nuisance or possibly trespass, an independent cause of action arises on each day during which the tort is committed, and the aggrieved party can recover for such proportion of the injury as lies within the limitation period, even though the wrong was first committed outside the period. Where the plaintiff is a minor or person suffering from mental disorder, the period of limitation does not run against him until his disability ends, i.e. on becoming eighteen or on becoming sane or on death. But once time has started to run, any subsequent disability will not stop it running.

However, a minor is only regarded as being under a disability if he is not in the custody of a parent when the cause of action accrues. If he is in the custody of a parent the parent is expected to commence an action within the limitation period and if he does not the minor's action may be statute barred. The meaning of "custody" has caused the Courts some difficulty, the problem being to decide whether "custody" means *legal custody* regardless of where the minor is living, or *factual control* of his life. The better view is that it means factual control. (*Brook* v. *Hoar*, 1967,[437] *Hewer* v. *Bryant*, 1969,[437a] and *Todd* v. *Davison*, 1970.)[437b]

The special periods of limitation in respect of actions against the estate of a deceased tortfeasor have already been considered on page 218. However, the Limitation Act, 1963, does not operate to extend the time within which an action must be brought against a deceased tortfeasor's estate.

The following special periods of limitations should be noted—

(i) Actions under the Fatal Accidents Acts; three years from the death. (1954 Act, Sect. 3.)

(ii) Actions arising out of collisions at sea; two years, subject to extension by the Court. (Maritime Conventions Act, 1911.)

(iii) A joint tortfeasor who wishes to recover a contribution must bring the action within two years from the date on which he admitted liability or judgment was entered against him. (Limitation Act, 1963, Sect. 4.)

(iv) Actions in respect of damage arising from nuclear incidents; thirty years. (Nuclear Installations Act, 1965.)

Public authorities and their officers have no special position and actions against them are governed by the same rules as any other action in tort.

It should also be noted that the defendant's *fraud* or *negligent concealment* may prevent his pleading the Statutes of Limitation. (*Beaman* v. *A.R.T.S.*, 1949,[438] *Eddis* v. *Chichester Constable*, 1969,[438a] and *Archer* v. *Moss*, 1970).[438b]

Assignment. It is against the rules of public policy to allow the assignment of rights of action in tort. However, such rights may pass to others by operation of law in the following circumstances—

(i) *Death*. Rights and liabilities in tort survive for the benefit or otherwise of the estate.

(ii) *Bankruptcy*. Rights of action in tort possessed by a debtor which relate to his *property* and which if brought will increase his assets will pass to his trustee in bankruptcy. Actions for *personal torts*, e.g. defamation, remain with the bankrupt.

(iii) *Subrogation*. An insurance company which compensates an insured person under a policy of insurance can step into his shoes and sue in respect of the injury.

TRESPASS, CONVERSION AND DETINUE

We shall next examine certain specific torts, beginning with the tort of trespass. There are three types of trespass: trespass to the person, trespass to land and trespass to goods. In considering trespass to goods we propose to deal with the allied torts of conversion (or trover) and detinue.

1. Trespass to the Person. This has several aspects.

(*a*) ASSAULT. An assault is an attempt or offer to apply unlawful force to the person of another. There must be an apparent present ability to carry out the threat, the basis of the wrong being that a person is put in present fear of violence. On general principles, pointing even an unloaded weapon at another, who does not know that it is unloaded, would amount to an assault. There must be some act, as words alone cannot constitute an assault, although they may prevent an assault coming into being. (*Turbervell* v. *Savage*, 1669.)[439] However, in *Fagan* v. *Metropolitan Police Commissioner*, 1968,[440] the court appears to have accepted that an assault can arise from an omission.

(*b*) BATTERY. This is the execution of the threat involved in an assault. The touching of a person in a hostile manner or against his will is the essence of the tort, and the slightest contact will suffice. Substantial damages will be awarded when the battery is an affront to personal dignity, e.g. the wrongful taking of a finger-print. The mere jostling which occurs in a crowd does not constitute battery, because there is presumed consent.

DEFENCES. There are certain defences to an action for trespass to the person—

(i) *Self-defence*. This is not merely the defence of oneself but also of those whom one has a legal or moral obligation to protect. It also applies to the protection of property, but no more than reasonable force must be used.

(ii) *Parental or Similar Authority*. Moderate chastisement inflicted on children by parents, and school masters by way of delegation of the parent's authority, is not actionable.

(iii) *Volenti non fit injuria*. As in the case of the players in a rugby match.

(iv) *Judicial Authority*. This includes the right to inflict proper punishment and to make lawful arrests.

(v) *Prosecution in a Magistrates' Court*. Assault and battery is a crime as well as a civil wrong. If the wrongdoer is prosecuted, and *summary* proceedings are taken and the accused is convicted and punished, or the case is dismissed and the magistrates award a certificate of dismissal, no further action or civil proceedings may be taken in respect of the particular wrong. (Offences against the Person Act, 1861.)

In a recent case it has been made clear that trespass to the person is not actionable in itself; the plaintiff must prove intention or negligence (*Fowler* v. *Lanning*, 1959)[441] though he need not prove damage. It is also settled that where the interference is *unintentional* the plaintiff's only cause of action lies in negligence. (*Letang* v. *Cooper*, 1964.)[436]

(*c*) FALSE IMPRISONMENT. This is the infliction of unauthorised bodily restraint without lawful justification. It is not necessarily a matter of bars and bolts, but any form of unlawful restraint might turn out to be false imprisonment. The imprisonment must be total, and if certain ways of exit are barred to a prisoner, but he is free to go off in another way, then there is no false imprisonment. (*Bird* v. *Jones*, 1845.)[442] If a person is on premises and is not given facilities to leave, then this does constitute false imprisonment, unless the refusal is merely the insistence on a reasonable condition. (*Herd* v. *Weardale Colliery*, 1915.)[443] It is not even essential that the plaintiff should be aware of the fact of his imprisonment, provided it is a fact. (*Meering* v. *Grahame White Aviation Co.*, 1919.)[444]

POWERS OF ARREST. The old distinction between felonies and misdemeanours was abolished by Sect. 1 of the Criminal Law Act, 1967, as from 1st January, 1968. The Act created a new class of "arrestable offence," i.e. offences for which the sentence is fixed by law, or for which a person (not previously convicted) may be sent to prison for five years, and attempts to commit such offences.

A private person may arrest without a warrant anyone who is, or whom he, with reasonable cause, suspects to be, *in the act* of committing an arrestable offence. (Criminal Law Act, 1967, Sect. 2 (2).) *Where an arrestable offence has been committed*, any person may arrest without warrant anyone who is, or whom he, with reasonable cause, suspects to be, guilty of the offence. (Criminal Law Act, 1967, Sect. 2 (3).)

A police constable is protected in respect of arrests made under the authority of a warrant. He may arrest without a warrant in the situations mentioned above. Furthermore he may arrest someone who is or is suspected, on reasonable grounds, to be *about to commit* an arrestable offence, and someone whom he suspects, on reasonable grounds, to be guilty of an arrestable offence even though the offence has *not* been committed. (Criminal Law Act, 1967, Sects. 2 (4) and (5).)

A police constable may also arrest without warrant for certain other offences by reason of special statutory powers.

At the time when an arrest is made the person arrested must be told the reason for his arrest, unless the reason is obvious, e.g. if he is caught in the act. (*Christie* v. *Leachinsky*, 1947,[445] *R.* v. *Kulynycz*, 1970, [445a] and *Wheatley* v. *Lodge*, 1970.)[445b] Furthermore, he must be taken before a magistrate or police officer as soon as possible. It was held in *Alderson* v. *Booth*, 1969,[446] that there may be an arrest by mere words provided the person arrested submits.

The *remedies* available against false imprisonment are self-help, i.e. breaking away, the writ of habeas corpus and an action for damages.

2. Trespass to Land. Trespass to land is interference with the possession of land. It is not enough that the plaintiff be the owner; he must also have possession. So where land is leased for a term of years, the lessee is the person entitled to sue in trespass, though the lessor may bring an action if the damage is such as to affect his reversion. However, when a person signs a contract for the purchase of land, he becomes entitled to possession of it, and if a trespass takes place before he actually takes possession, then he can sue in respect of that trespass when he does. His right to sue relates back to the date on which he became entitled to the land under the contract.

Interference with the possession of land may take many forms but it must be direct. (*Southport Corporation* v. *Esso Petroleum Co.*, 1954.)[447] For example, an unauthorised entry on land is a trespass. It is a trespass to place things on land, e.g. leaving a dead cat in a neighbour's garden. To remain on land after one's authority is terminated constitutes a trespass. So, if a friend invites you into his house for a meal, tires of your company and asks you to leave, then if you refuse you are a trespasser. If you abuse the purpose for which you are allowed to be on land you become a trespasser. In *Hickman* v. *Maisey*, [1900] 1 Q.B. 752, where the highway was used for making notes of the form of racehorses being tried out on adjoining land, this constituted a trespass, since the proper use of a highway is for passing and re-passing.

While trespass usually takes place above the surface, it may be underneath by means of tunnelling or mining. With regard to trespass in the air-space above land, the position is doubtful, since there is no good authority. It is probably only a trespass if it is either within the area of ordinary user, or if it involves danger or inconvenience. (*Kelson* v. *Imperial Tobacco Co.*, 1957,[448] and *Woollerton and Wilson Ltd.* v. *Richard Costain (Midlands) Ltd.*, 1969.)[448a]

The Civil Aviation Act, 1949, gives private aircraft complete immunity in trespass, and nuisance in respect of the flight of aircraft at a reasonable height, but makes owners of aircraft liable strictly for any damage caused.

There is in this branch of law a somewhat technical rule called trespass *ab initio* (from the beginning). The rule says that, where a person enters on land by virtue of a legal right and abuses the authority given to him, his original entry becomes an unlawful trespass. The abuse must take the form of a positive act, i.e. misfeasance, and must not be a failure to act or an omission, i.e. mere non-feasance. (*The Six Carpenters* Case, 1610.)[449] Further the right of entry must be conferred by law and not for example by contract. It is also necessary that the act be one which takes away all justification for entry. (*Elias* v. *Pasmore*, 1934.)[450] However, the Court of Appeal threw doubt on the existence of the rules of trespass *ab initio* in modern law. (*Chic Fashions (West Wales)* v. *Jones*, 1968.)[451] Cases similar to *Elias* and *Chic Fashions* continue to come before the courts but the doctrine of trespass *ab initio* is not the real basis of them. Instead the law is developing a series of rules relating to the power under the constitution of the police and other public officials to enter and search premises and seize chattels found thereon. In *Ghani* v. *Jones*, [1970] 1 Q.B. 693, the Court of Appeal decided that police officers who enter premises to search are not allowed to take property against the wishes of the owner unless that property is: (*a*) the fruit of crime; (*b*) the instrument of crime; or (*c*) material evidence to prove the commission of a crime. Thus in *Ghani* the police were not entitled to take and retain passports.

Problems have arisen where a plaintiff has entered the premises by virtue of a licence, contractual or otherwise, because at one time it was not certain whether this licence could be revoked so as to make the plaintiff a trespasser and permit his ejection.

The common law view was that, where a person paid for admission to premises, his licence to be on those premises could be revoked at any time, in spite of valuable consideration, so that he could then be ejected as a trespasser, the defendant being liable for breach of contract, but not for assault. (*Wood* v. *Leadbitter*, 1845.)[452]

On the other hand, Equity took the view that, if there was an enforceable contract not to revoke, express or implied, as where valuable consideration had been given, the licence could not be revoked so that if the plaintiff had been ejected he could sue for assault; he could not be made a trespasser by a mere attempt at revocation. (*Hurst* v. *Picture Theatres*, 1915.)[453]

The equitable view gave rise to certain problems because it seemed to confuse rights over land with mere contracts, but the matter may now be regarded as settled. In *Winter Garden Theatre* v. *Millenium Productions Ltd.*, 1948,[454] it was held by the House of Lords that, although a licence for value is contractual in its nature and cannot create a right over land itself (or a right *in rem* which will run with the land and affect third parties), yet, as between the parties to the contract it may be implied, even if it is not expressed, that the licence cannot unreasonably be revoked during the period for which the parties intended it to continue. This rule was applied in *Hounslow London Borough* v. *Twickenham Garden Development*, 1970.[454a]

There are certain extra-judicial remedies available to a person injured by a trespass. For example, *distress damage feasant* is the right to seize chattels which have done damage on land. There is no right to use or sell the chattels but merely to detain until the owner offers compensation. The remedy does not lie against Crown property, and the right to sue in trespass is postponed until the chattel is returned. Livestock may be detained subject to notice to the owner and police for compensation supported by a right of sale. (Animals Act, 1971.)

There is a further extra-judicial remedy, often referred to as *self-help*, whereby the person in possession of the land may eject the trespasser, using such force as is reasonably necessary. The trespasser must be asked to depart peacefully and given time in which to quit the land. (*Hemmings* v. *Stoke Poges Golf Club*, 1920.)[455] A trespasser who enters by *force* may be removed immediately and without a previous request to depart.

Trespass to land is actionable *per se* (in itself) and it is not necessary for the plaintiff to show actual damage in order to commence his action, although the damages would be nominal in the absence of real loss. Nevertheless it is possible to obtain an injunction without proof of loss.

3. Trespass to Goods, Conversion and Detinue. We propose to discuss the above torts by outlining the three basic features of each, i.e. the relationship between the plaintiff and the goods, the conduct of the defendant which the plaintiff must prove, and the principle of liability.

(a) TRESPASS TO GOODS

(i) *The relationship between the plaintiff and the goods.* Trespass to goods is a wrong against the possession of goods. Possession in English law is a difficult concept which is considered more fully on pp. 332–34. For the moment it will suffice to say that a person possesses goods when he has some form of *control* over them and has the *intention to exclude* others from possession and to hold the goods on his own behalf.

Possession must exist at the moment when the trespass is alleged to have been committed. Thus a bailee of goods can sue for a trespass to them, but a bailor cannot because, although he is the owner of the goods, he does not possess them at the time. Where there is a *bailment at will*, i.e. one which can be determined at any time, both bailee and bailor have possession so that either can sue for a trespass to the goods. Possession does not necessarily involve an actual grasp of the goods; often a lesser degree of control will suffice. (*The Tubantia*, 1924.)[456]

Difficulties have arisen over the requirement of the intention to exclude others as a necessary ingredient of possession. In regard to things found under or on land, it would appear that a person can have control of goods and the intention to exclude others sufficient to give him possession even when he does not know that the goods exist. (*Bridges* v. *Hawkesworth*, 1851,[451] *Elwes* v. *Brigg Gas Co.*, 1886,[458] *South Staffordshire Water Co.* v. *Sharman*, 1896,[459] *Corporation of London* v. *Appleyard*, 1963,[460] and *Hannah* v. *Peel*, 1945.)[461]

Since the plaintiff relies on possession and not on ownership or title, the defendant cannot set up the *jus tertii* (right of a third party), i.e. he cannot successfully defend an action by saying that some third party has a better right than either the plaintiff or himself. The defendant must set up his own title and not another's. (*Armory* v. *Delamirie*, 1722.)[462]

(ii) *The conduct of the defendant which the plaintiff must prove.* In trespass there must be a *direct* interference with the goods, and this may consist of moving a chattel or the throwing of something at it. A person who writes with his finger in the dust on the back of a car commits trespass, as does a person who beats another's animals or administers poison to them.

(iii) *The principle of liability.* In trespass to goods the liability would not now appear to be strict. The defence of inevitable accident would presumably be available to a defendant and it is possible that, since *Letang* v. *Cooper*, 1964,[436] the interference with the possession of goods must be intentional. Mere negligence may not suffice. This would follow a similar development in the tort of trespass to the person which began with the decision in *Fowler* v. *Lanning*, 1959.[441]

(*b*) CONVERSION OR TROVER

(i) *The relationship between the plaintiff and the goods.* It is often said that the right to sue in conversion depends on ownership, but this is not really true. To be able to sue for conversion the plaintiff must have had either possession or the immediate right to possess at the time the wrong was committed. Mere ownership without one of the above rights is not enough. Nor is the mere right to possess unless it is coupled with ownership. (*Jarvis* v. *Williams*, 1955.)[463]

With regard to the defence of *jus tertii* (the title of a third party) it is necessary to distinguish in conversion between two types of case—

(1) If the plaintiff bases his claim on *actual possession*, then the defendant cannot set up the *jus tertii*. (*Armory* v. *Delamirie*, 1722.)[462]

(2) If the plaintiff bases his claim not on actual possession but on the *right to possess*, the defendant may be able to set up the *jus tertii*. (*Leake* v. *Loveday*, 1842.)[464]

Certainly the *jus tertii* cannot generally be set up by a bailee where the bailor sues him for converting the goods bailed, because the bailee is estopped from denying the title of his bailor.

(ii) *The conduct of the defendant which the plaintiff must prove.* In conversion the defendant must do something which is a complete denial of, or is inconsistent with, the plaintiff's title to the goods; a mere interference with possession is not enough. (*Fouldes* v. *Willoughby*, 1841.)[465] Furthermore, conversion need not be a trespass. (*Oakley* v. *Lyster*, 1931.)[466]

Generally the conduct of the defendant must be an act rather than a failure to act. Thus, although the plaintiff may base his case on a demand for the goods followed by a refusal, he must still show a denial of title in the defendant. If, therefore, the defendant can show that he was retaining the goods in the exercise of a lien for (say) repair charges unpaid, the plaintiff will fail in his action. A defendant may also refuse temporarily to give up the goods while he takes steps to check the title of the plaintiff.

(iii) *The principle of liability.* In general, liability in conversion is strict and it is not necessary for the plaintiff to prove that the defendant had a wrong intention. Neither is it a defence for the defendant to say that he acted honestly. (*Elvin and Powell* v. *Plummer Roddis Ltd.*, 1933.)[467] However where the defendant has lost the goods by *negligence* there is no conversion and the plaintiff must sue in detinue.

(*c*) DETINUE

(i) *The relationship between the plaintiff and the goods.* The plaintiff must, as against the defendant, both be entitled to possession of the goods and also have a right of ownership or property in them. Once again the *jus tertii* is no defence in an action by a bailor against his bailee, neither can the defence be set up in other cases.

(ii) *The conduct of the defendant which the plaintiff must prove.* The plaintiff must show that the defendant wrongfully failed to comply with a demand for the restoration of the goods. It is a defence for the defendant to show that he has not got the goods, provided that he has not wrongfully parted with them or negligently lost them; and where the defendant is not the plaintiff's bailee, he may temporarily detain the goods in order to investigate the matter of title.

(iii) *The principle of liability.* The liability of the defendant is not strict. It is a defence if he has not got the goods, e.g. where the goods have been destroyed by fire without negligence on the part of the defendant.

REMEDIES. The three torts of trespass, conversion and detinue may also be differentiated by reference to the forms of relief primarily sought. In trespass the wrong does not necessarily involve dispossession, and the only remedy is damages, being the diminution in value to the plaintiff of the goods affected by the trespass. If the goods are returned intact, damages will be awarded, but they will be purely nominal. In conversion, where the defendant has denied the plaintiff's title, the measure of damages is normally the value of the goods as at the date of conversion, though damages have been awarded as at the date of judgment, particularly where the goods have appreciated in value and the plaintiff has not delayed in bringing his claim. The action does not lie for restitution, but for damages only.

Where the same wrongful act is both a conversion and a wrongful detention, the measure of damages is the same however the action is framed, but credit must be given to the defendant for any appreciation in value which is attributable to him. (*Munro* v. *Willmot*, 1949.)[468] A bailee can recover the *full value* from a third party and not merely the value of his interest. (*The Winkfield*, 1902.)[469] However, where the plaintiff and defendant *both* have an interest the plaintiff cannot recover more than the value of his *own* interest. (*Wickham Holdings Ltd.* v. *Brooke House Motors Ltd.*, 1967.)[470]

In detinue the primary remedy is not damages, but the specific restitution of goods wrongfully detained, or their value in lieu of this. A sum may also be claimed for the period of their detention (a sort of hiring fee). The value in lieu of restitution is normally calculated on the same basis as damages for conversion.

RECAPTION. A person who is entitled to the possession of goods of which he has been wrongfully deprived may retake them but must not use more than reasonable force. It is not clear whether he may enter upon the land of an innocent third party in order to recover the goods.

REPLEVIN. Goods which have been taken by what is alleged to be unlawful distress may be recovered by the owner giving security to the registrar of the county court that he will immediately bring an action to determine the legality of the distress.

NUISANCE

The tort of nuisance is of two types—public and private.

1. **Public Nuisance.** This is some unlawful act or omission endangering or interfering with the lives, comfort, property, or common rights of the public, e.g. the obstruction of a highway, or the keeping of dangerous premises near a highway. A public nuisance is a crime for which the remedy is criminal proceedings brought by the Attorney-General. But it is actionable as a tort at the suit of a private individual if he has suffered peculiar damage over and above that suffered by the public as a whole. (*Campbell* v. *Paddington Borough Council*, 1911.)[370]

Obstructions to the highway occur daily in our cities and towns, e.g. road repairs and scaffolding. However, these obstructions, being for reasonable purposes, are lawful unless they last for an excessive time. *Dangerous activities* carried on near to the highway may amount to a nuisance. Thus in *Castle* v. *St. Augustine's Links*, 1922,[471] damages were awarded against a golf club to a taxi-driver who lost an eye when a golf ball was sliced from the course on to the highway; the hole being sufficently close to the highway to constitute a public nuisance. With regard to *projections* on to the highway there is no liability for *things naturally on land*, e.g. trees, unless the person responsible for them knew, or ought to have known, that they were in a dangerous condition, as where a branch of a tree is rotten. However, liability appears to be strict in the case of *artificial projections*. (*Terry* v. *Ashton*, 1876.)[472]

2. **Private Nuisance.** This is an unlawful interference with a man's use of his property or with his health, comfort or convenience, and such interference may vary according to the standard existing in his neighbourhood. It is a wrongful act causing material injury to property or sensible personal discomfort. In this connection injuries to *servitudes* may amount to private nuisance as where the defendant obstructs a right of way, or interferes with the plaintiff's water supply, access of air, light or support.

In considering whether an act or omission is a nuisance, the following points are relevant.

(i) THERE NEED BE NO DIRECT INJURY TO HEALTH. It is enough that a person has been prevented to an appreciable extent from enjoying the ordinary comforts of life.

(ii) THE STANDARD OF COMFORT MUST BE EXPECTED TO VARY WITH THE DISTRICT. There is no uniformity of standard between Park Lane and Poplar, although there may be common ground in some matters, e.g. light, since it requires the same amount of light to read in either place. However, where the alleged nuisance has caused *actual damage to property* it is no defence to show that the district concerned is of any particular type.

(iii) A PERSON CANNOT TAKE ADVANTAGE OF HIS PECULIAR SENSITIVITY TO NOISE AND SMELLS. There must be some give and take, and a man cannot expect the same amenities in an industrial town as he might enjoy in the country.

(iv) THE UTILITY OF THE ALLEGED NUISANCE HAS NO BEARING ON THE QUESTION. Pigstyes and breweries may be regarded by the community as very necessary, but if they infringe a man's right to the ordinary comforts of life, they are nuisances. Consent cannot be implied from the fact that the plaintiff came to the premises knowing that the nuisance was in existence. (*Bliss* v. *Hall*, 1838.)[473] Nor is the fact that the nuisance arises out of the conferment of a public benefit a defence in the ordinary way. (*Adams* v. *Ursell*, 1913.)[474]

(v) THE MODES OF ANNOYANCE ARE INFINITELY VARIOUS, and may include such things as bell-ringing, circus performing, the excessive use of the radio, spreading tree roots and many others. (*Christie* v. *Davey*, 1893.)[475]

(vi) A NUISANCE MAY RESULT FROM THE ACTS OF SEVERAL WRONG-DOERS. Any one of them may be proceeded against, and he cannot plead in excuse that the nuisance was a joint effort, although he now has a right of contribution between joint tortfeasors for the damages which might be assessed against him.

(vii) DURATION OF THE ACT. Although the acts complained of in nuisance are usually continuous, e.g. the constant emission of pungent smells from a factory, an act may constitute a nuisance even though it is temporary or instantaneous as in the case of an explosion. (*British Celanese* v. *Hunt*, 1969.)[476] The duration of the act complained of has a bearing upon the remedy which is appropriate and the court will not often grant an injunction in respect of a temporary nuisance because damages are an adequate remedy. Furthermore, a temporary nuisance may be too trivial to be actionable.

(viii) SOMETIMES MALICE OR EVIL MOTIVE MAY BECOME THE GIST OF THE OFFENCE, since it may be evidence that the defendant was not using his property in a lawful way. (*Hollywood Silver Fox Farm* v. *Emmett*, 1936.)[477]

(ix) IT IS POSSIBLE TO ACQUIRE THE RIGHT TO CREATE A PRIVATE NUISANCE BY PRESCRIPTION, that is by twenty years' continuous operation since the act complained of first constituted a nuisance. There is no corresponding right in respect of a public nuisance. Since a public nuisance is a crime, no length of time will make it legitimate.

It seems that private nuisance is confined in its scope to injury caused to the use or enjoyment of land. A claim in private nuisance cannot be based solely upon personal injury, where an action would be in negligence.

Furthermore, the tort of nuisance refers to the unreasonable use of property and is not a matter of reasonable care (compare negligence). Thus the defendant's use of his property may be offensive and constitute a nuisance no matter how careful he is.

Parties to Sue or Be Sued. The occupant of the property affected by the nuisance is the person who should bring the action (*Malone* v. *Laskey*, 1907),[478] but a landlord may sue if the nuisance is effecting a permanent injury to his property, e.g. where the defendant is erecting a building which infringes the landlord's right to ancient lights.

Regarding liability, it is a general rule that the person who creates the nuisance is liable. But a landlord may be liable, as a joint tortfeasor with his tenant, (*a*) if he created the nuisance and then leased the property (*Wilchick* v. *Marks*, 1934,[479] and *Mint* v. *Good*, 1951); [480]or (*b*) where the nuisance was due to the landlord's authorising the tenant expressly or impliedly to create (*Harris* v. *James*, 1876)[481] or continue (*Brew Bros.* v. *Snax (Ross)*, 1969)[482] the nuisance; or (*c*) where the landlord knew or ought to have known of the nuisance before he let the premises. An occupier must abate a nuisance which was on the premises before he took them over, or is placed there afterwards, even by trespassers, provided that the occupier knows or ought to have known of the nuisance. (*Sedleigh-Denfield* v. *O'Callagan*, 1940.)[483] An occupier is also liable for nuisance arising out of the operations of an independent contractor engaged in work on the premises where there is a special danger of nuisance arising from the nature of the works being carried out, e.g. extensive tunnelling operations. (*Bower* v. *Peate*, 1876,[384] and *Padbury* v. *Holliday*, 1912.)[386]

Remedies. The remedies for nuisance are three in number—

(*a*) The injured party may abate the nuisance, that is, remove it, provided that no unnecessary damage is caused, that no injury arises to an innocent third party, e.g. a tenant, and that, where entry on the defendant's land is necessary, a notice requesting the removal of the nuisance has first been given.

(*b*) He may sue for damages.

(*c*) He may seek an injunction if (i) damages would be an insufficient remedy; and (ii) the nuisance is a continuing nuisance, e.g. smoke frequently emitted from a chimney.

Defences. Certain defences are available to a person who is charged with committing the nuisance—

(*a*) The injury is trivial. The legal maxim is: *De minimis non curat lex*. (The law does not concern itself with trifles.) Such a case would be an extremely short exposure to fumes from road repairs.

(*b*) The so-called nuisance arose from the lawful use of the land. (*Bradford Corporation* v. *Pickles*, 1895.)[357]

(*c*) The nuisance was covered by statutory authority, under the general principles elucidated under the defence of statutory authority.

(*d*) The person committing the alleged nuisance has acquired a prescriptive right through twenty years' user to do what is complained of. (*Sturges* v. *Bridgman*, 1879.)[484]

(*e*) The character of the neighbourhood is such that the act, while it might be a nuisance elsewhere, cannot be regarded as such in that particular district.

(*f*) Consent of the plaintiff is a possible defence but consent will not be implied simply because the plaintiff came to the premises knowing that the nuisance was in existence. (*Bliss* v. *Hall.* 1838.)[473]

Remoteness of Damage. For the purpose of deciding problems of remoteness of damage the Privy Council held in *The Wagon Mound* (No. 2), [1966] 2 All E.R. 709 (see p. 236), that in a case of nuisance, as of negligence, it is not enough that the damage was a *direct* result of the nuisance if the injury was not *foreseeable*. (*British Celanese* v. *Hunt*, 1969.)[476]

NEGLIGENCE

In ordinary language negligence may simply mean not done intentionally, e.g. the negligent publication of a libel. But while negligence may be one factor or ingredient in another tort, it is also a specific and independent tort with which we are now concerned.

The tort of negligence has three ingredients and to succeed in an action the plaintiff must show (i) the existence of a duty to take care which was owed to him by the defendant, (ii) breach of such duty by the defendant, and (iii) resulting damage to the plaintiff.

(i) THE DUTY OF CARE. Whether a duty of care exists or not is a question of law for the judge to decide, and it is necessary to know how this is done. The law of contract dominated the legal scene in the nineteenth century and this affected the law of torts. The judges, influenced by the doctrine of privity of contract, used it to establish the existence of a duty of care in negligence in those cases where a contract existed by laying down the principle that, if A is contractually liable to B, he cannot simultaneously be liable to C in tort for the same act or omission. (*Earl* v. *Lubbock*, 1905.)[485]

The House of Lords in *Donoghue* v. *Stevenson*, 1932,[354] dispelled the confusion caused by the application of the doctrine of privity of contract where physical injury is caused to the plaintiff by the defendant's negligent act. In this case Lord Atkin formulated what has now become the classic test for establishing a duty of care when he said—

> You must take reasonable care to avoid acts or omissions which you can reasonably foresee would be likely to injure your neighbour. Who then is my neighbour? The answer seems to be persons who are so closely and directly affected by my act that I ought reasonably to have them in contemplation as being affected when I am directing my mind to the acts or omissions which are called in question.

It will be seen, therefore, that the duty of care is established by putting in the defendant's place a hypothetical "reasonable man" and deciding whether the reasonable man would have foreseen the likelihood or probability of injury, not its mere possibility. The test is objective not subjective, and the effect of its application is that a person is not liable for every injury which results from his carelessness. There must be a duty of care. (*Bourhill* v. *Young*, 1943.)[431]

Although Lord Atkin's formula has been adopted as a broad general test, it has not been applied to all cases of carelessness. Thus there was, in general, no liability for damage caused by animals which strayed upon the highway, though the owner is now liable under the Animals Act, 1971. Furthermore, there may be no liability for damage caused by a *careless omission* or failure to act. (*East Suffolk Rivers Catchment Board* v. *Kent*, 1941.)[486]

In addition there is, in general, no liability where the defendant's act causes mere *economic* or *monetary loss* to the plaintiff unless the economic or monetary loss arises out of and is accompanied by foreseeable physical injury to the plaintiff or damage to his property. (*The World Harmony*, 1965,[487] *Weller & Co.* v. *Foot and Mouth Disease Research Institute*, 1965,[488] *Electrochrome Ltd.* v. *Welsh Plastics Ltd.*, 1968, [356] *British Celanese* v. *Hunt*, 1969,[476] and *S.C.M. (U.K.) Ltd.* v. *Whittall & Son Ltd.*, 1970.)[489]

Occasionally, however, mere economic or monetary loss may not be too remote. This appears to arise particularly in the special case of imposition of liability for negligently uttered false statements. (See p. 256.) However, as Lord Macmillan said in *Donoghue* v. *Stevenson*, 1932,[354] "the categories of negligence are never closed" and the courts do recognise extended forms of duties from time to time. (*Clay* v. *A. J. Crump & Sons Ltd. and others*, 1963,[490] and *Home Office* v. *Dorset Yacht Club Ltd.*, 1970.)[491]

(ii) BREACH OF THE DUTY. If a duty of care is established as a matter of law, whether or not the defendant was in breach of that duty is a matter of fact for the jury, if a jury is present, otherwise the matter is decided by the judge.

Here we are concerned with how much care the defendant must take. It is obvious that if motorists did not take out their cars many lives would be saved, and yet it is not negligent to drive a car. Once again the test is to place the "reasonable man" in the defendant's position. It is an objective test and was thus stated by Baron Alderson in *Blyth* v. *Birmingham Waterworks Co.* (1856), 11 Ex. 781

> Negligence is the omission to do something which a reasonable man guided upon those considerations which ordinarily regulate the conduct of human affairs would do, or doing something which a prudent and reasonable man would not do.

The standard required is not that of a particularly conscientious man but that of the average prudent man in the eyes of the jury. (*Daniels* v. *White and Sons*, 1938.)[492] It has been said that the reasonable man is the man on the Clapham omnibus, but it should not be thought that the average prudent man has a low standard of care. Most of us behave unreasonably from time to time, and if during one of these lapses a person suffers injury, it will be no good our pleading that we are usually reasonable men.

When a person has undertaken a duty which requires extraordinary skill, he will be expected to use a higher standard of care. For example, one would expect from a surgeon the degree of skill appropriate to a reasonably competent member of his profession. He may, therefore, be negligent even though he does his best. However, barristers provide an exception to this rule because no action lies against them for negligence in conducting a case. (*Rondel* v. *Worsley*, 1967.)[19]

It should be noted that if precautions are taken which would have been reasonable in the case of persons possessed of the usual faculties of sight and hearing, this will be sufficient to absolve a person who does injury to those not possessed of such faculties, so long as he was not aware of their infirmity. (*Paris* v. *Stepney Borough Council*, 1951.)[493] However, persons engaged on operations on the *highway* must act reasonably so as not to cause damage to those who are using the highway, including blind people. (*Haley* v. *London Electricity Board*, 1964.)[494] Furthermore, the court will take into account the importance of the object which the defendant was trying to achieve (*Watt* v. *Hertfordshire County Council*, 1954)[495] and whether it was practicable and necessary for the defendant to have taken the precautions which the plaintiff alleged should have been taken. (*Latimer* v. *A.E.C. Ltd.*, 1953.)[496]

(iii) RESULTING DAMAGE TO THE PLAINTIFF. It is necessary for the plaintiff to show that he has suffered some loss, since negligence is not actionable *per se* (in itself). The major problem arising here is the question of remoteness of damage which was dealt with earlier in the chapter. Where there is a jury trial, the jury decide the measure of general damages.

Although the burden of proof in negligence normally lies on the plaintiff, there is a principle known as *res ipsa loquitur* (the thing speaks for itself), and where the principle applies the court is prepared to lighten his burden. In some cases it is difficult for the plaintiff to show how much care the defendant has taken, and it is a common sense rule of evidence to allow the plaintiff to prove the result and not require him to prove any particular act or omission by the defendant.

Before the principle can apply two conditions must be satisfied—

(*a*) the thing or activity causing the harm must be wholly under the control of the defendant or his servants; and

(*b*) the accident must be one which would not have happened if proper care had been exercised. (*Byrne* v. *Boadle*, 1863.)[497]

There is no value in the principle where there is no indication of who is the person likely to have been negligent. (*Roe* v. *Minister of Health*, 1954.)[498]

It should be noted that just because the principle *res ipsa loquitur* applies, it is not certain that the plaintiff will succeed; the court is not bound to find the defendant negligent. The defendant may be able to prove how the accident happened and that he was not negligent. (*Pearson* v. *North Western Gas Board*, 1968.)[499] He may not know how the accident happened but he may be able to prove that it could not have arisen from his negligence. Finally, he may suggest ways in which the accident could have happened without his negligence, and the court may find his explanations convincing. If a tile falls off Y's roof and injures X who is lawfully on the highway below, this would probably be a situation in which *res ipsa loquitur* would apply. But if Y can show that at the time an explosion had occurred near by and this had probably dislodged the tile, and the court is impressed by this explanation of the event, the burden of proof reverts to X. However, it is not enough to offer purely hypothetical explanations (*Moore* v. *R. Fox and Sons*, [1956] 1 All E.R. 182), nor is it sufficient to explain how the accident happened unless the explanation also shows that the defendant was not negligent. (*Colville* v. *Devine*, [1969] 2 All E.R. 53.)

Sometimes when an accident occurs, both parties have been negligent and this raises the doctrine of *contributory negligence*. At one time a plaintiff guilty of contributory negligence could not recover any damages unless the defendant could, with reasonable care, have avoided the consequences of the plaintiff's contributory want of care. Thus the courts were often concerned to find out who had the last chance of avoiding the accident, and this led to some unsatisfactory decisions.

Now, however, under the Law Reform (Contributory Negligence) Act, 1945, liability is apportionable between plaintiff and defendant. The claim is not defeated but damages may be reduced according to the degree of fault of the plaintiff. A person may be in *fault* although not to *blame* for the accident. (*O'Connell* v. *Jackson*, 1971.)[653] It should be mentioned that a young child will seldom, if ever, be guilty of contributory negligence. (*Jones* v. *Lawrence*, 1969.)[500] Furthermore, the contributory negligence of an adult who happened to be with the child is no defence to an action brought by the child. (*Oliver* v. *Birmingham Bus Co.*, 1932.)[501]

It sometimes happens that a person is injured in anticipating negligence. If a passenger jumps off a bus which he believes to be out of control, and breaks his leg in so doing, he is not prejudiced by the fact that the driver later regains control and the anticipated accident is averted. He is not deprived of his remedy. This is sometimes referred to as the *doctrine of alternative danger*, and an act done in the agony of the moment cannot be treated as contributory negligence.

Statutory Duties. Sometimes a particular duty of care is laid upon a person by statute, e.g. the duty laid on an employer as to guarding machinery under the Factories Act. Such duties are high and very often absolute, though the employer can plead contributory negligence as a defence. In addition, where there is a breach of a statutory duty, it must be shown that the duty is owed to the plaintiff personally and not to the public as a whole. (*Atkinson* v. *Newcastle Waterworks Co.*, 1877.)[502]

A conditional statutory power saying that the person upon whom it is conferred may act, cannot be converted into a statutory duty which says he must act. (*East Suffolk Rivers Catchment Board* v. *Kent*, 1941.)[486] However, where a statute prescribes provision to prevent damage, if an action is to be brought, the harm resulting from the breach of duty must be of the type contemplated by the statute. (*Gorris* v. *Scott*, 1874,[503] and *Lane* v. *London Electricity Board*, 1955.)[25]

Liability for Misstatements. We have already considered the major principles of the *tort of deceit* in Chapter V (p. 158) but it is perhaps worth repeating that deceit occurs where there is a false statement of fact made knowing it to be false, or believing it to be false, or recklessly not caring whether it be true or false. If it is made with the intention that it should be acted upon by another and is so acted upon there are grounds for an action. (*Derry* v. *Peek*, 1889.)[193]

It should also be noted that fraudulent misrepresentations as to a person's *credit* are not actionable unless they are in writing and signed by the defendant. (*Lord Tenterden's Act*, 1828.)

Where monetary loss results from the defendant's negligent misstatements rather than his acts, it was, but is now no longer, necessary to prove the existence of a contract or fiduciary relationship in order to establish a duty of care (*Candler* v. *Crane, Christmas & Co.*, 1951,[504] and *Hedley Byrne & Co. Ltd.* v. *Heller & Partners Ltd.*, 1963),[194] and the same is true if the plaintiff receives physical injuries as a result of the defendant's careless instructions. (*Clayton* v. *Woodman & Son (Builders) Ltd.*, 1961.)[505] However, in the *Hedley Byrne*[194] case the House of Lords ruled that there must be a "special relationship" between the person making the statement and the person relying upon it before a duty of care can arise. Since this aspect of the law of negligence is still being developed it is unwise to be too dogmatic with regard to what constitutes this "special relationship." However, Lord Morris said of it in the *Hedley Byrne* case—

> I consider that it follows and that it should now be regarded as settled that if someone possessed of a special skill undertakes, quite irrespective of contract, to apply that skill for the assistance of another person who relies on such skill, a duty of care will arise. . . . Furthermore, if, in a sphere in which a person is so placed that others could reasonably rely on his judgment or his skill or on his ability to make careful inquiry, a person takes it on himself to give information or advice to, or allows his information or advice to be passed on to, another person who, as he knows or should know, will place reliance on it, then a duty of care will arise.

Lord Hodson also agreed with that view. However, in *Mutual Life Assurance* v. *Evatt*, 1971,[506] the Privy Council took a somewhat narrower view of this form of liability, though Lord Morris's statement is wide enough to cover the facts of *Evatt's* case. The Privy Council seems to have restricted the decision in *Hedley Byrne* to cases where the advice is given by a person who is or purports to be an expert, whereas if Lord Morris's view is accepted a person who gives advice, whether or not on a topic with which he is familiar and competent to deal could be responsible for damage resulting from that advice if given erroneously. The fact that less-informed persons rely on the advice of better-informed persons is well known and where this happens, at least in a business context, there should be a duty of care. Decisions of the Privy Council are not, of course, binding on English Courts so that the decision in *Evatt's* case would not prevent the Court of Appeal or the House of Lords from reaching wider conclusions in a subsequent case.

However, it is clear that professional men such as accountants and bankers are likely to be caught by the rule in the *Hedley Byrne*[194] case when they give reference or advice (and see *Dutton* v. *Bognor Regis U.D.C.*, 1971.)[654] The rule may also extend to barristers in respect of advice unrelated to litigation. (*Rondel* v. *Worsley*, 1967.)[19]

The maker of the statement can avoid liability by an express disclaimer. (*Hedley Byrne & Co. Ltd.* v. *Heller and Partners Ltd.*, 1963.)[194] Furthermore, Lord Tenterden's Act does not apply to negligent misstatements. (*Anderson (W. B.) and Sons* v. *Rhodes (Liverpool)*, 1967.)[507]

We have already seen in Chapter V (p. 161) that damages for negligent misstatements are also obtainable—

    (i) under the Misrepresentation Act, 1967, provided the parties are in a pre-contractual relationship;

    (ii) where the parties are in a fiduciary relationship, e.g. solicitor and client;

    (iii) under Sect. 43 of the Companies Act, 1948, promoters and directors are liable for negligent misstatements in prospectuses though they have certain defences.

Injurious falsehood, which is concerned with such matters as slander of goods, is briefly considered on p. 270.

OCCUPIER'S LIABILITY

The question of the liability of occupiers of premises to persons suffering injury thereon may be regarded as a further aspect of negligence. The occupier is the person who has *de facto* control of the premises or the possession of them; it is a question of fact in each case and does not depend entirely on title. It should also be noted that occupation may be *shared* between two or more persons. (*Wheat* v. *E. Lacon & Co. Ltd.*, 1966.)[508]

If a person, whilst on another's premises, suffers injury from some defect in the premises, the liability or otherwise of the occupier will vary according to the capacity in which such a person was there. This branch of the law has been affected by the Occupiers' Liability Act, 1957, but in order to understand the effect of the Act, it is necessary to consider in outline the former position at common law.

The common law divided entrants on to premises into three categories—

    (a) INVITEES. These were persons who entered premises on business which concerned themselves and the occupier, and at his express or implied invitation, e.g. workmen carrying out repairs on the premises, guests in an hotel, and the audience at a theatre or other place of entertainment. To an invitee the occupier owed a duty not to expose him to any unusual or unexpected dangers of which the occupier was aware, or would have been aware, if he had acted as a reasonable man.

(*b*) LICENSEES. These were persons entering premises by mere permission of the occupier granted gratuitously, e.g. guests in a private house or persons permitted to take a short cut across land or users of public parks. To licensees the occupier owed a duty to warn of any concealed danger of which he was aware, this liability being limited to dangers actually known to him.

It may be said then that the difference in the duty of care owed to an invitee and a licensee was that the occupier was liable to the former for dangers of which *he ought to have been aware*, and to the latter for dangers of which *he was in fact aware*, regardless of who created the danger.

The Occupiers' Liability Act, 1957. This Act was passed largely because of the anomalies which arose out of the attempts made by the courts to classify persons in the categories of invitees and licensees. Such persons are now called visitors, a term which includes anyone to whom the occupier has given, or is deemed to have given, an invitation or permission to use the premises. It includes some persons who enter the premises by right of law, such as inspectors, but not those who cross land in pursuance of a public or private right of way. Such rights of way must be taken as they are found. (*Greenhalgh* v. *British Railways Board*, [1969] 2 All E.R. 114.) Implied permission to enter premises is a matter of fact to be decided in the circumstances of each case, and the burden of proof is upon the person who claims implied permission. However, persons who enter upon premises for purposes of business which they believe will be of interest to the occupier have implied permission to enter even though their presence is distasteful to the occupier.

Under the Act, an occupier of premises owes to all visitors the duty to take such care as, in all the circumstances of the case, is necessary to see that the visitor will be reasonably safe in using the premises for the purpose for which he is invited or permitted to be there. If the visitor uses the premises for some other purpose, the occupier does not owe him the same duty; such a person is in effect a trespasser, and intrudes upon the property largely at his own risk.

The occupier may restrict or exclude his liability, by giving adequate warning or by contract, but a contractual exemption cannot affect third parties; so if a landlord exempts himself from liability in the lease with his tenant, this will not prevent a visitor to the tenant from suing the landlord in respect of injuries received because of defective stairways or lifts, where the landlord remains the occupier of these common services. However, an occupier cannot exclude his liability to a person who has entered in the exercise of a right conferred by law.

Where the accident has arisen through the defective work of an independent contractor, the occupier can avoid liability by showing that he behaved reasonably in the selection of the contractor and that, so far as he was able, he inspected the work done. (*Cook* v. *Broderip*, 1968.)[509]

The occupier may assume that persons who come on to his premises to exercise their calling will appreciate and guard against any special risks normally involved. The defence of *volenti non fit injuria* is available to the occupier, though he must show that the entrant assented to the risk, not that he merely knew of it: the entrant's knowledge is no longer a defence. (*Bunker* v. *Charles Brand & Son*, 1969.)[510]

The occupier may also raise the defence of *contributory negligence* by the entrant which, though not defeating his claim, may reduce damages.

Formerly, a trespasser took property as he found it in so far as his injuries were caused by the condition of the land or any structures erected on the land. However, an occupier must not set traps for trespassers and it would appear that in respect of injuries caused to trespassers by some *activity* carried out on the land by the occupier there is a duty of care towards a trespasser whose presence is reasonably foreseeable. (*Videan* v. *British Transport Commission*, 1963.)[399]

Dealings with children always demand a high degree of care, whether a person is sued in the capacity of an occupier of premises or not, (*Yachuk* v. *Oliver Blais & Co. Ltd.*, 1949.)[511] However, in the case of an occupier of premises, the duty towards children was rather different from the corresponding duty to adults. If, with knowledge of the trespass of children on his land, the occupier made no reasonable attempt to prevent such trespass, e.g. by repairing fences, and a child was injured by something on the land which was especially alluring to children, e.g. turntables, escalators, bright and poisonous berries, then the occupier in general was liable, even though the child was on the face of it a trespasser. (*Gough* v. *National Coal Board*, 1954,[512] and *Herrington* v. *British Railways Board*, 1971.)[512a] It should also be noted that what is adequate warning to an adult might not be so to a child. (*Mourton* v. *Poulter*, 1930.)[513]

The matter was fully considered by the House of Lords in *British Railways Board* v. *Herrington*, 1972.[655] The earlier decision of the Court of Appeal (see case 512[a]) was affirmed but on other grounds which alter the law.

HIGHWAY AUTHORITIES

A highway authority is liable for damage which is caused by its *active misfeasance* and, under the Highways (Miscellaneous Provisions) Act, 1961, Sect. 1(1), which arises from its failure to repair.

In an action for damages against a highway authority based upon its failure to repair, it is a defence to prove that the authority has in all the circumstances taken reasonable care to ensure that the highway was not dangerous (Sect. 1(2)). (*Griffiths* v. *Liverpool Corporation*, 1966.)[514]

NON-OCCUPIERS

If a person is injured as a result of defects in land or buildings sold or let by the defendant who then ceased to occupy the property, the defendant is not liable unless there is an express provision to this effect in the contract of sale or in a lease, unless he has acted fraudulently. However, a lessor of premises who, though not in occupation is responsible for repairs, owes a common duty of care to all persons lawfully on the premises. (Occupiers Liability Act, 1957, Sect. 4.)

The above rules do not, however, exclude the liability of persons other than the vendor or lessor, e.g. building contractors who have created a dangerous situation on the premises. (*A. C. Billings and Sons* v. *Riden*, [1958] A.C. 240 (see p. 548).)

Changes in this branch of the law are recommended by the Law Commission in a report entitled *Civil Liability of Vendors and Lessors for Defective Premises*. Under these recommendations, the maxim *caveat emptor* would no longer provide a defence to a claim of negligence against a vendor or lessor in respect of defects in the premises sold or let.

EMPLOYER'S NEGLIGENCE

Where a servant's case is based on his master's negligence *at common law*, he will have to prove that his injury was the result of the master's breach of a duty of care. The servant is assisted in this task because certain specific duties of a master were laid down by the House of Lords in the leading case of *Wilsons and Clyde Coal Co.* v. *English*, [1938] A.C. 57, and an employer must take reasonable care to provide—

  (i) *proper and safe plant and appliances* for the work;
 (ii) *a safe system of work* with adequate supervision and instruction;
(iii) *safe premises*; and
(iv) *a competent staff* of fellow servants.

The employer's duty is a personal one so that he remains liable even though he has delegated the performance of the duty to a competent independent contractor. Thus in *Paine* v. *Colne Valley Electricity Supply Co. Ltd.*, [1938] 4 All E.R. 803, an employer was held liable for injuries to his servant caused by the failure of contractors to install sufficient insulation in an electrical kiosk.

However, in *Davie* v. *New Merton Board Mills*, [1958] 1 All E.R. 67, the House of Lords decided that an employer was not liable for damage caused by a defective implement purchased from a reputable manufacturer. The employee was thus left to sue the manufacturer and this could prove difficult where the manufacturer had left the country or gone out of business or could not for any other reason be identified. Now the Employer's Liability (Defective Equipment) Act, 1969, provides that an employee who is injured because of a defect in his employer's equipment can recover damages from the employer if he can show that the defect is due to the fault of some person, e.g. the manufacturer, but if no one is at fault damages are not recoverable. Agreements by employees to contract out are void, and rights under the Act are *in addition* to common law rights. Thus, an injured employee can sue a third party such as a manufacturer if he wishes, e.g. as where the employer is insolvent, though the Employer's Liability (Compulsory Insurance) Act, 1969, requires employers to insure against their liability for personal injury to their employees. The injury must result from equipment provided for the employer's *business*. Thus, domestic servants injured by household equipment would not be covered.

There are numerous statutes which are designed to protect the health, and provide for the welfare and safety of employees and the Factories Act, 1961, covers the largest field of industrial activity.

The relevance of such statutes for our present purposes is that where the breach of a statutory duty, e.g. failure to fence a dangerous machine, has caused injury to a worker, he may be able to sue his employer for damages by using the breach of statutory duty to establish the duty of care under the principles already discussed.

TORTS AGAINST BUSINESS INTERESTS

It is a tort knowingly to induce a person to *break his contract* with a third party whereby that party suffers damage. It is also an actionable wrong for two or more persons to combine together (*or conspire*) for the purpose of wilfully causing damage to the plaintiff. Finally there is an action for *passing off* which occurs where A represents his goods or services to be those of B.

Inducement of Breach of Contract. If A induces B to break his contract with C, C can sue A. (*Daily Mirror Newspapers* v. *Gardner*, 1968.)[515] An action will lie even though the defendant is not aware of the precise terms of the contract. (*Emerald Construction Co. Ltd.* v. *Lowthian*, 1966.)[516] Interference with a contract may be *direct* (*Lumley* v. *Gye*, 1853)[517] or *indirect* (*J. T. Stratford & Son Ltd.* v. *Lindley*, 1964).[518] Furthermore, interference with a contract which hinders its execution but does not bring about a breach of it may be actionable. (*Torquay Hotel Co.* v. *Cousins*, 1969.)[519]

Trade union activity often involves interference with contract and in this connection the Trade Disputes Act, 1906, Sect. 3, provided that an act done in contemplation or furtherance of a *trade dispute* was not actionable *simply because* it induced another person to break a contract of employment. However, interference by *unlawful means* did not attract the protection of the Act.

Thus if A threatens to act unlawfully against B intending that B will act to the detriment of C, then A has committed the tort of intimidation, and if C suffers damage he will have a right of action against A. It is immaterial whether B's action in relation to C is or is not lawful. (*Rookes* v. *Barnard*, 1964.)[520] However, there is no action where A threatens a *lawful act* even though A's intention may be malicious. (*Allen* v. *Flood*, 1898.)[521]

Finally, under the provisions of the Trade Disputes Act, 1965, the object of which was to overrule *Rookes* v. *Barnard*, 1964,[520] an act done in contemplation or furtherance of a trade dispute was not actionable on the ground only that it consisted in *threatening to break or to procure the breach of a contract.* Threatening *other unlawful acts* is still actionable.

Conspiracy. Where two or more persons act without lawful justification for the purpose of wilfully causing damage to the plaintiff
and actual damage results, they commit the tort of conspiracy. The
tort was fully considered in *Crofter Hand Woven Harris Tweed Co. Ltd.*
v. *Veitch,* 1942,[522] where the following principles were laid down—

    (i) the tort covers acts which would be *lawful if done by one person;*
    (ii) the combination will be justified if the predominant motive
is self-interest or protection of one's trade rather than injury of the
plaintiff;
    (iii) damage to the plaintiff must be proved.

It should be noted that by the Trade Disputes Act, 1906, Sect. 1,
an act done in contemplation or furtherance of a trade dispute was not
actionable simply because it was done in consequence of an agreement
or combination.

The Industrial Relations Act, 1971, has, of course, very wide ramifications on industrial law but it must suffice to consider here the effect of
the Act on those aspects of law dealt with above.

In this connection, *provided the union is registered,* the former law relating
to immunities for unions and their officials will continue, the relevant
provisions quoted above being largely repeated in the 1971 Act. However, since the Trade Disputes Act, 1965, are repealed *a threat to strike* in
breach of employment contracts seems to be a possible ground of liability
in the N.I.R.C. and the High Court.

Passing off. Any person, company or other organisation which
carries on or proposes to carry on business under a name calculated to
deceive the public by confusion with the name of an existing concern,
commits the civil wrong of *passing off* and will be restrained by injunction from doing so. Other examples of passing off are the use of similar
wrappings, identification marks, and descriptions. The remedies other
than an injunction are an action for damages or for an account.

DEFAMATION

Defamation is the publication of a statement which tends to lower a
person in the estimation of right-thinking members of society generally,
or which tends to make them shun or avoid that person. (*Byrne* v.
Deane, 1937.)[523] In order to constitute a tort the statement must be
false. The criterion is the view which would be taken by the good and
worthy subject of the Queen.

The essence of the tort is the publication or communication of the
falsehood to at least one person other than the person defamed, and
other than the author's own husband or wife. Every successive repetition of the statement is a fresh commission of the tort. Hence a
defamatory statement written upon a postcard is published by the
sender not only to the ultimate recipient but also to the postal officials

through whose hands it may pass, and to every individual who legitimately handles the message, e.g. the secretary of the sender or the receiver. Similarly a libel contained in a newspaper is published by the reporter or author, and by the editor, the printer, the publisher, the proprietor, the wholesaler and the retail seller of that newspaper.

The third person who receives the defamatory statement must be capable of appreciating its significance. A written defamatory statement cannot be published to a blind man except in Braille. It is not publication to repeat a defamatory statement in a foreign language in the presence only of persons who cannot understand the tongue. But if X writes a defamatory statement to Y in (say) German, knowing that Y cannot understand it, X will be responsible for the publication which results from Y's showing it to a linguist for the purpose of translation. In addition, to constitute publication, the person to whom the statement is communicated must understand that it refers to the plaintiff.

No action lies at civil law for defaming a dead person, no matter how much it may annoy or upset his relatives. There may possibly be a prosecution for criminal libel if the necessary or natural effect of the words used is to render a breach of the peace imminent or probable.

Libel and Slander. The form of publication determines whether the tort committed is libel or slander. *Libel* is defamation in some permanent form; *slander* is a statement of a like kind in transient form. Pictures, effigies, writing and print are clearly libel. Speech is slander, and probably gestures and facial mimicry also. It has been held that a defamatory sound film was a libel (*Youssoupoff* v. *M.G.M. Pictures*, 1934),[524] and recent legislation has enacted that the broadcasting of defamatory matter is libel, whether sound or visual images are transmitted. (Defamation Act, 1952, Sect. 1.) (See also Theatres Act, 1968, p. 269.)

It is necessary to determine whether a tort is libel or slander for two reasons—

    (i) Libel may be a crime as well as a tort;

    (ii) Libel is actionable without the plaintiff having to prove special damage, i.e. pecuniary loss, whereas the plaintiff in an action for slander must as a general rule prove such special damage.

Slander is actionable without proof of special damage in the following cases—

    (*a*) Where there is an imputation that the plaintiff has been guilty of a criminal offence punishable with imprisonment.

    (*b*) Where there is an imputation of unchastity to any woman or girl (Slander of Women Act, 1891). This probably includes the case where a women is alleged to have been the victim of rape.

    (*c*) Where there is an imputation that the plaintiff is suffering from venereal disease, and possibly other contagious diseases, e.g. leprosy or plague, which might cause him to be shunned and avoided.

(*d*) Where there have been words calculated to disparage the plaintiff in any office, profession, business or calling, by imputing dishonesty, unfitness or incompetence. (Defamation Act, 1952, Sect. 2.)

A suggestion, therefore, that a clergyman has been guilty of immoral conduct, or that a solicitor knows no law is actionable without proof of special damage. Spoken words in a broadcast are now actionable *per se* since they are regarded as libel. (Defamation Act, 1952, Sect. 1.)

It is not enough that the words are abusive. To say of A, a bricklayer, that he is a legal ignoramus is not defamatory, though the same words would be defamatory if said of B, a solicitor. Difficulties might arise if the words were said of a chartered accountant who is required to have a knowledge of certain branches of the law.

To resolve problems such as these, two questions must be answered—

(i) Are the alleged words capable of bearing a meaning which is defamatory of the plaintiff? (This is a matter of law and is decided by the judge.)

(ii) If so, in this particular case are the words in fact defamatory of the plaintiff? (This is a matter of fact to be decided by the jury.)

Cases may arise where the words are not at first sight defamatory, and only appear as such when the surrounding circumstances have been explained. Again a statement may be ironical, or accompanied by a wink or a gesture, or it may be ambiguous, e.g. the statement that "X drinks." In such a case the plaintiff must show that the words contain an innuendo or hidden meaning and that reasonable persons could, and in fact would, interpret the *words* used in a defamatory sense. (*Cassidy* v. *Daily Mirror Newspapers Ltd.*, 1929.)[525] However, a newspaper article may be defamatory of a person whom readers only identify from their own knowledge of extrinsic facts. The defamation need not arise from words themselves. (*Morgan* v. *Odhams Press*, 1971.)[526] The judge decides as a matter of law whether the words are capable of bearing the innuendo alleged by the plaintiff, and the jury decides whether in fact the words do bear that meaning. (*Tolley* v. *Fry & Sons*, 1931.)[527] The meaning sought to be placed upon the words by the innuendo pleaded must be reasonable, and the court will not read into a statement a defamatory sense which is not there on a reasonable interpretation. (*Sim* v. *Stretch*, 1936.)[528]

If the judge decides that the words are capable of bearing a defamatory meaning, he must then consider whether the words are capable of referring to the plaintiff. This again is a question of law. If he finds the answer to be yes, he must leave to the jury the question: "Do the words in fact refer to the plaintiff?" This is a simple matter where the plaintiff has been referred to by name, and until recently the rule was that an author used a name at his peril if it turned out that it could reasonably be taken to refer to the plaintiff. Indeed the more obscure the name selected, the greater the chance of success of a plaintiff who bore that name should he sue for libel. (*Hulton & Co.* v. *Jones*, 1910.)[529] It is not uncommon to attach a disclaimer at the beginning of a work of fiction: "The persons and events described in this book are wholly imaginary," but it is doubtful whether this affects the author's liability.

The practical restriction on so-called "gold-digging" actions was the power of the jury to award contemptuous damages of a farthing, but the costs involved in defending an action might well lead a defendant to settle out of court for a substantial sum. The position has been modified by the Defamation Act, 1952, Sect. 4, which provides for an offer of amends which will be dealt with later.

It sometimes happens that a whole class of persons is the subject of a defamatory statement. Here a member of the class may only sue if he can show that he himself is the person pointed out by the defamatory statement. (*Knupffer* v. *London Express Newspaper Ltd.*, 1944.)[530]

Words may, of course, be defamatory of the plaintiff without his being mentioned by name, if the statement can be shown to apply to him. (*Youssoupoff* v. *M.G.M.*, 1934.)[524]

The defendant's motives are generally immaterial. The most laudable motives will not by themselves prevent a defamatory statement from being actionable. But where the defendant puts his motives in issue, as where he pleads fair comment or qualified privilege, or relies on Sect. 4 of the Defamation Act, 1952 (unintentional defamation), the plaintiff may then prove the malice of the defendant, or improper motive, to rebut the defence.

Defences. There are certain special defences which are peculiar to an action for defamation, but these defences do not preclude a defendant from denying in addition that the words are defamatory, or asserting that they do not refer to the plaintiff, or that they were not published.

1. JUSTIFICATION. As the essence of defamation is a false statement, a defendant may always plead the truth of the statement as a defence in civil proceedings (but not in an action for criminal libel, where the rule is: "The greater the truth, the greater the libel," since true libels are more likely to inflame passions). If the statement is true, no injury is done to the plaintiff's reputation; it is simply reduced to its true level.

In the defence of justification the defendant asserts that the statements are "true both in substance and in fact." He must show not merely that the words are literally true, but also that there are no significant omissions which would affect the truth of the statement taken as a whole. If, however, the statement is essentially true, an incidental inaccuracy will not deprive the defendant of his right to justify. (*Alexander* v. *N. E. Railway Co.*, 1865.)[531] Proof that the plaintiff has been convicted of an offence will not justify a statement that he committed that offence. (*Goody* v. *Odhams Press Ltd*, 1966.)[532]

The defence of justification really amounts to a positive charge against the plaintiff, and if it fails the damages may be increased, since the original wrong has been aggravated. The defendant's honest belief that the statement is true is no justification, though it may reduce damages. Nor is it a justification to prove that a quoted statement was made, if the quotation cannot be proved to be true. Suppose a statement is made: "Mrs. A tells me that Dr. B has been committing adultery with a woman patient." It is no justification to show that Mrs. A made the statement to the defendant; he must show that Dr. B is actually guilty of the conduct alleged.

In connection with this defence, it is important to note Sect. 5 of the Defamation Act, 1952, which provides that in an action for libel and slander in respect of words containing two or more distinct charges against a plaintiff, a defence or justification shall not fail by reason only that the truth of every charge is not proved if the words not proved to be true do not materially injure the plaintiff's reputation having regard to the truth of the remaining charges.

2. Fair Comment on a Matter of Public Interest. Here the defendant must show that the statement alleged to be defamatory is in fact legitimate comment. The statement must be comment, i.e. the speaker's opinion of a true state of affairs; it must not be an assertion of facts, but a comment on known facts. (*London Artists* v. *Littler*, 1969.)[533] The comment must be fair, that is, honestly believed in by the defendant, and made without any malicious or improper motive.

Comment is the individual reaction to facts, and the court and the jury require to be satisfied only of the defendant's honesty. The test is: "Would any honest man, however prejudiced he may be, however exaggerated or obstinate his views, have said that which this criticism has said of what is criticised?" If the answer is, "yes," the comment is fair for the purposes of raising this defence.

The matter upon which the comment is made must be one of legitimate public interest such as the conduct of Parliament, the Government, local authorities and other public authorities, or the behaviour of a trade union whose actions affect supplies and services to the public. Further, a matter may become the subject of public interest because the plaintiff has voluntarily submitted himself and his affairs to public criticism. A person who makes a public speech, or publishes a book, or presents a play thereby submits the subject matter of such thing for public comment, and cannot complain if the comment is adverse.

It should also be noted that the facts relied on to support a plea of fair comment must be facts existing at the time of the comment and not facts which have occurred some time before the comment was made. (*Cohen* v. *Daily Telegraph*, [1968] 2 All E.R. 407.)

3. Privilege. This defence protects statements made in circumstances where the public interest in securing a free expression of facts or opinion outweighs the private interests of the person about whom the statements are made. Privilege may be absolute—such a statement is

never actionable—or qualified, when privilege may be defeated by proof of the defendant's malice.

Absolute Privilege. The Bill of Rights, 1689, protects statements in either House of Parliament. The Parliamentary Papers Act, 1840, affords a similar protection to reports, papers, etc., published by order of either House, e.g. *Hansard* and Government White Papers. The Defamation Act, 1952, Sect. 9, protects verbatim broadcasts and newspaper reports of Parliamentary proceedings but Parliament itself can fine or imprison those who abuse this privilege.

With regard to the courts, statements by the judge, members of the jury, counsel, and the parties or witnesses are absolutely privileged, as are Orders of Court. Thus an Order of Court for divorce, including a finding of adultery against a woman, is not actionable even though reversed on appeal. A statement made by a witness is not actionable even though the judge finds it untrue and malicious. The abuse of the above privilege is checked by (*a*) the law of perjury (in the case of untrue statements by witnesses), (*b*) the power of the judge to report improper behaviour on the part of counsel to the Benchers of his Inn, and (*c*) the judge's general power to commit persons to prison for contempt of court.

Communications between senior and responsible public officers in the course of their duty are absolutely privileged.

Qualified Privilege. Where such privilege exists, a person is entitled to communicate a defamatory statement so long as he does so honestly and reasonably with regard to the words used and the means of publication, and without malice. Qualified privilege has been held to arise in the following cases—

(i) Common interest, i.e. where a statement is made by a person who is under a legal or moral duty to communicate it to a person who has a similarly legitimate interest in receiving it. This covers testimonials or references to prospective employers, or to trade protection societies whose function it is to investigate the creditworthiness of persons who are the objects of their enquiry. (*London Association for the Protection of Trade* v. *Greenlands*, 1916.)[534]

(ii) Statements in protection of one's private interests are privileged. (*Osborn* v. *Thos. Boulter and Son*, 1930.)[535]

(iii) Statements by way of complaint to a proper authority, e.g. petitions to Parliament and complaints to officials of local authorities and professional bodies. (*Beach* v. *Freeson*, 1971.)[536]

(iv) Professional confidential communications between solicitor and client on legal advice.

(v) Newspaper reports on various public matters. The Defamation Act, 1952, Sect. 7, confers qualified privilege upon fair and accurate newspaper reports of various matters of public interest and importance. These are of two classes—

(*a*) Those which are privileged without any explanation or contradiction being issued, e.g. reports of public proceedings of colonial or dominion legislatures, reports of public proceedings of the United Nations Organisation, of the International Court of Justice, or of British courts martial, and fair and accurate copies of and extracts from British public registers and notices.

(b) Those which are privileged only if the newspaper concerned is prepared, on the plaintiff's request, to publish a reasonable letter or statement in explanation or contradiction of the original report, e.g. semi-judicial findings of the governing bodies of learned societies, professional and trade associations, or authorities controlling games and sports. This also applies to fair and accurate reports of public meetings, meetings of local and public authorities, and the meetings of public companies.

(vi) Fair and accurate reports of Parliamentary proceedings are the subject of qualified privilege whether contained in a newspaper or not.

(vii) Fair and accurate reports of public judicial proceedings are privileged. This does not protect reports of proceedings in domestic tribunals, e.g. The Law Society, unless the report is in a newspaper. Such reports will not be privileged if the court has forbidden publication, as is often done in cases affecting children, or if the matter reported is obscene or scandalous. It is also a criminal offence to report indecent matter relating to judicial proceedings. (Judicial Proceedings Act, 1926; Domestic and Appellate Proceedings etc. Act, 1968.

Qualified privilege may be rebutted by proof of malice or some improper motive, and proof of actual spite or illwill in the publication will defeat it. An improper motive may be inferred from the tone of the statement or from the circumstances attending its publication, and malice may also be inferred from abuse of the privilege, such as the giving of excessive publicity to statements protected by qualified privilege. But where a person without malice joins with a malicious person in publishing a libel in circumstances of qualified privilege, the person without malice is not liable to the person defamed. (*Egger* v. *Viscount Chelmsford*, 1964.)[537]

4. OFFER OF AMENDS. The Defamation Act, 1952, provides that the publisher of "innocent defamation" may make an offer of amends as defined in the Act. (Sect. 4.) The words shall be treated as published innocently if the words were not defamatory on the face of them, and if the publisher did not know of circumstances by virtue of which they might be understood to be defamatory of the plaintiff, and if reasonable care was exercised in relation to the publication. Given that the above circumstances exist the defendant can apparently make an offer of amends, supported by an affidavit setting out the facts relied on to show that his publication was innocent.

An offer of amends requires the publication of a suitable apology to the party aggrieved and a suitable correction. The offeror must also take steps to notify persons to whom copies have been distributed that the words used are alleged to be defamatory of the party aggrieved.

The High Court decides how the offer shall be carried into effect unless the parties have agreed on the matter.

It is a defence in any proceedings for defamation that the defendant's offer (i) has been accepted and performed, or (ii) that it has been refused, after having been made as soon as practicable after the defendant received notice that the words were or might be defamatory of the plaintiff, and that the offer has not been withdrawn.

If the plaintiff rejects the offer because he does not think the publication was innocent, or because the section of the Act has not been complied with, and fails to establish this at the trial, there seems no way of later enforcing the offer of amends.

5. CONSENT OF THE PLAINTIFF TO PUBLICATION. If the plaintiff has agreed to publication, he cannot subsequently sue in respect of that statement. (*Chapman* v. *Lord Ellesmere*, 1932.)[538] Consent may be given in respect of a particular publication, or it may be general.

Theatres Act, 1968. Sect. 4 of the Theatres Act, 1968, amends the law of defamation (including the law relating to criminal libel) by providing that the publication of words (including pictures, visual images, gestures, and the like) in the public performance of a play shall be treated as publication in permanent form, i.e. libel. Performances given on a domestic occasion in a private dwelling house are exempt (Sect. 7(1)) and so are rehearsals and performances for broadcast or recording purposes (Sect. 7(2)) provided such rehearsals and performances are attended only by the persons *directly* connected with the giving of them.

Sect. 5 of the Act creates an offence of incitement to racial hatred by presenting or directing the public performance of a play though again, rehearsals and performances attended only by persons directly concerned are exempt. Prosecution under Sect. 5 is with the consent of the Attorney General (Sect. 8).

It is of interest to note also that Sect. 1 of the Act abolishes the power of the Lord Chamberlain to censor plays.

Damages. Although many slanders are actionable only on proof of special damage to the plaintiff, actual damages awarded by the court will not be confined to the special damage so proved. For example, if as a result of defamation a man loses his employment, he can prove special damage in this connection, but the actual damages awarded may take in much more than this particular loss. Damages for defamation tend to be high. Juries are often used in such cases, and they are concerned with the *quantum* of damages. The damages awarded for loss of reputation may often be higher than damages awarded for the loss of life. However, damages should be compensatory and not punitive (*Rookes* v. *Barnard*, 1964,[529] and *Davis* v. *Rubin*, 1967),[539] though they may be *aggravated* by mental suffering arising from the defamation, or *mitigated* by a full apology, provocation by the plaintiff, or the plaintiff's bad reputation. (*Goody* v. *Odhams Press Ltd.*, 1966.)[532]

Injunctions. Apart from damages a defamed person may seek an

injunction restraining further publication. Such injunctions are of two
kinds—

    (*a*) *A perpetual injunction*, which is usually granted at the trial, and
    (*b*) *an interim injunction* (or interlocutory injunction), which is
granted pending the trial, and may be *quia timet*, that is before the
wrong is actually done.

However, publication of an article will not be restrained merely
because it is defamatory where the defendant says he intends to justify
it or make fair comment on a matter of public interest. (*Fraser* v. *Evans*,
[1969] 1 All E.R. 8.

Before concluding the tort of defamation we should notice also the
separate tort of *injurious falsehood*. Just as defamation is an attack on a
man's reputation, so injurious falsehood is an attack on his goods. To
say that A's goods are inferior in quality to B's may be an injurious
falsehood. To say that A sells inferior goods as goods of superior
quality may, on the other hand, be a defamatory statement.

THE RULE IN *Rylands* v. *Fletcher*

This celebrated rule was stated in the case of *Rylands* v. *Fletcher*, 1868—

> Where a person for his own purposes brings and keeps on land in his
> occupation anything likely to do mischief if it escapes, he must keep it in at
> his peril, and if he fails to do so he is liable for all damage naturally accruing
> from the escape.

The rule has been held to apply whether the things brought on the land
be "beasts, water, filth or stenches." The rule also applies to fire.
(*Emanuel* v. *Greater London Council*, 1970.)[540] It does not apply to the
pollution of beaches by oil because, *inter alia*, the oil does not escape
from *land* but from the sea.

The duty is an absolute one and does not depend on negligence
provided the use of the land is not natural use. (*British Celanese* v. *Hunt*,
1969.)[476] In the case which gave rise to the rule, the defendant had
constructed a reservoir on his land, employing competent workmen for
the purpose. Water escaped from the reservoir and percolated through
certain old mine shafts, which had been filled with marl and earth, and
eventually flooded the plaintiff's mine. The defendant was held liable
in that he had collected water on his land, the water not being naturally
there, and it had escaped and done damage. Since the defendant employed competent workmen, it follows that the liability is absolute and
does not depend on negligence, and in any case the defendant's action
was quite innocent as there was no reason why he should know of, or
even suspect the existence of, the disused shafts.

In order for the rule to apply, there must be an escape of the thing
which inflicts the injury from a place over which the defendant has
occupation or control to a place which is outside his occupation or
control. (*Read* v. *Lyons*, 1947.)[541]

The rule is not confined to wrongs between owners of adjacent land and does not depend on ownership of land (*Charing Cross Electricity Supply Co.* v. *Hydraulic Power Co.*, 1914),[542] but the plaintiff must have *some* interest in the land. (*Weller* v. *Foot and Mouth Disease Research Institute*, 1965.)[488] Neither is it confined to the escape of water, but may cover the escape of any offensive or dangerous matter arising out of abnormal use of land. (*Attorney-General* v. *Corke*, 1933.)[543] It seems doubtful at the moment whether the rule extends to personal injuries, and it may be that proof of negligence is always necessary in an action of this kind. (*Read* v. *Lyons*, 1947,[541] and *Perry* v. *Kendricks Transport*, 1956.)[544]

In general there is no liability under the rule for damage caused by the escape of things naturally on the land (*Giles* v. *Walker*, 1890),[545] though there may be an action in nuisance (*Davey* v. *Harrow Corporation*, 1957)[546] or in negligence.

Although *Rylands* v. *Fletcher* imposes strict liability, the following defences are still open to the defendant—

(*a*) That the escape was the plaintiff's fault. It should also be noted that there is no reason why the Law Reform (Contributory Negligence) Act, 1945, should not apply where the plaintiff is partly to blame.

(*b*) That it was an Act of God (*Nichols* v. *Marsland*, 1876),[402] though the defence is not often pleaded. (*Greenock Corporation* v. *Caledonian Railway Co.*, 1917.)[547]

(*c*) That the escape was due to the wrongful act of a stranger. (*Rickards* v. *Lothian*, 1913,[548] and *Emanuel* v. *Greater London Council*, 1970.)[540]

(*d*) That the damage was caused by artificial works done for the common benefit of the plaintiff and the defendant. (*Peters* v. *Prince of Wales Theatre (Birmingham) Ltd.*, 1943.)[549]

(*e*) That there was statutory authority for the act of the defendant, provided that the defendant was not negligent. It should be noted that the defence of statutory authority is not available in respect of reservoirs. (Reservoirs (Safety Provisions) Act, 1930.)

CHAPTER VII

THE LAW OF PROPERTY

ENGLISH law divides property into real property and personal property. Real property includes only freehold interests in land, and personal property comprises all other proprietary rights, whether in land or chattels. This classification is not identical with the obvious distinction between immoveables and moveables, and this is the result of the attitude of early law to the nature of a lease.

THE NATURE OF PROPERTY

Actions in respect of property fall into two kinds: actions *in rem* or real actions, and actions *in personam* or personal actions. An action *in rem* in English law is an action in which a specific thing is recovered; an action *in personam* gives damages only.

It so happened that in early days the courts would allow a real action or *actio realis* only for the specific recovery of land. If an owner was dispossessed of other forms of property, the person who had taken the property had a choice; he could either restore the property taken or pay damages to the rightful owner. Hence land became known as real property or *realty*, and all other forms of property were called personal property or *personalty*. So far the distinction corresponds to that between moveables and immoveables, but this convenient classification was disturbed by the lease for a term of years.

Although a lease of land was an interest in immoveable property, the real action was not available to the dispossessed tenant. Leases did not fit into the feudal system of landholding by tenure but were regarded as personal business arrangements whereby one man allowed another the use of the land for a period in return for a rent.

These transactions were personal contracts and created rights *in personam* between the parties, and not rights *in rem* which could affect feudal status. It was not an uncommon form of investment to buy land and let it out on lease to obtain an income on capital invested, and such transactions were more akin to commercial dealings than to landholding as it was understood in early days. Moreover the system had its advantages, since a lease was immune from feudal burdens and could be bequeathed by will at a time when dispositions by will of other land were still not permitted.

Leaseholds, therefore, come under the heading of personal property or chattels, but because they partake so strongly of the character of land, they are often referred to as *chattels real* to distinguish them from pure personalty, e.g. a watch or a fountain pen. Since the property legislation of 1925 this distinction has lost much of its importance, but it is still true that if in his will a testator says "All my personalty to P and all my realty to R," P would get the leaseholds.

Pure personalty itself comprises two different kinds of property known as *choses in possession* and *choses in action*. Choses in possession denote chattels, such as jewellery and furniture, which are tangible objects and can be physically possessed and enjoyed by their owner. Choses in action are intangible forms of property which are incapable of physical possession, and their owner is usually compelled to bring an action if he wishes to enforce his rights over property of this kind. Examples of choses in action are debts, patents, copyrights, trade marks, shares, and negotiable instruments.

Up to now we have been considering in the main rights which one has in one's own things. However it is possible to have rights over the things of another. We have already mentioned the lease, which is the right to possess another's land for a term in return for a rent, but in addition it is possible to become the owner of a *servitude* over the land of another, e.g. a right of way, a right of light, or a right to the support of buildings. A servitude may also be a right to take something from the land of another, e.g. the right to fish or collect firewood. Rights of the first class are called *easements*, and of the second *profits à prendre*. Further, a person may raise a loan on the security of his property either real or personal, and the lender has certain rights over the property so used as a security if the loan is not repaid.

The above, then, is an outline of the nature of property in English law and we must now consider certain aspects of property law in more detail.

ESTATES IN LAND

Since the Norman Conquest absolute ownership of land has been impossible. William the Conqueror considered himself owner of all land in England and parcelled it out to his barons who became his tenants. In return for this "honour" the barons had to render to the Crown certain services, either of a military or other public nature, but an exception was made in the case of land held by the Church. The ecclesiastics were not able to provide military services, and special spiritual tenures were introduced.

In order to assist themselves in supplying the services required by the King, the barons began to subgrant part of the land, and a series of tenures sprang up, all persons holding as tenants of the Crown in the last analysis.

It is outside our scope to pursue the rise and fall of the system of tenures, but all land is now held on a single tenure called "common socage," and all obligations to the Crown have disappeared, except for certain ceremonials preserved because of their antiquity. Even today, however, a person does not own land; he holds an estate in land. The *tenure* answers the question "How is the land held?" The term *estate* answers the question "For how long is the land held?"

Before 1926 there were the following estates in land—

Estates of Freehold. These estates were divided as follows—

(1) THE ESTATE IN FEE SIMPLE. This was granted *to A and his heirs* or *to A in fee simple*. The exact words used above were essential, and indeed only the latter formula was valid after the Conveyancing Act, 1881. A grant in fee simple confers full rights of possession, enjoyment and disposition during life and by will. If the owner of the estate dies intestate, the land passes to the relatives entitled under statute in that event. Only in the event of the owner dying intestate and without relations will the estate come to an end and the land pass to the Crown.

(2) THE ESTATE TAIL. (From the French "tailler," cut down.) This is an estate less than a fee simple, e.g. granted *to A and the heirs of his body* or *to A in tail*. The tenant in tail has full rights of possession and enjoyment and the estate does not come to an end at his death; it passes to his heirs but only to a limited class of heirs, the heirs of his body or his descendants. The line of descent may be further restricted by making the estate *in tail male*, i.e. descending only through males, or conceivably *in tail female*, descending through females. There is also an *estate in special tail* inheritable only by the issue of the tenant by a certain wife or husband.

Before 1926 a tenant in tail had no power to dispose of his estate by will, but a tenant in tail in possession could in his lifetime, and still can, bar the entail by deed. (The Law of Property Act, 1925, extending the Fines and Recoveries Act, 1833.) A disentailing deed operates to convert the entail into a fee simple estate. The tenant can now bar the entail by will by referring in the will to the entailed property or to entailed property generally. If the estate is not in possession, as where there is a grant to A for life and then to B in tail, A is the "protector of the settlement" and B cannot wholly bar the entail without A's consent.

(3) THE ESTATE FOR LIFE. This is granted *to A for life* or other period of uncertain duration, e.g. during widowhood. Such an estate was held only for the life of the grantee, so that it was not possible for him to leave it by will or to give rights to another *inter vivos* for longer than his own life.

(4) THE ESTATE *pur autre vie*. This is for the life of another, e.g. a grant *to A so long as B shall live*. This estate is similar to the life estate except that the duration of the estate depends on the life of a person other than the grantee.

Estates Less than Freehold. Such estates were of the nature of leaseholds and were divided as follows—

1. ESTATES FOR YEARS, such as existed under leases, and including a tenancy from year to year.

2. ESTATES AT WILL, where the tenancy is determinable at will by either the lessor or the lessee.

3. ESTATES BY SUFFERANCE, where a person who had held a lawful title continued in possession after his title had ended.

Any of these estates might be either a legal estate or an equitable interest arising under a trust. Further these estates, whether legal or equitable, were either (i) in possession, thus carrying the right of present enjoyment, or (ii) in expectancy, being in reversion or remainder. Thus where there was a grant *to A for life and then to B*, B's interest was said to be *in remainder*, because his estate became effective only on the expiration of the estate of the previous owner. An example of a *reversion* is where A, who has a fee simple of Blackacre, grants B a life estate in the land but makes no further disposition of it. On B's death Blackacre will revert to A, and A is said to have a *reversionary interest* in Blackacre. A reversion is similar to a remainder in that the right to enjoy the land is postponed to a future date, but where there is a reversion the land eventually returns to the grantor, whereas with a remainder the land goes to some other person.

THE LEGISLATION OF 1925

The existence of so many estates in land made the transfer of land most complicated. There might be a large number of legal owners of the same piece of land, and before the land could be conveyed to a purchaser all the interests had to be got in. Other problems arose on intestacy, because the rules for intestate succession were not the same for realty and personalty. In 1925 a thorough reform of land law was undertaken and was eventually achieved by the following statutes: The Law of Property Act, 1925; The Settled Land Act, 1925; The Administration of Estates Act, 1925; The Land Charges Act, 1925; and the Land Registration Act, 1925.

The Law of Property Act, 1925, reduced the number of legal estates which can exist over land to two, and the number of legal interests or charges in or over land to five. All other estates, interests, and charges in or over land take effect as equitable interests, and can exist only behind a trust, the trustees having the legal fee simple estate.

The difference between a legal estate and a legal interest is that the owner of the legal estate is entitled to the enjoyment of the whole of the property, either in possession or receiving rents, whereas the owner of a legal interest has a limited right in or over the land of another.

The two legal estates possible today are—

1. *A fee simple absolute in possession;* and
2. *A term of years absolute.*

The word *fee* implies that the estate is an estate of inheritance, and the word *simple* shows that the fee is capable of descending to the general class of heirs, and is not restricted, as in an estate tail, to heirs of a particular class. The word *absolute* distinguishes a fee simple which will continue for ever, from a fee which may be determinable. The fee simple must be *in possession*, although this does not imply only physical possession but also the right to receive rents and profits.

Even if a landlord has granted a lease he may still have a fee simple in possession because he is entitled to the rent reserved by the lease.

The *term of years absolute* is what is normally understood by a lease. But a term of years includes a term for less than a year, or for a year or years and a fraction of a year, or even a tenancy from year to year. The essential characteristic is that a term of years has a minimum period of certain duration. It seems, therefore, that a lease for life is no longer a legal estate; nor is a tenancy at will or sufferance since there is no certainty as to the period of their continuance. A term of years may be absolute notwithstanding that it may be determined by notice, re-entry, or operation of law or other event.

TYPES OF FEE SIMPLE. The fee simple absolute in possession is the only fee simple which can exist as a legal estate. Any other form is necessarily an equitable interest only. Such may be—

(*a*) A fee simple absolute but not in possession, e.g. in expectancy .
(*b*) A fee simple not absolute which may be either a determinable fee, a conditional fee or a base fee.

A *determinable fee* is one limited to determine on the happening of some event which may never occur. If the event happens, the interest automatically reverts to the grantor, unless there is a gift over to someone. If the event becomes impossible, the fee becomes absolute, e.g. a grant to A in fee simple until B marries (and B dies a bachelor). If the event is one which must happen some time, the fee is not a determinable fee, e.g. a grant to A in fee simple until B dies (since B is bound to die); here A has an estate *pur autre vie*.

A *conditional fee* is a fee simple subject to either—

(i) *a condition precedent*, where the interest does not commence unless and until some event occurs, e.g. to A in fee simple when or if he attains the age of twenty-one years; or
(ii) *a condition subsequent*, where the interest is liable to determine from the happening of some event, e.g. to A in fee simple, provided he never sells out of the family.

The difference between a determinable fee and a conditional fee is primarily one of language. The words *while*, or *until*, or *during*, or *so long as*, usually create a determinable fee. A grant to a school in fee simple until it ceases to publish annual accounts would be a limitation creating a determinable fee; but a grant to a school in fee simple upon condition that it publishes annual accounts would create a conditional fee.

There is, however, one case where a fee simple upon a condition subsequent can exist as a legal estate. Before 1926 it was a common practice, more particularly in Lancashire, upon a sale of freeholds to reserve a perpetual rentcharge called a chief rent, instead of taking a lump sum of purchase money, with a right to re-enter and determine the fee simple for default of payment of rent. When the Law of

Property Act, 1925, became law, the unfortunate purchasers of such property would not have a fee simple absolute and therefore no legal estate. The Law of Property (Amendment) Act, 1926, added to the 1925 Act a provision that a fee simple subject to a right of re-entry should be a fee simple absolute for the purposes of the Act.

The system of legal rentcharges has recently been examined by the Law Commission, which notes that there is still some tendency towards the creation of new rentcharges in estate development. Largely because of the extra work and costs involved in conveyancing where there are rentcharges, the Commission proposes that no new rentcharges should be capable of creation and that a satisfactory method should be found of extinguishing existing ones.

A base fee arises in the following circumstances. Suppose property is left to A for life with remainder to B in tail. It is possible for B to bar the entail, but if he wishes to do this during A's lifetime he must obtain A's consent. If this is not forthcoming, he can only bar the entail so as to defeat his own descendants, thus creating a base fee. He cannot prevent a reversion to the grantor without obtaining A's consent when the entail is barred. If then B's heirs fail at any time in the future, the land would revert to the grantor.

LEGAL INTERESTS AND CHARGES. We have seen that there are, since 1926, only two possible legal estates: a fee simple absolute in possession and a term of years absolute, but the Law of Property Act, 1925, also lays down five possible legal interests in land—

(i) An easement, right or privilege for an interest equivalent to either of the above estates. Thus an easement for life would not be a legal interest.

(ii) A rentcharge in possession, either perpetual or for a term of years absolute. A rentcharge is a right which is independent of any lease or mortgage, and gives the owner a right to a periodical sum of money, e.g. where the fee simple owner of Blackacre charges the land with a payment of £100 per annum payable to R.

(iii) A charge by way of legal mortgage.

(iv) Land tax or other charge not created by any instrument, e.g. created by statute.

(v) Rights of entry over or in respect of a term of years absolute, and annexed for any purpose to a legal rentcharge.

EQUITABLE INTERESTS

All estates, interests or charges over land except those outlined above take effect as equitable interests only and must exist behind a trust. Life interests are equitable and so are entails. Reversions and remainders, together with conditional interests, are also equitable.

Settled Land and Trusts for Sale. A settlement was designed to provide for successive interests in property. There are two methods of settling land: (*a*) the Strict Settlement and (*b*) the Trust for Sale.

The aim of a strict settlement was to keep the land in the family. On marriage a man would convey his property to trustees to carry out the terms of the settlement which were usually to give *a life interest* to the husband, *an entail* to his eldest son, a provision for the wife (called *a jointure*), other children being provided for by *portions* raised out of the property in the settlement.

By such a settlement the land became substantially inalienable, at least until the eldest son reached the age of twenty-one and was able to bar the entail. At twenty-one the son S usually barred the entail with the consent of his father F, and S's fee simple was resettled so that, after the death of F, S would receive a life interest with remainder to his own son in tail. This tied up the land for another generation when the process could be repeated. In this way, by means of settlement and resettlement, persons of full age never had more than a life estate.

A trust for sale had a somewhat different objective. Here the land was conveyed to trustees who were to sell it and invest the proceeds in order to provide the income for the beneficiaries under the trust. It was an essential characteristic of a trust for sale that the trustees had not merely a power but a binding duty to sell. However, it was usual to provide that the trustees should have power to postpone sale at their discretion, and manage the land until they deemed it prudent to sell.

Settlements. Where settlements are created after 1925 other than by will, the Settled Land Act, 1925, requires two deeds to be executed—the vesting deed and the trust instrument. The vesting deed must contain a description of the settled land, a statement that the settled land is vested in the tenant for life upon the trusts for the time being affecting the settled land, the names of the trustees of the settlement, and a statement of any larger powers granted to the tenant for life in addition to his statutory powers.

The trust instrument must contain the appointment of the trustees, the names of the persons entitled to appoint new trustees, a statement of any additional powers conferred by the settlement in extension of the statutory powers, and the trusts of the settlement. Where a settlement is created by will, the will is regarded as the trust instrument, and the personal representatives must execute a vesting instrument, vesting the legal estate in the tenant for life. Thus a purchaser of settled land is only concerned with the vesting deed or assent, since it is from such documents that he derives his title. The trusts can remain secret since the trust instrument need not be produced on sale.

Under the settlement the person obtaining the benefit from the estate is usually an adult with a life interest and he is called the *tenant for life*. It is his function to manage the estate and he has power to sell or exchange the settled land or any part of it with an adjustment of any difference in value in the case of exchange. He may grant leases subject to certain restrictions, but in the absence of a contrary provision in the settlement, he has no power to mortgage or charge the legal estate for his own benefit, although he can mortgage or assign his own beneficial life interest.

He has other powers which he can only exercise with the consent of the settlement trustees or the court, e.g. the power to sell or otherwise dispose of the principal mansion house, the power to cut and sell timber, the power to compromise claims and sell settled chattels. He has the power to make improvements at his own expense, or the cost may be borne by the capital money if he complies with the provisions of the Act. He has also power to select investments for capital money.

The tenant for life is in a strong position, for he is subject to no control in the exercise of his powers except that he must give notice to the trustees of his intention to exercise the most important ones, he must obtain the consent of the trustees or leave of the court in certain cases, and he is in fact himself a trustee for the other beneficiaries. There may be joint tenants for life under a settlement and, where this is so, they must usually agree as to the exercise of their joint powers. The court will exercise a power, e.g. by ordering a sale of property, but only if the joint tenant who does not agree to sell is acting in bad faith. (*Barker* v. *Addiscott*, [1969] 3 All E.R. 685.)

It is clear that under a settlement a proper balance must be preserved between the tenant for life and the persons who will be entitled to the land or the proceeds of the land after his death. He is not allowed, therefore, to run down the estate during his lifetime in order to increase his own income, but is only allowed to take from the land the current income and must pass on the estate substantially unimpaired.

Trusts for Sale. A trust for sale is an immediate binding trust for sale whether or not exercisable at the request or with the consent of any person, and with or without a power at discretion to postpone the sale. Such a trust for sale may be either express or by operation of law. Trusts for sale are governed by the Law of Property Act, 1925, and not by the Settled Land Act, 1925.

An express trust for sale is almost always created by two documents —a conveyance on trust for sale and a trust instrument. But even where a trust for sale is embodied in a single document, a purchaser of the legal estate is not concerned with the trusts affecting the rents and profits of the land until sale, or with the proceeds of the sale.

There are cases where a trust for sale is imposed by statute. These are—

(*a*) where a person dies intestate,

(*b*) where two or more persons are entitled to land as joint tenants or tenants in common,

(*c*) where trustees lend money on mortgage and the property becomes vested in them free from the right of redemption.

It should, of course, be borne in mind that in addition to settlements deliberately created as such the setting up of an entailed or life interest *automatically creates a settlement*. Thus each of the following limitations will create a settlement—

(*a*) "to A for life;"
(*b*) "to A in tail;"
(*c*) "to A for life, remainder to B in tail."

In each of these cases A is the tenant for life as defined by Sects. 19 and 20 of the Settled Land Act, 1925. (In effect these two sections provide that generally a person entitled to possession under the settlement is the tenant for life.) In each of the above cases the legal estate will be conveyed to A by a vesting deed and A will hold the legal estate on the limitations or trusts set out in the trust instrument, i.e. for himself for life or in tail, or for himself for life with remainder for B in tail.

CO-OWNERSHIP

Two persons may own land simultaneously. In such a case they are either joint tenants or tenants in common. Where they are joint tenants there is no question of a share of the property—each is the owner of the whole. Where there is a tenancy in common, each is regarded as owning an individual share in the property, but that share has not positively been marked out. Tenants in common hold property in undivided shares.

A joint tenancy arises where land is conveyed to two or more persons and no words of severance are used. A tenancy in common arises when there are words of severance. Thus a conveyance "to A and B" would create a joint tenancy, whilst a conveyance "to A and B equally" would create a tenancy in common. The right of survivorship or *jus accrescendi* is a distinguishing feature of joint tenancies, and upon the death of one joint tenant, his share in the property passes to the survivors until there is only one person left and he becomes the sole owner of the property. The *jus accrescendi* does not apply to tenancies in common and such a tenant may dispose of his share by will.

Both types of co-ownership have advantages and disadvantages. The *jus accrescendi* as applied to joint tenancies prevents too many interests being created in the land, because a joint tenant cannot leave any part of the property by will and so the number of interests decreases. When the land is sold the number of signatures on the conveyance will not be excessive. On the other hand joint tenancies are unfair in that eventual sole ownership depends merely on survival. Where there is a tenancy in common, each tenant can leave his interest by will possibly by dividing it between two or more persons, thus the number of interests increases and on sale many interests must be got in.

The common law preferred the joint tenancy, but Equity preferred the tenancy in common and would in certain circumstances treat persons as tenants in common rather than joint tenants regardless of words of severance. For instance, where two persons lend money on mortgage, Equity regards them as tenants in common of the interest in the land subject to the mortgage; also where joint purchasers of land put up the purchase money in unequal shares; and in the case of partnership land, the partners are treated as tenants in common in Equity.

The Law of Property Act, 1925, has combined the best features of both types of co-ownership by providing that where land is owned by two or more persons they, or the first four of them if there are more than four, should be treated as holding the legal estate as trustees and joint tenants, for the benefit of themselves and other co-owners (if any) in Equity. Thus a purchaser of the property is never required to get more than four signatures on the conveyance, and the trusts attach to the purchase money for the benefit of the co-owners. The statutory trusts on which the property is held are: to sell the property with power to postpone the sale; and to hold the proceeds of sale, and the rents and profits until sale, for those benefically entitled under the trust.

It should be noted that although the provisions set out in the above paragraph deal with the problems which formerly arose in conveying land which was in joint ownership, *it is still possible to create a joint tenancy in both the land and the proceeds of sale*. Where such a joint tenancy exists the *jus accrescendi* will apply to the equitable interests of the joint tenants in the proceeds of sale, unless there has been a severance of the joint tenancy since the creation of the estate. Severance is possible under Sect. 36 (2) of the Law of Property Act, 1925, which provides that—

> . . . where a legal estate (not being settled land) is vested in joint tenants beneficially, and any tenant desires to sever the joint tenancy in Equity, he shall give to the other joint tenants a notice in writing of such desire or do such other acts or things as would, in the case of personal estate, have been effective to sever the tenancy in Equity, and thereupon under the trust for sale affecting the land the net proceeds of sale, and the net rents and profits until sale, shall be held upon the trusts which would have been requisite for giving effect to the beneficial interest if there had been an actual severance.

A notice of severance may be regarded as properly served if sent by post even if it not received by the addressee. (*Re 88 Berkeley Road, London N.W.*9; *Rickwood* v. *Turnsek*, [1971] 1 All E.R. 254.)

Severance of a joint tenancy may, as provided by Sect. 36 (2), be effected other than by giving notice. (*Re Draper's Conveyance*, 1967.)[550]

A LEASEHOLD OR A TERM OF YEARS

The major characteristics of a term of years are that the lessee is given exclusive possession of the land and that the period for which the term is to endure is fixed and definite. It is open to the parties to decide whether their agreement shall be a lease or licence, though the words used by the parties are not conclusive. If there is no right to exclusive possession then there is a mere licence and not a lease. (*Shell-Mex* v. *Manchester Garages*, 1971.)[551] For example, a guest in a hotel does not normally have a lease, because the proprietor retains general control over the room.

The Duration of Leases. Leases may be for a fixed period of time, and in this case the commencement and termination of the lease must be ascertainable before the lease takes effect. Thus a lease "for the life of X" would not come under this heading. A lease may be for an indefinite period in the sense that it is to end when the lessor or lessee gives notice. Even so such an arrangement would operate as a valid lease, since the duration of the term can be made certain by the parties giving notice.

In the absence of agreement, the period of a lease may be determined by reference to the payment of rent. Thus if a person takes possession of the premises with the owner's consent for an indefinite period, but the owner accepts rent paid say weekly, monthly, quarterly or annually, then the term may be based on that period, though from early times there has been a presumption that the payment and acceptance of rent shows an intention to create a yearly tenancy but not if the rent is received by mistake. (*Legal and General Assurance Society* v. *General Metal Agencies*, 1969.)[161] A yearly tenancy requires half a year's notice to terminate it if there has been no agreement on the matter. Other periodical tenancies, in the absence of agreement, are determined by notice for the full period. Even where there has been a definite term, a periodical tenancy can arise. Where X is granted a lease of twenty-one years and stays on after the expiration of that term with the owner's consent, then there is a new implied term based on the period of payment of rent.

However, where the tenant is permitted to stay in possession on the understanding that there are to be negotiations for a new lease there is a *tenancy at will*.

A *tenancy at will* may also arise *by agreement* where a person takes possession of property with the owner's consent, the arrangement being that the term can be brought to an end by either party giving notice. If there is no agreement as to rent, the tenancy can become a periodical tenancy if the tenant pays and the owner accepts rent paid at given periods of time. A tenancy at will may also arise *by implication* from the conduct of the parties. For example, a prospective purchaser of land who is allowed to take possession before completion occupies the property as a tenant at will until completion.

Where a tenant stays on after the expiration of his term without the consent of the owner, there is a *tenancy by sufferance*. No rent is payable under such a tenancy, but the tenant must compensate the owner by a payment in respect of the use and occupation of the land. This compensation is referred to as *mesne profits*. Such a tenancy can be brought to an end at any time, though it may become a periodical tenancy if the owner accepts a payment of rent at given intervals of time.

It should be noted that the law bases the duration of a periodic tenancy on the intervals of time at which the rent has been paid and accepted, on the ground that this is evidence of the parties' intention. If there is other evidence of intention, then the court will also take this into account, e.g. there may be a prior lease which negatives the intention to create the sort of periodic tenancy which the payment of rent suggests.

Creation of Leases. Leases are normally created by a document under seal. However, where the lease is not to exceed three years, a written or oral lease will suffice, so long as the lease takes effect in possession at once at the best rent obtainable. Where a tenancy is in excess of three years then, if the agreement is not under seal, it will operate at common law as a yearly tenancy if the tenant enters into possession and pays rent on a yearly basis, i.e. by reference to a year, even if the rent is paid in quarterly instalments.

The position in Equity is rather different. In Equity, if a person has entered into an agreement for a lease but has no document under seal, then, if he has entered and paid rent or carried out repairs, i.e. if there is a sufficient act of part performance, Equity will insist that the owner of the property execute a formal lease under seal. The equitable maxim, "Equity looks upon that as done which ought to be done," applies. This principle is known as the Rule in *Walsh* v. *Lonsdale,* 1882.[552]

It may seem that this rule makes an agreement for a lease as effective as a lease under seal, and certainly, as between the parties to the agreement, absence of a seal is not vital.

However, the rights of the tenant under the rule are equitable and not legal rights, and the tenant can be turned out by a third party to whom the landlord sells the legal estate, if the third party purchases the property for value and without notice of the existence of the lease.

Nevertheless, since the property legislation of 1925, the tenant can register the agreement as an Estate Contract, and, once the agreement is so registered, all subsequent purchasers of the legal estate are deemed to have notice of the lease and are bound to honour it. (See further, p. 328.)

Rights and Liabilities of Landlord and Tenant. The rights and liabilities of the parties depend largely upon the lease though a landlord has a special right at common law to distrain for rent, i.e. to move in on the tenant's personal property and remove it for sale to satisfy the amount owing for rent. Where the lease is by deed, the deed will usually fix the rights and liabilities by express clauses which are called covenants. Certain covenants are also implied by law where there is no provision in the lease. The most usual express covenants are covenants to pay rent, covenants regarding repairs and renewals, and a covenant that the tenant will not assign or sub-let. The following covenants are implied where appropriate. The landlord covenants that he will not disturb the tenant's quiet enjoyment of the property, or make the use or enjoyment of the land difficult or impossible, i.e. the landlord undertakes not to *derogate from the grant*. In the case of furnished houses, the landlord covenants that the property is fit for human habitation, and under the Housing Act, 1957, Sect. 6., where any house was let before 6th July, 1957, at a rent of £40 or less in London or £26 or less elsewhere, or where any house was let on or after 6th July, 1957, at a rent of £80 or less in London or £52 or less elsewhere, there is an implied condition that the premises are fit for human habitation at the time of letting, and will be maintained in that state. Tenants whose rent is in excess of the amounts laid down by the Act of 1957 may be able to take advantage of the implied covenants in Sect. 32 of the Housing Act, 1961, which requires the lessor to keep in repair the structure and exterior of the dwelling house, including drains, gutters and external pipes. The Act applies only to the lease of a dwelling house for a term of less than seven years granted on or after 24th October, 1961. The following tenant's covenants are implied by Law: a covenant to pay rent, rates and certain taxes, and to repair. The tenant must in general keep the premises wind- and water-tight, and must not commit waste, i.e. he must not do deliberate damage to the premises.

The Leasehold Reform Act, 1967. The main purpose of this legislation was to deal with the problems caused by the imminent expiration of the leases of many old houses, the problem being particularly acute in South Wales. Many leaseholders were faced with two alternatives—

(i) to be evicted; or
(ii) to buy the freehold, often at a price which they could not afford.

The Act has important commercial implications because—

(i) there are large leasehold estates in many English cities and towns and banks and other business organisations such as building societies and insurance companies are mortgagees of some of these properties;
(ii) banks and other business organisations may be approached with regard to lending money to a leaseholder to enable him to purchase the freehold of his property.

Under the provisions of the act (as amended), occupants of leasehold houses are *offered the right either to buy the freehold, or to have the lease extended by fifty years*, provided the following conditions are satisfied—

(i) the lease must be of the *whole house*, though the Act still applies where there has been sub-letting (it does not, however, apply to leaseholders of maisonettes or flats). However, the lessee of a house divided into flats will be entitled to buy the freehold of the whole house so long as he lives in one of the flats. The same applies if a leasehold house consists of a shop with a flat above so long as the lease includes the whole house and the lessee lives in the flat. It does not matter that part is used for business purposes. (*Lake* v. *Bennett,* [1970] 1 All E.R. 457.)

(ii) the rateable value of the house must not exceed £200 (£400 in Greater London). (Sect. 1 (1).) This means, in effect, that expensive houses are excluded.

(iii) the lease must have been granted for a term of more than twenty-one years (Sects 1 (1) and 3 (1));

(iv) the house must have been occupied by the leaseholder as his main or only residence for the last five years or for periods amounting to five years in the last ten years (Sect. 1 (1) and (2));

(v) the yearly ground rent must not amount to more than two-thirds of the annual rateable value of the whole house. In London, this would be £260 per annum and £133 per annum elsewhere.

RIGHT TO PURCHASE FREEHOLD (i.e. ENFRANCHISE). A leaseholder who wishes to buy the freehold must give notice to the freeholder who will arrange for the property to be surveyed at the expense of the lease-holder. (Sect. 9 (4).) Notice must be served before the existing lease comes to an end, otherwise the existing leaseholder loses his rights under the Act. The form of notice is somewhat complicated and has given rise to a number of cases in Court. The advice of a solicitor should be sought.

The price of the freehold depends solely upon the value of the land on which the house stands. The value of the house itself is not taken into account. The site value is also diminished because the freeholder has to wait for possession for the remainder of the existing lease and notionally for a further fifty years.

Where the leaseholder and freeholder cannot agree on a price ascertained on the above assumptions, the Lands Tribunal will settle the matter. (Sect. 21 (1).) The prices fixed by the Tribunal have varied between £300 and £1,000.

RIGHT TO EXTEND THE LEASE. A fifty-year extension of the lease involves the payment of a revised ground rent from the time when the extended term begins. (Sect. 14.) The revised ground rent must represent the letting value of the site for the uses to which the property has been put since the beginning of the existing tenancy, nothing being included for the value of buildings on the site. (Sect. 15.)

If the parties cannot reach agreement the rent will be fixed by the Lands Tribunal (Sect. 21 (1)), and the new rent, whether fixed by agreement or otherwise, may be reviewed and revised after twenty-five years if the freehold owner so wishes. (Sect. 15 (2).)

The effect of the above provisions is likely to be a substantial increase in ground rent. It should also be noted that the right to buy the freehold is lost when the original lease expires and the right to purchase the freehold cannot be exercised at any time during the extension. (Sect. 16 (1).)

Where the leaseholder has died before taking advantage of this Act, his widow or other member of his family who was living with the leaseholder for more than five years before his death need not wait a further five years but may buy the freehold as soon as he or she inherits the lease. Furthermore, it does not matter if one of two joint lessees does not live in the house. This is especially useful to a wife who is not living with her husband if the lease is in their joint names.

In practice it is better to buy the freehold than to seek an extension of the lease. A tenant can lose the extended lease if a landlord can prove that he wants to develop the property. The tenant would receive compensation for the loss of his lease but would lose his home.

SERVITUDES

Servitudes are rights over the property of another and may be either *easements* or *profits à prendre*.

Easements. An easement may be defined as a right to use or restrict the use of the land of another person in some way. There are various classes of easements and these include—

    (*a*) rights of way,
    (*b*) rights of light,
    (*c*) rights to abstract water,
    (*d*) rights to the support of buildings.

To be valid an easement must satisfy the following conditions—

1. THERE MUST BE A DOMINANT AND SERVIENT TENEMENT. The land in respect of which, and for the benefit of which, the easement exists is called the dominant tenement, and the land over which the right is exercised is called the servient tenement. A valid easement cannot exist "in gross," i.e. without reference to the holding of land (*Hill* v. *Tupper*, 1863),[553] and the grant of a right of way over his land by a landowner to be exercised by the grantee personally, and without reference to any land capable of deriving benefit from the right of way, is merely a licence and not an easement.

2. THE EASEMENT MUST ACCOMMODATE THE DOMINANT TENEMENT. The easement must confer some benefit on the land itself so as to make it a better and more convenient property; it is not enough that the owner obtains some personal advantage. A right of way over contiguous land generally benefits the dominant tenement, and an easement can exist even where two tenements do not actually adjoin, provided it is clear that the easement benefits the dominant tenement.

3. THE DOMINANT TENEMENT AND THE SERVIENT TENEMENT MUST NOT BE BOTH OWNED AND OCCUPIED BY THE SAME PERSON. Thus, if P owns both Blackacre and Whiteacre and habitually walks over Blackacre to reach Whiteacre, he is not exercising a right of way in respect of Blackacre, but merely walking from one part of his land to another. For this rule to apply, P must have simultaneously both ownership and possession of the two properties concerned. It is not enough that he owns the two if they are leased to different tenants, or that he be tenant of both if they are owned by different owners.

4. THE EASEMENT MUST BE CAPABLE OF FORMING THE SUBJECT OF A GRANT. This means that the right must be sufficiently definite. (*Bass* v. *Gregory*, 1890.)[554] There must be a capable grantor and a capable grantee, and the right must be within the general nature of the rights capable of existing as easements. An easement is a right to use or restrict the use of a neighbour's land which should not normally involve him in doing any work or spending any money, though in *Crow* v. *Wood*, 1970,[555] the Court of Appeal recognised an easement of fencing.

The categories of easements are not closed and new rights have from time to time been recognised as easements (*Re Ellenborough Park*, 1956),[556] though in general the courts are still reluctant to extend the categories. (*Phipps* v. *Pears*, 1965.)[557]

Profits à prendre. A profit à prendre is the right to take something of legal value from the land of another, e.g. shooting, fishing, and grazing rights; the right to cut turf or take wood for fuel. The exception is a right to take water from a stream which is treated as an easement because running water cannot be privately owned and is not therefore a thing of legal value.

A profit necessarily involves a servient tenement but there may or may not be a dominant tenement, for a profit can exist *in gross*. A profit may be a several profit, where enjoyment is granted to an individual as is often the case with shooting and fishing rights; or a profit may be in common which may be enjoyed by more than one person, as is often the case with grazing rights and the right to take various materials for use as fuel.

Acquisition of Servitudes. Servitudes may be acquired (*a*) by Statute, (*b*) by Express or Implied grant, (*c*) by Prescription.

Easements created by statute are usually in connection with local Acts of Parliament.

When land is sold, a servitude may be expressly reserved in favour of another tenement of the seller, or may be expressly granted in similar circumstances by deed; and under the Law of Property Act, 1925, Sect. 62, a conveyance, if there is no contrary express intention operates to convey servitudes appertaining to the land conveyed. (*Crow* v. *Wood*, 1970.)[555]

Where an owner of two plots conveys one of them, then certain easements are implied. These are *easements of necessity*, as where the piece of land would be completely surrounded and inaccessible without a right of way; *intended easements*, which would be necessary to carry out the common intentions of the parties; *ancillary easements*, which would be necessary in view of the right granted, as the grant of the use of water implies the right of way to reach the water. Where part of a tenement is granted, then the grantee acquires easements over the land which are continuous and apparent, are necessary to the reasonable enjoyment of the land granted, and have been and are used by the grantor for the benefit of the part granted. (*Ward* v. *Kirkland*, 1966.)[558] An example of this is a window enjoying light.

Prescription. Prescription may be based on a presumed grant or alternatively may be established by user as of right.

Prescription at common law depended on user since time immemorial, which at law means since 1189. Clearly in most cases it is out of the question to show continuous user for this period, and so the courts were prepared to accept twenty years' continuous user as raising the presumption of a grant. This presumption may be rebutted by showing that at some time since 1189 the right could not exist, and it follows that an easement of light cannot be claimed by prescription at common law in a building erected since 1189. This serious difficulty was met in part by the presumption of a lost modern grant, and juries were told that if there had been user during living memory or even for twenty years, they might presume a lost grant or deed, and this ultimately became mandatory, even though neither judge nor jury had any belief that such instrument had ever existed. (*Tehidy Minerals* v. *Norman*, 1971.)[559]

The position is now clear under the Prescription Act, 1832, which was passed to deal with the difficulties arising under the common law. Under this Act, which supplements the common law, we must distinguish easements other than light from easements of light and easements from profits.

(*a*) EASEMENTS OTHER THAN LIGHT. Twenty years' uninterrupted user as of right will establish an easement. User as of right means *nec vi, nec clam, nec precario,* i.e. without force, stealth or permission. If the owner of the so-called servient tenement can prove that he has given verbal permission, i.e. that the easement is *precario,* then it cannot be claimed. Nevertheless forty years' similar user will establish the easement, and in this case, if the owner of the servient tenement wishes to prove that the right was exercised by permission, he must produce a written agreement to that effect.

(*b*) EASEMENTS OF LIGHT. These can be established by twenty years' user, the defences being that the owner of the servient tenement gave permission and that there is a deed or written agreement to this effect, or that the owner of the servient tenement interrupted the enjoyment of the right for a continuous period of a year by erecting something which blocked the light. Under the Rights of Light Act, 1959, it is no longer necessary to erect something of this nature; the owner of the servient land may now register on the local land charges register a statutory notice indicating where he would have put up a screen, and this operates as if the access of light had been restricted for one year. User as of right is not necessary, and oral consent will not bar the claim even if the claimant has made regular money payments for the use of the right.

The right can only be claimed having regard to the type of room affected. A bedroom does not require the amount of light that other rooms do, and if the claimant has used the bedroom to repair watches for twenty years, he will still only be able to claim that amount of light appropriate to a bedroom. There is no right to receive unlimited light but in *Ough* v. *King*, [1967] 3 All E.R. 859, the Court of Appeal held that in determining whether there was an infringement of a right to light regard must be had to the nature of the locality and to the higher standard of lighting required in modern times. There is no claim to a view or a prospect which can be seen from a window.

(*c*) PROFITS A PRENDRE. The general period for prescription here is thirty years under the Act of 1832, though twenty years is enough if the Court is presuming a lost modern grant. (*Tehidy Minerals* v. *Norman*, 1971.)[559]

If an easement is denied or threatened, it would be necessary to ask the court for an injunction to prevent the owner of the servient tenement from acting contrary to the easement, and its existence would have to be proved under one of the headings given above. The court may then—

(*a*) find the easement not proved; or

(*b*) grant an injunction to restrain the owner of the servient tenement from acting contrary to it; or

(*c*) if the infringement is not serious the court may award once for all damages, in which case the servient owner will have bought his right to act contrary to the easement.

Termination or Extinguishment of Servitudes. Servitudes may be extinguished by statute, or by express or implied release. At law a deed is necessary for express release, but in Equity an informal release will be effective if it would be inequitable for the dominant owner to claim that the right still exists.

If the dominant owner shows by his conduct an intention to release an easement, it will be extinguished. The demolition of a house to which an easement of light attaches may amount to an implied release, but not if it is intended to replace the house by another building. Mere non-user is not enough, although it may be some evidence of intention to abandon the right. (*Tehidy Minerals* v. *Norman*, 1971.)[559] There is no fixed time but twenty years' non-user usually constitutes abandonment.

We have already seen that an easement is extinguished when the dominant and servient tenements come into simultaneous ownership and possession of the same person, since a man cannot have an easement over his own land.

RESTRICTIVE COVENANTS

A restrictive covenant is essentially a contract between two owners of land whereby one agrees to restrict the use of his land for the benefit of the other. We are not concerned here with covenants in leases, which are governed by separate rules already outlined.

Such covenants were not adequately enforced by the common law because the doctrine of privity of contract applied, and as soon as one of the parties to the covenant transferred his land, the covenant was not enforceable by the transferee because he had not been a party to the original contract. However, the common law realised that this was rather too rigid and went so far as to allow a transferee to enforce the benefit of the covenant against the original party to it. Thus if A, the owner of Blackacre, agreed with B, the owner of Whiteacre, that he would not use Blackacre for the purposes of trade, then if B sold Whiteacre to C, C could enforce the covenant against A. However, if A sold Blackacre to D, C could not enforce the covenant against D, because the common law would not allow D to bear the burden of a covenant he did not make.

Equity takes a different view, and allows C to enforce the sort of covenant outlined above by injunction, if the following conditions are fulfilled—

(i) THE COVENANT MUST BE SUBSTANTIALLY NEGATIVE. Much depends upon the words used in the covenant, and an undertaking which seems *prima facie* to be positive may imply a negative undertaking and this may then be enforced. (*Tulk* v. *Moxhay*, 1848.)[118] A covenant to use a house as a dwelling house implies that it will not be used for other purposes, and would be enforceable in the negative sense. If the covenant requires the covenantor to spend money, it is not a negative covenant.

(ii) THE COVENANT MUST BENEFIT THE LAND. It is often said that the covenant must "touch and concern" the land and must not be merely for the personal benefit of the claimant. Restrictive covenants usually endeavour to keep up the residential character of the district and benefit the land by preserving value and amenities as a residential property.

(iii) THE PERSON CLAIMING THE BENEFIT MUST RETAIN LAND WHICH CAN BENEFIT FROM THE COVENANT TAKEN. (*Kelly* v. *Barrett*, 1924.)[560] If X owns a piece of land which he splits up into two plots, selling one plot to Y and taking a restrictive covenant in favour of the plot he has retained, then he can enforce the covenant so long as he retains the land to be benefited. If X now sells the plot he had retained, he will not be able to enforce the covenant for the future, although the purchaser from X will be able to do so.

There is an exception to this rule in the case of *building schemes* involving an estate of houses. Here the covenants are taken by the owner of the land from each person purchasing a house, and although the owner does not retain any of the land, the covenants may be enforced by the purchasers as between themselves. However, a building scheme will not be implied simply because there is a common vendor and the existence of common covenants. It was at one time thought that there must be a defined area and evidence of laying out in lots (*Re Wembley Park Estate Co. Ltd's Transfer*, [1968] 1 All E.R. 457). However, in *Re Dolphin's Conveyance*, [1970] 2 All E.R. 664, Stamp, J., held that so long as the covenants held in the conveyances were, as a matter of construction, intended to give the purchasers of the parcels mutual rights, this was sufficient to make them enforceable and there was no need, in particular, to consider lotting.

Since restrictive covenants are in general enforceable only in Equity, the question of notice arises. So if X sells a piece of land which is subject to a covenant to a purchaser who has no notice of the covenant, the purchaser is not bound. However, it is now possible to register restrictive covenants under the Land Charges Act and this operates as notice to all purchasers. Under Sect. 84 of the Law of Property Act, 1925 (as amended by Sect. 28(6) of the Law of Property Act, 1969), the Lands Tribunal has power, on the application of any person interested, to discharge or modify a restrictive covenant.

THE TRANSFER OF LAND

It is usual, when a disposition of land is contemplated, to draw up a contract. For a contract of sale to be valid both parties must have contractual capacity, the contract must be legal, there must be clear agreement on all the essential terms, and acceptance of the offer must be unconditional. Where one accepts an offer to sell "subject to contract," no contract is effected until a formal contract is approved.

Under Sect. 40 of the Law of Property Act, 1925, it is provided that no action may be brought upon any contract for the sale or other disposition of land, or any interest in land, unless the agreement upon which such action is brought, or some memorandum or note thereof, is in writing and signed by the party to be charged or some other person lawfully authorised. In the absence of a note or memorandum the contract is unenforceable, though the equitable doctrine of part performance may sometimes be invoked.

When a valid contract for sale exists, the purchaser acquires an equitable interest in the property and the vendor is in effect a qualified trustee for him. Thus if the property increases in value between contract and completion, the purchaser is entitled to the increase and similarly he must bear any loss. This is particularly important in cases where property is destroyed by fire between contract and completion, since the purchaser would still have to pay the purchase money, even although he only received a conveyance of the land with the useless buildings on it. It is now provided by Sect. 47 of the Law of Property Act, 1925, that in such a case the purchaser may become entitled to money payable on an insurance policy maintained by the vendor.

The vendor has a lien on the property sold to the extent of the unpaid purchase money and may enforce this by an order for sale; this lien may be registered as a general equitable charge. The purchaser has a similar lien in respect of money paid under the contract prior to conveyance.

On a sale of land it is usual to use a standard form of contract prepared by The Law Society since this saves much trouble in drafting. In what is called an open contract for the sale of land the vendor must under Sect. 23 of the Law of Property Act, 1969, show a title for at least fifteen years, beginning with a good "root of title," i.e. a document dealing with the whole legal and equitable interests in the land. It may be necessary to go back more than fifteen years in order to find such a document. The vendor prepares an abstract of title, listing all the relevant documents in connection with its establishment, and he must produce these documents in order to justify the abstract of title he has prepared. It should be noted that all the above matters are attended to by the parties' solicitors.

A contract for the sale of land will normally contain a completion date which is the time by which the transaction must be concluded. The transfer of land involves the following stages—

(*a*) The preparation of the contract.

(*b*) The exchange of contracts between the vendor's and purchaser's solicitors, when the purchaser pays a deposit, usually ten per cent of the purchase money.

(*c*) The delivery by the vendor's solicitors of an abstract of title.

(*d*) The examination of this title by the purchaser's solicitors and the checking of the abstract against the actual deeds to see that it is correct.

(*e*) After all outstanding queries have been solved, a conveyance is prepared by the purchaser's solicitors which is sent to the vendor's solicitors for approval. The draft conveyance may be exchanged a number of times before agreement is reached. Where the land is registered, a simpler form of transfer deed is used.

(*f*) Just before completion the purchaser's solicitors will make the necessary searches in the Land Charges Register and in the Register maintained by the appropriate local authority to see what encumbrances are registered in respect of the property.

(*g*) An appointment is then arranged for completion and the purchaser hands over the money, the vendor handing over the conveyance, which he has signed, together with the title deeds. This brings the transaction to a conclusion.

PERSONAL PROPERTY

We have already mentioned that personal property is divided into two classes—*choses in action* and *choses in possession*, the latter being divided into *chattels real* (i.e. leaseholds) and *chattels personal*. We have already dealt with leaseholds, and the sale of chattels personal has been codified by the Sale of Goods Act, 1893, a study of which would not be appropriate to a book of this nature. The assignment of choses in action will now be dealt with.

ASSIGNMENTS

The common law does not recognise assignments of choses in action, but Equity does and so does statute.

1. **Assignment by Act of Parties.** There are four possible categories—

(*a*) A LEGAL ASSIGNMENT OF A LEGAL CHOSE UNDER SECT. 136 OF THE LAW OF PROPERTY ACT, 1925. (This provision was originally contained in the Judicature Act, 1873.) To be effective such an assignment, e.g. the goodwill of a business, must be absolute and not partial; must be in writing signed by the assignor; and must be notified in writing to the debtor, generally by the assignee. If the above requirements are complied with, the assignee can sue the debtor without making the assignor a party to the action. Failure to give notice to the debtor means that there is no legal assignment; the debtor can validly pay the assignor, and the assignee is liable to be postponed to a later assignee for value who notifies the debtor. However, it is not necessary for the date of the assignment to be given in the notice of assignment as long as the letter, or other form of written notice, states clearly that there has been an assignment and identifies the assignee. *Van Lynn Developments Ltd.* v. *Pelias Construction Co. Ltd, The Times*, 10th October, 1968.

(*b*) EQUITABLE ASSIGNMENTS OF LEGAL CHOSES.

(*c*) EQUITABLE ASSIGNMENTS OF EQUITABLE CHOSES.

The difference between a legal and an equitable chose is historical in that an equitable chose is a right which, before 1875, could only be enforced in the Court of Chancery, e.g. the interest of a beneficiary under a trust fund.

In equitable assignments of legal choses the assignor must be made a party in any action against the debtor, but if the chose is equitable this is not necessary. No particular form is required; all that is necessary is evidence of intention to assign. Notice should be given to the debtor or the trustees, as the case may be, in order to preserve priority as outlined above.

Thus the transfer of a debt by word of mouth, although invalid under statute, may nevertheless be good and enforceable in Equity.

(*d*) EQUITABLE ASSIGNMENTS OF MERE EXPECTANCIES. These are mere hopes of future entitlement, e.g. a legacy under the will of a living testator. The rules regarding such assignments are the same as those set out in (*b*) and (*c*) above, but no notice to the debtor can be given because there is none. Value is not needed for assignments within Sect. 136 of the Law of Property Act, 1925, or for equitable assignments of equitable choses in action. It is probably not needed for an equitable assignment of a legal chose, though the position is not clear. Value is needed for the assignment of mere expectancies; a document under seal is not enough. Value is also needed to support an agreement to assign an equitable chose, but if the assignee lawfully takes delivery of the property assigned, the assignor cannot recover it.

Assignments are said to be "subject to equities"; the person to whom the right is assigned takes it subject to any right of set off which was available against the original assignor. So if X assigns to Z a debt of £10 due from Y, and X also owes Y £5, then in any action brought by Z for the money, Y can set off the debt of £5. But the assignee is not subject to purely personal claims which would have been available against the assignor, e.g. damages for fraud, though the remedy of rescission is available against the assignee where the assignor obtained the contract by fraud.

Assignments of certain choses in action are governed by special statutes so that the rules outlined above do not apply. In such cases the special statute must be complied with. Examples are—

(*a*) Bills of Exchange and Promissory Notes—Bills of Exchange Act, 1882.

(*b*) Shares in companies registered under the Companies Act, 1948, and previous Acts—The Companies Act, 1948.

(*c*) Policies of Life Assurance—Policies of Assurance Act, 1867.

Rights of a personal nature under a contract cannot be assigned. If X contracts to write newspaper articles for a certain newspaper, it cannot assign its rights under the contract to another. The right to recover damages in litigation cannot be assigned, for reasons of public policy. Liabilities under a contract cannot be assigned; the party to benefit cannot be compelled by mere notice to accept the performance of another, though a liability can be transferred by a novation (a new contract), if the party to benefit agrees.

2. Assignment by Operation of Law. The involuntary assignment of rights and liabilities arises in the case of death and bankruptcy.

(i) DEATH. The personal representatives of the deceased acquire his rights and liabilities, the latter to the extent of the estate. Contracts of personal service are discharged.

(ii) BANKRUPTCY. The trustee in bankruptcy has vested in him all the rights of the bankrupt, except for actions of a purely personal nature which in no way affect the value of the estate, e.g. actions for defamation. The trustee is liable to the extent of the estate for the bankrupt's liabilities, though the trustee has a right to disclaim onerous or unprofitable contracts.

NEGOTIABLE INSTRUMENTS

To rank as a negotiable instrument, a document must be recognised as such either by statute, or by the custom of merchants (*Goodwin* v. *Robarts*, 1875)[10] arising out of the Law Merchant (*Crouch* v. *Credit Foncier of England*, 1873),[11] and accepted as valid by the courts.

The major characteristics of a negotiable instrument are as follows—

(*a*) The rights represented by the instrument are transferable merely by delivering it to another, though bills made payable to order require indorsement.

(*b*) Unlike the assignee of an ordinary contractual right, the transferee of a negotiable instrument does not take subject to equities, and he is not affected by defects in the title of his predecessor provided he is what is known as a *holder in due course*.

(*c*) The acceptor of a bill of exchange, or the banker in the case of a cheque, is under a duty to pay the *holder for the time being* of the instrument. So, upon transfer of the instrument, there is no need to notify the acceptor or the banker of a change of ownership, as there is on a legal assignment of other choses in action under the Law of Property Act, 1925.

(*d*) The holder of a bill of exchange can sue upon it in his own name. This can be done with a legal assignment, but not with an equitable one.

Types of Instrument. The most important negotiable instruments are bills of exchange, promissory notes and cheques, and these three types are the subject-matter of the Bills of Exchange Act, 1882. Nevertheless, certain other instruments are negotiable namely—

(1) TREASURY BILLS, i.e. bills issued by the British Government subject to the provisions of the Treasury Bills Act, 1877, amended by the National Debt Act, 1889, and by subsequent regulations.

(2) SHARE WARRANTS, if they are to bearer but not otherwise.

(3) DIVIDEND WARRANTS.

(4) BONDS issued by English companies are negotiable if payable to *bearer*, and bonds issued by a foreign government, or indeed by a foreign corporation, may be negotiable if they are negotiable in the country of issue and also negotiable by custom in England.

(5) DEBENTURES payable to bearer.

(6) BEARER SCRIP, e.g. where debentures or debenture stock are allotted under terms that they shall be paid for by instalments provisional bearer scrip certificates may be issued to subscribers to be exchanged for proper debentures or stock certificates when all instalments have been paid.

Postal orders, money orders, I.O.U.s, Share Certificates and Share Transfers are not negotiable instruments, nor is a bill of lading.

THE BILLS OF EXCHANGE ACT, 1882

The law relating to bills of exchange has been codified in the Bills of Exchange Act, 1882, and *all section references on this subject are to this Act unless otherwise indicated.*

The Nature of a Bill of Exchange. A bill of exchange is an unconditional order in writing, addressed by one person to another, signed by the person giving it, requiring the person to whom it is addressed to pay on demand, or at a fixed or determinable future time, a sum certain in money to, or to the order of, a specified person, or to bearer. (Bills of Exchange Act, 1882, Sect. 3.)

The example on p. 296 is a bill of exchange which is addressed by Richard Brown to G. Green, and requires him to pay £400 to J. White, or his order, six months after the date of the bill which is 1st January, 1972. Richard Brown is called the *drawer*, G. Green is called the *drawee*, and J. White is called the *payee*.

The Advantages of a Bill of Exchange. Before proceeding to discuss in detail the law relating to Bills of Exchange it is worth examining why they are used at all.

(1) **A bill of exchange provides a creditor with a better remedy.** Once a bill of exchange has been accepted, it settles the amount of the debt owing, and makes a legal remedy easier to obtain than would be the case under an ordinary contract.

(2) **Bills of exchange may be discounted.** Thus anybody who holds the bill, and is entitled to claim the money on the due date, can discount the bill by taking it to a bank or discounting house. The bank will, in many cases, be willing to take the bill off the holder's hands, pay the holder the present value of the bill and collect the money when due.

(3) **A bill may be negotiated.** Anyone who holds a bill of exchange can transfer it to a creditor in payment and White could, if he chose, use the bill in this manner to settle a debt with Gray.

THE PARTIES

The parties to the bill are Brown, the *drawer*; Green, the *drawee*; and White, the *payee*. If Green signs the bill he becomes the *acceptor*, and if White indorses the bill over to Gray, White becomes an *indorser* and Gray an *indorsee* and holder of the bill. Indorsement is effected by signing the bill on the back.

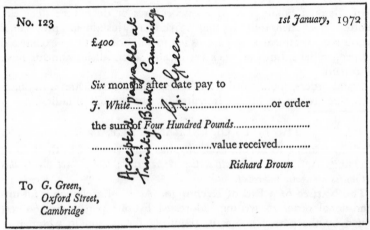

No. 123   1st January, 1972

£400

Six months after date pay to

J. White...or order

the sum of Four Hundred Pounds...........................

....value received............

                                        Richard Brown

To   G. Green,
     Oxford Street,
     Cambridge

Accepted payable at Trinity Bank, Cambridge. G. Green

Each of the parties to a bill makes certain promises which are implied by law. The *drawer* on signing the instrument promises that, if the bill is dishonoured, he will pay the amount thereof to the holder and that, if an indorser is called upon to pay the holder, he (the drawer) will indemnify that indorser.

The *indorser* on signing undertakes that, if the bill is dishonoured, he will pay the amount thereof to the holder and that, if a subsequent indorser is called upon to pay the holder, he (the prior indorser) will indemnify the subsequent indorser.

The *acceptor* on signing promises that he will pay the amount of the bill to the holder on maturity.

There are now three signatures on the specimen bill above: those of Brown as drawer, Green as acceptor, and White as indorser. The bill matures when six months have elapsed, i.e. on 1st July, 1972. (Banking and Financial Dealings Act, 1971.) On this date Gray, the holder, will present it to Green and demand payment. If Green pays, all parties are satisfied; but if Green dishonours the bill by non-payment, Gray has the following remedies—

(*a*) He can sue for the enforcement of Green's promise to pay when the bill matures;

(*b*) He can sue for the enforcement of Brown's promise to pay if the bill is dishonoured;

(*c*) He can sue for the enforcement of White's promise to pay if the bill is dishonoured.

Gray has thus three rights of action to obtain the money due to him. If he chooses to sue White, then White can recover from Brown on his promise to indemnify any indorser who has to pay the holder.

A bill may get into circulation without being accepted. If it is subsequently presented for acceptance and acceptance is refused, this amounts to dishonour, and the parties whose names appear on the bill can be sued on their implied promises. Since the drawee has not become the acceptor, his signature will not appear so there is no promise of his on which he could be sued.

HOLDERS. A person is a *holder* for the purposes of the Act only if he is either a payee in possession, or an indorsee in possession, or a person in possession of a bearer bill. A *holder for value* is a person in possession as above of a bill for which at any time value has been given. He is a holder for value as regards all parties prior to himself.

A *holder in due course* is a holder (as defined above) who has taken the bill complete and regular on the face of it (*Arab Bank Ltd.* v. *Ross*, 1952);[561] before it was overdue; for value and in good faith; without notice of any defect in the title of his transferor; and if it has been dishonoured, then without notice of dishonour. Every one of these requirements must be satisfied if a holder is to be a holder in due course.

A *bill is deemed overdue* in the following circumstances—

(*a*) If it has been drawn so that it is payable a fixed number of days, weeks or months after date, the bill is overdue when the relevant period has expired. Days of grace are not now added. (Banking and Financial Dealings Act, 1971.)

(*b*) If the bill is payable a fixed number of days, weeks or months after sight, the period is calculated from the date on which the bill is presented for acceptance. The bill is overdue when the relevant period has expired, and no days of grace are now to be added.

(c) If the bill is payable at sight, or on demand, it is overdue when it has been in circulation for an unreasonable length of time. What is unreasonable has never been legally defined, but with regard to cheques it has been suggested that they are stale, from the point of view of taking free from equities, after ten days. With regard to payment by a banker, a cheque is usually held stale after six months, though the drawer is still liable to the holder for the limitation period of six years; the holder may in such a case have taken "subject to equities."

Value must be given for a bill, so a person to whom the bill was negotiated as a gift cannot be a holder in due course. However, if a bill is negotiated to a holder in settlement of a past debt or liability, the holder is deemed to have given value and may be a holder in due course, since the Act provides that past consideration will support a bill of exchange. Furthermore, there is nothing in the Act of 1882 which requires that value should have been given *directly* by the holder to the drawer so long as value has been given. (*Diamond* v. *Graham*, 1968.)[562] Every holder of a bill is *prima facie* deemed to be a holder in due course unless it is proved that it is affected by fraud, duress or illegality, when the holder is put to proof of his position.

ORDER IN WRITING

A bill of exchange is an unconditional order in writing addressed by one person to another. We will now consider these elements.

A bill of exchange is a *written document* and in this context writing includes print. (Sect. 2.) The person who originates it is called the *drawer*, and he must have capacity to incur liability and this is co-extensive with capacity to contract. (Sect. 22.)

The order must be unconditional, and an instrument which orders any act to be done in addition to the payment of money is not a bill of exchange. (Sect. 3 (2).) An order to pay out of a particular fund is not unconditional, e.g. out of the money due to me from P when received. An unqualified order to pay, coupled with an indication of a particular fund out of which the drawee is to re-imburse himself, or a particular account to be debited with the amount, is regarded as unconditional, e.g. a cheque drawn on No. 2 A/c. (Sect. 3 (3).)

The bill of exchange must be signed, and no person is liable as drawer, indorser, or acceptor of a bill, who has not signed it as such. The following cases should be noted—

(1) Where a person signs a bill in a trade or assumed name, he is liable on it as if he had signed in his own name.

(2) The signature of the name of a firm is equivalent to the signature

by the person so signing of the names of all the persons liable as partners in that firm. (Sect. 23.)

(3) A signature by procuration (e.g. per pro B. Brown, J. Jones), operates as notice that the agent has a limited authority to sign, and the principal is only bound by such signature if the agent so signing was acting within the actual limits of his authority. (Sect. 25.)

Where a person signs a bill as a drawer, indorser, or acceptor, and adds words to his signature indicating that he signs for or on behalf of a principal or in a representative character, he is not personally liable thereon; but the mere addition to his signature of words describing him as an agent, or as filling a representative character, does not exempt him from personal liability. (*Childs* v. *Monins and Bowles*, 1821.)[563]

(4) Sect. 108 of the Companies Act, 1948, has effect upon representative signatures on behalf of companies. The relevant law is illustrated by *Durham Fancy Goods Ltd.* v. *Michael Jackson (Fancy Goods) Ltd.*, 1968.[127]

Where a signature on a bill is forged or unauthorised, it is wholly inoperative and no rights can be acquired through or under that signature, unless the party against whom it is sought to retain or enforce payment of the bill is *precluded* from setting up the forgery or want of authority. However, an unauthorised signature not amounting to a forgery may be ratified. (Sect. 24.)

Nevertheless there are the following exceptions—

(1) *The acceptor of a bill*, by accepting it, is precluded from denying to a holder in due course the existence of the drawer, the genuineness of his signature, and his capacity and authority to draw the bill (Sect. 54 (2));

(2) *The indorser of a bill*, by indorsing it, is precluded from denying to a holder in due course the genuineness and regularity in all respects of the drawer's signature and all previous indorsements (Sect. 55 (2));

(3) If a signature on a bill has been forged and the party whose signature it purports to be gets to know of the forgery, he may, if he does not inform the holder within a reasonable time, be estopped from asserting it (*Greenwood* v. *Martins Bank Ltd.*, 1933;)[564]

(4) If an acceptor has admitted the authenticity of his signature, he cannot at a later date refuse to honour it on the ground that it is a forgery.

ACCEPTANCE

When the drawee signs the bill he becomes the acceptor, and promises to pay the holder the amount of the bill on maturity provided the acceptance is unqualified. *A general acceptance* assents without qualification to the order of the drawer.

An acceptance must not express that the drawee will perform his promise by any other means than the payment of money, and the acceptance must be written on the bill and signed by the drawee. The drawee's signature without additional words is sufficient and he need not sign with his own hand; the signature may be written by some other person by or under his authority.

A bill may be accepted before it has been signed by the drawer or while otherwise incomplete. (Sect. 18 (1).) Incompleteness does not invalidate a bill and a bill is not invalid by reason (*a*) that it is not dated; (*b*) that it does not specify the value given, or that any value has been given therefor; (*c*) that it does not specify the place where it is drawn or the place where it is payable. (Sect. 3 (4).)

When a bill lacks a material particular, the person in possession of it has *prima facie* authority to fill up the omission in any way he thinks fit.

QUALIFIED ACCEPTANCE. The acceptor may qualify his acceptance. In the case of a bill for £100 drawn six months after date, the acceptor may introduce a *qualification as to amount:* "Accepted for fifty pounds only." The acceptor can then only be sued for £50. He may also sign thus: "Accepted nine months after date." The acceptor cannot then be sued until nine months have expired, and this is known as a *qualification as to time.* An acceptance "Payable at my office and there only" would amount to a *qualification as to place.* Finally, an acceptance "subject to security being provided" would be a *general conditional acceptance.*

Qualified acceptance amounts to dishonour and gives a right of action against the parties immediately, but the person presenting the bill may agree to the qualification. In this case, if he wishes to retain his rights against the drawer and prior indorsers, he must obtain their assent, except in the case of qualification as to amount when he need only serve notice on them.

ACCOMMODATION BILLS. Sometimes a bill is what is called an *accommodation bill,* and an accommodation party to such a bill is one who has signed it as drawer, acceptor, or indorser, without receiving value for it. His object is to lend his name and credit to some other person.

An accommodation party is liable on the bill to a holder for value; and it is immaterial whether, when such a holder took the bill, he knew the party to be an accommodation party or not. (Sect. 28.) Where a drawee accepts a bill for the accommodation of the drawer, it is understood that the drawer will make available funds to meet the bill on maturity, and, if he does not do so, and the acceptor has to pay the bill, the drawer must indemnify the acceptor.

Presentment for Acceptance. Where a bill expressly stipulates that it shall be presented for acceptance, or where a bill is drawn payable elsewhere than at the residence or place of business of the drawee, it must be presented for acceptance before it can be presented for payment. When a bill is payable after sight presentment is clearly necessary in order to fix the maturity of the instrument. The presentment must be made *by or on behalf of the holder to the drawee, or to some person authorised to accept or refuse acceptance on his behalf,* at a reasonable hour on a business day and before the bill is overdue.

When a bill is duly presented for acceptance and is not accepted within the customary time (usually twenty-four hours), the person presenting it must treat it as dishonoured by non-acceptance.

In case of such dishonour, the holder has an immediate right of recourse against the drawer and indorsers, and no presentment for payment is necessary. He must, however, give them notice of dishonour without delay otherwise they are discharged not only from liability on the bill but also on the consideration given for it.

PAYMENT

Where a bill is not payable to bearer, *the payee* must be named or otherwise indicated therein with reasonable certainty. A bill may be made payable to two or more payees, jointly or in the alternative, to one of two, or to one or some of several payees. A bill may also be made payable to the holder of an office for the time being. Where the payee is a fictitious or non-existent person, the bill may be treated as payable to bearer. (Sect. 7.) (*Bank of England* v. *Vagliano Bros.*, 1891.)[565]

The sum payable by a bill is a *sum certain* although it is required to be paid with interest, by stated instalments, or according to an indicated rate of exchange. (Sect. 9 (1).)

Where the sum payable is expressed in words and also in figures, and there is a discrepancy between the two, the sum denoted by the words is the amount payable. (Sect. 9 (2).)

Presentment for Payment. A bill must be duly presented for payment, otherwise the drawer and indorsers are discharged from liability.

(*a*) Where the bill is not payable on demand, presentment must be made on the day it falls due.

(*b*) Where the bill is payable on demand, presentment must be made within a reasonable time after its issue in order to render the drawer liable, and within a reasonable time after its indorsement to render the indorser liable.

The bill must be presented by the holder or by some person authorised to receive payment on his behalf, at a reasonable hour on a business day, at the proper place. Where it is authorised by agreement or usage, a presentment through the post office is sufficient. (Sect. 45.)

Presentment for payment is dispensed with—

(*a*) Where, after the exercise of reasonable diligence, it cannot be effected;
(*b*) Where the drawee is a fictitious person;
(*c*) Where the acceptor is an accommodation party;
(*d*) By waiver of presentment, express or implied.

Time of Payment. *A bill is payable on demand* (*a*) which is expressed to be payable on demand, or at sight, or on presentation; or (*b*) in which no time for payment is expressed.

A bill is payable at a fixed or determinable future time when it is expressed to be payable (i) at a fixed period after date or sight; (ii) on or at a fixed period after the occurrence of a specified event which is certain to happen, though the time of happening may be uncertain. An instrument expressed to be payable on a contingency is not a bill, and the happening of the event does not cure the defect. (Sect. 11.) Suppose a bill runs "Pay B. Brown or Order Five Hundred Pounds on the marriage of his daughter Jane to William Smith." This would not be a valid bill, even though the wedding took place shortly afterwards.

A bill is not invalid by reason only of the fact that it is ante-dated, post-dated, or dated on a Sunday. (Sect. 13.)

Where a bill expressed to be payable at a fixed period after date is issued undated, or where the acceptance of a bill payable at a fixed period after sight is undated, any holder may insert therein the true date of issue or acceptance, and the bill will be payable accordingly.

Where the holder in good faith and by mistake inserts the wrong date, and in every case where a wrong date is inserted and the bill comes into the hands of a holder in due course, the bill is valid and the date so inserted is deemed to be the true one. (Sect. 12.)

In calculating the due date of a bill not payable on demand the period is determined by excluding the day from which time begins to run and including the day of payment. The Act provides for the case where a bill becomes due on a non-business day i.e., Saturday, Sunday or a Bank Holiday. (See Sect. 92 of the 1882 Act and Sect. 3 Banking and Financial Dealings Act, 1971.)

NEGOTIABILITY

When a bill contains words prohibiting transfer, or indicating an intention that it should not be transferable, it is valid as between the parties thereto, but is not negotiable. An example of this would be a bill made payable to *G. Green only*. Where a bill is negotiable, it may be payable either to order or to bearer, and a bill is payable to bearer which is expressed to be so payable, or on which the only or last indorsement is an indorsement in blank.

A bill is negotiated when it is transferred from one person to another in such a manner as to constitute the transferee the holder of the bill. *A bill payable to bearer is negotiated by delivery; a bill payable to order is negotiated by the indorsement of the holder completed by delivery.*

Where a bill is negotiable in its origin, it continues to be negotiable until it has been (*a*) restrictively indorsed; or (*b*) discharged by payment or otherwise. *Where an overdue bill is negotiated*, it can only be negotiated subject to any defects of title affecting it at maturity, and thenceforward no person who takes it can acquire or give a better title than that which the person from whom he took it had. *Future holders cannot be holders in due course.*

Valid Indorsement. An indorsement, in order to operate as a negotiation, must comply with the following conditions, namely—

(1) *It must be written on the bill itself* and be signed by the indorser. The simple signature of the indorser on the bill, without additional words, is sufficient. An indorsement on a copy of the bill, in countries where copies are recognised, is valid.

(2) *It must be an indorsement of the entire bill.* A partial indorsement which purports to transfer to an indorsee a part only of the amount payable, or which purports to transfer the bill to two or more indorsees severally, does not operate as a negotiation of the bill.

(3) Where a bill is payable to the order of *two or more payees* or indorsees who are not partners, *all must indorse* unless the one indorsing has authority to indorse for the others.

(4) Where, in a bill payable to order, the *payee or indorsee is wrongly designated*, or his name is mis-spelt, he may indorse the bill as therein described adding, if he wishes, his proper signature.

(5) *Where there are two or more indorsements* on the bill, each indorsement is deemed to have been made in the order in which it appears on the bill until the contrary is proved.

(6) *An indorsement may be made in blank or special.* It may also contain terms making it restrictive. (Sect. 32.)

(*a*) CONDITIONAL INDORSEMENT. Where a bill purports to be indorsed conditionally, the condition may be disregarded by the payer, and a payment made to the indorsee is valid whether the condition has been fulfilled or not. Nevertheless the indorsee is bound by the condition and holds the money in trust for the indorser until the condition is fulfilled.

(*b*) SPECIAL INDORSEMENT. An indorsement in blank specifies no indorsee, and a bill so indorsed becomes payable to bearer. *A special indorsement* specifies the person to whom, or to whose order, the bill is to be payable. When a bill has been indorsed in blank, any holder may convert the blank indorsement into a special indorsement, by writing above the indorser's signature a direction to pay the bill to, or to the order of, himself or some other person. (Sect. 34.)

(*c*) RESTRICTIVE INDORSEMENT. An indorsement is restrictive which prohibits the further negotiation of the bill, or which expresses that it is a mere authority to deal with the bill as thereby directed and not a transfer of the ownership thereof, e.g. "Pay D only." or "Pay D for the Account of Y." or "Pay D or order for collection."

Delivery. The implied promises made by the parties to a bill are not enforceable unless each signatory has made delivery of the bill to some other person. If A signs a bill as acceptor, and the bill is stolen from his desk and is negotiated to B, B cannot sue A as acceptor because A did not deliver the bill and he is still at liberty to cancel his signature. (*Baxendale* v. *Bennett*, 1878.)[566] It should be noted that if B is a holder in due course he *will* be able to sue A, because *delivery is conclusively presumed in* favour of a holder in due course. (Sect. 21.)

DISCHARGE

A bill of exchange is discharged in the following ways—

(*a*) *By payment in due course* by or on behalf of the acceptor.

(*b*) *By express waiver*, where the holder absolutely and unconditionally renounces his rights against the acceptor. The waiver
must be in writing unless the bill is delivered up to the acceptor.

(*c*) *By material alteration*, except as against a party who has
himself made, authorised, or assented thereto, and against subsequent indorsers.

The following alterations are material, namely (i) any alteration of the
date, the sum payable, the time of payment, the place of payment;
and (ii) the addition of a place of payment without the acceptor's
assent, where a bill has been accepted generally. (Sect. 64 (2).) An
alteration may be material even if the change is beneficial. (*Gardner* v.
Walsh, 1855.) [567]

Examples of immaterial alterations are (i) changing a bill payable to
Jones or Bearer into *Jones or Order*; (ii) striking out of the words *or
Order*; (iii) the alteration of the drawee's name, when it is wrong, to
agree with a name correctly signed by way of acceptance.

(*d*) *By intentional and apparent cancellation* by the holder or his
agent.

(*e*) *By negotiation back to the acceptor*, sometimes called merger.
Suppose A has accepted a bill for £100 and has sold goods worth
£100 to H. If a subsequent indorser I negotiates the bill to H, and
H negotiates it back to A in settlement, the bill is discharged.

(*f*) *By the bill becoming statute barred*. A bill of exchange is a
simple contract and becomes statute barred six years from the cause
of action, i.e. dishonour.

DISHONOUR

A bill may be dishonoured by non-acceptance or by non-payment,
and the holder can sue prior parties on their implied promises. A
bill is dishonoured by non-payment—

(*a*) When it is duly presented for payment and payment is refused
or cannot be obtained; and

(*b*) When presentment is excused and the bill is overdue and
unpaid. When a bill is dishonoured by non-payment, an immediate
right of recourse against the drawer and indorsers accrues to the
holder. (Sect. 47.)

Notice of Dishonour. When a bill has been dishonoured by non-
acceptance or by non-payment, notice of dishonour must be given to
the drawer and each indorser, and any drawer or indorser to whom
such notice is not given is discharged. Notice, in order to be valid and

effectual, must be given in accordance with the rules laid down in the Bills of Exchange Act, 1882.

(*a*) Where the notice is given on behalf of the holder it operates for the benefit of subsequent holders, and all prior indorsers who have a right of recourse against the party to whom it is given.

If D is the drawer, P the payee, I_1, I_2, I_3, subsequent indorsers and H the holder, then if H gives notice to P, this would retain the liability of P, not only to H and subsequent holders, but also to I_1, I_2 and I_3, *although these latter three would not be liable to H.*

(*b*) Where notice is given by or on behalf of an indorser entitled to give notice, it operates for the benefit of the holder, and all indorsers subsequent to the party to whom notice is given.

If I_2 gives notice to P, then P is liable to I_1, I_2, I_3, H and subsequent holders.

(*c*) Actually if H gives notice to I_3, the chances are that I_3 will give notice to I_2, I_2 to I_1, I_1 to P, and P to D, since otherwise the person breaking the chain would lose his right of recourse though remaining liable himself. However, since one of these might fail to give notice and lose the right of recourse both for himself and for subsequent parties, the safest way is for H to notify all prior parties.

Noting and Protesting. It is convenient at this point to mention that, when a bill is dishonoured, it is sometimes obligatory and often desirable to *note* and *protest* the bill for non-acceptance or non-payment. Many solicitors carry out the office of *notary public*, and this office is universally recognised throughout the world.

In order to *note* the bill, the notary makes a formal demand upon the drawee for acceptance, or upon the acceptor for payment, as the case may be, and if the demand is refused, he writes a minute on the face of the bill consisting of the date, the noting charges, a reference to his register, and his initials. He also attaches to the bill a ticket giving the answer received to the request for acceptance or payment. To evidence these transactions the notary makes in his register a full copy of the bill, and a note of the answer, if any, received to his request.

The *protest* is against any loss sustained by the non-acceptance or non-payment of the bill, and is embodied in a solemn declaration made on behalf of the holder by a *notary public* who signs it. Where it is necessary to protest a bill and no notary is available, the function can be performed by a householder or substantial resident who gives a certificate of dishonour attested by two witnesses.

A *protest* must contain a copy of the instrument and must state the person who has requested the protest, the place and date of the protest, the reason for the protest, the demand made and the answer received, if any. Alternatively it may state that the drawee or acceptor cannot be found, if this is the case. The protest must be signed by the notary.

It is not necessary to note or protest inland bills, but there are certain advantages derived from noting a bill, and the costs of noting are recoverable as damages. The notary knows clearly what measures must be taken when a bill is dishonoured; he is the best witness at a trial that proper steps were taken; and his minute on the bill is the best record of dishonour for the purpose of notifying parties to the bill that they have acquired liability.

PROMISSORY NOTES

Definition. A promissory note is an unconditional promise in writing, made by one person to another, signed by the maker, engaging to pay, on demand or at a fixed or determinable future time, a sum certain in money to, or to the order of, a specified person or to bearer. (Sect. 83 (1).)

A promissory note is inchoate and incomplete until delivery is made to the payee or to bearer.

Such an instrument has only two parties—the maker and the payee —and does not require acceptance. The relevant rules governing bills of exchange are applicable to promissory notes.

CHEQUES

A cheque is defined in Sect. 73 of the Bills of Exchange Act, 1882, as "A bill of exchange drawn on a banker payable on demand." The relevant provisions of the Act applicable to bills of exchange payable on demand apply also to cheques. However, the provisions regarding acceptance have no application to cheques and the rules relating to crossings on cheques do not apply to other bills. Further, a delay in presenting a cheque for payment will not, in itself, discharge the drawer. (Sect. 74.) If a banker pays a cheque bearing a forged or unauthorised indorsement he is nevertheless discharged, although in a similar case the acceptor of a bill would not be. There are also certain special obligations which arise in the case of cheques because of the contract between banker and customer.

The words "on demand" are not usually printed on cheques but under the provisions of Section 10 (1) (*b*) they are implied.

A cheque need not take any particular form unless there is a contrary agreement between banker and customer. A mere printed statement on the cheque-book cover is not enough. (*Burnett* v. *Westminster Bank*, 1965.)[568]

RELATIONSHIP OF BANKER AND CUSTOMER

The relationship between a banker and a customer is that of *debtor and creditor* and is not fiduciary. Where a customer deposits money in a bank, this money is under the control of the banker and is not held by the banker in the form of a trust although he has obligations in connection with it.

Banker's Obligation to Repay. The banker can invest the money and deal with it as he pleases, but he is answerable for the amount deposited by the customer, and is under an obligation to pay it on demand, or to pay it to third parties on the order of the customer. The banker is not an agent or a factor, he is a debtor who promises to repay the money or any part of it at the branch of the bank where the account is kept, during banking hours, against the written order of the customer presented at, or addressed to, the bank at that branch. The bank must honour a customer's cheques up to the amount of the customer's deposit or alternatively up to the amount of an agreed overdraft.

The banker is under *no obligation to pay cheques in part*, and if a customer with a deposit or agreed overdraft of £400 draws against it a cheque for £500, the bank is not empowered to pay it as to £400, but should either pay it in full or refuse payment altogether.

Banker's Obligation not to Disclose. The bank has a further contractual obligation not to disclose information concerning the customer's affairs. (*Tournier* v. *National Provincial and Union Bank of England*, 1924.)[569] The obligation extends to all facts discovered by the banker while acting in that capacity and is not confined merely to the state of the account. Failure to comply with this obligation will render the banker liable to damages which will, however, be nominal unless actual loss can be proved.

The duty of non-disclosure is not absolute but qualified. On principle disclosure is excusable—

(*a*) *Under compulsion of law*, for example, under Sect. 7 of the Bankers' Books Evidence Act, 1879, the court may by order authorise a party to an action to inspect and copy entries in a banker's books, although the power is exercised with caution.

(*b*) *Where there is a duty to the public to disclose*, as where the account concerned is that of a person suspected of being a spy and receiving payments from a foreign government.

(*c*) *Where the interests of the bank require disclosure*, as where the bank is in the process of enforcing an overdraft.

(*d*) Where the disclosure is made with the express or implied consent of the customer. (*Sunderland* v. *Barclays Bank Ltd.*, 1938.)[570]

There is a growing practice of making credit enquiries, and banker's references are commonly given and asked for. If the customer gives the bank's name as a reference, the position is clear enough, but in the absence of the customer's express or implied consent the general practice may not be justifiable merely on the ground that it is an existing usage to supply such information to another bank. A misleading and negligent reference may render the banker liable in damages. (*Hedley Byrne & Co. Ltd.* v. *Heller and Partners Ltd.*, 1964.)[194]

Customer's Obligation of Care. The customer on his part undertakes to exercise reasonable care in drawing up his written orders so as not to mislead the bank or facilitate forgery. (*London Joint Stock Bank Ltd.* v. *Macmillan and Arthur*, 1918;[571] *C. H. Slingsby* v. *District Bank*, 1931.)[572]

Although a customer receives from time to time a bank statement he is not under a duty to check it and is not bound by any errors in it which he does not find. However, a bank may, by reason of estoppel, have to pay a cheque drawn by a customer who has relied upon an incorrect credit balance on his bank statement.

Wrongful Dishonour. A banker has a duty to honour a customer's cheques up to the amount of his credit balance or agreed overdraft. This duty is owed to the customer only and not to any other party. If a banker wrongfully dishonours the cheque of a customer, and if the customer is a man of business, the harm to his credit might lead to the award of substantial sums in an action for damages. Where, however, the customer is not in business, he will only receive nominal damages unless he can prove special damage. (*Gibbons* v. *Westminster Bank Ltd.*, 1940.)[573] In certain cases there may indeed be a possible action for libel against the bank. (*Davidson* v. *Barclays Bank Ltd.*, 1940,[574] and *Jayson* v. *Midland Bank Ltd*, 1968.)[575]

Presentment of Cheque for Payment. Since a cheque is payable on demand against funds which are already provided, presentment for acceptance is quite unnecessary and would indeed have no significance. The cheque must, however, be presented for payment, and if not so presented within a reasonable time of its issue, and if the drawer or the person on whose account it is drawn had the right at the time of such presentment as between him and the banker to have the cheque paid, and suffers actual damage through the delay, he is discharged to the extent of such damage. In determining what is a reasonable time regard is had to the nature of the instrument, the usage of trade and of bankers, and the facts of the particular case.

The holder of such cheque as to which such drawer or person is discharged shall be a creditor, in lieu of such drawer or person, of such banker to the extent of such discharge, and is entitled to recover the amount from him. (Sect. 74.)

The effect of Sect. 74 is that the drawer of a cheque is liable on it for the usual limitation period of six years, but he will be discharged before then if the holder does not present it for payment within a reasonable time and the drawer suffers actual damage because of the delay.

For example, if D has £500 in his banking account and draws a cheque in favour of P for £300, and P is dilatory in presenting it so that before he does so D's bank goes into liquidation and is only able to pay ten shillings in the pound, D will be regarded as a creditor of the bank for £200 and P for £300. Thus D will receive £100 and P £150 in the liquidation. It is obviously, therefore, in the interest of payees to present cheques for payment without undue delay. Quite apart from the question of loss on liquidation a cheque may go *stale*. In some banks a cheque goes stale after six months; in others it is as long as twelve months, and a bank might be reluctant to pay a stale cheque since such a payment would not be in the usual course of business.

Revocation of Banker's Authority. The duty and authority of a banker to pay a cheque drawn on him by his customer are determined by—

(1) Countermand of payment;
(2) Notice of the customer's death. (Sect. 75.)

Countermand of payment must be brought to the notice of the banker in unambiguous terms if it is to be effective. (*Curtice* v. *London, City and Midland Bank Ltd.*, 1908.)[576] Moreover, it must be clear to the bank that the order for taking such a serious step comes from the person entitled to give the order. In this sense a telegram countermanding payment of a cheque might be acted upon by the bank to the extent of postponing honouring the cheque until further enquiries could be made. To countermand a cheque by an unauthenticated telegram would involve the bank in a certain amount of risk.

If a bank were to cash a cheque within a few minutes after the three o'clock closing time, and were to receive a countermand of payment before the opening of business at ten a.m. next day, the payment would nevertheless be in order from the bank's point of view. The bank would not be able to dishonour a cheque after closing hours, but is entitled, within a reasonable business margin of its advertised time of closing, to deal with a cheque, not to dishonour it, but to do what it is asked to do, namely, to pay it. If the bank closes its doors at 3 p.m. there may still be customers in the bank whose wishes have not yet been attended to.

It should be noted that a countermand notice sent to one branch of a bank does not operate as notice to another branch. (*Burnett* v. *Westminster Bank*, 1965.)[568]

A banker's authority to pay a cheque is determined by notice of the customer's death, and to this may be added notice of the customer's mental disorder, notice of an act of bankruptcy on which a bankruptcy petition could be presented against him, or that a receiving order has been made, or that he is an undischarged bankrupt, or on service of a garnishee order nisi. Garnishee proceedings may be taken by a judgment creditor where the judgment debtor (in this case the customer) is himself owed money by a third party (in this case the bank). The order nisi binds the debt in the hands of the bank and cheques drawn by the customer cannot be paid. The bank will usually open a new account for subsequent receipts and payments. Where the customer is a limited company, notice of a petition for compulsory winding up or a resolution for voluntary winding up will terminate the banker's duty to honour cheques. The banker need not, as we have seen, pay cheques where a customer has an insufficient balance to cover the cheque, or has not previously arranged an adequate overdraft, and the banker should not pay if he has notice of any defect in the title of the person presenting the cheque.

Payment without Authority. A banker is liable for wrongfully dishonouring the cheques of his customers but may also be liable if he pays a cheque when he should not have done so. Thus, a banker will not be able to debit the customer's account if he pays a countermanded cheque, a cheque void for material alteration, or a cheque on which the drawer's signature is forged.

However, where the customer has been *negligent* in drawing up his cheque so as to mislead the bank or facilitate forgery, the bank may debit his account. (*London Joint Stock Bank* v. *Macmillan and Arthur*, 1918.)[571] Further, if the drawer's signature has been forged and he gets to know of the forgery, he may, if he does not inform the bank promptly and the bank is put to loss, be *estopped* from asserting the forgery. (*Greenwood* v. *Martins Bank*, 1933.)[564]

Where the wrongful payment by the bank actually satisfies a debt due from a customer to his creditor, the customer would make a profit by reason of the restoration rule. For example, if the bank paid a countermanded cheque which A, a customer, had drawn in favour of B, to whom A owed money, the result of the restoration rule would be that A's debt to B would be satisfied and A's balance at the bank would have to be restored. To prevent this profit being made the bank, on restoring A's account, is *subrogated* to B's rights against A, and can recover from A by this means.

Limitation. The six-year limitation period applicable to simple contract debts does not run against the customer of a bank from the date of payment in, for there is no cause of action until the customer demands the money and the demand is not met. For example, if A deposited £100 with his bank in 1965 and did not draw cheques against the account until 1972, there would be no question of the bank pleading the Limitation Act as an excuse for not paying it. However, if the cheque was not paid by the bank time would then begin to run against A and he would have to sue the bank in respect of their failure to pay within six years.

Joint Accounts. In *Brewer* v. *Westminster Bank*, 1952,[577] McNair, J., decided that in the case of a joint account, the bank's duties were owed to the account holders *jointly* and not *severally*. The result of this decision was that where one account-holder forged the other's signature on cheques drawn on the account and then added his own signature, the innocent account-holder had no action against the bank.

However, in *Jackson* v. *White and Midland Bank Ltd.*, [1967] 2 Lloyd's Rep. 68, where one joint-account-holder forged the signature of the other, Park, J., declined to follow *Brewer's* case, holding that where there was a joint account with, say, A and B, the bank in effect agreed with A and B *jointly* that it would honour cheques signed by them both and with A *separately* that it would not honour cheques unless signed by him, and with B *separately* that it would not honour cheques unless signed by him. Thus, where the bank honours a cheque on which B has forged A's signature, A should be able to sue the bank because it is in breach of the separate agreement with him.

It should be noted that *Jackson's* case cannot overrule *Brewer's* case because both are decisions at first instance. However, the decision in *Brewer's* case has received much criticism and it is likely that the reasoning in *Jackson's* case will be applied in future.

Generally. Banks often accept valuable property for safe custody and are liable as ordinary bailees in this respect, i.e. they must take reasonable care for the safety of the property. Should the banker misdeliver the goods to the wrong person, then he is liable in conversion even though there was no negligence on his part.

Bankers nowadays often give advice on investment to customers and potential customers and, if the giving of such advice forms part of the banker's business, he will be liable in damages if his advice is negligent. (*Woods* v. *Martins Bank*, 1958.)[578] If such advice is not part of the business of a particular banker, the person who gave the advice might be personally liable for negligence. (*Hedley Byrne & Co. Ltd.* v. *Heller & Partners Ltd.*, 1963.)[194]

In the absence of express instructions, it is not part of a banker's duty to consider a customer's tax liability when crediting an account with a dividend. (*Schioler* v. *Westminster Bank Ltd.*, 1970.)[579]

CROSSED CHEQUES

Nature of Crossing. The Act provides—

(1) Where a cheque bears across its face an addition of—

(*a*) The words "and company" or any abbreviation thereof between two parallel transverse lines, either with or without the words "not negotiable"; *or*

(*b*) Two parallel transverse lines simply, either with or without the words "not negotiable," *that addition constitutes a crossing and the cheque is crossed generally.* (Sect. 76 (1).)

Where there is a general crossing the banker must pay the cheque to another banker and must not cash the cheque across the counter.

(2) Where a cheque bears across its face an addition of the name of a banker, either with or without the words "not negotiable," that addition constitutes a crossing, and *the cheque is crossed specially and to that banker.* (Sect. 76(2).) Where there is a special crossing the cheque must be paid to the banker named in the crossing.

General and special crossings give additional protection to holders in the case of theft, for the thief may not have a bank account and, even if he has, the extra time involved in clearing the crossed cheque may enable the drawer or holder to stop payment.

In addition to the crossings specified in the Act, it is not uncommon for the drawer to add the words "Account payee," and this is regarded as an instruction to the collecting banker to collect only for the account of that payee, an instruction which he neglects at his peril.

Crossing Procedure. Sect. 77 of the Act lays down the following rules—

(1) A cheque may be crossed generally or specially by the drawer.

(2) Where a cheque is uncrossed, the holder may cross it generally or specially.

(3) Where a cheque is crossed generally, the holder may cross it specially.

(4) Where a cheque is crossed generally or specially, the holder may add the words "not negotiable."

(5) Where a cheque is crossed specially, the banker to whom it is crossed may again cross it specially to another banker for collection.

EXAMPLES OF CROSSINGS ON CHEQUES

(6) Where an uncrossed cheque, or a cheque crossed generally, is sent to a banker for collection, he may cross it specially to himself. (Sect. 77.)

There is no reason why the payee cannot also add "Account payee."

A crossing authorised by the Act is a material part of the cheque and it is not lawful for any person to obliterate or, except as authorised by the Act, to add to or alter the crossing. (Sect. 78.)

Duties of Banker as to Crossed Cheques. Sect. 79 provides that if a paying banker receives a cheque—

(i) crossed specially to more than one banker he must not pay it; however, if one of the bankers named is acting as an agent for collection for the other, the cheque may be paid to the agent bank; collection through an agent is rare today, but was more frequent when there were a number of small banks using a major London bank as agents for collection;

(ii) crossed specially to a named banker, he must pay only the named banker (or the named banker's agent for collection, if any);

(iii) crossed generally, it cannot be paid except through a banker, though payment through any banker will suffice.

If a banker fails to observe the above rules he is liable to the true owner for loss incurred because the cheque was not paid as directed by the crossing. There are two possible sets of circumstances to consider.

(*a*) *The banker may, in fact, have paid the true owner* in which case there can be no claim against him. However, Lord Cairns once said of such a cheque ". . . the drawers might refuse to be debited with it as having been paid contrary to their mandate." (*Smith* v. *Union Bank of London* (1875), 1 Q.B.D. 31 at p. 36.)

(*b*) *Payment may have been made to a person who is not the true owner.* In the case of an uncrossed cheque, the banker may be protected by Sect. 59 of the Act if the person he pays is the holder, and by Sect. 60 if the person to whom payment was made was in possession under a forged or unauthorised indorsement.

Thus, if a bearer cheque is stolen from its owner by T, and the drawee bank pays him, it has no liability to the true owner because T is the holder and Sect. 59 applies. Furthermore, if A draws a cheque on his bank payable to C and it is stolen by T who forges C's indorsement and negotiates it to E, who is paid by the bank in good faith and in the ordinary course of business, Sect. 60 will apply and the bank will not be liable to the true owner, C.

However, if, in the examples given above, the cheque had been crossed and the banker had not observed the instructions on the crossing, he would be liable to the true owner in each case and could not derive protection from Sects. 59 and 60.

Protection against Alterations and Obliterations. Where a cheque is presented for payment which does not at the time of presentment *appear to be crossed,* or to have had a crossing which has been obliterated, or to have been added to or altered otherwise than as authorised by the Act, *the banker paying the cheque in good faith and without negligence shall not be responsible or incur any liability.* Nor shall the payment be questioned *even if the cheque had been crossed,* or if the crossing had been obliterated or been added to or altered otherwise than as authorised by the Act, or if payment had been made otherwise than to a banker or to the banker to whom the cheque was crossed, or to his agent for collection being a banker, as the case may be. (Sect. 79.)

Effect of Crossing "Not Negotiable." Where a person takes a crossed cheque which bears on it the words "not negotiable," he shall not have and shall not be capable of giving a better title to the cheque than that which the person from whom he took it had. (Sect. 81.)

While the words "not negotiable" do not prevent the cheque from being transferred, they do have a serious effect on the title of subsequent holders.

(1) ORDER CHEQUES. To negotiate an order cheque, an appropriate indorsement must be made. If such a cheque were lost or stolen, then any such indorsement would be forged and no subsequent holder could obtain a title. The addition of the words "not negotiable" does not affect the position.

(2) BEARER CHEQUES. A bearer cheque is negotiable by transfer without indorsement and a person taking such a cheque might have a title as a holder in due course even if a previous holder had none. The addition of the words "not negotiable" to a bearer cheque protects the rights of the true holder against a subsequent holder, and if such a cheque were stolen and transferred to an innocent third party who obtained payment, the true owner could demand restitution within the limitation period of six years.

The words "not negotiable" can be written on a crossed cheque when making the crossing or subsequently. A cheque crossed "not negotiable" is still transferable subject to defects in title. A bill of exchange so crossed is not even transferable. If the words "not negotiable" appear on a cheque otherwise than as part of the crossing, the better view is that they are of no effect.

Account Payee. We have seen that, although such a crossing is not authorised by the Act, it is not uncommon for the drawer of a cheque to include in the crossing the words "A/c payee" or "A/c payee only." This is an *instruction to the collecting banker and not to the paying banker*. It will be in order for the paying banker to pay the amount of the cheque to the collecting banker, leaving it to the latter to ensure that this instruction on the cheque is carried out. It would, no doubt, be negligence in the banker if he collected the money for some other account, but the point is rather academic for bankers do not normally collect for any account except that of the payee. The words "Account payee" or "Account payee only" do not prevent a cheque from being negotiated. The holder of such a cheque, not being the payee, might find it difficult to persuade a bank to collect the cheque for him, but he could collect the money himself from the drawer who would certainly be liable on such a cheque to a holder in due course.

Application of Crossings Rules. The crossing rules apply not only to cheques but also—

(i) to the instruments other than cheques specified in Sect. 4 of the Cheques Act, 1957 (see below, p. 316); and

(ii) to dividend warrants. (Sect. 95, Bills of Exchange Act, 1882).

BANKER'S PROTECTION

Paying Bankers. If a banker pays one of his customer's cheques to the wrong person then he is liable to the true owner in conversion for the face value of the cheque and he cannot debit the customer's account. However, the following statutory provisions may provide the banker with a defence—

(*a*) *Under Sect.* 59 payment by the banker to the holder at or after maturity in good faith and without notice of any defect in his title discharges the bill, frees the banker from all liability and enables him to debit the customer's account. However, the person paid *must be the holder*, and a person holding an order bill by means of a forged or unauthorised indorsement is not a holder. Therefore payment to him would not discharge the bill or free the banker from liability. The Section would provide a defence where a banker paid the bearer of a bearer cheque.

(*b*) *Under Sect.* 60 if a banker on whom a cheque is drawn pays it, in good faith and in the ordinary course of business, he is deemed to have paid it in due course and is not prejudiced by the fact that the *indorsement* was forged or made without authority The Section applies only to indorsements on cheques and does not apply where the drawer's signature has been forged, nor where the cheque is void for material alteration.

(*c*) *Where a cheque is crossed.* Where the banker, on whom a crossed cheque is drawn, in good faith and without negligence pays it, if crossed generally, to a banker, and if crossed specially, to the banker to whom it is crossed (or his agent for collection being a banker), *the banker* paying the cheque, *and,* if the cheque has come into the hands of the payee, *the drawer shall* respectively be entitled to the same rights and *be placed in the same position as if payment of the cheque had been made to the true owner* thereof. (Sect. 80.)

For example, A draws a cheque on the B Bank payable to C. C, on receipt of the cheque, crosses it generally. The cheque is then stolen by T who opens an account at the Z Bank in the name of C. The Z Bank presents the cheque to the B bank which pays in good faith and without negligence. The B Bank is protected by Sect. 80 from liability to C, and C cannot sue A.

(*d*) *Cheques Act,* 1957, *Sect.* 1. Although cheques are bills of exchange, most of them have a very short life, being sent by the drawers to the payees who promptly pay them straight into their banking accounts. Prior to the Act, although there was no transfer by the payee to an indorsee, such cheques required indorsement, a laborious and rather useless process.

Sect. 1 of the Cheques Act, 1957, provides—

Where a *paying banker* in good faith and in the ordinary course of business pays a cheque drawn on him which is not indorsed or is irregularly indorsed, he does not, in doing so, incur any liability by reason only of the absence of, or irregularity in, indorsement, and he is deemed to have paid it in due course.

The same protection is extended to him if he pays—

(i) A document issued by a customer of the bank which, though not a bill of exchange, is intended to enable a person to obtain from the bank the sum mentioned in the document; or

(ii) A draft payable on demand drawn by him on himself, whether payable at the head office or some other office of the bank.

The Committee of London Clearing Bankers announced, shortly after the Act was passed, that they would still require indorsement of cheques other than those paid into a banking account for the credit of the payee. Accordingly, if the payee pays a cheque into his own account there is no need for him to indorse it. However, if a payee or indorsee presents a cheque for payment over the counter (the cheque being uncrossed), the person receiving payment will have to indorse it. Where a crossed cheque is negotiated and paid into a bank by the last indorsee, the banker will require the indorsement of all indorsers but not that of the last indorsee who is paying in.

Whilst the decisions of the Committee of London Clearing Bankers are not law, it is thought that a banker who pays a cheque without obtaining an indorsement where the Committee says he should would not be acting in the ordinary course of business and would not, therefore, be protected by Sect. 1 of the Cheques Act, 1967, nor by Sect. 60 of the Bills of Exchange Act, 1882. He would probably also be negligent and be unable to claim the protection of Sect. 80.

Further, it is assumed that where the Committee requires an indorsement it must be a regular indorsement, and payment of a cheque with an irregular indorsement would be negligent and not in the ordinary course of business, so that there could be no statutory protection if there was a wrongful payment.

Bankers Collecting Cheques. The Cheques Act, 1957, Sect. 4, extends protection to *bankers who collect payment* on the following instruments—

(i) Cheques.

(ii) Any document issued by a customer of a banker which, though not a bill of exchange, is intended to enable a person to obtain payment from that banker of the sum mentioned in the document.

(iii) Any document issued by a public officer which is intended to enable a person to obtain payment from the Paymaster General or the Queen's and Lord Treasurer's Remembrancer of the sum mentioned in the document but which is not a bill of exchange.

(iv) Any draft payable on demand drawn by a banker upon himself, whether payable at the head office or some other office of the bank. (Sect. 4 (2).)

Where a banker, *in good faith and without negligence—*

(*a*) receives payment for a customer of one of the above instruments; or

(*b*) having credited a customer's account with the amount of such an instrument receives payment thereof for himself;

and the customer has no title, or a defective title, to the instrument, the banker does not incur any liability to the true owner of the instrument by reason only of having received payment thereof. (Sect. 4 (1).)

A banker is not to be treated for the purposes of the section as having been negligent by reason only of his failure to concern himself with absence of, or irregularity in, indorsement of an instrument. (Sect. 4 (3).)

This section repeals, replaces and extends Sect. 82 of the Bills of Exchange Act, 1882, and provides *protection for the collecting banker against an action for conversion* if he collects for someone with no, or a defective, title.

Sect. 4 applies to all cheques, whether crossed or not, and also extends to a range of other instruments. However, an instrument on which the drawer's signature is forged is not a cheque nor is an instrument which has become void for material alteration, and no protection is given in respect of the collection of such instruments.

The Section applies only where the banker collects payment for a *customer* and acts without negligence, and in the matter of negligence the onus of proof is on him. Thus there must be an account, but it seems to be enough that the customer has opened it with the cheque which is in dispute.

A banker may be negligent on many counts, for example where he has failed to obtain or follow up the references of a customer opening an account, if this failure was to some extent responsible for the wrongful collection. Failure to inquire as to a new customer's employer is negligence if the banker knows that the customer is in a position which might enable him to misappropriate his employer's cheques, as where he is a cashier. A banker should not collect, without inquiry, cheques for employees or partners or officials which are drawn on their firm or company, nor should he collect a cheque marked "Account Payee" for another account. Finally, a banker will be held to have been negligent in any case where it appears to the court that inquiries should have been made. (*Lloyds Bank Ltd.* v. *E. B. Savory & Co.*, 1933.)[580]

It should be noted, however, that the above decision represents the high-water mark of judicial severity in the matter of bankers' negligence and in two recent cases, *Orbit Mining and Trading Co.* v. *Westminster Bank*, 1962,[581] and *Marfani & Co.* v. *Midland Bank*, 1967.[582] the judiciary seems to have accepted that bank employees cannot be highly inquisitive if they are to deal promptly with the large number of cheques which are cleared every day, and the standard of care required has been lowered, possibly too far.

Collecting Banker as Holder in Due Course. Where a banker collects payment of a cheque for a person who is not the true owner. he may be liable in conversion although, as we have seen, he may derive protection from Sect. 4 of the Cheques Act, 1957. However, he may also escape liability if he can prove that he has become a holder in due course of the cheque. Where this is so the banker will obtain a good title to the cheque even if the title of the transferee was non-existent or defective, and in spite of his own negligence, if any.

A banker, like any other person, must give *value* before he can become a holder in due course, and this may happen in *three* ways—

(i) where the customer pays in a cheque to reduce his overdraft, if the banker forgoes interest;

(ii) where there is an express or implied agreement between banker and customer under which the customer can and does draw against the cheque before it has been cleared: where there is no prior agreement it seems that the banker does not give value; and

(iii) where the banker cashes a cheque for a person who is not a customer and therefore *buys* it from that person rather than *collecting* it for him.

A banker cannot become a holder in due course if an *essential* indorsement is forged but he can, by virtue of Sect. 2 of the Cheques Act, 1957, become the holder in due course of an order cheque, even though it is not indorsed to him. The banker will, therefore, have the right to sue the drawer if the cheque is dishonoured.

The Section provides that a *collecting banker* who gives value for, or has a lien on, a cheque payable to order which the holder delivers to him for collection without indorsing it, has such (if any) rights as he would have had if, upon delivery, the holder had indorsed in blank.

The Section provides an exception to Sect. 31 of the Bills of Exchange Act, 1882, in that it allows an order cheque to be negotiated without indorsement. It should also be noted that the Section applies only to cheques and not to analogous instruments, as do Sects. 1 and 4, and that it does not deal with the case in which an indorsement exists and is irregular. Presumably, where this is so the cheque is not complete and regular on the face of it and the banker will not be a holder in due course. The cases of *Westminster Bank Ltd.* v. *Zang*, 1965,[583] and *Barclay's Bank Ltd.* v. *Astley Industrial Trust Ltd.*, 1970,[584] are illustrative of some of the problems arising out of the operation of Sect. 2.

Unindorsed Cheques as Evidence of Payment. Sect. 3 of the Cheques Act provides that an unindorsed cheque which appears to have been paid by the banker on whom it is drawn is evidence of the receipt by the payee of the sum payable by the cheque. Prior to the Act such an indorsed cheque was *prima facie* but not conclusive evidence that the payee had received the sum payable; the Act merely confirms that in future an unindorsed cheque can fulfil the same function.

Nevertheless, by drawing attention to this virtue of a cheque, it has led to a widespread practice among business men of dispensing with the issue of receipts where payment is by cheque, with a consequent saving in effort, time and money.

SECURITIES

A security is some right or interest in property given to a creditor so that, if the debt is not paid, the creditor can obtain the amount of the debt by exercising certain remedies against the property, rather than by suing the debtor by means of a personal action on his promise to pay. Securities, therefore, create rights over the property of another, and here we shall discuss liens, mortgages of land, chattels and choses in action.

LIEN

A lien is a right over the property of another which arises by operation of law and independently of any agreement. It gives a creditor the right (a) to retain possession of the debtor's property until he has paid or settled the debt, or (b) to sell the property in satisfaction of the debt in those cases where the lien is not possessory. Where the parties agree that a lien shall be created, such agreement will effectively create one.

1. Possessory or Common Law Lien. To exercise this type of lien the creditor must have actual possession of the debtor's property, in which case he can retain it until the debt is paid or settled. It should be noted that creditor cannot ask for possession of the debtor's goods in order to exercise a lien.

A common law lien may be particular or general—

(a) PARTICULAR LIEN. This gives the possessor the right to retain goods until a debt arising in connection with these goods is paid.

(b) GENERAL LIEN. This gives the possessor the right to retain goods not only for debts specifically connected with them, but also for all debts due from the owner of the goods however arising.

The law favours particular rather than general liens.

If X sends a clock to R to be repaired at a cost of 50p, R may retain the clock under a particular lien until the 50p is paid. If, however, X owed R 75p for the earlier repair of a watch, R cannot retain the clock to enforce the payment of 125p unless, as is unlikely, he can claim a general lien.

The following are cases of *particular lien*—

(i) A carrier can retain goods entrusted to him for carriage until his charges are paid.

(ii) An innkeeper has a lien over the property brought into the inn by a guest and also over property sent to him while there, even if it does not belong to him. (*Robins* v. *Gray*, 1895.)[585] The lien does not extend to motor cars or other vehicles, or to horses or other animals.

(iii) A shipowner has a lien on the cargo for freight due.

(iv) In a sale of goods, the unpaid seller has a lien on the goods, if still in his possession, to recover the price.

(v) Where a chattel is bailed in order that work may be done on it or labour and skill expended in connection with it, it may be retained until the charge is paid. Such liens may arise in favour of a car repairer over the car repaired; by an arbitrator on the award; by an architect over plans he has prepared; by a miller over corn for the cost of grinding; and innumerable other instances of this character.

A *general lien* may arise out of contract or custom, and the following classes of persons have a general lien over the property of their customers or clients—factors, bankers, solicitors, stockbrokers, and in some cases insurance brokers.

Although a common law lien normally gives no power of sale, there are some exceptional cases in which a right of sale is given by statute. Such a right is given to innkeepers (Innkeepers Act, 1878), unpaid sellers of goods (Sale of Goods Act, 1893), and bailees who accept goods for repair or other treatment for reward (Disposal of Uncollected Goods Act, 1952). Briefly, the latter Act provides for the sale of goods accepted for repair or other treatment which are ready for delivery if the bailee has given the bailor twelve months' notice that they are ready, and the bailor at the end of twelve months takes no action to collect the goods. The bailee may then sell the goods by public auction, provided that he gives the bailor fourteen days' notice of his intention to do so, and accounts to the bailor for the balance of the proceeds of sale *after* deduction of charges and expenses.

It should also be noted that the High Court has a discretion to order the sale of goods if it is just to do so, e.g. where the goods are perishable and see *Larner* v. *Fawcett*, 1950.[586]

A common law lien is discharged—

(a) by payment of the sum owing;
(b) by parting with the possession of the goods;
(c) by an agreement to give credit for the amount due;
(d) by accepting an alternative security for the debt owing.

2. Maritime Lien. A maritime lien does not depend on possession. It is a right which attaches to a ship in connection with a maritime liability. It travels with the ship and may be enforced by the arrest and the sale of the ship through the medium of a court having Admiralty jurisdiction. Examples of such liens are—

(a) Liens of salvors.
(b) The lien of seamen for their wages.
(c) The lien of a master for his outgoings.
(d) Liens which arise from damage due to collision.
(e) Liens of bottomry bond holders.

The order of attachment is important and depends on circumstances. Successive salvage liens attach in inverse order, later ones being preferred to earlier ones, since the earlier lien would be useless if the later salvage had not preserved the ship from loss. Claims for collision damage are treated as of equal rank. Liens for wages, in the absence of salvage liens, have priority over other liens; however, liens for wages earned before a salvage operation are postponed to the lien for salvage, since the value of such a lien has been preserved by the salvage operation.

If a ship which is subject to lien is sold, the purchaser takes it subject to the lien and is responsible for discharging it.

3. Equitable Lien. An equitable lien is an equitable right, conferred by law, whereby one man acquires a charge on the property of another until certain claims have been met. It differs from a common law lien which is founded on possession and does not confer a power of sale. An equitable lien is independent of possession and may be enforced by a judicial sale.

An equitable lien may arise out of an express provision in a contract or from the relationship between parties, e.g. as between the partners in a firm, or between the vendor and purchaser of property for the purchase money.

An equitable lien can, like all equitable rights, be extinguished by the owner selling the property to a *bona fide* purchaser for value who has no notice of the lien.

An equitable lien differs from a mortgage. A mortgage as we shall now see is always created by the act of parties, an equitable lien may arise by operation of law.

4. Banker's Lien. At common law a banker has a general possessory lien on all securities, such as bills of exchange, promissory notes and bonds, deposited with him by customers in the ordinary course of business unless there is an agreement, express or implied, to the contrary. The lien does not extend to property or securities deposited for safe custody. However, a customer may deposit a security as collateral for a loan, in which case the banker has rights over it, but the transaction is an equitable mortgage rather than a lien.

A banker's lien gives a right of sale, at least of negotiable securities subject to the lien, because Sect. 27 of the Bills of Exchange Act, 1882, provides that a person having a possessory lien over a bill is deemed a holder for value to the extent of the lien, and can, therefore, sell and transfer the bill.

MORTGAGES OF LAND

Legal Mortgage of Freeholds. Under the 1925 legislation the mortgagor (the borrower) does not divest himself of his legal estate, but grants to the mortgagee (the lender) a demise for a term of years absolute. Thus, if X owns Blackacre and borrows money on mortgage from Y, he will grant Y a term of usually three thousand years in Blackacre, both agreeing that the term of years will end when the loan is repaid. X will also agree to pay interest on the loan at a stipulated rate.

Alternatively, under the provisions of Sect. 87 of the Law of Property Act, 1925, it is possible to create a legal mortgage of freeholds by means of a short deed stating that a charge on the land is created. Such a charge does not give a term of years, but the mortgagee has the same rights and powers as if he had received a term of years under a mortgage by demise.

Before 1926 mortgages were created by conveying the freehold to the mortgagee. Since 1925 an attempt to create a mortgage by this method operates as a grant of a mortgage lease of 3,000 years, subject to cesser on redemption. (Sect. 85, Law of Property Act, 1925.)

Legal Mortgages of Leaseholds. If X, the owner of a ninety-nine years lease of Blackacre, borrows money on mortgage from Y, he may grant Y a sub-lease of (say) ninety-nine years less ten days, both agreeing that when the loan is repaid the term shall cease. X also agrees to pay interest. Such a term is known as a *mortgage by demise*.

Alternatively a legal mortgage of leaseholds may be created by a charge by way of legal mortgage under Sect. 87 of the Law of Property Act, 1925, if made by deed. No sub-lease is created but the remedies of the mortgagee are the same as if it had been.

. When a person has borrowed money by mortgaging property, he may still be able to borrow further sums, if the amount of the charge is not equal to the full value of the property and there seems to be adequate security for further loans. The owner of freehold land may grant a term of three thousand years plus one day to another mortgagee, whilst the owner of a lease may grant a second sub-lease of (say) ninety-nine years less nine days. Alternatively, a second charge by way of legal mortgage may be created by a further deed.

The only limit to further borrowing on second and subsequent mortgages is that of finding a lender who is prepared to become a second, third, or fourth mortgagee.

Equitable Mortgages. A mortgagee who receives a mere equitable interest in the land is said to have an equitable mortgage. Thus if the borrower's interest is equitable, e.g. a life interest, then any mortgage of it is necessarily equitable. Such an interest may be mortgaged by lease or charge, as in legal mortgages, or by a deposit of title deeds with the lender, usually accompanied by a memorandum explaining the transaction. Such mortgages must be in writing and signed by the borrower or his agent. (Sect. 53, Law of Property Act, 1925.)

An informal mortgage of a legal estate or interest creates an equitable mortgage, e.g. an attempt to create a legal mortgage otherwise than by deed.

Where there is a binding agreement to create a legal mortgage, but the formalities necessary to do so have not been carried out, Equity regards the agreement as an equitable mortgage. The agreement can be enforced by specific performance so that the mortgagee can obtain a legal mortgage from the borrower under the Rule in *Walsh* v. *Lonsdale*, 1882.[552] Before there is a binding agreement there must be either written evidence of the agreement, signed by the borrower or his agent, or a sufficient act of part performance by the lender.

Rights of the Mortgagor or Borrower. The main right of the mortgagor is the right to redeem (or recover) the land. Originally at common law the land became the property of the lender as soon as the date decided upon for repayment had passed, unless during that time the loan had been repaid. However, Equity regarded a mortgage as essentially a security, and gave the mortgagor the right to redeem the land at any time on payment of the principal sum, plus interest due to the date of payment. What is more important, this rule applied even though the common law date for repayment had passed. This right, which still exists, is called the *Equity of Redemption*, and there are two important rules connected with it—

(*a*) ONCE A MORTGAGE ALWAYS A MORTGAGE. This means that Equity looks at the real purpose of the transaction and does not always have regard to its form. If Equity considers that the transaction is a mortgage, the rules appertaining to mortgages will apply, particularly the right to redeem the property even though the contractual date for repayment has passed, or has not yet arrived. In the latter case, however, the mortgagor must generally give six months' notice of his intention to redeem, or pay six months' interest in lieu, so that the mortgagee may find another investment. However, if the parties contract at arm's length, and there is no evidence of oppression by the mortgagee, the court will endeavour to uphold the principle of sanctity of contract and will enforce any reasonable restriction on the right to redeem. (*Knightsbridge Estates Trust Ltd.* v. *Byrne*, 1939.)[587]

(*b*) THERE MUST BE NO CLOG ON THE EQUITY OF REDEMPTION. This means—

(i) that the court will not allow postponement of the repayment period for an unreasonable time; and

(ii) the property mortgaged must, when the loan is repaid, be returned to the borrower in the same condition as when it was pledged. (*Noakes* v. *Rice*, 1902.)[588]

Nevertheless, particularly in modern times, so long as the parties are at arm's length when the loan is negotiated, Equity will allow a collateral transaction. (*Kreglinger* v. *New Patagonia Meat and Cold Storage Co.*, 1914,[589] and *Cityland and Property (Holdings) Ltd.* v. *Dabrah*, 1967.)[590]

It is worth noting that the mortgagor may, where he is in possession of the land, grant leases to third parties subject to any special agreement to the contrary.

Powers and Remedies of the Legal Mortgagee. A legal mortgagee (the lender) has the following concurrent powers and remedies—

(*a*) To TAKE POSSESSION. This right does not depend upon default by the mortgagor, but the mortgagee will normally only enter into possession of the property under the term of years granted to him, or under the charge by way of legal mortgage, when he is not being paid the sum due, and when he wishes to pay himself from the proceeds of the property. This is not a desirable remedy, however, because when the mortgagee takes possession he is strictly accountable to the mortgagor, not only for what he has received but for what he might have received with the exercise of due diligence and proper management. (*White* v. *City of London Brewery Co.*, 1889.)[591] If the mortgagee is simply concerned to intercept rents, where the mortgaged property is let and the mortgagor is a landlord, he will do better to appoint a receiver under the Law of Property Act, 1925, Sect. 109. Most mortgagees who ask for a possession order do so in order to sell with vacant possession. The Administration of Justice Act, 1970, which is concerned, amongst other things, with mortgage possession actions, reinstates the old practice of the Chancery masters by allowing the Court to make an order adjourning the proceedings, or suspending or postponing a possession order provided it appears that the mortgagor is likely to be able to pay within a reasonable time any sums due under the mortgage (Sect. 36). The Act applies wherever a mortgage includes a dwelling house even though part may be used for business purposes. Sect. 36 does not apply to a foreclosure action in which a claim for possession is also made.

(*b*) FORECLOSURE. The mortgagee may obtain an order from the court if the mortgagor fails to pay for an unreasonable time. The first order is a *foreclosure order nisi* providing that the debt must be paid within a stated time. If it is not so paid, the order is made *absolute* and the property becomes that of the mortgagee, the mortgagor's equity of redemption being barred, and the property vesting in the mortgagee, free from any right of redemption either in law or Equity. Such orders are seldom used, for it is still open to the court to re-open the foreclosure, i.e. to give the mortgagor a further opportunity to redeem.

(*c*) RIGHT OF SALE. Normally this is the most valuable right of the mortgagee. Subject to certain conditions he can, on the default of the mortgagor, sell and convey to a purchaser the whole of the mortgaged property, and recoup himself out of the proceeds. Unless the mortgagee is a building society (Building Societies Act, 1962, Sect. 36), he is not a trustee of the power of sale for the benefit of the mortgagor. He is not only under a duty to act in good faith but must also take reasonable care to obtain the true market value of the property at the time when he chooses to sell (*Cuckmere Brick Co. Ltd.* v. *Mutual Finance*, [1971] 2 All E.R. 633.) A building society must get the best price obtainable. A mortgagee cannot sell to himself or to his nominee.

(*d*) To SUE FOR THE MONEY OWING. The mortgage is a pledge for the repayment of the money, but mortgagors almost invariably give a personal covenant to repay. This is of value should the property be destroyed or lose its value. When the date fixed for redemption is passed, the mortgage money is due and the mortgagee can sue for it. He will rarely do so, for in most cases the other remedies will be more satisfactory.

(*e*) THE RIGHT TO APPOINT A RECEIVER. The Law of Property Act, 1925, Sect. 109, gives the mortgagee the right to appoint a receiver to receive the rents and profits on the mortgagee's behalf in order to pay the money due. The receiver is deemed to be the agent of the mortgagor, who is liable for his acts and defaults unless otherwise provided by the mortgage. The mortgagee thus avoids the disadvantage of strict accountability to which he would be subject if he entered himself.

Remedies of Equitable Mortgagees. Where the mortgage is equitable and is created by deed, then the mortgagee has virtually the same remedies as have been set out above. Otherwise, if the mortgage is by a mere deposit of title deeds, then the mortgagee must ask the court—

(*a*) for an order to sell; or
(*b*) for an order appointing a receiver.

Other Rights of Mortgagees. A mortgagee has other rights and he may, where the mortgage is created by deed, insure the mortgaged property against loss by fire up to two-thirds of its value, and charge the premiums on the property in the same way as the mortgage money.

A mortgagee has a right to the title deeds of the property, and if the mortgage is redeemed by the mortgagor, the mortgagee must return the deeds to him in the absence of notice of a second or subsequent mortgage, in which case the deeds should be handed to the next mortgagee.

There are two other important rights which a mortgagee may exercise in appropriate circumstances—the right to consolidate and the right to tack.

CONSOLIDATION. Where a person has two or more mortgages, he may refuse to allow one mortgage to be redeemed unless the other or others are also redeemed. This right is particularly valuable where property might fluctuate in value, and where a mortgagor might redeem one mortgage where the security was more than adequate, leaving the mortgagee with a debt on the other property not properly secured.

Consolidation is only possible if the right to consolidate was reserved in one of the mortgage deeds, or if the mortgage was contracted prior to 1882. The contractual date for redemption must have passed on all mortgages and they must have been created by the same mortgagor, though not necessarily in favour of the same mortgagee. Nevertheless in such cases, where it is proposed to consolidate two mortgages, both the mortgages must have been vested in one person at the same time as both the equities of redemption were vested in another.

TACKING. The right to tack may bring about a modification of the priority of mortgages. It is now confined to the tacking of further advances. Thus, where a man has lent money on a first mortgage and there are second and third mortgages, if the first mortgagee agrees to advance a further sum, he may tack this to his first mortgage and thus get priority over the second and third, which would normally rank before the tacked mortgage. This can now only be done if the intervening mortgagees agree, or if the further advance is made without notice of an intervening mortgage, or if the prior mortgage imposed an obligation to make further advances.

ATTORNMENT CLAUSE. Many mortgages contain an attornment clause by which the borrower attorns or acknowledges himself as a tenant at will, or from year to year, of the lender at a nominal rent such as a peppercorn. The advantage of such a clause was that it entitled the lender to evict the borrower for failure to pay the mortgage instalments and so obtain possession more speedily. However, changes in the rules of court from 1933–37 made a speedy procedure available to mortgagees as such, and there is now no substantial advantage in an attornment clause.

Priority of Mortgages. The Land Charges Act, 1925, introduced the principle of registering charges on land. The object of searching the Land Charges Register is to discover the rights, if any, of third parties which are enforceable against the land. It is a general principle that a purchaser or mortgagee of land is deemed to have actual notice of all third-party rights capable of registration and actually registered, whereas he acquires his interest in the land free from third-party rights capable of registration and not registered. There are five separate registers kept at the Land Charges Department of the Land Registry in London. Search may be made in person, but is usually done by filling in an appropriate form and sending it to the Land Charges Superintendent in London. This results in an *official search certificate*.

Where there is a mortgage of a legal estate with deposit of title deeds, the mortgage ranks from the date of its creation and such a mortgage cannot be registered.

Where there is a mortgage of legal estate without deposit of title deeds, the mortgage ranks from its date of registration as a land charge.

Regarding mortgages of equitable interests, the question of priority is based on the rule in *Dearle* v. *Hall* (1828), 3 Russ. 1, and such mortgages rank from the date on which the mortgagee gave notice of his mortgage to the trustees of the equitable interest, though such notice will not postpone a previous mortgage of which the mortgagee giving notice was aware.

The Leasehold Reform Act, 1967. Where, under the provisions of this Act, a leaseholder buys the freehold, the conveyance automatically discharges the premises from any mortgage even though the lender is not a party to the conveyance. (Sect. 12 (1).) However, the leaseholder must apply the money which he is using to buy the freehold, in the first instance, in or towards the payment (or redemption) of the mortgage. (Sect. 12 (2).) If the lender raises difficulties the tenant may, in order to protect his interest, pay the money into court. (Sect. 13.) The lender (or mortgagee) must accept not less than three months' notice to pay off the whole or part of the principal secured by the mortgage, together with interest to the date of payment regardless of any provisions to the contrary in the mortgage (Sect. 12 (4).)

The court is also given power, under Sect. 36, to alter the rights of the parties to a mortgage in order to mitigate any financial hardship which may arise as a result of the purchase of a freehold under the provisions of the Act.

If it is desired that a mortgage of the former leasehold interest should be extended to cover the freehold, this may be done by requesting the borrower to execute a deed of substituted security. If a tenant acquires an extended lease a lender is entitled to possession of the documents of title relating to the new lease (Sect. 14 (6)) and should ask for them when the borrower obtains an extended lease. The borrower should also be required to execute a mortgage of the extended lease.

REGISTRATION OF LAND CHARGES

The Land Charges Act, 1925, introduced the principle of registering charges on land. The object of searching the Land Charges Register is to discover the rights, if any, of third parties which are enforceable against the land. It is a general principle that a purchaser or mortgagee of land is deemed to have actual notice of all third-party rights capable of registration and actually registered, whereas he acquires his interest in the land free from third-party rights capable of registration and not registered.

The injustice to a purchaser of this rule lay in the fact that in practice there is no investigation of the title prior to the formation of the contract. In consequence, if a vendor did not actually disclose to a purchaser that there were charges over the land, then, if the charges were registered, the purchaser was unable to rescind the contract since he was deemed to know that they existed. In future, under Sect. 24 of The Law of Property Act, 1969, the purchaser will be affected *as against his vendor* only by land charges of which he had *actual* knowledge at the time of entering into the contract. If he completes the contract the purchaser remains bound by registered land charges *as against the holder of the charge* whether or not he has actual knowledge of them.

The most important search is in the Registers of the Land Charges Department of the Land Registry in London, though local landcharges may appear in registers kept by local authorities. Search may not now be in person, but is done by filling in the details of the appropriate form and sending it to the Land Charges Superintendent in London. This results in an *official search certificate*.

It is now possible to ask for search by telephone or telex provided this is followed by a normal search in written form. The Land Registration and Land Charges Act, 1971, introduces a number of changes designed to simplify the procedure. These include changes made necessary by computerisation.

The registers are registers of names, not properties. Thus a charge affecting Whiteacre, a property situated in Birmingham and owned by John Jones, will be indexed under John Jones, provided he was owner of Whiteacre when the charge was created.

There are five separate registers—

1. A Register of Pending Actions. These are actions which are being pursued with regard to the land, e.g. a petition in bankruptcy.

2. A Register of Annuities. This Register contains annuities registered before 1926. Other annuities are registered as Class C Land Charges.

3. A Register of Writs and Orders Affecting Land. These are various orders enforcing judgments, e.g. a receiving order in bankruptcy.

4. A Register of Deeds of Arrangement. These are assignments of property for the benefit of creditors generally.

5. A Register of Land Charges. The most important classes are as follows—

CLASS A. Charges created as a result of the application of some person under the provisions of an Act of Parliament, e.g. a charge under Sect. 72 of the Agricultural Holdings Act, 1948, by the provisions of which a tenant of agricultural land has a charge against the land in respect of the value of improvements he has carried out.

CLASS C. Such charges are subdivided as follows—

(i) *Puisne Mortgages*. These are legal mortgages of a legal estate in land where the mortgagee does not obtain the title deeds. They are invariably second or third mortgages.

(ii) *Limited Owners' Charges*. These are equitable charges which a tenant for life acquires by discharging out of his own pocket liabilities due from the property. The commonest example is death duties.

(iii) *General Equitable Charges* (except those arising under a settlement or trust for sale. These are not registrable because the object of the law is to allow them to be over-reached). The most usual example is an equitable mortgage of a legal estate. Annuities created after 1925 are registrable here, but not if they arise under a settlement or trust for sale.

(iv) *Estate Contracts*. These may be defined as "any contract by an estate owner or by a person entitled at the date of the contract to have a legal estate conveyed to him, to convey or create a legal estate." Thus if the owner of the legal estate in Whiteacre enters into an agreement for the sale thereof, this contract is registrable as an estate contract. However, the contract must be binding on the parties so that an agreement "subject to contract" would not be capable of registration. (*Thomas* v. *Rose*, [1968] 3 All E.R. 765.)

CLASS D. This class may be subdivided as follows—

(i) *Death Duties.* The Commissioners of Inland Revenue may register a charge for estate duty.

(ii) *Restrictive Covenants.* These are any covenants or agreements entered into after 1925 which restrict the use of land and are not between lessor and lessee.

(iii) *Equitable Easements created after* 1925.

CLASS F. The Matrimonial Homes Act, 1967, creates a new type of land charge registrable under this class. The Act was passed to restore the legal position to what it was before the decision of the House of Lords in *National Provincial Bank Ltd.* v. *Ainsworth*, [1965] 2 All E.R. 472. In that case it was decided that a deserted wife had no special right or "equity" to continue to occupy the matrimonial home though there had formerly been such a right. The effect of the decision in *Ainsworth's Case* was that a husband who was the owner of the matrimonial home could, having deserted his wife and children, sell or mortgage the house to a third party who would in most cases be able to get an order for possession in order to enforce his rights. In these circumstances the deserted wife and children would have to give up occupation of the matrimonial home and find other accommodation.

The Act provides that where one spouse owns or is the tenant of the matrimonial home, the other spouse has certain "rights of occupation" (Sect. 1(1)) and cannot be evicted without an order of the court. Where a spouse is not in occupation of the matrimonial home he or she has a right, with the leave of the court, to enter and occupy the house. However, the court may order a spouse who is occupying the matrimonial home by reason of the Act to make periodical payments to the other spouse in respect of that occupation. It should be noted that the Act protects husbands as well as wives.

The Act provides that the rights of occupation provided for in Sect. 1(1) are a charge on the estate or interest of the other spouse (Sect. 2(1)), registrable as a new type of land charge (Class F) under the Land Charges Act, 1925. Where the land is registered land a notice or caution must be registered under the Land Registration Act, 1925. A purchaser or mortgagee is deemed to have notice of rights of occupation which have been properly registered. Rights of occupation may be registered on marriage though in most cases registration will not take place unless and until the marriage breaks down.

Where a spouse registers rights of occupation, the house is unlikely subsequently to be an acceptable security for a loan because the rights of occupation represent a prior charge on the property which cannot be sold with vacant possession. However, a spouse who is entitled to rights of occupation may, under Sect. 6(3) of the Act, agree in writing that any other charge shall rank in priority to his or her charge.

Searching applies to unregistered land, but in many parts of the country land registration is compulsory, e.g. in London, Middlesex and Surrey. Here the landowner receives a land certificate, and on the sale of the land he has only to make out a transfer deed, and have the purchaser's name entered on the Land Register instead of his own so that no chain of ownership is established and searching for title is not necessary.

The compulsory registration system will, broadly speaking, be extended to all urban areas of England and Wales by the summer of 1973 and to the rest of the country by 1980. However, registration only occurs when a particular property changes hands. This phases the work and means that a property which is not sold or leased stays unregistered.

MORTGAGES OF PERSONAL CHATTELS

Just as land can be used as a means of securing debts, so also can personal chattels. There are two principal ways in which this can be done—

(*a*) *by mortgage*: in this case the borrower retains possession of his goods but transfers their ownership to the lender to secure the loan.

This raises a problem because, since the borrower retains the chattels, he also retains an appearance of wealth, and this may mislead others into giving him credit. Accordingly the Bills of Sale Acts, 1878–91, were passed, and under the statutory provisions, where chattels are retained by the mortgagor, a bill of sale must be made out. Where ownership of the chattel passes to the mortgagee conditionally upon its being reconveyed to the mortgagor on repayment of the loan, the Bill of Sale is called a conditional bill. An absolute Bill of Sale is one which transfers completely the ownership in chattels by way of sale, gift or settlement.

All Bills of Sale must be attested and registered within seven days of execution. Registration is in the Central Office of the Supreme Court. Conditional Bills of Sale must be re-registered every five years if they are still operative.

A conditional Bill of Sale is totally void if it is not registered, whilst an unregistered absolute Bill of Sale is void against the trustee in bankruptcy and judgment creditors of the grantor so that the chattels represented by the Bill are available to pay the grantor's debts.

(*b*) *By pledge*, or "*pawn*": in this case the lender obtains possession of the goods, the borrower retaining ownership. Thus there is no danger that the borrower will obtain credit on the strength of his possession of the chattels, and the law relating to pledges is mainly concerned to protect the interests of the borrower (or pledger) against dishonest pawnbrokers.

MORTGAGES OF CHOSES IN ACTION

It is possible to use a chose in action as security for a loan, and mortgagees frequently take life assurance policies as security, e.g. a bank in the case of an overdraft. However, shares in companies are perhaps the commonest chose in action to be used as security.

Shares may be made subject to a legal mortgage, but here the shares must actually be transferred to the mortgagee so that his name may appear on the company's share register. An agreement is made out in which the mortgagee agrees to re-transfer the shares to the mortgagor when the loan is repaid.

It is also possible to have an equitable mortgage of company shares, and this is in fact the usual method adopted. The share certificate is deposited with the mortgagee, together with a blank transfer signed by the registered holder, the name of the transferee being left blank. The shares are not actually transferred, but the agreement accompanying the transaction allows the mortgagee to sell the shares by completing the form of transfer and registering himself as the legal owner if the mortgagor fails to repay the loan.

OWNERSHIP

Ownership is a term used to express the relationship which exists between a person and certain rights which are vested in him. Ownership is the greatest right or collection of rights—the ultimate right—which a person can have over or in a thing.

For example, X may own a fee simple in Blackacre and may lease the land to Y, so giving up possession. But however long the lease, the ultimate right of ownership is in X, and eventually the right to possess, which he has for the moment forfeited, will return to him or to his estate if he is dead. Z may have a right of way over Blackacre. This is not ownership of Blackacre, but is ownership of a right over it which limits X's enjoyment of the land. B may have lent money to X on the security of the land, so that B is a mortgagee and, therefore, the owner of a right in Blackacre, but this does not constitute ownership of the land; it is a mere encumbrance attached to it, limiting X's enjoyment to the extent of the rights given to B as mortgagee. Nevertheless the supreme right is vested in X, and this right is called ownership of Blackacre.

Ownership is a *de jure* relationship; there is no need to possess the thing. Possession tends to be *de facto*, i.e. evidenced by physical possession, although, as we shall see, physical possession is not necessary in order to have legal possession.

It may be said that in a general sense all rights are capable of ownership, which is of many kinds—

(*a*) CORPOREAL, i.e. the ownership of a thing or chose in possession such as a watch or a fountain pen.

(*b*) INCORPOREAL, i.e. the ownership of a right only, e.g. the right to recover a debt of £20 from X by an action at law, or the ownership of a chose in action. A share certificate is a chose in action, and ownership of it is incorporeal, for it is ownership of certain rights: the right to dividends as and when declared, the right to vote at meetings, and so on.

(*c*) SOLE OWNERSHIP, as where X is the sole owner of Blackacre.

(*d*) CO-OWNERSHIP, as where X and Y are simultaneously owners of Blackacre, as joint tenants or tenants in common.

(*e*) LEGAL OR EQUITABLE OWNERSHIP. Thus a grant giving X the fee simple absolute in possession of Blackacre constitutes him the legal owner. But a grant giving X a life interest only constitutes him an equitable owner, whose interest can exist only behind a trust, the legal estate being vested in trustees.

(*f*) TRUST OR BENEFICIAL OWNERSHIP. In the grant set out above giving X a life interest, the trustees hold the legal estate but not beneficially; the beneficial interest is in X and Equity will protect it.

(*g*) VESTED OR CONTINGENT OWNERSHIP. In a grant to X for life, with remainder to Y if he attains the age of twenty-one years, X's interest is equitable and vested, Y's interest is equitable and contingent since he must satisfy the requirement of majority before his interest vests.

POSSESSION

The physical control of a thing by a person is what is normally known as possession, and if the idea of possession had remained wedded to physical control, the position would have been simple enough. But the widening sphere of legal activity made it necessary to attribute to persons who were not actually in physical control some or all of the advantages enjoyed by persons who were.

There are three possible situations at law—

(i) A man can have physical control without legal possession, as in the case of a porter carrying a traveller's suitcase in a station.

(ii) A man can have possession and its advantages without actual physical control, e.g. a man may have books at home which are still in his possession even when he is away on holiday.

(iii) He can have both physical control and possession, e.g. a watch in his pocket or a pen in his hand.

Possession, therefore, has acquired a technical legal meaning, and the separation of possession from physical control has given the concept a high degree of flexibility.

The old theory of possession, derived from the Roman Law, relies upon (i) *corpus*, i.e. physical control, and (ii) *animus*, i.e. the intention to exclude others. But although these concepts help in deciding possession, they do not provide the complete answer. Indeed as Viscount Jowitt has said: "In truth English law has never worked out a completely logical and exhaustive definition of possession." The handing over of a key may be sufficient by itself to pass the possession of the contents of a room or box if it provides the effective means of control over the goods.

Trespass to Property. In the law of torts, trespass to property is an invasion of possession. The policy of this branch of the law is to compensate the party whose interests have been affected, and in order to enable such persons to recover, the court has contrived to attribute possession to them.

A bailee is a person who gets possession of a chattel from another with his consent. A bailment may be at will, i.e. revocable by the bailor at any time, or it may be for a term, i.e. for a fixed period of time. Where a bailment is at will, the bailee, who by definition has possession, can sue a third party in trespass. Since the bailment is revocable at will, the bailor also has an interest worth protecting, and in order that he too may bring an action in trespass, his right to possess is treated as possession itself. Where, on the other hand, the bailment is for a term, only the bailee can bring trespass and not the bailor, although, where the bailee brings the action, he will normally have to account to the bailor for any damages obtained.

Where a master has temporarily handed a thing to his servant, possession remains with the master and the servant takes only custody. Thus a master can sue in trespass for an injury to the goods by a third party.

A person who loses a thing retains his ownership in it, and for the purpose of suing in conversion someone who has taken it, his right to regain possession will suffice, and the same is probably true of an action in trespass. But for the purpose of claiming from an insurance company for loss, he will be regarded as having lost possession, within the terms of the contract, if the thing cannot in fact be found.

Trespass by relation is another example of the artificial manipulation of the concept of possession to provide a remedy in trespass to one who needs to be compensated. When a person, with a right to possess, enters in pursuance of that right, he is deemed to have been in possession from the time when his right originally accrued, e.g. from the time when he made the original contract for a purchase or a lease. He can, therefore, sue for any trespass that has been committed between the accrual of the right and the actual entry.

The owner of land possesses everything attached to or under the land, particularly if the place is one to which the public is not admitted. (*Elwes* v. *Brigg Gas Co.*, 1886,[458] *South Staffordshire Water Co.* v. *Sharman*, 1896),[459] and *Corporation of London* v. *Appleyard*, 1963.[460] Things lying loose on the land are not in the possession of the landowner but fall into the possession of the first finder, at any rate if he is lawfully on the land and the public is generally admitted thereto. (*Bridges* v. *Hawkesworth*, 1851,[457] and *Hannah* v. *Peel*, 1945.)[461]

However, it should be noted that unless an owner of chattels can be shown to have *abandoned* or *sold* them he remains their owner and has a better title than a finder or a person on whose property they are found. (*Moffat* v. *Kazana*, 1968.)[592]

Adverse Possession. A person may sometimes acquire the owner-ship of land by adverse possession. This arises from the occupation and use of land without the permission of, or any interference from, the true owner, as where a stranger encloses and cultivates a portion of a neighbour's land or occupies another's house. Adverse possession for a period of twelve years will give the possessor a title (*Hayward* v. *Challoner*, 1967),[593] but such adverse possession must take the form of overt acts which are inconsistent with the title of the owner, and in this case possession is viewed much more strictly than in the others we have been considering above. (*Littledale* v. *Liverpool College*, 1900.)[594]

BAILMENT

Bailments are concerned with pure personalty and not with real property.

The bailment may or may not originate in a contract and a minor may be a bailee of goods even though he obtained them under a void contract. (*Ballett* v. *Mingay*, 1943.)[361]

Possession. An essential feature of a bailment is the transfer of possession to the bailee. There is no precise definition of possession, but the basic features are *control* and *an intention to exclude others*. However, a person can have possession of chattels which he does not know exist (*South Staffordshire Water Co.* v. *Sharman*, 1896).[459] A servant who receives goods from his master to take to a third party has mere *custody;* possession remains with the master and the servant is not a bailee. If a third party hands goods to a servant for his master the servant obtains possession and is the bailee.

In a bailment for a *fixed term* the bailee has possession to the exclusion of the bailor, and is, therefore, the only person who can sue a third party for trespass or conversion if there is interference with possession. In a bailment at will, i.e. one which the bailor can terminate at will, the bailor retains either possession or an immediate right to possess and the actions of trespass and conversion are available to him as well as to the bailee. A bailee can sue a third party in tort for loss of or damage to the goods even though the bailee is not liable to the bailor for the loss or damage. (*The Winkfield*, 1902.)[469]

Bailment and Licence. The problem of distinguishing between bailment and licence has arisen mainly in connection with the parking of vehicles. If a vehicle is parked on land, either gratuitously or even on payment of a charge, the transaction may amount to a mere licence and not a bailment which gives rise to duties of care. (*Ashby* v. *Tolhurst*, 1937.)[595] The decisions in *Ultzen* v. *Nicols*, 1894,[596] and *Deyong* v. *Shenburn*, 1946,[597] are illustrative of the problems involved in distinguishing bailment and licence.

Finders and Involuntary Recipients. To constitute a bailment, the person who is given possession of goods must be entrusted with them for a particular purpose, e.g. to use and return as in the case of loan or hire, or to take from one place to another as in carriage. A banker is not a bailee of money paid into a customer's account, for his obligation is to return an equivalent sum and not the identical notes and coins. However, a banker is a bailee of property deposited with him for safe custody.

A finder is not a true bailee because he is not entrusted with the goods for a particular purpose. However, if he takes them into his possession he will be liable for loss or damage resulting from his negligence. (*Newman* v. *Bourne and Hollingsworth*, 1915.)[598]

A person cannot be made a bailee against his will. (*Neuwirth* v. *Over Darwen Industrial Co-operative Society*, 1894.)[599] Where the receipt of the goods is involuntary it is unlikely that the recipient is under any higher duty than to refrain from intentional damage. However, he must not convert the goods, but although liability for conversion is usually strict, an involuntary recipient will only be liable if he acts intentionally or negligently. (*Elvin and Powell Ltd.* v. *Plummer Roddis Ltd.*, 1933.)[467]

The Unsolicited Goods and Services Act, 1971, is relevant in this connection. The Act is designed to deal with selling techniques involving the sending of unsolicited goods, thus rendering the recipient an involuntary bailee. The Act provides for fines to be made on persons making demands for payment for goods they know to be unsolicited. If the demand is accompanied by threats a higher scale of fines applies. Furthermore, unsolicited goods may be kept by the recipient without payment *after a period of thirty days* provided the recipient gives notice to the sender asking that they be collected, or *after six months* even if no notice has been given.

Obligations of the Bailor. Where the bailment is gratuitous it has been said that the limit of the liability of the bailor is to communicate to the bailee defects in the article lent *of which he is aware*. However, the principle in *Donoghue* v. *Stevenson*, 1932,[354] may apply to gratuitous bailments so that the bailor would be liable if he had not taken reasonable care to ensure that the goods bailed were not dangerous, even though he had no actual knowledge of a defect in the chattels lent.

When the bailment is for reward there is an implied warranty on the part of the bailor that he has a title to the goods so that the bailee's possession will not be disturbed, and that the goods are fit and suitable for the bailee's purpose. This does not mean that the bailee is liable for all defects but only for those which skill and care can guard against. (*Hyman* v. *Nye*, 1881,[600] *Reed* v. *Dean*, 1949.)[601] However, the warranty as to fitness and suitability does not apply where the defect is apparent to the bailee and he does not rely on the skill or judgment of the bailor.

Obligations of the Bailee. When Lord Holt, in *Coggs* v. *Bernard*, 1703,[103] established the liability of the bailee in negligence he laid down different duties of care for different kinds of bailments. Thus, in a bailment for the sole benefit of the bailee, such as a gratuitous loan, the bailee's duty of care was much higher than in a bailment for the benefit of both parties such as a hiring. However, in recent times there has been disapproval of Lord Holt's different standards of care (*Houghland* v. *R. Low* (*Luxury Coaches*) *Ltd.*, 1962),[602] and it is now the better view that the standard of care required of a bailee is to take reasonable care in all the circumstances of the case, which equates his duty with that owed by any person in the law relating to negligence, though the burden of disproving negligence is on the bailee. (*Global Dress Co.* v. *Boase & Co.*, 1966.)[603]

The *main* circumstances which the court is likely to consider when deciding the question of negligence in a bailee are—

(*a*) *The type of bailment.* Although some current legal opinion is against a doctrinal distinction between bailment for reward and gratuitous bailment, reward or lack of reward will continue to be an *important circumstance* in the matter of the bailee's negligence. A gratuitous bailee must take the same care of the property bailed as a reasonable man would take of his own property. It is no defence for a bailee to show that he kept the goods with as much care as his own because the test of reasonableness is objective. (*Doorman* v. *Jenkins*, 1834.)[604] In a bailment for reward the duty of care tends to be somewhat higher. (*Brabant* v. *King*, 1895.)[605]

(*b*) *The expertise of the bailee.* If the bailee's profession or situation implies a certain expertise he will be liable if he fails to show it. (*Wilson* v. *Brett*, 1843.)[606]

(*c*) *The property bailed.* If the goods bailed are, to the knowledge of the bailee fragile or valuable, a high standard of care will be expected. (*Saunders* (*Mayfair*) *Furs* v. *Davies*, 1965.)[607]

A bailee may be liable in negligence if he does not give notice to the bailor of a loss or try to recover lost or stolen property. (*Coldman* v. *Hill*, 1919.)[608]

A bailee is vicariously liable for the torts of his servants, but a servant who became a thief was not regarded as acting within the scope of his employment. (*Cheshire* v. *Bailey*, 1905.)[609] However, in *Morris* v. *C. W. Martin & Sons Ltd.*, 1965,[381] it was held that a bailee for reward cannot necessarily escape liability for loss of goods stolen by his servant because theft may be regarded as being in the course of employment.

A bailee may attempt to exclude his liability by an exemption clause in the contract of bailment. This matter must now be considered in the light of the *Suisse Case.*[226] and the rules of construction of contracts (pp. 167–69).

Delegation by Bailee. Whether a bailee can delegate performance of the contract to another depends upon the nature of the bailment and the particular contract which may authorise delegation. Contracts involving the carriage, storage, repair or cleaning of goods often assume personal performance by the bailee. (*Davies* v. *Collins*, 1945;[610] *Edwards* v. *Newland*, 1950.)[611] Where there is a delegation, even though unknown to the bailee, the delegate is a bailee and owes a duty of care directly to the bailor. (*Learoyd Bros.* v. *Pope*, 1966.)[612]

Estoppel and Interpleader. A bailee is estopped at common law from denying the title of his bailor and if the bailor demands the return of the goods it is no defence for the bailee to plead that the bailor is not the owner. However, a bailee may defend an action for non-delivery of the goods—

(*a*) by showing that he has delivered them under an authorisation by the bailor;

(*b*) by showing that he has not got the goods because he has been dispossessed by a person with a better title, as in a bailment of stolen goods which are reclaimed by the owner;

(*c*) if he still retains possession he may allege that a third party has a better title but he must defend the action on behalf of, and with the authority of, the true owner. (*Rogers, Sons & Co.* v. *Lambert & Co.*, 1891.)[613]

Where adverse claims are made against the bailee by the bailor and a third party, the bailee should take interpleader proceedings under the Rules of the Supreme Court. The effect of this will be to bring the bailor and the third party together in an action which will decide the validity of their claims. The bailee can then hand over the goods to whichever party has established his claim and will not risk liability in detinue or conversion.

Lien. A bailee may, in certain circumstances, have a lien on the goods and the general nature of a lien is described on pp. 319–21.

CHAPTER VIII

THE LAW OF TRUSTS

A TRUST is an equitable obligation which imposes upon a person (called a trustee) a duty of dealing with property over which he has control (called the trust property) for the benefit of persons (called the beneficiaries or *cestuis que trust*) of whom he may himself be one, and any of whom may enforce the obligation. Generally speaking all kinds of property, whether real or personal, may be held on trust, but the property most frequently so held includes land, stocks and shares.

THE NATURE OF A TRUST

A trust must be distinguished from other legal concepts—

1. CONTRACTS. Consideration is not necessary to a trust unless it is incompletely constituted; it is, however, necessary to a contract not under seal. A contract can be terminated by the parties; trusts can only be terminated before coming to their natural conclusion—

(*a*) by the agreement of all possible beneficiaries (where there are possible beneficiaries who are as yet unborn a trust cannot be varied or brought to an end by agreement);

(*b*) by the settlor or the trustees if a specific power to do so is conferred by the trust; or

(*c*) by the court under the Variation of Trusts Act, 1958.

Under the Act the court can, for example, approve arrangements designed to increase the powers of trustees, to vary investment clauses and the beneficial interests, and to reduce the incidence of taxation. The court may also approve the deletion of a forfeiture provision provided such a deletion is for the benefit of all the beneficiaries on whose behalf the court is concerned to approve the arrangement. (*Re Remnant's Trusts*, 1970.)[614]

However, in regard to minors or unborn children, the court should consider not merely the financial benefits of a variation but also the educational and social benefits. (*Re Weston's Settlements*, 1968.)[615] The court can also consent to alterations on behalf of minors and unborn persons, though if an adult beneficiary does not consent to the proposed arrangement, the court cannot approve it under the statute. Subject to certain statutory exceptions contracts can only be enforced by the parties; trusts can be enforced by any beneficiary, whether a party or not to the creation of the trust.

2. BAILMENTS. A bailor retains property rights over the property bailed; a settlor does not retain such rights over the trust property. Only chattels can be bailed, whereas trusts can be made over any property. A bailee exercises rights in his own name; a trustee exercises them in favour of the beneficiaries.

3. POWERS. A power is the authority given to a person to dispose of property which is not his. The person who confers the power is known as the donor, and the recipient of the power as the donee. A general power imposes no restrictions of choice on the donee, and he may appoint the property which is the subject of the power to anyone, even to himself. An example of a general power is: "To A for life, remainder as he shall appoint." A has a life interest and a general power of appointment. A special power restricts the donee to appointing the property to a limited class known as the objects of the power, e.g. power to appoint among his issue, or among the children of X.

A power must be distinguished from a trust since it is discretionary, whereas a trust is mandatory and must be carried out. A power in the nature of a trust arises where the wording of the instrument creating the power is so construed that there is an obligation to make payments to the objects of the power, though the donee has power to select among those objects if he wishes to do so. If the power of selection is not exercised, the objects take equally. If there is a gift over in default of the exercise of the power, there cannot be a power in the nature of a trust. If there is no such gift over, there may be. A legal power can exist, e.g. a power of attorney; trusts on the other hand must be equitable. The donee of a power has no title over the interests he can appoint, whereas a trustee has a title over the trust property.

It was at one time thought that the requirements of certainty of objects were much stricter for trusts than they were for powers. It was said that with a trust it must be possible to enumerate the beneficiaries and that if this was difficult or impossible the trust was void. It was, however, accepted that in the case of a power less certainty would suffice. (*Re Gibbard's Will Trusts*, 1966.)[616] Nevertheless, in *McPhail* v. *Doulton*, 1970,[617] the House of Lords decided that the test to be applied to ascertain the validity of a trust ought to be similar to that accepted for powers, namely that the trust was valid if it could be said with certainty that any given individual was or was not a member of the class of beneficiaries designated.

4. AGENCY. An agent has no property rights as such in the subject matter of the agency; a trustee has property rights over the subject matter of the trust. An agent is entirely controlled by his principal; trustees are only partially controlled by the beneficiaries, and not at all by the settlor or creator of the trust. An agent can involve his principal in liability; a trustee cannot involve either the settlor or the beneficiaries in personal liability.

CLASSIFICATION OF TRUSTS

There are several methods of classification, but the following is thought to be a suitable one for most purposes—

1. **Public and Private Trusts.** Public trusts are enforceable by the Attorney-General as charities. Private trusts comprise all noncharitable trusts.

2. Express Trusts. These trusts are set out in writing, or made orally by the settlor, and in some cases are created by statute. Suppose X conveys land in fee simple to his six children, A, B, C, D, E and F. The Law of Property Act, 1925, provides that in such a case A, B, C and D hold the legal estate in the land on trust for themselves and E and F in Equity. The trusts imposed by the statute are known as statutory trusts and give power to sell the property and divide the proceeds among the persons entitled to the equitable interests, though the trustees may postpone sale.

3. Constructive Trusts. This classification is sometimes used to cover all other trusts, but is more commonly applied to trusts arising by operation of law irrespective of the parties' intentions. Secret profits or other benefits obtained by a trustee by virtue of his control of the trust property are held under a constructive trust. (*Keech* v. *Sandford*, 1726,[618] and *Protheroe* v. *Protheroe*, 1968.)[618a]

4. Implied Trusts. These are non-express trusts based on the presumed intention of the parties. For example, if X leaves property by will on trust to pay therefrom an annuity of £500, and the residue of the income of the property is undisposed of, the balance of the income reverts to X's estate, since the law assumes that a settlor intends to keep what he has not effectively disposed of. This form of trust is called a resulting trust.

A useful illustration of the concept of the resulting trust operating in a commercial situation is provided by *Barclays Bank Ltd.* v. *Quistclose Investments Ltd.*, 1968.[619] In addition, it may be used to recover money donated to a non-charitable fund for a particular purpose where that purpose has failed (*Re West Sussex Constabulary's Widows, Children and Benevolent* (1930) *Fund Trusts*, 1970).[620] (See also p. 350 for provisions of The Charities Act, 1960, where the fund has charitable objects.)

5. Trusts of Perfect Obligation. These are trusts where there are persons, including the Attorney-General for charities, who can enforce them.

6. Trusts of Imperfect Obligation. These are trusts for non-charitable purposes which have no human beneficiaries who can enforce them directly. (*Re Shaw*, 1957.)[621] However, there are some anomalous exceptions, e.g. trusts for the upkeep of tombs and trusts for the upkeep of animals. The validity of these cases is doubtful, but where the court is prepared to allow them, they must be limited to what is known as the perpetuity period, i.e. they can only operate for a period of a life or lives in being plus a period of twenty-one years thereafter. If they are valid, their effect is that the trustees may carry them out if they wish, but if they fail to do so, the trustees must account to the persons who would have been entitled if the trust had failed.

FORMALITIES

By Sect. 53 of the Law of Property Act, 1925, re-enacting the earlier provisions of the Statute of Frauds, 1677, declarations of trust over land must be evidenced in writing. This provision only applies to express and not to constructive or implied trusts. Settled land is subject to the formal requirements of the Settled Land Act, 1925, and this matter is dealt with in the chapter on property. Dispositions of existing equitable interests must be in writing; written evidence is not enough. A direction to trustees, who hold property on trust "for X absolutely," to hold that property on new trusts is such a disposition and must be in writing.

With regard to trusts set up by will, the will must conform with the Wills Act, 1837, which means that it must usually be in writing, signed by the testator and attested by two competent witnesses. Subject to the requirements relating to wills, trusts of personal property may be declared orally.

The formal requirements above referred to must not be used as a cloak for fraud. Thus where absence of writing would assist the defendant in defrauding the plaintiff, the statutory provision will provide no defence, and oral evidence will be admissible to prove the trust. (*Bannister* v. *Bannister*, 1948,[622] and *Hodgson* v. *Marks*, 1970.)[235]

It is on this doctrine that secret trusts depend, and these are of two main kinds—

(*a*) fully secret trusts; and
(*b*) half-secret trusts.

They arise where a testator leaves property in his will to persons who are not expected to hold it for their own benefit, but to hold it for the benefit of others who have been named to them by the testator, although they are not mentioned in the will. Strictly speaking such trusts would be inoperative except that it would amount to a fraud to ignore them.

(*a*) FULLY SECRET TRUSTS. If, although there appears to be an absolute gift by will or on intestacy, the gift was in fact made and left unchanged in reliance on a promise by the donee to the deceased before death to hold the gift on trust, that trust will be enforceable notwithstanding the provisions of the Wills Act, 1837. If the donee agreed before the death to hold on trust, but the exact beneficial interests were not revealed, the donee holds on a resulting trust for the deceased's estate. If the donee did not agree to hold the property on any trust, he takes beneficially.

The trusts in a fully secret trust have nothing really to do with the will: they are binding on the legatee's conscience because of his agreement with the testator. It follows that a beneficiary under a secret trust can, therefore, witness the will and still take under the trust, and that there is no lapse if the secret beneficiary pre-deceases the testator, the property going into the deceased beneficiary's estate.

Sometimes a gift is made by will to two persons, but notification of the trusts has been made to only one before the death of the testator. If such a gift is made to A and B as tenants in common, and the trusts are communicated to A at any time before the death, A holds on trust and B takes beneficially. If a gift by will is made to A and B as joint tenants, and the trusts are communicated to either of them at or before the date of the will, both hold on trust. But if the trust is communicated to A between the date of the will and the testator's death, then A will hold on trust and B will take beneficially.

(*b*) HALF-SECRET TRUSTS. There is a half-secret trust where the existence of a trust is revealed on the face of the will but its terms are not, e.g. "To A £6,000 on the trusts I have told him." If there is communication at or before the date of the will, the trust is enforceable. If not, the donee will hold on a resulting trust for the testator's estate. (*Re Pugh's Will Trusts*, 1967.)[623] He cannot take beneficially unless the will itself states that there is to be no binding obligation upon him, even if he can show that the testator told him he was to take beneficially.

If, in a will, property is left to X "on the trusts I shall reveal," the trust will fail even if in fact there has been communication before the will. This rule is justified on the ground that a testator cannot, by means of a valid will, impose a trust without creating beneficial interests, and then by his words reserve to himself the right to infringe the Wills Act, 1837, by creating those interests by means of an informal non testamentary document. (*Re Bateman's Will Trusts*, 1970.)[624] Where a sealed envelope is handed to a secret trustee, this counts as communication from that date, and not from the time of opening.

THE THREE CERTAINTIES OF A TRUST

For the valid creation of a trust three things are essential and these are called the three certainties: certainty of words, certainty of subject matter, and certainty of objects.

1. Certainty of Words. The words should be imperative, but sometimes precatory words are used, e.g. "I leave my property to B in the full confidence that he will make provision for C." At one time a trust would be quite readily inferred from such expressions, but the more modern tendency is in the opposite direction. (*Re Adams and the Kensington Vestry*, 1884.)[625] No trust will now be inferred unless the instrument as a whole manifests such intention, or unless the precatory words are identical with words held to have created a trust in a previously reported decision.

2. Certainty of Subject Matter. This implies two things—

(i) that the property which is the subject of the trust must be certain; and
(ii) that the interests of the beneficiaries are ascertainable.

If a testator were to leave in his will "a nice round sum in trust for my brothers, George and John," this would fail for uncertainty.

3. Certainty of Objects. The persons whom the trust is intended to benefit (the objects of the trust) must be identified with sufficient certainty. (*Sale* v. *Moore*, 1827,[626] and *Re Pugh's Will Trusts*, 1967.)[623]

Nevertheless a settlor can confer a power of appointment amongst a class, and if the class of beneficiaries is certain, but the shares which they are to take are not, then the beneficiaries will take equally.

As we have seen, it was at one time thought that the requirements of certainty of objects were much stricter for trusts than they were for powers. However, as a result of the decision of the House of Lords in *McPhail* v. *Doulton*, 1970,[617] it appears that the test for both trusts and powers is similar, i.e. in a trust for a class, as in a power to appoint among a class, it is sufficient if one can tell whether any given person is within the class or not.

The effect of the lack of one or more of the certainties is as follows. If there is a lack of certainty of subject matter, the whole transaction fails. If there is a lack of certainty of words, the donee takes beneficially if the subject matter can be ascertained, except where the court decides that a precatory trust is enforceable. If there is uncertainty of objects, the donee holds on a resulting trust for the settlor, or, if he is dead, his residuary legatee or devisee, or the person entitled on intestacy as the case may be.

THE PARTIES TO A TRUST

The parties to a trust are the settlor, the trustee or trustees, and the beneficiaries or the *cestuis que trust*.

1. The Settlor. Any person who is competent to deal with either the legal estate or the equitable interest in property may create a trust, and such a person is generally known as the settlor.

2. The Trustees. Generally speaking any person of natural capacity and legal ability to execute a trust, and domiciled within the jurisdiction of a court of Equity, can be a trustee. The following classes, however, require special consideration—

(*a*) CORPORATIONS. By the Bodies Corporate (Joint Tenancies) Act, 1889, a body corporate was empowered to hold land in joint tenancy with an individual or other body corporate. Corporations formerly needed either statutory authority or licence in mortmain in order that they might hold land. In early times, when land was conveyed to a corporation, it was deemed to be a conveyance into mortmain (the dead hand). Since a corporation did not die, the benefits accruing to the feudal lord on the death of his tenant were lost if the land was conveyed to a corporation. Consequently, to restrict such holdings, corporations were required to obtain a licence in mortmain.

Statutory authority was given to certain types of corporations so that they might hold land without such a licence, e.g. registered companies under the Companies Act, 1948. The Charities Act, 1960, abolishes the law of mortmain altogether, and this restriction on the holding of land by corporations no longer applies.

(*b*) TRUST CORPORATIONS. Many banks and insurance companies now undertake trusteeship work for profit. The Public Trustee Act,

1906, authorises the Public Trustee to undertake trusteeship with the financial backing of the Treasury.

(*c*) MARRIED WOMEN. All disabilities on the holding of trust property by married women were removed by Sect. 170 of the Law of Property Act, 1925.

(*d*) MINORS. By Sect. 20 of the Law of Property Act, 1925, the appointment of a trustee who is a minor is void. Where a person named as a trustee is a minor, another trustee can be appointed in his place under Sect. 36 of the Trustee Act, 1925. A minor can hold property on an implied, constructive or resulting trust.

(*e*) AN ALIEN is allowed by the Status of Aliens Act, 1914, to hold real or personal property of every description, except a British ship, and he can, therefore, be a trustee in most cases.

(*f*) BANKRUPTS. They may be appointed trustees, and if a trustee becomes bankrupt, the trust property does not vest in his trustee in bankruptcy.

(*g*) BENEFICIARIES. Beneficiaries and other interested persons are not incapable of being appointed trustees, but in view of the conflict which may arise between their duty and their interest, such an appointment is undesirable, and will never be made by the court, but such an appointment made out of court may be valid. Relatives of beneficiaries should not normally be appointed, although the rules as to this are much less stringent, and in certain cases the court itself has appointed such a person.

3. Beneficiaries. All persons who can hold a legal estate can *prima facie* hold a beneficial interest. A minor can hold an equitable interest although he cannot hold a legal estate. The Crown and other corporations may be beneficiaries. If an express private trust is to be upheld there must be a beneficiary who can apply to the court to compel performance of the obligation in his favour. (*Re Shaw*, 1957.)[621]

EXECUTED AND EXECUTORY TRUSTS

An express trust may be either *executed* or *executory*, the words referring to the creation of the trust and not its carrying out.

The difference between the two is that, in the case of an *executed* trust, all that is necessary for its declaration is done at the outset, whereas, in the case of an *executory* trust, some further instrument is necessary. The following examples will make the distinction clear—

(*a*) X vests property in trustees on trust for Y for life, and on Y's death for Z absolutely. This is an *executed* trust.

(*b*) X, in his will, directs his executors to use certain funds to buy land and settle it on Y and his children. This is an *executory* trust.

COMPLETELY AND INCOMPLETELY CONSTITUTED TRUSTS

A trust becomes constituted when the trust property is vested in the trustees on the trusts. Until then a trust is incompletely constituted.

All trusts in wills are completely constituted since the testator's property vests automatically in his personal representatives, though trusts in wills may be executed or executory. An incompletely constituted trust can only be enforced in Equity by a person who is within the consideration for its creation. A completely constituted trust, whether voluntary or made for consideration, can be enforced by any beneficiary.

Once a trust becomes completely constituted it is irrevocable unless there is an express power of revocation in the trust. A voluntary and incompletely constituted trust is revocable. At common law even a volunteer (a person who gives no consideration) can enforce by way of damages a voluntary agreement under seal if he is a party to the deed. So if X agrees under seal to transfer certain property to trustees, it would seem *prima facie* to be possible for the trustees to sue X for damages for breach of the deed if he refuses to transfer the property into trust and so completely constitute it. However, where trustees are parties to a voluntary agreement of this kind, the court may direct them not to sue for damages at common law on behalf of their beneficiaries.

There are three ways of completely constituting a trust—

1. BY A TRANSFER OF THE TRUST PROPERTY TO TRUSTEES. If the settlor has the legal property to give, it will be enough for him to do everything necessary to transfer the property to the trustees. (*Re Rose*, 1952.)[627] He must comply with any legal requirements for its transfer, e.g. the requirements of statute in the case of a transfer of shares (*Antrobus* v. *Smith*, 1805),[628] or a conveyance under seal in the case of land. If the settlor only has an equitable interest, he can assign it informally to trustees; all that matters is that the assignment be in writing and the intention to assign should be plain. (*Kekewich* v. *Manning*, 1851.)[629]

2. BY A DECLARATION THAT THE SETTLOR WILL HOLD HIS PROPERTY ON CERTAIN TRUSTS. No formalities are required except where land is involved when the declaration must be in writing. An unsuccessful attempt to transfer property to trustees will not be construed as a declaration of trust so as to convert the settlor into his own trustee (*Jones* v. *Lock*, 1865),[630] except under the Settled Land Act, 1925, and where the settlor has done all that is necessary on his part as in *Re Rose*[627] above.

3. BY A DECLARATION TO TRUSTEES TO HOLD THE PROPERTY ON NEW TRUSTS. This must be in writing but otherwise no formality is required.

There are the following exceptions to the rule that an incompletely constituted trust cannot be enforced in Equity by a volunteer—

(*a*) Under the rule in *Strong* v. *Bird* (1874), 18 Eq. 315, if a donor intends to, but does not actually give, property to a donee, and the donee becomes the personal representative of the donor, the gift is automatically constituted and is effective.

(*b*) If a settlement under the Settled Land Act, 1925, is not made in the form required by the Act, it does not transfer the legal estate but operates as a trust instrument.

(c) A conveyance to an infant of land operates as an agreement for value to make a settlement in favour of the infant.

(d) A *donatio mortis causa*, i.e. a transfer of property, or something representing it, such as a key to a jewel case, in contemplation of, or conditionally upon, death is enforceable, although it would not have been effective as a gift *inter vivos*.

The enforceability of incompletely constituted trusts depends upon valuable consideration having been given by the beneficiary. In addition to consideration which would be enough to support a contract, marriage, in so far as it concerns the spouse and the issue of the marriage, is valuable consideration in pre-nuptial settlements, and in post-nuptial settlements made pursuant to ante-nuptial agreements. Children of a previous marriage are not included, nor are relatives more remote than children, e.g. cousins.

PROTECTIVE AND DISCRETIONARY TRUSTS

Determinable and Conditional Interests. A determinable interest contains the determining event in the limitation itself, e.g. "To X until he is thirty-five, and then to Y." A conditional interest arises where an interest is defeasible by a separate condition, e.g. "To X absolutely, but if he reaches the age of thirty-five, to Y." Any interest subject to a condition defeating it on bankruptcy passes to the trustee in bankruptcy, notwithstanding the condition. An interest determinable on bankruptcy will determine thereon and will not pass to the trustee unless the settlement was created by the bankrupt himself.

Discretionary Trusts. There is a discretionary trust where trustees are bound to pay the income to one or more of a defined class, but are not bound to pay anything to any particular member of the class. There is thus a trust and a power in the same instrument. Each object of the discretion has only a hope and no right to anything (*Gartside* v. *I.R.C.* (1967), 111 S.J. 982), and if he goes bankrupt nothing passes to his trustees in bankruptcy, unless the trustees in control of the trust exercise their discretion in favour of the bankrupt. If all possible objects of a discretion combine in disposing of their interests, the disposition is effective, since together they are absolutely entitled.

The effect of the *Gartside* decision, at least in respect of the payment of estate duty, has been reversed by Sect. 36(2) of the Finance Act, 1969. Before this Act the trust fund was not dutiable on the death of any but the last of the class of discretionary beneficiaries. The precise provisions are too complex for a book of this nature, but in broad terms a charge to duty is now imposed on the trust fund on the death of any object of the discretionary trust. This form of trust will, therefore, be less popular in future.

Protective Trusts. These are a combination of (a) a determinable interest, and (b) a discretionary trust. Under such a trust the interest of the principal beneficiary is to determine on (say) bankruptcy, or an attempted sale of the interest, and then a discretionary trust arises in favour of the principal beneficiary and certain other persons. Instead of expressly drafting such a trust, it has become common for settlors to take advantage of the form given in Sect. 33 of the Trustee Act, 1925, which operates if the words "on protective trusts" are used.

Under this section, the determinable interest of the principal beneficiary determines if he does anything which under the section deprives him of the income, e.g. goes bankrupt. If this happens a discretionary trust begins, the objects of which are (i) the principal beneficiary, his spouse and issue, or (ii) if he has no spouse or issue, the principal beneficiary and the persons who would be entitled if he were then dead. The determinable interest ceases on bankruptcy, on mortgaging the property, on assignment of the future income, or on the impounding of income by the trustees to make good a breach of trust instigated by the principal beneficiary.

CHARITABLE TRUSTS

In order to decide whether the objects of a trust are charitable, it has been the practice of the courts to rely on the objects laid down in the preamble to the Statute of Charitable Uses, 1601, and this in spite of the fact that the statute was repealed by the Mortmain and Charitable Uses Act, 1888, which in its turn has been repealed by the Charities Act, 1960. Even so it seems possible that this preamble will still be referred to in cases of difficulty. However, the classic description of charities is contained in the judgment of Lord Macnaghten in *Commissioners of Income Tax* v. *Pemsel*, [1891] A.C. 531. According to this definition *there are four classes of charitable trusts*—

    (i) for the relief of poverty;
   (ii) for the advancement of education;
  (iii) for the advancement of religion; and
  (iv) for certain other purposes beneficial to the community.

There must be an element of public benefit in all charitable trusts except to a large extent those for the relief of poverty which will be dealt with last.

Education. Trusts which have as their object the education of the public are charitable, but certain problems have arisen in this sphere. If the test for ascertaining the objects of a trust for education is a contract of service between one employer and his employees, the trust is not charitable however numerous the employees may be. (*Oppenheim* v. *Tobacco Securities*, 1951.)[631] Nor is it charitable if the test is a blood relationship to one person. On the other hand, a general trust to prefer the employees of a named company with regard to seventy-five per cent of the fund's income was held charitable. (*Re Koettgen*, 1954.)[632]

Religion. For a religious trust to be charitable there must be an ascertainable benefit, such as the provision of services for a class at least as wide as the followers of the religion in question. Any religion, so long as it is not subversive of public order or morality, will qualify. But a trust for the purposes of a monastic order whose objects are limited to prayer and self-sanctification is not charitable, because the benefits to the public cannot be proved, i.e. such things are not capable of judicial proof in the generally accepted manner. (*Gilmour* v. *Coates*, 1949.)[633]

It was held in *Re Banfield*, [1968] 2 All E.R. 276, that the fact that a religious community opens its doors to those of all creeds and to those who have no creed does not prevent it being a valid religious charity. Alternatively, if such a community cannot be regarded as a religious charity it may be regarded as within the fourth class of charitable purposes laid down in *Pemsel's* case.

Other Purposes Beneficial to the Community. The trust must be within the spirit and intendment of the Statute of Charitable Uses, 1601, and here it is suggested that the courts will still refer to the statute in spite of its repeal. Although such purposes must be of a public nature, the trust can serve a locality, e.g. a parish. Where no purposes are defined a trust for a locality will be assumed to be charitable, but the mere restriction of a trust to a locality will not make what would otherwise be a non-charitable trust into a charitable one. (*Re Gwyon*, 1930.)[634] A trust beneficial to a limited class of persons, even to the adherents of a particular religion, is not charitable where it is not a trust for religious purposes. (*Inland Revenue Commissioners* v. *Baddeley*, 1955.)[635]

As a result of the decision of the House of Lords in the above case, Parliament passed the Recreational Charities Act, 1958, which lays down that it is charitable to provide facilities for recreation or leisure time occupations, if the facilities improve the conditions of life of the persons for whom they are primarily intended. These persons must have need of these facilities by reason of age, youth, infirmity, disablement, poverty, or social or economic circumstances. Failing this the facilities are to be available to the members of the public at large, though trusts in favour of Women's Institutes would be valid, enabling a trust to be restricted to the female members of the public.

In *Scottish Burial Reform and Cremation Society* v. *Glasgow City Corporation*, [1967] 3 All E.R. 215, the House of Lords held that a non-profit-making society whose principal object was the promotion of cremation could be regarded as a charity.

In addition, it was held in *The Incorporated Council of Law Reporting for England and Wales* v. *Attorney-General*, [1971] 1 All E.R. 436, that the Council could be registered as a charity since the provision of accurate law reports was a purpose beneficial to the community. Without them, the administration and development of the law would be difficult. The objects of the Council fell within the spirit and intendment of the Act of 1601.

Poverty. In order to be classed as charitable, trusts to relieve poverty need only be to a limited exsent for the public benefit. Thus a trust for the relief of poor relations, or of the poor employees of one particular company, has been held to be charitable. (*Re Scarisbrick*, 1951.)[636] Where gifts are made on trust to officials or bodies with charitable functions, such gifts are assumed to be charitable if no purposes are expressed. Where the trusts are outlined it is then a question of construction whether such trusts are charitable; the trustees' purposes are then to some extent irrelevant. Thus a gift to a vicar and the churchwardens for parish work was held not to be charitable, because "for parish work" gives rise to interpretation, and not all such work is charitable. If the words "for parish work" had been left out, the gift would presumably have been charitable. On the other hand, a gift to the vicar "for his work in the parish" was held to be charitable because the vicar's work is the advancement of religion.

A trust to be charitable must be exclusively charitable. If it is possible for all the trust property to be applied to non-charitable purposes, the trust is not a charitable trust. (*Chichester* v. *Simpson*, 1944,[637] and *Re Wootton's Will Trusts*, 1968.)[637a] If part only of the trust property can be applied for non-charitable purposes and the non-charitable purpose is invalid, then the property will be divided equally between the charitable and non-charitable purposes. (*Re Scarisbrick*, 1951.)[636] A purely ancillary non-charitable purpose in a good charitable trust will be upheld as charitable. (*Re Coxen*, 1948.)[638]

However, it is not essential that those benefiting under the trust should receive those benefits free from any charge. Thus, in *Re Payling's Will Trusts*, [1969] 3 All E.R. 698, it was held by Buckley, J., that a gift of a house offering rent-free accommodation for the aged constituted a valid charitable trust even though those residing in the home might be called upon to pay for food and other services.

The Charitable Trusts (Validation) Act, 1954, validates retrospectively certain trust dispositions which came into operation before 16th December, 1952, and under which property was to be applied partly for charitable and partly for non-charitable purposes, thus saving the charitable aspect of the trust. Little use seems to have been made of the statute.

THE CHARITIES ACT, 1960

The above Act abolishes the law of mortmain altogether, and provides for three Charity Commissioners together with a staff forming a department under the Home Secretary. The Commissioners have a duty to promote the effective use of charitable resources, to advise trustees and to check abuses. They are also required to maintain a Register of Charities and to inspect and audit accounts. They may devise new charitable schemes, and authorise dealings with property which forms part of the permanent endowment of the charity, though certain charities are exempt from this provision, e.g. the British Museum and some universities and colleges. The commissioners also authorise legal proceedings regarding charities where they have not dealt with the matter themselves. The Act also defines the operation of the *cy-près* doctrine.

There are certain basic differences between charitable and non-charitable trusts—

Certainty of Objects. Charitable trusts never fail for uncertainty of objects, so property left "on charitable trusts" would be good. If necessary a scheme is directed to carry them into effect, the scheme being prepared or approved by the Charity Commissioners.

Cy-près Doctrine. The *cy-près* doctrine applies to charitable trusts only. Under this doctrine, if a charitable trust cannot in practice be carried out consistently with the spirit of the gift, and the donor or testator has shown a "general charitable intention," it is the duty of the trustees to take steps, usually by applying to the court, to have the property applied *cy-près*, i.e. for a similar charitable purpose. Under the old law the *cy-près* doctrine would only be applied if it was impossible or impracticable to carry out the trusts and the settlor had expressed a general charitable intention. The Charities Act, 1960, makes it unnecessary to decide the question of impossibility or impracticability. Instead the *cy-près* doctrine can be applied wherever there was a general charitable intention and where—

(*a*) the original purpose in whole or in part—

    (i) has been fulfilled as far as possible; or
    (ii) cannot be carried out; or

(*b*) the original purpose does not provide entire use for the gift; or
(*c*) the available property and other property applicable to similar purposes can be more effectively used in conjunction and applied to common purposes; or
(*d*) the original purpose referred to some area or class of persons which has now ceased to be suitable or practical in administering the the gift; or
(*e*) the original purposes either wholly or in part have since—

    (i) been adequately provided for by other means;
    (ii) ceased, as being useless or harmful to the community, to be charities in law;
    (iii) ceased to be a suitable method of using property in accordance with the spirit of the gift.

It should be noted that the more precisely the donor defines the charitable purpose intended by him, the harder it is to discover a general charitable intention. Therefore the Charities Act also provides that property may be applied *cy-près* as if it were given with a general charitable intention if it was given for a specific charitable object which failed, and the donor cannot be found or has disclaimed in writing his right to have his property returned to him. This provision will enable the court to apply street or house-to-house collections to other charitable purposes where the fund raised is not exhausted by the payments out of it, or where it fails.

Before the Act, the courts had decided that in such a case there was a resulting trust in favour of the persons who had provided the money, but since it was difficult to ascertain who they were, large funds remained in court. There must be reasonable advertisement or inquiry to ascertain the donors, though the court can declare the property to belong to unidentified owners where, as in the case of a collection, ascertainment of the donors would be unreasonable. Where there has been an advertisement for donors, a donor may claim the return of his gift within twelve months after the date of the *cy-près* scheme, subject to the right of the charity trustees to deduct proper expenses.

Rule against Perpetuities. Charities are exempt from some aspects of the rule against perpetuities. The rule is designed to prevent property from being tied up for an indefinite period of time and has two branches—

(a) THE RULE AGAINST REMOTENESS OF VESTING. Property must become absolutely vested in the persons entitled to it within a period of a life or lives in being when the instrument making the gift takes effect plus a period of twenty-one years after the end of the life or lives in being. A period of gestation may be added at the beginning or end of the perpetuity period. For example, suppose Y leaves property on trust for the eldest son (as yet unborn) of X, provided he reaches twenty-one. Under the rule the property must vest in the eldest son of X (if it vests at all) within the period, since if X has a son, he must reach the age of twenty-one within the period of X's life, or within twenty-one years thereafter, and if he is *en ventre sa mère* when X dies, the period of gestation will be added. If, however, Y leaves property to the eldest son (as yet unborn) of X provided he becomes a barrister, the gift is void under the rule, because although the property may vest within the period, there is a possibility that it may not, since the eldest son of X might not be called to the Bar until thirty years after his father's death. The gift is void if there is a possibility of it not vesting within the period, unless it is covered by the "wait and see" rule contained in the Perpetuities and Accumulations Act, 1964. (See below.)

(b) THE RULE AGAINST INALIENABILITY. Under this branch of the rule property cannot be tied up for ever. So if X leaves freehold land on trust to be used for ever for the purposes of a private tennis club, then the trust would be void for perpetuity, since there is no power to dispose of the property, which may be held on trust for longer than the perpetuity period.

The Perpetuities and Accumulations Act, 1964. This does not affect the Rule against Inalienability, nor the law relating to Trusts of Imperfect Obligation. (See p. 340.) However, Sect. 1 of the Act does enable a testator to specify a period of years not exceeding *eighty* as the perpetuity period instead of a life or lives in being plus twenty-one years if he wishes to do so.

Under the Rule against Remoteness of Vesting as it applied before the Perpetuities and Accumulations Act, 1964, came into force, the gift was void if there was a *mere possibility* of it not vesting within the period. There was no question of waiting to see what happened. Sect. 3 of the 1964 Act established a "wait and see" rule and in certain cases the interest will not be treated as void for remoteness until it becomes established that it must vest (if at all) after the end of the perpetuity period.

The 1964 Act came into force on 16th July, 1964, and in general applies only to instruments taking effect after that date. The Act also binds the Crown.

Charities are subject to the rule against remoteness of vesting so that a gift to Charity X when the first man lands on the planet Venus would be void under the rule. There is an exception in the case of a gift over from one charity to another. So where a person gives "to Charity A £10,000, but if my tomb falls into disrepair to Charity B," the gift to Charity B is not void even though it may vest outside the perpetuity period.

Charities are not subject to the rule against inalienability. There is no objection to the giving of property to trustees to apply the income for ever in favour of a charity. Non-charitable trusts, including gifts to unincorporated associations, are subject to this rule and are void unless the capital is freely alienable within the perpetuity period. If the association could spend the funds tomorrow such a trust would be valid even although in fact they do not spend them. Unless such freedom is given the trust must be limited to the perpetuity period.

Gifts for the upkeep of a tomb or grave not in a church are not charitable, but can be made effective in several ways. A gift to Charity A with a gift over to Charity B if at any time the grave falls into disrepair is valid, but there must be no trust imposed on the charity actually to maintain the grave, since this would make the gift non-charitable. It must be an inducement, not a trust. A gift of income to a corporation determinable on its failure to maintain the grave, with a gift over on such failure to the testator's residuary estate has been held good. A gift for the upkeep of a whole churchyard is charitable. The result may also be achieved by a contract as where X leaves money to his trustees so that they might enter into a contract with a Cemetery Corporation to maintain the grave for as long as they are prepared to do so for a given sum of money. The perpetuity rule does not apply to contracts.

Finally, charities are exempt from income tax and have certain exemptions from stamp duty and local rates. Charitable trustees can act by a majority whereas other trustees must be unanimous. This is because it is quite common to have a large number of trustees in a charitable trust.

THE APPOINTMENT OF TRUSTEES

Trustees are usually appointed by the instrument which sets up the trust, but a trustee may also be appointed by a person acting under an express power in the trust instrument, or by a person acting under the power contained in the Trustee Act, 1925. In the latter case, subject to any contrary provisions in the trust instrument, a trustee may be appointed to replace one who—

(i) is dead;
(ii) remains outside the United Kingdom for over one year (whether willing to be replaced or not);
(iii) desires to be discharged;
(iv) refuses or is unfit to act;
(v) is incapable of acting; or
(vi) is a minor.

Such appointment must be in writing and may be made by—

(*a*) the person named in the trust instrument, and in default of such person;
(*b*) the continuing trustees (including one who retires voluntarily if willing, but excluding one who is removed under section (ii) above), and in default of such person;
(*c*) the personal representatives of the last surviving trustee.

Additional trustees may be appointed (so long as the number of four is not exceeded) even where no trustee is replaced, and the court has wide powers of appointing new trustees under the Trustee Act, 1925. It will not exercise them if the appointment can easily be made out of court.

There is no general rule as to the number of trustees but it is usual to have at least two, and where land is settled or held on trust for sale, the Trustee Act, 1925, Sect. 34 lays down a maximum of four trustees. Sect. 14 also provides that two trustees are required to give a purchaser of land which is held on trust a valid receipt for the purchase money so as to over-reach the equitable interests which the beneficiaries have in the trust property. A trust corporation can act as sole trustee and give valid receipts under Sect. 14. Thus there are advantages in appointing the Public Trustee or other trust corporation, since it cannot die or retire and is unlikely to abscond with the trust funds. In the case of the Public Trustee the State is liable for breaches of trust (if any).

A trustee is not bound to accept office. He may revoke expressly or by implication, e.g. by failing to take up his duties. If all the trustees fail to act or revoke, the settlor is the trustee if the trust is created *inter vivos*. If created by will, his personal representatives act as trustees. If a trustee dies, his duties devolve on the survivors since the trustees are joint tenants of the trust property. If a sole surviving trustee dies, the duties can be exercised by his personal representatives. No trust can fail for the lack of a trustee, since there is an equitable maxim: "Equity never wants for a trustee."

A trustee who wishes to retire may obtain his discharge by obtaining the consent of his co-trustees and the person (if any) who is empowered to appoint new trustees, so long as there remain at least two trustees or a trust corporation to perform the duties under the trust.

The Judicial Trustee Act, 1896, Sect. 1, authorises the court, on application by a trustee or beneficiary, to appoint a person called a *judicial trustee* to be a trustee of the trust either jointly with any other person, or as sole trustee and, if good cause is shown, in place of all or any of the existing trustees. This provision is a useful one in cases where the administration of the estate by ordinary trustees has broken down.

There is no legal bar to the appointment of a foreign resident as a trustee of an English trust. Thus, in *Re Whitehead's Will Trusts, The Times*, 23rd April, 1971, where the beneficiary had been settled in Jersey for more than ten years and intended to stay there permanently it was held by Pennycuick, V.C., that there were exceptional circumstances making proper the appointment of new trustees all resident in Jersey.

Vesting Declarations. Retirement of a trustee is normally effected by deed, though a deed is not essential under Sect. 36 of the Trustee Act, 1925. However, a deed is normally used in order to take advantage of the provisions of Sect. 40 which provides for the automatic vesting in new trustees of property subject to the trust. The section does not apply—

(*a*) *to mortgages* (except debentures) held by the trustees (such mortgages must be transferred expressly to the new trustees);

(*b*) *to land held under a lease containing a covenant against assignment without consent of the lessor* (this is to prevent accidental forfeiture of the lease);

(*c*) *to stocks and shares in companies*, where the usual method of transfer must be used since the share register of a company is evidence of membership and the names must therefore be brought up to date.

THE DUTIES OF TRUSTEES

The trustees have the following duties—

1. *To administer the trust prudently.*
2. *To comply strictly with the terms of the trust.*
3. *To invest within the range of investments authorised* by the Trustee Investments Act, 1961, or as provided by the trust instrument if this provides for a different range of investment.

The 1961 Act allows trustees to invest in the equity share capital of companies and repeals Sect. 1 of the Trustee Act, 1925. The trust property must be divided into two equal parts and one part may be invested in what are called "narrower-range" investments; these are not so very different from the list of investments under the Trustee Act. The other part may be invested in "wider-range" investments and these include Equity share capital of companies subject to certain safeguards regarding share capital and dividends.

4. *Not to vary the trusts*, although the beneficiaries, if they are all ascertained and *sui juris* (adult and sane) can authorise a variation, and under the Variation of Trusts Act, 1958, the court too can sanction variations.

5. *Not to delegate duties under the trust*, although trustees can employ professional men, e.g. accountants and solicitors who are paid out of the trust estate. (See also p.359.)

6. *To keep accounts*. The Trustee Act, 1925, allows an audit once in three years and the fees may be paid out of income or capital at the discretion of the trustees.

In general trustees must carry out their duties and exercise their discretions free from the control of the beneficiaries, e.g. as to whom to appoint as a new trustee. However, all the beneficiaries, if *sui juris* and acting together, may as we have seen direct the trustee how to dispose of the trust property, and they may also direct trustees who hold shares on trust how to exercise their voting rights. Any beneficiary may at any time obtain an injunction to restrain a trustee from acting in breach of trust, and where some of the beneficiaries (but not all) become absolutely entitled to part of the trust property, they can generally demand to be paid their share where the trust property consists of personalty, but cannot do so where the trust property consists of land.

The court can also exercise control over trustees, and where an administration order is made by the court, nothing can be done without the consent of the court. The court has power to decide questions of interpretation of trust instruments, and will interfere with the exercise by the trustees of a discretion—

(*a*) where the trustees surrender their discretion to the court; or
(*b*) refuse to exercise their discretion at all; or
(*c*) exercise it otherwise than in good faith.

The court can also sanction administrative acts which are unauthorised by the trust, and under the Variation of Trusts Act, 1958, may approve arrangements varying or revoking trusts or enlarging the administrative powers of trustees on behalf of persons who cannot consent, i.e.

(i) minors and persons under disability;
(ii) unascertained persons and persons who may become beneficially entitled in the future;
(iii) unborn persons;
(iv) objects of a discretionary class under protective trusts.

The trustees have no right to be paid for their services unless the trust instrument so provides, but they are entitled to the reimbursement of their expenses in connection with the trust. The Public Trustee has a statutory right to payment. Trustees are personally liable for breaches of trust, e.g. losses arising out of investing money in risky investments which fail, and cannot set off losses against profits, but must make good each individual loss, leaving the profits in trust. A trustee has a right to be indemnified by a beneficiary who has instigated the breach and has benefited thereby, and has a right of contribution from his co-trustees, if any. In addition the court has power to relieve a trustee from personal liability where he has acted honestly and reasonably, but it is doubtful whether this would protect a bank or other professional trustee.

Trustees are not permitted to make a profit from their trust, and any such profit will be held on trust for the beneficiaries. (*Protheroe* v. *Protheroe*, 1968.)[618a] If a trustee uses the trust property for his own benefit he is accountable both for any profits and for any loss, and if he uses his legal control of the trust property to gain appointments or contracts for himself or his firm, he is accountable for the profits. Thus, where a trustee holds shares in a company and is appointed a director by using the voting power attached to the shares, he will be accountable for his director's fees except where the trust instrument allows him to retain them, or unless he would have been appointed even if he had used the trust shares to vote against his appointment.

There is a definite prohibition against his purchasing the trust property, however fair the purchase may be, except where the contract for an option to purchase existed before the trusteeship began. The bar extends to sales to an agent for a trustee, or to companies of which the trustee is virtually sole shareholder. However, a trustee may purchase the beneficiary's interest if he can show that the transaction was beneficial to the beneficiary, that full information was given to him, and that no confidence was reposed in the purchasing trustee by the beneficiary, i.e. that there was no undue influence.

MAINTENANCE AND ADVANCEMENT

Where minors are beneficiaries under a trust, the question often arises as to whether any provision can be made for them either—

(*a*) *out of income* for maintenance, e.g. holidays, education and living expenses; or

(*b*) *out of capital* for their advancement, e.g. the purchase of a house on marriage.

Trustees may be given power to apply income towards the beneficiary's maintenance or capital towards his advancement—

(*a*) by the trust instrument; or

(*b*) by statute in Sections 31 and 23 of the Trustee Act, 1925, which apply unless a contrary intention is expressed in the trust instrument.

These statutory provisions do not impose a duty on trustees, they merely give a *power* to apply trust monies for maintenance or advancement.

BREACH OF TRUST

Where an action of a trustee causes loss of capital, the measure of damages is the loss actually caused, but where a trustee advances funds on a mortgage which is only a breach of trust because of the amount lent, the trustee is only liable for the excess lent by him over the sum he could properly have lent, namely two-thirds of the valuation. Failure to get a valuation as required by Sect. 28 of the Trustee Act does not by itself disentitle him to this benefit. If a trustee sells an authorised investment in order to purchase an unauthorised one, the beneficiaries have the option of making the trustee replace the authorised investment sold, or the money produced by its sale. A fraudulent breach of trust is a crime.

A trustee has certain defences to a breach of trust. The court has jurisdiction to release trustees from liability for a breach of trust when they have acted honestly and reasonably and should in the circumstances be released. But honesty, stupidity or ignorance of the law is not *prima facie* reasonable. There is no limitation period for the actions by beneficiaries against trustees if the trustee is guilty of fraud, or if they wish to recover trust property which he has converted to his own use and is in his possession. Subject to these exceptions, actions are barred after six years or, if the action is to recover land or is in respect of a claim to the personal estate of a deceased person, twelve years. The time runs from the breach, irrespective of the beneficiaries' knowledge, but time does not run against a reversioner or a person subject to a disability until the reversion falls in or the disability ends.

A beneficiary who is *sui juris*, who has full knowledge of the facts, and has not been subject to the influence of the trustee, has no action if he has assented to, or joined or acquiesced in a breach of trust. A trustee is not liable for the acts of his co-trustees as opposed to their joint acts unless he is guilty of wilful default, and he is not liable for breaches committed after he has ceased to be a trustee, unless he retired to enable that particular breach to be committed. As trustees are jointly and severally liable for breaches committed, one may be made liable to repair the whole of the damage caused by a breach committed by him and several others. In such a case he is entitled to a contribution from his co-trustees so that they share the burden equally.

Anyone knowingly meddling with trust property or who is knowingly a party to a breach of trust is liable as a trustee for any loss caused. But an agent for trustees is only liable for a breach if he acted dishonestly or outside the scope of his authority on his own initiative.

If any beneficiary is indebted to the trust, any interest he may have under the trust will be impounded to discharge the liability to it. A trustee who has overpaid a beneficiary is entitled to adjust the account out of future payments, but not if the effect will be to pay himself in his capacity as beneficiary, where he is a beneficiary.

In the administration of estates of deceased persons, if one beneficiary can show that another was paid too much, the overpaid beneficiary is personally liable to refund the overpayment. It is not settled whether this rule applies to trusts generally. These rules apply to a beneficiary who is innocently overpaid; anyone who takes property with notice that he is not entitled to receive it acts as a constructive trustee for the rightful owner.

Trust property can be followed or traced. If a trustee converts trust property, it remains subject to the trust and the beneficiaries can adopt the transaction or compel a reconversion, whereupon the trustees will be liable for any loss or profit. If the trustee has mixed trust property with his own, the beneficiaries cannot adopt the transaction and take the mixed asset, but they have a lien on it and can enforce a sale. If the trust property has disappeared altogether, the beneficiaries are limited to a personal claim against the trustee.

REVOCATION OF TRUSTS

Trusts may be revoked or set aside in certain cases—

1. **By the Settlor.** A settlor can revoke a settlement if he expressly reserves the power to do so, and he can also revoke it if he can show that it was procured by fraud, duress, mistake, or undue influence, but only if the parties can be restored to something approximating to their position before the settlement was made. Marriage settlements cannot be set aside since the parties cannot be restored to their original position, but a settlement can be set aside if made for a consideration which wholly fails, e.g. a marriage settlement where the marriage is a nullity.

2. **By the Settlor's Creditors.** There are two separate statutory jurisdictions—

(*a*) UNDER SECT. 172 OF THE LAW OF PROPERTY ACT, 1925. Conveyances made with intent to defraud creditors are voidable by the persons prejudiced, but no-one who gives good or valuable consideration without notice of the intent to defraud can have any benefit taken away from him. Thus a marriage settlement, whereby a man who is heavily in debt settles a substantial sum on his intended wife and children, cannot be set aside under this section against the children who necessarily have no notice of intent to defraud, and can only be set aside against the wife if she can be proved to have such notice.

(*b*) UNDER SECT. 42 OF THE BANKRUPTCY ACT, 1914. All voluntary dispositions made within two years of bankruptcy are void against the trustee in bankruptcy if he takes steps to have them set aside. The settlor's or donor's intentions are immaterial, but the exercise of a general power of appointment is not within this section.

Persons giving value to a voluntary donee from the bankrupt are protected if they had no notice of the bankruptcy, so the section would seem to make such dispositions voidable rather than void.

Voluntary dispositions within ten years of bankruptcy are similarly affected unless the beneficiaries can show—

(i) that the settlor or donor could then pay his debts without using the property given away; and

(ii) that the property was transferred to the trustee or donee at the date of the settlement or gift.

Persons who give value are protected so long as they have no notice of an act of bankruptcy.

Powers of Attorney Act, 1971—Delegation of Trusts. Under Sect. 9 of the above Act, a trustee can delegate for a period not exceeding twelve months the execution or exercise of all or any of the trusts, powers and discretions vested in him as trustee, either alone or jointly with any other person or persons. The trustee concerned must give written notice to every person who has power to appoint new trustees and to each of his fellow trustees. This power is *not* restricted to cases where the trustee is going or remaining abroad.

CHAPTER IX

THE LAW OF SUCCESSION

IN English law a person of full age and sound mind has unrestricted power of disposition over property which is at his death, or subsequently becomes, part of his estate. A will is ambulatory; it takes effect at the testator's death in respect of property of which he is then competent to dispose, but meanwhile it is inoperative and remains revocable either in whole or in part.

THE GENERAL NATURE OF A WILL

Testamentary Capacity. Subject to the following exceptions, any person, including an alien, and a married woman, can make a valid will disposing of either real or personal property—

(i) An minor cannot make a will unless he or she is entitled to make a nuncupative will, e.g. an informal serviceman's will.

(ii) Persons of unsound mind are also incapacitated, but such a person may make a valid will during a lucid interval, and subsequent unsoundness of mind does not invalidate a will already made.

Infirmity, old age or illness may in law be equivalent to unsoundness of mind. There can be partial insanity, i.e. unsoundness of mind always existing but only occasionally manifest and, in this connection, a general duty lies on any person setting up a will to show that it is the will of a competent testator.

If a will, rational on the face of it, is proved to be properly executed and attested, it will be presumed to have been made by a competent testator. If there is evidence of circumstances which are contrary to the presumption of sanity, the court will pronounce against the will, unless on the evidence as a whole the court is satisfied that the testator was of sound mind when he made it.

If the testator has been certified the onus is upon the person propounding the will to show that it was executed during a lucid interval. Similarly when a will is prepared under circumstances which raise a well-grounded suspicion that it does not express the testator's intention, the court will not pronounce in favour of the will unless the suspicion is removed.

To avoid the injustice which might arise from inability to make a valid will the Court of Protection may direct a settlement or gift of the property of a mental patient whose affairs it is managing (Sect. 103 Mental Health Act, 1959). The Administration of Justice Act, 1969, adds a new paragraph to Sect. 103 empowering the Court of Protection to direct the execution of a will or codicil on behalf of a patient as well as directing a settlement or gift. The will would normally be made by the patient's professional advisors and the court may authorise someone to sign it. The signature is witnessed in the usual way and the will is sealed with the official seal of the Court of Protection.

(iii) A will may be wholly or partially invalidated if the testator has been induced to execute it by coercion, whether mental or physical, or through fear or fraud or excessive importunity.

Where a sick husband made a will in a particular way at the behest of a nagging wife, the will was held invalid; but honest persuasion or flattery, by which one person induces another to make a will in his favour, will not invalidate it, if there is no element of actual coercion. Even undue influence, which would be a ground for setting aside a contract or other transaction *inter vivos*, will not invalidate a will if there has been no coercion. And there is no presumption of undue influence arising from fiduciary relationships as there is in the case of *inter vivos* transactions. Thus the relationships of solicitor and client, doctor and patient, are not in themselves relevant in the law of succession.

However, under the Administration of Justice Act, 1970, Sect. 1(4), probate business (other than non-contentious or common form probate business) is assigned to the Chancery Division and it will be interesting to see whether the Chancery judges deal differently with wills whose execution is alleged to have been procured by undue influence. Certainly there is a much greater tendency for *gifts* to be set aside in Chancery on the grounds of undue influence (see p. 171).

FORMALITIES NECESSARY FOR A WILL

1. **Writing.** The Wills Act, 1837, Sect. 9, requires that a will be in writing, but writing includes print and typescript, and a will written on an eggshell has been admitted to probate.

2. **Signature.** The will must be signed "at the foot or end thereof by the testator or by some other person in his presence and by his direction." (Wills Act, 1837, Sect. 9.) Initials or even a partial signature will suffice, and the signature may be made by a mark, such as a cross, or even an inked thumbprint. However, a mere seal, being appropriate only to a deed, has been held to be insufficient.

The provision of the Wills Act, 1837, as to the position of the signature caused much difficulty, so the Wills Act Amendment Act, 1852, provided that a signature should be valid if so placed, at or after or following or under or beside or opposite to the end of the will, that it appeared on the face of the will that the testator intended by his signature to give effect to the writing as his will. But a signature cannot operate to give effect to any part of the will which is written below it, or inserted subsequently in point of time.

These problems arise mainly in home-made wills. The will of a testator who signed at the top of the page, because there was no room at the bottom, was held invalid. But there may be circumstances enabling the court to decide that the signature is valid, as where the dispositions in the will continued from the bottom of the page up the margin, and the signature was in the margin but at the top of the page; and, even more remarkable, where the signature was in the middle of the will; and where a will made on a printed form and signed on its face page was in the circumstances held to include dispositions written on the back.

A will has been held duly executed where the testator signed the envelope in which the will was sealed, as in the *Estate of Mann*, [1942] P. 146, but in the *Estate of Bean*, [1944] P. 83, the signature in the same circumstances was held to be bad. It is clear that precedent is not so important in succession, since so much depends on the circumstances of each case.

3. Attestation. Sect. 9 of the Wills Act, 1837, provides—"Such signature shall be made or acknowledged by the testator in the presence of two or more witnesses present at the same time." In general a person of sufficient understanding, even if under twenty-one, is a competent witness; but not a blind man.

It is not essential that the witnesses should know that the document is a will; they are simply witnesses to a signature. Both witnesses must be present together when the testator actually signs or acknowledges his signature. It should be noted that the testator may sign his will before the witnesses come on the scene, and then simply acknowledge the signature in front of them. (*Re Groffman*, 1969.)[639] Finally, Sect. 9 requires that such witnesses shall attest and subscribe the will in the presence of the testator, and provides that no special form of attestation shall be necessary. Each witness must, therefore, subscribe in the presence of the testator, and must do so after and not before the testator has signed or acknowledged. It is not necessary, however, that a witness should subscribe in the presence of another witness but he usually does so.

If the witnesses have attested and subscribed properly, the absence of an attestation clause does not invalidate the will, but it is advisable and usual to insert one in order to raise a presumption that the will was duly executed, and to avoid the necessity for an affidavit of due execution by one of the witnesses on obtaining probate. The usual form of attestation clause is as follows—

> Signed and declared by the said X.Y. the Testator as
> and for his last Will in the presence of us both present at
> the same time, who at his request, in his presence,
> and in the presence of each other, have hereunto
> subscribed our names as Witnesses.
>
> Signed: P.Q.
> R.S.

The following shorter form has been held good—"Signed by the above-named testator in our joint presence and by us in his."

If a witness is a person to whom or to whose spouse a gift is made by the will, his attestation is valid but the Wills Act, 1837, Sect. 15, made the gift void. Furthermore, it was held by the Court of Appeal in *Re Bravda*, [1968] 1 W.L.R. 479, that Sect. 15 precluded a beneficiary who had signed the will from benefiting under it *even where the will was also witnessed by two or more persons who did not receive gifts under it.*

The Wills Act, 1968, overrules the decision in *Re Bravda* and amends Sect. 15 of the Wills Act, 1837, by providing that "the attestation of a will by a person to whom or to whose spouse there is given or made any such disposition as is described in that Section shall be disregarded if the will is duly executed without his attestation and without that of any other such person."

The provisions of the Act of 1968 will apply to anyone dying after the passing of the Act (i.e. 30th May, 1968), whenever his will was made. Thus, if there are two or more signatures of people entirely disinterested, the beneficiaries will be entitled under the will even though they have witnessed it, but if there are three signatures, two of whom are given legacies, they will both fail to be entitled to receive them, though the attestation will be valid.

4. Informal or Nuncupative Wills. The Wills Act, 1837, Sect. 11, enables any soldier being in actual military service, or any mariner or seaman being at sea, to make an informal will of personal property, i.e. either in writing without a witness, or orally before a witness.

The Wills (Soldiers and Sailors) Act, 1918, declares that the privilege has always extended to minors. In addition it extended the privilege. to cover real property, and has enabled a mariner or seaman who is a member of the naval or marine forces of the Crown to make an informal will, not only when at sea, but also when so circumstanced that, if he were a soldier, he would be regarded as being in actual military service. The term "soldier" has been held to include an army nurse and a member of the W.A.A.F.; a lady typist employed on an ocean liner has been held to be a mariner or seaman.

Actual military service means that any soldier, sailor or airman can make an informal will if actually serving, or called up for service, with the armed forces in connection with operations of war which are or have been taking place or are imminent, and even during a period of training. (*Re Wingham*, 1949[640] and *Re Newland*, 1952.)[641]

REVOCATION OF WILLS

A will is said to be ambulatory, a term derived from the Latin word *ambulo*—I walk. It is not static until death, and an agreement by the testator not to revoke his will does not prevent him from doing so. But if valuable consideration for the promise has been given, the other party can obtain damages against the testator's estate, but not specific performance.

There are three methods of revocation: by making a subsequent will or codicil, by destruction with intent to revoke, and by subsequent marriage.

1. Revocation by Subsequent Will or Codicil. A soldier or sailor entitled to make an informal will may revoke a previous will, whether formal or informal, by an informal declaration. If however the soldier returns to civil life, he cannot revoke a former will by informal declaration, even if the will was made informally. A soldier or sailor who is a minor and who is entitled to make and does make an informal will, and then returns to civil life, cannot revoke it at all unless he has attained majority.

Revocation may be express or implied. A will usually contains an express revocation clause, usually the first, which runs—"I hereby revoke all previous wills, etc." The fact that a later will is described as the testator's last will does not of itself revoke an earlier will. If an earlier and later will are inconsistent in any respect, the later will be regarded as impliedly revoking the earlier to the extent that it is inconsistent with it. Thus, if a testator by his will gives all his property to A and then by codicil gives all his property to B, the codicil impliedly revokes the will unless for any reason the gift to B is invalid, e.g. if B for instance has witnessed the codicil.

2. Destruction with Intent to Revoke. Under the Wills Act, 1837, Sect. 20, three conditions are necessary—

(a) *Burning, tearing or otherwise destroying the will.* Partial destruction is sufficient if it is clear that cancellation of the will was intended, as by the tearing off of the signature and attestation clause. A mere intention to revoke without destruction is not enough. As was said by James, L.J., "All the destroying in the world without intention will not revoke a will, nor intention without destroying, there must be the two." (*Cheese* v. *Lovejoy,* 1877.)[642]

(b) *Destruction by the testator or some other person in his presence and by his direction* Destruction of the will at the testator's request but not in his presence is ineffectual. A testator wrote to his solicitor asking him to tear up his will, which the solicitor did but not in the presence of the testator. This was held not to be a valid revocation. Further, destruction by another person in the testator's presence does not revoke a will, unless it is done by his direction. (*Gill* v. *Gill,* 1909.)[643] This rule is necessary because a person who has not received what he thought to be his proper entitlement under a will might well destroy it. A will being destroyed without being revoked can be proved by secondary evidence, i.e. by a copy or a draft, or even by oral evidence.

(c) *Animus revocandi or intention to revoke on the part of the testator.* If a will remains in the custody of the testator until death, but cannot be found after death, he is presumed to have destroyed it with intention to revoke, but the presumption may be rebutted. (*Sugden* v. *Lord St. Leonards,* 1876.)[644] Even an express revocation clause in a will is not effectual to revoke an earlier will if there is positive proof that the testator had no *animus revocandi,* but the burden of proof is heavy.

Conditional or Dependent Relative Revocation. Revocation may be conditional, in which case, under the doctrine of dependent relative revocation, revocation does not take effect unless the condition is fulfilled. (*In the Estate of Bridgewater*, 1965.)[645] Where revocation of an existing will was conditional on the execution of a new will, and the testator died before the new will was made, the original was not revoked. And where a testator revoked by destruction a will in favour of his wife, in the mistaken belief that if he died intestate she would get everything, the doctrine of dependent relative revocation applied and the will remained valid. Similarly, a revocation clause in a second will was held ineffectual to revoke entirely an earlier will because the revocation was conditional upon the later will being completed, which in fact it was not.

Revocation of a will is absolute unless it is shown to be conditional and the burden of proof lies on the person seeking to show that a revocation is conditional. (*Re Surridge, Sparks* v. *Kingdon* (1970), 114 S.J. 208.)

3. Revocation by Marriage. The Wills Act, 1837, provides in effect that the will of a man or woman is revoked by his or her marriage. But the Law of Property Act, 1925, Sect. 177, provides that a will made in contemplation of marriage shall not be revoked by the solemnisation of the marriage contemplated. The section applies to wills made or confirmed by codicil after 1925. It appears that where a will asserts that it is made in contemplation of marriage, the mere mention of marriage and not marriage to a named person does not bring the section into operation, and a subsequent marriage revokes the will. (*Sallis* v. *Jones*, 1936,[646] and *In the Estate of Langston*, 1953.)[647] It seems that the one safe way to ensure that a will is not revoked by marriage is to see that it is made "in contemplation of my marriage to Mary Jones."

CLASSES OF TESTAMENTARY DISPOSITION

Testamentary dispositions of freehold land are called devises and are either (*a*) specific, e.g. a gift of a specified real estate, or (*b*) residuary, e.g. a gift of all T's real estate or of all that remains after specific devises. Thus—"I devise Blackacre to X and the remainder of my realty to Y."

Dispositions of personal property, including leaseholds, are called bequests or legacies. Legacies are of four kinds—

(*a*) Specific. A gift of a specified thing, or a specified part of T's personal estate, e.g. "my gold watch" or "all my personal chattels" is a specific legacy. A specific legacy has certain advantages. (i) It will be paid in priority to general legacies. (ii) It will not be sold to pay debts until the undisposed-of property and residue are exhausted. On the other hand, unlike a general legacy, a specific legacy may be adeemed if it is destroyed or disposed of by the testator during his lifetime.

(*b*) Demonstrative Legacies. The term is applied to personal estate, and such a legacy is general and not specific, although it is directed to be paid out of a particular part of the testator's estate. An example is "A legacy of £1,000 out of my five per cent Defence Bonds."

A demonstrative legacy is more beneficial than a specific legacy because it is not liable to ademption, and is therefore payable out of the general estate where the particular fund does not exist at T's death; and it is more beneficial than a general legacy because, being payable out of a specific fund, it does not abate with the general legacies so long as the fund is sufficient. Thus a gift to X of £1,000 would abate before the gift outlined above.

(c) A GENERAL LEGACY. This term is applied to personalty and is given without specifying a particular item, e.g. a gold watch or £1,000 worth of shares in the X Co. It is not essential that T should possess at his death property of the kind indicated, but if such property cannot be obtained within twelve months of death, the legatee is entitled to its value as at the date of death, plus interest at four per cent.

A general legacy is more beneficial than a specific legacy because it is not liable to be adeemed but it is less beneficial than a specific legacy because it is liable to abate, and is liable to be used to pay debts and expenses before the specific legacies are touched.

(d) PECUNIARY LEGACIES. A pecuniary legacy is a sum of money with no mention of a particular fund out of which it is payable. A pecuniary legacy is, of course, a general legacy, but a general legacy is not necessarily pecuniary, e.g. a gold watch. Similarly, a demonstrative legacy may be but need not be a pecuniary legacy, e.g. one of my black horses.

RESIDUARY GIFTS. A residuary gift is a gift of residue of the estate or part of it. The residue of an estate is that part of it left over after all other gifts have been made and all debts and expenses paid.

CLASS GIFTS. "A gift is said to be to a class of persons when it is to all those who come within a certain category or description defined by a general or collective formula and who, if they take at all, are to take one divisible subject in certain proportionate shares" (*per* Lord Selborne, L.C., in *Peaks* v. *Mosely* (1880), A.C. 714 at p. 723). Thus, a gift "to those of my nephews who shall be living at the death of both of my daughters and if more than one in equal shares" would be a class gift. The essential characteristic of a class gift is therefore the identification of the beneficiaries by description as a group rather than by nomination as individuals. Thus, the following would not be a class gift; "Equally between my five daughters." (In *re Smith's Trusts* (1878), 9 Ch. 117.) The most significant feature of class gifts for our purposes is that should one of the members of the class pre-decease the testator the potential share attributable to that person will not *lapse* and fall into residue or be property undisposed of. Instead it will remain in the fund to be divided among those members of the class who survive the testator.

THE FAILURE OF LEGACIES

Legacies may fail in several ways—

(a) LAPSE. Normally a devise or legacy lapses or fails if the intended donee predeceases the testator (but see class gifts above). Then the property falls into residue (if there is one), or where the gift is a gift of residue or a share of residue, it is undisposed of and passes as on intestacy.

(*b*) ADEMPTION. This occurs when something which is the subject of a specific bequest perishes or is sold between the time the will is executed and the death. If A bequeaths "My horse, Black Bess" to B, and the horse dies or is sold before A's death, then B is entitled to nothing. In legal language the legacy is adeemed.

(*c*) ABATEMENT. This occurs when there is not enough property to satisfy all beneficiaries after the debts and expenses have been paid. In such a case the beneficiaries must lose some of their gifts. Gifts abate in the following order—

(i) residuary gifts;
(ii) general gifts;
(iii) specific gifts.

Demonstrative gifts will not abate unless the fund out of which they are expressed to be payable is itself exhausted. If that happens, they will be treated as general gifts and will abate with them.

FAMILY PROVISION

The Inheritance (Family Provision) Act, 1938, as amended by the Intestate's Estates Act, 1952, and the Family Provision Act, 1966, gives the court the power in its discretion to order maintenance out of the deceased's net estate for the benefit of dependants.

The Act applies if a person dies domiciled in England leaving—

(i) a spouse; or
(ii) a daughter who has not married (including a daughter whose marriage has been annulled. *Re Rodwell*, [1969] 3 All E.R. 1363); or
(iii) a daughter who is incapable of maintaining herself owing to physical or mental disability; or
(iv) an infant son; or
(v) a son similarly incapacitated.

Son or daughter includes an adopted child, a child *en ventre sa mère* at the deceased's death, and presumably also a legitimated son or daughter. It should be noted that a deserted married daughter is not provided for. The Family Law Reform Act, 1969, Sect. 18, has entitled illegitimate children to apply in the case of a person dying on or after 1st January, 1970. However, grandchildren and nephews to whom the deceased might have been in *loci parentis* are still not included. The right of an "infant" son to apply under the 1938 Act continues until he is 21, despite the lowering of the age of majority for most purposes by the Act of 1969.

Any of the above dependants may apply to the court which, if it is of the opinion that the disposition of the deceased's estate by his will or by the law of intestacy or by a combination of both, does not make reasonable provision for the applicants, may order reasonable provision for their maintenance, on such conditions, if any, as the court thinks fit. The court may order maintenance as from a future date in the case of a very young child not requiring maintenance for some time.

The provision may be made by way of a lump-sum payment or by periodical payments out of income, or partly by lump-sum payment and partly by periodical payments (*Re Canderton* (1970), 114 S.J. 208) and the court order must provide for the termination of payments not later than—

(i) in the case of a spouse, remarriage;

(ii) in the case of a daughter who is not married, marriage or cesser of disability whichever is the later;

(iii) in the case of an infant son, his majority; in the case of a son under disability, cesser of the disability;

(iv) the death of the dependant.

An order for maintenance may provide for payments—

(*a*) of a specified amount; or

(*b*) equal to the whole or part of the income of the net estate; or

(*c*) to be determined in any other way which the court thinks fit.

The court will take into account the following circumstances. Provision will not be ordered if it will result in a sacrificial sale of property. The court will take into account past, present or future income or capital of the applicant from any source, including Social Security benefits (*Re Canderton* (1970), 114 S.J. 208), his conduct in relation to the deceased, and any other circumstances the court thinks relevant or material. It will consider the deceased's reasons, so far as ascertainable, for making the dispositions in his will, or for not disposing of all or part of his estate, or for not making provision for any particular dependant.

A provision in a will may be reasonable although it does not enable the applicant to live in a former style, and an application by a surviving husband will rarely be entertained except as where a husband had given up his job to act as housekeeper, and was well advanced in years.

In order to sustain a claim, application to the court must be made within six months from the date when the first grant of representation to the deceased's estate is taken out, However, the court may extend the time and is not restricted as formerly to cases in which the six months' limit would operate unfairly, e.g. as where a will or codicil is discovered which makes a substantial change in the distribution of the estate.

Under the Matrimonial Causes Act, 1965, as amended by the Family Provision Act, 1966, any *former spouse* who has not remarried can apply to the court, *within six months* of the date of probate being granted or letters of administration being taken out, for an order for payments to be made from the estate until remarriage or death. Application may be made after six months if the court gives leave.

The court has discretion in the matter and will make an order only if it would be reasonable in the circumstances for the deceased to have made some provision for the former spouse. The court will consider, *inter alia*, the conduct of the deceased and the former spouse, the income of the former spouse, and any capital sums received by the former spouse from the deceased during his lifetime. The rules relating to lump sum and periodical payments under the 1965 Act are the same as those set out above which relate to the Act of 1938, as amended.

Sect. 6 of the Family Provision Act, 1966, enables the court to make interim orders for payment of such sums at such intervals as it thinks fit under either the 1938 or 1965 Act where on an application for maintenance it appears—

(i) that the applicant is in immediate need of financial assistance but it is not yet possible to determine what order (if any) should be made; and

(ii) that property comprised in the net estate is, or can be made, available to meet the applicant's need.

Any subsequent order may provide that sums paid on an interim order shall be treated as having been paid on account of maintenance provided by the subsequent order.

A personal representative who pays any sum under an interim order is not liable if the estate is insufficient to make the payment unless at the time of making the payment he has reasonable cause to believe that the estate is not sufficient.

If the Court decides to make an award under the Act, then it has also to consider how the burden of that award is to be borne as between the beneficiaries entitled to the deceased's estate. The Act of 1938 covers this point by conferring in Sect. 3 (as amended) a wide power on the court to give such directions as it thinks fit.

Sect. 7 of the Act of 1966 makes provision for the extension to the county court of jurisdiction both for original and further proceedings under the 1938 and 1965 Acts where it is shown to the satisfaction of the court that the value of the net estate does not exceed £5,000 or such larger sum as may be fixed by order made by the Lord Chancellor.

PERSONAL REPRESENTATIVES

When a person dies he usually has debts outstanding and creditors to be satisfied, and the claims of these have to be dealt with. There are also the conflicting claims of the beneficiaries. In order that the estate may be wound up, the debts settled, and the appropriate beneficiaries may receive what is due to them under a will or intestacy, personal representatives are necessary. These are of two kinds; executors or administrators.

Executors. Subject to the following qualifications, executors can be appointed only by the testator himself—

(i) If there is only one executor (not being a trust corporation) and a life or minority interest arises under the Will, the court can appoint an additional executor. (Judicature Act, 1925, Sect. 160.)

(ii) The court may appoint a special or additional executor if there is settled land under the will. (Administration of Estates Act, 1925, Sect. 23.)

(iii) The executor of a sole or last surviving executor of a testator becomes the executor of that testator. Thus if T dies, leaving only one executor E1, who dies leaving only one executor E2, who dies leaving only one executor E3, this constitutes a chain of representation and E1, E2 and E3 can act successively as executors. If, however, E1 dies intestate, administrators will be appointed to administer his estate, but they will not become the executors of T. In such a case it is necessary to apply for Letters of Administration *de bonis non* (in respect of unadministered property).

(iv) An executor *de son tort* (of his own wrong), i.e. one who intermeddles with an estate, may find himself saddled with the burdens of executorship.

Persons who may be Appointed Executors. A testator may appoint any person, including an alien, or a bankrupt, but probate will not be granted (*a*) to a person of unsound mind; or (*b*) to a minor during his minority.

A corporation sole appears to have been always capable of being appointed and of taking probate as executor, but if before the Administration of Justice Act, 1920, a corporation aggregate was appointed executor, the practice was to grant administration with the will annexed to a syndic (agent or representative) nominated by the corporation. The Act empowered the court to grant probate to a corporation itself as executor, if its principal place of business was within the United Kingdom. This Act was repealed by the Administration of Estates Act, 1925, which enables probate to be granted to a trust corporation, but if a non-trust corporation is appointed executor, the position would presumably be the same as it was before the Act of 1920. By a Trust Corporation is meant the Public Trustee, or any corporation which is either appointed a trustee by the court in any particular case, or is qualified to act as custodian trustee under the Public Trustee (Custodian Trustee) Rules, 1926, e.g. banks.

Difficulties can arise in regard to the appointment of a firm of solicitors as executors. Appointment of a partnership firm as such is not valid because a partnership is not a legal entity, so that there may be uncertainty as to which of the partners is to act. The following formula was adopted by Latey, J., in *Re Hogan (dec'd)*, [1969] 3 All E.R. 1570.

(I appoint the partners at the date of my death in the firm of . . . of . . . or the firm which at that date has succeeded to and carries on its practice to be the executors and trustees of this my will and I express the wish that two and only two of them shall prove my will and act initially in its trusts).

Mode of Appointment. Normally executors are expressly nominated by the will or codicil, but an appointment can be implied as where a testator after nominating his sister as executrix, requested his nephews X and Y to help her, and where a named person was, in another case, directed to pay the testator's debts. In such instances the executor is said to be an executor according to the tenor, but the court will not grant probate to a person as executor according to the tenor, unless it is possible to collect from the will an intention that the person named should pay the debts and generally administer the estate; and, of course, every case depends upon its own particular facts.

Number of Executors. A testator need not appoint more than one executor, and a sole executor, even if he is not a Trust Corporation, is competent to act for all purposes, including the sale of land and the giving of a valid receipt for the proceeds of sale—in contrast with a trust for sale, where the sole trustee cannot do so. Probate will not be granted to more than four persons. If more than four are nominated, then probate will be granted to the first four who are *sui juris* (of full age and sound mind) and willing to act.

Acceptance of Office. A person named as an executor and who has not intermeddled with the estate may refuse to act, but a refusal must be in the form of a renunciation in writing recorded in the Probate Registry. There is a prescribed form of renunciation in which the executor takes an oath that he has not intermeddled, because an executor who has intermeddled cannot renounce. The effect of renunciation is as if the executor had never been appointed. Such renunciation may be withdrawn only if it can be shown to be for the benefit of the estate or the persons interested in it, not otherwise. An executor to whom probate has once been granted can never resign (as a trustee can).

Public Trustee. The Public Trustee is a corporation sole set up by the Public Trustee Act, 1906, and is a trust corporation for the purposes of the Trustee Act, 1925, and for any other purposes. He may be appointed executor alone or with any person or persons not exceeding three.

He cannot accept office (*a*) if the testator was not domiciled in England or Wales; or (*b*) if the estate is known or believed to be insolvent; or, (*c*) if the administration of the estate involves the carrying on of a business, except with a view to the sale thereof or where the consent of the Treasury is obtained. The Public Trustee can renounce a probate in any case except on the ground of the smallness of the estate. It is not necessary that the will should contain any provision for the payment of the Public Trustee's fees as these are provided for by statute. This is not so in the case of other trust corporations such as banks, where a specific provision for payment must be included in the will. Solicitor-executors must also ensure that the will contains a charging clause if they are to recover for work done on behalf of the estate.

Title of the Executor. An executor appointed by will derives his title from the will, and all the testator's real and personal property vests in the executor as from the moment of death. An executor who is competent to take probate (i.e. *sui juris*), may, before the probate, validly do any act in relation to the administration of the estate, except an act for which proof of his executorial capacity is necessary, e.g. commencing an action or the conveyance of land. A sole surviving executor can deal alone with land, but if there are two or more proving executors who are surviving, all must concur in dealing with freehold or leasehold land. In regard to pure personalty the powers of executors are joint and several, so that the act of one of them will bind the others, e.g. giving a receipt for money collected.

PROBATE

Probate Registries. The principal Probate Registry is at Somerset House. Application for probate may be made there in any case, and must be made there if the testator died domiciled abroad; otherwise application may be made to any of the district registries.

The Administration of Estates (Small Payments) Act, 1965, raises to a uniform amount of £500 the limits contained in many statutory provisions which permit the distribution of small sums due to deceased persons *without a grant of probate or letters of administration*. The Act does not alter the position of private individuals holding small sums due to deceased persons. A satisfactory discharge can be obtained only from the legal personal representatives of the deceased and there is an element of risk involved in paying to anyone else. However, government and other bodies, e.g. co-operative societies who pay out under various statutory powers, are protected.

Probate Courts. In all contentious matters concerning the grant of probate or administration, jurisdiction lies with the Chancery Division of the High Court. Non-contentious matters are heard in the Family Division. The County Court of the district in which the deceased had a fixed abode at the time of his decease, is empowered to exercise jurisdiction if the estate does not exceed £1,000. Appeal from of these courts is to the Court of Appeal.

Probate in Common Form. A grant of probate obtained from a registry without application to the court is called Probate in Common Form. The executors must either apply in person, or through a solicitor, and not by any other person, e.g. if a wife is an executor she cannot send her husband. All that is required is the production of the necessary documents, and the payment of fees, stamps and death duties. The necessary documents are—

(*a*) THE EXECUTOR'S OATH. The names of the executors must appear in full in the same order as in the will. The full name and address and domicil of the deceased must be given, and any difference between his true name and that in the will, and any change of address. The oath also sets out the gross value of the estate, and states whether there was any settled land vested in the deceased which remains settled after his death. The oath is in the form of an affidavit, sworn before a commissioner for oaths, and declaring that the executor believes the will to be the last will of the deceased.

(*b*) INLAND REVENUE AFFIDAVIT AND ESTATE ACCOUNT. These are official forms obtainable from any Collector of Taxes or the Estate Duty Office, and the value of the real and personal estate for duty purposes must be fully set out, together with debts and funeral expenses. All the executors swear to an affidavit before a commissioner. In order to speed up the issue of grants, the Inland Revenue has, in general, dispensed with the examination and assessment of Inland Revenue affidavits by the Estate Duty Office prior to the issue of a grant in favour of a system of assessment by solicitors.

(*c*) THE ORIGINAL WILL. This must be signed by all the executors and the commissioner on the first page of the will and along the margin. It is important that in other respects the will should be in the condition in which the deceased left it, and that it should not be perforated by pins, etc., which might lead to the conclusion that something had been torn off. It is not now necessary, as it formerly was, to lodge a copy of the will, as a photostat copy will normally be made in the Registry.

(*d*) RENUNCIATION. An executor who does not wish to act may renounce. However, if he does not prove and does not renounce, power to prove subsequently will be reserved to him.

(*e*) WHERE THE EXECUTOR IS A TRUST CORPORATION OTHER THAN THE PUBLIC TRUSTEE, A SEALED RESOLUTION OF THE DIRECTORS MUST BE LODGED APPOINTING SOME OFFICIAL OF THE CORPORATION TO ACT ON ITS BEHALF. On depositing the above documents at the appropriate Registry, and after payment of fees and estate duty on the personalty, probate will eventually issue.

Probate in Solemn Form. This is advisable where the validity of the will is open to question, or where there is a possibility of dispute as to any codicil, or where there is reason to doubt the testator's capacity. It entails the hearing of evidence and is in effect an action in the Chancery Division.

Apart from the executor's discretion to apply for Probate in Solemn Form in these cases, he may be compelled to do so by somebody opposing his application for Probate in Common Form. It is said that he may even be called upon to prove in Solemn Form within thirty years of the grant in Common Form. (*Williams on Executors and Administrators*, Vol 1.) However, a claim by a beneficiary under a will or an intestacy must be brought within twelve years of the date when the benefit accrued. (Limitation Act, 1939.) A creditor can never require Probate in Solemn Form, because he will be paid in any event if the estate is sufficient.

Administrators. Where a person dies intestate his personal representatives are called administrators, and must apply for a grant of letters of administration. The following priorities apply—

1. The Surviving Spouse. If a spouse survives, but dies before obtaining a grant, his or her personal representatives will have the first right.

2. Children or other issue of the intestate, including illegitimate, legitimated or lawfully adopted children or their issue.

3. Father or mother of the deceased.

4. Brothers and sisters of the whole blood or their issue.

5. Brothers and sisters of the half-blood or their issue.

6. Grandparents.

7. Uncles and aunts of the whole blood or their issue.

8. Uncles and aunts of the half-blood or their issue.

9. The Crown (if beneficially entitled).

10. Creditors.

If several persons have an equal claim, grant is normally made to the first to apply, subject to notice to the others. In case of dispute the court decides on the most suitable person or persons. A grant will not be made to (*a*) a bankrupt, (*b*) a person of unsound mind, or (*c*) a syndic or nominee on behalf of a corporation. A grant is made to not more than four persons and not fewer than two if a life or minority interest arises under the intestacy.

Administration with the Will Annexed. This will be granted if the deceased made a will but appointed no executor; or if the person appointed refuses to act or fails to appear when cited to take out probate; or where he is incapable of acting, or pre-deceases the testator, or survives the testator but dies before proving. The order of priority of persons entitled to apply for administration differs from that on intestacy, and the persons having first priority are the residuary legatees or devisees under the will.

Administration *de bonis non*. This is *de bonis non administratis*—with reference to unadministered property.

It is granted when all the persons, to whom probate or administration to the estate of a deceased person has been granted, die without having administered the whole estate, and the chain of representation does not continue. To justify such a grant the following conditions must exist—

(i) Part of the deceased's estate must remain unadministered.

(ii) The chain of representation must be broken, as where a sole or last surviving executor dies after proving and without himself leaving a proving executor.

If an executor dies without having proved, his executor (if any) will not become the original testator's executor, and in that case a grant with the will annexed is necessary and not a grant *de bonis non*.

Administration *durante minore aetate*. (For the duration of minority.) Administration to an adult may be granted *durante minore aetate* if the person appointed sole executor is an infant. Administration *cum testamento annexo* will be granted to the guardian, or such other person as the court thinks fit; but if there is a life interest or any infant beneficiary, at least two persons or a trust corporation must be appointed. A grant *durante minore aetate* will also be made where all persons otherwise entitled to apply for a grant of administration are infants, as may happen on intestacy.

Obtaining Administration with or without a Will. To obtain a grant the following documents are necessary—

(*a*) INLAND REVENUE AFFIDAVIT. This is made by the proposed administrator in similar form to that mentioned above in regard to executors.

(*b*) OATH OF PROPOSED ADMINISTRATOR. This oath relates to the death and the character in which the applicant applies.

(*c*) BOND FOR DUE ADMINISTRATION. One significant distinction between executors and administrators was the requirement that an administrator should give a bond, usually with sureties, for the due administration of the estate. The bond caused some delay and expenses in the proceedings and put a burden on the administrator which was not, in many cases, necessary. The Administration of Estates Act, 1971, abolishes the need for a bond and sureties except in a limited number of cases, e.g. application by a person not normally resident in the U.K., or in special circumstances when the Registrar deems it desirable.

Revocation. It is possible to revoke a grant of Probate or of Letters of Administration.

PROBATE CAN BE REVOKED—

   (i) where a grant has been obtained by fraud;

   (ii) where a later will has been discovered;

   (iii) where the testator proves to be alive;

   (iv) where a grant has been made to the wrong person, e.g. where a later codicil is discovered appointing someone else;

   (v) where the executor called upon to prove in solemn form fails to establish the will;

   (vi) where a grant was irregularly issued;

   (vii) where one of several executors dies before the grant, or becomes incapable of acting and the grant is nevertheless issued in ignorance of the fact.

If one of several executors becomes of unsound mind after grant, the grant is revoked and a new grant is made to the same executors excluding the insane person.

LETTERS OF ADMINISTRATION CAN BE REVOKED—

   (i) where a grant was improperly obtained, e.g. within less than fourteen days of the death.

   (ii) where the grant was to the wrong persons, e.g. to a reputed wife.

   (iii) where the administrator becomes of unsound mind, or otherwise incapable of acting, or cannot be found.

   (iv) where the intestate proves to be alive.

Nevertheless all conveyances of any interests in real or personal estate to a purchaser by a person to whom probate or administration has been granted are valid, notwithstanding any revocation of the grant. (Administration of Estates Act, 1925, Sect. 37.)

INTESTACY

Under the Administration of Estates Act, 1925, as amended by the Intestates' Estates Act, 1952, and the Family Provision Act, 1966, with respect to deaths on or after 1st January, 1967, the estate is held by the administrators, after payment of funeral and testamentary expenses and debts, on trust for sale and conversion, with power to postpone the sale, and with it the distribution of the residue, among the statutory next of kin. The extended rights of succession given to an illegitimate child by the Family Law Reform Act, 1969, are dealt with on p. 377–8.

Distribution of the Estate

1. Where there is a surviving spouse (if there is no issue, parent, brother or sister of the whole blood, or issue of such brother or sister) the spouse takes the whole estate absolutely. It should be noted that under Sect. 40 of the Matrimonial Proceedings and Property Act, 1970, a party to a decree of judicial separation is not entitled, while the decree is in force and the separation is continuing, to share in the intestacy of the other party. The rule does not apply where the separation order was made by magistrates.

2. If there is issue surviving, the spouse takes all *personal* chattels, i.e. the personal belongings of the deceased, £15,000, free of death duties and costs, with interest at 4 per cent until payment or appropriation, and a life interest in half the residue. The issue take on statutory trusts, half the residue at once, and the other half on the death of the spouse.

3. If there is no issue but there is surviving a parent, brother or sister of the whole blood, or issue of such brother or sister, the spouse takes all the personal chattels as above, £40,000 as a statutory legacy with interest as above, and half the residue absolutely. The surviving parent or parents take equally the other half of the residue absolutely. If no parent survives, the brothers and sisters of the whole blood take the other half of residue on trust until attaining eighteen or marrying, when they take equally. Children of the issue of an intestate take *per stirpes*, by stocks of descent, if their parents have predeceased the intestate, as do children of persons other than issue. *Per stirpes* means they take their parent's share between them.

4. Where there is no surviving spouse, if the issue of the intestate survive and attain eighteen or marry, they take on the statutory trusts. (Sect. 47 of the Administration of Estates Act, 1925.) If no issue survive, but either or both parents survive they take absolutely and equally if both survive.

When assessing the share of a child where there is a *total* intestacy it is necessary under Sect. 47 of the Administration of Estates Act, 1925, to take into account advances (if any) made to him by the deceased during his lifetime. Such advances are brought into hotchpot before the shares of the children are calculated. For example, suppose X dies leaving three children, a daughter A and two sons B and C, and they are together entitled to £18,000; X's wife having predeceased him and the children being over eighteen or married. In the absence of the hotchpot rule, each child would receive £6,000. But suppose that X had before his death given his daughter £2,000 on the occasion of her marriage, and his son B £4,000 to enable him to start a business. Under the hotchpot rule the sums so given are added to the £18,000 making £24,000. The children are now entitled to £8,000 each. However since A has already received £2,000 she will take £6,000, and since B has received £4,000 he will take £4,000. C who has received nothing will take £8,000.

5. If the intestate leaves no spouse and no issue or parent, then his estate will be held in trust for certain relations who become entitled in the following order: brothers and sisters of the whole blood; brothers and sisters of the half-blood; grandparents; uncles and aunts of the whole, and then of the half-blood. For all these persons (except grandparents who take absolutely) the residuary estate is held on the statutory trusts.

On a failure of the prescribed classes, the estate of the intestate goes to the Crown as *bona vacantia*. Power is reserved to the Crown to provide for dependants not entitled as above.

When the residue includes a dwelling house in which the surviving spouse was resident at the deceased's death, the surviving spouse may require such interest to be made part of the interest he or she takes under the intestacy, subject to conditions set out in the Second Schedule of the Act of 1952.

An adopted person is, for the purposes of devolution of property on intestacy, treated as if he or she were the child of the adopter, born in lawful wedlock and not the child of any other person. (Adoption Act, 1958, Sect. 16.)

A legitimated person is entitled to an interest in the estate of an intestate dying after the date of legitimation in like manner as if he had been born legitimate. (Legitimacy Act, 1926, Sect. 3.) Where the legitimated person or his issue dies intestate the same persons are entitled to take interests in the estate as if he had been born legitimate. (*Ibid*, Sect. 4.) These rules are unchanged by the Family Law Reform Act, 1969. However, if the intestate died *before* the legitimation, the person involved will have the extended rights of any other illegitimate person under the 1969 Act.

Rights of Succession of Illegitimate Children. Until the Family Law Reform Act, 1969, an illegitimate person *had no rights on intestacy* nor could his parents take on his intestacy except that under Sect. 9 of the Legitimacy Act, 1926, if his mother died without leaving any legitimate children surviving her, an illegitimate child could take on her intestacy and so could his issue if he was dead. Furthermore, his mother could participate in his intestacy as if he had been legitimate.

The position is now changed by Sect. 14 of the 1969 Act as regards the intestacy of any person dying on or after 1st January, 1970. The section provides that on the intestacy of either of his parents an illegitimate child and, if he is dead, his issue takes the same interest he would have taken had he been legitimate. In addition, if an illegitimate person dies intestate, both his parents take the same interest which they would have taken had he been legitimate.

It should be noted that the Act gives rights only as between the parent and the illegitimate child and his issue. An illegitimate person cannot take on his brother's intestacy or vice versa, nor can a grandparent take on the intestacy of an illegitimate grandchild.

It was a well-known rule of English law that in construing a *will or other disposition*, e.g. a trust, any reference to a "child" or other relation included only legitimate children or relatives traced through legitimate children *unless the contrary was proved*. Sect. 15 of the 1969 Act has reversed this rule by providing that in any disposition made on or after 1st January, 1970, a reference to a beneficiary who is a child of any person or is related in some other way to any other person includes an illegitimate child or a person who is illegitimate or whose relationship is traced through an illegitimate person, *subject to a contrary intention in the disposition*. In consequence a gift "to my children" would, under Sect. 15, include the testator's illegitimate children. The construction of the word "heir" is not affected, however, so that entailed interests and property with a title go only to legitimate children or persons. Sect. 33 of the Wills Act, 1837, which relates to *lapse* (see p. 366) did not operate through illegitimate or legitimated relationships. Under Sect. 16 of the 1969 Act it does operate through such persons who may now benefit.

Sect. 17 of the 1969 Act gives some *protection to trustees and personal representatives* as a result of the difficulties which they may experience in tracing illegitimate relatives particularly those of men. They are allowed to distribute property without taking certain active steps, e.g. advertising, to find illegitimate connections.

Commorientes. It sometimes happens that two persons die together in circumstances where it is doubtful or impossible to ascertain which died first, as when a man and wife are both killed in a car or aeroplane crash. This difficulty is removed by Sect. 184 of the Law of Property Act, 1925. In so far as it concerns questions of title to property, the elder is presumed to have died first and wills take effect in that order. This rule still applies even where the evidence suggests that they died simultaneously.

However, the Intestates' Estates Act, 1952, prevents the above rule coming into operation on intestacy. Where an intestate and his or her spouse die in such circumstances that it is uncertain which survived the other, the spouse is presumed to have died first (regardless of the seniority rule) for the purposes of intestacy. Thus if A and B are married and childless and both die intestate the relatives of A will not inherit from B and those of B will not inherit from A.

Partial Intestacy. When the deceased does not entirely dispose of his property the foregoing provisions apply to the property not disposed of, subject to any provisions of the will which may apply. The spouse and children must bring into account property received under the will and advances made during the deceased's lifetime; other relatives need not do so.

GIFTS *INTER VIVOS*

A person may make dispositions of his property with the intention that they should become operative during his lifetime. A transfer of property where the giver (the donor) receives no valuable consideration from the recipient (the donee) is a gift. A gift in English law is irrevocable in spite of subsequent ingratitude on the part of the donee; but it may be conditional where the gift is to determine if a certain event happens or does not happen.

A gift may be made by deed, in which case it is not necessary to deliver the property though the donee can refuse the gift. Where a gift is not made by deed there must be a transfer or delivery of the property to the donee coupled with an intention that the donee should become the owner and not merely the possessor.

DONATIO MORTIS CAUSA

A *donatio mortis causa* is the delivery of property in contemplation of the donor's death on condition that the gift is not to be absolute until he dies. It is immaterial that the death results from a cause different from that contemplated, and if a donor is suffering from cancer but dies from pneumonia the gift is nevertheless good. Contemplation of suicide is not sufficient.

The gift must be conditional on death, that is, it must be revocable during the donor's lifetime, and it must be a present gift to take effect in the future, i.e. on death, and not a future gift such as "You are to have this if anything happens to me."

Revocation of the gift is automatic if the donor recovers from his illness, or may be express if the donor resumes possession of the property or tells the donee that the gift is revoked. A *donatio* cannot be revoked by will because the donee's title is complete at the donor's death.

In the absence of delivery, oral or written words of gift are not enough. In the case of a chattel, or of a chose in action which is transferable by delivery, either the thing itself must be handed over or something which deprives the owner of access to it and enables the donee to get it, e.g. the delivery of the key to a safe. The delivery of one of two or more keys is not enough since the owner has not deprived himself of access to the gift. In the case of choses in action not transferable by delivery, there must be delivery of such a document as will entitle the donee to obtain the property.

Anything capable of passing by mere delivery can be the subject of a *donatio*, e.g. a Post Office Savings Book; National Savings Certificates; Victory Bonds; A Trustee Savings Book, and a Bank Deposit Pass Book. Freehold or leasehold land cannot pass by *donatio*, neither can Premium Bonds (by the terms of issue).

A *donatio* differs from a legacy in that it takes effect conditionally before death and no assent by the personal representatives is necessary. Further it cannot be revoked by will, as a legacy can, because a *donatio* takes effect notionally before the will does.

APPENDIX

THE DEVELOPMENT OF ENGLISH LAW

1. The Earl of Oxford's case (1615), 1 Rep. Ch. 1

Merton College, Oxford, had been granted a lease of Covent Garden for 72 years at £9 a year, and some 50 years later sold the lease to the Earl for £15 a year. Later the college retook possession of part of it, on the ground that a statute of Elizabeth prevented the sale of ecclesiastical and college lands so that the conveyance to the Earl was void. The Earl brought an action to eject the college from the land, and the common law judges found in favour of the college, saying that they were bound by the statute. The Earl filed a Bill in Equity for relief, and Lord Ellesmere granted it, stating that the claim of the college was against all good conscience. This brought law and Equity into open conflict and resulted in the ruling of James I that, where common law and Equity are in conflict, Equity shall prevail.

2. Cheney v. Conn, [1968] 1 All E.R. 779

Cheney objected to his tax assessments under the Finance Act, 1964, on the ground that the government was applying part of the tax collected to the making of nuclear weapons. Cheney alleged that this was contrary to the Geneva Conventions—which had been incorporated into the Geneva Conventions Act, 1957—and conflicted with international law. *Held*—that even if there was a conflict between the 1964 and 1957 Acts, the 1964 Act gave clear authority to collect the taxes in question and being later in time prevailed. "It is not for the court to say that a parliamentary enactment, the highest law in this country, is illegal." (*Per* Ungoed-Thomas, J.)

3. Prince of Hanover v. Attorney-General, [1956] Ch. 188

A statute of Anne in 1705 provided for the naturalisation of Princess Sophia, Electress of Hanover, and the issue of her body. The statute was repealed by the British Nationality Act, 1948, Sect. 34 (3), but by Sect. 12 a person who was a British subject immediately before the commencement of the Act (1st January, 1949) became a citizen of the United Kingdom and Colonies. The plaintiff was born in 1914 in Hanover and was lineally descended from the Electress. He now claimed a declaration that he was a British subject immediately before the commencement of the British Nationality Act. It was necessary for him to establish this in order to make a claim on a fund, put up by the Polish Government, to compensate Britons who had lost property in Poland because of nationalisation. Vaisey, J., held at first instance that the statute had not lost its force merely because of its age, but thought that, although the statute was unqualified and plain in its meaning, its words taken alone produced an absurd result, since, under the statute, the Kaiser would have been a British subject. Parliament must, therefore, have intended some limitation on the operation of the words used. By referring to the preamble it seemed possible to draw the conclusion that the purpose of the Act was to be effected in the lifetime of Anne, and that after that time its purpose was spent and the plaintiff was not entitled to his declaration. On reaching the Court of Appeal, *it was held* that the appellant was a British subject under the statute of Anne which had remained law until repealed by the 1948 Act, the statute being so clear in its meaning that it was unnecessary to apply rules of interpretation to it. Rules of interpretation were to be used only in case of ambiguity or doubt as to meaning.

4. Vauxhall Estates Ltd. *v.* Liverpool Corporation, [1932] 1 K.B. 733

In 1928 the Minister of Health made a Street Improvement Scheme Order for a certain area of Liverpool. The Order required the compulsory purchase of property, and the question of compensation payable to owners arose. Under Sect. 2 of the Acquisition of Land (Assessment of Compensation) Act, 1919, the plaintiffs would receive £2,370, but if Sect. 46 of the Housing Act, 1925, applied, the plaintiffs would receive £1,133. A provision in the Act of 1919 stated that other statutes inconsistent with the 1919 Act were not to have effect. *Held*—The 1925 Act impliedly repealed the 1919 Act in so far as it was inconsistent with it. Compensation was to be assessed under the latest enactment.

5. Beckett (A. F.) Ltd. *v.* Lyons, [1967] 1 All E.R. 833

A foreshore between Seaham and West Hartlepool was held partly by the plaintiff company and partly by the local authority. The plaintiff company had a right to collect coal from the local authority's part of the beach in return for a rent of £3,500 per annum. The plaintiffs sued the defendants for trespass because they had been removing sea coal from the foreshore, these coals having been washed by the tide on to the foreshore from submarine outcrops off the Durham coast. The defendants did not raise questions of title to the foreshore but set up an alleged lawful custom in favour of the inhabitants of the County Palatine. Their witnesses included two elderly persons who had been resident in a near-by village since 1886 who said that people had taken bags of coal from the foreshore for their own use and for sale during the last five years of the last century, and other witnesses gave evidence of coal being carried away from 1912 to 1914 and again in the 1920's. There was also evidence that after the closure of the beaches during the second world war of 1939-45 commercial exploitation started, coal being removed by inhabitants of the Palatinate, including residents in neighbouring villages, with the aid of motor-lorries. *Held*—by the Court of Appeal—the defendants had no right to remove sea-borne coal from the foreshore because—

(i) the evidence was insufficient to establish the existence of a custom supporting a right in the inhabitants of so large an area, since the evidence of removal extended in substance only to inhabitants of villages near to the foreshore who could remove it in buckets and wheelbarrows, and not to the inland area of the country where transport by lorry was required;

(ii) the practice of taking the sea-borne coal was not necessarily of right and might be explained by tolerance on the part of the foreshore owner of what was, at least in earlier times, an unimportant and non-commercial activity;

(iii) the present commercial exploitation of the coal by motor lorries was quite different from the old practice;

(iv) the right was a profit-à-prendre and not an easement (see pp. 286–7) and a fluctuating body of persons such as the inhabitants of a county could not acquire a right of that nature by custom.

6. Simpson v. Wells (1872), L.R. 7 Q.B. 214

The appellant had been charged with obstruction of a public footpath by setting up a refreshment stall. In his defence he alleged that he had done so by virtue of a custom which dated back to the fairs, called Statute Sessions, which were held for the purpose of hiring servants and deciding current rates of wages. The custom of setting up such stalls had been in existence for at least fifty years. Evidence showed that Statute Sessions were authorised by the Statutes of Labourers, the first of which was passed in the reign of Edward III (1327–77), and the custom could not, therefore, have existed in 1189. The appellant's defence failed.

7. Mercer v. Denne, [1904] 2 Ch. 534

The plaintiffs sued on behalf of themselves and all other persons carrying on the trade or business of fishermen in the parish of Walmer in the county of Kent, claiming a customary right for the purpose of the said trade or business to dry their nets on the beach ground of Walmer, and for that purpose to spread their nets on the beach. The defendant owned a section of the beach ground and wished to build on it, and the plaintiffs asked for an injunction to prevent this. The defence was that the so-called custom was exercised only occasionally and discontinuously, and at great and irregular intervals, and that prior to 1799 and for many years thereafter the beach ground was below the high-water mark, and until recent times was wholly unsuitable and incapable of being used for drying nets. *Held*—The custom was a valid custom and was not unreasonable. The fluctuations in user were due, amongst other things, to the fact that the action of the wind and tide made the amount of beach available a variable quantity. Nevertheless the fishermen had always claimed the right to use whatever ground was available, and so the custom extended to the additional ground now made available by the recession of the sea.

8. Mills v. Colchester Corporation (1867), L.R. 2 C.P. 476

The owners of an oyster fishery which had been in existence since the time of the first Queen Elizabeth held courts for the purpose of granting fishing licences. The plaintiff applied for a licence and was refused, and he now claimed a customary right to fish. *Held*—He could not set up a customary right because the right to fish had always depended on the grant of a licence (i.e. permission).

9. Bryant v. Foot (1868), L.R. 3 Q.B. 497

A clergyman claimed a customary fee of thirteen shillings for every marriage which he celebrated. Evidence showed that the fee had been collected for a period of forty-eight years, and this would normally have been enough to raise a presumption of antiquity. However, the court *held* that, since the sum of thirteen shillings would manifestly have been an unreasonable fee in 1189, the custom could not be admitted.

10. Goodwin v. Robarts (1875), L.R. 10 Exch. 337

In 1873 the Russian Government raised loans by means of bonds through Messrs. Rothschilds who were London bankers. Rothschilds issued a document of title called scrip to purchasers, the scrip to be exchanged in due course for bonds. In February, 1874, the plaintiff purchased £500 worth of scrip and left it in the hands of his broker who was to await the plaintiff's instructions. The broker pledged the scrip with the defendants as security for a loan of £800 on

27th February, 1874. In April he was declared a defaulter on the Stock Exchange, was made bankrupt, and absconded, not having repaid the loan of £800. The defendants, in ignorance of the plaintiff's claim, sold the scrip for £471 5s. If the scrip could be considered negotiable, then the defendants were entitled as against the plaintiff, for a major characteristic of such an instrument is that it passes from one party to another free of previous defects in title. It was proved that it was a custom of merchants all over Europe to treat such scrip as negotiable, and so the court was prepared to recognise it as negotiable by the common law of England.

11. Crouch *v.* Credit Foncier of England (1873), L.R. 8 Q.B. 374

The defendants were a limited company registered under an Act of 1862. In May, 1869, they sold to a person named Macken a document under the seal of the company, and signed by two directors and the secretary. The document was called a debenture. In July, 1869, the bond was stolen from Macken, and in October, 1871, this bond came up for payment under a system whereby certain bonds were drawn for payment at intervals of time. The plaintiff had purchased the bond from a person named Stanley who had since absconded. The defendants having notice of the theft refused to pay the plaintiff on the bond, and he brought this action claiming that he was the lawful bearer of the bond, and that the instrument had been treated by merchants as negotiable, so that he could acquire a good title even from a thief. *Held*—It was impossible to add to the common law of England by recent custom of merchants. This custom must have been recent, since the document was a company debenture bond, and companies of this kind had only been in existence since 1844. The custom could not, therefore, have been part of the Law Merchant. The plaintiff's claim failed, the court holding that the instrument was not negotiable at law or by statute.

N.B. Company Bearer Debentures are now negotiable under the provisions of the Companies Act, 1948.

12. Boys *v.* Blenkinsop, *The Times*, 25th June, 1968.

Mrs. Nellie Blenkinsop was charged at Lewes with having "permitted" her son Donald to drive a car without third-party insurance contrary to Sect. 201 of the Road Traffic Act, 1960. The registered owner of the car was the driver's father whose insurance policy did not cover driving by his son. However, it appeared that the son had asked his mother's permission to drive and she had given it and had said she was the owner when asked by a constable. The defence submitted that there was no case to answer because only the registered owner could permit use of the vehicle. The prosecution submitted that this was wrong because Mrs. Blenkinsop might have been, if not joint owner, at any rate responsible for care, management or control of the car within *Lloyd* v. *Singleton*, [1953] 1 All E.R. 291. The prosecuting inspector had asked the justices to refer to *Wilkinson's Road Traffic Offences* (5th ed. 1965, p. 202) which in relation to that case stated "A person may 'permit' though he is not the owner." Counsel for the defence objected that unless the justices were referred to the case itself they were not allowed to look at the textbook. The inspector did not have a report of the case with him. The justices dismissed the case and the prosecution appealed to the Divisional Court. The Court allowed the appeal and remitted the case to the justices to continue the hearing of it. Parker, L.C.J., said "They are entitled to and should look at the textbook;

and if they then feel in doubt they should, of their own motion, send for the authority, and if necessary, adjourn for it to be obtained."

THE COURTS OF LAW

13. R. *v.* London County Council, ex parte The Entertainments Protection Association Ltd., [1931] 2 K.B. 215

The county council granted a new licence, under Sect. 2 of the Cinematograph Act, 1909, in respect of a cinema called the Streatham Astoria. One of the conditions contained in the Act was that the premises were not to be opened on Sundays, Christmas Day or Good Friday. Subsequent to the grant of the licence, a committee of the council considered an application that the Streatham Astoria be allowed to open on the above-mentioned days. The committee resolved that "no action be taken for the present in the event of the premises being opened . . . on Sundays, Christmas Day and Good Friday," subject to the applicants paying a sum of money to a selected charity. The Association challenged the ruling of the committee by *certiorari*. *Held*—The council was usurping its jurisdiction in breaking a condition of the licence, and that this was prohibited by the Act of 1909. *Certiorari* lay to quash the committee's ruling.

14. R. *v.* Deal Justices, ex parte Curling (1881), 45 L.T. 439

Justices, who were subscribers to the Society for the Prevention of Cruelty to Animals, had taken part in the conviction of the appellant for the offence of cruelty to a horse, the prosecution having been brought by the society. The appellant sought to quash the conviction by *certiorari*. *Held*—*Certiorari* must be refused. Subscribers to the society had no authority over prosecutions which were instituted by Central Office in London, and the society never accepted penalties taken from offenders, so that there was no bias.

15. Dimes *v.* Grand Junction Canal (1852), 3 H.L.C. 759

Dimes was the Lord of a manor through which the canal passed, and he had been concerned in a case with the proprietors of the canal in which he disputed their title to certain land. Dimes had obtained an order of ejectment, but the canal company approached the Lord Chancellor (Lord Cottenham) to prevent Dimes enforcing the order and to confirm the company's title. The Lord Chancellor granted the relief sought. Dimes now appealed to the House of Lords on the ground that the Lord Chancellor was a shareholder in the company and was therefore biased. *Held*—The Lord Chancellor's order granting the relief must be quashed because, although there was no evidence that his pecuniary interest had influenced him, yet it should not appear that any court had laboured under influences of this nature.

16. R. *v.* Metropolitan Police Commissioner, ex parte Parker, [1953] 1 W.L.R. 1150

The Commissioner had revoked Parker's cab licence under powers given to him in the London Cab Order, 1934, on the ground that the cab had been used for the purpose of prostitution. The Order gave the Commissioner power to revoke a licence if satisfied that the licensee was not a fit person to hold one. He was not bound to hold an inquiry or hear evidence. Having made up his mind to revoke the licence, the Commissioner directed that Parker should appear before the licensing committee, and that if the committee saw any reason why the Commissioner should change his mind on the matter of revocation, they should report to him. Parker denied the allegations of the police and wished to call evidence in support of his denial at the committee but was not allowed to do so. The committee reported to the Commissioner that he should not alter his decision, and the licence was revoked. Parker asked for *certiorari* to quash the order of revocation. *Held—Certiorari* did not lie. The Commissioner and the committee were exercising administrative, not judicial or quasi-judicial functions. Therefore they need not observe the rules of natural justice by granting Parker a full hearing. However, if the Commissioner had set up the committee to hear evidence and report its findings so that he could decide whether or not to revoke the licence, then the committee would have been exercising judicial functions and must observe the rules of natural justice.

16*a*. *Ridge v. Baldwin*, [1963] 2 All E.R. 66

Mr. Ridge, who was the Chief Constable of Brighton, had been acquitted on a charge of conspiring with other police officers to obstruct the course of justice, though the trial judge, Donovan, J., said that Mr. Ridge had not given the necessary professional or moral leadership to the Brighton Police Force. The Brighton Watch Committee subsequently dismissed Mr. Ridge from his post as Chief Constable under a power in the Municipal Corporations Act, 1882, giving them a right to dismiss "any constable whom they think negligent in the discharge of his duty or otherwise unfit for the same". Ridge was not given a chance to answer the charges or appear before the Watch Committee. *Held*—by the House of Lords—the dismissal was void; Mr. Ridge should have been heard.

16*b*. *R. v. Aston University Senate, ex parte Roffey*, [1969] 2 Q.B. 538

Two students, Roffey and Partridge, failed their university examinations in June, 1967, and again in September, 1967. They were required to withdraw from the University. This decision was reached by the board of examiners who considered personal matters relating to the students but did not give them a hearing. The students applied in July, 1968, for an order of *certiorari* to quash the decision ordering them to withdraw. *Held*—the students should have been heard but because of the delay in applying for what was a discretionary order it would not be granted.

17. Pett *v*. The Greyhound Racing Association Ltd., [1968] 2 All E.R. 145

The plaintiff held a licence to train greyhounds, issued to him by the defendant organisation, whose rules gave disciplinary powers to track stewards. But there were no rules relating to the procedure to be followed at inquiries. A greyhound owned by the plaintiff and entered for a race was found to have traces of barbiturates in its urine and the stewards ordered an inquiry and granted the plaintiff an adjournment so that he might be legally represented, but later told the plaintiff that they would not allow such representation because it would cause delay and frustration. The plaintiff sought a declaration from the Court that he was entitled to representation and an injunction to restrain the holding of the inquiry if he was not. An interlocutory injunction was granted and the defendants appealed against it. *Held*—by the Court of Appeal—that where a person has a right of audience before a tribunal on a matter concerning his reputation and livelihood, he is entitled to be represented by an agent, including a lawyer, unless the rules of the tribunal expressly exclude that right. The appeal was dismissed.

The view of the Court of Appeal was obiter and given in interlocutory proceedings. At the trial Lyell, J., did not follow the Court of Appeal saying that a domestic tribunal was not acting contrary to natural justice by refusing legal representation. The better view is that the decision of the Court of Appeal is the correct one.

N.B. In *Pett* v. *Greyhound Racing Association Ltd.* (No. 2), [1970] 1 All E.R. 243, the Association told the Court that they had made new rules permitting trainers to be legally represented at inquiries. The plaintiff would therefore be permitted legal representation and no issue remained between the parties.

18. Enderby Town Football Club Ltd. *v.* The Football Association Ltd., [1971] 1 All E.R. 215

The football club, which had been censured by a local county football association for negligent administration, appealed to the F.A. and asked for legal representation. Two rules of the F.A. were brought into question. One was rule 38(*b*) which excluded legal representation and the other was rule 40(*b*) which said that legal proceedings should only be taken as a last resort and then only with the consent of the Council of the Association. The football club asked for an injunction restraining the hearing of the appeal unless the club was allowed legal representation. It was *held*—by the Court of Appeal—

(*a*) the points of law raised in the appeal were difficult and could be brought before the ordinary courts of law for a declaration of rights. These courts were the most appropriate place for such matters to be litigated. Rule 40(*b*) did not prevent this course of action. It was invalid since it attempted to oust the jurisdiction of the courts, but;

(*b*) if the Club did not want to go to the ordinary courts but chose to raise the matter before the F.A., then it must abide by rule 38(*b*) and could not have legal representation.

19. Rondel *v.* Worsley, [1967] 3 All E.R. 993

The appellant was charged with causing grievous bodily harm and was tried and convicted. He was represented at the trial by the respondent barrister who had appeared on a "dock brief." The appellant later issued a writ and statement of claim against the respondent claiming damages for professional negligence in the respondent's presentation of the case and in his dealing with the evidence. The statement was ordered to be struck out by the Master as disclosing no cause of action and this order was upheld by Lawton, J., and the Court of Appeal. On further appeal to the House of Lords it was *held* that the appeal must be dismissed. A barrister's conduct and management of litigation either in court or at an earlier stage could not give rise to a claim for professional negligence. This ruling arose out of public policy in that—

(*a*) a barrister should be able to carry out *his duty to the court* independently and without fear;

(*b*) actions against barristers would amount in effect to a retrial of the case in which it was suggested negligence arose; this would prolong litigation contrary to the public interest; and

(*c*) barristers are obliged to accept any client if a proper fee is paid and cannot refuse clients on any other ground.

Lords Reid, Morris of Borth-y-Gest and Upjohn were of the opinion that public policy did not require the extension of this immunity to the non-litigious aspects of a barrister's work, and along with Lord Pearce thought that a solicitor should be given the same immunity in litigious work which could have been done by a barrister as the latter would have had if engaged.

LAW IN ACTION

20. Hotel and Catering Industry Training Board *v.* Automobile Proprietory Ltd., [1969] 2 All E.R. 582

This was a test case brought by the Board to decide whether the Industrial Training (Hotel and Catering Board) Order 1966 made by the Minister of Labour pursuant to powers conferred upon him by the Industrial Training Act 1964, was *ultra vires* in so far as it purported to extend to any members' clubs. If the order was *ultra vires*, the R.A.C. club in Pall Mall was not liable to pay a levy to the Board by reason of its activities in providing midday and evening meals and board and lodging for reward. The relevant order was made under Sect. 1(1) of the Act of 1964, which provides that the Minister may "for the purpose of making better provision for . . . training . . . for employment in any activities of industry or commerce" make an order specifying "those activities," and establishing a board to exercise the functions of an industrial training board. The 1966 order specified "the activities" as including the supply of main meals and lodging for reward by a members' club. *Held*—by the House of Lords—The general object of the Act of 1964 was to provide employers in industry and commerce with trained personnel and to finance the training by a levy on employers in the industry, and that it was not intended to allow a levy to be made on private institutions like members' clubs. Although such institutions might pursue activities not unlike those of an hotel keeper, they could not be regarded as within the phrase "activities of industry or commerce."

21. Denithorne *v.* Davies, [1967] 2 Lloyd's Rep. 489

Fishermen were charged with using edible crab as bait in their lobster pots contrary to a by-law made by the Eastern Sea Fisheries Joint Committee under the Sea Fisheries Regulation Acts, 1888 to 1894. The by-law prohibited the use of any edible crab of whatever size for bait but under the general law only the taking of crabs under four-and-a-half inches in width is prohibited. However, the by-law was made because the breaking of the crab's shell before using it for bait made it impossible to tell what size it had been before being used as bait. The accused contended that the by-law was unreasonable and therefore unenforceable because only edible crab of less than four-and-a-half inches in width required protection. The justices accepted this contention. The prosecution appealed to the Divisional Court of Queen's Bench which allowed the appeal and directed the justices to convict. A court should only interfere with the by-laws of a public body if they were patently oppressive. The magistrate's finding that the difficulty in proving that edible crabs under four-and-a-half inches in width had been used as bait was an insufficient justification for the absolute prohibition could not be supported in the light of *Kruse* v. *Johnson*, [1898] 2 Q.B. 91, because although drastic it was not unreasonable. *N.B.* in *Kruse* v. *Johnson*, Lord Russell of Killowen laid it down that a court will not treat the by-laws of a public authority as unreasonable unless they are manifestly oppressive.

22. R. *v.* Gould (1968), 112 S.J. 69.

The appellant was convicted of bigamy although when he remarried he believed on reasonable grounds that a decree nisi of divorce in respect of his previous marriage had been made absolute which it had not, so that he was still married at the time of the second ceremony. The Court of Criminal Appeal in *R.* v. *Wheat and Stocks*, [1921] 2 K.B. 119, had decided on similar facts that a reasonable belief in the dissolution of a previous marriage was no defence. In this appeal to the Court of Appeal (Criminal Division) the court quashed the conviction *holding* that in spite of the decision in *R.* v. *Wheat and Stocks*, a defendant's honest belief on reasonable grounds that at the time of his second marriage his former marriage had been dissolved was a good defence to a charge of bigamy. Diplock, L.J., giving the judgment of the court, said that in its criminal jurisdiction the Court of Appeal does not apply the doctrine of *Stare decisis* as rigidly as in its civil jurisdiction, and if it is of the opinion that the law has been misapplied or misunderstood it will depart from a previous decision.

23. Gardiner *v.* Sevenoaks R.D.C. (1950), 66 T.L.R. 1091

The local authority served a notice under the Celluloid and Cinematograph Film Act, 1922, on the occupier of a cave where film was stored, requiring him to comply with certain safety regulations. The cave was described in the notice as "premises." Gardiner, who was the occupier, appealed against the notice on the ground that a cave could not be considered "premises" for the purpose of the Act. *Held*—Whilst it was not possible to lay down that every cave would be "premises" for all purposes, the Act was a safety Act and was designed to protect persons in the neighbourhood and those working in the place of storage. Therefore, under the "Mischief Rule" this cave was "premises" for the purposes of this Act.

24. Evans *v.* Cross, [1938] 1 K.B. 694

The appellant was charged with having driven a car on the outside of a white line when overtaking on a bend in the road. He was charged under the Road Traffic Act, 1930, Sect. 49, with ignoring a traffic sign and was convicted by the justices. He now appealed on the ground that a white painted line on a road was not a traffic sign within the meaning of the Act. Sect. 48 (1) of the Act defines a traffic sign as "all signals, warning signposts, direction posts, signs or other devices." *Held*—The last three words must be construed as something *ejusdem generis* with the preceding words and, therefore, a white painted line on a road was not a traffic sign. The appropriate charge would have been careless or dangerous driving.

25. Lane *v.* London Electricity Board, [1955] 1 All E.R. 324

The plaintiff was an electrician employed by the defendants to instal additional lighting in one of their sub-stations. While inspecting the sub-station, he tripped on the edge of an open duct and fell, sustaining injuries. The plaintiff claimed that the defendants were in breach of their statutory duty under the Electricity (Factories Act) Special Regulations in that the part of the premises where the accident occurred was not adequately lighted to prevent "danger." *Held*—It appeared that the word "danger" in the regulations meant "danger from shock, burn or other injury." Danger from tripping was not *ejusdem generis*, since the specific words related to forms of danger resulting from contact with electricity.

26. Muir *v.* Keay (1875), L.R. 10 Q.B. 594

Sect. 6 of the Refreshment Houses Act, 1860, stated that all houses, rooms, shops or buildings, kept open for public refreshment, resort and entertainment during certain hours of the night, must be licensed. The defendant had premises called "The Cafe," and certain persons were found there during the night when the cafe was open. They were being supplied with cigars, coffee and ginger beer which they were seen to consume. The justices convicted the defendant because the premises were not licensed. He appealed to the divisional court by case stated, suggesting that a licence was required only if music or dancing was going on. The divisional court, applying the *noscitur a sociis* rule, *held*—That "entertainment" meant matters of bodily comfort, not matters of public enjoyment such as music and dancing, so that the justices were right to convict.

SOME FUNDAMENTAL LEGAL CONCEPTS

27. Henderson v. Henderson, [1965] 1 All E.R. 179

In December, 1962, Mrs. Henderson presented a petition for divorce against Mr. Henderson, and he challenged the right of the English court to hear the petition on the ground that he was domiciled in Scotland at the time the petition was presented. The respondent was born in England in 1932, his father being domiciled at that time in Scotland. However, his father had acquired an English domicil by the time the respondent reached his majority. On the question of the respondent's domicil of origin, it was held that the domicil of dependence at the date of birth and not at majority fixed the domicil of origin, and that the domicil of origin was therefore Scottish. With regard to the present domicil of the respondent the court had the following facts to consider. It appeared that from 1932 until 1952 the respondent had lived in England and that in 1952 he took a job for a few months in the Far East. In 1953, when he reached his majority, he was in England, but in 1954 he took a temporary job in Scotland for health reasons. In 1955 he was married to the petitioner who was an English girl. In 1956 they both left Scotland and lived in Canada for three years. In 1959 they returned to England and had remained there since, apart from holidays in Scotland in 1961 and 1962. The facts could be divided as follows—

(*a*) *In favour of a Scottish Domicil*: (i) Scotland attracted him and suited his health; (ii) he had chosen Scotland for his holidays; (iii) it also appeared that he had given his son a Scottish Christian name.

(*b*) *In favour of an English Domicil*: (i) his wife was English; (ii) it appeared that the parents of both the parties were settled in Surrey; (iii) he had spent only two years of his life in Scotland, this being perhaps the most important factor of all. *Held*—Since his domicil at age twenty-one was dependent on his father, he was domiciled in England on attaining his majority, and the evidence was not strong enough to suggest that he had abandoned this dependent domicil in favour of another. The court, therefore, had jurisdiction to hear the petition.

28. Re Beaumont, [1893] 3 Ch. 490

A widow had several children, all of whom were domiciled in Scotland. The widow remarried and came to live in England where she acquired an English domicil. There was issue of the second marriage. One of her children by her first marriage was Catherine Beaumont. She was sixteen years of age when her mother went to live in England, but stayed on in Scotland in the care of an aunt. She died at twenty-two years of age being a spinster and intestate. She was entitled at her death to an interest in a settlement set up on the first marriage of her mother, and the question of entitlement to that interest depended on whether she died domiciled in England or Scotland. If she had a Scottish domicil, neither her mother nor her brother or sisters of the half-blood would, as the law of Scotland then stood, be entitled to any share in her estate on intestacy, and presumably she would not have wished that her property should go to her relatives of the half-blood. *Held*—The domicil of an infant where the father is dead does not necessarily follow that of its mother. The better view was that her mother had abstained from exercising her power to change the domicil of the children of her first marriage, so that Catherine Beaumont was domiciled in Scotland at her death. Further, the continued residence of Catherine Beaumont in Scotland after attaining majority was evidence of her intention to reside there permanently.

29. Harrison *v.* Harrison, [1953] 1 W.L.R. 865

The respondent, Mr. Harrison, was born in England of English parents. In 1948, when Harrison was eighteen, his parents emigrated to South Australia. Harrison stayed on in England. Later he went to New Zealand, and in 1950 married the petitioner when still under age, intending to settle in New Zealand. However, in 1951, while he was still under twenty-one, he and his wife came temporarily to England so that he might undergo training for his business as a trainer of horses, and in June of that year Harrison attained full age. In January 1953, whilst the couple were still in England, his wife filed a divorce petition. The court had jurisdiction if the parties were domiciled in England. The court *held* that they were, but since no reasons were given the arguments of counsel must have been accepted. Counsel's arguments were as follows: (i) Harrison's domicil of origin was England. (ii) When his parents emigrated to South Australia, Harrison's domicil changed to South Australia. (iii) Although he resided in New Zealand he still retained his dependent domicil, which he kept until he came of age in June 1951. (iv) At that time he was in England and intended to return and settle in New Zealand, but since he was not then resident in New Zealand, he could not acquire domicil there. Harrison had therefore lost his dependent domicil but had not acquired a domicil of choice. Thus there was a gap in domicil, and Harrison's domicil of origin filled that gap. Since his domicil of origin was England, the English court had jurisdiction.

30. R. *v.* Kemp, [1957] 1 Q.B. 399

The accused struck his wife with a hammer and was charged with causing grievous bodily harm. He was an elderly man of good character who suffered from arteriosclerosis. Medical opinions differed as to the precise effects of this disease on his mind. It was *held* that, whichever medical opinion was accepted, arteriosclerosis was a disease capable of affecting the mind, and was thus a disease of the mind within the M'Naghten Rules, whether or not it was recognised medically as a mental disease.

31. Salomon *v.* Salomon & Co., [1897] A.C. 22

Salomon carried on business as a leather merchant and boot manufacturer. In 1892 he formed a limited company to take over the business. The Memorandum of Association was signed by Salomon, his wife, daughter and four sons. Each subscribed for one share. The company paid £30,000 to Salomon for the business and the mode of payment was to give Salomon £10,000 in debentures, secured by a floating charge, and 20,000 shares of £1 each. The company fell on hard times and a liquidator was appointed. The debts of the unsecured creditors amounted to nearly £8,000, and the company's assets were approximately £6,000. The unsecured creditors claimed all the remaining assets on the ground that the company was a mere alias or agent for Salomon. *Held*—The company was a separate and distinct person. The debentures were perfectly valid and therefore Salomon was entitled to the remaining assets in part payment of the secured debentures held by him.

32. Jenkin *v.* Pharmaceutical Society, [1921] 1 Ch. 392

The defendant society was incorporated by Royal Charter in 1843 for the purpose of advancing chemistry and pharmacy and promoting a uniform system of education of those who should practise the same, and also for the protection of those who carried on the business of chemists or druggists. *Held*—The expenditure of the funds of the society in the formation of an industrial committee, to attempt to regulate hours of work and wages and conditions of work between masters and employee members of the society, was *ultra vires* the charter, because it was a trade union activity which was not contemplated by the Charter of 1843. Further, the expenditure of money on an insurance scheme for members was also not within the powers given in the charter, for it amounted to converting the defendant society into an insurance company. The plaintiff, a member of the society, was entitled to an injunction to restrain the society from implementing the above schemes.

THE LAW OF CONTRACT

33. Vincent *v.* Premo Enterprises (Voucher Sales) Ltd. and Others, [1969] 2 All E.R. 941

The plaintiffs, Mr. Vincent and his sister Miss Vincent, owned a freehold house in Central Road, Yeovil. They let four rooms on the first floor to Darch and Willcox Ltd. who kept two of the rooms for themselves and sublet the other two rooms to the first defendants, Premo Enterprises. The tenancy of Darch and Willcox Ltd. was due to end on 25th March, 1967, whereupon the subtenancy of Premo Enterprises would also end. However, negotiations took place whereby Premo Enterprises were to take a tenancy of the whole floor direct from the plaintiffs.

The terms of the agreement were set out in two letters from which it appeared that Premo Enterprises were to take a tenancy of the whole first floor for five years from 25th March, 1967, at a rent of £250 per annum subject to the lease being prepared and signed.

On 25th March, 1967, Darch and Willcox Ltd. vacated their accommodation and moved into premises across the road, Mr. Willcox taking the key saying to Premo's two girl employees that they could have the key whenever they required it. It was accepted by the court that the girls did not ask for the key until 1st May, 1967, which was regarded as the date when Premo's went into possession of the whole of the first floor.

The plaintiffs signed, sealed and delivered the lease and handed it to their solicitors. Premo's signed and sealed the counterpart on condition that the date when they took vacant possession should be agreed and that no rent should be payable in respect of the time before they took vacant possession, i.e. between 25th March, 1967, and 1st May, 1967. Before the solicitors exchanged the documents Premo's sought to withdraw from the transaction. The plaintiffs claimed that the lease was binding and sued in the Yeovil County Court for rent from 25th March, 1967. Premo's said in defence that the deed had not been delivered but was an escrow and that the conditions had not been fulfilled. At the hearing in the County Court the plaintiffs agreed to give credit for the period 25th March, 1967, to 1st May, 1967, but the judge held that the lease was not binding on Premo's, being an escrow, and that it was too late for the plaintiffs to say that the condition had been fulfilled at the hearing. He rejected the plaintiffs' claim and they appealed. *Held*—by the Court of Appeal—since the first defendants intended to be bound subject only to the date of possession being agreed, the deed was delivered as an escrow. However, it was not too late to fulfil the condition at the hearing and the deed was therefore binding on the first defendants.

> The question is whether this deed was 'delivered' at all, or whether it was delivered subject to a condition, i.e. as an 'escrow'. . . . The defendants did intend to be bound, but subject to the date of possession being agreed. That makes it, I think, an escrow. . . . This deed was signed, sealed and delivered by the first defendants, subject only to the condition that the date on which possession was given should be ascertained and the rent adjusted accordingly. The next question is whether the condition was fulfilled. I think it was fulfilled at the hearing before the county court when the date of possession was ascertained by the judge to be 1st May, 1967; and the plaintiffs agreed to adjust the rent accordingly. The judge thought it was too late. He did not think the condition could be fulfilled after the action was brought. I do not share his view. . . . I see nothing in this case to debar the plaintiffs from insisting on their legal rights. They did not know of this condition imposed by the defendants to their solicitors until the defence was pleaded; and they acted quite reasonably from that time onwards. The deed having been delivered, the condition having been fulfilled, the defendants are bound.

(*Per* Lord Denning, M. R.)

34. Wilson *v.* Wilson, [1969] 3 All E.R. 945

In 1961 the defendant wished to buy a freehold property in Battersea but his income was not sufficient to qualify him for a building society loan. Accordingly his brother, the plaintiff, joined him in the application to the building society but paid no part of the purchase price, nor any of the costs and expenses, or the mortgage repayments. The transfer of the property declared that the plaintiff and defendant were joint owners and the title was registered in their joint names as was the charge in favour of the building society.

In March, 1967, the plaintiff commenced an action claiming a half share in the property. The defendant alleged that it was never intended that he and his brother should be beneficial joint owners but that the property was held on trust by the defendant and his brother for the sole benefit of the defendant. The defendant asked, amongst other things, for rectification of the deed of transfer. *Held*—by Buckley, J.—that the court would order rectification of the deed by striking out that part of it which declared beneficial interests so as to show the true intention of the parties, i.e. that the beneficial ownership of the property was in the defendant alone. In the course of his judgment Buckley, J., said ". . . where a deed is rectifiable (that it to say, ought to be rectified), the doctrine of estoppel by deed will not bind the parties to it . . ."

35. Carlill *v.* Carbolic Smoke Ball Co., [1893] 1 Q.B. 256

The defendants were proprietors of a medical preparation called "The Carbolic Smoke Ball." They inserted advertisements in various newspapers in which they offered to pay £100 to any person who contracted influenza after using the ball three times a day for two weeks. They added that they had deposited £1,000 at the Alliance Bank, Regent Street "to show our sincerity in the matter." The plaintiff, a lady, used the ball as advertised, and was attacked by influenza during the course of treatment, which in her case extended from 20th November, 1891, to 17th January, 1892. She now sued for £100 and the following matters arose out of the various defences raised by the company. (*a*) It was suggested that the offer was too vague since no time limit was stipulated in which the user was to contract influenza. The court said that it must surely have been the intention that the ball would protect its user during the period of its use, and since this covered the present case it was not necessary to go further. (*b*) The suggestion was made that the matter was an advertising "puff" and that there was no intention to create legal relations. Here the court took the view that the deposit of £1,000 at the bank was clear evidence of an intention to pay claims. (*c*) It was further suggested that this was an attempt to contract with the whole world and that this was impossible in English law. The court took the view that the advertisement was an offer to the whole world and that, by analogy with the reward cases, it was possible to make an offer of this kind. (*d*) The company also claimed that the plaintiff had not supplied any consideration, but the court took the view that using this inhalant three times a day for two weeks or more was sufficient consideration. It was not necessary to consider its adequacy. (*e*) Finally the defendants suggested that there had been no communication of acceptance but here the court, looking at the reward cases, stated that in contracts of this kind acceptance may be by conduct.

36. Pharmaceutical Society of Great Britain *v.* Boots Cash Chemists (Southern) Ltd., [1953] 1 Q.B. 401

The defendants' branch at Edgware was adapted to the "self service" system. Customers selected their purchases from shelves on which the goods were displayed and put them into a wire basket supplied by the defendants. They then took them to the cash desk where they paid the price. One section of shelves was set out with drugs which were included in the Poisons List referred to in Sect. 17 of the Pharmacy and Poisons Act, 1933, though they were not dangerous drugs and did not require a doctor's prescription. Sect. 18 of the Act requires that the sale of such drugs shall take place in the presence of a qualified pharmacist. Every sale of the drugs on the Poison List was supervised at the cash desk by a qualified pharmacist, who had authority to prevent customers from taking goods out of the shop if he thought fit. One of the duties of the society was to enforce the provisions of the Act, and the action was brought because the plaintiffs claimed that the defendants were infringing Sect. 18. *Held*—The display of goods in this way did not constitute an offer. The contract of sale was not made when a customer selected goods from the shelves, but when the company's servant at the cash desk accepted the offer to buy what had been chosen. There was, therefore, supervision in the sense required by the Act at the appropriate moment of time.

37. Spencer *v.* Harding (1870), L.R. 5 C.P. 561

The defendants had sent out a circular in the following terms: "We are instructed to offer to the wholesale trade for sale by tender the stock-in-trade of Messrs. Gilbeck and Co., amounting as per stock-book to £2,503 13s. 1d. and which will be sold at a discount in one lot. Payment to be made in cash. The stock may be viewed on the premises up to Thursday the 20th instant, on which day, at 12 o'clock noon precisely, the tenders will be received and opened at our offices." The plaintiffs suggested that the circular was an offer to sell the stock to the person who made the highest bid for cash, and that they had sent the highest bid which the defendants had refused to accept. *Held*—The circular was an invitation to treat and not an offer, and the defendants need not accept a tender unless they wished to do so. Willes, J., said of the circular: "It is a mere attempt to ascertain whether an offer can be obtained within such a margin as the sellers are willing to accept."

38. Partridge *v.* Crittenden, [1968] 2 All E.R. 421

Mr. Partridge inserted an advertisement in a publication called *Cage and Aviary Birds* containing the words "Bramblefinch cocks, bramblefinch hens, 25s. each." The advertisement appeared under the general heading "Classified Advertisements" and in no place was there any direct use of the words "offer for sale." A Mr. Thompson answered the advertisement enclosing a cheque for 25s. and asking that a "bramblefinch hen" be sent to him. Mr. Partridge sent one in a box, the bird wearing a closed ring.

Mr. Thompson opened the box in the presence of an R.S.P.C.A. inspector, Mr. Crittenden, and removed the ring without injury to the bird. Mr. Crittenden brought a prosecution against Mr. Partridge before the Chester magistrates alleging that Mr. Partridge had offered for sale a brambling contrary to Sect. 6 (1) of the Protection of Birds Act, 1954, the bird being other than a close-ringed specimen bred in captivity and being of a species which was resident in or visited the British Isles in a wild state.

The justices were satisfied that the bird had not been bred in captivity but had been caught and ringed. A close-ring meant a ring that was completely closed and incapable of being forced or broken except with the intention of damaging it; such a ring was forced over the claws of a bird when it was between three and ten days old, and at that time it was not possible to determine what the eventual girth of the leg would be so that the close-ring soon become difficult to remove. The ease with which the ring was removed in this case indicated that it had been put on at a much later stage and this, together with the fact that the bird had no perching sense, led the justices to convict Mr. Partridge.

He appealed to the Divisional Court of the Queen's Bench Division where the conviction was quashed. The Court accepted that the bird was a wild bird, but since Mr. Partridge had been charged with "offering for sale," the conviction could not stand. The advertisement constituted in law an invitation to treat, not an offer for sale, and the offence was not, therefore, established. There was of course a completed sale for which Mr. Partridge could have been successfully prosecuted but the prosecution in this case had relied on the offence of "offering for sale" and failed to establish such an offer.

39. Harvey *v.* Facey, [1893] A.C. 552

The plaintiffs sent the following telegram to the defendant: "Will you sell us Bumper Hall Pen? Telegraph lowest cash price." The defendant telegraphed in reply: "Lowest price for Bumper Hall Pen £900." The plaintiffs then telegraphed: "We agree to buy Bumper Hall Pen for £900 asked by you. Please send us your title deeds in order that we may get early possession." The defendant made no reply. The Supreme Court of Jamaica granted the plaintiffs a decree of specific performance of the contract. On appeal the Judicial Committee of the Privy Council *held* that there was no contract. The second telegram was not an offer, but was in the nature of an invitation to treat at a minimum price of £900. The third telegram could not therefore be an acceptance resulting in a contract.

40. Clifton *v.* Palumbo, [1944] 2 All E.R. 497

The plaintiff who was the owner of a very large estate wrote to the defendant as follows: "I am prepared to offer you or your nominee my Lytham estate for £600,000. I also agree that a reasonable and sufficient time shall be granted to you for the examination and consideration of all the data and details necessary for the preparation of the Schedule of Completion." The defendant purported to accept this offer, but later the plaintiff thought the price too low and brought this action for a declaration that there was no binding contract between himself and the defendant. The defendant counterclaimed for specific performance. *Held*—The plaintiff's letter was an invitation to treat and not an offer, so that the defendant's purported acceptance did not give rise to a binding contract between the parties. Findlay, L.J. (following Lord Green, M.R.), said of the plaintiff's letter: "It is quite possible for persons on a half-sheet of notepaper, in the most informal and unorthodox language, to contract to sell the most extensive and most complicated estate that can be imagined. That is quite possible, but, having regard to the habits of the people in this country, it is very unlikely."

41. Harris *v.* Nickerson (1873), L.R. 8 Q.B. 286

The defendant, an auctioneer, advertised in London newspapers that a sale of office furniture would be held at Bury St. Edmunds. A broker with a commission to buy furniture came from London to attend the sale. Several conditions were set out in the advertisement, one being: "The highest bidder to be the buyer." The lots described as office furniture were not put up for sale but were withdrawn, though the auction itself was held. The broker sued for loss of time in attending the sale. *Held*—He could not recover from the auctioneer. There was no offer since the lots were never put up for sale, and the advertisement was simply an invitation to treat.

42. Brogden *v.* Metropolitan Railway (1877), 2 App.Cas. 666

The plaintiff had been a supplier of coal to the Railway Company for a number of years, though there was no formal agreement between them. Eventually the plaintiff suggested that there ought to be one, and the agents of the parties met and a draft agreement was drawn up by the Railway Company's agent and sent to the plaintiff. The plaintiff inserted several new clauses into the draft, and in particular filled in the name of an arbitrator to settle the parties' differences under the agreement should any arise. He then wrote the word "Approved" on the draft and returned it to the Railway Company's agent. There was no formal execution, the draft remaining in the agent's desk. However, coal was supplied according to the prices mentioned in the draft, though these were not the market prices, and prices were reviewed from time to time in accordance with the draft. The parties then had a disagreement and the plaintiff refused to supply coal to the Railway Company on the grounds that, since the Railway Company had not accepted the offer contained in the amended draft, there was no binding contract. *Held*—

(i) The draft was not a binding contract because the plaintiff had inserted new terms which the Railway Company had not accepted; but

(ii) the parties had indicated by their conduct that they had waived the execution of the formal document and agreed to act on the basis of the draft. There was, therefore, a binding contract arising out of conduct, and its terms were the terms of the draft.

43. Williams *v.* Carwardine (1833), 5 C. & P. 566

The defendant published a handbill by the terms of which he promised to pay the sum of £20 to any person who should give information, leading to the discovery of the murderer of Walter Carwardine. Two persons were tried for the murder at Hereford Assizes and were acquitted. Shortly afterwards the plaintiff, who was living with one Williams, was severely beaten by him and, believing that she was going to die and to ease her conscience, she gave information leading to the conviction of the man Williams for the murder. In an action to recover the reward the jury found that the plaintiff was not induced to give the information by the reward offered, but by motives of spite and revenge. *Held*—She was nevertheless entitled to the reward, for she had seen the handbill and had given information. Patteson, J., said: "We cannot go into the plaintiff's motives."

44. Winn *v.* Bull (1877), 7 Ch. D. 29

The defendant had entered into a written agreement with the plaintiff for the lease of a house, the term of the lease and the rent being agreed. However, the written agreement was expressly made "subject to the preparation and approval of a formal contract." It appeared that no other contract was made between the parties. The plaintiff now sued for specific performance of the agreement. *Held*—The written agreement provided a memorandum sufficient to satisfy Sect. 4 of the Statute of Frauds, 1677 (now Sect. 40 of the Law of Property Act, 1925), but there was no binding contract between the parties because, although certain covenants are normally implied into leases, it is also true that many and varied express covenants are often agreed between the parties. The words "subject to contract" indicated that the parties were still in a state of negotiation, and until they entered into a formal contract there was no agreement which the Court could enforce.

45. Filby *v.* Hounsell, [1896] 2 Ch. 737

Property had been offered for sale by auction but had not been sold. An offer was then made to buy the property, stating that if the offer was accepted the purchaser would sign a contract "on the auction particulars." This offer was accepted "subject to contract as agreed." *Held*—The parties were bound by a contract drafted on the auction particulars, although they had not signed a formal contract.

46. Chillingworth and another *v.* Esche, [1923] All E.R. Rep. 97

By a document, dated 10th July, 1922, Chillingworth and Cummings agreed to purchase the defendant's nursery gardens at Cheshunt, Herts., for £4,800 "subject to a proper contract to be prepared by the vendor's solicitors." The plaintiffs paid a deposit of £240. After the solicitors on both sides had agreed on the terms of a contract the plaintiffs refused, without reason, to go on and claimed a declaration that the document of 20th July, 1922, was not binding and that the deposit must be repaid. *Held*—by the Court of Appeal—that the document was nothing more than a conditional offer and a conditional acceptance and would only ripen into a binding agreement when a formal document was signed. Further, on the construction of the documents and in the circumstances, the plaintiffs were entitled to the repayment of the deposit. The plaintiffs' solicitors were not agents of their clients, so as to bind them, when they agreed with the defendant's solicitors on the terms of the contract.

47. Goding v. Frazer, [1966] 3 All E.R. 234

An estate agent had arranged, on behalf of a vendor, the sale of the latter's land "subject to contract." The agent accepted a deposit from the potential purchaser, but there was no mention of the capacity in which he received it, i.e. either as agent for the vendor or as stake-holder. At a later stage the purchaser withdrew and, the estate agent being insolvent, claimed the return of his deposit from the vendor. *Held*—when an estate agent receives a deposit on a subject-to-contract sale, he receives it as agent for the vendor, unless there is an agreement to the contrary, and the vendor remains liable for returning the said deposit. The purchaser succeeded in his claim.

47a. Burt v. Claude Cousins & Co. Ltd., and Shaw (1971), 115 S.J. 207

The plaintiff paid a ten per cent deposit of £2,075 to an estate agent in respect of the purchase price of an hotel "subject to contract". The sale fell through and the estate agent went into liquidation having put the deposit into the bank and used it. *Held*—by the Court of Appeal following *Goding* v. *Frazer*—that the vendor Shaw was liable to repay the deposit although he had never received it. Lord Denning, M. R., dissented saying an estate agent in this situation is a stake holder not an agent in respect of the deposit and that the vendor should not be liable to repay, but see now case number 648.

48. Branca v. Cobarro, [1947] 2 All E.R. 101

The defendant agreed to sell to the plaintiff the lease and goodwill of a mushroom farm. The contract ended with the words "This is a provisional agreement until a full legalised agreement, drawn up by a solicitor and embodying all the conditions herewith stated is signed." The defendant alleged that the agreement was not binding on him but it was *held*—by the Court of Appeal—that the words "provisional" and "until" were not appropriate words to indicate conditional assent. They indicated that the parties intended a binding agreement which would remain in force until superseded by a more formal contract between the parties.

49. Tomlin v. Standard Telephones and Cables Ltd., [1969] 3 All E.R. 201

The plaintiff was a fitter employed to help on board H.M. telecommunications Ship *Alert*. In the course of his duties he strained his back and claimed against the defendants, his employers, for damages in respect of that accident. The plaintiff's solicitor and the employers' insurers negotiated an agreement that liability would be accepted on a 50 per cent basis. In this action the defendants alleged that they were not bound by the agreement entered into by their representatives the insurers, because it appeared that the letters constituting the agreement were headed "Without Prejudice." *Held*—by the Court of Appeal—that on a proper construction of the letters written by the defendants' representatives there was a definite and binding agreement to pay half the damages though the actual amount was left for further negotiation.

A point that arises is that all the letters written by the agent of the insurance company bore the words "Without Prejudice". The point is taken that, by reason of those words, there could not be any binding agreement between the parties . . . *Walker* v. *Wilsher* (1889), 23 Q.B.D. 335. . . . Lindley, L.J., said at p. 337 "What is the meaning of the words 'without prejudice'? I think they mean without prejudice to the position of the writer of the letter if the terms he proposes are not accepted. If the terms proposed in the letter are accepted a complete contract is established and the letter, although written without prejudice, operates to alter the old state of things and to establish a new one." That statement of Lindley, L.J., is of great authority and seems to me to apply exactly to the present case if in fact there was a binding agreement, or an agreement intended to be binding, reached between the parties; and, accordingly, it seems to me that not only was the court entitled to look at the letters although they were nearly all described as "Without Prejudice", but it is quite possible (and in fact the intention of the parties was) that there was a binding agreement contained in that correspondence.

(*Per* Danckwerts, L.J.)

50. Hillas & Co. Ltd. *v.* Arcos Ltd., [1932] All E.R. Rep. 494

The plaintiffs had entered into a contract with the defendants under which the defendants were to supply the plaintiffs with "22,000 standards of soft wood (Russian) of fair specification over the season 1930." The contract also contained an option allowing the plaintiffs to take up 100,000 standards as above during the season 1931. The parties managed to perform the contract throughout the 1930 season without any argument or serious difficulty in spite of the vague words used in connection with the specification of the wood. However, when the plaintiffs exercised their option for 100,000 standards during the season 1931, the defendants refused to supply the wood, saying that the specification was too vague to bind the parties, and the agreement was therefore inchoate as requiring a further agreement as to the precise specification. *Held*—by the House of Lords—that the option to supply 100,000 standards during the 1931 season was valid. There was a certain vagueness about the specification, but there was also a course of dealing between the parties which operated as a guide to the Court regarding the difficulties which this vagueness might produce. Since the parties had not experienced serious difficulty in carrying out the 1930 agreement, there was no reason to suppose that the option could not have been carried out without difficulty had the defendants been prepared to go on with it. Judgment was given for the plaintiffs.

51. Foley *v.* Classique Coaches Ltd., [1934] 2 K.B. 1

F owned certain land, part of which he used for the business of supplying petrol. He also owned the adjoining land. The company wished to purchase the adjoining land for use as the headquarters of their charabanc business. F agreed to sell the land to the company on condition that the company would buy all their petrol from him. An agreement was made under which the company agreed to buy its petrol from F "at a price to be agreed by the parties in writing and from time to time." It was further agreed that any dispute arising under the agreement should be submitted "to arbitration in the usual way." The agreement was acted upon for three years. At this time the company felt it could get petrol at a better price, and the company's solicitor wrote to F repudiating the contract. *Held*—Although the parties had not agreed upon a price, there was a contract to supply petrol at a reasonable price and of reasonable quality, and although the agreement did not stipulate the future price, but left this to the further agreement of the parties, a method was provided by which the price could be ascertained without such agreement, i.e. by arbitration. An injunction was therefore granted requiring the company to take petrol from F as agreed.

A similar problem arose in *F. & S. Sykes (Wessex) v. Fine-Fare, The Times,* 17th November, 1966. In that case producers of broiler chickens agreed with certain retailers to supply between 30,000 and 80,000 chickens a week during the first year of the agreement and afterwards "such other figures as might be agreed." The agreement was to last for not less than five years, and it was agreed that any differences between the parties should be referred to arbitration. Eventually the retailers contended that the agreement was void for uncertainty. *Held*—by the Court of Appeal—it was not, because in default of the further agreement envisaged the number of chickens should be such reasonable number as might be decided by the arbitrator.

52. Scammell (G.) and Nephew Ltd. *v.* Ouston, [1941] A.C. 251

Ouston wished to acquire a new motor van for use in his furniture business. Discussions took place with the company's sales manager as a result of which the company sent a quotation for the supply of a suitable van. Eventually Ouston sent an official order making the following stipulation, "This order is given on the understanding that the balance of the purchase price can be had on hire-purchase terms over a period of two years." This was in accordance with the discussions between the sales manager and Ouston, which had taken place on the understanding that hire purchase would be available. The company seemed to be content with the arrangement and completed the van. Arrangements were made with a finance company to give hire-purchase facilities, but the actual terms were not agreed at that stage. The appellants also agreed to take Ouston's present van in part exchange, but later stated that they were not satisfied with its condition and asked him to sell it locally. He refused and after much correspondence he issued a writ against the appellants for damages for non-delivery of the van. The appellants' defence was that there was no contract until the hire-purchase terms had been ascertained. *Held*—The defence succeeded; it was not possible to construe a contract from the vague language used by the parties.

N.B. If there is a trade custom, business procedure or previous dealings between the parties, which assist the court in construing the vague parts of an agreement, then the agreement may be enforced. Here there was no such evidence.

53. The Moorcock (1889), 14 P.D. 64

The appellants in this case were in possession of a wharf and a jetty extending into the River Thames, and the respondent was the owner of the steamship *Moorcock*. In November, 1887, the appellants and the respondent agreed that the ship should be discharged and loaded at the wharf and for that purpose should be moored alongside the jetty. Both parties realised that when the tide was out the ship would rest on the river bed. In the event the *Moorcock* sustained damage when she ceased to be waterborne owing to the centre of the vessel settling on a ridge of hard ground beneath the mud. There was no evidence that the appellants had given any warranty that the place was safe for the ship to lie in, but it was *Held*—by the Court of Appeal—that there was an implied warranty by the appellants to this effect, for breach of which they were liable in damages.

> Now, an implied warranty, or, as it is called, a covenant in law, as distinguished from an express contract or express warranty, really is in all cases founded on the presumed intention to the parties, and upon reason. The implication which the law draws from what must obviously have been the intention of the parties, the law draws with the object of giving efficacy to the transaction and preventing such a failure of consideration as cannot have been within the comtemplation of either side; and I believe if one were to take all the cases, and they are many, of implied warranties or covenants in law, it will be found that in all of them the law is raising an implication

from the presumed intention of the parties with the object of giving to the transaction such efficacy as both parties must have intended that at all events it should have. In business transactions such as this, what the law desires to effect by the implication is to give such business efficacy to the transaction as must have been intended at all events by both parties who are business men; not to impose on one side all the perils of the transaction, or to emancipate one side from all the chances of failure, but to make each party promise in law as much, at all events, as it must have been in the contemplation of both parties that he should be responsible for in respect of those perils or chances.

(*Per* Bowen, L.J.)

54. Nicolene Ltd. *v.* Simmonds, [1953] 1 All E.R. 882

The plaintiffs alleged that there was a contract for the sale to them of 3,000 tons of steel reinforcing bars and that the defendant seller had broken his contract. When the plaintiffs claimed damages the seller set up the defence that, owing to one of the sentences in the letters which constituted the contract, there was no contract at all. The material words were "We are in agreement that the usual conditions of acceptance apply". In fact there were no usual conditions of acceptance so that the words were meaningless but the seller nevertheless suggested that the contract was unenforceable since it was not complete. *Held*— by the Court of Appeal—that the contract was enforceable and that the meaningless clause could be ignored.

In my opinion a distinction must be drawn between a clause which is meaningless and a clause which is yet to be agreed. A clause which is meaningless can often be ignored, whilst still leaving the contract good; whereas a clause which has yet to be agreed may mean that there is no contract at all, because the parties have not agreed on all the essential terms. . . . In the present case there was nothing yet to be agreed. There was nothing left to further negotiation. All that happened was that the parties agreed that "the usual conditions of acceptance apply." That clause was so vague and uncertain as to be incapable of any precise meaning. It is clearly severable from the rest of the contract. It can be rejected without impairing the sense or reasonableness of the contract as a whole, and it should be so rejected. The contract should be held good and the clause ignored. The parties themselves treated the contract as subsisting. They regarded it as creating binding obligations between them; and it would be most unfortunate if the law should say otherwise. You would find defaulters all scanning their contracts to find some meaningless clause on which to ride free.

(*Per* Denning, L.J.)

55. Hyde *v.* Wrench (1840), 3 Beav. 334

The defendant offered to sell his farm for £1,000. The plaintiff's agent made an offer of £950 and the defendant asked for a few days for consideration, after which the defendant wrote saying he could not accept it, whereupon the plaintiff wrote purporting to accept the offer of £1,000. The defendant did not consider himself bound, and the plaintiff sued for specific performance. *Held*—The plaintiff could not enforce this "acceptance" because his counter offer of £950 was an implied rejection of the original offer to sell at £1,000.

55a. Neale v. Merrett, [1930] W.N. 189

The defendant offered to sell land to the plaintiff for £280. The plaintiff replied, purporting to accept the offer and enclosing £80, promising to pay the balance by monthly instalments of £50 each. *Held*—The plaintiff could not enforce the acceptance because it was not unqualified, since he had introduced a system of deferred payment.

55*b*. *Northland Airlines Ltd.* v. *Dennis Ferranti Meters Ltd.* (1970), 114 Sol. J. 845

Ferranti offered to sell Northland an aircraft by a telegram in the following terms—"Confirming sale to you—aircraft—£27,000 fob Winnipeg. Please remit £5,000 for account of . . . (a bank account was named)."

Northland replied by telegram as follows—"This is to confirm your cable and my purchase—aircraft on terms set out in your cable. Price £27,000 delivered fob Winnipeg. £5,000 forwarded your bank in trust for your account pending delivery. Balance payable on delivery. Please confirm delivery to be made 30 days within this date". Ferranti did not regard this as an acceptance and disposed of the aircraft elsewhere. Northland sued for damages for breach of contract. *Held*—by the Court of Appeal—that the second telegram was not an acceptance because the deposit was not paid over outright as requested but left in trust pending delivery and Northland had inserted a delivery date whereas the offer did not mention one. These were new terms so that the second telegram was a counter offer and not an acceptance.

56. Stevenson v. McLean (1880), 5 Q.B.D. 346

The defendant offered to sell to the plaintiffs a quantity of iron "at 40s. nett cash per ton till Monday." On Monday the plaintiffs telegraphed asking whether the defendant would accept 40s. for delivery over two months, or if not what was the longest limit the defendant would give. The defendant received the telegram at 10.1 a.m. but did not reply, so the plaintiffs, by telegram sent at 1.34 p.m., accepted the defendant's original offer. The defendant had already sold the iron to a third party, and informed the plaintiffs of this by a telegram despatched at 1.25 p.m. arriving at 1.46 p.m. The plaintiffs had therefore accepted the offer before the defendant's revocation had been communicated to them. If, however, the plaintiffs' first telegram constituted a counter offer, then it would amount to a rejection of the defendant's original offer. *Held*—The plaintiffs' first telegram was not a counter offer, but a mere inquiry which did not amount to a rejection of the defendant's original offer, so that the offer was still open when the plaintiffs accepted it.

57. Trollope & Colls Ltd. v. Atomic Power Constructions Ltd., [1962] 3 All E.R. 1035

The plaintiffs were sub-contractors for the civil engineering aspects of the building of a new power station. The defendants were the main contractors, the Central Electricity Board being the employing authority. The plaintiffs had submitted a tender in 1959 in which they had said that the price for their part of the work would be nine million pounds. Part A of this tender contained a price adjustment clause allowing the plaintiffs to adjust the price tendered according to variations, if any, in the cost of labour and materials during the course of completing the work. Numerous changes were made in this part of the tender and in the price adjustment clause by the Central Electricity Board, but at a meeting of the parties on 11th April, 1960, the tender as amended was agreed by the plaintiffs. The plaintiffs had by this time already done a considerable amount of work on the site.

Later the plaintiffs regretted the agreement of 11th April, 1960, and claimed that they were free to terminate operations at any time and asked for a *quantum meruit* for their services up to 11th April, 1960. The Board claimed that a binding contract existed between themselves and the plaintiffs on the terms of the agreement of 11th April, 1960, and that this agreement, when made, operated retrospectively to cover the work done by the plaintiffs up to 11th April and subsequently. The plaintiffs then alleged that the agreement of 11th April could only operate for the future, and that work done up to 11th April, 1960, should be assessed by the Court on a *quantum meruit*, or alternatively be based on an implied contract on the terms of the tender of 1959 before amendments. *Held*—The agreement of 11th April, 1960, operated retrospectively so that the plaintiffs were entitled to payment for work done prior to 11th April only on the basis of the amended tender and were also bound to operate for the future on the same basis.

N.B. The action was one in which many parties were joined, and the Central Electricity Board was in fact one of the defendants.

58. Great Northern Railway *v.* Witham (1873), L.R. 9 C.P. 16

The company advertised for tenders for the supply for one year of such stores as they might think fit to order. The defendant submitted a tender in these words: "I undertake to supply the company for twelve months with such quantities of (certain specified goods) as the company may order from time to time." The company accepted the tender, and gave orders under it which the defendant carried out. Eventually the defendant refused to carry out an order made by the company under the tender, and this action was brought. *Held*—The defendant was in breach of contract. A tender of this type was a standing offer which was converted into a series of contracts as the company made an order. The defendant might revoke his offer for the remainder of the period covered by the tender, but must supply the goods already ordered by the company.

59. Powell *v.* Lee (1908), 99 L.T. 284

The defendants were managers of a school and wished to appoint a headmaster. Powell applied for the position and together with two other applicants was selected for the final choice of the managers. The managers passed a resolution appointing Powell but gave no instructions that this decision was to be communicated to him, although D (one of the managers) was instructed to inform one of the other candidates (Parker) that he had not been appointed. D, without authority, also informed Powell that he had been selected. The matter was then re-opened and Parker was properly appointed. Lee then informed the plaintiff that this appointment had been made. The plaintiff now sued the six managers for damages for breach of contract. *Held*—There was no contract because there was no authorised communication of the intention to contract by the managers.

60. Felthouse *v.* Bindley (1862), 11 C.B.(N.S.) 869

The plaintiff had been engaged in negotiations with his nephew John regarding the purchase of John's horse, and there had been some misunderstanding as to the price. Eventually the plaintiff wrote to his nephew as follows: "If I hear no more about him I consider the horse is mine at £30 15s." The nephew did not reply but, wishing to sell the horse to his uncle, he told the defendant, an autioneer who was selling farm stock for him, not to sell the horse as it had already been sold. The auctioneer inadvertently put the horse up with the rest of the stock and sold it. The plaintiff now sued the auctioneer in conversion, the basis of the claim being that he had made a contract with his nephew and the property in the animal was vested in him (the uncle) at the time of the sale. *Held*—The plaintiff's action failed. Although the nephew intended to sell the horse to his uncle, he had not communicated that intention. There was, therefore, no contract between the parties, and the property in the horse was not vested in the plaintiff at the time of the auction sale.

61. Eliason *v.* **Henshaw** (1819), 4 Wheat. 225 (Supreme Court U.S.A.)

Eliason offered to buy flour from Henshaw. The offer was sent by a wagoner employed by Eliason, there being a stipulation that any reply to the offer should be sent by the wagoner who brought the offer. Henshaw sent his reply accepting the offer by post, his letter arriving some time after the wagoner had returned to Eliason's premises. Eliason, assuming that Henshaw was not interested in his offer, had purchased the flour he needed elsewhere. *Held*—There was no contract. Eliason had specified a mode of acceptance and his wishes must be respected, particularly since the wagoner had arrived before Henshaw's letter.

62. Manchester Diocesan Council for Education *v.* **Commercial and General Investments Ltd.,** [1969] 3 All E.R. 1593

The plaintiffs, a corporate body, were the owners of a freehold property known as Hesketh Fletcher Senior Church of England School. The property was vested in the plaintiffs on a condition that it could be sold subject "to the approval of the purchase price" by the Secretary of State for Education and Science. Late in 1963 the plaintiffs decided to sell the property by tender, the conditions requiring that tenders be sent to the plaintiffs' surveyor by 27th August, 1964. Clause 4 of the form of tender stated "The person whose tender is accepted shall be the purchaser and shall be informed of the acceptance of his tender by letter sent to him by post addressed to the address given in the tender . . .." The following events then occurred—

(i) On 25th August, 1964, the defendants completed the form of tender and stated that they agreed to its conditions.

(ii) On 26th August, 1964, the completed tender was sent to the plaintiffs' surveyor.

(iii) On 1st September, 1964, the plaintiffs' surveyor informed the defendants' surveyor that he would recommend acceptance of the defendants' offer and would write again as soon as he had formal instructions.

(iv) On 14th September, 1964, the defendants' surveyor replied saying that he looked forward to receiving formal acceptance and naming the solicitors who would act for the defendants.

(v) On 15th September, 1964, the plaintiffs' solicitor acknowledged this letter by correspondence with the defendants' surveyor which also stated that the "sale has now been approved," and that instructions had been given to obtain the approval of the Secretary of State.

(vi) On 18th November, 1964, the approval of the Secretary of State was obtained.

(vii) On 23rd December, 1964, the plaintiffs' solicitors wrote to the defendants' solicitors stating that the contract was now binding on both parties.

(viii) The defendants' solicitors replied to the effect that they did not agree that there was any binding contract.

(ix) On 7th January, 1965, the plaintiffs' solicitors wrote to the defendants at the address given in the tender giving formal notice of acceptance.

The question in issue in this case was whether the offer contained in the tender lapsed before 7th January, 1965, by reason of lapse of time between 25th August, 1964, and 7th January, 1965. It was *held*—by Buckley, J.—

(i) That the letter of 15th September, 1964, looked at in the light of earlier correspondence, was communication to the defendants that their offer had been accepted. The failure to inform the defendants of the acceptance in the manner laid down in Clause 4 did not nullify acceptance of the offer since Clause 4 did not say that a letter addressed to the address given in the tender was the only mode of acceptance and acceptance by any other equally advantageous method was valid. (*Tinn* v. *Hoffman* (1873), 29 L.T. 271 applied.)

(ii) Alternatively, if the letter of September, 1964, did not constitute an acceptance, the offer had not lapsed because the plaintiffs had not by any conduct refused the offer. In fact the letter of 15th September, 1964, showed a continuing intention to accept and there was no evidence of a change of mind before 7th January, 1965. Thus the offer was still open to be accepted on 7th January, 1965. (*Ramsgate Victoria Hotel Co.* v. *Montefiore*, 1866,[70] *distinguished*.)

63. Entores Ltd. *v.* Miles Far Eastern Corporation, [1955] 2 Q.B. 327

The plaintiffs, who conducted a business in London, made an offer to the defendants' agent in Amsterdam by means of a teleprinter service. The offer was accepted by a message received on the plaintiffs' teleprinter in London. Later the defendants were in breach of contract and the plaintiffs wished to sue them. The defendants had their place of business in New York and in order to commence an action the plaintiffs had to serve notice of writ on the defendants in New York. The Rules of Supreme Court allow service out of the jurisdiction when the contract was made within the jurisdiction. On this point the defendants argued that the contract was made in Holland when it was typed into the teleprinter there, stressing the rule relating to posting. *Held*—Where communication is instantaneous, as where the parties are face to face or speaking on the telephone, acceptance must be received by the offeror. The same rule applied to communications of this kind. Therefore the contract was made in London where the acceptance was received.

N.B. The suggestion was made that the doctrine of estoppel may operate in this sort of case so as to bind the offeror, e.g. suppose X telephones his acceptance to Y, and Y does not hear X's voice at the moment of acceptance, then Y should ask X to repeat the message, otherwise Y may be estopped from denying that he heard X's acceptance and will be bound in contract.

64. Household Fire Insurance Company *v.* Grant (1879), 4 Ex.D. 216

The defendant handed a written application for shares in the company to the company's agent in Glamorgan. The application stated that the defendant had paid to the company's bankers the sum of £5, being a deposit of one shilling per share on an application for one hundred shares, and also agreed to pay nineteen shillings per share within twelve months of the allotment. The agent sent the application to the company in London. The company secretary made out a letter of allotment in favour of the defendant and posted it to him in Swansea. The letter never arrived. Nevertheless the company entered the defendant's name on the share register and credited him with dividends amounting to five shillings. The company then went into liquidation and the liquidator sued for £94 15s., the balance due on the shares allotted. It was *held* by the Court of Appeal that the defendant was liable. Acceptance was complete when the letter of allotment was posted on the ground that, in this sort of case, the Post Office must be deemed the common agent of the parties, and that delivery to the agent constituted acceptance. Bramwell, L.J., in a dissenting judgment, regarded actual communication as essential. If the letter of acceptance does not arrive, an unknown liability is imposed on the offeror. If actual communication is required the *status quo* is preserved, i.e. the parties have not made a contract.

65. Re London and Northern Bank, ex parte Jones, [1900] 1 Ch. 220

Dr. Jones, who lived in Sheffield, applied for shares in the bank. He then sent a letter of revocation which was received by the bank at 8.30 a.m. on 27th October. The bank's letter of allotment was taken to the G.P.O. at St. Martins-le-Grand at 7 a.m. on 27th October, but was handed to a postman. Evidence showed that the letter did not go straight into the system. The allotment letter to Jones was delivered at 7.30 p.m. on 27th October, the postmark showing that it was posted at a branch office, not at the G.P.O. If the letter had been posted at 7.30 a.m., it would have gone to Sheffield on the 10 a.m. train. Evidence showed that it went by the 12 o'clock train. *Held*—The letter was not posted when it was handed to the postman. The evidence did not show with any clarity when the letter was posted, but, since the burden of proof was on the company, it was possible to say that they had not shown the letter of acceptance was posted before 8.30, or even before 9.30 a.m., when the bank's secretary opened the letter of revocation.

An additional point is that evidence given for the Post Office showed that, under the terms of the Post Office Guide, a town postman is not allowed to take letters in this way, and would be disciplined if he did. The position may be different in the country where the custom of taking letters in this way is perhaps better established.

66. Adams *v.* Lindsell (1818), 1 B. & A. 681

The defendants were wool dealers in business at St. Ives, Huntingdon. By letter dated 2nd September they offered to sell wool to the plaintiffs who were wool manufacturers at Bromsgrove, Worcestershire. The defendants' letter asked for a reply "in course of post" but was misdirected, being addressed to Bromsgrove, Leicestershire. The offer did not reach the plaintiffs until 7 p.m. on 5th September. The same evening the plaintiffs accepted the offer. This letter reached the defendants on 9th September. If the offer had not been misdirected, the defendants could have expected a reply on 7th September, and accordingly they sold the wool to a third party on 8th September. The plaintiffs now sued for breach of contract. *Held*—Where there is a misdirection of the offer, as in this case, the offer is made when it actually reaches the offeree, and not when it would have reached him in the ordinary course of post. The defendants' mistake must be taken against them and for the purposes of this contract the plaintiffs' letter was received "in course of post."

N.B. The position may be different if the fact of delay is obvious to the offeree so that he is put on notice that the offer has lapsed, e.g. A writes to B offering to sell him certain goods and saying that the offer is open until 30th June. If A misdirects the offer so that it does not reach B until 2nd July, it is doubtful whether B could accept it.

67. Byrne *v.* Van Tienhoven (1880), 5 C.P.D. 344

On 1st October the defendants in Cardiff posted a letter to the plaintiffs in New York offering to sell them tinplate. On 8th October the defendants wrote revoking their offer. On 11th October the plaintiffs received the defendants' offer and immediately telegraphed their acceptance. On 15th October the plaintiffs confirmed their acceptance by letter. On 20th October the defendants' letter of revocation reached the plaintiffs who had by this time entered into a contract to resell the tin plate. *Held*—(*a*) that revocation of an offer is not effective until it is communicated to the offeree, (*b*) the mere posting of a letter of revocation is not communication to the person to whom it is sent. The rule is not, therefore, the same as that for acceptance of an offer. Therefore the defendants were bound by a contract which came into being on 11th October.

68. Dunmore (Countess) *v.* Alexander (1830), 9 Sh (Ct. of Sess.) 190

In this case a letter accepting an offer of employment was followed by a further letter withdrawing the acceptance. Both letters were received by the offerer by the same post. *Held*—The acceptance was validly cancelled.

69. Dickinson *v.* Dodds (1876), 2 Ch.D. 463

The defendant offered to sell certain houses by letter stating, "This offer to be left over until Friday, 9 a.m." On Thursday afternoon the plaintiff was informed by a Mr. Berry that the defendant had been negotiating a sale of the property with one Allan. On Thursday evening the plaintiff left a letter of acceptance at the house where the defendant was staying. This letter was never delivered to the defendant. On Friday morning at 7 a.m. Berry, acting as the plaintiff's agent, handed the defendant a duplicate letter of acceptance explaining it to him. However, on the Thursday the defendant had entered into a contract to sell the property to Allan. *Held*—Since there was no consideration for the promise to keep the offer open, the defendant was free to revoke his offer at any time. Further Berry's communication of the dealings with Allan indicated that Dodds was no longer minded to sell the property to the plaintiff and was in effect a communication of Dodds' revocation. There was therefore no binding contract between the parties.

70. Ramsgate Victoria Hotel Co. *v.* Montefiore (1866), L.R. 1 Exch. 109

The defendant offered by letter dated 8th June, 1864, to take shares in the company. No reply was made by the company, but on 23rd November, 1864, they allotted shares to the defendant. The defendant refused to take up the shares. *Held*—His refusal was justified because his offer had lapsed by reason of the company's delay in notifying their acceptance.

71. Financings Ltd. *v.* Stimson, [1962] 3 All E.R. 386

On 16th March, 1961, the defendant saw a motor car on the premises of a dealer and signed a hire-purchase form provided by the plaintiffs (a finance company), this form being supplied by the dealer. The form was to the effect that the agreement was to become binding only when the finance company signed the form. It also carried a statement to the effect that the hirer (the defendant) acknowledged that before he signed the agreement he had examined the goods and had satisfied himself that they were in good order and condition, and that the goods were at the risk of the hirer from the time of purchase by the owner. On 18th March the defendant paid the first instalment and took possession of the car. However, on 20th March, the defendant being dissatisfied with the car, he returned it to the dealer though the finance company were not informed of this. On the night of 24th–25th March the car was stolen from the dealer's premises and was recovered badly damaged. On 25th March the finance company signed the agreement accepting the defendant's offer to hire the car. The defendant did not regard himself as bound and refused to pay the instalments. The finance company sold the car, and now sued for damages for the defendant's breach of the hire-purchase agreement. *Held*—The hire purchase agreement was not binding on the defendant because—

(i) he had revoked his offer by returning the car, and the dealer was the agent of the finance company to receive notice;

(ii) there was an *implied* condition in the offer that the goods were in substantially the same condition when the offer was accepted as when it was made.

72. Bradbury *v.* Morgan (1862), 1 H. & C. 249

The defendants were the executors of J. M. Leigh who had entered into a guarantee of his brother's account with the plaintiffs for credit up to £100. The plaintiffs, not knowing of the death of J. M. Leigh, continued to supply goods on credit to the brother, H. J. Leigh. The defendants now refused to pay the plaintiffs in respect of such credit after the death of J. M. Leigh. *Held*— The plaintiffs succeeded, the offer remaining open until the plaintiffs had *knowledge* of the death of J. M. Leigh.

N.B. This was a continuing guarantee which is in the nature of a standing offer accepted piecemeal whenever further goods are advanced on credit. Where the guarantee is not of this nature, it may be irrevocable. However, in *Lloyds* v. *Harper* (1880), 16 Ch.D. 290, the defendant, while living, guaranteed his son's dealings as a Lloyds underwriter in consideration of Lloyds admitting the son. It was *held* that, as Lloyds had admitted the son on the strength of the guarantee, the defendant's executors were still liable under it, because it was irrevocable and was not affected by the defendant's death. It continued to apply to defaults committed by the son after the father's death.

73. *Re* Cheshire Banking Co., Duff's Executors' Case (1886), 32 Ch.D. 301

In 1882 the Cheshire and Staffordshire Union Banking Companies amalgamated, and Duff received a circular asking whether he would exchange his shares in the S Bank for shares in the C Bank which took the S Bank over. Duff held 100 £20 shares on which £5 had been paid, but he did not reply to the circular and died shortly afterwards. The option was exercised on behalf of his executors, Muttlebury, Bridges and Watts, and a certificate was made out in their names and an entry made in the register in which they were entered as shareholders, described as "executors of William Duff, deceased." The executors objected to having the share certificate in their names, so the directors of the Cheshire Banking Co. cancelled the certificate and issued a fresh one in the name of William Duff. On 23rd October, 1884, the company went into voluntary liquidation, and on 26th October it was ordered that the winding up should be under supervision. *Held*—The liquidator acted rightly when he restored the executors' names to the register. The executors wished to enter into a new contract which had not previously existed. They could not make a dead man liable and so could only make themselves personally liable. Their names were improperly removed and must be restored. Although they had a right of indemnity against the estate, they were personally liable for the full amount outstanding on the shares, regardless as to whether the estate was adequate to indemnify them.

74. Balfour *v.* Balfour, [1919] 2 K.B. 571

The defendant was a civil servant stationed in Ceylon. In November, 1915, he came to England on leave with his wife, the plaintiff in the present action. In August, 1916, the defendant returned alone to Ceylon because his wife's doctor had advised her that her health would not stand up to a further period of service abroad. Later the husband wrote to his wife suggesting that they should remain apart, and in 1918 the plaintiff obtained a decree nisi. In this case the plaintiff alleged that before her husband sailed for Ceylon he had agreed, in consultation with her, that he would give her £30 per month as maintenance, and she now sued because of his failure to abide by the said agreement. The Court of Appeal *held* that there was no enforceable contract because the parties did not intend to create legal relations. The provision for a flat payment of £30 per month for an indefinite period with no attempt to take into account changes in the circumstances of the parties did not suggest a binding agreement. Duke, L.J., seems to have based his decision on the fact that the wife had not supplied any consideration.

75. Spellman *v.* Spellman, [1961] 2 All E.R. 498

The parties were husband and wife and relations between them were very strained and the husband promised to buy a car for his wife in an effort to bring about a reconciliation. In May, 1960, the husband had a car delivered to the matrimonial home, saying that he had bought it for his wife. The registration book was put in the name of the wife, though the husband's reasons for doing this were not clear, although it had something to do with insurance. Relations between the parties continued to be strained, and eventually the husband left the matrimonial home taking the car with him, the wife keeping the registration book. The car was the subject of a hire-purchase agreement under which the husband was liable for the instalments. The Court of Appeal *held* that the husband was entitled to the car and that the wife should transfer the log book to him. The points of interest raised by the case are as follows—

(i) The wife claimed that the husband had made her a gift of the car. This was rejected by the court because, under the hire-purchase agreement, the title in the car was in the hire-purchase company. Therefore the car was not the husband's to give.

(ii) The wife also claimed that there had been an equitable assignment of the car to her. This was rejected because, although no formalities are required for an equitable assignment, intention to assign must be shown and there was insufficient evidence of this. Danckwerts, L.J., held the view that, although the hire-purchase agreement prohibited assignment, this would not have been fatal in the face of intention to assign by the husband. Willmer, L.J., thought it would.

(iii) A further claim by the wife was that, when the husband put the registration book in her name, he had declared a trust over it for her and held it on trust. The court rejected this view, stating that there was not sufficient evidence of declaration of trust.

(iv) The court applied the principle in *Balfour* v. *Balfour*[74] and held that there was no intention to create legal relations on the ground that domestic arrangements between spouses were not within the cognisance of the law.

76. Merritt *v.* Merritt (1970), *The Times*, 28th April

After a husband had formed an attachment for another woman and had left his wife, a meeting was held between the parties on 25th May, 1966, in the husband's car. The husband agreed to pay the wife £40 per month maintenance and also wrote out and signed a document stating that in consideration of the wife paying all charges in connexion with the matrimonial home until the mortgage repayments had been completed, he would agree to transfer the property to her sole ownership. The wife took the document away with her and had herself paid off the mortgage. The husband did not subsequently transfer the property to his wife and she claimed a declaration that she was the sole beneficial owner and asked for an order that her husband should transfer the property to her forthwith. The husband's defence was that the agreement was a family arrangement not intended to create legal relations. *Held*—by the Court of Appeal—

(i) That the agreement, having been made when the parties were not living together in amity, was enforceable. (*Balfour* v. *Balfour*, 1919,[74] *distinguished.*)

(ii) The contention that there was no consideration to support the husband's promise could not be sustained. The payment of the balance of the mortgage was a detriment to the wife and the husband had received the benefit of being relieved of liability to the building society.

Accordingly the wife was entitled to the relief she claimed.

77. Gould *v.* Gould, [1969] 3 All E.R. 728

On 15th May, 1966, the appellant left his wife for the second time agreeing to pay her £15 per week as maintenance for herself and the two children of the marriage. The agreement was made orally and was subject to the qualification that the appellant would pay "as long as I can manage it." He kept to the agreement until October, 1967, when he began to fall behind with his payments. In February, 1968, he told the wife that he could not pay the full amount in the future. The wife then issued a writ claiming the balance outstanding for the period up to 17th February, 1968. She claimed 13 weeks at £15 per week but gave credit for payments made by the appellant in January and February of £60, making a total claim of £135. The appellant put in a defence denying that he had agreed to pay his wife maintenance as alleged or at all. The County Court judge at Exeter County Court found the agreement proved and enforceable, there being an intention to create legal relations. The husband appealed to the Court of Appeal where it was *held* that it had not been within the contemplation of the parties to make a legally binding agreement. The uncertainty of the terms and the absence of any consideration from the wife, such as an undertaking not to seek maintenance if the payments were kept up, precluded that result.

Lord Denning, M.R. dissented and would have held the agreement to be legally binding, saying with regard to the uncertainty of the agreement—

> I think a good meaning can be given to the husband's statement by implying a term that, if the husband found that he could not manage to keep up the payments, he could, on reasonable notice, determine the agreement. That is a perfectly

intelligible term. If it were included in a written document, I have no doubt the court would enforce it. I should also do so when it is included in an oral agreement.

On the matter of consideration he said—

There is ample consideration for such agreement. First, there is the consideration that neither is insisting on the matrimonial right to live together. Second, whilst the payments are being made, she cannot complain of wilful neglect to maintain. Third, the agreement means that she has no authority to pledge his credit at common law for necessaries. See now Matrimonial Proceedings and Property Act, 1970.

78. Simpkins *v.* Pays, [1955] 3 All E.R. 10

The defendant and the defendant's granddaughter made an agreement with the plaintiff, who was a paying boarder, that they should submit in the defendant's name a weekly coupon, containing a forecast by each of them, to a Sunday newspaper fashion competition. On one occasion a forecast by the granddaughter was correct and the defendant received a prize of £750. The plaintiff sued for his share of that sum. The defence was that there was no intention to create legal relations but that the transaction was a friendly arrangement binding in honour only. *Held*—There was an intention to create legal relations. Far from being a friendly domestic arrangement, the evidence showed that it was a joint enterprise and that the parties expected to share any prize that was won.

79. Parker *v.* Clark, [1960] 1 All E.R. 93

The plaintiffs, Mr. & Mrs. Parker, were a middle-aged couple and lived in their own cottage in Sussex. The defendants, Mr. & Mrs. Clark, who were aged 77 and 78 respectively, lived in a large house in Torquay. Mrs. Parker was the niece of Mrs. Clark. In 1955 the plaintiffs visited the defendants and, as a result of certain conversations held at that time, Mrs. Clark wrote to Mrs. Parker suggesting that the plaintiffs should come to live in the defendants' house in Torquay, setting out detailed financial terms as to the sharing of expenses. Mrs. Clark also suggested that the plaintiffs' cottage might be sold and the proceeds invested, and that the defendants would leave the house in Torquay, and its major contents, to Mrs. Parker, her sister and her daughter. Mrs. Parker wrote accepting this offer and the cottage was sold. After the mortgage was paid off, £2,000 of the remaining money was lent to their daughter to enable her to buy a flat. The plaintiffs then moved into the defendants' house in Torquay. For a time all went well and Mr. Clark executed a will leaving the property as agreed. In 1957 differences between the parties arose, and after much unpleasantness Mr. Clark told the plaintiffs to go and they left in December, 1957. The plaintiffs claimed damages for breach of contract. *Held*—There was an intention to create legal relations arising from the circumstances. In view of the fact that the plaintiffs had sold their home and lent £2,000 to their daughter, it was obvious that, having "burned their boats," they must have relied on the agreement. The letter from Mrs. Clark was an offer sufficiently precise and detailed; it was not merely a statement of terms for a future agreement. Further it was a sufficient memorandum to satisfy Sect. 40 of the Law of Property Act, 1925. Finally, the fact that Mr. Clark had altered his will indicated that he regarded the agreement as binding.

The damages awarded were divided as follows—

(i) Damages of £1,200 plus costs, in favour of the parties jointly, based on the value per annum of living rent free in the house. (£300 multiplied by four because of the expectation of life of the defendants.)

(ii) Damages of £3,400, in favour of Mrs. Parker separately, in respect of the value to her of inheriting a share in the defendants' house on their death.

80. Jones *v.* Padavatton, [1969] 2 All E.R. 616

In 1962 the plaintiff, Mrs. Jones, who lived in Trinidad, made an offer to the defendant Mrs. Padavatton, her daughter, to provide maintenance for her at the rate of £42 a month if she would leave her job in Washington in the United States and go to England and read for the Bar. Mrs. Padavatton was at that time divorced from her husband having the custody of the child of that marriage. The agreement was an informal one and there was uncertainty as to its exact terms. Nevertheless the daughter came to England in November 1962, bringing the child with her, and began to read for the Bar, her fees and maintenance being paid for by Mrs. Jones. In 1964 it appeared that the daughter was experiencing some discomfort in England occupying one room in Acton for which she had to pay £6 17s. 6d. per week. At this stage Mrs. Jones offered to buy a large house in London to be occupied partly by the daughter and partly by tenants, the income from rents to go to the daughter in lieu of maintenance. Again there was no written agreement but the house was purchased for £6,000 and conveyed to Mrs. Jones. The daughter moved into the house in January, 1965, and tenants arrived, it still being uncertain what precisely was to happen to the surplus rent income (if any) and what rooms the daughter was to occupy. No money from the rents was received by Mrs. Jones and no accounts were submitted to her. In 1967 Mrs. Jones claimed possession of the house from her daughter, who had by that time married again, and the daughter counter-claimed for £1,655 18s. 9d. said to have been paid in connection with running the house. At the hearing the daughter still had one subject to pass in Part I of the Bar examinations and also the whole of Part II remained to be taken.

Held—by the Court of Appeal—

(i) That the arrangements were throughout family agreements depending upon the good faith of the parties in keeping the promises made and not intended to be rigid binding agreements. Furthermore, the arrangements were far too vague and uncertain to be enforceable as contracts. (*Per* Danckwerts and Fenton Atkinson, L.J.)

(ii) That although the agreement to maintain while reading for the Bar might have been regarded as creating a legal obligation in the mother to pay (the terms being sufficiently stated and duration for a reasonable time being implied), the daughter could not claim anything in respect of that agreement which must be regarded as having terminated in 1967, five years being a reasonable time in which to complete studies for the Bar. The arrangements in relation to the home were very vague and must be regarded as made without contractual intent. (*Per* Salmon, L.J.)

The mother was therefore entitled to possession of the house and had no liability under the maintenance agreement. The counter-claim by the daughter was left to be settled by the parties, Salmon, L.J., saying—

If this reference is pursued, it will involve an account being meticulously taken of all receipts and expenditure from December, 1964, until the date on which the daughter yields up possession. This will certainly result in a great waste of time and money, and can only exacerbate ill-feeling between the mother and the daughter. With a little goodwill and good sense on both sides, this could and should be avoided by reaching a reasonable compromise on the figures. I can but express the hope that this may be done, for it would clearly be to the mutual benefit of both parties.

81. Buckpitt *v.* Oates, [1968] 1 All E.R. 1145

The plaintiff and the defendant, both aged 17 years, were in the habit of riding together in each other's cars. Neither of them had insurance cover against injury to passengers. The defendant had a notice affixed to the facia panel of his car stating that any passenger travelled at his own risk, and it was found as a fact that the plaintiff was aware of this notice. On a drive from Paignton to Newton Abbot the defendant, at the plaintiff's request, carried him as a passenger in his (the defendant's) car. The car struck a wall due to the defendant's negligence and the plaintiff was injured. The plaintiff had paid 10*s.* towards the cost of the petrol (which in fact cost less). The plaintiff claimed damages for personal injuries and it was *held* dismissing the claim—

(i) there was no legal contract of carriage, the arrangement between the parties being one not intended to create a legal relationship;
(ii) the plaintiff had agreed to be carried at his own risk and, though an infant in law, could not enforce a right which he had voluntarily waived or or abandoned. The defence of *volenti non fit injuria* succeeded.

John Stephenson, J., said "No man—and it seems to me, no infant—can enforce a right which he has voluntarily waived or abandoned . . . . Of course the court will always consider with great care whether a particular plaintiff had the means and the knowledge and experience to appreciate fully and freely the risk and what he was consenting to." See case number 390.

82. Jones *v.* Vernon's Pools Ltd., [1938] 2 All E.R. 626

The plaintiff said that he had sent to the defendants a football coupon on which the penny points pool was all correct. Defendants denied having received it and relied on a clause printed on every coupon. The said clause provided that the transaction should not "give rise to any legal relationship . . . or be legally enforceable . . . but . . . binding in honour only." The court *held* that this clause was a bar to any action in a court of law.

N.B. This case was followed by the Court of Appeal in *Appleson* v. *Littlewood Ltd.*, [1939] 1 All E.R. 464, where the contract contained a similar clause.

83. Rose and Frank Co. *v.* Crompton (J. R.) & Brothers Ltd., [1925] A.C. 445

In 1913 the plaintiffs, an American firm, entered into an agreement with the defendants, an English company, whereby the plaintiffs were appointed sole agents for the sale in the U.S.A. of paper tissues supplied by the defendants. The contract was for a period of three years with an option to extend that time. The agreement was extended to March, 1920, but in 1919 the defendants terminated it without notice. The defendants had received a number of orders for tissues before the termination of the contract, and they refused to execute them. The plaintiffs sued for breach of contract and for non-delivery of the goods actually ordered. The agreement of 1913 contained an "Honourable Pledge Clause" drafted as follows: "This arrangement is not entered into nor is this memorandum written as a formal or legal agreement and shall not be subject to legal jurisdiction in the courts of the United States of America or England . . ." It was *held* by the House of Lords that the 1913 agreement was not binding on the parties, but that in so far as the agreement had been acted upon by the defendants' acceptance of orders, the said orders were binding contracts of sale. Nevertheless the agreement was not binding for the future.

84. Mountstephen v. Lakeman (1871), L.R. 7 Q.B. 196

The defendant was chairman of the Brixham Local Board of Health. The plaintiff, who was a builder and contractor, was employed in 1866 by the board to construct certain main sewage works in the town. On 19th March, 1866, notice was given by the board to owners of certain homes to connect their house drains with the main sewer within twenty-one days. Before the expiration of the twenty-one days Robert Adams, the surveyor of the board, suggested to the plaintiff that he should make the connections. The plaintiff said he was willing to do the work if the board would see him paid. On the 5th April, 1866, i.e. before the expiration of the twenty-one days, the plaintiff commenced work on the connections. However, before work commenced it appeared that the plaintiff had had an interview with the defendant at which the following conversation took place—

Defendant: "What objection have you to making the connections?"

Plaintiff: "I have none, if you or the board will order the work or become responsible for the payment."

Defendant: "Go on Mountstephen and do the work and I will see you paid."

The plaintiff completed the connections in April and May, 1866, and sent an account to the board on 5th December, 1866. The board disclaimed responsibility on the ground that they had never entered into any agreement with the plaintiff nor authorised any officer of the board to agree with him for the performance of the work in question. It was *held*—that Lakeman had undertaken a personal liability to pay the plaintiff and had not given a guarantee of the liability of a third party, i.e. the board. In consequence Lakeman had given an indemnity which did not need to be in writing under Sect. 4 of the Statute of Frauds, 1677. The plaintiff was therefore entitled to enforce the oral undertaking given by the defendant.

85. Carr v. Lynch, [1900] 1 Ch. 613

The defendant was lessor of the Warden Arms, Kentish Town, which was leased to Charles Smith. In September, 1898, the premises were assigned to Arthur Jayne for the residue of the term. On the expiration of the lease Jayne applied to the defendant to grant him a further lease, and the defendant consented on condition that Jayne paid him £50. When Jayne paid the money he produced a memorandum which he had prepared and the defendant signed it. The memorandum read as follows: "Dear Sir, In consideration of you having this day paid me the sum of £50, I hereby agree to grant you or your assigns a further lease of 24 years." Before the new lease was to commence Jayne assigned the lease to the plaintiff, Arthur Carr, but the defendant refused to grant the new lease to Carr. This action was for specific performance of the agreement for a lease, and the defence was that the memorandum did not satisfy the Statute of Frauds because it did not sufficiently identify the parties. *Held*—The plaintiff succeeded. The memorandum was sufficient because the defendant had admitted that Jayne had paid him £50 on the day in question and the person who had paid was the person to get the lease according to the document. Therefore Jayne was adequately identified, and Carr, being Jayne's assignee, was entitled to a lease.

86. F. Goldsmith (Sicklesmere), Ltd. v. Baxter, [1969] 3 All E.R. 733

By an agreement dated 9th April, 1968, the defendant agreed to purchase a piece of land, cottage and buildings known as "Shelley," Stanstead, Suffolk from the plaintiff company. The memorandum of agreement was signed by a Mr. Brewster, one of the company's directors, "for and on behalf of Goldsmith Coaches (Sicklesmere) Limited." Mr. Brewster thought that this was the company's name and it did carry on business under that description. The property known as "Shelley" was described in the particulars of sale and the memorandum of agreement stated that the vendor company, described as Goldsmith Coaches (Sicklesmere) Ltd., was the beneficial owner of it. The defendant's solicitors were subsequently unable to trace a company called Goldsmith Coaches (Sicklesmere) Ltd. and the defendant refused to complete by conveying the property on the ground that since there was no vendor there was no contract. The company thereupon sued for specific performance. *Held*—by Stamp, J.— that specific performance would be granted. A contract was to be construed by reference to the surrounding circumstances or in the light of known facts. Accordingly it was clear that the name inserted in the memorandum of sale as being that of the vendor was merely an inaccurate description of the plaintiff company which was therefore a party to the contract and could easily be identified as such by reference to other characteristics.

Looking at the memorandum alone, and without regard to the surrounding circumstances, I find that the person—the persona ficta—said to be the vendor has the following characteristics:

(i) it is named Goldsmith Coaches (Sicklesmere), Ltd.;
(ii) its registered office is said to be at Sicklesmere;
(iii) it has an agent called Brewster who claims to act for it;
(iv) it is the beneficial owner of "Shelley."

Then, applying the rule that a contract is to be construed by reference to the surrounding circumstances, or in the light of the known facts, I find first, that there is no limited company which in law has the name Goldsmith Coaches (Sicklesmere), Ltd., but that the plaintiff company is often known as "Goldsmith Coaches" and carries on business as a bus and coach contractor, and does so at Sicklesmere. Then I find, secondly, that the plaintiff company's registered office is at Sicklesmere, in the very place at which it carries on the bus and coach business. Thirdly, I find that the plaintiff company has an agent called Brewster; and, fourthly, that it is the beneficial owner of "Shelley". I find in addition that there is no other company having those characteristics. Applying this process, if it be permissable, I conclude beyond peradventure that Goldsmith Coaches (Sicklesmere), Ltd., is no more, nor less, than an inaccurate description of the plaintiff company, F. Goldsmith (Sicklesmere), Ltd. . . . In the absence of authority constraining me to do so—and none has been cited—I would find it impossible to hold that a company incorporated under the Companies Acts has no identity but by reference to its correct name, or that, unless an agent acts on its behalf by that name, or a name so nearly resembling it that it is obviously an error for that name, he acts for nobody. A limited company has in my judgment characteristics other than its name by reference to which it can be identified: for example, a particular business, and a particular place or places where it carries on business, particular shareholders, and particular directors.

87. Hawkins *v.* Price, [1947] Ch. 645

On 31st January, 1946, the plaintiff and defendant entered into a bargain for the sale of a freehold bungalow and land. The plaintiff paid a deposit of £100, and the defendant signed a deposit receipt thus: "Received of H.H. the sum of £100 being deposit on bungalow named 'Oakdene,' Station Road, Stoke Mandeville, Bucks, sold for £1,000." The plaintiff now sued for specific performance of the agreement, and it was discovered that there was a term that vacant possession be given by 31st March, 1946. This term was not mentioned in the deposit receipt. Nevertheless the plaintiff claimed that the said receipt was a sufficient memorandum to satisfy Sect. 40 of the Law of Property Act, 1925. *Held*—It was not, because—

(i) The deposit receipt did not contain reference to the fact that the sale was with vacant possession. Although it is not necessary that the memorandum should contain every term, it must at least contain all material terms. In the view of the court the question of vacant possession was material and not collateral.

(ii) The plaintiff suggested that since the term was solely for his benefit he could waive it. The court decided that the term was not solely for his benefit because, although it governed the date on which he could take possession, it also informed Mrs. Price of how long she might remain in possession.

(iii) It was difficult for the plaintiff to waive the term because he was suing for specific performance with vacant possession.

87a. *Scott* v. *Bradley*, [1971] 1 All E.R. 538

The plaintiff and defendant agreed that the defendant would sell her freehold property to the plaintiff for £5,000. The plaintiff agreed to pay half the defendant's legal costs but this was not recorded on the receipt. The plaintiff sought to enforce the contract and offered to pay half the defendant's legal costs of the sale. *Held*—by Plowman, J.—that on making this offer the plaintiff could enforce the contract.

88. Caton *v.* Caton (1867), L.R. 2 H.L. 127

A Mr. Caton and a Mrs. Henley proposed to marry, and decided to enter into a marriage settlement. A document was drafted as a basis for the marriage settlement and the names Caton and Henley appeared in it, but only for the purpose of showing what Mr. Caton was to do and what Mrs. Henley was to have under the agreement. The document was not signed by either of the parties. At the time when this action was brought a marriage settlement had to be evidenced in writing under the provisions of the Statute of Frauds, 1677, and this document was produced as a memorandum. *Held*—It was not a sufficient memorandum because, although the names of the parties appeared in the document, they did not appear as signatures intended to subscribe it.

89. Pearce *v.* Gardner, [1897] 1 Q.B. 688

The plaintiff brought this action to recover damages for breach of a contract by the defendant under the terms of which the defendant had agreed to sell the plaintiff certain gravel which was *in situ* on the land. At the trial the plaintiff put in evidence a letter signed by the defendant and commencing "Dear Sir." The letter did not contain the plaintiff's name. The plaintiff then put in evidence an envelope which had been used to post the letter, which showed the plaintiff's name and address. *Held*—The letter and the envelope together provided a memorandum sufficient to satisfy the Statute of Frauds.

N.B. Before documents can be connected so as to provide a memorandum, they must be *prima facie* connected as in the case of a letter and an envelope. See *Williams* v. *Lake* (1860), 2 E. & E. 349. In this case the plaintiff put in evidence as a memorandum a letter similar to the one put forward in the above case. He was not able to produce an envelope, however, and the court *held* that the letter was not a memorandum sufficient to satisfy the Statute of Frauds.

90. Timmins v. Moreland Street Property Ltd., [1958] Ch. 110

The defendants agreed to buy certain property belonging to the plaintiff for £39,000 and gave him a cheque for £3,900 as a deposit, the cheque being made payable to his solicitors. The plaintiff made out a signed deposit receipt which stated that the sum of £3,900 was a deposit for the purchase of the property which was adequately described, and that the plaintiff agreed to sell for £39,000. Subsequently the defendants stopped the cheque and repudiated the contract. The plaintiff sued for breach of contract and the defendants pleaded absence of a memorandum under Sect. 40 of the Law of Property Act, 1925. The plaintiff claimed that a sufficient memorandum existed if the deposit receipt were read together with the cheque containing the defendants' signature. *Held*—The two documents could not be connected, because the cheque was made payable to the plaintiff's solicitors and there was no necessary connection between it and the deposit receipt.

91. Griffiths v. Young, [1970] 3 W.L.R. 246

Following an agreement concerning the sale of land by the defendant to the plaintiff the plaintiff's solicitor wrote to the defendant's solicitor stating a price "subject to contract." A telephone conversation between the solicitors followed and later there was a letter from the defendant's solicitor confirming the defendant's instructions to sell for an agreed price. *Held*—by the Court of Appeal— the letters constituted a sufficient memorandum and the phrase "subject to contract" did not render the first letter defective in view of later events.

92. Monnickendam v. Leanse (1923), 39 T.L.R. 445

The plaintiff orally agreed to buy a house from the defendant and paid a deposit of £200. Later the plaintiff refused to go on with the contract and pleaded lack of memorandum in writing, though the defendant was always willing to complete. The plaintiff now sued to recover the deposit. *Held*— He could not recover the deposit.

N.B. The case illustrates that the difficulties arising out of the absence of a memorandum in writing are procedural rather than substantive. The contract, though unenforceable, is not wholly without effect, for in the above case the contract was raised as a defence to an action for the deposit. It is essential of course that the vendor be prepared to complete the bargain; he cannot deny the enforceability of the contract and yet claim its existence as a defence to the action for recovery of the deposit.

93. Rawlinson v. Ames, [1925] 1 Ch. 96

The defendant orally agreed to take a lease of the plaintiff's flat. The plaintiff carried out alterations in the flat at the defendant's request and under her supervision. She then refused to take the lease and pleaded absence of memorandum required by the Statute of Frauds. The plaintiff claimed specific performance of the contract on the grounds that the alterations made in the flat were unequivocal acts of part-performance. *Held*—The plaintiff succeeded. The alterations were not in themselves unequivocal in that the plaintiff might have been altering the flat for some other purpose, but the fact that the defendant supervised and approved of the alterations indicated that she was then minded to take the lease.

94. Broughton *v.* Snook, [1938] 1 Ch. 505

The plaintiff orally agreed to purchase an inn from X and gave an undertaking not to disturb the sitting tenant until the tenant's lease expired. Before the end of his term the tenant vacated the inn and let the plaintiff take possession with X's knowledge. The plaintiff thereupon effected substantial improvements. X died and his executors advertised the sale of the inn. The plaintiff claimed specific performance of the oral agreement. *Held*—Although the plaintiff had gone into possession, this did not constitute an act of part performance because it might have referred to an agreement with the tenant. However, the improvements he had made were unequivocal and constituted part performance. Specific performance was granted.

95. Daniels *v.* Trefusis, [1914] 1 Ch. 788

The defendant orally agreed to buy land from the plaintiff. In the course of negotiations the plaintiff's solicitors, in accordance with the agreement, gave notice to two weekly tenants of the plaintiff so that the defendant might have vacant possession on completion. The tenants gave up possession and then the defendant refused to complete the contract, pleading absence of memorandum in writing. The plaintiff now claimed specific performance of the contract on the grounds of part performance. *Held*—Notice to the tenants was an act of part performance, and their subsequent eviction was an act referable to the contract. It would be a fraud on the plaintiff for the defendant to plead absence of memorandum. Specific performance was granted.

96. Wakeham *v.* MacKenzie, [1968] 2 All E.R. 783

Some two years after his wife's death a widower aged 72 orally agreed with the plaintiff, a widow of 67, that if she would move into his house and look after him for the rest of his life she should have the house (of which he was the owner) together with the contents on his death. It was also agreed that the plaintiff should pay her own board and buy her own coal.

The plaintiff gave up her council flat and moved into the widower's house and looked after him as agreed, paying for her board and coal. He died in February, 1966, but did not leave the house or contents to her. The executor of the widower's estate contended that if there was a contract no action could be brought upon it at common law because there was no memorandum in writing as required by Sect. 40 of the Law of Property Act, 1925, which was accepted. However in respect of the plaintiff's claim for the equitable remedy of specific performance the adequacy of her acts of part performance was in question. On this matter Stamp, J., *held*—

> I conclude from *Kingswood Estate Co. Ltd.* v. *Anderson* first that it is not the law that the acts of part performance relied on must be not only referable to a contract such as that alleged, but referable to no other title, the doctrine to that effect laid down by Warrington, L.J., in *Chaproniere* v. *Lambert* having been exploded; and secondly that the true rule is that the operation of acts of part performance requires only that the acts in question be such as must be referred to some contract and may be referred to the alleged one; that they prove the existence of some contract and one consistent with the contract alleged.

His Lordship accordingly made an order for specific performance of the oral agreement on which the plaintiff relied.

97. Maddison *v.* Alderson (1883), 8 App. Cas. 467

The plaintiff had been employed as a housekeeper to Thomas Alderson for a number of years. At one period Alderson was pressed for money, and asked the plaintiff whether she would be willing to carry on working as housekeeper for the rest of his life without wages, in return for which he would leave her a life interest in a farm by his will. Alderson made a will in those terms but unfortunately it was not properly attested, and on his death it was declared void. The plaintiff brought this action against Alderson's executor who relied on absence of memorandum as required by the Statute of Frauds. The plaintiff claimed that the work she had carried out without payment constituted part performance, which entitled her to specific performance of the contract. *Held*— The work she had carried out was equivocal. There were many reasons why the plaintiff might have worked without wages. It did not follow that she was entitled to a life interest in the farm.

98. **Congresbury Motors Ltd.** *v.* **Anglo-Belge Finance Co. Ltd.,** [1969] 3 All E.R. 545

In January, 1965, the plaintiffs borrowed £46,000 from the defendants, Anglo-Belge Finance Co. Ltd., to finance the purchase of a filling station and garage. Later they borrowed another £4,000 from the defendants who were registered moneylenders. In this action the plaintiffs were claiming—

(i) a declaration that their undertaking to repay the loans was unenforceable since there was not a sufficient note or memorandum of the transaction as required by Sect. 6 of the Moneylenders Act, 1927. The mortgage deed used to secure the loan which might have been regarded as a sufficient memorandum did not in fact show the date on which the loan was made;

(ii) an injunction to restrain the defendants from enforcing the mortgage; and

(iii) an order for the cancellation and delivery up of the mortgage deed.

In effect the plaintiffs were claiming to retain their garage without paying for it.

The defendants counterclaimed—

(i) for payment under the mortgage and alternatively;

(ii) for a declaration that the plaintiffs held the money in trust for them, and in the further alternative;

(iii) a declaration that they were entitled to a lien on the property for the money paid to the vendors of the property; and

(iv) an order for sale.

It was *Held*—by Plowman, J., and the Court of Appeal—that the plaintiffs' undertaking to repay the loan was unenforceable because there was not a sufficient note or memorandum under Sect. 6 (2) of the Moneylenders Act, 1927, the date on which the loan was made having been omitted. However, the defendants' claim for a lien on the property succeeded. The money borrowed was actually used to acquire the property and in these circumstances the moneylenders became entitled to the lien on the property which the vendors would have had if the purchase price remained unpaid. In other words the moneylenders acquired by subrogation the usual lien of the unpaid seller of land. The claim that the property was held in trust for the moneylenders failed. This claim was based on the case of *Barclays Bank Ltd.* v. *Quistclose Investments Ltd.*, [1968] 3 All E.R. 651, where it was held that if money is lent for a specific purpose which is not carried out the money is held on trust for the lenders. However, the present case was distinguished because the purpose had not failed, the borrowers having actually purchased the filling station and garage.

N.B. Bankers, properly so called, are exempt from the Moneylenders Acts.

99. Dunlop v. Selfridge, [1915] A.C. 847

The appellants were motor tyre manufacturers and sold tyres to Messrs. Dew & Co. who were motor accessory dealers. Under the terms of the contract Dew & Co. agreed not to sell the tyres below Dunlop's list price, and as Dunlop's agents, to obtain from other traders a similar undertaking. In return for this undertaking Dew & Co., were to receive special discounts. Some of which they could pass on to retailers who bought tyres. Selfridge & Co. accepted two orders from customers for Dunlop covers at a lower price. They obtained the covers through Dew & Co. and signed an agreement not to sell or offer the tyres below list price. It was further agreed that £5 per tyre so sold should be paid to Dunlop by way of liquidated damages. Selfridge's supplied one of the two tyres ordered below list price. They did not actually supply the other, but informed the customer that they could only supply it at list price. The appellants claimed an injunction and damages against the respondents for breach of the agreement made with Dew & Co., claiming that Dew & Co. were their agents in the matter. *Held*—There was no contract between the parties. Dunlop could not enforce the contract made between the respondents and Dew and Co. because they had not supplied consideration. Even if Dunlop were undisclosed principals, there was no consideration moving between them and the respondents. The discount received by Selfridge was part of that given by Dunlop to Dew & Co. Since Dew & Co. were not bound to give any part of their discount to retailers the discount received by Selfridge operated only as consideration between themselves and Dew & Co. and could not be claimed by Dunlop as consideration to support a promise not to sell below list price. (See now Restrictive Trade Practices Act, 1956, Sect. 25 and Resale Prices Act, 1964.)

100. Haigh v. Brooks (1839), 10 A. & E. 309

The defendant had guaranteed a debt of £10,000 which a firm named John Lees and Son owed to the plaintiffs. Subsequently the plaintiffs agreed to give up the document and release Brooks from liability on it if Brooks would undertake to pay at maturity certain bills of exchange which had already been accepted by John Lees and Son. The bills amounted to £9,666 13s. 7d. Brooks gave the required undertaking but failed to pay the bills when they matured, and the plaintiffs brought this action. The defence was that the plaintiffs had not supplied consideration for Brooks' promise to pay the bills because the guarantee from which he had been released was in any case unenforceable, since the memorandum evidencing the guarantee did not contain a statement of the consideration as required by the Statute of Frauds. (See now Mercantile Law Amendment Act, 1856, Sect. 3.) *Held*—Even if the guarantee was not binding, the surrender of it was sufficient consideration to support the defendant's promise to pay the bills. He had got what he had bargained for, i.e. his release from the guarantee, and it did not matter that the consideration was inadequate.

101. White v. Bluett (1853), 23 L.J. Ex. 36

This action was brought by White who was the executor of Bluett's father's estate. The plaintiff, White, alleged that Bluett had not paid a promissory note given to his father during his lifetime. Bluett admitted that he had given the note to his father, but said that his father had released him from it in return for a promise not to keep on complaining about the fact that he had been disinherited. *Held*—The defence failed and the defendant was liable on the note. The promise not to complain was not sufficient consideration to support his release from the note.

102. Chappell & Co. Ltd. *v.* Nestlé Co. Ltd., [1959] 2 All E.R. 701

The plaintiffs owned the copyright in a dance tune called "Rockin' Shoes," and the defendants were using records of this tune as part of an advertising scheme. A record company made the records for Nestlés who advertised them to the public for 1s. 6d. each but required in addition three wrappers from their 6d. bars of chocolate. When they received the wrappers they threw them away. The plaintiffs sued the defendants for infringement of copyright. It appeared that under the Copyright Act of 1956 a person recording musical works for *retail* sale need not get the permission of the holder of the copyright, but had merely to serve him with notice and pay 6¼ per cent of the retail selling price as royalty. The plaintiffs asserted that the defendants were not retailing the goods in the sense of the Act and must therefore get permission to use the musical work. The basis of the plaintiffs' case was that retailing meant selling entirely for money, and that as the defendants were selling for money plus wrappers, they needed the plaintiffs' consent. The defence was that the sale was for cash because the wrappers were not part of the consideration. *Held*— The plaintiffs succeeded because the wrappers were part of the consideration and the question of their adequacy did not arise.

103. Coggs *v.* Bernard (1703), 2 Ld. Ray. 909

The defendant had agreed to take several hogsheads of brandy, belonging to the plaintiff, from the cellar of one inn to another. One of the casks was broken and the brandy lost and the plaintiff alleged that this was due to the defendant's carelessness. The defendant denied liability on the grounds that there was no consideration to support the agreement to move the casks. *Held*—the plaintiff's claim succeeded. The court made an attempt to find consideration by saying that when the plaintiff entrusted the goods to the defendant this was sufficient consideration to oblige him to be careful with them. However, it is hard to see how such a "trusting" can amount to consideration for it was not a benefit to the defendant, nor was it a detriment to the plaintiff because he wished his goods to be carried. It does not appear to have been the price of any promise and the case seems to have been decided on the ground that once the relationship of bailor and bailee is established certain duties fall upon the bailee independently of any contract.

103a. *Gilchrist Watt and Sanderson Pty.* v. *York Products Pty.*, [1970] 1 W.L.R. 1262

Two cases of German clocks were bought by the respondents and shipped to Sydney. The shipowners arranged for the appellant stevedores to unload the ship. The goods were put in the appellants' shed but when the respondents came to collect them one case of clocks was missing. It was admitted that this was due to the appellants' negligence. *Held*—by the Privy Council— that the appellants were liable. Although there was no contract between the parties an obligation to take due care of the goods was created by delivery and voluntary assumption of possession under the sub-bailment.

104. Collins *v.* Godefroy (1831), 1 B. & Ad. 950

The plaintiff was subpoenaed to give evidence for the defendant in an action to which the defendant was a party. The plaintiff now sued for the sum of six guineas which he said the defendant had promised him for his attendance. *Held*—The plaintiff's action failed because there was no consideration for the promise. Lord Tenterden said: "if it be a duty imposed by law upon a party regularly subpoenaed to attend from time to time to give his evidence, then a promise to give him any remuneration for loss of time incurred in such attendance is a promise without consideration."

105. Vanbergen *v.* St Edmunds Properties Ltd., [1933] 2 K.B. 223

The plaintiff owed the defendants £208 and the defendants had issued a bankruptcy notice to be served on 7th July. On 6th July the plaintiff told the defendants' solicitors that he hoped to raise the money at Eastbourne, but that he could not do so until 8th July. The solicitors agreed to put off the service of the notice until noon on 8th July, in return for the plaintiff's promise to pay the money into an Eastbourne bank by that time. The plaintiff paid the money in as directed on 7th July, but his letter advising the solicitors went astray. They thereupon served the bankruptcy notice. The plaintiff now sued for damages for breach of contract. *Held*—The action could not be sustained because the plaintiff was already bound to pay the sum of £208 long before 8th July and was not supplying consideration by paying it into the bank on 7th July. The solicitors were in order in serving the notice.

106. Stilk *v.* Myrick (1809), 2 Camp. 317

A sea-captain, being unable to find any substitutes for two sailors who had deserted, promised to divide the wages of the deserters among the rest of the crew if they would work the ship home shorthanded. *Held*—The promise was not enforceable because of absence of consideration. In sailing the ship home the crew had done no more than they were already bound to do. Their original contract obliged them to meet the normal emergencies of the voyage of which minor desertions were one. *c/f. Hartley v. Ponsonby* (1857), 7 E. & B. 872, where a greater remuneration was promised to a seaman to work the ship home when the number of deserters was so great as to render the ship unseaworthy. *Held*—This was a binding promise because the sailor had gone beyond his duty in agreeing to sail an unseaworthy ship. In fact the number of desertions was so great as to discharge the remaining seamen from their original contract, leaving them free to enter into a new bargain.

107. Ward *v.* Byham, [1956] 2 All E.R. 318

An unmarried mother sued to recover a maintenance allowance by the father of the child. The defence was that, under Sect. 42 of the National Assistance Act, 1948, the mother of an illegitimate child was bound to maintain it. However, it appeared that in return for the promise of an allowance the mother had promised—

> (*a*) to look after the child well and ensure that it was happy; and,
> (*b*) to allow it to decide whether it should live with her or the father.

Held—There was sufficient consideration to support the promise of an allowance because the promises given in (*a*) and (*b*) above were in excess of the statutory duty, which was merely to care for the child.

108. Shadwell v. Shadwell (1860), 9 C.B. (N.S.) 159

The plaintiff was engaged to marry a girl named Ellen Nicholl. In 1838 he received a letter from his uncle, Charles Shadwell, in the following terms: "I am glad to hear of your intended marriage with Ellen Nicholl and, as I promised to assist you at starting, I am happy to tell you that I will pay you one hundred and fifty pounds yearly during my life and until your income derived from your profession of Chancery barrister shall amount to six hundred guineas, of which your own admission will be the only evidence that I shall receive or require." The plaintiff duly married Ellen Nicholl and his income never exceeded six hundred guineas during the eighteen years his uncle lived after the marriage. The uncle paid twelve annual sums and part of the thirteenth but no more. On his death the plaintiff sued his uncle's executors for the balance of the eighteen instalments to which he suggested he was entitled. *Held*—The plaintiff succeeded even though he was already engaged to Ellen Nicholl when the promise was made. His marriage was sufficient consideration to support his uncle's promise, for, by marrying, the plaintiff had incurred responsibilities and changed his position in life. Further the uncle probably derived some benefit in that his desire to see his nephew settled had been satisfied.

109. Roscorla v. Thomas (1842), 3 Q.B. 234

The plaintiff bought a horse from the defendant and, after the sale had been completed, gave an undertaking that the horse was sound and free from vice. The horse was in fact a vicious horse, and the plaintiff sued on the express warranty which he alleged had been given to him. *Held*—If the warranty had been given at the time of the sale it would have been supported by consideration and therefore actionable, but since it had been given after the sale had taken place, the consideration for the warranty was past, and no action could be brought upon it. Further, no warranty could be implied from the circumstances of the sale.

110. Re McArdle, [1951] Ch. 669

Certain children were entitled under their father's will to a house. However, their mother had a life interest in the property and during her lifetime one of the children and his wife came to live in the house with the mother. The wife carried out certain improvements to the property, and, after she had done so. the children signed a document addressed to her stating: "In consideration of your carrying out certain alterations and improvements to the property . . . at present occupied by you, the beneficiaries under the Will of William Edward McArdle hereby agree that the executors, the National Provincial Bank Ltd., . . . shall repay to you from the said estate when so distributed the sum of £488 in settlement of the amount spent on such improvements . . ." On the death of the testator's widow the children refused to authorise payment of the sum of £488, and this action was brought to decide the validity of the claim. *Held*— Since the improvements had been carried out before the document was executed, the consideration was past and the promise could not be enforced.

111. Re Casey's Patents, Stewart v. Casey, [1892] 1 Ch. 104

Patents were granted to Stewart and another in respect of an invention concerning appliances and vessels for transporting and storing inflammable liquids. Stewart entered into an arrangement with Casey whereby Casey was to introduce the patents. Casey spent two years "pushing" the invention and then the joint owners of the patent rights wrote to him as follows: "In consideration of your services as the practical manager in working both patents we hereby agree to give you one-third share of the patents." Casey also received the letters patent. Some time later Stewart died and his executors claimed the letters patent from Casey, suggesting that he had no interest in them because the consideration for the promise to give him a one-third share was past. *Held*—The previous request to render the services raised an implied promise to pay. The subsequent promise could be regarded as fixing the value of the services so that Casey was entitled to a one-third share of the patent rights.

112. Dungate *v.* Dungate, [1965] All E.R. 818

The plaintiff lent £500 with interest at 5 per cent to his brother George and George's business partner, a Mr. Elson. The loan was acknowledged in writing dated 12th October, 1953. The plaintiff also lent further sums of money to George in 1956 and 1957 although these loans were without interest.

George paid the interest of £25 per annum by quarterly instalments until 13th April, 1957. On 23rd February, 1962, George wrote to the plaintiff saying, among other things, "Keep a check on totals and amounts I owe you and we will have account now and then." The letter did not say how much was owed. George died on 30th May, 1963, and on 16th October, 1964, the plaintiff sued George's widow and administratrix of his estate for the repayment of the loans. The defendant pleaded that the plaintiff's claim was statute barred. *Held*—The defence failed and the claim was not statute barred because the letter of 23rd February, 1962, made it clear that George owed money to the plaintiff. Although no amount was stated it was sufficient acknowledgement of the plaintiff's claim to make time run again from 23rd February, 1962, and not from the date of the loans.

113. Tweddle *v.* Atkinson (1861), 1 B. & S. 393

William Tweddle the plaintiff was married to the daughter of William Guy. In order to provide for the couple, Guy promised the plaintiff's father to pay the plaintiff £200 if the plaintiff's father would pay the plaintiff £100. An agreement was accordingly drawn up containing the above mentioned promise, and giving William Tweddle the right to sue either promisor for the sums promised. Guy did not make the promised payment during his lifetime and the plaintiff now sued Guy's executor. *Held*—The plaintiff's action failed because he had not given any consideration to Guy in return for the promise to pay £200. The provision in the agreement allowing William Tweddle to sue was of no effect without consideration.

114. Dunlop *v.* New Garage & Motor Co. Ltd., [1915] A.C. 79

The facts of this case are somewhat similar to case 99 mentioned above except that here the wholesalers obtained an undertaking from the respondents by means of a written agreement in which the wholesalers were clearly described as the agents of Dunlop. There was therefore a direct contractual relationship between the parties, and the appellants could enforce the agreement not to sell below the list price. The case is also concerned with the distinction between liquidated damages and a penalty, because it was suggested that the sum of £5 per tyre was not recoverable because it was not a genuine pre-estimate of loss, but it was inserted to compel performance by the respondents. There is, of course, a presumption that where a single sum is payable on the occurrence of one or more or all of several events then the sum stipulated is a penalty because it is unlikely that all the events can attract the same loss. The contract in this case listed five events on the occurrence of which the sum of £5 was payable. Even so the House of Lords *held* that the presumption need not always apply, and that it did not apply in this case. Where precise estimation is difficult as it was here, then any contractual provision is likely to represent the parties' honest attempt to provide for breach, and the court will follow it.

Certain points of interest arise out of the two cases—

(i) In neither case did the court regard a re-sale price maintenance agreement as illegal because it was in restraint of trade.

(ii) *Dunlop* v. *Selfridge*[99] illustrates that restrictive covenants do not run with chattels though they may with land. (Compare *Tulk* v. *Moxhay*.)[118]

115. Les Affréteurs Réunis Société Anonyme v. Walford, [1919] A.C. 801

The respondent Walford was a broker and he had negotiated a charter party between the owners of a ship the S.S. *Flore* and a fuel oil company. One of the clauses in the charter party stated that the owners of the ship promised the charterers that they would pay the broker (Walford) a certain commission on a figure estimated to be the gross amount of hire. In an action for the commission it was *held*—Although Walford was not a party to the contract, which was between the owners and the charterers, there was nevertheless a trust created in his favour and the commission was recoverable.

N.B. The case was, with the agreement of the appellants, dealt with as if the charterers were co-plaintiffs though they had not in fact been joined.

116. Shamia v. Joory, [1958] 1 Q.B. 448

The defendant, an Iraqi merchant having a business in England, employed the plaintiff's brother as an agent in Baghdad. At the end of 1952 the defendant admitted that he owed his agent £1,300, and was requested, and agreed, to pay £500 of this as a gift to the plaintiff, who was the agent's brother and a student in England. The agent informed his brother of the defendant's promise. The plaintiff then wrote to confirm this promise, and the defendant sent a cheque which was not paid because it was not properly drawn. The defendant asked for the return of the cheque to correct it, but shortly afterwards repudiated all liability to the plaintiff having, by this time, reason to doubt the account presented by the plaintiff's brother. The plaintiff now sued to recover the sum of £500 as money had and received to his use (an action in quasi-contract) and Barry, J., *held*—He must succeed.

117. Smith and Snipes Hall Farm Ltd. v. River Douglas Catchment Board, [1949] 2 K.B. 500

In 1938 the defendants entered into an agreement with eleven persons owning land adjoining a certain stream, that, on the landowners paying some part of the cost, the defendants would improve the banks of the stream and maintain the said banks for all time. In 1940 one landowner sold her land to Smith, and in 1944 Smith leased the land to Snipes Hall Farm Ltd. In 1946, because of the defendants' negligence, the banks burst and the adjoining land was flooded. *Held*—The plaintiffs could enforce the covenant given in the agreement of 1938 even though they were strangers to it. The covenants were for the benefit of the land and affected its use and value and could therefore be transferred with it.

118. Tulk *v.* Moxhay (1848), 2 Ph. 774

The plaintiff was the owner of several plots of land in Leicester Square and in 1808 he sold one of them to a person called Elms. Elms agreed, for himself, his heirs and assigns, "to keep the Square Garden open as a pleasure ground and uncovered with buildings." After a number of conveyances, the land was sold to the defendant who claimed a right to build on it. The plaintiff sued for an injunction preventing the development of the land. The defendant, whilst admitting that he purchased the land with notice of the covenant, claimed that he was not bound by it because he had not himself entered into it. *Held*—An injuction to restrain building would be granted because there was a jurisdiction in Equity to prevent, by way of injunction, acts inconsistent with a restrictive covenant on land, so long as the land was acquired with notice of that covenant, and the plaintiff retains land which can benefit from the covenant.

N.B. Such notice may now be constructive where the covenant is registered under the Land Charges Act, 1925.

119. Beswick *v.* Beswick, [1967] 2 All E.R. 1197

A coal merchant agreed to sell the business to his nephew in return for a weekly consultancy fee of £6 10s. payable during his lifetime, and after his death an annuity of £5 per week was to be payable to his widow for her lifetime. After the agreement was signed the nephew took over the business and paid his uncle the sum of £6 10s. as agreed. The uncle died on 3rd November, 1963, and the nephew paid the widow one sum of £5 and then refused to pay her any more. On 30th June, 1964, the widow became the administratrix of her husband's estate, and on 15th July, 1964, she brought an action against the nephew for arrears of the weekly sums and for specific performance of the agreement for the future. She sued in her capacity as administratrix of the estate and also in her personal capacity. Her action failed at first instance and on appeal to the Court of Appeal, [1966] 3 All E.R. 1, it was decided amongst other things that—

(i) specific performance could in a proper case be ordered of a contract to pay money;

(ii) 'property' in Sect. 56 (i) of the Law of Property Act, 1925, included a contractual claim not concerned with realty and that therefore a third party could sue on a contract to which he was a stranger. The widow's claim in her personal capacity was therefore good (*per* Denning, M.R., and Danckwerts, L.J.);

(iii) the widow's claim as administratrix was good because she was not suing in her personal capacity but on behalf of her deceased husband who had been a party to the agreement;

(iv) that no trust in her favour could be inferred.

There was a further appeal to the House of Lords, though not on the creation of a trust, and there it was *held* that the widow's claim as administratrix succeeded, and that specific performance of a contract to pay money could be granted in a proper case. However, having decided the appeal on these grounds their Lordships went on to say that the widow's personal claim would have failed because Sect. 56 of the Law of Property Act, 1925, was limited to cases involving realty. The 1925 Act was a consolidating not a codifying measure, so that if it contained words which were capable of more than one construction, effect should be given to the construction which did not alter the law. It was accepted that when the present provision was contained in the Real Property Act, 1845, it had applied only to realty. Although Sect. 205 (i) of the 1925 Act appeared to have extended the provision to personal property, including things in action, it was expressly qualified by the words: "unless the context otherwise requires," and it was felt that Parliament had not intended to sweep away the rule of privity by what was in effect a sidewind.

120. Charnock v. Liverpool Corporation and Another (1968), 118 New L.J. 612

The plaintiff took his car, which had been damaged in an accident, to the second defendants' garage for repair. On 25th June there was a meeting at the garage between the plaintiff, an assessor employed by the plaintiff's insurance company and the second defendants' service manager. It was agreed that the insurance company would pay the cost of the repairs, and on 25th June the insurance company sent a letter to the second defendants saying: "We confirm that it is in order for you to proceed with the repairs as per your estimate. Please forward your final account to this office."

The garage company took eight weeks to repair the car and were paid by the insurance company. The plaintiff was awarded damages against the garage company for unreasonable delay in repairing the car. The garage company appealed on the ground that there was no contract between them and the plaintiff and that their contract was with the insurance company. *Held*—by the Court of Appeal—that a reasonable time for effecting the repairs would have been five weeks. Furthermore, the plaintiff was entitled to sue because there were two contracts, one between the plaintiff and the garage company, the other between the insurance company and the garage company. Accordingly the plaintiff was entitled to claim damages for delay in effecting repairs.

121. Foakes v. Beer (1884), 9 App. Cas. 605

Mrs. Beer had obtained a judgment against Dr. Foakes for debt and costs. Dr. Foakes agreed to settle the judgment debt by paying £500 down and £150 per half-year until the whole was paid, and Mrs. Beer agreed not to take further action on the judgment. Dr. Foakes duly paid the amount of the judgment plus costs. However, judgment debts carry interest by statute, and while Dr. Foakes had been paying off the debt, interest amounting to £360 had been accruing on the diminishing balance. In this action Mrs. Beer claimed the £360. *Held*—She could do so. Her promise not to take further action on the judgment was not supported by any consideration moving from Dr. Foakes.

122. D. & C. Builders Ltd. v. Rees, [1965] 3 All E.R. 837

D. & C. Builders, a small company, did work for Rees for which he owed £482 13s. 1d. There was at first no dispute as to the work done but Rees did not pay. In August and October, 1964, the plaintiffs wrote for the money and received no reply. On 13th November, 1964, the wife of Rees (who was then ill) telephoned the plaintiffs, complained about the work, and said, "My husband will offer you £300 in settlement. That is all you will get. It is to be in satisfaction." D. & C. Builders, being in desperate straits and faced with bankruptcy without the money, offered to take the £300 and allow a year to

Rees to find the balance. Mrs. Rees replied: "No, we will never have enough money to pay the balance. £300 is better than nothing." The plaintiffs then said: "We have no choice but to accept." Mrs. Rees gave the defendants a cheque and insisted on a receipt "in completion of the account." The plaintiffs, being worried, brought an action for the balance. The defence was bad workmanship and also that there was a binding settlement. The question of settlement was tried as a preliminary issue and the judge, following *Goddard* v. *O'Brien*, [1880] 9 Q.B.D. 33, decided that a cheque for a smaller amount was a good discharge of the debt, this being the generally accepted view of the law since that date. On appeal it was *held* (per The Master of the Rolls, Lord Denning) that *Goddard* v. *O'Brien* was wrongly decided. A smaller sum in cash could be no settlement of a larger sum and "no sensible distinction could be drawn between the payment of a lesser sum by cash and the payment of it by cheque." In the present case there was no true accord. The debtor's wife had held the creditors to ransom, and there was no reason in law or Equity why the plaintiffs should not enforce the full amount of the debt.

123. Good v. Cheesman (1831), 2 B. & Ad. 328

The defendant had accepted two bills of exchange of which the plaintiff was the drawer. After the bills became due and before this action was brought, the plaintiff suggested that the defendant meet his creditors with a view perhaps to an agreement. The meeting was duly held and the defendant entered into an agreement with his creditors whereby the defendant was to pay one-third of his income to a trustee to be named by the creditors, and that this was to be the method by which the defendant's debts were to be paid. It was not clear from the evidence whether the plaintiff attended the meeting, though he certainly did not sign the agreement. There was, however, evidence that the agreement had been in his possession for some time and it was duly stamped before the trial. No trustee was in fact appointed, though the defendant was willing to go on with the agreement. *Held*—The agreement bound the plaintiff and the action on the bills could not be sustained. The consideration, though not supplied to the plaintiff direct, existed in the forbearance of the other creditors. Each was bound in consequence of the agreement of the rest.

The better view is that the basis of this decision is to be found not in the law of contract but in tort, in the sense that once an agreement of this kind has been made it would be a *fraud* on the other creditors for one of their number to sue the debtor separately.

124. Welby v. Drake (1825), 1 C. & P. 557

The plaintiff sued the defendant for the sum of £9 on a debt which had originally been for £18. The defendant's father had paid the plaintiff £9 and the plaintiff had agreed to take that sum in full discharge of the debt. *Held*—The payment of £9 by the defendant's father operated to discharge the debt of £18.

N.B. Here again the basis of the decision is that it would be a fraud on the third party to sue the original debtor. "If the father did pay the smaller sum in satisfaction of this debt, it is a bar to the plaintiff's now recovering against the son; because by suing the son, he commits a fraud on the father, whom he induced to advance his money on the faith of such advance being a discharge of his son from further liability." (*per* Lord Tenterden, C.J.)

125. Combe *v.* Combe, [1951] 2 K.B. 215

The parties were married in 1915 and separated in 1939. In February, 1943, the wife obtained a decree *nisi* of divorce, and a few days later the husband entered into an agreement under which he was to pay his wife £100 per annum, free of income tax. The decree was made absolute in August, 1943. The husband did not make the agreed payments and the wife did not apply to the court for maintenance but chose to rely on the alleged contract. She brought this action for arrears under that contract. Evidence showed that her income was between £700 and £800 per annum and the defendant's was £650 per annum. Byrne, J., at first instance, held that, although the wife had not supplied consideration, the agreement was nevertheless enforceable, following the decision in the *High Trees*[126] case, as a promise made to be acted upon and in fact acted upon. *Held*—(i) That the *High Trees*[126] decision was not intended to create new actions where none existed before, and that it had not abolished the requirement of consideration to support simple contracts. In such cases consideration was a cardinal necessity. (ii) In the words of Birkett, L.J., the doctrine was "a shield not a sword," i.e. a defence to an action, not a cause of action. (iii) The doctrine applied to the modification of existing agreements by subsequent promises and had no relevance to the formation of a contract. (iv) It was not possible to find consideration in the fact that the wife forbore to claim maintenance from the court, since no such contractual undertaking by her could have been binding even if she had given it. Therefore this action by the wife must fail because the agreement was not supported by consideration.

126. Central London Property Trust Ltd. *v.* High Trees House Ltd., [1947] K.B. 130

In 1937 the plaintiffs granted to the defendants a lease of ninety-nine years of a new block of flats at a rent of £2,500 per annum. The lease was under seal. During the period of the war the flats were by no means fully let owing to the absence of people from the London area. The defendant company, which was a subsidiary of the plaintiff company, realised that it could not meet the rent out of the profits then being made on the flats, and in 1940 the parties entered into an agreement which reduced the rent to £1,250 per annum, this agreement being put into writing but not sealed. The defendants continued to pay the reduced rent from 1941 to the beginning of 1945, by which time the flats were fully let, and they continued to pay the reduced rent thereafter. In September, 1945, the receiver of the plaintiff company investigated the matter and asked for arrears of £7,916, suggesting that the liability created by the lease still existed, and that the agreement of 1940 was not supported by any consideration. The receiver then brought this friendly action to establish the legal position. He claimed £625, being the difference in rent for the two quarters ending 29th September and 25th December, 1945. *Held*—(i) A simple contract can in Equity vary a deed (i.e. the lease), though it had not done so here because the simple contract was not supported by consideration. (ii) As the agreement for the reduction of rent had been acted upon by the defendants, the plaintiffs were estopped in Equity from claiming the full rent from 1941 until early 1945 when the flats were fully let. After that time they were entitled to do so because the second agreement was only operative during the continuance of the conditions which gave rise to it. To this extent the limited claim of the receiver succeeded.

N.B. The rule established by the case seems to be that where a person has indicated by a promise that he is not going to insist upon his strict rights, as a result of which the other party alters his position by acting on that promise, then the law, although it does not give a cause of action in damages if the promise is broken, will require it to be honoured to the extent of refusing to allow the promissor the right to act inconsistently with it, even though the promise is not supported by consideration. The doctrine has been called "equitable estoppel," "quasi-estoppel," and "promissory estoppel," in order to distinguish it from estoppel at common law. At common law estoppel arises when the defendant by his conduct suggests that certain existing facts are true. Here the estoppel was based on a promise not conduct, and the promise related to future conduct not to existing facts.

127. Durham Fancy Goods Ltd. *v.* Michael Jackson (Fancy Goods) Ltd., [1968] 2 All E.R. 987

On 18th September, 1967, the plaintiffs drew a bill of exchange on the first defendants in the following form, "M. Jackson (Fancy Goods) Co." The bill was signed by Mr. Jackson who was the director and company secretary. The bill was dishonoured and the plaintiffs brought an action against Mr. Jackson contending that by signing the form of acceptance he had committed a criminal offence under Sect. 108 of the Companies Act. 1948, and had made himself personally liable on the bill because he should either have returned the bill with a request that it be re-addressed to Michael Jackson (Fancy Goods) Ltd., or he should have accepted it "M. Jackson (Fancy Goods) Ltd. p.p. Michael Jackson (Fancy Goods) Ltd., Michael Jackson." It was *held*—by Donaldson, J.—that the misdescription was in breach of Sect. 108 of the Companies Act, 1948, and that Mr. Jackson was personally liable, under the section, to pay the bill. However, since the error was really that of the plaintiffs they were estopped from enforcing Mr. Jackson's personal liability. The principle of equity upon which the promissory estoppel cases were based was applicable and barred the plaintiff's claim. That principle was formulated by Lord Cairns in *Hughes* v. *Metropolitan Railway Co.* (1877), 2 App. Cas. 439, p. 448, and although in his enunciation Lord Cairns assumed a pre-existing contractual relationship between the parties, that was not essential provided that there was a pre-existing legal relationship which could in certain circumstances give rise to liabilities and penalties. Such a relationship was created by Sect. 108.

N.B. A holder other than the plaintiffs might have been able to bring an action against Mr. Jackson under Sect. 108 since such a holder would not have been affected by the equity in that he would not have drawn the bill in an incorrect name.

N.B. Sect. 108 provides: "(1) every company . . . (c) shall have its name mentioned in legible characters . . . in all bills of exchange . . . purporting to be signed by or on behalf of the company . . . (4) If an officer of the company or any person on his behalf . . . (b) signs . . . on behalf of the company any bill of exchange . . . wherein its name is not mentioned in manner aforesaid . . . he shall be liable to a fine not exceeding £50, and shall further be personally liable to the holder of the bill of exchange . . . for the amount thereof unless it is duly paid by the company."

128. Ajayi *v.* Briscoe (Nigeria) Ltd., [1964] 3 All E.R. 556

The plaintiff claimed hire-purchase instalments due on Seddon Tipper lorries supplied to the defendant. The defendant claimed the equitable principle of promissory estoppel because, when the lorries could not be used by reason of servicing difficulties, the plaintiff had promised to service the vehicles and had also said, "we are agreeable to you withholding instalments due on Seddon Tippers as long as they are withdrawn from active service." The defendant could not establish that he had changed his position because of the promise. He was not using the lorries when they went for service and still did not use them after the plaintiffs had repaired them. He was not able to show that he had had to re-organise his business in any way, but in spite of this still did not pay the instalments. *Held*—by the Privy Council—that the plaintiff's action succeeded. The defence of promissory estoppel did not apply.

129. Mighell *v.* Sultan of Johore, [1894] 1 Q.B. 149

The Sultan, who was a foreign sovereign, was living in England as a private person under an assumed name. He made a promise of marriage to the plaintiff. *Held*—the promise was not actionable.

130. Coutts & Co. *v.* Browne-Lecky, [1947] K.B. 104

The first defendant, an infant, had been permitted to overdraw his account with the plaintiffs, who were bankers. The overdraft was guaranteed by the second and third defendants, who were adults. The overdraft was not repaid and the plaintiffs now sued the adult guarantors. *Held*—Since the loan to the infant was void under the Infants Relief Act, 1874, the infant could not be in default because he was not liable to repay the loan. Since the essence of a guarantee is that the guarantor is liable for the default or miscarriage of the principal debtor, it followed that the adult guarantors could not be liable. The action therefore failed.

N.B. Had the contract been one of indemnity the adult defendants would have been liable, because, under a contract of indemnity, the person giving the indemnity is in effect the principal debtor and his liability does not depend on the default of any other person. (*Yeoman Credit Ltd.* v. *Latter*, [1961] 1 W.L.R. 828.)

131. R. *v.* Wilson (1879), 5 Q.B.D. 28

Wilson was charged with, and convicted of, feloniously leaving England with intent to defraud his creditors. His conviction was quashed because his debts were void under the Infants' Relief Act, 1874, and in law he had no creditors.

132. Nash *v.* Inman, [1908] 2 K.B. 1

The plaintiff was a Savile Row tailor and the defendant was an infant undergraduate at Trinity College, Cambridge. The plaintiff sent his agent to Cambridge because he had heard that the defendant was spending money freely, and might be the sort of person who would be interested in high-class clothing. As a result of the agent's visit, the plaintiff supplied the defendant with various articles of clothing to the value of £145 0s. 3d. during the period October, 1902, to June, 1903. The clothes included eleven fancy waistcoats. The plaintiff now sued the infant for the price of the clothes. Evidence showed that the plaintiff's father was in a good position, being an architect with a town and country house, and it could be said that the clothes supplied were suitable to the defendant's position in life. However, his father proved that the defendant was amply supplied with such clothes when the plaintiff delivered the clothing now in question. *Held*—The plaintiff's claim failed because he had not established that the goods supplied were necessaries.

133. Elkington *v.* Amery, [1936] 2 All E.R. 86

The defendant was an infant and the son of a former cabinet minister. He purchased from the plaintiffs an engagement ring and an eternity ring, the court treating the latter as a wedding ring. He also purchased a lady's gold vanity bag. The Court of Appeal treated the two rings as being necessaries, but did not accept that the vanity bag was a necessary because there was no evidence to show that it was purchased in respect of the engagement.

134. Roberts *v.* Gray, [1913] 1 K.B. 520

The defendant wished to become a professional billiards player and entered into an agreement with the plaintiff, a leading professional, to go on a joint tour. The plaintiff went to some trouble in order to organise the tour, but a dispute arose between the parties and the defendant refused to go. The plaintiff now sued for damages of £6,000. *Held*—The contract was for the infant's benefit, being in effect for his instruction as a billiards player. Therefore the plaintiff could sustain an action for damages for breach of contract, and damages of £1,500 were awarded.

135. Chaplin *v.* Leslie Frewin (Publishers), [1965] 3 All E.R. 764

The plaintiff, the infant son of a famous father, made a contract with the defendants under which they were to publish a book written for him and telling his life story. The plaintiff sought to avoid the contract on the ground that the book gave an inaccurate picture of his approach to life. *Held*—Amongst other things—that the contract was binding if it was for the infant's benefit. The time to determine that question was when the contract was made and at that time it was for the infant's benefit and could not be avoided.

N.B. In *Denmark Productions* v. *Boscobel Productions* (1967), 111 S.J. 715, Widgery, J., held that a contract by which an infant appoints managers and agents to look after his business affairs is, in modern conditions, necessary if he is to earn his living and rise to fame, and if it is for his benefit it will be upheld by analogy with a contract of service.

136. De Francesco *v.* Barnum (1890), 45 Ch. D. 430

Two infants bound themselves in contract to the plaintiff for seven years to be taught stage dancing. The infants agreed that they would not accept any engagements without his consent. They later accepted an engagement with Barnum and the plaintiff sued Barnum for interfering with the contractual relationship between himself and the infants, and also to enforce the apprenticeship deed against the infants and to obtain damages for its breach. The contract was, of course, for the infants' benefit and was *prima facie* binding on them. However, when the court considered the deed in greater detail, it emerged that there were certain onerous terms in it. For example the infants bound themselves not to marry during the apprenticeship; the payment was hardly generous, the plaintiff agreeing to pay them 9d. per night and 6d. for matinee appearances for the first three years, and 1s. per night and 6d. for matinee performances during the remainder of the apprenticeship. The plaintiff did not undertake to maintain them whilst they were unemployed and did not undertake to find them engagements. The infants could also be engaged in performances abroad at a fee of 5s. per week. Further the plaintiff could terminate the contract if he felt that the infants were not suitable for the career of dancer. It appeared from the contract that the infants were at the absolute disposal of the plaintiff. *Held*—The deed was an unreasonable one and was therefore unenforceable against the infants. Barnum could not, therefore, be held liable, since the tort of interference with a contractual relationship presupposes the existence of an enforceable contract.

137. Clements *v.* L. & N.W. Railway, [1894] 2 Q.B. 482

Clements became a porter with the railway company and agreed to join the company's insurance scheme and to forgo his rights under the Employers' Liability Act, 1880. He sustained an injury at work and claimed under the company's scheme. He now made a claim under the Act on the grounds that the contract was not for his benefit since it deprived him of an action under the Act. The company's scheme was on the whole a favourable one because it covered more injuries than the statute but the scale of compensation was lower. *Held*—The contract as a whole was for the infant's benefit and was binding on him. He had no claim under the Act.

138. Mercantile Union Guarantee Corporation *v.* Ball, [1937] 2 K.B. 498

The purchase on hire-purchase terms of a motor lorry by an infant carrying on business as a haulage contractor was *held* not to be a contract for necessaries, but a trading contract by which the infant could not be bound.

N.B. It would be possible for the owner to recover the lorry because a hire-purchase contract is a contract of bailment not a sale. Thus, ownership does not pass when the goods are delivered.

139. Steinberg *v.* Scala (Leeds) Ltd., [1923] 2 Ch. 452

The plaintiff, Miss Steinberg, purchased shares in the defendant company and paid certain sums of money on application, on allotment and on one call. Being unable to meet future calls, she repudiated the contract whilst still an infant and claimed—

(*a*) Rectification of the Register of Members to remove her name therefrom, thus relieving her from liability on future calls; and

(*b*) The recovery of the money already paid.

The company agreed to rectify the register and issue was joined on the claim to recover the money paid.

Held—The claim under (*b*) above failed because there had not been total failure of consideration. The shares had some value and gave some rights, even though the plaintiff had not received any dividends and the shares had always stood at a discount on the market.

140. Davies *v.* Beynon-Harris (1931), 47 T.L.R. 424

An infant took a lease of a flat a fortnight before attaining his majority. Three years later he was sued for arrears of rent and claimed that he could avoid the contract. *Held*—He was liable to pay the rent because the lease was voidable not void, and was now binding on him because he had not repudiated it during minority or within a reasonable time thereafter.

N.B. An infant cannot take a legal estate in land, Sect. 1 (6), Law of Property Act, 1925. This prevents him from taking a lease at law. However, he does obtain an equitable interest and must observe the covenants in the lease so long as he retains a beneficial interest in the property.

141. Goode *v.* Harrison (1821), 5 B. & Ald. 147

An infant partner, who took no steps to avoid a partnership contract upon attaining his majority, was *held* liable for the debts of the firm incurred after he came of age.

142. Coxhead *v.* Mullis (1878), 3 C.P.D. 439

Mullis whilst an infant offered to marry the plaintiff and she accepted him. After Mullis came of age he continued to recognise the engagement and wrote affectionate letters to the plaintiff and paid visits to her but made no fresh promise to marry her. In an action by the plaintiff for breach of promise it was *held* that the defence of infancy succeeded in view of Sect. 2 of the Infants Relief Act, 1874. Although ratification might have been enough at common law the section no longer allowed ratification to be effective.

143. Northcote *v.* Doughty (1879), 4 C.P.D. 385

The defendant offered marriage to the plaintiff and she agreed to accept him if he obtained his parents' consent. The defendant later wrote to the plaintiff saying that he had told his mother and father all about it and that their reaction was favourable. When he came of age he wrote to the plaintiff saying that he would now marry her as soon as he could. It was *held* that there was sufficient evidence from which the jury could infer a fresh promise to marry after age.

144. Pearce *v.* Brain, [1929] 2 K.B. 310

Pearce an infant, exchanged his motor-cycle for a motor-car belonging to Brain. The infant had little use out of the car, and had in fact driven it only a short distance when it broke down because of serious defects in the back axle. Pearce now sued to recover his motor-cycle, claiming that the consideration had wholly failed. *Held*—(*a*) That a contract for the exchange of goods, whilst not a sale of goods, is a contract for the supply of goods, and that if the goods are not necessaries, the contract is void if with an infant. (*b*) The car was not a necessary good and therefore the contract was void. (*c*) Even so the infant could only recover the motor-cycle in the same circumstances as he could recover money paid under a void contract, i.e. if the consideration had wholly failed. The court considered that the infant had received a benefit under the contract, albeit small, and that he could not recover the motor-cycle.

145. Corpe *v.* Overton (1833), 10 Bing. 252

An infant agreed to enter into a partnership and deposited £100 with the defendant as security for the due performance of the contract. The infant rescinded the contract before the partnership came into being. *Held*—He could recover the £100 because he had received no benefit, having never been a partner.

146. Stocks *v.* Wilson, [1913] 2 K.B. 235

An infant obtained furniture from the plaintiff by falsely stating that he was of full age. *Held*—The property in the furniture passed to the infant, under the Infants Relief Act, 1874. Even if he sold the property the infant could not be sued in conversion. The infant had sold part of the furniture to a third party for £30, and Lush, J., *held* that the plaintiff could recover this sum by applying the equitable principle of restitution.

N.B. Pearce v. *Brain*,[144] supports *Stocks* v. *Wilson* because, if the property in the car had not passed to the infant, there would have been total failure of consideration, thus enabling him to recover his motor-cycle.

147. Leslie (R) Ltd. *v.* Sheill, [1914] 3 K.B. 607

Sheill an infant borrowed £400 from R. Leslie, Ltd., moneylenders, by fraudulently representing that he was of full age. The contract was void under Sect. 1 of the Infants Relief Act, 1874, and the plaintiffs sued for the return of the money, either as damages for the tort of deceit, or as money had and received to the plaintiff's use. *Held*—Neither claim could succeed because they were attempts to circumvent the Act and the infant was entitled to retain the money advanced. With regard to the equitable doctrine of restitution, it was suggested that, since the money had been spent and could not be precisely traced, restitution was not possible; for to order restitution would mean that the infant would have to pay an equivalent sum out of his present or future resources, and this would be closer to enforcing a void contract than to granting equitable restitution. It was also suggested that *Stocks* v. *Wilson*,[146] was wrongly decided in so far as Lush, J., granted restitution of the £30 which the infant had received by selling the property to a third party. The court in this case suggested that "Restitution ends where repayment begins," i.e. unless the actual property passing under the contract can be recovered, the remedy of restitution does not lie to recover money or property received in its stead.

148. Burnard *v.* Haggis (1863), 14 C.B.N.S. 45

Haggis was an undergraduate and hired the plaintiff's mare for riding. The plaintiff warned the defendant that the mare was not to be used for "jumping or larking." The defendant allowed a friend to ride the mare and the latter put the mare at a fence, in consequence of which the mare was impaled on a stake and died. The plaintiff sued the defendant in trespass. *Held*—The infant was liable, though the trespass actually happened because there had been a contract, yet the act of jumping the mare was just as distinct from the contract as if the defendant had run a knife into her and killed her. Therefore the defendant's infancy, which might have been a defence in contract, did not apply in this action for pure tort.

149. Ashbury Railway Carriage & Iron Co. *v.* Riche (1875), L.R. 7 H.L. 653

The company bought a concession for the construction of a railway system in Belgium, and entered into an agreement whereby Messrs. Riche were to construct a railway line. Messrs. Riche commenced the work, and the company paid over certain sums of money in connection with the contract. The company later ran into difficulties, and the shareholders wished the directors to take over the contract in a personal capacity, and indemnify the shareholders. The directors thereupon repudiated the contract on behalf of the company, and Messrs. Riche sued for breach of contract. The case turned on whether the company was engaged in an *ultra vires* activity in building a complete railway system, because if so, the contract it had made with Messrs. Riche would be *ultra vires* and void, and the claim against the company would fail. The objects clause of the company's memorandum stated that it was established—

"to make or sell or lend on hire railway carriages, wagons and all kinds of railway plant, fittings, machinery and rolling stock; to carry on the business of mechanical engineers and general contractors, to purchase and sell as merchants timber, coal, metal and other materials, and to buy and sell such materials on commission or as agents."

The House of Lords *held* that the purchase of the concession to build a complete railway system from Antwerp to Tournai was *ultra vires* and void because it was not within the objects of the company. The words empowering the company to carry on the business of general contracting must be construed *ejusdem generis* with the preceding words, and must therefore be restricted to contracting in the field of plant, fittings and machinery only. The contract with Messrs. Riche was therefore void, and the directors were entitled to repudiate it. It was also stated that even if all the shareholders had assented to the contract, it would still have been void because there can be no ratification of an *ultra vires* contract.

150. Re Jon Beauforte, [1953] Ch. 131

The company was authorised by its memorandum to carry on the business of costumiers, tailors, drapers, haberdashers, milliners and the like. It decided to manufacture veneered wall panels, and for this purpose had a factory erected, and ordered and was supplied with veneers. It was clear that the contracts for the erection of the factory and supply of veneers were *ultra vires* and void, but one of the questions before the court was whether the liquidator of the company had been correct in disallowing a claim made by a supplier of coke. The supplier argued that the coke might have been used in the good side of the business, and that he did not know that the coke was to be used for an *ultra vires* purpose. The court decided against him because the order for coke was given on headed paper describing the company as "veneered panel manufacturers." From this the coke supplier was deemed to know that the contract was *ultra vires*, because everyone is deemed to know the contents of the memorandum of association of a registered company, which is registered at the Companies' Registry, London, and can be inspected.

N.B. This doctrine of constructive notice of a company's objects is now well established and yet it is based on the assumption that, because inspection is possible, it should always be made before contracts are entered into. However, business would grind to a halt if this sort of inquiry were made every time a contract was made; it does not accord, therefore, with normal business practice.

151. Deuchar *v.* The Gas Light and Coke Co., [1925] A.C. 691

The plaintiff was a shareholder in the defendant company and was also the secretary of a company which supplied the defendants with caustic soda. The plaintiff sought a declaration from the court that the manufacture of caustic soda and chlorine by the defendants, and the erection of a factory for the purpose, was *ultra vires* the company. He also asked for an injunction to restrain the defendants from manufacturing caustic soda and chlorine. Astbury, J., at first instance, had found that the activities were fairly incidental to the powers given in the objects clause, and the Court of Appeal affirmed this decision. On appeal to the House of Lords it appeared that the defendants derived their powers from a special Act of Parliament, the Gas Light and Coke Companies Act, 1868, which gave them power to make and supply gas and deal with and sell by-products. The Act authorised the conversion of the by-products into a marketable state. One of the residuals of gas-making was naphthalene which could be converted into beta-naphthol and profitably sold, conversion being by the use of caustic soda. The company had formerly purchased this from the company of which the plaintiff was secretary, but later erected a factory on their land and began to make it themselves, though they only made what they required for their own use and did not make caustic soda for resale. Chlorine was a by-product of the manufacture of caustic soda, and the chlorine, it was admitted, was converted into bleaching powder and sold. The House of Lords *held* that the manufacture of caustic soda was fairly incidental to the company's powers, and although the sale of the bleaching powder was not incidental, the matter was trivial and on the basis of the maxim *de minimis non curat lex* (the law does not concern itself with trifles) the court would not interfere.

152. Cotman *v.* Brougham, [1918] A.C. 514

The parties to this action were liquidators. Cotman was liquidator of the Essequibo Rubber Estates Ltd., and Brougham was liquidator of Anglo-Cuban Oil Co. It appeared that E underwrote the shares in A-C although the main clause of E's objects clause was to develop rubber estates abroad. However, a sub-clause allowed E to promote companies and deal in the shares of other companies and gave numerous other powers. The final clause of E's objects clause said in effect that each sub-clause should be considered as an independent main object. The E Company, not having paid for the shares which it had agreed to underwrite, was put on the list of contributories of A-C, and E's liquidator asked that his company be removed from that list because the contract to underwrite was *ultra vires* and void. *Held*, by the House of Lords, that it was not, and that the E Company was liable to pay for the shares underwritten. The final clause of E's objects clause meant that each object could be pursued alone, because the Registrar had accepted the memorandum in this form and had registered the company. All the judges of the House of Lords deplored the idea of companies being registered with an objects clause in this wide form, and thought that the matter ought to have been raised by mandamus by the Registrar refusing to register the company. However, since the certificate of incorporation had been issued, it was conclusive; and matters concerning the company's registration could not be gone into.

153. Introductions Ltd. *v.* National Provincial Bank Ltd., [1969] 1 All E.R. 887

Introductions Ltd. was incorporated in 1951 and the objects of the company were to promote and provide entertainment and accommodation for overseas visitors. This business was not successful and in November, 1960, the company embarked on a new business, pig farming. The company ran short of cash and arranged to borrow money from the defendants. The company executed certain debentures in favour of the bank for its indebtedness, which at the time of the winding up order in November, 1965, was £29,571.

The bank now wished to enforce its security under the debentures and recover the loan. The liquidators of the company claimed that the loan was *ultra vires* and void, and the bank did not dispute that it was aware that the company's business was that of pig breeding and had notice of the company's objects. However, one of the sub-clauses of the memorandum related to borrowing and the bank said it was entitled to lend money on the strength of the sub-clause alone as it formed one of the objects of the company. There was a proviso to the memorandum which clearly stated that all sub-clauses of the memorandum were to be treated as separate and independent objects. *Held*—by the Court of Appeal—that the loan was *ultra vires* and void. The bare power to borrow contained in the sub-clause could not legitimately stand alone.

The company must have had in view purposes to which the money was to be applied, i.e. for the purposes of the objects of the company. This being so the sub-clause did not authorise the raising or borrowing of money for something which was not an object of the company. However if the bank had not known the purpose for which the money was required the loan would have been valid because the bank was not bound to inquire as to its purpose.

154. Bell Houses Ltd. *v.* City Wall Properties Ltd., [1966] 2 All E.R. 674

The plaintiff company claimed £20,000 as commission under an alleged contract with the defendant company for the introduction of the latter to a financier who would lend the defendant company £1,000,000 for property development. As a preliminary issue the defendant company alleged that the contract was *ultra vires* and could not be enforced against them.

The principal business of the plaintiff company was the development of housing estates, and therefore the occasional raising of finance formed a necessary part of its activities. In consequence the company had obtained valuable knowledge of various sources of finance and because of this the company was able to arrange finance for the defendants. The defendants contended that the plaintiff company, in arranging finance for an outside organisation, was, in effect, embarking on a new type of business, i.e. "mortgage broking," and since this was not expressly included in the objects, nor reasonably incidental thereto, it was *ultra vires*. One of the sub-clauses in the objects clause of the plaintiff company was as follows: "To carry on any other trade or business *whatsoever* which can *in the opinion of the board of directors* be *advantageously* carried on by (the company) in connection with, or as ancillary to, any of the above businesses or the general business of the (company)." *Held*— by the Court of Appeal—that the alleged contract was *intra vires* in particular because of the clause set out above. In the court's view the *bona fide* opinion of the board, in this case represented by the managing director who arranged the finance, that the contract could be advantageously carried on with the company's principal business, was enough no matter how unreasonable in the *objective* sense that opinion might seem to be.

155. Sharp Bros. and Knight *v.* Chant, [1917] 1 K.B. 771

Landlord and tenant agreed that the rent of a certain small house should be increased by the sum of 6d. per week. The tenant paid this increased rent for some time and it was then discovered that Rent Restriction legislation prevented the landlord from recovering any increase in rent he might make on certain properties of which the small house in question was one. *Held*—The tenant had paid the extra rent under a mistake of law, and could not sue for its return or deduct it from future payments of rent.

156. Solle v. Butcher, [1950] 1 K.B. 671

Butcher had agreed to lease a flat in Beckenham to Solle at a yearly rental of £250, the lease to run for seven years. Both parties had acted on the assumption that the flat, which had been substantially reconstructed so as to be virtually a new flat, was no longer controlled by the Rent Restriction legislation then in force. If it were so controlled, the maximum rent payable would be £140 per annum. Nevertheless Butcher would have been entitled to increase that rent by charging 8 per cent of the cost of repairs and improvements which would bring the figure up to about £250 per annum, the rent actually charged, if he had served a statutory notice on Solle before the new lease was executed. No such notice was in fact served. Actually they both for a time mistakenly thought that the flat was decontrolled when this was not the case. Solle realised the mistake after some two years, and sought to recover the rent he had over-paid and to continue as tenant for the balance of the seven years as a statutory tenant at £140 per annum. Butcher counterclaimed for rescission of the lease in Equity. It was *held* by a majority of the Court of Appeal that the mistake was one of *fact* and not of law, i.e. the fact that the flat was still within the pro-visions of the Rent Acts, and this was a bilateral mistake as to quality which would not invalidate the contract at common law. However, on the counter-claim for rescission, it was *held* that in spite of the decisions in *Seddon* v. *North Eastern Salt Co.* (1905)[200] and *Angel* v. *Jay* (1911),[201] the lease could be rescin-ded even though it had been executed. In order not to dispossess Solle, the court offered him the following alternatives—

(*a*) to surrender the lease entirely; or

(*b*) to remain in possession as a mere licensee until a new lease could be drawn up after Butcher had had time to serve the statutory notice which would allow him to add a sum for repairs to the £140 which would bring the lawful rent up to £250 per annum.

157. Cooper *v.* Phibbs (1867), L.R. 2 H.L. 149

Cooper agreed to take a lease of a fishery from Phibbs. Unknown to either party the fishery already belonged to Cooper who now brought the action to set aside the lease and for delivery up of the lease. *Held*—The agreement must be set aside on the grounds of common or identical bilateral mistake. However, since Equity has the power to give ancillary relief, Phibbs was given a lien on the fishery for the improvements he had made to it during the time he believed it to be his. This lien could be discharged by Cooper paying Phibbs the value of the improvements.

158. Foster *v.* Mackinnon (1869), L.R. 4 C.P. 704

The plaintiff was a person entitled to receive payment on a bill of exchange for £3,000; the defendant was an endorser of the bill and was *prima facie* liable on it. The evidence showed that the defendant was an old man of feeble sight, and that he had signed the bill under the mistaken impression that it was a guaran-tee. *Held*—The defendant was not in the circumstances negligent in signing the bill and his plea of mistake was successful so that he was not liable on it. This plea is commonly called *non est factum*.

159. Carlisle and Cumberland Banking Co. *v.* Bragg, [1911] 1 K.B. 489

Two persons named Rigg and Bragg were drinking together. Rigg showed a paper to Bragg and said that it was a duplicate of an insurance document signed by Bragg on the previous day. Rigg asserted that the original document had become wet and blurred by rain, and asked Bragg to sign the duplicate, which Bragg did. Actually it was a continuing guarantee of Rigg's current account with the bank, and by forging the signature of a witness Rigg obtained an over-draft. The bank now sued Bragg on the guarantee. *Held*—Although Bragg was negligent in signing the document, he was able to plead mistake so that the guarantee was not enforceable against him.

N.B. The Court of Appeal, in *Muskham Finance Ltd.* v. *Howard*, [1963] 3 All E.R. 81, and *Gallie* v. *Lee* (1969)[160] suggested that this decision should be reconsidered, implying that negligence in signing the document might estop the signer from pleading that the document was mistakenly signed. (See now *Saunders* v. *Anglia Building Society*, 1970.)[160a]

160. Gallie *v.* Lee and Another, [1968] 2 All E.R. 322

The plaintiff, a widow aged 78 years, signed a document which Lee told her was a deed of gift of her house to her nephew. She did not read the document but believed what Lee had told her. In fact the document was an assignment of her leasehold interest in the house to Lee and Lee later mortgaged that interest to a building society. In an action by the plaintiff against Lee and the building society it was *held*—(i) that the assignment was void and did not confer a title on Lee, (ii) although the plaintiff had been negligent she was not estopped from denying the validity of the deed against the building society for she owed it no duty. The Court of Appeal, in allowing an appeal by the building society, *held* that the plea of *non est factum* was not available to the plaintiff. The transaction intended and carried out was the same, i.e. an assignment.

160(*a*). *Saunders* v. *Anglia Building Society*, [1970] 3 All E.R. 961

This appeal to the House of Lords was brought by the executrix of Mrs. Gallie's estate. The House of Lords affirmed the decision of the Court of Appeal but took the opportunity to restate the law relating to the avoidance of documents on the ground of mistake as follows—

(*a*) The plea of *non est factum* will rarely be available to a person of full capacity who signs a document apparently having legal effect without troubling to read it.

(*b*) A mistake as to the identity of the person in whose favour the document is executed will not normally support a plea of *non est factum* though it may do if the court regards the mistake as fundamental (Lord Reid and Lord Hodson). Neither judge felt that the personality error made by Mrs. Gallie was sufficient to support the plea.

(*c*) The distinction taken in *Howatson* v. *Webb*, [1908] 1 Ch. 1 that the mistake must be as to the class or character of the document and not merely as to its contents was regarded as confusing and illogical. A better test would be whether the document which was in fact signed was "fundamentally different," "radically different" or "totally different." This test is more flexible than the character/contents one and yet it still restricts the operation of the plea of *non est factum*.

(*d*) *Carlisle and Cumberland Banking Co.* v. *Bragg*, 1911,[159] was overruled. Henceforth carelessness on the part of a person signing a document will prevent him from raising the plea. In addition the person claiming to have taken proper care bears the burden of proving that he did.

161. Legal and General Assurance Society *v.* General Metal Agencies, [1969] 113 S.J. 876

Legal and General, who were the landlords of General Metal Agencies, served a statutory notice of termination of the tenancy. General Metal applied to the County Court for a new tenancy but Legal and General opposed the application on the grounds of persistent late payment of rent and it was dismissed. However, Legal and General subsequently sent by mistake a computerised demand for the next quarter's rent in advance over the signature of their general manager. General Metal sent a cheque for the rent and this was presented to the bank and paid. In this action Legal and General claimed possession of the premises and General Metal contended that Legal and General by demanding and accepting the next quarter's rent in advance had by implication created a new tenancy. It was *Held*—by Fisher, J.—

(i) that Legal and General were entitled to show that the demand was sent and the rent received by mistake. There was no intention to create a new tenancy, the use of a computer making no difference to the established common law principle;

(ii) that, in consequence, Legal and General were entitled to possession of the premises.

162. Higgins (W.) Ltd. *v.* Northampton Corporation, [1927] 1 Ch. 128

The plaintiff entered into a contract with the corporation for the erection of dwelling houses. The plaintiff made an arithmetical error in arriving at his price, having deducted a certain sum twice over. The corporation sealed the contract, assuming that the price arrived at by the plaintiff was correct. *Held*— The contract was binding on the parties. Rectification of such a contract was not possible because the power of the court to rectify agreements made under mistake is confined to common not unilateral mistake. Here, rectification would only have been granted if fraud or misrepresentation had been present.

163. Cundy *v.* Lindsay (1878), 3 App. Cas. 459

The respondents were linen manufacturers with a business in Belfast. A fraudulent person named Blenkarn wrote to the respondents from 37 Wood Street, Cheapside, ordering a quantity of handkerchiefs but signed his letter in such a way that it appeared to come from Messrs. Blenkiron, who were a well-known and solvent house doing business at 123 Wood Street. The respondents knew of the existence of Blenkiron but did not know the address. Accordingly the handkerchiefs were sent to 37 Wood Street. Blenkarn then sold them to the appellants, and was later convicted and sentenced for the fraud. The respondents sued the appellants in conversion claiming that the contract they had made with Blenkarn was void for mistake, and that the property had not passed to Blenkarn or to the appellants. *Held*—The respondents succeeded; there was an operative mistake as to the party with whom they were contracting.

164. King's Norton Metal Co. Ltd. *v.* Edridge, Merrett & Co. Ltd. (1897), 14 T.L.R. 98

The plaintiffs were metal manufacturers in Worcestershire, the defendants being metal manufacturers at Birmingham. In 1896 the plaintiffs received a letter from a firm called Hallam & Co., Soho Wire Works, Sheffield. The letter was written on headed paper, the heading depicting a large factory, and in one corner was a statement that the company had depots and agencies at Belfast, Lille and Ghent. The letter requested a quotation for the supply of brass rivet wire, and a quotation was sent and later an order was received and the goods dispatched. These goods were never paid for. It later emerged that a person named Wallis had set up in business as Hallam & Co. and had fraudulently obtained the goods by the above methods. Wallis sold the goods to the defendants who bought *bona fide* and for value. The plaintiffs had previously done business with Wallis's firm, Hallam & Co., and had been paid by cheque signed Hallam & Co. The plaintiffs sued the defendants in conversion, regarding this as a better action than the one for fraud against Wallis. In order to sustain the action in conversion, the plaintiffs had to establish that the contract with Hallam & Co. was void for mistake, and that because of this the defendants had no title to the wire. *Held*—The plaintiffs' claim failed because the contract with Hallam & Co. was voidable for fraud but not void for mistake. The firm Hallam & Co. was a mere alias for Wallis, and since there was no other firm of Hallam & Co. with whom the plaintiffs had previously done business, they were really dealing with one person who from time to time used different names, i.e. Wallis or Hallam & Co. Although the contract was voidable for fraud, it had not been avoided when the goods were sold to the defendants; their title was good and they were not liable in conversion.

165. Phillips *v.* Brooks Ltd., [1919] 2 K.B. 243

A fraudulent person named North went into the plaintiff's jeweller's shop and selected goods to the value of £3,000. He then asked whether he could take away one of the items (a ring) which he said he wanted for his wife's birthday. He said, no doubt to reassure the jeweller, that he was Sir George Bullough of St. James's Square. The plaintiff had heard of the name and, on referring to a directory and finding the address was correct, he allowed North to take away the ring in return for a cheque. Then North, using the name Firth, pledged the ring with the defendants, who were pawnbrokers. They took the ring in good faith and advanced £350 upon it. North was subsequently convicted of obtaining the ring by false pretences, and this action was brought by the plaintiff who claimed that he was mistaken in his contract with North, and that since the contract was void the property had not passed. He, therefore, asked that the ring be returned to him or that he be paid £450, its value. *Held*—The contract between Phillips and North was not void for mistake and Brooks obtained a good title to the ring. The representation by North that he was Sir George Bullough only affected the taking away of the ring and the acceptance by Phillips of the cheque. By that time the sale had taken place and so far as the sale was concerned the identity of the purchaser was not important to Phillips.

166. Ingram and others *v.* Little, [1961] 1 Q.B. 31

The plaintiffs, three ladies, were the joint owners of a car. They wished to sell the car and advertised it for sale. A fraudulent person, introducing himself as Hutchinson, offered to buy it. He was taken for a drive in it and during conversation said that his home was at Caterham. Later the rogue offered £700 for the car but this was refused, though a subsequent offer of £717 was one which the plaintiffs were prepared to accept. At this point the rogue produced a cheque book and one of the plaintiffs, who was conducting the negotiations, said that the deal was off and that they would not accept a cheque. The rogue then said that he was P. G. M. Hutchinson, that he had business interests in Guildford, and that he lived at Stanstead House, Stanstead Road, Caterham. One of the plaintiffs checked this information in a telephone directory and, on finding it to be accurate, allowed him to take the car in return for a cheque. The cheque was dishonoured, and in the meantime the rogue had sold the car to the defendants and had disappeared without trace. The plaintiffs sued for the return of the car, or for its value as damages in conversion, claiming that the contract between themselves and the rogue was void for mistake, and that the property had not passed. At the trial judgment was given for the plaintiffs, Slade, J., finding the contract void. His judgment was affirmed by the Court of Appeal, though Devlin, L.J., dissented, saying that the mistake made was as to the credit-worthiness of the rogue, not as to his identity since he was before the plaintiffs when the contract was made. A mistake as to the substance of the rogue would be a mistake as to quality and would not avoid the contract. Devlin, L.J., also suggested that legislation should provide for an apportionment of the loss incurred by two innocent parties who suffer as a result of the fraud of a third. (See now *Lewis* v. *Averay*, 1971.)[649]

167. Webster *v.* Cecil (1861), 30 Beav. 62

The parties had been negotiating for the sale of certain property. Later Cecil offered by letter to sell the property for £1,250. Webster was aware that this offer was probably a slip because he knew that Cecil had already refused an offer of £2,000, and in fact Cecil wished to offer the property at £2,250. Webster accepted the offer and sued for specific performance of the contract. The court refused to grant the decree.

168. Couturier *v.* Hastie (1856), 5 H.L.C. 673

Messrs. Hastie dispatched a cargo of corn from Salonica and sent the charter-party and bill of lading to their London agents so that the corn might be sold. The London agents employed Couturier to sell the corn and a person named Callander bought it. Unknown to the parties the cargo had become over-heated, and had been landed at the nearest port and sold, so that when the contract was made the corn was not really in existence. Callander repudiated the contract and Couturier was sued because he was a *del credere* agent, i.e. an agent who, for an extra commission, undertakes to indemnify his principal against losses arising out of the repudiation of the contract by any third party introduced by him. *Held*—The claim against Couturier failed because the contract presupposed that the goods were in existence when they were sold to Callander.

169. McRae *v.* The Commonwealth Disposals Commission, [1951] Argus L.R. 771

The defendants had invited tenders for the purchase of a tanker, said to be lying on the Jourmand Reef off Papua, together with the oil it was said to contain. The plaintiff submitted a tender of £285 which the defendants accepted. The plaintiff went to considerable trouble and expense to modify a ship which he owned for salvage work, and also bought equipment and engaged a crew. In fact there was no tanker anywhere near the latitude and longitude given by the defendants, and there was no such place as the Jourmand Reef. The plaintiff sued for damages for breach of contract. The High Court of Australia *held* that the plaintiff succeeded because the defendants had impliedly warranted that the goods existed. The court distinguished *Couturier* v. *Hastie* (1856)[168] on the ground that in that case the goods had existed but had perished whereas in the present case the goods had never existed at all.

N.B. The implied term solution is not too sound because when the court implies a term it generally does so on the ground that the parties would have included it had they addressed themselves to the matter. It is by no means certain in this case that the defendants would have agreed to such a term. However, there would now be a possible solution in tort if the plaintiff chose to sue in negligence because since the decision of the House of Lords in *Hedley Byrne* v. *Heller and Partners* (1963),[194] it would appear that there is a liability for careless misstatements resulting in monetary loss.

170. Cochrane v. Willis (1865), 1 Ch. App. 58

Cochrane was the trustee in bankruptcy of Joseph Willis who was the tenant for life of certain estates in Lancaster. Joseph Willis had been adjudicated bankrupt in Calcutta where he resided. The remainder of the estate was to go to Daniel Willis, the brother of Joseph, on the latter's death, with eventual remainder to Henry Willis, the son of Daniel. Joseph Willis had the right to cut the timber on the estates during his life interest, and the representative of Cochrane in England threatened to cut and sell it for the benefit of Joseph's creditors. Daniel and Henry wished to preserve the timber and so they agreed with Cochrane through his representatives to pay the value of the timber to Cochrane if he would refrain from cutting it. News then reached England that when the above agreement was made Joseph was dead, and therefore the life interest had vested in Daniel. In this action by the trustee to enforce the agreement it was *held* that Daniel was making a contract to preserve something which was already his and the Court found, applying the doctrine of *res sua*, that the agreement was void for an identical or common mistake.

171. Bell v. Lever Bros. Ltd., [1932] A.C. 161

Lever Bros. had a controlling interest in the Niger Company. Bell was the chairman, and a person called Snelling was the vice-chairman, of the Niger Company's Board. Both directors had service contracts which had some time to run. They became redundant as a result of amalgamations and Lever Bros. contracted to pay Bell £30,000 and Snelling £20,000 as compensation. These sums were paid over and then it was discovered that Bell and Snelling had committed breaches of duty during their term of office by making secret profits on a cocoa pooling scheme. They could, therefore, have been dismissed without compensation. Lever Bros. sought to set aside the payments on the ground of mistake. *Held*—The contract was not void because Lever Bros. had got what they bargained for, i.e. the cancellation of two service contracts which, though they might have been terminated, were actually in existence when the cancellation agreement was made. The mistake was as to the quality of the two directors and such mistakes do not avoid contracts.

N.B. The case also illustrates that the contract of service is not of utmost good faith. A servant is not bound to disclose his wrongdoing to his master, so that the silence of the two directors did not amount to a misrepresentation which could assist Lever Bros. in the setting aside of the agreement.

172. Leaf v. International Galleries, [1950] 2 K.B. 86

In 1944 the plaintiff bought from the defendants a drawing of Salisbury Cathedral for £85. The defendants said that the drawing was by Constable. Five years later the plaintiff tried to sell the drawing and was told that this was not so. He now sued for rescission of the contract. The decision in the county court was that rescission could not be granted because the representation was innocent and the contract had been executed. The appeal to the Court of Appeal was concerned with the question of the right to rescind; no claim for damages was made. The following points of interest emerged: (i) It was possible to restore the *status quo* by the mere exchange of the drawing and the purchase money so that rescission was not affected by inability to restore the previous position. (ii) The mistake made by the parties in assuming the drawing to be a Constable was a mistake as to quality and did not avoid the contract. (iii) The statement that the drawing was by Constable could have been treated as a warranty giving rise to a claim for damages, but it was not possible to award damages because the appeal was based on the plaintiff's right to rescind. (iv) The court, therefore, treated the statement as a representation and, finding it to be innocent, refused to rescind the contract because of the passage of time since the purchase. (v) Denning, L.J., criticised the rule in *Seddon* v. *North Eastern Salt Company*[200] and suggested that rescission was not always lost merely because the contract was executed. Evershed, M.R., whilst not suggesting that *Seddon* v. *North-Eastern Salt Company* was good law, thought that it ought not to be lightly disregarded because it had stood as law since 1905.

Note the effect that the Misrepresentation Act, 1967, would have on certain parts of this decision.

173. Jones *v.* Clifford (1876), 3 Ch.D. 779

Clifford agreed to buy from Jones some freehold and leasehold land, thinking that Jones was the owner. Before Clifford actually completed the contract, he entered into an agreement with a sub-purchaser for the sale of the property. The sub-purchaser discovered, whilst searching the title, that Clifford was in fact the true owner of the property, having derived his title from a conveyance to one of his ancestors in 1781. Clifford, on learning this, refused to complete, and Jones now sued for specific performance. *Held*—Specific performance would not be granted because the contract was affected by an identical bilateral or common mistake. The court also ordered an investigation into the title.

174. Magee *v.* Pennine Insurance Co. Ltd., [1969] 2 All E.R. 891

In 1961 the plaintiff, a man of 58, acquired an Austin car. He also signed a proposal form for insurance in which he said that the car belonged to him. He was asked to give details of his driving licence and of all other persons who, to his present knowledge, would drive the car. He gave the necessary details to a Mr Atkinson at the garage where he bought the car and it appeared that Mr. Atkinson did not write them down correctly on the proposal form. However, the details given were that the vehicle would be driven by the plaintiff as a provisional licence holder, his elder son, who had an annual licence, and his younger son, John aged 18, who was shown as a provisional licence holder. In fact the plaintiff was buying the car for John and it transpired that the plaintiff had never held a licence, not even a provisional one. Thus, although the trial judge later found that the plaintiff was not fraudulent, a misrepresentation had been made and on the faith of it being true the defendants granted an insurance policy to the plaintiff. The plaintiff was also required by the defendants to sign the following declaration—

I do hereby declare that the Car described is and shall be kept in good condition and that the answers above given are in every respect true and correct and I hereby agree that this Declaration shall be the basis of the Contract of Insurance between the Company and myself.

This normally has the effect of making all the statements in the proposal form conditions of the contract. (See *Dawsons Ltd.* v. *Bonnin* [1922], 2 A.C. 413.)

The policy was renewed each year and the premiums paid and in 1964 the car was replaced by another. The policy was renewed for the new car without anything further being said about the drivers or the ownership. At 4 a.m. on 25th April, 1965, John Magee was driving the new car when he ran into a shop window. The plate glass was smashed and the car was a complete wreck. The insurance company sent an engineer to look at the car and he pronounced it a write-off, whereupon the insurers offered to pay the plaintiff £385 and this offer was accepted by him. Afterwards the insurance company made further enquiries and on discovering that the statements in the proposal form of 1961 were untrue refused to pay. The plaintiff then sued the insurers and was given judgment for £385 in the County Court. The insurers appealed to the Court of Appeal where it was *held* in allowing the appeal—

(i) (*Per* Lord Denning, M.R.) that although the acceptance by the plaintiff of the insurance company's offer constituted a contract of compromise that contract was made under circumstances of common mistake which rendered the contract voidable in equity. (*Solle* v. *Butcher*, 1950,[156] applied);

(ii) (*Per* Fenton Atkinson, L.J.—referring to the misapprehension as a mutual mistake) that on the basis of certain statements in *Bell* v. *Lever Bros*, 1932,[171] the contract could be avoided at common law, where, as in this case, the misapprehension was on a fundamental matter (*N.B.* Lord Denning, M.R., and Winn, L.J., did not take this view of the decision in *Bell* v. *Lever Bros*, 1932[171]);

(iii) (*Per* Winn, L.J., dissenting) that following *Bell* v. *Lever Bros.*, 1932,[171] the contract was binding on the insurers—no reference was made by Winn, L.J., to *Solle* v. *Butcher*, 1950.[156]

175. Grist v. Bailey, [1966] 2 All E.R. 875

In September, 1954, the defendant agreed to sell to the plaintiff a freehold dwelling house for £850 "subject to the existing tenancy." Both parties believed at that time that the property was occupied by a tenant who was protected by the Rent Acts. In fact both the tenant and her husband had died before the contract was made and since the rent had always been paid to the vendor's agent he was not aware of the true position. The house was occupied by the son of the former tenant, but he was not protected by the Rent Acts and gave up possession. The plaintiff sought specific performance of the contract of sale and the defendant asked for rescission. *Held*—by Goff, J.—applying the dictum of Denning, L.J., in *Solle* v. *Butcher*, 1950,[156]— there was a jurisdiction in Equity to set aside an agreement for common mistake of a fundamental fact. Had the defendant known the true state of affairs she would not have agreed to sell at such a low price. However, being a case of equitable relief it could be granted unconditionally or on terms, and a term offered by the defendant was imposed, i.e. that, if required, she would enter into a fresh contract with the plaintiff at a proper price for vacant possession.

176. Joscelyne v. Nissen (1970), 2 W.L.R. 509

The plaintiff, Mr. Joscelyne, sought rectification of a written contract made on 18th June, 1964, under which he had made over his car-hire business to his daughter, Mrs. Margaret Nissen. It had been expressly agreed that in return for the car-hire business Mrs. Nissen would pay certain expenses including gas, electricity and coal bills but the agreement on these matters was not expressly incorporated into the written contract.

Mrs. Nissen failed to pay the bills and the plaintiff brought an action in the Edmonton County Court claiming amongst other things a declaration that Mrs. Nissen should pay the gas, electricity and coal bills and alternatively that the written agreement of 18th June, 1964, should be rectified to include a provision to that effect. The County Court judge allowed the claim for rectification and Mrs. Nissen appealed to the Court of Appeal on the ground that the judge had misdirected himself, in ordering rectification, in view of his finding that there was no complete antecedent agreement between the parties on the issue of payment of the expenses. The Court of Appeal, after considering different expressions of judicial views upon what was required before a contractual instrument might be rectified by the court, *held* that the law did not require a complete antecedent concluded agreement provided there was some outward expression of agreement between the contracting parties.

177. Frederick Rose (London) Ltd. *v.* William Pim & Co. Ltd., [1953] 2 Q.B. 450

The plaintiffs received an order from an Egyptian firm for feveroles (a type of horse bean). The plaintiffs did not know what was meant by feveroles and asked the defendants what they were and whether they could supply them. The defendants said that feveroles were horse beans and that they could supply them, so the plaintiffs entered into a written agreement to buy horse beans from the defendants which were then supplied to the Egyptian firm under the order. In fact there were three types of horse beans: feves, feveroles and fevettes, and the plaintiffs had been supplied with feves, which were less valuable than feveroles. The plaintiffs were sued by the Egyptian firm and now wished to recover the damages they had had to pay from the defendants. In order to do so they had to obtain rectification of the written contract with the defendants in which the goods were described as "horsebeans." The word "horsebeans" had to be rectified to "feveroles," otherwise the defendants were not in breach.

Held—

(i) Rectification was not possible because the contract expressed what the parties had agreed to, i.e. to buy and sell horsebeans. Thus the supply of any of the three varieties would have amounted to fulfilment of the contract.

(ii) The plaintiffs might have rescinded for misrepresentation but they could not restore the *status quo*, having sold the beans.

(iii) The plaintiffs might have recovered damages for breach of warranty, but the statement that "feveroles are horsebeans and we can supply them" was oral, and warranties in a contract for the sale of goods of £10 and upwards had in 1953 to be evidenced in writing. (Sale of Goods Act, 1893, Sect. 4.) The plaintiff would now have a remedy under the Law Reform (Enforcement of Contracts) Act, 1954. (See p. 132.)

(iv) The defence of mistake was also raised, i.e. both buyer and seller thought that all horsebeans were feveroles. This was an identical bilateral or common mistake, but since it was not a case of *res extincta* or *res sua* it had no effect on the contract.

178. Henkel *v.* Pape (1870), L.R. 6 Ex. 7

The parties to this action had been negotiating for the sale of certain rifles. No contract was made but later the purchaser ordered three rifles by telegram. Owing to the telegraph clerk's negligence the message was transmitted as "the" rifles. From previous negotiations this was understood to mean fifty rifles and that number was dispatched. *Held*—there was no contract between the parties.

179. Wood *v.* Scarth (1858), 1 F. & F. 293

The plaintiff was suing for damages for breach of contract alleging that the defendant had entered into an agreement to grant the plaintiff a lease of a public house, but had refused to convey the property. It was shown in evidence that the defendant intended to offer the lease at a rent, and also to include a premium on taking up the lease of £500. The defendant had told his agent to make this clear to the plaintiff, but the agent had not mentioned it. After discussions with the agent the plaintiff wrote to the defendant proposing to take the lease "on the terms already agreed upon" to which the defendant replied accepting the proposal. There was a mutual or non-identical bilateral mistake. The defendant thought that he was agreeing to lease the premises for a rent plus a premium, and the plaintiff thought he was taking a lease for rental only because he did not know of the premium. The plaintiff had sued for specific performance in 1855, and the court in the exercise of its equitable jurisdiction had decided that specific performance could not be granted in view of the mistake, as to grant it would be unduly hard on the defendant. However, in this action the plaintiff sued at common law for damages, and damages were granted to him on the ground that in mutual or non-identical mistake the court may find the sense of the promise and regard a contract as having been made on these terms. Here it was quite reasonable for the plaintiff to suppose that there was no premium to be paid. Thus a contract came into being on the terms as understood by the plaintiff, and he was entitled to damages for breach of it.

180. Raffles *v.* Wichelaus (1864), 2 H. & C. 906

The defendants agreed to buy from the plaintiffs 125 bales of cotton to arrive "*ex Peerless* from Bombay." There were two ships called *Peerless* sailing from Bombay, one in October and one in December. The defendants thought they were buying the cotton on the ship sailing in October, and the plaintiffs meant to sell the cotton on the ship sailing in December. In fact the plaintiffs had no cotton on the ship sailing in October. The defendants refused to take delivery of the cotton when the second ship arrived and were now sued for breach of contract. *Held*—Since there was a mistake as to the subject matter of the contract there was in effect no contract between the parties.

181. Scriven Bros. & Co. *v.* Hindley & Co., [1913] 3 K.B. 564

An auctioneer was selling bales of tow and hemp. Hindley's agent bid £17 per ton for certain bales which had been put up for sale. The bid was about right for hemp but extravagant for tow. The auctioneer knew that the bales were of tow but he accepted the bid. Hindley & Co. refused to take delivery of the tow and were sued for breach of contract. *Held*—There was no contract between the parties since there was no consensus; and there was no negligence on the part of the agent in mistaking the lot offered, because the markings in the catalogue were such that such a mistake might be made. In fact the ship which had brought the tow normally brought hemp, and buyers were given to assuming that all her cargo was hemp.

182. Tamplin *v.* James (1880), 15 Ch.D. 215

James purchased a public house at an auction sale. The property was adequately described in the particulars of sale and by reference to a plan. James thought he knew the property and did not bother to refer to the particulars. In fact a field which had been occupied by the publican, and which James thought to be included in the sale, was held under a separate lease and was not part of the lot offered. Tamplin sued for specific performance and James raised this mistake as a defence. *Held*—Specific performance would be granted. Although the parties were not at one on the question of the subject matter, James had by his conduct raised an implication that he was prepared to buy the property offered.

183. Edgington *v.* Fitzmaurice (1885), 29 Ch.D. 459

The plaintiff was induced to lend money to a company by representations made by its directors that the money would be used to improve the company's buildings and generally expand the business. In fact the directors intended to use the money to pay off the company's existing debts as the creditors were pressing hard for payment. When the plaintiff discovered that he had been misled, he sued the directors for damages for fraud. The defence was that the statement they had made was not a statement of a past or present fact but a mere statement of intention which could not be the basis of an action for fraud. *Held*—The directors were liable in deceit. Bowen, L.J., said: "There must be a misstatement of an existing fact; but the state of a man's mind is as much a fact as the state of his digestion. It is true that it is very difficult to prove what the state of a man's mind at a particular time is, but if it can be ascertained, it is as much a fact as anything else. A misrepresentation as to the state of a man's mind is, therefore, a misstatement of fact."

184. Smith *v.* Land and House Property Corporation (1884), 28 Ch.D. 7

The plaintiffs put up for sale on 4th August, 1882, the Marine Hotel, Walton-on-the-Naze, stating in the particulars that it was let to "Mr. Frederick Fleck (a most desirable tenant) at a rental of £400 for an unexpired term of $27\frac{1}{2}$ years." The directors of the defendant company sent the Secretary, Mr. Lewin, to inspect the property and he reported that Fleck was not doing much business and that the town seemed to be in the last stages of decay. The directors, on receiving this report, directed Mr. Lewin to bid up to £5,000, and in fact he bought the hotel for £4,700. Before completion Fleck became bankrupt and the defendant company refused to complete the purchase, whereupon the plaintiffs sued for specific performance. It was proved that on 1st May, 1882, the March quarter's rent was wholly unpaid; that a distress was then threatened, and that Fleck paid £30 on 6th May, £40 on 13th June, and the remaining £30 shortly before the sale. No part of the June quarter's rent had been paid. The chairman of the defendant company said that the hotel would not have been purchased but for the statement in the particulars that Fleck was a most desirable tenant. *Held*—specific performance would not be granted. The description of Fleck as a most desirable tenant was not a mere expression of opinion, but contained an implied assertion that the vendors knew of no facts leading to the conclusion that he was not. The circumstances relating to the unpaid rent showed that Fleck was not a desirable tenant and there was a misrepresentation. Bowen, L.J., said—

It is material to observe that it is often fallaciously assumed that a statement of opinion cannot involve the statement of a fact. In a case where the facts are equally well known to both parties, what one of them says to the other is frequently nothing but an expression of opinion. The statement of such opinion is in a sense a statement of a fact about the condition of the man's own mind, but only of an irrelevant fact, for it is of no consequence what the opinion is. But if the facts are not equally known to both sides, then a statement of opinion by the one who knows the facts best involves very often a statement of a material fact, for he impliedly states that he knows facts which justify his opinion.

185. Curtis *v.* Chemical Cleaning and Dyeing Co., [1951] 1 K.B. 805

The plaintiff took a wedding dress, with beads and sequins, to the defendant's shop for cleaning. She was asked to sign a receipt which contained the following clause: "The company is not liable for damage howsoever arising." The plaintiff asked what the effect of the document was, and the assistant told her that it exempted the company from liability in certain ways, and particularly that in her case she would have to take the risk of damage to beads and sequins. Thereupon the plaintiff signed the document without reading it. The dress was returned stained, and the plaintiff sued for damages. The company relied on the clause. *Held*—The company could not rely on the clause because the assistant had misrepresented the effect of the document so that the plaintiff was merely running the risk of damage to the beads and sequins.

185a. Mendelssohn v. Normand Ltd., [1969] 2 All E.R. 1215

The plaintiff left his car in the defendants' garage as he had done before. He was about to lock it as he had done on previous occasions when the attendant said that he could not do so. The plaintiff explained that there was a suitcase containing jewellery on the back seat and the attendant agreed to lock the car when he had moved it. He gave the plaintiff a ticket on the back of which was printed a statement that the proprietors would not "accept responsibility for any loss sustained . . . no variation of these conditions will bind the (proprietors) unless made in writing signed their duly authorised manager". A conspicuous written notice at the reception desk exempted the defendants from loss or damage to the vehicle or its contents. When he returned the plaintiff found the car unlocked and the key in the ignition. It was later discovered that the suitcase had been stolen while the car was in the defendants' garage. In an action by the plaintiff for damages it was held—by the Court of Appeal—that

(a) The notice at the reception desk was of no effect. It was not seen by a driver until he came to collect his car. The plaintiff had seen it before but had not read it.

(b) The plaintiff must be taken to have agreed to the conditions on the ticket which were incorporated in the contract; but

(c) the defendants could not rely upon the ticket because—

(i) the attendant had ostensible authority to promise to lock the car and thus to see that the contents were safe. This promise was repugnant to and took priority over the printed condition; and

(ii) the defendants had through their employee agreed to keep the car locked and left it unlocked so performing the contract in an entirely different way from the manner agreed. The defendants were therefore liable.

186. With *v.* O'Flanagan, [1936] Ch. 575

The defendant was a medical practitioner who wished to sell his practice. The plaintiff was interested and in January, 1934, the defendant represented to the plaintiff that the income from the practice was £2,000 a year. The contract was not signed until May, 1934, and in the meantime the defendant had been ill and the practice had been run by various other doctors as *locum tenentes*. In consequence the receipts fell to £5 per week, and no mention of this fact was made when the contract was entered into. The plaintiff now claimed rescission of the contract. *Held*—He could do so. The representation made in January was of a continuing nature and induced the contract made in May. The plaintiff had a right to be informed of a change in circumstances, and the defendant's silence amounted to a misrepresentation.

187. Tate *v.* Williamson (1866), 2 Ch. App. 55.

An extravagent Oxford undergraduate who was being pressed for money by his creditors sought financial advice from Williamson who recommended the sale of the undergraduate's estate in Staffordshire. Williamson then offered to buy it himself for £7,000 without disclosing the existence of minerals under the land which made the undergraduate's interest worth at least £14,000. The offer was accepted and a conveyance executed but some years later the sale was set aside by the Court at the instance of the undergraduate's heir. Williamson had been guilty of constructive fraud in that he had exploited to his own advantage the confidence placed in him.

188. Peek *v.* Gurney (1873), L.R. 6 H.L. 377

Peek purchased shares in a company on the faith of statements appearing in a prospectus issued by the respondents who were directors of the company. Certain of the statements were false and Peek sued the directors. It appeared that Peek was not an original allottee, but had purchased the shares on the market, though he had relied on the prospectus. *Held*—Peek's action failed because the statements in the prospectus were only intended to mislead the original allottees. Once the statements had induced the public to be original subscribers, their force was spent.

189. Gross *v.* Lewis Hillman Ltd. and Another, [1969] 3 All E.R. 1476

Mrs. Gross instructed property dealers Grace Rymer Investments to find a suitable shop for her to purchase as an investment. Lewis Hillman Ltd. owned a shop which they had leased and Henry James and partners had been instructed to sell the shop. Lewis Hillman Ltd. was controlled by a Mr. Edward James who also controlled the firm of Henry James and Partners. Edward James had arranged to let the shop to a dormant wool company, H.G. Somers & Sons Ltd. whose shares had recently been bought by two brothers planning to set up a chain of wool shops. Henry James and Partners introduced the shop to Grace Rymer by two letters the first of which said that the shop had been let to H. G. Somers and Sons Ltd. on a twenty-one years' full repairing and insuring lease at £800 p.a. exclusively for the sale of wool and hosiery and that the company had branches in Liverpool, Blackpool and Southport. Grace Rymer asked for tenants' references and in a second letter Henry James and Partners replied that H. G. Somers and Sons Ltd. was incorporated in 1928, had a paid up capital of £5,000 and enclosed a bankers reference relating to the letting of another shop to H. G. Somers & Sons Ltd. at a rent of £3,000 p.a.

Grace Rymer believing as a result of the letters that H. G. Somers was a going concern agreed to purchase the shop on its own behalf and recommended Mrs. Gross to purchase it offering to let her have the benefit of Grace Rymer's contract for a commission of 2¼ per cent of the purchase price. Mrs. Gross purchased the shop and it was conveyed directly by Lewis Hillman Ltd. to whom she paid the purchase price at the request of Grace Rymer. Three months later H. G. Somers & Sons Ltd. became insolvent and went into liquidation. In an action by Mrs. Gross against Lewis Hillman Ltd. to rescind the conveyance and against both Lewis Hillman Ltd. and Henry James & Partners for damages for deceit on the ground of fraudulent misrepresentation Mrs. Gross relied upon the representations in the two letters relating to the status of H. G. Somers & Sons Ltd. *Held*—by the Court of Appeal—that although the letters if read together might have amounted to fraudulent misrepresentation the trial judge had acquitted Edward James of any intention to deceive and the court would not interfere with that finding not having seen or heard James. Neither would the court order a new trial since even if there was fraudulent misrepresentation Mrs. Gross could not rescind the contract on the strength of it. The right to rescind for misrepresentation was not an equity which ran with the land and any misrepresentation to Mrs. Gross was spent when her agents, Grace Rymer, bought the property on their own behalf prior to selling it to her. Had Grace Rymer remained her agents throughout the misrepresentations made to them as agents would have been, in effect, made to Mrs. Gross who could then have rescinded the contract.

190. Redgrave *v.* Hurd (1881), 20 Ch.D. 1

The plaintiff was a solicitor who wished to take a partner into the business. During negotiations between the plaintiff and Hurd the plaintiff stated that the income of the business was £300 a year. The papers which the plaintiff produced showed that the income was not quite £200 a year, and Hurd asked about the balance. Redgrave then produced further papers which he said showed how the balance was made up, but which only showed a very small amount of income making the total income up to about £200. Hurd did not examine these papers in any detail, but agreed to become a partner. Later Hurd discovered the true position and refused to complete the contract. The plaintiff sued for breach and Hurd raised the misrepresentation as a defence, and also counter-claimed for rescission of the contract. *Held*—Hurd had relied on Redgrave's statements regarding the income and the contract could be rescinded. It did not matter that Hurd had the means of discovering their untruth; he was entitled to rely on Redgrave's statement.

191. Smith *v.* Chadwick (1884), 9 App. Cas. 187

This action was brought by the plaintiff, who was a steel manufacturer, against Messrs. Chadwick, Adamson and Collier, who were accountants and promoters of a company called the Blochairn Iron Co. Ltd. The plaintiff claimed £5,750 as damages sustained through taking shares in the company which were not worth the price he had paid for them because of certain mis-representations in the prospectus issued by the defendants. The action was for fraud. Among the misrepresentations alleged by Smith was that the prospectus stated that a Mr. J. J. Grieves, M.P., was a director of the company, whereas he had withdrawn his consent the day before the prospectus was issued. It was *held* that the statement regarding Mr. Grieves was untrue but was not material to the plaintiff, because the evidence showed that he had never heard of Mr. Grieves. His action for damages failed.

192. Horsfall *v.* Thomas (1862), 1 H. & C. 90

Thomas asked Horsfall to make him a gun and agreed to pay for it by means of two bills of exchange. Horsfall made the gun, and at the third trial by Thomas the gun flew to pieces. Evidence showed that the breech was defective and that a plug of metal had been driven into the breech to conceal the defect. Horsfall sued on one of the bills and Thomas pleaded fraud. *Held*—Horsfall succeeded and the defence failed because it appeared that Thomas had never inspected the gun so that any attempt to conceal the defect could not have had any operation on his mind. Even if the plug had not been put into the breech the defendant's position would have been the same.

193. Derry *v.* Peek (1889), 14 App. Cas. 337

The Plymouth, Devonport and District Tramways Company had power under a special Act of Parliament to run trams by animal power, and with the consent of the Board of Trade by mechanical or steam power. Derry and the other appellants were directors of the company and issued a prospectus, inviting the public to apply for shares in it, stating that they had power to run trams by steam power, and claiming that considerable economies would result. The directors had assumed that the permission of the Board of Trade would be granted as a matter of course, but in the event the Board of Trade refused permission except for certain parts of the tramway. As a result the company was wound up and the directors were sued for fraud. The court *decided* that the directors were not fraudulent but honestly believed the statement in the prospectus to be true.

N.B. This case gave rise to the Directors' Liability Act, 1890, now Sect. 43 of the Companies Act, 1948, which makes directors liable to pay compensation for misrepresentation in a prospectus, subject to a number of defences.

194. Hedley Byrne & Co. Ltd. *v.* Heller & Partners Ltd., [1963] 2 All E.R. 575

The appellants were advertising agents and the respondents were merchant bankers. The appellants had a client called Easipower Ltd. who were customers of the respondents. The appellants had contracted to place orders for advertising Easipower's products on television and in newspapers, and since this involved giving Easipower credit, they asked the respondents, who were Easipower's bankers, for a reference as to the creditworthiness of Easipower. The respondents said that Easipower Ltd. was respectably constituted and considered good, though they said that the statement was made without responsibility on their part. Relying on this reply, the appellants placed orders for advertising time and space for Easipower Ltd., and the appellants assumed personal responsibility for payment to the television and newspaper companies concerned. Easipower Ltd. went into liquidation, and the appellants lost over £17,000 on the advertising contracts. The appellants sued the respondents for the amount of the loss, alleging that the respondents had not informed themselves sufficiently about Easipower Ltd. before writing the statement, and were therefore liable in negligence. *Held*—In the present case the respondents' disclaimer was adequate to exclude the assumption by them of the legal duty of care, but, in the absence of the disclaimer, the circumstances would have given rise to a duty of care in spite of the absence of a contract or fiduciary relationship. The dissenting judgment of Denning, L.J., in *Candler* v. *Crane, Christmas*, 1951,[504] was approved, and the majority judgment in that case was disapproved.

195. Doyle *v.* Olby (Ironmongers) Ltd. and Others, [1969] 2 All E.R. 119

In 1963 the plaintiff wished to buy a business. He saw an advertisement in *Dalton's Weekly* and obtained particulars of an ironmonger's business in Epsom belonging to the first defendants. The price asked for the lease, the business and goodwill was £4,500, the stock to be taken at valuation. In 1964 after negotiations with various members of the Olby family the plaintiff purchased the business paying £4,500 covering goodwill and fixtures and fittings, and £5,000 for the stock. He also needed a longer lease and so surrendered the existing lease taking on a longer one at an increased rent. The owner of the shop who benefited from this transaction was another member of the Olby family. In order to pay the money the plaintiff put up all the cash he had, i.e. £7,000 and borrowed £3,000 on mortgage. When he went into occupation he discovered that the defendants had made a number of false statements relating to the business. In particular the plaintiff discovered that half the trade was wholesale which could only be obtained by employing a traveller to go round to the customers. The plaintiff could not afford to employ a traveller and all the wholesale trade was lost. The second defendant had told the plaintiff in the course of negotiations that all the trade was over the counter.

The plaintiff was most dissatisfied and in May, 1964, he brought an action for damages for fraud and conspiracy against Olby (Ironmongers) Ltd. and several members of the Olby family who had been involved in the sale of the Epsom business. At the trial the judge awarded damages on a contractual basis as if the statement "the trade is all over the counter. There is no need to employ a traveller" had been a term of the contract. In consequence the judge accepted that the proper measure of foreseeable damage was, in accordance with *Hadley* v. *Baxendale* 1854,[331] the reduction in the value of goodwill due to the misstatement. The goodwill was valued at £4,000 and since 50 per cent of the turnover was wholesale goodwill would have been reduced by 35 to 40 per cent giving £1,500 as a round figure for damages.

In the Court of Appeal Lord Denning, M.R., said on this point:

On principle the distinction seems to be this: in contract, the defendant has made a promise and broken it. The object of damages is to put the plaintiff in as good a position, as far as money can do it, as if the promise had been performed. In fraud, the defendant has been guilty of a deliberate wrong by inducing the plaintiff to act to his detriment. The object of damages is to compensate the plaintiff for all the loss he has suffered, so far, again, as money can do it. In contract, the damages are limited to what may reasonably be supposed to have been in the contemplation of the parties. In fraud, they are not so limited. The defendant is bound to make reparation for all the actual damage directly flowing from the fraudulent inducement. The person who has been defrauded is entitled to say: "I would not have entered into this bargain at all but for your representation. Owing to your fraud, I have not only lost all the money I have paid you, but, what is more, I have been put to a large amount of extra expense as well and suffered this or that extra damages." All such damages can be recovered: and it does not lie in the mouth of the fraudulent person to say that they could not reasonably have been foreseen. For instance, in this very case the plaintiff has not only lost the money which he paid for the business, which he would never have done if there had been no fraud; he put all that money in and lost it; but also he has been put to expense and loss in trying to run a business which has turned out to be a disaster for him. He is entitled to damages for all his loss, subject, of course, to giving credit for any benefit that he has received. There is nothing to be taken off in mitigation: for there is nothing more that he could have done to reduce his loss. He did all that he could reasonably be expected to do.

Accordingly damages were assessed by the Court of Appeal at £5,500 being made up as follows—

	£	£	
Cost of acquiring business		4,500	
Cost of acquiring stock		5,000	
		9,500	
Less: Cash received by Doyle when business sold in 1967	3,500		
Cash received on sale of stock	800		
Value of living accommodation during the three years	2,500	7,000	(as a round figure)
Loss		2,500	
Additional damages for strain and worry and interest on loans and bank overdraft		3,000	
Damages awarded		£5,500	

196. Mafo *v.* Adams, [1969] 3 All E.R. 1404

In July, 1965, the plaintiff, a Nigerian, was granted a weekly tenancy in Richmond by the defendant, a West Indian. On 10th December, 1965, the defendant gave the plaintiff notice to quit though the plaintiff appeared to have been a good tenant. The plaintiff then claimed the benefit of the Rent Acts and refused to leave. On 15th February, 1966, the plaintiff was invited to see alternative accommodation at Norbury and saw a lady who posed as Mrs. Williams. The plaintiff arranged to move into the accommodation at Norbury and paid Mrs. Williams £6 10s. representing two weeks' rent in advance, though the cheque was never cashed. The plaintiff and his pregnant wife then left the Richmond tenancy but were unable to obtain entry to the Norbury accommodation. It later emerged that Mrs. Williams was in fact Adams' wife, from whom he was separated, and that he and she had combined in a piece of trickery to get the plaintiff out of the Richmond tenancy. The plaintiff was unable to resume possession of the Richmond accommodation and subsequently suffered physical inconvenience but no financial damage although it appeared that the accommodation he found was unlikely to be as securely protected by the Rent Acts as the Richmond flat had been. On appeal by the landlord from an award to the tenant of £100 for breach of covenant of quiet enjoyment and £100 exemplary damages for deceit it was *Held*—by the Court of Appeal—

(i) £100 was a proper figure for compensatory damages;

(ii) that Lord Devlin's statements in *Rookes* v. *Barnard*, [1964] 1 All E.R. 367, at p. 411, that "Exemplary damages can properly be awarded whenever it is necessary to teach a wrongdoer that tort does not pay" might well have extended the number of cases in which exemplary damages could potentially be awarded. However, assuming that exemplary damages could be awarded in an action for deceit, the plaintiff was not entitled to them because there was no finding that the landlord had acted in such a way as to bring himself within Lord Devlin's statement. Exemplary damages are in the main to be awarded in cases where the defendant realises that he is breaking the law, and that damages may be awarded against him, but nevertheless makes what has been described as a cynical calculation of profit and loss and says that he will flout the powers of the court because on a purely cash basis he can show a profit. Where exemplary damages were claimed the court must be careful to see that the case for punishment was as well established as in other penal proceedings. The plaintiff was not therefore entitled to exemplary damages.

197. Car & Universal Finance Co. Ltd. *v.* Caldwell, [1963] 2 All E.R. 547

On 12th January, 1960, Mr. Caldwell sold a motor car to a firm called Dunn's Transport, receiving a cheque signed "for and on behalf of Dunn's Transport, W. Foster, F. Norris." Caldwell presented the cheque to the bank but it was dishonoured, and so he went to see the police and asked them to recover the car. He also saw officials of the Automobile Association and asked them to trace the car by their patrols. The car was found on 20th January, 1960, in the possession of a director of a firm of car dealers called Motobella & Co. Ltd. The company claimed to have bought it on 15th January from Norris and to have a good title. On 29th January, the defendant's solicitors demanded the car from Motobella and at the same time Norris was arrested and pleaded guilty to obtaining the car by false pretences. The defendant sued Motobella & Co. Ltd. for the return of the car and obtained judgment, but when he tried to repossess the car, a finance house, Car & Universal Finance Co. Ltd., claimed that it belonged to them. It appeared that Motobella had transferred the ownership to a finance house called G. & C. Finance on 15th January, 1960, and they had transferred it to the plaintiffs on 3rd August, 1960, the latter company taking the vehicle in good faith. In this action the plaintiffs claimed the car. It was *held* that Caldwell was entitled to it because, amongst other things, he had avoided the contract of sale to Norris when he asked the police to get the car back for him so that later sales of the car to Motobella and to G. & C. Finance did not pass the property.

198. Long *v.* Lloyd, [1958] 2 All E.R. 402

The plaintiff and the defendant were haulage contractors. The plaintiff was induced to buy the defendant's lorry by the defendant's misrepresentation as to condition and performance. The defendant advertised the lorry for sale at £850, the advertisement describing the vehicle as being in "exceptional condition." The plaintiff saw the lorry at the defendant's premises at Hampton Court on a Saturday. During a trial run on the following Monday the plaintiff found that the speedometer was not working, a spring was missing from the accelerator pedal, and it was difficult to engage top gear. The defendant said there was nothing wrong with the vehicle except what the plaintiff had found. He also said at this stage that the lorry would do 11 miles to the gallon.

The plaintiff purchased the lorry for £750, paying £375 down and agreeing to pay the balance at a later date. He then drove the lorry from Hampton Court to his place of business at Sevenoaks. On the following Wednesday, the plaintiff drove from Sevenoaks to Rochester to pick up a load, and during that journey the dynamo ceased to function, an oil seal was leaking badly, there was a crack in one of the road wheels, and he used 8 gallons of petrol on a journey of 40 miles. That evening the plaintiff told the defendant of the defects, and the defendant offered to pay half the cost of a reconstructed dynamo, but denied any knowledge of the other defects. The plaintiff accepted the offer and the dynamo was fitted straight away. On Thursday the lorry was driven by the plaintiff's brother to Middlesbrough, and it broke down on the Friday night. The plaintiff, on learning of this, asked the defendant for his money back, but the defendant would not give it to him. The lorry was subsequently examined and an expert said that it was not roadworthy. The plaintiff sued for rescission. *Held*—at first instance, by Glyn-Jones, J.—that the defendant's statements about the lorry were innocent and not fraudulent because the evidence showed that the lorry had been laid up for a month and it might therefore have deteriorated without the defendant's precise knowledge. The Court of Appeal affirmed this finding of fact and made the following additional points—

(1) The journey to Rochester was not affirmation because the plaintiff was merely testing the vehicle in a working capacity.

(2) However, the acceptance by the plaintiff of the defendant's offer to pay half the cost of the reconstructed dynamo, and the subsequent journey to Middlesbrough, did amount to affirmation, and rescission could not be granted to the plaintiff.

The Court was non-committal on the validity of the decisions in *Seddon* v. *North-Eastern Salt Co.* (1905)[200] and *Angel* v. *Jay* (1911)[201] which were relevant since the contract had been executed. However, it was said in the judgments that if the plaintiff's action was not barred by the decisions in these two cases, there was affirmation, and it was on the ground of affirmation that rescission was not granted. Presumably the Court would not treat the defendant's statements as warranties because he was not a dealer in lorries but merely a user.

N.B. Damages could now be obtained for negligent misrepresentation under the Misrepresentation Act, 1967, Sect. 2(1), for how could the seller say he had reasonable grounds for believing that the lorry was in first-class condition?

199. Clarke *v.* Dickson (1858), E.B. & E. 148

In 1853 the plaintiff was induced by the misrepresentation of the three defendants, Dickson, Williams and Gibbs, to invest money in what was in effect a partnership to work lead mines in Wales. In 1857 the partnership was in financial difficulty and with the plaintiff's assent it was converted into a limited company and the partnership capital was converted into shares. Shortly afterwards the company commenced winding-up proceedings and the plaintiff, on discovery of the falsity of the representations, asked for rescission of the contract. *Held*—Rescission could not be granted because capital in a partnership is not the same as shares in a company. The firm was no longer in existence, having been replaced by the company, and it was not possible to restore the parties to their original positions.

N.B. It should be noted that in addition to the problem of restoration, third-party rights, i.e. creditors, had accrued on the winding up of the company and this is a further bar to rescission.

200. Seddon *v.* North Eastern Salt Co. Ltd., [1905] 1 Ch. 326

The plaintiff agreed to purchase certain company shares from the defendants. The shares were transferred to him in October, 1903. It emerged that the defendants had misled him as to certain losses made by the company, though there was no suggestion of fraud. The plaintiff retained the shares until January, 1904, and then asked for rescission of the contract. *Held*—The contract to take the shares had been executed and in the absence of fraud it could not be rescinded.

201. Angel *v.* Jay, [1911] 1 K.B. 666

The plaintiff agreed to take a lease of a dwelling house from the defendant, the lease to be for three years. During the negotiations the defendant innocently misrepresented that the drains were in good order when in fact they were not. The plaintiff was in possession for six months and then brought this action for rescission of the contract. *Held*—The contract to take the lease having been executed, it could not be rescinded.

202. Henderson & Co. *v.* Williams, [1895] 1 Q.B. 521

The plaintiffs were sugar merchants at Hull. The defendant was a warehouseman at Hull and Goole. On 3rd June, 1894, a fraudulent person named Fletcher, posing as the agent of one Robinson, negotiated a purchase of sugar from Messrs. Grey & Co., who were Liverpool merchants. The sugar was lying in the defendant's warehouse at Goole, and Messrs. Grey & Co. sent a telegram and later a letter advising the defendant that the sugar was to be held to the order of Fletcher, and the defendant entered the order in his books. Robinson was a reputable dealer and a customer of Messrs. Grey & Co., and of course Fletcher had no right to act on Robinson's behalf. Fletcher sold the goods to the plaintiffs who, before paying the price, got a statement from the defendant that the goods were held to the order of Fletcher. The defendant later discovered Fletcher's fraud and refused to release the sugar to the plaintiffs who now sued in conversion. *Held*—The defendant was estopped from denying Fletcher's title and was liable in damages based on the market price of the goods at the date of refusal to deliver. Further the true owners, Messrs. Grey & Co., could not set up their title to the sugar against that of the plaintiffs, since they had allowed Fletcher to hold himself out as the true owner.

203. Whittington *v.* Seale-Hayne (1900), 82 L.T. 49

The plaintiffs were breeders of prize poultry and they took a lease of the defendant's premises. The defendant innocently misrepresented that the premises were in a sanitary condition but in fact the water supply was poisoned, and this caused the illness of the plaintiff's manager. In addition, certain of their poultry died or became valueless for breeding purposes. The local authority required the plaintiffs to carry out certain work in order to render the premises sanitary, the plaintiffs having agreed in the lease to do such work if it became necessary. The plaintiffs now asked for rescission of the contract and for an indemnity against the following losses: Stock lost, £750; loss of profit on sales, £100; loss of breeding season, £500; removal of stores and rent, £75; medical expenses, £100. *Held*—The lease could be rescinded, but the plaintiffs' indemnity was restricted to the losses necessarily incurred by taking a lease of the premises, i.e. rent, rates and the cost of the repairs ordered by the local authority.

N.B. The reason for restricting the indemnity in this sort of case seems to be based on the fact that although Equity is prepared to rescind contracts for innocent misrepresentation, thus providing a remedy where the common law does not, Equity will not circumvent the law by making an indemnity (the object of which is to help restore the *status quo*) the equivalent of damages for fraud.

204. Pym *v.* Campbell (1856), 6 E & B 370

An agreement for the sale of a patent was drawn up and signed. It was also agreed at the time that the written agreement was not to be binding unless a third party approved of the invention. In an action on the written agreement evidence was admitted to show that the third party had not approved and therefore the agreement was not effective.

205. Quickmaid Rental Services Ltd. *v.* Reece (1970), *The Times*, 21st April, 1970

In 1967 a salesman named Burbridge persuaded Mr. Reece to install on his service station premises in Ashton New Road, Manchester, a Quickmaid machine which supplied coffee, tea and other beverages to travellers by putting coins into a slot. Mr. Reece was asked to sign two written agreements, one for the machine itself and the other for a canopy. It was to be for five years. Mr. Reece paid £37 10s. deposit for the machine and was to pay monthly rentals thereafter. But before he agreed or signed anything Mr. Burbridge made an important statement to him. He said that he would not install any other such machine on Ashton New Road. That stipulation induced Mr. Reece to sign the documents. Mr. Burbridge realized that any other machine would affect Mr. Reece's business considerably. Later he made a memorandum saying he would not sell any more machines in that particular road.

However in May, 1968 Mr. Reece discovered that in January the company, through another salesman, had installed another machine up the road. That was within two and a half months of the promise to him; and the second machine was in a more advantageous position for getting custom. On discovering that, Mr. Reece, who had had trouble with his machine, stopped his banker's order for the rental. The company thereupon sued Mr. Reece in the County Court for £73 15s., being the instalments from June to October, 1968. *Held*—by the Court of Appeal—that the company's claim failed. The proper way to approach the case was to regard it as a contract made partly in writing by the signed documents and partly by word of mouth, by what was said at the time. The stipulation about no other machine being in the road was most important; it was a term which amounted to a condition; and when it was broken it was broken in a manner which went to the root of the contract. It destroyed the profitable basis of the contract. Breach of that condition gave Mr. Reece the right to say he would no longer go on; nor on the evidence did he affirm the contract after discovering the breach. The appeal should be dismissed. (*Per* Lord Denning, M.R.)

206. Bannerman *v.* White (1861), 10 C.B.(N.S.) 844

The defendant was intending to buy hops from the plaintiff and he asked the plaintiff whether sulphur had been used in the cultivation of the hops, adding that if it had he would not even bother to ask the price. The plaintiff said that no sulphur had been used, though in fact it had. It was *held* that the plaintiff's assurance that sulphur had not been used was a term of the contract and the defendant was justified in raising the matter as a defence to an action for the price.

207. Oscar Chess Ltd. *v.* Williams, [1957] 1 W.L.R. 370

In May, 1955, Williams bought a car from the plaintiffs on hire-purchase terms. The plaintiffs took Williams's Morris car in part exchange. Williams described the car as a 1948 model and produced the registration book, which showed that the car was first registered in April, 1948, and that there had been several owners since that time. Williams was allowed £290 on the Morris. Eight months later the plaintiffs discovered that the Morris car was a 1939 model, there being no change in appearance in the model between 1939 and 1948. The allowance for a 1939 model was £175 and the plaintiffs sued for £115 damages for breach of warranty that the car was a 1948 model. Evidence showed that some fraudulent person had altered the registration book but he could not be traced, and that Williams honestly believed that the car was a 1948 model. *Held*—The contract might have been set aside in Equity for misrepresentation but the delay of eight months defeated this remedy. The mistake was a mistake of quality which did not avoid the contract at common law and in order to obtain damages the plaintiffs must prove a breach of warranty. The court was unable to find that Williams was in a position to give such a warranty, and suggested that the plaintiffs should have taken the engine and chassis number and written to the manufacturers, so using their superior knowledge to protect themselves in the matter. The plaintiffs were not entitled to any redress. Morris, L.J., dissented, holding that the statement that the car was a 1948 model was a fundamental condition.

208. D'Mello *v.* Loughborough College of Technology (1970), *The Times,* June 17th, 1970

In 1961 the college advertised a one-year postgraduate course in economics and administration in the oil industry. The plaintiff, who was then working for an oil company in India saw the advertisement and wrote asking for further details. The college sent him a prospectus containing a syllabus of the course and a college calendar for 1961/62 and 1962/63 together with an application form. In due course the college accepted him for the course and in September, 1963, he joined four other students who had already begun their studies. All the other students completed the course but D'Mello gave up early in 1964 because he said that the course was different from the one in the prospectus and in particular did not have sufficient relevance to the oil industry. He now claimed damages for breach of contract. *Held*—by O'Connor, J.—that the prospectus was part of the contract but the plaintiff failed in that he had not shown that the college was in breach of it. It was a matter for the College authorities to decide as a matter of skill and judgment how to conduct the course and there was no evidence to show that they were in breach of their duty to the plaintiff in this regard.

209. De Lassalle *v.* Guildford, [1901] 2 K.B. 215

A person who was intending to take a lease of a house refused to execute the lease unless the lessor would first give him an assurance that the drains were in good condition. The lessor gave this undertaking and the lessee signed the lease, though the lessor's assurance regarding the drains was not incorporated in it. Even so *the lessor was held liable* when the drains were found to be out of order on the grounds that he was in breach of a collateral contract.

210. Shanklin Pier, Ltd. *v.* Detel Products, Ltd., [1951] 2 All E.R. 471

The plaintiffs owned a pier and made a contract with a firm to have the pier repainted with bituminous paint. A director of the defendant company went to Shanklin and persuaded the plaintiffs to use paint, called D.M.U., made by the defendant company. The director assured the plaintiffs that D.M.U. would have a life of at least seven to ten years. The plaintiffs then approached the contractors who were to do the work and the specification regarding the type of paint to be used was altered and D.M.U. substituted. The contractors applied D.M.U. to the pier but it was unsatisfactory and lasted about three months. The plaintiffs sued the defendants for breach of warranty that the paint would last at least seven to ten years. Judgment was given for the plaintiffs by McNair, J., who said "Counsel for the defendants submitted that in law a warranty could give rise to no enforceable course of action except between the same parties as the parties to the main contract in relation to which the warranty was given. In principle, this submission seems to me to be unsound. If, as is elementary, the consideration for the warranty in the usual case is the entering into of the main contract in relation to which the warranty is given, I see no reason why there may not be an enforceable warranty between A and B supported by the consideration that B should cause C to enter into a contract with A or that B should do some other act for the benefit of A."

211. Harling *v.* Eddy, [1951] 2 K.B. 739

The plaintiff purchased a heifer at an auction sale. The auction sale was subject to certain conditions which were printed in the catalogue issued to potential buyers. One of the conditions stated that no warranties were given regarding animals purchased unless such warranties appeared on the purchaser's account. When the heifer was brought into the ring, potential buyers showed little interest, and no bids were made until the auctioneer, with the authority of the owner, said: "There is nothing wrong with her. I will guarantee her in every respect and I will take her back if she is not what I say she is." The plaintiff thereupon purchased the animal, no warranties being given on the account. The heifer gave little milk and died of tuberculosis four months after purchase. The plaintiff sued for damages and the defence was the exemption clause in the auctioneer's catalogue. *Held*—The plaintiff succeeded. The following points arise out of the judgment in the Court of Appeal—

(*a*) A statement that an animal is sound in every respect would *prima facie* have been no more than a warranty, but the auctioneer's statement that he would take the animal back implied a right in the purchaser to reject the animal, thus making the statement a condition and not a warranty so that the exemption clause was not effective to exclude it. However, since the plaintiff had sued for breach of warranty, it was necessary also to treat the statement of the auctioneer as a warranty in which case it was possible to take the view that the statement was not incorporated into the original contract but was a collateral contract. This conclusion could be reached by bearing in mind the initial silence which greeted the entry of the animal into the ring; and the fact that the bidding only began when the statement had been made suggested that the defendants were not contracting on the auction particulars but on the auctioneer's statement. (*per* Evershed, M.R.)

(*b*) Denning, L.J., proceeded on the assumption that the statement was a warranty and held that, even so, the exemption clause did not exclude it because "the party who is liable in law cannot escape liability by simply putting up a printed notice or using a printed catalogue containing exempting conditions. He must go further and show affirmatively that it is a contractual document and accepted as such by the party affected."

212. Behn *v.* Burness (1863), 3 B. & S. 751

A ship, the *Martaban*, was chartered to carry coal from Newport to Hong Kong. The charter party described the ship as "now in the port of Amsterdam" whereas in fact the ship was at Niewdiep about 62 miles from Amsterdam. She was late in arriving at Newport and the charterers refused to load her. *Held*— The charterers were justified in their refusal. In a charter party the situation of the ship when the charter was made was a term of great commercial importance and must be treated as a condition.

213. Poussard *v.* Spiers and Pond (1876), 1 Q.B.D. 410

Madame Poussard had entered into an agreement to play a part in an opera, the first performance to take place on 28th November, 1874. On 23rd November Madame Poussard was taken ill and was unable to appear until 4th December. The defendants had hired a substitute, and discovered that the only way in which they could secure a substitute to take Madame Poussard's place was to offer that person the complete engagement. This they had done, and they refused the services of Madame Poussard when she presented herself on 4th December. The plaintiff now sued for breach of contract. *Held*—The failure of Madame Poussard to perform the contract as from the first night was a breach of condition, and the defendants were within their rights in regarding the contract as discharged.

214. Bettini *v.* Gye (1876), 1 Q.B.D. 183

The plaintiff was an opera singer. The defendant was the director of the Royal Italian Opera in London. The plaintiff had agreed to sing in Great Britain in theatres, halls and drawing rooms for a period of time commencing on 30th March, 1875, and to be in London for rehearsals six days before the engagement began. The plaintiff was taken ill and arrived on 28th March, 1873, but the defendant would not accept the plaintiff's services, treating the contract as discharged. *Held*—The rehearsal clause was subsidiary to the main purposes of the contract, and its breach constituted a breach of warranty only. The defendant had no right to treat the contract as discharged and must compensate the plaintiff, but he had a counterclaim for any damage he had suffered by the plaintiffs' late arrival.

215. Chapelton *v.* Barry Urban District Council, [1940] 1 K.B. 532

The plaintiff Chapelton wished to hire deck chairs and went to a pile owned by the defendants, behind which was a notice stating: "Hire of chairs 2d. per session of three hours." The plaintiff took two chairs, paid for them, and received two tickets which he put into his pocket after merely glancing at them. One of the chairs collapsed and he was injured. A notice on the back of the ticket provided that "The council will not be liable for any accident or damage arising from hire of chairs." The plaintiff sued for damages and the council sought to rely on the clause in the ticket. *Held*—The clause was not binding on Chapelton. The board by the chairs made no attempt to limit the liability, and it was unreasonable to communicate conditions by means of a mere receipt.

216. Thompson *v.* L.M.S. Railway, [1930] 1 K.B. 41

Thompson, who could not read, asked her niece to buy her an excursion ticket, on the front of which were printed the words, "Excursion. For conditions see back." On the back was a notice to the effect that the ticket was issued subject to the conditions in the company's timetables, which excluded liability for injury however caused. Thompson was injured and claimed damages. *Held*—Her action failed. She had constructive notice of the conditions which had, in the court's view, been properly communicated to the ordinary passenger.

N.B. The Transport Act, 1962, Sect. 42(7), provides that the British Railways Board as it is now called shall not carry passengers by rail on conditions which purport directly or indirectly to exclude the Board's liability in respect of death or bodily injury to passengers other than passengers travelling on a free pass. On its own facts, therefore, the above case is of historical interest only, though it is still relevant on the question of constructive notice.

217. Richardson Steamship Company Ltd. *v.* Rowntree, [1894] A.C. 217

Rowntree booked a passage on the appellants' ship travelling from Philadelphia to Liverpool. The ticket was folded so that no writing was visible until it was opened. A clause printed on the ticket limited the appellants' liability for injury or damage to passengers or their luggage to $100. The clause was printed in rather small type and was rendered less obvious by a red ink stamp on the ticket. *Held*—Rowntree was not bound by the clause as she did not know of its existence, and there was no constructive notice because the shipowner had not given reasonable notice of the condition.

218. L'Estrange *v.* Graucob (F.), [1934] 2 K.B. 394

The defendant sold to the plaintiff a slot machine, inserting in the order form the following clause: "Any express or implied condition, statement or warranty, statutory or otherwise, is hereby excluded." The plaintiff signed the order form but did not read the relevant clause, and she now sued in respect of the unsatisfactory nature of the machine supplied. *Held*—The clause was binding on her, although the defendants made no attempt to read the document to her nor call her attention to the clause.

219. Olley *v.* Marlborough Court Ltd., [1949] 1 K.B. 532

Husband and wife arrived at an hotel as guests and paid for a room in advance. They went up to the room allotted to them; on one of the walls was the following notice: "The proprietors will not hold themselves responsible for articles lost or stolen unless handed to the manageress for safe custody." The wife closed the self-locking door of the bedroom and took the key downstairs to the reception desk. A third party took the key and stole certain of the wife's furs. In the ensuing action the defendants sought to rely on the notice as a term of contract. *Held*—The contract was completed at the reception desk and no subsequent notice could affect the plaintiff's rights.

N.B. As was pointed out in *Spurling* v. *Bradshaw*, [1956] 1 W.L.R. 461, if the husband and wife had seen the notice on a previous visit to the hotel it would have been binding on them.

219a. *Thornton* v. *Shoe Lane Parking Ltd.*, [1971] 1 All E.R. 686

The plaintiff suffered physical injuries when taking his car out of a multi-storey car park and sued the proprietors for these injuries. They claimed that they were not liable by reason of an exclusion clause on a ticket issued to the plaintiff. The sequence of relevant events was as follows—

(*a*) The plaintiff drove up to the automatic barrier where there was a notice saying "All cars parked at owner's risk." This did not cover physical injury. Most people would think it referred to the car or its contents.

(*b*) An automatic device issued a ticket at the barrier. This referred to further conditions which were displayed inside the premises. These conditions exempted the defendants from a number of possible liabilities including physical injury. The plaintiff did not read these and had not used the park before.

Held—by the Court of Appeal—the terms of the offer were those contained in the notice at the ticket machine. The plaintiff was not bound by the conditions inside the premises to which the ticket referred because the ticket came too late in the transaction to incorporate them.

220. Adler *v.* Dickson, [1955] 1 Q.B. 158

The plaintiff was travelling as a first-class passenger on the Peninsular and Orient Company's liner *Himalaya*. The ticket contained the following term: "Passengers are carried at passengers' risk . . . The company will not be responsible for any injury whatsoever to the person of any passenger arising from, or occasioned by, the negligence of the company's servants." The plaintiff fell from the gangway on to the wharf and was injured. Since the exemption clause exempted the company from liability, the plaintiff brought an action for negligence against the master and boatswain of the ship. *Held*—The plaintiff succeeded. The master and boatswain were not parties to the contract and could not claim the benefit of the exemption clause.

221. McCutcheon *v.* David MacBrayne, [1964] 1 All E.R. 430

McCutcheon wished to have his motor car transported from Islay to the Scottish mainland, and McCutcheon's agent made a contract of carriage on behalf of McCutcheon with the respondent company. The ship sank owing to the respondents' negligent navigation and the appellant sued for damages. The respondents contended that they were not liable because of certain exemption clauses displayed on a notice in the booking office and also contained in a "risk note" which was normally given to each customer, though one was not given to the appellant's agent in this case. However, on previous occasions when the parties had done business, "risk notes" containing exemptions had sometimes been given either to the appellant or his agent. The appellant and his agent knew that some conditions were attached to the respondents' contracts, but did not know specifically what they were. *Held*, by the House of Lords, allowing the appellant's appeal, that since this was an oral contract, the conditions relied on were not incorporated into it so as to exempt the respondents from liability in negligence. Lord Devlin was of opinion that previous dealings are relevant only if they prove actual and not constructive knowledge of the terms and also prove assent to them.

222. Akerib *v.* Booth, [1961] 1 All E.R. 380

The defendants were the owners of premises where they carried on business as packers and forwarders of goods. They made a contract with the plaintiff under which they agreed to pack the plaintiff's goods and also to lease to him six rooms in the premises to be used partly as an office and partly as a store by the plaintiff. Because of the defendants' negligence water escaped from a cistern on the top floor of the premises, and this damaged the plaintiff's goods and some office material in the rooms which he was leasing. The plaintiff sued for damages, and the defendants pleaded a paragraph in the schedule to the contract which said that the defendants were not in any circumstances to be responsible for damage caused by water to any goods whether in the possession of the defendants or not. The Court was concerned to decide the meaning and scope of these words. Taken as they stood and read in isolation, the words applied to all goods without any restriction. However, the plaintiff argued that if the words were read in the context of the whole contract, the *main* purpose of which was to cover the defendants in the process of packing, the words must be confined to goods which had been handed over to the defendants for this purpose. The Court of Appeal *held* that either interpretation was possible. However, since the words were ambiguous they must be construed against the defendants who had drafted the contract and put the term into it. The immunity must, therefore, be confined to goods handed over to the defendants for packing, and the plaintiff succeeded.

N.B. This is really an aspect of the *contra proferentem* rule which construes all ambiguous statements in written contracts against the draftsman and in favour of the other party.

223. Karsales (Harrow) Ltd. *v.* Wallis, [1956] 2 All E.R. 866

The defendant inspected a Buick car which a Mr. Stanton wished to sell him. The defendant found it to be in excellent condition and agreed to pay £600 for it, effecting the purchase through a finance company. The car was badly damaged before it was delivered to Wallis; the new tyres which were on the car when Wallis saw it had been replaced by old ones; the radio had been removed; the cylinder head was off; all the valves were burnt; and the engine had two broken pistons. Wallis would not agree to take delivery of the car but it was towed to his place of business and left there. The finance company originally involved assigned its rights under the agreement with Wallis to Karsales, and in this action Karsales were trying to recover the instalments due under the agreement. In so doing they relied on the following clause in the agreement assigned to them: "No condition or warranty that the vehicle is roadworthy, or as to its age condition or fitness for any purpose, is given by the owner or implied herein." The county court judge decided that the exemption clause was effective and ordered Wallis to pay. Wallis now appealed. The Court of Appeal held that Wallis was not liable because exemption clauses, no matter how widely expressed, only avail the party who includes them when he is carrying out his contract in its essential respects. Here there was a breach of a fundamental term amounting to non-performance. As Birkett, L.J., said: "A car that will not go is not a car at all."

224. Alexander *v.* Railway Executive, [1951] 2 All E.R. 442

Alexander was a magician who had been on a tour together with an assistant. He left three trunks at the parcels office at Launceston station, the trunks containing various properties which were used in an "escape illusion." The plaintiff paid 5d. for each trunk deposited and received a ticket for each one. He then left saying that he would send instructions for their dispatch. Some weeks after the deposit and before the plaintiff had sent instructions for the dispatch of the trunks, the plaintiff's assistant persuaded the clerk in the parcels office to give him access to the trunks, though he was not in possession of the ticket. The assistant took away several of the properties and was later convicted of larceny. The plaintiff sued the defendants for damages for breach of contract, and the defendants pleaded the following term which was contained in the ticket and which stated that the Railway Executive was "not liable for loss misdelivery or damage to any articles where the value was in excess of £5 unless at the time of the deposit the true value and nature of the goods was declared by the depositor and an extra charge paid." No such declaration or payment had been made. *Held*—The plaintiff succeeded because, although sufficient notice had been given constructively to the plaintiff of the term, the term did not protect the defendants because they were guilty of a breach of a fundamental obligation in allowing the trunks to be opened and things to be removed from them by an unauthorised person.

N.B. Devlin, J., said that a deliberate delivery to the wrong person did not fall within the meaning of "misdelivery," and this may be regarded as the real reason for the decision, as it involves the application of the *contra proferentum* rule.

225. Hunt and Winterbotham (West of England) Ltd. *v.* B.R.S. (Parcels) Ltd., [1962] 1 All E.R. 111

The defendants entered into a contract with the plaintiffs under the terms of which the defendants were to carry 15 parcels of woollen goods to Manchester. In fact only 12 parcels arrived and the plaintiffs now sued for damages for the value of the three parcels lost. The defendants pleaded an exemption clause excluding their liability for loss "however sustained." The plaintiffs based their claim on negligence and did not plead breach of a fundamental obligation. There was no evidence as to how the parcels had been lost, the defendants being unable to offer an explanation. In view of this the Court of Appeal gave judgment for the defendants saying that if they were negligent, the exemption clause would protect them. The plaintiffs had not alleged breach of a fundamental obligation and had produced no evidence to suggest that the defendants were in breach of a fundamental obligation which would have been essential if such a breach were alleged.

226. Suisse Atlantique Société D/Armament Maritime S.A. *v.* N.V. Rotterdamsche Kolen Centrale, [1966] 2 All E.R. 61

The plaintiffs were shipowners and the defendants chartered a ship from them for "two years' continuous voyages." Under the contract, demurrage of $1,000 per day had to be paid by the charterers to the owners if the ship was detained in port longer than the loading time permitted and specified by the contract. There were substantial delays and the demurrage was paid, but the shipowner's loss of freight was greater than the demurrage they had received and they claimed general damages over and above the demurrage. It was suggested for the owners that the delay was deliberate and enabled them to regard the contract as *repudiated* so that the demurrage provisions did not apply and they could recover their full loss. The owners further argued that because of the cases relating to fundamental breach and exemption clauses the demurrage clause could not cover a breach as serious as this. The House of Lords, after consideration of the fundamental breach cases, *Held*—that—

(*a*) a fundamental breach no longer automatically nullifies an exemption clause. The matter is one of construction of the contract.

(*b*) The demurrage clause was not so much an exemption clause as a provision for liquidated damages, but was wide enough to cover the breaches complained of.

(*c*) Even if the charterer's conduct had given the owners the right to treat the contract as repudiated, they had not done so and the contract including the demurrage clause remained in force.

227. Harbutt's Plasticine Ltd. *v.* Wayne Tank and Pump Co. Ltd., [1970] 1 All E.R. 225

In 1961 the defendants agreed to install certain equipment in the plaintiff's factory for the purpose of storing, heating and dispensing wax for certain manufacturing processes. A clause of the contract provided that until the installation was taken over by the plaintiff the defendant would indemnify the plaintiff for any damage caused by the negligence of the defendant's servants, but that the total liability should not exceed £2,330. Owing to the negligent switching on of the machine by the defendant's servants it became overheated, caught fire and destroyed the factory. *Held*—

(i) The defendants were liable for the full amount of loss (£146,581). There had been a fundamental breach of the contract and in the circumstances the exclusion clause limiting the damage to £2,330 did not apply.

(ii) In order to determine whether a breach of contract was fundamental not only the breach itself but also the events resulting from the breach must be considered. In this case the breaches by the defendants and the consequences of them were so fundamental as to bring the contract to an end.

(iii) Where the defendant had been guilty of such a fundamental breach that the contract was automatically at an end so that the innocent party had no chance of an election whether to continue or not the guilty party could not rely on an exclusion or limitation clause when sued for damages for breach.

(iv) Where the innocent party with knowledge of a fundamental breach can and does treat the contract as continuing and sues for damages, the application of an exclusion clause exempting the defendant from liability depends upon the relevant rules of construction of contracts.

(v) The proper measure of damages was the cost of building a new factory, even though the new factory was in many ways better than the old one. However, the money received by the plaintiffs from their insurance company should go in relief of the damages paid by the defendants and reduce them by the relevant amount.

227*a*. *Farnworth Finance Facilities Ltd.* v. *Attryde*, [1970] 2 All E.R. 774

Mr. Attryde bought a motor-cycle on hire purchase. The contract which was not covered by the Hire Purchase Acts contained a clause to the effect that the vehicle was supplied "subject to no conditions or warranties whatsoever express or implied." The machine had many faults and although Mr. Attryde always complained about them he did drive the machine for some 4,000 miles before deciding to repudiate the contract. He was then sued by the finance company who claimed that the exemption clause applied to exclude liability for defects. *Held*—by the Court of Appeal—that it did not. There was a rule of construction which provided that in general terms an exclusion clause was not effective to exclude a fundamental breach which was what had occurred in this case. The defects taken together amounted to a fundamental breach. Mr. Attryde had not affirmed the contract by using the machine. He had always complained about the defects and had indicated that he would only finally accept the machine if they were remedied. It should be noted that Lord Denning appears in his judgment to have tried to square the decision with both *Harbutt*[227] and *Suisse*[226] as follows—

We have in this case to apply the principles about fundamental breach, which were recently considered by this court in *Harbutt's Plasticine Ltd.* v. *Wayne Tank and Pump Co. Ltd.* The first thing to do, is, no doubt, to construe the contract, remembering always the proposition of Pearson, L.J., which was approved by the House of Lords in *Suisse Atlantique Société d'Armement Maritime S.A.* v. *N.V. Rotterdamsche Kolen Centrale:* ". . . there is a rule of construction that normally an exception or exclusion clause or similar provision in a contract should be construed as not applying to a situation created by a fundamental breach of contract." That rule of construction applies here. It means that we must see if there was a fundamental breach of contract. If there was, then the exempting condition should not be construed as applying to it. We look, therefore, to the terms of the contract, express or implied (apart from the exception clauses) and see which of them were broken. If they were broken in a fundamental respect, the finance company cannot rely on the exception clauses. (See also *Kenyon etc.* v. *Baxter Hoare Ltd.*, 1971.)[651]

228. Polloch & Co. *v.* Macrae, [1922] S.C. (H.L.) 192

The defendants entered into a contract to build and supply marine engines. The contract carried an exemption clause which was designed to protect the defendant from liability for defective materials and workmanship. The engines supplied under the contract had a great many defects and could not be used. *Held*—by the House of Lords—that on a true construction of the contract the exemption clause did not apply because it was repugnant to the main purpose of the contract. Lord Dunedin said: "Now, when there is such a congeries of defects as to destroy the workable character of the machine I think this amounts to a total breach of contract, and that each defect cannot be taken by itself separately so as to apply the provisions of the conditions of guarantee and make it impossible to claim damages."

229. Thomas National Transport (Melbourne) Pty. Ltd. and Pay *v.* May and Baker (Australia) Pty. Ltd., [1966] 2 Lloyd's Rep. 347

The owners of certain packages made a contract with carriers under which the packages were to be carried from Melbourne to various places in Australia. The carriers employed a sub-contractor to collect the parcels and take them to the carriers' depot in Melbourne. When the sub-contractor arrived at the Melbourne depot it was locked and so he drove the lorry full of packages to his own house and left it in a garage there. There was a fire and some of the packages were destroyed. The owners sued the carriers who pleaded an exemption clause in the contract of carriage. *Held*—by the High Court of Australia—that the plaintiffs succeeded. There had been a fundamental breach of contract. The intention of the parties was that the goods would be taken to the carriers' depot and not to the sub-contractors' house, in which case the carriers could not rely on the clause. The decision in the *Suisse Case* was applied.

230. Hutton *v.* Warren (1836), 150 E.R. 517

The plaintiff was the tenant of a farm and the defendant the landlord. At Michaelmas, 1833, the defendant gave the plaintiff notice to quit on the Lady Day following. The defendant insisted that the plaintiff should cultivate the land during the period of notice which he did. The plaintiff now asked for a fair allowance for seeds and labour of which he had no benefit having left the farm before harvest. It was proved that by custom a tenant was bound to farm for the whole of his tenancy and on quitting was entitled to a fair allowance for seeds and labour. *Held*—the plaintiff succeeded.

> We are of opinion that this custom was, by implication, imported into the lease. It has long been settled, that, in commercial transactions, extrinsic evidence of custom and usage is admissable to annex incidents to written contracts, in matters with respect to which they are silent. The same rule has also been applied to contracts in other transactions of life, in which known usages have been established and prevailed; and this has been done upon the principle of presumption that, in such transactions, the parties did not mean to express in writing the whole of the contract by which they intended to be bound, but a contract with reference to those known usages.
> (*Per* Parke, B.)

231. Lister *v.* Romford Ice and Cold Storage Co. Ltd., [1957] 1 All E.R. 125

The defendants' lorry driver negligently reversed the company's vehicle into another servant of the company (his father) who received damages from the company under the doctrine of vicarious liability. The defendants were insured against this liability and the insurance company paid the damages and, under the doctrine of subrogation, sued the lorry driver in the name of the company to recover what they had paid. It was unanimously *held* by the House of Lords that the lorry-driver, as a servant of the company, owed them a duty to perform his work with reasonable care and skill, and that a servant who involves his master in vicarious liability by reason of negligence is liable in damages to the master for breach of contract. This liability arises out of an implied term in the contract of service to indemnify the master for loss caused to him by the servant's negligence. The damages will in such a case amount to a complete indemnity in respect of the amount which the employer has been held vicariously liable to pay the injured plaintiff.

232. Cumming *v.* Ince (1847), 11 Q.B. 112

An old lady was induced to settle property on one of her relatives by the threat of unlawful confinement in a private mental home. *Held*—The settlement could be set aside on the ground of duress, i.e. the threat of false imprisonment.

233. Williams *v.* Bayley (1866), L.R. 1 H.L. 200

A father agreed to make a mortgage of property to a bank in consideration of the return by the bank of certain promissory notes forged by his son. The banker concerned had suggested in conversation with the father that the son would be prosecuted if some agreement were not reached. The promise to make the mortgage was held invalid because of undue influence which, though not presumed in this case, had been proved.

234. Lancashire Loans Ltd. *v.* Black, [1934] 1 K.B. 380

A daughter married at eighteen and went to live with her husband. Her mother was an extravagant woman and was in debt to a firm of moneylenders. When the daughter became of age, her mother persuaded her to raise £2,000 on property in which the daughter had an interest, and this was used to pay off the mother's debts. Twelve months later mother and daughter signed a joint and several promissory note of £775 at eighty-five per cent interest in favour of the moneylenders, and the daughter created a further charge on her property in order that the mother might borrow more money. The daughter did not understand the nature of the transaction, and the only advice she received was from a solicitor acting for the mother and the moneylenders. The moneylenders brought this action against the mother and daughter on the note. *Held* —The daughter's defence that she was under undue influence of her mother succeeded, in spite of the fact that she was of full age and married with her own home.

235. Hodgson *v.* Marks, [1970] 3 All E.R. 513

Mrs. Hodgson, who was a widow of 83, owned a freehold house in which she lived. In 1959 she took in a Mr. Evans as a lodger. She soon came to trust Evans and allowed him to manage her financial affairs. In June, 1960, she transferred the house to Evans, her sole reason for so doing being to prevent her nephew from turning Evans out of the house. It was orally agreed between Mrs. Hodgson and Evans that the house was to remain hers although held in the name of Evans. Evans later made arrangements to sell the house without the knowledge or consent of Mrs. Hodgson. The house was bought by Mr. Marks and Mrs. Hodgson now asked for a declaration that he was bound to transfer the property back to her. The following questions arose.—

(*a*) Whether Evans held the house in trust for Mrs. Hodgson. It was *held* by Ungoed—Thomas, J., that he did. The absence of written evidence of the trust as required by Sect. 53 of the Law of Property Act, 1925, was not a bar to Mrs. Hodgson's claim. The Act was not intended to assist a fraud.

(*b*) Whether Evans had exercised undue influence. It was *held* that he had and a presumption of undue influence was raised. Although the parties were not in the established categories Evans had a relationship of trust and confidence with Mrs. Hodgson of a kind which raised a presumption of undue influence.

However, Mrs. Hodgson lost the case because Mr. Marks was protected by Sect. 70 of the Land Registration Act, 1925, which gives rights to a purchaser of property for value in respect of interests in that property of which the purchaser is not aware. Mrs. Hodgson's appeal succeeded. To ensure a good title a purchaser must, in spite of Sect. 70, pay heed to the possibility of rights in all occupiers. ([1971] 2 All E.R. 684.)

236. Allcard *v.* Skinner (1887), 36 Ch.D. 145

In 1868 the plaintiff joined a Protestant institution called the sisterhood of St. Mary at the Cross, promising to devote her property to the service of the poor. The defendant Miss Skinner was the Lady Superior of the Sisterhood. In 1871 the plaintiff ceased to be a novice and became a sister in the order, taking her vows of poverty, chastity and obedience. By this time she had left her home and was residing with the sisterhood. The plaintiff remained a sister until 1879 and, in compliance with the vow of poverty, she had by then given property to the value of about £7,000 to the defendant. The plaintiff left the order in 1879 and became a Roman Catholic. Of the property she had transferred, £1,671 remained in 1885 and the plaintiff sought to recover this sum, claiming that it had been transferred in circumstances of undue influence. *Held*—The gifts had been made under pressure of an unusually persuasive nature, particularly since the plaintiff was prevented from seeking outside advice under a rule of the sisterhood which said, "Let no sister seek the advice of any extern without the superior's leave." However, the plaintiff's claim was barred by her delay because, although the influence was removed in 1879, she did not bring her action until 1885.

237. Goodinson *v.* Goodinson, [1954] 2 All E.R. 255

A contract made between husband and wife, who had already separated, provided that the husband would pay his wife a weekly sum by way of maintenance in consideration that she would indemnify him against all debts incurred by her, would not pledge his credit, and would not take matrimonial proceedings against him in respect of maintenance. The wife now sued for arrears of maintenance under this agreement. The last promise was admittedly void since its object was to oust the jurisdiction of the courts, but it was *held* that this did not vitiate the rest of the contract; it was not the sole or even the main consideration, and the wife's action for arrears succeeded.

238. Dann *v.* Curzon (1911), 104 L.T. 66

An agreement was made for advertising a play by means of collusive criminal proceedings brought as a result of a pre-arranged disturbance at the theatre. The plaintiffs, who agreed to create the disturbance and did in fact do so, sued for the remuneration due to them under the agreement. *Held*—The action failed because it was an agreement to commit a criminal offence and was therefore against public policy.

239. Anderson Ltd. *v.* Daniel, [1924] 1 K.B. 138

Sellers of artificial fertilisers were required by statute to give purchasers an invoice stating the percentages of chemical substances contained in the fertiliser. Any seller who failed to give such an invoice was liable to a fine. Here the sellers had delivered ten tons of artificial fertiliser without complying with the statute. *Held*—They could not recover the price. The purpose of the statute was to protect a section of the public, i.e. the purchasers of artificial manure, and the sellers had carried out the contract in an illegal way.

240. Shaw *v.* Groom, [1970] 1 All E.R. 702

Mrs. Groom was the tenant of a room in North London and Mrs. Shaw was her landlord. The tenancy was a controlled one and Mrs. Groom had occupied the room for some twenty years at a rent of 7s. 11d. per week plus 2s. 6d. for electricity. Mrs. Groom fell into arrears with her rent and Mrs. Shaw brought this action to recover the money owing to her. Unfortunately Mrs. Shaw had failed, during the tenancy, to comply with Sect. 4 of the Landlord and Tenant Act, 1962, which required that the tenant be provided with a rent book. Mrs. Groom now alleged that Mrs. Shaw could not recover the arrears of rent because her failure to provide a rent book was illegal performance of the contract. *Held*—by the Court of Appeal—that Mrs. Shaw succeeded. The intention of the legislature was not to preclude the landlord from recovering rent due or to impose on him any forfeiture beyond the fines stipulated in the Act of 1962. It was accepted that the requirement of a rent book was to protect a class of persons of whom Mrs. Groom was one. This did not, however, automatically prevent Mrs. Shaw's claim. The rule that an illegal contract cannot be enforced by the guilty party must be sensibly restricted in its operation.

241. Smith *v.* Mawhood (1845), 14 M. & W. 452

It was held in this case that a tobacconist could recover the price of tobacco sold by him even though he did not have a licence to sell it and had not painted his name on his place of business. Here the statutory penalty was £200, but the object of the statute was not to affect the contract of sale but to impose a fine on the offender for the purpose of revenue.

242. Brogden *v.* Marriott (1863), 3 Bing. (N.C.) 88

In this case the parties had agreed to buy and sell a horse, the price to be £200 if it transpired that the horse could trot at eighteen miles per hour within a month of purchase. If this speed was not attained the price was to be a shilling. The horse did not achieve this speed and the purchaser claimed it for a shilling. *Held*—There was no claim because the contract was in fact a wager.

243. Rourke *v.* Short (1856), 5 E. & B. 904

The two parties were making a contract for the sale of certain rags but could not agree on the price that had been paid on a previous sale between them. It was eventually agreed that if the seller's memory was correct the rags should be sold for six shillings per cwt. and if not the price should be three shillings per cwt. The seller's memory proved to be correct but the buyer would not take delivery of the rags. This action by the seller failed because the previous selling price was in fact the subject of a wager, the difference in the prices being a stake.

244. Pearce *v.* Brooks (1866), L.R. 1 Exch. 213

The plaintiffs hired a carriage to the defendant for a period of twelve months during which time the defendant was to pay the purchase price by instalments. The defendant was a prostitute and the carriage, which was of attractive design, was intended to assist her in obtaining clients. One of the plaintiffs knew that the defendant was a prostitute but he said that he did not know that she intended to use the carriage for purposes of prostitution. The evidence showed to the contrary. The jury found that the plaintiffs knew the purpose for which the carriage was to be used and thereupon the court *held* that the plaintiffs' claim for the sum due under the contract failed for illegality.

245. Foster *v.* Driscoll, [1929] 1 K.B. 470

Several persons entered into what was in effect a partnership contract to equip a ship and load it with six different varieties of whisky. The ship was then to be sent to the U.S.A. and the whisky was to be sold either in the U.S.A. or on its borders to persons who would then dispose of it in violation of the U.S.A.'s prohibition laws. This action was brought on a bill of exchange which had been accepted by members of the syndicate or partnership as a method of paying for the whisky. *Held*—The contract of partnership was void as against public policy because it had been formed to procure an act which was illegal by the law of a foreign but friendly country, and no action was possible in respect of any matter arising out of the scheme.

246. Regazzoni *v.* K. C. Sethia Ltd., [1958] A.C. 301

The defendants agreed to sell and deliver jute bags to the plaintiff, both parties knowing and intending that the goods would be shipped from India to Genoa so that the plaintiff might then send them to South Africa. Both parties knew that the law of India prohibited the direct or indirect export of goods from India to South Africa, this law being directed at the policy of apartheid adopted by South Africa. The defendants did not deliver the jute bags as agreed and the plaintiff brought this action in an English court, the contract being governed by English law. *Held*—Although the contract was not illegal in English law, it could not be enforced because it had as its object the violation of the law of a foreign and friendly country in which part of the contract was to be carried out.

247. John *v.* Mendoza, [1939] 1 K.B. 141

The defendant owed the plaintiff £852 15s. 6d. The defendant was made bankrupt and the plaintiff was intending to prove for his debt in the bankruptcy. The defendant asked him not to do so, but to say that the £852 15s. 6d. was a gift whereupon the defendant would pay the plaintiff in full regardless of the sum received by other creditors. In view of the defendant's promise the plaintiff withdrew his proof, but in the event all the other creditors were paid in full and the bankruptcy was annulled. The plaintiff now sued for the debt. *Held*—There was no claim, for the plaintiff abandoned all right to recover on failure to prove in the bankruptcy, and the defendant's promise to pay in full was unenforceable, being an agreement designed to defeat the bankruptcy laws.

248. Parkinson *v.* The College of Ambulance Ltd. and Harrison, [1925] 2 K.B. 1

The first defendants were a charitable institution and the second defendant was the secretary. Harrison fraudulently represented to the plaintiff, Colonel Parkinson, that the charity was in a position to obtain some honour (probably a knighthood) for him if he would make a suitable donation to the funds of the charity. The plaintiff paid over the sum of £3,000 and said he would pay more if the honour was granted. No honour of any kind was received by the plaintiff and he brought this action to recover the money he had donated to the College. *Held*—The agreement was contrary to public policy and illegal. No relief could be granted to the plaintiff.

249. Napier *v.* National Business Agency Ltd., [1951] 2 All E.R. 264

The defendants engaged the plaintiff to act as their secretary and accountant at a salary of £13 per week plus £6 per week for expenses. Both parties were aware that the plaintiff's expenses could never amount to £6 a week and in fact they never exceeded £1 per week. Income Tax was deducted on £13 per week, and £6 per week was paid without deduction of tax as reimbursement of expenses. The plaintiff, having been summarily dismissed, claimed payment of £13 as wages in lieu of notice. *Held*—The agreement was contrary to public policy and illegal. The plaintiff's action failed.

250. Alexander *v*. Rayson, [1936] 1 K.B. 169

The plaintiff was the lessee of certain flats in Piccadilly. He let one of the flats to Mrs. Rayson by granting her an underlease at £450 a year. Another agreement was made whereby Mrs. Rayson was to pay £750 a year for certain services provided by the plaintiff. The defendant paid both sums for a time, but later paid a quarter's rent under the underlease, i.e. £112 10s., refusing to pay for services on the ground that they had not been rendered. The plaintiff sued in respect of the sum owing for services. The defendant alleged, amongst other things, that the contract for services was illegal since it was designed to defraud the Westminster City Council, the latter having assessed the rateable value of the flat on the basis of a rental of £450 a year, which was the income under the lease shown to the assessment committee. *Held*—The agreement for services could not be enforced because it was illegal. In any case there was no consideration moving from the plaintiff in respect of the services, for it emerged that he was already bound to carry out the services under his own lease.

251. Edler *v*. Auerbach, [1950] 1 K.B. 359

The defendant leased premises to the plaintiff for use as offices. The lease was contrary to the provisions of the Defence Regulations of 1939, since the premises had previously been used as residential accommodation and should have been let as such. The local authority discovered the illegal use and would not allow it to continue. The plaintiff now sued for rescission of the lease together with rent paid under it. The defendant counterclaimed for rent due and for damage done to the premises, including the removal of a bath. *Held*— The landlord could not enforce the illegal lease but was entitled to damages for the plaintiff's failure to replace the bath.

252. Bowmakers Ltd. *v*. Barnet Instruments Ltd., [1944] 2 All E.R. 579

Bowmakers bought machine tools from a person named Smith. This contract was illegal because it contravened an Order made by the Minister of Supply under the Defence Regulations, Smith having no licence to sell machine tools. Bowmakers hired the machine tools to Barnet Instruments under hire-purchase agreements which were also illegal because Bowmakers did not have a licence to sell machine tools. Barnet Instruments failed to keep up the instalments, sold some of the machine tools and refused to give up the others. Bowmakers sued, not on the illegal hire-purchase contracts, but in conversion, and judgment was given for Bowmakers. The Court of Appeal declared the contracts illegal but, since Bowmakers were not suing under the contracts but as owners, their action succeeded. The wrongful sales by Barnet Instruments terminated the hire-purchase contracts.

N.B. Although the contract between Smith and Bowmakers was illegal ownership passed to Bowmakers by reason of delivery. When goods are delivered the person receiving them has some evidence of title by reason of possession and need not necessarily plead a contract. Where, in an illegal situation, the goods have not been delivered there may be difficulty in establishing ownership without relying on the illegal contract. Nevertheless, ownership was established without delivery in *Belvoir Finance Co. Ltd*. v. *Stapleton*, [1970] 3 W.L.R. 530. In this case A (a dealer) sold certain cars to B (a finance company) which let them on hire purchase to C (a car-hire firm). C did not pay the minimum deposit required by regulation to B; thus the hire-purchase contract was illegal. Later, C's manager, S, sold the cars to innocent purchasers. C did not pay the hire-purchase instalments and B sued S in conversion, the company C having gone into liquidation. It was *held* by the Court of Appeal that B succeeded. They were the owners of the cars and S had converted their property. The decision is of interest since B (the finance company) had never taken delivery of the cars; they were sent direct from A to C as is usual in these transactions. Nevertheless B was accepted as owner although the only means of proving ownership open to B seems to have been the illegal hire purchase contract with C. This was the only document which showed how B came to acquire ownership of the cars.

253. Fielding and Platt Ltd. *v.* Najjar, [1969] 2 All E.R. 150

The plaintiffs entered into an agreement with a Lebanese company to make and deliver an aluminium press. Payment was to be made by six promissory notes given at stated intervals by the defendant personally. The defendant, who was the managing director of the Lebanese company, told the plaintiffs that they ought to invoice the goods as part of a rolling mill, his intention being to deceive the Lebanese import authorities into believing that the import of the press was authorised whereas in fact it was not. The first promissory note was dishonoured and the plaintiffs stopped work on the press and cabled a message to the Lebanese company to that effect. The second promissory note was then dishonoured and the plaintiffs sued upon the notes. It was *held*—by the Court of Appeal—that

(i) since the first note covered work in progress there was no defence based on failure of consideration;

(ii) any illegality in connection with the importing of the press was not part of the contract or agreed to by the plaintiffs;

(iii) the plaintiffs' claim was not, therefore, affected by illegality;

(iv) since the plaintiffs had repudiated the contract before the second note was dishonoured they had no claim for the amount of the note as such but could only sue for damages—the defendant was not liable on the second note.

254. Atkinson *v.* Denby (1862), 7 H. & N. 934

The plaintiff was in financial difficulties and offered to pay his creditors the sum of 5s. in the £ as a full settlement. All the creditors except the defendant agreed to this. The defendant said that he would agree only if the plaintiff paid him £50. Afraid that the scheme would not go through without the defendant's co-operation, the plaintiff made the payment. *Held*—He could recover it because he had been coerced into defrauding his creditors.

255. Hughes *v.* Liverpool Victoria Legal Friendly Society, [1916] 2 K.B. 482

John Henry Thomas, a grocer, had originally taken out five policies on customers who owed him money. It was agreed that Thomas had an insurable interest in the customers because they were his debtors. Thomas let the policies drop and an agent of the defendant company persuaded a Mrs. Hughes to take them up, assuring her that she had an insurable interest which she had not. She now brought this action to recover the premiums paid. *Held*—The contract was illegal but the plaintiff could recover the premiums. She had been induced to take up the policies by the fraud of the defendants' agent.

256. Kiriri Cotton Co. *v.* Dawani, [1960] A.C. 192

A tenant paid a premium to his landlord in order to get possession of a flat. The acceptance of the premium was an offence under Sect. 3 (2) of the Uganda

Rent Restriction Ordinance, and the Ordinance did not provide for recovery of the premium. Both parties were ignorant of the Ordinance. In this action to recover the premium the Judicial Committee of the Privy Council *held* that the premium paid by the tenant must be recoverable because the object of the statute was to protect tenants.

257. Taylor *v.* Bowers (1876), 1 Q.B.D. 291

The plaintiff was under pressure from his creditors and in order to place some of his property out of their reach he assigned certain machinery to a person named Adcock. The plaintiff then called a meeting of his creditors and tried to get them to settle for less than the amount of their debts, representing his assets as not including the machinery. The creditors would not and did not agree to a settlement. The plaintiff now sued to recover his machinery from the defendants who had obtained it from Adcock. *Held*—The plaintiff succeeded because the illegal fraud on the creditors had not been carried out.

258. Kearley *v.* Thomson (1890), 24 Q.B.D. 742

The plaintiff had a friend who was bankrupt and wished to obtain his discharge. The defendant was likely to oppose the discharge and accordingly the plaintiff paid the defendant £40 in return for which the defendant promised to stay away from the public examination and not to oppose the discharge. The defendant did stay away from the public examination but before an application for discharge had been made the plaintiff brought his action claiming the £40. *Held*—The claim failed because the illegal scheme had been partially effected.

259. Bigos *v.* Bousted, [1951] 1 All E.R. 92

The defendant was anxious to send his wife and daughter abroad for the sake of the daughter's health, but restrictions on currency were in force so that a long stay abroad was impossible. In August, 1947, the defendant, in contravention of the Exchange Control Act, 1947, made an agreement under which the plaintiff was to supply £150 of Italian money to be made available at Rapallo, the defendant undertaking to repay the plaintiff with English money in England. As security, the defendant deposited with the plaintiff a share certificate for 140 shares in a company. The wife and daughter went to Italy but were not supplied with currency, and had to return sooner than they would have done. The defendant, thereupon, asked for the return of his share certificate but the plaintiff refused to give it up. This action was brought by the plaintiff to recover the sum of £150 which she insisted she had lent to the defendant. He denied the loan, and counter-claimed for the return of his certificate. In the course of the action the plaintiff abandoned her claim, but the defendant proceeded with his counter-claim saying that, although the contract was illegal, it was still executory so that he might repent and ask the court's assistance. *Held*—The court would not assist him because the fact that the contract had not been carried out was due to frustration by the plaintiff and not the repentance of the defendant. In fact his repentance was really want of power to sin.

260. Fisher *v.* Bridges (1854), 188 E.R. 713

The plaintiff agreed to sell the defendant certain land which the defendant intended to use as a prize in a lottery. The use of land for lotteries was forbidden by statute but the land was conveyed and the purchase price all but

£630 was paid. Later the defendant entered into a deed with the plaintiff under the terms of which he agreed to pay the £630 and the plaintiff now sued upon that deed. *Held*—No action lay on the deed. Jervis, C.J., said: "It is clear that the covenant was given for the payment of the purchase money. As it springs from, and is the creature of the illegal agreement, and as the law would not enforce the original illegal contract, so neither will it allow the parties to enforce a security for the purchase money which, by the original bargain, was tainted with illegality."

261. Southern Industrial Trust *v.* Brooke House Motors (1968), 112 S.J. 798

A customer wished to buy a car from the defendants who were dealers. The dealers and the customer inserted incorrect figures relating to price and deposit in the hire-purchase agreement so that it became illegal under statutory provisions then applying to such agreements. The car was then sold to the plaintiff finance company which was unaware of the true position. The finance company hired it out to the customer under the falsified hire-purchase agreement. The dealers had represented both to the customer and the finance company that the car was a 1962 model whereas in fact it was registered in 1958. When the customer discovered this he refused to pay any further instalments to the finance company and the company sued the dealers for breach of a warranty in the contract of sale to them, i.e. that the car was a 1962 model. It was *held*— by the Court of Appeal—that damages were recoverable notwithstanding the illegality of the hire-purchase agreement between the plaintiffs and the customer. The sale by the dealers to the finance company was collateral to that and was not tainted by the illegality in the other agreement.

262. Kaufman *v.* Gerson, [1904] 1 K.B. 591

The defendant's husband had misappropriated money entrusted to him by the plaintiff, his employer. The defendant made a contract in writing with the plaintiff under which she agreed to make good the loss, the plaintiff agreeing not to prosecute. The events took place in France and the agreement was governed by French law, which did not regard the element of coercion in the case as a vitiating element. Nevertheless, the action being brought on the contract in an English court, it was dismissed because it was contrary to public policy for an English court to enforce a contract obtained in this way.

263. Cowan *v.* Milbourn (1867), L.R. 2 Ex. 230

A person hired a hall to deliver blasphemous lectures and then was refused possession of it. His action claiming possession was refused on the grounds that no relief could be granted by the court where the purpose of the contract was illegal.

264. Berg *v.* Sadler and Moore, [1937] All E.R. 637

The plaintiff was a hairdresser and sold tobacco and cigarettes. He was a member of the Tobacco Trade Association, the Association having as its object the prevention of price cutting. Manufacturers would supply tobacco to traders who agreed not to sell at less than the fixed retail price. The plaintiff sold tobacco at cut prices and was put on the manufacturers' stop list which meant that he could not obtain supplies. The plaintiff made contact with a person named Reece who was a member of the Association and Reece agreed to obtain goods from manufacturers and hand them over to the plaintiff, in return for which Reece was to receive a commission from the plaintiff. One such transaction was carried out. On a later occasion the plaintiff's assistant and a representative of Reece went to defendant's premises to obtain a supply of cigarettes. The plaintiff's assistant handed over £72 19s. od. to Moore, who had some doubt about the matter and said he would send the goods direct to Reece's shop. Thereupon the plaintiff's assistant demanded the return of the money, Moore refused to give it back, and this action was brought to recover it. *Held*—This was an attempt by the plaintiff to obtain goods by false pretences and, since no action arises out of a base cause, the plaintiff's action failed.

265. Clay v. Yates (1856), 1 H. & B. 73

The plaintiff made an agreement with the defendant under which he was to print for the defendant 500 copies of a treatise to which a dedication was to be prefixed. The plaintiff began printing the book and later the dedication. The dedication was defamatory and the plaintiff omitted it from the book, and the defendant refused to pay for the book without the dedication. *Held*— The plaintiff was justified in refusing to print defamatory matter and was entitled to payment for so much of his work as was lawful.

266. Strongman Ltd. v. Sincock, [1955] 2 Q.B. 525

The defendant, who was an architect, employed the plaintiffs, who were builders, to modernise certain property. It was illegal at the time to carry out such work without the necessary licences. The defendant did get licences for part of the work, but the builders also did work for him which was £3,459 in excess of what was covered by licence. The defendant now refused to pay for the work, claiming that the contract was illegal. *Held*—The plaintiffs had acted in good faith but the contract, being illegal, could not be sued upon. However, they were entitled to damages up to the value of the unlicensed work on the basis of the defendant's breach of a collateral warranty that he would get the licences required.

267. Marles v. Trant (Philip) & Sons Ltd., [1954] 1 Q.B. 29

The defendants innocently sold wheat as spring wheat to the plaintiff. The wheat was in fact winter wheat but had been sold to the defendants as spring wheat. The contract with the plaintiff was not illegal as formed but was illegal as performed because the defendants did not comply with a statutory provision which required an invoice to be delivered with the goods. The plaintiff discovered that the seed was winter wheat and sued the defendants for breach of contract. *Held*—In spite of the illegality of the performance the plaintiff, could, being the innocent party, receive damages.

268. Re Davstone Estates Ltd., [1969] 2 All E.R. 849

The plaintiffs were landlords of a block of flats in St. Albans. The plaintiffs agreed with the tenants to keep the common parts of the block in good repair and the tenants agreed to pay £15 a year to the plaintiffs for this service. The tenants were also required to agree to a clause which provided that if the tenants' proportionate share of the actual cost of repairs incurred by the plaintiffs should exceed £15 in any year the tenants would pay the excess. A certificate by the plaintiffs' surveyor was to be conclusive as to the tenants liability to pay any excess. The plaintiffs had to make good many structural defects as distinct from repairs and maintenance and the court was required as a matter of construction of the tenancy agreement to say whether any of these costs were recoverable from the tenants. In the course of his judgment Ungoed—Thomas, J. *held* that the provision as to the finality of the plaintiffs' surveyor's certificate ousted the jurisdiction of the court and was void as contrary to public policy.

269. Horwood *v.* Millar's Timber Co., [1917] 1 K.B. 305

The plaintiff was a moneylender and he had lent money to a person named Bunyon who was employed as a clerk by the defendants. Bunyon owed £42 together with a sum of £31 as interest. Bunyon assigned to the plaintiff a policy of assurance on his life worth £100, and all the salary or wages due or to become due to him with the defendants or any other employer. The plaintiff attached certain conditions to the agreement and under these Bunyon agreed not to leave his job without the plaintiff's permission; to do nothing to get himself dismissed; not to borrow; not to sell, pledge or otherwise dispose of his property, and not to obtain credit. If Bunyon was in breach of any of the conditions the whole sum was immediately payable. The plaintiff now sued Bunyon's employers in respect of the salary assigned. *Held*—The contract was illegal, being against public policy, and it was therefore unenforceable. That part of the contract which dealt with the assignment of salary was not severable from the rest and so the action failed.

270. Denny's Trustee *v.* Denny, [1919] 1 K.B. 583

A young man with dissolute habits had fallen into the hands of moneylenders. A deed was entered into under the terms of which the son transferred all his property to the father, who agreed to pay all his debts and to make him a reasonable allowance. The deed provided that the son should not go within eighty miles of Piccadilly Circus without his father's consent, otherwise the annuity would be forfeited. The son became bankrupt and his trustee, wishing to set aside the deed and claim the property for the benefit of creditors, suggested that the deed constituted an illegal restraint. *Held*—The deed was good and could not be set aside; its purpose was to reform the son.

271. Neville *v.* Dominion of Canada News Co. Ltd., [1915] 3 K.B. 556

The plaintiff was a director of a land company engaged in property deals in Canada and the defendants were newspaper proprietors who owed the plaintiff a certain sum of money. Other newspapers had made adverse comments on certain of the plaintiff's land deals and had refused to accept his advertisements. The plaintiff agreed with the defendants to accept less than the sum owed to him, if the defendants would undertake not to comment unfavourably on his dealings. The defendants did publish such comment in spite of the agreement and the plaintiff sought to enforce the contract. *Held*—His action failed because the restraint was against public policy. It was the ordinary and proper business of a newspaper to comment on fraudulent schemes.

272. Wallis *v.* Day (1837), 2 M. & W. 273

The plaintiff was in business as a carrier and he sold that business to the defendant. The plaintiff agreed in return for a weekly salary of £2 3s. 10d. to serve the defendant as assistant for life and further agreed that except as assistant he would not for the rest of his life exercise the trade of carrier. This action was brought by the plaintiff to recover eighteen weeks' arrears of salary.

The defence was that the contract was void as being an unlawful restraint of trade and that no part of it was enforceable. It was unnecessary to decide this point because the court *held* that the restraint was reasonable but Lord Abinger, dealing with the defence, said: "The defendants demurred on the ground that the covenant being in restraint of trade was illegal and therefore the whole contract was void. I cannot however accede to that conclusion. If a party enters into several covenants one of which cannot be enforced against him he is not therefore released from performing the others, and in the present case the defendants might have maintained an action against the plaintiff for not rendering them the services he covenanted to perform, there being nothing illegal in that part of the contract."

273. Hermann v. Charlesworth, [1905] 2 K.B. 123

C agreed that he would introduce gentlemen to Miss Hermann with a view to marriage. She agreed to make an immediate payment of £52 and a payment of £250 on the day of the marriage. He introduced her to several gentlemen and corresponded with others on her behalf but no marriage took place. Miss Hermann now sued for the return of the £52 and succeeded. Although the claim succeeded at common law on the ground of total failure of consideration, Sir Richard Henn-Collins said in the course of his judgment that he could have granted the return of the money by the use of Equity even after a marriage had taken place.

274. Kenyon v. Darwin Cotton Manufacturing Co., [1936] 2 K.B. 193

The plaintiff was employed by the defendants and joined a scheme under which the employees were to finance the company by taking up shares in it. Payment for the shares was to be made by deductions from wages and the employees signed documents agreeing to take the shares and authorising a sum of money to be deducted from their wages. This second document was illegal under the Truck Act, 1831. The plaintiff now sued to recover that part of her wages which had been applied in paying for shares, and the defendants counterclaimed for the amount due on the shares. The plaintiff succeeded because her action was a statutory one under the Truck Act of 1831. The defendants claimed that the agreement to take the shares was legal and should be severed from the part of the agreement dealing with the method of payment. *Held*—There could be no severance because that would leave a contract in which the employees agreed to pay for the shares not out of their wages but out of their assets generally, and this was an agreement which they did not intend to make.

275. Nordenfelt v. Maxim Nordenfelt Guns and Ammunition Co., [1894] A.C. 535

Nordenfelt was a manufacturer of machine guns and other military weapons. He sold the business to a company, giving certain undertakings which restricted his business activities. This company was amalgamated with another company and Nordenfelt was employed by the new concern as managing director. In his contract Nordenfelt agreed that for twenty-five years he would not manufacture guns or ammunition in any part of the world, and would not compete with the company in any way. *Held*—The covenant regarding the business sold was valid and enforceable, even though it was world-wide, because the business connection was world-wide and it was possible in the circumstances to sever this undertaking from the rest of the agreement. However, the further undertaking not to compete in any way with the company was unreasonable and void.

276. Morris & Co. *v.* Saxelby, [1916] 1 A.C. 688

On leaving school Saxelby entered the drawing office of a company engaged in the manufacture of lifting machinery, pulley blocks and travelling cranes. The company had its head office and works in Loughborough and branch offices in eight large cities. Eventually Saxelby became head of one of the company's departments at a salary of £3 17s. 6d. a week. He had entered into a covenant not to engage in a similar business in the United Kingdom for a period of seven years from the date of leaving the company's service. In this action the company sought to enforce that covenant and it was *held* by the House of Lords that it was unreasonably wide, having regard to Saxelby's interests because it would "deprive him for a lengthened period of employing, in any part of the United Kingdom, that mechanical and technical skill and knowledge which, as I have said, his own industry, observation, and intelligence have enabled him to acquire in the very specialized business of the appellants, thus forcing him to begin life afresh, as it were, and depriving him of the means of supporting himself and his family:" per Lord Atkinson.

Furthermore, their Lordships were unanimously of the opinion that the covenant was wider than was necessary to protect those interests which the company was entitled to protect, being aimed at securing the appellants against all competition from Saxelby.

277. Esso Petroleum Co. Ltd. *v.* Harper's Garage (Stourport) Ltd., [1967] 1 All E.R. 699

The defendant company owned two garages with attached filling stations, the Mustow Green Garage, Mustow Green, near Kidderminster, and the Corner Garage at Stourport-on-Severn. Each garage was tied to the plaintiff oil company, the one at Mustow Green by a solus supply agreement only with a tie clause binding the dealer to take the products of the plaintiff company at its scheduled prices from time to time. There was also a price-maintenance clause which was no longer enforceable and a "continuity clause" under which the defendants, if they sold the garage, had to persuade the buyer to enter into another solus agreement with Esso. The defendants also agreed to keep the garage open at all reasonable hours and to give preference to the plaintiff company's oils. The agreement was to remain in force for four years and five months from 1st July, 1963, being the unexpired residue of the ten-year tie of a previous owner. At the Corner Garage there was a similar solus agreement for twenty-one years and a mortgage under which the plaintiffs lent Harpers £7,000 to assist them in buying the garage and improving it. The mortgage contained a tie covenant and forbade redemption for twenty-one years. In August, 1964, Harpers offered to pay off the loan but Esso refused to accept it. Harpers then turned over all four pumps at the Corner Garage to V.I.P. and later also sold V.I.P. at Mustow Green. The plaintiff company now asked for an injunction to restrain the defendants from buying or selling fuels other then Esso at the two garages during the subsistance of the agreements. *Held*—by the House of Lords—that the rule of public policy against unreasonable restraints of trade applied to the solus agreements and the mortgage. The shorter period of four years and five months was reasonable so that that tie was valid but the other tie for twenty-one years in the solus agreement and the mortgage was invalid, so that the injunction asked for by the plaintiffs could not be granted.

277a. *Cleveland Petroleum Co. Ltd.* v. *Dartstone Ltd.*, [1969] 1 All E.R. 201

The owner of a garage and filling station at Crawley in Sussex leased the property to Cleveland and they in turn granted an underlease to the County Oak Service Station Ltd. The underlease contained a convenant under which all motor fuels sold were to be those of Cleveland. There was power to assign in the underlease and a number of assignments took place so that eventually Dartstone Ltd. became the lessees, having agreed to observe the covenants in the underlease. They then challenged the covenant regarding motor fuels and Cleveland asked for an injunction to enforce it. The injunction was granted. Dealing in the Court of Appeal with *Harper's Case*[277] Lord Denning, M.R., said

> . . . it seems plain to me that in three at least of the speeches of their Lordships a distinction is taken between a man who is *already* in possession of the land before he ties himself to an oil company and a man who is *out* of possession and is let into it by an oil company. If an owner in possession ties himself for more than five years to take all his supplies from one company, that is an unreasonable restraint of trade and is invalid. But if a man, who is out of possession, is let into possession by the oil company on the terms that he is to tie himself to that company, such a tie is good.

278. Rother *v.* Colchester Corporation, [1969] 2 All E.R. 600

The Corporation as landlords convenanted with Mr. Rother as a tenant of a hardware shop on an estate in Colchester that they would not let any other shop on the estate for the purpose of a general hardware merchant and ironmonger. They let a shop to the local Co-operative Society as a food hall, the lease stating that they were not to sell any commodity or item which might cause the landlord to commit a breach of any of his covenants for the benefit of tenants of adjacent shops. The premises were used by the Society mainly as a food hall but items usually sold by hardware merchants were on display for sale. In this action by Mr. Rother for breach of the covenant it was *held* by Megarry, J, that a covenant not to let premises for a particular purpose could not be enlarged into a convenant not to permit the premises to be used for that purpose. A restrictive covenant must be construed strictly so as not to create a wider obligation than is imputed by the actual words.

279. George Silverman Ltd. *v.* Silverman [1969], *The Times*, 3rd July, 1969.

Mr. David Silverman, a young dress designer, and his father held shares in George Silverman Ltd., a company by which David Silverman was employed. They sold their shares to Cope Allman International Ltd. as part of a package deal under which that company acquired the ownership and goodwill of George Silverman Ltd. and the services of David Silverman under a contract of employment. The contract of employment provided that if David Silverman left the service of George Silverman he would not for a period of two years thereafter have any interest, either on his own account or as shareholder, director, servant, advisor, or agent of any person, firm, or company, in any business similar to or competing with the business carried on by George Silverman Ltd. in any part of the United Kingdom or Eire. He was later found guilty of possessing cannabis and discharged by the company. The company then asked for an injunction to restrain him from competing with its business according to the terms of the restraint. *Held*—by the Court of Appeal—an injunction could be granted restraining David Silverman. Although the restraint appeared in a contract of service and might in other circumstances have been too wide, David and his father had been paid £90,000 for their shares with a further £20,000 which they would get in the future. The restraint had to be looked at as if it was between vendor and purchaser of a business. The Cope Allman company was entitled to protect its investment in George Silverman Ltd. for the two-year period of the restraint.

280. Attwood *v.* Lamont, [1920] 3 K.B. 571

Attwood carried on business as a draper, tailor and general outfitter in a shop at Kidderminster. The business was organised into different departments, each with a manager. Lamont was appointed as head cutter and manager of the tailoring department, and in his contract of service he agreed that he would not at any time, whether on his own account or on behalf of anybody else, carry on the trades of tailor, dressmaker, general draper, milliner, hatter, haberdasher, gentlemen's, ladies', or children's outfitter at any place within ten miles of Kidderminster. Some time later Lamont asked Attwood to release him from the covenant or to make him a partner, but Attwood refused to do this. Lamont left his employment and set up in business at Worcester, which was outside the ten-mile limit. However, he did do business with Attwood's customers and took orders in Kidderminster. Attwood now asked for an injunction to restrain Lamont in respect of his tailoring activities, claiming that that part of the covenant was severable, though admitting the covenant as a whole was too wide. *Held*—The part of the agreement concerning tailoring was not severable; and even if severable was invalid because it was a covenant against competition. Lamont was a rival largely because of his skill and not because of trade connection.

281. Fitch *v.* Dewes, [1921] 2 A.C. 158

A solicitor at Tamworth employed a person who was successively his articled clerk and managing clerk. In his contract of service, the clerk agreed, if he left the solicitor's employment, never to practise as a solicitor within seven miles of Tamworth Town Hall. *Held*—The agreement was good because during his service the clerk had become acquainted with the details of his employer's clients, and could be restrained even for life from using that knowledge to the detriment of his employer.

282. G. W. Plowman and Son *v.* Ash, [1964] 2 All E.R. 10

The plaintiffs, who were corn merchants, asked for an interlocutory injunction to restrain a former salesman from soliciting orders from customers or former customers in breach of an undertaking in his contract of service that he would not "canvass or solicit for himself or any other person or persons any farmer or market gardener who shall at any time during the employment of the employee hereunder have been a customer of the employers." *Held*—by the Court of Appeal—Since there was an implied limitation in the clause relating to the goods which were the subject of the employment, an interlocutory injunction should be granted. A covenant in restraint of trade regarding solicitation in a contract of service may be good provided its duration is reasonable, even though it covers customers whom the employee did not know and persons who were but have ceased to be customers and it is unlimited as to area.

282a. Home Counties Dairies Ltd. v. Skilton, [1970] 1 All E.R. 1227

Skilton, a milk roundsman employed by the plaintiffs, agreed amongst other things not "to serve or sell milk or dairy produce" to persons who within six months before leaving his employment were customers of his employers. Skilton left his employment with the plaintiffs in order to work as a roundsman for Westcott Dairies. He then took the same milk-round as he had worked when he was with the plaintiffs. *Held*—by the Court of Appeal —a flagrant breach of agreement. The words "dairy produce" were not too wide. On a proper construction they must be restricted to things normally dealt in by a milkman on his round.

A further point was taken that the customer restriction would apply to anyone who had been a customer within the last six months of the employment and had during that period ceased so to be, and it was said that the employer could have no legitimate interest in such persons. I think this point is met in the judgment in *G. W. Plowman & Son Ltd.* v. *Ash*, 1964,[282] where it was said that a customer might have left temporarily and that his return was not beyond hope and was therefore a matter of legitimate interest to the employer.

Per Harman, L.J.

283. Gledhow Autoparts *v.* Delaney, [1965] 3 All E.R. 288

The defendant, a commercial traveller, was employed by a company under a contract of service which provided that for three years from the termination of his employment he would not "solicit or seek to obtain orders . . . from any person firm or company situate or carrying on business within the districts in which the traveller had operated during the course of this agreement or during any periods of employment with" the company.

The defendant sold parts for the lighting systems of cars and was required to call at garages in various districts in Southern England. However, there were many garages in this area which were not, and never had been, the plaintiffs' customers, and on which the defendant did not call. After leaving his employment the defendant continued to solicit orders on his own account from garages in the districts in which he had worked for the company. An injunction to restrain him from so doing was granted at first instance. The traveller appealed to the Court of Appeal where it was *held* that the injunction should not have been granted. The condition was invalid as being in unreasonable restraint of trade. Where an employer imposes a restraint which is to last three years and which extends to many persons, firms or companies which are not customers, and on whom the employee does not call, the restraint is wider than is reasonably necessary for the protection of the employer's business.

N.B. According to Sellers and Diplock, L.JJ., the restraint would have been reasonable if it had included—

(*a*) Actual customers.
(*b*) Persons on whom the traveller had called in the course of his work, even though they were not his employer's customers.

284. Scorer *v.* Seymour Jones, [1966] 3 All E.R. 347

Under a contract dated 2nd June, 1964, between an estate agent and one of his unqualified employees who was the estate agent's clerk and negotiator, the employee agreed that he would not, for three years after leaving his employment, carry on or be employed or interested in the business of an auctioneer, surveyor or estate agent within five miles of the employer's premises at Kingsbridge and Dartmouth. The employee was the manager of the branch office at Kingsbridge and there were recurring customers at this branch. The employee was unsatisfactory and was dismissed in November, 1964; thereafter he practised on his own account as an estate agent in Salcombe within five miles of Kingsbridge, but outside a five-mile radius of Dartmouth. The employer Scorer asked for an injunction restraining his former employee Seymour Jones from practising within five miles of the Kingsbridge office. The injunction was granted at Kingsbridge County Court, and on appeal by the employee against the granting of an injunction it was *held* by the Court of Appeal that the injunction was rightly granted because the employer had many recurring clients and the restraint on practising within five miles of the Kingsbridge office was reasonable. Further, the restriction on practising within five miles of the Dartmouth office was not reasonable restraint but was severable. *Per* Sellers, L.J., in considering whether the restriction was contrary to the public interest, it was proper to take into account the fact that the employee was unqualified and not controlled by professional rules.

285. Printers and Finishers *v.* Holloway (No. 2), [1964] 3 All E.R. 731

The plaintiffs brought an action against Holloway, their former works manager, and others, including Vita-Tex Ltd., into whose employment Holloway had subsequently entered, claiming injunctions against Holloway and other defendants based, as regards Holloway, on an alleged breach of an implied term in his contract of service with the plaintiffs that he should not disclose or make improper use of confidential information relating to the plaintiff's trade secrets. Holloway's contract did not contain an express covenant relating to non-disclosure of trade secrets. The plaintiffs were flock-printers and had built up their own fund of "know-how" in this field. The action against Vita-Tex arose because Holloway had, on one occasion, taken a Mr. James, who was an employee of Vita-Tex Ltd., round the plaintiff's factory. Mr. James's visit took place in the evening and followed a chance meeting between himself and Holloway. However, the plant was working and James did see a number of processes. It also appeared that Holloway had, during his employment made copies of certain of the plaintiff's documentary material and had taken these copies away with him when he left their employ. The plaintiffs sought an injunction to prevent the use or disclosure of the material contained in the copies of documents made by Holloway.

Held—by Cross, J.—

(a) The plaintiffs were entitled to an injunction against Holloway so far as the documentary material was concerned, although there was no express term in his contract regarding non-disclosure of trade secrets.

(b) No injunction would be granted restraining Holloway from putting at the disposal of Vita-Tex Ltd. his memory of particular features of the plaintiffs' plant and processes. He was under no express contract not to do so and the Court would not extend its equitable jurisdiction to restrain breach of confidence in this instance. Holloway's knowledge of the plaintiffs' trade secrets was not readily separable from his general knowledge of flock printing.

(c) An injunction would be granted restraining Vita-Tex Ltd. from making use of the information acquired by James on his visit.

286. Robb *v.* Green, [1895] 2 Q.B. 315

The plaintiff was a dealer in live game and eggs. The major part of his business consisted of procuring the eggs, and the hatching, rearing and sale of game birds. For the purpose of carrying on this business, the plaintiff occupied game farms at Liphook in Hampshire, and at Elstead near Godalming. His customers were numerous and for the most part were country gentlemen and their gamekeepers. The plaintiff kept a list of these customers in his order book. The defendant, who was for three years the plaintiff's manager, copied these names and addresses, and after leaving the plaintiff's employ set up in a similar business on his own and sent circulars both to the plaintiff's customers and their gamekeepers inviting them to do business with him. The plaintiff sought damages and an injunction. *Held*—by the Court of Appeal (affirming the judgment of Hawkins, J.)—Although there was no express term in the defendant's contract to restrain him from such activities, it was an implied term of the contract of service that the defendant would observe good faith towards his master during the existence of the confidential relationship between them. The defendant's conduct was a breach of that contract in respect of which the plaintiff was entitled to damages of £150 and an injunction.

287. Sanders *v.* Parry, [1967] 2 All E.R. 803

In January, 1964, the defendant was engaged by the plaintiff solicitor as assistant solicitor. The defendant had been told by the plaintiff that he was to undertake the legal work of an important client, Mr. Tully. The defendant took up his employment on 16th March, 1964. During August or September, 1964, the defendant and Tully agreed that the defendant would set up in practice on his account whereupon Tully would transfer all his legal business from the plaintiff to the defendant and this was done. In an action for damages for breach of an implied term of the contract that the defendant would serve the plaintiff faithfully, the defendant admitted the term but said that he was not in breach of it because the agreement between him and Tully had been initiated by Tully and he had merely accepted an offer which Tully had made. *Held*—That even if the agreement had not been initiated by the defendant, he had, in accepting the offer during the substance of his agreement with the plaintiff, acted contrary to the interests of the plaintiff and was in breach of the implied term of fidelity.

288. Hivac Ltd. *v.* Park Royal Scientific Instruments Ltd., [1946] 1 All E.R. 350

The plaintiffs were manufacturers of midget valves used in deaf aids, the work requiring a high degree of skill. The defendants were newcomers to the trade and concerned themselves mainly with the assembly of hearing aids. The plaintiffs' employees worked a five and a half day week, having Sunday free. Five such employees worked on Sundays for the defendants, assisting in the assembly of midget valves. The plaintiffs asked for an injunction to restrain their employees from carrying out such work. *Held*—In the special circumstances of the case an injunction would be granted, not because of any specific contractual restraint but because the conduct of the particular employees constituted a breach of the duty of fidelity which every servant owes to his master.

289. Commercial Plastics v. Vincent, [1964] 3 All E.R. 546

The plaintiffs employed Vincent, a plastics technologist, to co-ordinate research and development in the production of their P.V.C. (Poly-vinyl-chloride) calendered sheeting, which was made up into adhesive tape. Vincent's contract forbade him to seek employment with any of the plaintiffs' competitors in the P.V.C. calendering field for one year after leaving their employment. Vincent had access to secret material, including certain mixing specifications recorded in code and, although, he could not remember these, he could probably remember, in relation to any matter concerning adhesive tape, what was the problem and what was the solution, what experiments were made and whether the results were positive or negative. Vincent left his employment with the plaintiffs and proposed to take up employment with a competitor. The plaintiffs asked for an injunction to restrain Vincent from breaking the restraining term in his contract with them. *Held*—by the Court of Appeal—An injunction could not be granted. Although what Vincent could remember was sufficiently definite to be capable of protection by an appropriate condition or covenant,the term in the agreement was excessive. It was world-wide in scope, although the plaintiffs did not, on the facts of the case, require protection outside the United Kingdom. Furthermore, the term extended to the plaintiff's competitors in the whole field of P.V.C. whereas they required protection, so far as Vincent was concerned, only in relation to calendered sheeting for adhesive tape.

290. Kores Manufacturing Co. Ltd. v. Kolok Manufacturing Co. Ltd., [1959] Ch. 108

The two companies occupied adjoining premises in Tottenham and both manufactured carbon papers, typewriter ribbons and the like. They made an agreement in which each company agreed that it would not, without the written consent of the other, "at any time employ any person who during the past five years shall have been a servant of yours." The plaintiffs' chief chemist sought employment with the defendants, and the plaintiffs were not prepared to consent to this and asked for an injunction to enforce the agreement. *Held*—by the Court of Appeal—

  (*a*) A contract in restraint of trade cannot be enforced unless—
     (i) it is reasonable as between the parties, *and*
     (ii) it is consistent with the interests of the public.

  (*b*) The mere fact that the parties are dealing on equal terms does not prevent the court from holding that the restraint is unreasonable in the interests of those parties.

  (*c*) The restraint in this case was grossly in excess of what was required to protect the parties and accordingly was unreasonable in the interests of the parties.

  (*d*) The agreement therefore failed to satisfy the first of the two conditions set out in (*a*) above and was void and unenforceable.

291. General Billposting Co. Ltd. v. Atkinson, [1909] A.C. 118

Atkinson was manager to a Newcastle billposting company for a number of years upon terms that he should hold office subject to termination at twelve months' notice by either party, and with a restriction on his right to trade after termination of his employment. The restriction on trade was that he should not, whilst in the employment of the company or within two years afterwards, carry on a similar business within a certain radius of Newcastle without the company's permission. In 1906 Atkinson was dismissed without notice and he successfully sued the company for wrongful dismissal. Having recovered damages he began to trade as a billposter on his own account within the prohibited area. The General Billposting Co. Ltd., having taken over the company with which Atkinson was employed, brought an action for an injunction and for damages for breach of contract. *Held*—by the House of Lords—Atkinson was entitled to treat the dismissal as a repudiation of the contract and to sue for damages for breach of contract, and was no longer bound by the restriction on trade.

292. Bromley *v.* Smith, [1919] 2 K.B. 235

The plaintiff was a baker at Clacton and it was his practice to send carts containing bread on various rounds to visit boarding houses and shops. In 1895 the plaintiff required an assistant to undertake what was known as the town round and by means of an advertisement he came into communication with the defendant, a young man of eighteen years, who lived some miles away at a place called Great Baddow. The defendant had since the age of twelve been engaged in the bakery trade. On 18th November, 1895, the plaintiff and defendant entered into an agreement under which the defendant agreed that he would not at any time within the space of three years after the date of leaving the plaintiff's service engage or be engaged in the business of miller, baker, hay, straw or corn dealer, or restaurant keeper, or in the manufacture of flour meal. Eventually the defendant terminated his employment by giving notice to the plaintiff and then in partnership with a man named Green he took over premises in Clacton, three miles from the plaintiff's premises, and commenced business as a baker and confectioner. Both before and after he left the plaintiff's employment the plaintiff, on his own admission, canvassed the plaintiff's customers and some of these customers gave their custom to the defendant. At the time of the agreement the plaintiff did not carry on any business other than that of a baker and confectioner but he was contemplating an extension of his business and was considering opening a restaurant. *Held*—by Channell, J.—The restraint must coincide with what is necessary for the protection of the existing business of the employer and restriction relating to the business of restaurant keeper went further than was necessary. However, the restraint was severable because each of the prohibited trades was stated separately and those relating to the business of baker or confectioner were enforceable. Furthermore, the contract as severed was enforceable, even though the defendant was an infant when he made it. It was a contract for his benefit even though it contained restraints. "A contract which contains only terms on which an infant can reasonably expect employment must, I think, be for his benefit."

293. Bull *v.* Pitney-Bowes, [1956] 3 All E.R. 384

The plaintiff was employed by the defendant and it was a term of that employment that the plaintiff should belong to a non-contributory pension scheme. It was also provided that any retired member of the pension scheme who took employment in any activity in competition with, or detrimental to, the defendant's interests would forfeit his rights under the pension scheme unless he discontinued the activity when required to do so. The plaintiff retired and took up employment with one of the defendant's competitors. He was requested to discontinue this activity but refused to do so, and he sued his former employer and the committee and custodian trustee of the pension fund for declarations that the forfeiture provision was void and that he was entitled to a pension. *Held*—by Thesiger, J.—that the declarations should be made; the forfeiture clause was void as an unreasonable restraint of trade.

294. Lyne-Pirkis *v.* Jones, [1969] 3 All E.R. 738

The plaintiff and the defendant were medical practitioners in practice at Godalming. A clause in the partnership deed stated that if any partner retired he should not "for a period of five years immediately following such retirement . . . engage in practice as a medical practitioner whether alone or jointly with any other person within a radius of ten miles of the Market House in Godalming." The defendant terminated the partnership and the plaintiff asked for an injunction to prevent him from practising within the stated area. The patients of the partnership all lived within a radius of five miles. *Held*—by the Court of Appeal—that the covenant was not enforceable. It was wider than was reasonably necessary to restrict competition because it used the phrase "medical practitioner" which could include medical consultant and was not limited to general practice. In these circumstances there was no need for the court to decide whether a radius of ten miles was too wide though Russell, L.J., thought it was.

295. Pharmaceutical Society of Great Britain *v.* Dickson, [1968] 2 All E.R. 686

The Society passed a resolution to the effect that the opening of new pharmacies should be restricted and be limited to certain specified services, and that the range of services in existing pharmacies should not be extended except as approved by the Society's council. The purpose of the resolution was clearly to stop the development of new fields of trading in conjunction with pharmacy. Mr. Dickson, who was a member of the Society and retail director of Boots Pure Drug Company Ltd., brought this action on the grounds that the proposed new rule was *ultra vires* as an unreasonable restraint of trade. A declaration that the resolution was *ultra vires* was made and the Society appealed to the House of Lords where the appeal was dismissed, the following points emerging from the judgment.

(i) Where a professional association passes a resolution regulating the conduct of its members the validity of the resolution is a matter for the courts even if binding in honour only, since failure to observe it is likely to be construed as misconduct and thus become a ground for disciplinary action.

(ii) A resolution by a professional association regulating the conduct of its members is *ultra vires* if it is not sufficiently related to the main objects of the association. The objects of the society in this case did not cover the resolution, being "to maintain the honour and safeguard and promote the interests of the members in the exercise of the profession of pharmacy."

(iii) A resolution by a professional association regulating the conduct of its members will be void if it is in unreasonable restraint of trade.

296. Re. Chocolate and Sugar Confectionery Reference, [1967] 3 All E.R. 261

The Restrictive Practices Court was asked to make an order exempting chocolate, sugar confectionery, and related types of goods from the general ban on resale price maintenance. The case for the suppliers, i.e. virtually all of the major manufacturers, was that without resale price maintenance there would be a major shift in trade from confectionery shops to supermarkets as a result of price cutting. This would lead to a loss of sales since chocolate and similar goods were often bought on impulse from small outlets. This would lead to loss of variety and higher prices in the longer term.

That price cutting by supermarkets would take place was accepted by the Court but the consequences were not regarded as inevitably those put forward by the suppliers. A normal shopper would not, for example, travel more than a short distance to buy a bar of chocolate for say, one new penny less than the recommended price. Some shops would go out of business, probably to the extent of 10 per cent of outlets, but in the view of the Court this reduction would not cause the public significant inconvenience. Accordingly the Court ruled that the suppliers had not established their case and that resale price maintenance for chocolates and sweets was unlawful.

A significant feature of the case was the acceptance by the Court of evidence of economic principles and statistics. It marks the first real sign of co-operation between lawyers and economists; the arguments were economic and statistical rather than legal.

297. Moore & Co. *v.* Landauer & Co., [1921] 2 K.B. 519

The plaintiffs entered into a contract to sell the defendants a certain quantity of Australian canned fruit, the goods to be packed in cases containing 30 tins each. The goods were to be shipped "per S.S. *Toromeo*." The ship was delayed by strikes at Melbourne and in South Africa, and was very late in arriving at London. When the goods were discharged about one half of the consignment was packed in cases containing 24 tins only, instead of 30, and the buyers refused to accept them. *Held*—Although the method of packing made no difference to the market value of the goods, the sale was by description under Sect. 13 of the Sale of Goods Act, 1893, and the description had not been complied with. Consequently the buyers were entitled to reject the whole consignment by virtue of the provisions of Sect. 30 (3) of the Sale of Goods Act.

298. Cutter *v.* Powell (1795), 6 Term Rep. 320

The defendant was the master of a ship called the *Governor Parry* and the plaintiff was the second mate on that ship. The ship sailed from Jamaica on 2nd August, 1793, and Cutter sailed in her and carried out all his duties as second mate. However, he died on 20th September, 1793, i.e. before the ship completed her voyage to Liverpool on 9th October, 1793. The contract under which Cutter rendered the services was worded as follows—

"Ten days after the ship Governor Parry my self master arrives at Liverpool I promise to pay to Mr. T. Cutter the sum of 30 guineas provided he proceeds, continues and does his duty as second mate in the said ship from hence to the port of Liverpool. Signed at Kingston, 31st July, 1793."

Cutter's widow now sued to recover a proportionate part of his wages, but Lord Kenyon, C.J., held that the contract was entire and there could be no claim on a *quantum meruit* for partial performance.

N.B. The Merchant Shipping Act, 1970, now provides for the payment of wages for partial performance in such cases, and the Law Reform (Frustrated Contracts) Act, 1943, would also have assisted the widow to recover, because the sailor had conferred a benefit on the master of the ship prior to his death (which would now frustrate the contract) giving the widow the right to sue the master for the benefit of Cutter's work up to the time of his death.

299. Sumpter *v.* Hedges, [1898] 1 Q.B. 673

The plaintiff entered into a contract with the defendant under the terms of which the plaintiff was to erect some buildings for the defendant on the defendant's land for a price of £565. The plaintiff did partially erect the buildings up to the value of £333, and the defendant paid him a part of that figure. The plaintiff then told the defendant that he could not finish the job because he had run out of funds. The defendant then completed the work by using material belonging to the plaintiff which had been left on the site. The plaintiff now sued for work done and materials supplied, and the Court gave him judgment for materials supplied, but would not grant him a sum of money by way of *quantum meruit* for the value of the work done prior to his abandonment of the job. The reason was given that, before the plaintiff could sue successfully on a *quantum meruit*, he would have to show that the defendant had voluntarily accepted the work done, and this implied that the defendant must be in a position to refuse the benefit of the work as where a buyer of goods refuses to take delivery. This was not the case here; the defendant had no option but to accept the work done, so his acceptance could not be presumed from conduct. There being no other evidence of the defendant's acceptance of the work, the plaintiff's claim for the work done failed.

300. De Barnardy *v.* Harding (1853), 8 Exch. 822

The plaintiff agreed to act as the defendant's agent for the purpose of preparing and issuing certain advertisements and notices designed to encourage the sale of tickets to see the funeral procession of the Duke of Wellington. The plaintiff was to be paid a commission of 10 per cent upon the proceeds of the tickets actually sold. The plaintiff duly issued the advertisements and notices, but before he began to sell the tickets, the defendant withdrew the plaintiff's authority to sell them and in consequence the plaintiff did not sell any tickets and was prevented from earning his commission. The plaintiff now sued upon a *quantum meruit* and his action succeeded.

301. Hoenig *v.* Isaacs, [1952] 2 All E.R. 176

The defendant employed the plaintiff who was an interior decorator and furniture designer to decorate a one-room flat owned by the defendant. The plaintiff was also to provide furniture, including a fitted bookcase, a wardrobe and a bedstead, for the total sum of £750. The terms of the contract regarding payment were as follows—"Net cash as the work proceeds and the balance on completion." The defendant made two payments to the plaintiff of £150 each, one payment on the 12th April and the other on the 19th April. The plaintiff claimed that he had completed the work on 28th August, and asked for the balance, i.e. £450. The defendant asserted that the work done was bad and faulty, but sent the plaintiff a sum of £100 and moved into the flat and used the furniture. The plaintiff now sued for the balance of £350, the defence being that the plaintiff had not performed his contract, or in the alternative that he had done so negligently, unskilfully and in an unworkmanlike manner.

The Official Referee assessed the work that had been done, and found that generally it was properly done except that the wardrobe door required replacing and that a bookshelf was too short and this meant that the bookcase would have to be remade. The defendant claimed that the contract was entire and that it must be completely performed before the plaintiff could recover. The Official Referee was of opinion that there had been substantial performance, and that the defendant was liable for £750 less the cost of putting right the above-mentioned defects, the cost of this being assessed at £55 18s. 2d. The Court accordingly gave the plaintiff judgment for the sum of £294 1s. 10d.

302. Narbeth v. James: (the Lady Tahilla), [1967] 1 Lloyds' Rep. 591

The plaintiff sold his motor-yacht to the defendant in April, 1960, for a price of £8,000. The defendant paid £5,000 and it was agreed that the balance be met at the defendant's option in one of three ways—(i) by allowing the plaintiff free use of the yacht for one month during each of the years 1962, 1963 and 1964, subject to the plaintiff giving the defendant three months' notice of the month in which he required the yacht; (ii) by paying the plaintiff £1,000 for any year in which the yacht was not available for use under method (i); (iii) by payment in cash if the vessel was disposed of by the defendant. In April, 1960, the defendant secured the balance due from him by executing a mortgage in favour of the plaintiff. In 1966 the plaintiff sued the defendant for the whole balance with interest under the mortgage. The defendant denied liability and contended that the yacht was made available for the plaintiff in 1962, 1963 and 1964, but the plaintiff had not given notice of the month he required her. *Held*—By Brandon, J.,—that the plaintiff was entitled to the £3,000 plus interest. As a general proposition where A had an option to perform a contract in more than one way and the obligations of B depended on which way A chose and could only be effectively performed by B if he had notice beforehand, then A would be under an implied obligation to give B proper notice. Thus in the present case in order to give business efficacy to the contract it was necessary to imply a term that the defendant would give the plaintiff reasonable prior notice whether or not he was choosing method (i) in respect of any of the three relevant years. No notice had been given, therefore the mortgage remained undischarged and the plaintiff was entitled to the judgment.

303. Bowes v. Shand (1877), 2 App. Cas. 455

The action was brought for damages for non-acceptance of 600 tons (or 8,200 bags) of Madras rice. The sold note stated that the rice was to be shipped during "the months of March and/or April 1874." 8,150 bags were put on board ship on or before February 28th, 1874, and the remaining 50 bags on March 2nd, 1874. The defendants refused to take delivery because the rice was not shipped in accordance with the terms of the contract. *Held*—The bulk of the cargo was shipped in February and therefore the rice did not answer the description in the contract and the defendants were not bound to accept it.

304. Chas. Rickards Ltd. v. Oppenheim, [1950] 1 K.B. 616

The defendant ordered a Rolls-Royce chassis from the plaintiffs, the chassis being delivered in July, 1947. The plaintiffs found a coach builder prepared to make a body within six or at the most seven months. The specification for the body was agreed in August, 1947, so that the work should have been completed in March, 1948. The work was not completed by then but the defendant still pressed for delivery. On 29th June, 1948, the defendant wrote to the coach-builders saying that he would not accept delivery after 25th July, 1948. The body was not ready by then and the defendant bought another car. The body was completed in October, 1948, but the defendant refused to accept delivery and counterclaimed for the value of the chassis which he had purchased. *Held*—Time was of the essence of the original contract, but the defendant had waived the question of time by continuing to press for delivery after the due date. However, by his letter of 29th June he had again made time of the essence, and had given reasonable notice in the matter. Judgment was given for the defendant on the claim and counterclaim.

305. Elmdore Ltd. *v.* Keech (1969), 113 S.J. 871

The plaintiffs agreed to print an advertisement in their plastic telephone directory cover which they said would be distributed within 120 days. The covers were distributed eleven days late. It was *Held*—by the Court of Appeal—that since this was a mercantile contract the general rule that time was of the essence applied unless the circumstances showed otherwise. There were no special circumstances on the facts of the case and the plaintiffs' action for the price must be dismissed.

306. Deeley *v.* Lloyds Bank Ltd., [1912] A.C. 756

A customer of the bank had mortgaged his property to the bank to secure an overdraft limited to £2,500. He then mortgaged the same property to the appellant for £3,500, subject to the bank's mortgage. It is the normal practice of bankers, on receiving notice of a second mortgage, to rule off the customer's account, and not to allow any further withdrawals, since these will rank after the second mortgage. In this case the bank did not open a new account but continued the old current account. The customer thereafter paid in moneys which at a particular date, if they had been appropriated in accordance with the rule in *Clayton's* case, would have extinguished the bank's mortgage. Even so the customer still owed the bank money, and they sold the property for a price which was enough to satisfy the bank's debt but not that of the appellant. *Held*—The evidence did not exclude the rule in *Clayton's* case, which applied, so that the bank's mortgage had been paid off and the appellant, as second mortgagee, was entitled to the proceeds of the sale.

307. Hochster *v.* De la Tour (1853), 2 E. & B. 678

The defendant agreed in April, 1852, to engage the plaintiff as a courier for European travel, his duties to commence on 1st June, 1852. On 11th May, 1852, the defendant wrote to the plaintiff saying that he no longer required his services. The plaintiff commenced an action for breach of contract on 22nd May, 1852, and the defence was that there was no cause of action until the date due for performance, i.e. 1st June, 1852. *Held*—The defendant's express repudiation constituted an actionable breach of contract.

308. Omnium D'Entreprises and Others *v.* Sutherland, [1919] 1 K.B. 618

The defendant was the owner of a steamship and agreed to let her to the plaintiff for a period of time and to pay the second plaintiffs a commission on the hire payable under the agreement. The defendant later sold the ship to a

purchaser, free of all liability under his agreement with the plaintiffs. *Held*—
The sale by the defendant was a repudiation of the agreement and the plaintiffs
were entitled to damages for breach of the contract.

309. Maredelanto Compania Naviera S.A. *v.* Bergbau-Handel GmbH. the Mihalis Angelos, [1970] 3 All E.R. 125

The vessel Mihalis Angelos, which was owned by Maredelanto, was chartered
by Bergbau-Handel under a charter party dated 25th May, 1965. The charter-
party provided—

(*a*) that the vessel should be ready to load about 1st July, 1965; and
(*b*) that if it was not ready to load on or before 20th July, 1965, the charterers should have the option of cancelling the contract.

The purpose of the charterparty was for the charterers to load mineral ore
(apatite) in Haiphong in North Vietnam and transport it to Hamburg or
another port in Europe. Sometime before 12th July, 1965, the railway which
was to bring the ore to Haiphong was allegedly destroyed by American bombing.
However, the Mihalis Angelos was in Hong Kong on 23rd July and could not
have reached Haiphong before 27th July. Instead of waiting until 20th July
when they could have cancelled the contract legitimately, the charterers decided
to repudiate it on 17th July on the grounds of *force majeure* because they thought
the railway had been destroyed so that the apatite ore could not be transported
to Haiphong, thus rendering the charterparty useless to them. The shipowners
did not accept that *force majeure* applied and they sued for £4,000 being damages
for loss of the charter. At first instance Mocatta, J., held that the charterers were
not entitled to repudiate on 17th July. The situation was not necessarily one of
force majeure at that time. They were therefore in breach on 17th July and the
owners were entitled to sue at that time. In addition they were entitled to
damages of £4,000 and it did not matter that they would have been unable to
perform the contract at the due date, i.e. 20th July. In the Court of Appeal,
however, it was decided that the owners were only entitled to nominal damages.
The fact that the owners could not have performed the contract on 20th July
was a contingency which had to be taken into account.

310. Avery *v.* Bowden (1855), 5 E. & B. 714

The defendant chartered the plaintiff's ship and agreed to load her with a
cargo at Odessa within forty-five days. The ship went to Odessa and remained
there for most of the forty-five-day period. The defendant told the captain of
the ship that he did not propose to load a cargo and that he would do well to
leave, but the captain stayed on at Odessa, hoping that the defendant would
change his mind. Before the end of the forty-five-day period the Crimean War
broke out so that performance of the contract would have been illegal. *Held*—
The plaintiff might have treated the defendant's refusal to load a cargo as an
anticipatory breach of contract but his agent, the captain, had waived that
right by staying on at Odessa, and now the contract had been discharged by
something which was beyond the control of either party.

311. White and Carter (Councils) Ltd. *v.* McGregor, [1961] 2 W.L.R. 17

The respondent was a garage proprietor on Clydebank and on 26th June,
1957, his sales manager, without specific authority, entered into a contract
with the appellants whereby the appellants agreed to advertise the respondent's business on litter bins which they supplied to local authorities. The

contract was to last for three years from the date of the first advertisement display. Payment was to be by instalments annually in advance, the first instalment being due seven days after the first display. The contract contained a clause that, on failure to pay an instalment or other breach of contract, the whole sum of £196 4s. became due. The respondent was quick to repudiate the contract for on 26th June, 1957, he wrote to the appellants asking them to cancel the agreement, and at this stage the appellants had not taken any steps towards carrying it out. The appellants refused to cancel the agreement and prepared the advertisement plates which they exhibited on litter bins in November, 1957, and continued to display them during the following three years. Eventually the appellants demanded payment, the respondent refused to pay, and the appellants brought an action against him for the sum due under the contract. *Held*—The appellants were entitled to recover the contract price since, although the respondent had repudiated the contract, the appellants were not obliged to accept the repudiation. The contract survived and the appellants had now completed it.

N.B. Although the respondent's agent had no actual authority, he had made a similar contract with the appellants in 1954, and it was not disputed that he had apparent authority to bind his principal.

312. Allen *v.* Robles (Compagnie Parisienne de Guarantie Third Party), [1969] 3 All E.R. 154

The defendant, Mr. Robles, drove his car in a negligent fashion and ran into the plaintiff's house. In an action at Nottingham Assizes the judge awarded the plaintiff damages against Mr. Robles and the question arose as to whether Mr. Robles could claim on his insurance policy with the French insurance company which was joined as third party in this action. Mr. Robles was in breach of his contract of insurance because that contract provided that he must notify the insurance company of any claim made against him within five days of the claim. This he had not done. In fact he failed to inform the insurance company of the claim by the plaintiff until two months after he knew it had been made. On the other hand the insurance company did not repudiate their liability until some four months after Mr. Robles informed them of the claim. It was *held*—by the Court of Appeal—that the insurance company had not lost its right to repudiate the contract. The delay was not so long as to indicate that they had accepted liability and it had in no way changed the circumstances of the case. It had not, for example, increased Mr. Allen's loss or altered Mr. Robles liability. There was thus no prejudice to those concerned.

313. Davis Contractors Ltd., *v.* Fareham U.D.C., [1956] A.C. 696

In July, 1946, the plaintiff contracted with the defendants to build seventy-eight houses for £92,425 within a period of eight months. Owing to lack of adequate supplies of labour and building materials, it took the plaintiffs twenty-two months to complete the work. There was no provision in the contract regarding such eventualities. The extra expense incurred by the plaintiffs was £17,651, and they claimed that the original contract with the council was frustrated and that they were entitled to recover the total cost on a *quantum meruit*. *Held*—Events had made the contract more onerous to the plaintiffs but had not frustrated the contract. The eventuality should have been provided for. The only claim the plaintiffs had was for the sum agreed in the contract; *quantum meruit* was not available in the absence of frustration.

314. Re. Shipton, Anderson & Co. and Harrison Bros.' Arbitration, [1915] 3 K.B. 676

A contract was made for the sale of wheat lying in a warehouse in Liverpool. Before the seller could deliver the wheat, and before the property in it had passed to the buyer, the Government requisitioned the wheat under certain emergency powers available in time of war. *Held*—Delivery being impossible by reason of lawful requisition by the Government, the seller was excused from performance of the contract.

315. Storey *v.* Fulham Steel Works (1907), 24 T.L.R. 89

The plaintiff was employed by the defendants as manager for a period of five years. After he had been working for two years he became ill, and had to have special treatment and a period of convalescence. Six months later he was recovered, but in the meantime the defendant had terminated his employment. The plaintiff now sued for breach of contract, and the defendants pleaded that the plaintiff's period of ill-health operated to discharge the contract. *Held*— The plaintiff's illness and absence from duty did not go to the root of the contract, and was not so serious as to allow the termination of the agreement.

316. Taylor *v.* Caldwell (1863), 3 B. & S. 826

The defendant agreed to let the plaintiff have the use of a music hall for the purpose of holding four concerts. Before the first concert was due to be held the hall was destroyed by fire, and the plaintiff now sued for damages because of the defendant's breach of contract in not having the premises ready for him. *Held*—The contract was impossible of performance and the defendant was not liable.

317. Krell *v.* Henry, [1903] 2 K.B. 740

The plaintiff owned a room overlooking the proposed route of the Coronation procession of Edward VII, and had let it to the defendant for the purpose of viewing the procession. The procession did not take place because of the King's illness and the plaintiff now sued for the agreed fee. *Held*—The fact that the procession had been cancelled discharged the parties from their obligations, since it was no longer possible to achieve the real purpose of the agreement.

318. Herne Bay Steamboat Co. *v.* Hutton, [1903] 2 K.B. 683

The plaintiffs agreed to hire a steamboat to the defendant for two days, in order that the defendant might take paying passengers to see the naval review at Spithead on the occasion of Edward VII's Coronation. An official announcement was made cancelling the review, but the fleet was assembled and the boat might have been used for the intended cruise. The defendant did not use the boat, and the plaintiffs employed her on ordinary business. This action was brought to recover the fee of £200 which the defendant had promised to pay for the hire of the boat. *Held*—The contract was not discharged, as the review of the fleet by the sovereign was not the foundation of the contract. The plaintiffs were awarded the difference between £200 and the profits derived from the use of the ship for ordinary business on the two days in question.

319. Joseph Constantine Steamship Line Ltd. *v.* Imperial Smelting Corporation Ltd., [1942] A.C. 154

The respondents chartered a steamship to proceed to Port Pirie, Australia, to load a cargo. On the day before the ship was due to load her cargo, and whilst she was lying in the roads off Port Pirie, there was an explosion in one of her boilers. She was therefore unable to perform the charter as agreed, although she could have done so after rather extensive repairs. The respondents claimed damages for breach of contract. *Held*—The explosion frustrated the contract and the appellants were not liable. The cause of the explosion was unknown, and negligence could not be proved against the appellants; otherwise they would have been liable on the ground that the frustrating event would have been self-induced.

320. Jackson *v.* Union Marine Insurance Co. (1874), L.R. 10 C.P. 125

The plaintiff was the owner of a ship which had been chartered to go with all possible dispatch from Liverpool to Newport, and there load a cargo of iron rails for San Francisco. The plaintiff had entered into a contract of insurance with the defendants, in order that he might protect himself against the failure of the ship to carry out the charter. The vessel was stranded in Caernarvon Bay whilst on its way to Newport. It was not re-floated for over a month, and could not be fully repaired for some time. The charterers hired another ship and the plaintiff now claimed on the policy of insurance. The insurance company suggested that since the plaintiff might claim against the charterer for breach of contract there was no loss, and the court had to decide whether such a claim was possible. *Held*—The delay consequent upon the stranding of the vessel put an end, in the commercial sense, to the venture, so that the charterer was released from his obligations and was free to hire another ship. Therefore, the plaintiff had no claim against the charterer and could claim the loss of the charter from the defendants.

321. Maritime National Fish Ltd. *v.* Ocean Trawlers Ltd., [1935] A.C. 524

The respondents were the owners and the appellants the charterers of a steam trawler, the *St. Cuthbert*. The *St. Cuthbert* was fitted with, and could only operate with, an otter trawl. When the charter party was renewed on 25th October, 1932, both parties knew that it was illegal to operate with an otter trawl without a licence from the Minister. The appellants operated five trawlers and applied for five licences. The Minister granted only three and said that the appellants could choose the names of three trawlers for the licences. The appellants chose three but deliberately excluded the *St. Cuthbert* though they could have included it. They were now sued by the owners for the charter fee, and their defence was that the charter party was frustrated because it would have been illegal to fish with the *St. Cuthbert*. It was *held* that the contract was not frustrated, in the sense that the frustrating event was self-induced by the appellants and that therefore they were liable for the hire.

322. Cricklewood Property and Investment Trust Ltd. *v.* Leighton's Investment Trust Ltd., [1945] A.C. 221

In May, 1936, a building lease was granted between the parties for 99 years, but before any building had been erected war broke out in 1939 and government restrictions on building materials and labour meant that the lessees could not erect the buildings as they intended, these buildings being in fact shops. Leighton's sued originally for rent due under the lease and Cricklewood, the builders, said the lease was frustrated. The House of Lords *held* that the doctrine of frustration did not apply because the interruption from 1939 to 1945 was not sufficient in duration to frustrate the lease, and so they did not deal specifically with the general position regarding frustration of leases, basing their judgment on the question of the degree of interruption. In so far as they did deal with the general position this was *obiter*, but Lord Simon thought that there could be cases in which a lease would be frustrated, and the example that he quoted was a building lease where the land was declared a permanent open space before building took place; here he thought that the fundamental purpose of the transaction would be defeated. Lord Wright took much the same view on the same example. Lord Russell thought frustration could not apply to a lease of real property, and Lord Goddard, C.J., took the same view. Lord Porter expressed no opinion with regard to leases generally and so this case does not finally solve the problem.

323. Hillingdon Estates Co. *v.* Stonefield Estates Ltd., [1952] Ch. 627

By a contract dated 13th January, 1938, the vendors, Stonefield, and the plaintiffs, Hillingdon, who were the purchasers, agreed to buy and sell a freehold. The purchasers were to take a conveyance on 31st January, 1939, and the use of the land was to be for building an estate only. The completion was delayed by the outbreak of war and on 11th October, 1948, the contract was still not completed by a conveyance, and at that time the Middlesex County Council compulsorily purchased the land, leaving the *owners* with the compensation which would, of course, be less than the market value in 1948. The plaintiffs said that the contract was discharged. They did not ask for rescission but for a declaratory judgment to this effect and the defendants claimed specific performance. It was *held* that the plaintiffs failed and the defendants succeeded and specific performance was granted, the plaintiffs' claim being refused. It would appear therefore that the doctrine of frustration does not apply to a contract for the sale of land once a legal or equitable estate has passed.

324. Chandler *v.* Webster, [1904] 1 K.B. 493

The defendant agreed to let the plaintiff have a room for the purpose of viewing the Coronation procession on 26th June, 1902, for £141 15s. The contract provided that the money be payable immediately. The procession did not take place because of the illness of the King and the plaintiff, who had paid £100 on account, left the balance unpaid. The plaintiff sued to recover the £100 and the defendant counter-claimed for £41 15s. It was held by the Court of Appeal that the plaintiff's action failed and the defendant's counter-claim succeeded because the obligation to pay the rent had fallen due before the frustrating event.

325. The Fibrosa Case, [1942] 2 All E.R. 122

An English company (Fairburn) agreed to sell to a Polish firm (Fibrosa), machinery for £4,800, one-third to be paid with the order. Delivery of the machinery was to be made within three or four months of the settlement of final details at a place called Gdynia in Poland. Only £1,000 was paid with the order and on 3rd September, 1939, Britain declared war on Germany. On 23rd September, Gdynia was occupied by the Germans, the machinery was not delivered and the Polish company sued for the return of the £1,000. It was held by Mr. Justice Tucker and the Court of Appeal that the contract was frustrated under the rule in *Chandler* v. *Webster* (1904)[324] and that the action failed. The House of Lords, however, *held* that the money was recoverable, not because the contract was void *ab initio*, but in quasi contract on the grounds that there had been a total failure of consideration. Lord Simon said that under the law relating to the formation of contracts, a promise to do something provides consideration (thus a promise supports a promise), but under the law relating to failure of consideration, the promise is not enough, the performance of the promise is looked to. Here the money was paid to secure performance and there was no performance.

326. Lynn v. Bamber, [1930] 2 K.B. 72

In 1921 the plaintiff purchased some plum trees from the defendant, and was given a warranty that the trees were "Purple Pershores." In 1928 the plaintiff discovered that the trees were not "Purple Pershores" and sued for damages. The defendant pleaded that the claim was barred by the Statutes of Limitation. *Held*—The defendant's fraudulent misrepresentation and fraudulent concealment of the breach of warranty provided a good answer to this plea, so that the plaintiff could recover.

327. Wilson v. United Counties Bank, [1920] A.C. 102

A business man left his business affairs in the hands of the bank whilst he went to serve in the war of 1914–18. The bank mismanaged his affairs, and he was eventually adjudicated bankrupt. The trader and his trustee brought this action against the bank for breach of their contractual duty. Damages of £45,000 were awarded for loss of estate, and of £7,500 for the injury caused to the trader's credit and business reputation. With regard to the damages the court *held* that the £45,000 belonged to the trustee for the benefit of creditors, and the £7,500 went to the trader personally.

328. Sunley & Co. Ltd. v. Cunard White Star Ltd., [1940] 1 K.B. 740

The defendants agreed to carry a machine, belonging to the plaintiffs, to Guernsey, but because of delays for which the defendants were responsible, the machine was delivered a week late. The plaintiffs were not able to show that they had an immediate use for the machine, and could not prove loss of profit. However, it was *held* that, to compensate the plaintiffs for the defendant's breach of contract, they should recover £20 as one week's depreciation of the machine, and the sum of £10 as interest on the capital cost.

329. Chaplin v. Hicks, [1911] 2 K.B. 786

The defendant organised a beauty contest inviting the readers of certain newspapers to select fifty girls from whom the defendant would select twelve. The twelve successful entrants were to be offered theatrical engagements. The plaintiff was one of the fifty girls selected by the newspaper readers, but the defendant did not invite her to the final selection. She now claimed damages for breach of contract, and the defendant pleaded that, even if he had invited her to the final selection, it was by no means certain that she would have been one of the successful twelve, and therefore, the damages should be nominal. *Held*—Although it was difficult to assess damages, yet the plaintiff was entitled to an assessment, whereupon the jury awarded her £100.

330. Beach v. Reed Corrugated Cases Ltd., [1956] 2 All E.R. 652

This was an action brought by the plaintiff for wrongful dismissal by the defendants. The plaintiff was the managing director of the company and he had a fifteen-year contract from 21st December, 1950, at a salary of £5,000 per annum. His contract was terminated in August, 1954, when he was fifty-four years old and the sum of money that he might have earned would have been £55,000, but the general damages awarded to him were £18,000 after the court had taken into account income tax, including tax on his private investments.

N.B. The same principle has been applied to damages recoverable in tort for loss of earnings (*B.T.C.* v. *Gourley*, [1956] A.C. 185).

331. Hadley v. Baxendale (1854), 9 Exch. 341

The plaintiff was a miller at Gloucester. The driving shaft of the mill being broken, the plaintiff engaged the defendant, a carrier, to take it to the makers at Greenwich so that they might use it in making a new one. The defendant delayed delivery of the shaft beyond a reasonable time, so that the mill was idle for much longer than should have been necessary. The plaintiff now sued in respect of loss of profits during the period of additional delay. The court decided that there were only two possible grounds on which the plaintiff could succeed—(i) That in the usual course of things the work of the mill would cease altogether for want of the shaft. This the court rejected because, to take only one reasonable possibility, the plaintiff might have had a spare. (ii) That the special circumstances were fully explained, so that the defendant was made aware of the possible loss. The evidence showed that there had been no such explanation. In fact the only information given to the defendant was that the article to be carried was the broken shaft of a mill, and that the plaintiff was the miller of that mill. *Held*—That the plaintiff's claim failed, the damage being too remote.

However, loss of profits for non-delivery or delayed delivery are recoverable if foreseeable as a consequence of the breach. Thus in *Victoria Laundry Ltd.* v. *Newman Industries Ltd.*, [1949] 1 All E.R. 997, the defendants agreed to deliver a new boiler to the plaintiffs by a certain date but failed to do so with the result that the plaintiffs lost (a) normal business profits during the period of delay, and (b) profits from dyeing contracts which were offered to them during the period. It was *held* that (a) but not (b) were recoverable as damages. In *Czarnikow Ltd.* v. *Koufos*, [1967] 3 All E.R. 686, shipowners carrying sugar from Constanza to Basrah delayed delivery at Basrah for nine days during which time the market in sugar there fell and the charterers lost more than £4,000. It was *held* that they could recover that sum from the shipowners because the very existence of a "market" for goods implied that prices might fluctuate and a fall in sugar prices was reasonably foreseeable by the shipowners.

332. Horne v. Midland Railway Co. (1873), L.R. 8 C.P. 131

The plaintiff had entered into a contract to sell 4,595 pairs of boots to the French Army at a price above the market price. The defendants were responsible for a delay in the delivery of the boots, and the purchasers refused to accept delivery, regarding time as the essence of the contract. The plaintiff's claim for damages was based on the contract price, namely 4s. per pair, but it was *held* that he could only recover the market price of 2s. 9d. per pair unless he could show that the defendants were aware of the exceptional profit involved, and that they had undertaken to be liable for its loss.

333. Pinnock Brothers *v.* Lewis and Peat Ltd., [1923] 1 K.B. 690

The plaintiffs bought from the defendants some East African Copra Cake which, to the defendants' knowledge, was to be used for feeding cattle. The cake was adulterated with castor oil and was poisonous. The plaintiffs resold the cake to other dealers, who in turn sold it to farmers, who used it for feeding cattle. Cattle fed on the cake died, and claims were made by the various buyers against their sellers, the whole liability resting eventually on the plaintiffs. In this action the plaintiffs sued for the damages and costs which they had been required to pay. Two major defences were raised, the first being an exemption clause saying that the goods were not warranted free from defects, and the other that the damage was too remote. The court dismissed the exemption clause and *held* that, when a substance is quite different from that contracted for, it cannot merely be defective. Further the damage was not too remote, since it was in the implied contemplation of the defendants that the cake would at some time be fed to cattle.

334. Charter *v.* Sullivan, [1957] 2 Q.B. 117

The plaintiffs, who were motor dealers, agreed to sell a Hillman Minx car to the defendant for £773 17s., which was the retail price fixed by the manufacturers. The defendant refused to complete the purchase and the plaintiffs resold the car a few days later to another purchaser at the same price. The plaintiffs sued for breach of contract and the measure of damages claimed was £97 15s., the profit the plaintiffs would have made on the sale if it had gone through. Evidence showed that the plaintiffs could have sold to a second purchaser another Hillman Minx which could have been ordered from the manufacturers' stock had the defendant taken the first Hillman Minx as agreed. The plaintiff's sales manager said in his evidence "we can sell all the Hillman Minx cars we can get." This evidence was accepted by the trial judge. The plaintiffs were really suggesting that but for the defendant's refusal to complete they would have sold two cars and not one, and in so doing would have made double the profit. *Held*—An award of nominal damages (i.e. forty shillings) would be made. The plaintiff's sales manager said the plaintiffs could always find a purchaser for every Hillman Minx car they could get from the manufacturers, and so the plaintiffs must have sold the same number of cars and made the same number of fixed profits as they would have made if the defendant had duly carried out his promise.

335. Thompson (W. L.) Ltd. *v.* Robinson (Gunmakers) Ltd., [1955] Ch. 177

On 4th March, 1954, the defendants agreed in writing with the plaintiffs, who were motor car dealers, to purchase from them a Standard Vanguard car. On 5th March, 1954, the defendants said that they were not prepared to take delivery. The plaintiffs returned the car to their suppliers who did not ask for any compensation. The plaintiffs now sued for damages for breach of contract. The selling price of a Standard Vanguard was fixed by the manufactures and the plaintiff's profit would have been £61 1s. 9d. When the agreement was made there was not sufficient demand for Vanguards in the locality as would absorb all such cars available for sale in the area, but evidence did not show that there was no available market in the widest sense, i.e. in the sense of the country as a whole. It was *held* that the plaintiffs were entitled to compensation for the loss of their bargain, i.e. the profit they would have made (being £61 1s. 9d.) because they had sold one car less than they would have done.—The decision depends to a large extent on the fact that in Yorkshire, at the time the contract was made, the supply of Standard Vanguards did exceed the demand.

336. Luker v. Chapman (1970), 114 S.J. 788

The plaintiff lost his right leg below the knee as a result of a traffic accident in which his motor cycle was in collision with the defendant's sports car. The accident was partly caused by the defendant's negligence. After the accident the plaintiff was unable to continue with his employment as a telephone engineer and refused a clerical job, taking up teacher training instead. *Held*—by Browne, J.—that the plaintiff was required to mitigate damages and should have accepted the clerical job. The defendant was not liable for the loss of income involved in the period of teacher training.

337. Ford Motor Co. (England) Ltd. v. Armstrong (1915), 31 T.L.R. 267

The defendant was a retailer who received supplies from the plaintiffs. As part of his agreement with the plaintiffs the defendant had undertaken—

(i) not to sell any of the plaintiffs' cars or spares below list price;
(ii) not to sell Ford cars to other dealers in the motor trade;
(iii) not to exhibit any car supplied by the company without their permission.

The defendant also agreed to pay £250 for every breach of the agreement as being the agreed damage which the manufacturer will "sustain." The defendant was in breach of the agreement and the plaintiffs sued. It was *held* by the Court of Appeal that the sum of £250 was in the nature of a penalty and not liquidated damages. The same sum was payable for different kinds of breach which were not likely to produce the same loss. Furthermore its size suggested that it was not a genuine pre-estimate of loss.

338. Cellulose Acetate Silk Co. Ltd. v. Widnes Foundry Ltd., [1933] A.C. 20

The Widnes Foundry entered into a contract to erect a plant for the Silk Co. by a certain date. It was also agreed that the Widnes Foundry would pay the Silk Co. £20 per week for every week they took in erecting the plant beyond the agreed date. In the event the erection was completed thirty weeks late, and the Silk Co. claimed for their actual loss which was £5,850. *Held*—The Widnes Foundry were only liable to pay £20 per week as agreed.

339. Craven-Ellis v. Canons Ltd., [1936] 2 K.B. 403

The plaintiff was employed as managing director by the company under a deed which provided for remuneration. The Articles provided that directors must have qualification shares, and must obtain these within two months of appointment. The plaintiff and other directors never obtained the required number of shares so that the deed was invalid. However, the plaintiff had rendered services, and he now sued on a *quantum meruit* for a reasonable sum by way of remuneration. *Held*—He succeeded on a *quantum meruit*, there being no valid contract.

340. Gilbert and Partners v. Knight, [1968] 2 All E.R. 248

The respondent Knight, agreed, in August, 1965, to pay Gilbert, who was a member of the appellant firm of surveyors, a fee of £30 to supervise specified building work estimated to cost £600. In May, 1966, when the builder started work, the respondent ordered some additional work which brought the cost to £2,238. Gilbert supervised this additional work but made no request for an additional payment until the work was completed. He then rendered an account for £135 being the agreed £30 plus a scale fee of 100 guineas for supervising the additional work. The respondent paid only the agreed £30 and would not pay more. Gilbert and Partners' action against Knight was dismissed and they appealed. It was *held* by the Court of Appeal, dismissing the appeal, that the firm was entitled to £30 only. No *quantum meruit* claim lay for supervising the additional work unless a new contract to pay for that work had been made because the parties never discharged the original contract for one lump-sum fee of £30.

341. Metropolitan Electric Supply Co. v. Ginder, [1901] 2 Ch. 799

The defendant entered into a contract with the plaintiffs in which he agreed to take all the electricity he required from them. The plaintiffs sued for an injunction to prevent the defendant from obtaining energy elsewhere. *Held*— The plaintiffs succeeded since the agreement was in essence an undertaking not to take supplies of electricity from elsewhere, and could be enforced by injunction.

342. Whitwood Chemical Co. v. Hardman, [1891] 2 Ch. 416

The defendant entered into a contract of service with the plaintiffs and agreed to give the whole of his time to them. In fact he occasionally worked for others, and the plaintiffs tried to enforce the undertaking in the service contract by injunction. *Held*—An injunction could not be granted because there was no express negative stipulation. The defendant had merely stated what he would do, and not what he would not do, and to read into the undertaking an agreement not to work for anyone else required the court to imply a negative stipulation from a positive one. No such implication could be made.

343. Warner Brothers Pictures Incorporated v. Nelson, [1937] 1 K.B. 209

The defendant, the film actress Bette Davis, had entered into a contract in which she agreed to act exclusively for the plaintiffs for twelve months. She was anxious to obtain more money and so she left America, and entered into a contract with a person in England. The plaintiffs now asked for an injunction restraining the defendant from carrying out the English contract. *Held*—An injunction would be granted. The contract contained a negative stipulation not to work for anyone else, and this could be enforced. However, since the contract was an American one, the court limited the operation of the injunction to the area of the court's jurisdiction, and although the contract stipulated that the defendant would not work in any other occupation, the injunction was confined to work on stage or screen.

344. Ryan v. Mutual Tontine Westminster Chambers Association, [1893] 1 Ch. 116

The defendants leased a residential flat to the plaintiff and also agreed to employ a porter who would be resident on the premises. The porter was to clean the flats and deliver parcels, take in articles for safe custody, and take charge of keys. The defendants appointed a porter but the man concerned was also a chef at a club in Westminster and was absent from the flats each day from 11 a.m. to 3 p.m., carrying out his duties as a chef. While he was away his duties were carried out in a most indifferent fashion by a number of boys and a charlady. These persons were not resident. The plaintiff now sued for breach of contract and asked for specific performance of the promise to appoint a full time porter. *Held*—Specific performance could not be granted because the court could not supervise the day-to-day performance of an such obligation. The plaintiff's remedy was an action for damages.

345. Page One Records Ltd. *v.* Britton, [1967] 3 All E.R. 822

By a written contact made in 1966 the defendants, a group of four musicians ("The Troggs"), appointed the plaintiffs to manage their professional careers for five years, they being persons of no business experience who were unlikely to survive as a "pop" group without the services of a manager. The contract was world-wide. The plaintiffs agreed to use all their resources of knowledge and experience to advance the defendants' careers, and the contract further provided that the defendants would not engage any other person to act as manager or agent for them, and that they would not act themselves in such capacity. The plaintiffs were to receive twenty per cent of all moneys earned by the defendants during the period of the contract. The Troggs became an established group, earning as much as £400 per night. In 1967 the defendants signified their intention to repudiate the management contract, but the court held that there had been no breaches of duty by the plaintiffs to justify the repudiation. In fact the plaintiffs had supported the group in the fullest measure and were to a large extent responsible for the success of the group. The plaintiffs sued for damages for breach of contract and applied also for an interlocutory injunction restraining the defendants until trial from engaging any person, firm or corporation, other than the plaintiffs, as their manager. *Held*—by Stamp, J. that the injunction must be refused because—

(i) The defendants had no business experience and had to have a manager. If an injunction was granted it would *compel* not merely *encourage* the defendants to carry out their contract with the plaintiffs. *Warner Bros.* v. *Nelson*, 1937,[343] was distinguishable because Bette Davis was a person of intelligence, capacity and means and if she had chosen not to act at all, rather than for Warner Bros., she would have been able to employ herself both usefully and remuneratively in other spheres of activity. Other similarly remunerative employment was not available to the "Troggs."

(ii) The injunction, if granted, would also have the effect of enforcing a contract for personal services of a fiduciary nature, because the plaintiffs were managers and it would be necessary for them to see, and be friendly with, the defendants for a further four years. In *Warner Bros.* v. *Nelson*, 1937, the obligation of the plaintiffs was largely to pay money to Miss Davis; they were not involved in the much more intimate relationship of managing her career.

346. Brook's Wharf and Bull Wharf Ltd. *v.* Goodman Bros, [1936] 3 All E.R. 696

The plaintiff company had agreed to store in its warehouse goods imported by the defendants. The defendants were liable by Act of Parliament to pay customs duties but the Act also allowed the authorities to recover these duties from the warehouseman. The goods were stolen before the defendants had paid the customs duties and they refused to do so. The authorities claimed the duties from the plaintiffs who paid them. *Held*—by the Court of Appeal—that the plaintiffs could recover the sums paid by way of duty from the defendants in quasi-contract.

347. Metropolitan Police District Receiver *v.* Croydon Corporation, [1957] 1 All E.R. 78

A policeman had recovered damages for an accident resulting from the defendants' negligence. The injuries were received while the policeman was on duty and his wages were paid while he was unfit by the Police Receiver who was required by Act of Parliament to make these payments. In this action the Receiver was seeking to recover the amount paid in wages on the ground that the defendants would have had to pay more in damages to the policeman if he had not received his pay. *Held*—by the Court of Appeal—that the action failed. The defendants were not under a common and legal obligation to pay the policeman's wages so that quasi-contract did not apply.

348. Rowland *v.* Divall, [1923] 2 K.B. 500

In April, 1922, the defendant bought an "Albert" motor car from a man who had stolen it from the true owner. One month later the plaintiff, a dealer, purchased the car from the defendant for £334, repainted it, and sold it for £400 to Colonel Railsdon. In September, 1922, the police seized the car from Colonel Railsdon and the plaintiff repaid him the £400. The plaintiff now sued the defendant for £334 on the grounds that there had been a total failure of consideration since the plaintiff had not obtained a title to the car. *Held*— The defendant was in breach of Sect. 12 of the Sale of Goods Act, 1893, which implies conditions and warranties into a sale of goods relating to the seller's right to sell, and there had been a total failure of consideration in spite of the fact that the car had been used by the plaintiff and his purchaser. The plaintiff contracted for the property in the car and not the mere right to possess it. Since he had not obtained the property, he was entitled to recover the sum of £334 and no deductions should be made for the period of user.

N.B. Although the court purported to deal with this case as a breach of Sect. 12 (1) of the Act, it would appear that in fact they operated on common law principles and gave complete restitution of the purchase price because of total failure of consideration arising out of the seller's lack of title. The condition under Sect. 12 (1) had by reason of the plaintiff's use of the car and the passage of time become a warranty when the action was brought and if the court had been awarding damages for breach of warranty it would have had to reduce the sum of £334 by a sum representing the value to the plaintiff of the use of the vehicle which he had had.

349. Cox *v.* Prentice (1815), 3 M. & S. 344

The defendant wished to sell a bar of silver to Cox but before the sale the bar was weighted by an assay master. Cox paid £88 for the bar on the basis of the weight ascribed to it by the assay master. It was later discovered that the weight was less than certified by the assay master who had made a mistake in the weighing. *Held*—Cox could recover the excess from Prentice since the money had been paid under a mistake of fact.

350. Lovell *v.* Lovell, [1970] 1 W.L.R. 1451

In the course of an action based on a claim for money lent fourteen years before the issue of a writ, the plaintiff served interrogatories on the defendant. This is allowed as part of civil procedure in order to ascertain facts material to the claim. Two of the questions were—"On (a certain date) did you owe (the plaintiff) £2,300?" and "If not £2,300 did you owe her any sum and if so, what sum?" *Held*—by the Court of Appeal—the questions need not be answered. To allow interrogatories of this kind would mean that no one could ever rely on the Limitation Act since he would be forced to give an acknowledgement of the debt on which an action could subsequently be brought.

351. Initial Services *v.* Putterill, [1967] 3 All E.R. 145

The first defendant was employed by the plaintiff launderers as their sales manager but he resigned and took a number of the plaintiff's documents which he handed to reporters of the *Daily Mail*, who were the second defendants. He also gave the reporters of the same newspaper information about the company's affairs. The newspaper published articles alleging a liaison system between launderers to keep up their prices, and that the plaintiffs had increased their prices after the imposition of the Selective Employment Tax ostensibly to offset that tax, when in fact they were getting substantial extra profit. On the plaintiff's action for breach of an implied term of the defendant's contract of service that he would not disclose to strangers confidential information obtained by him in the course of his employment, the defendant pleaded that the plaintiffs had agreements which ought to have been registered under the Restrictive Trade Practices Act, 1956, that they ought to have been referred to the Monopolies Commission, and that they had issued misleading circulars about their reasons for raising their prices. *Held*—

(i) The servant was under no obligation not to disclose information which ought, in the public interest, to be disclosed to a person having a proper interest to receive it;

(ii) it was at least arguable that the information supplied by the defendant was in the above category;

(iii) the allegations in the defence could not be said to be so invalid that they ought to be struck out.

There was argument on the question as to whether the press was the proper authority for the receipt of confidential information but this doubt was not enough to invalidate the defence at this stage.

LAW OF TORTS

352. Perera *v.* Vandiyar, [1953] 1 All E.R. 1109

The plaintiff was the tenant of a flat in Tooting, and the defendant was the landlord. On 8th October, 1952, the landlord cut off the supply of gas and electricity to the flat in order to induce the plaintiff to leave. As a result, the plaintiff was forced to move out of the flat and lived elsewhere until the services were restored on 15th October, 1952. The plaintiff claimed damages for breach of implied covenant for quiet enjoyment, and also for eviction. *Held*— The plaintiff was entitled to damages for breach of the implied covenant, but punitive damages on the purported tort of eviction were not recoverable because the defendant had not committed a tort. It had not been necessary for the defendant to trespass on any part of the demised premises in order to cut off the services, and mere intention to evict was not a tort.

353. Hargreaves *v.* Bretherton, [1958] 3 W.L.R. 463

The plaintiff pleaded that the defendant had falsely and maliciously and without just cause or excuse committed perjury as a witness at the plaintiff's trial for certain criminal offences, and that as a result the plaintiff had been convicted and sentenced to eight years' preventive detention. A point of law arose because the plaintiff's action was in effect based on the purported tort of perjury. *Held*—No action lay on this cause, since there was no tort of perjury, and therefore the plaintiff's claim must be struck out.

353a. Roy v. Prior, [1969] 3 All E.R. 1153

The plaintiff, a doctor, sued the defendant, a solicitor, for damages alleging, amongst other things, that the defendant had caused his arrest and forcible attendance at court to give evidence in a criminal case by saying falsely in court that the plaintiff was evading a witness summons. The action failed. Lord Denning, M.R., saying the course of his judgment—

> It is settled law that, if a witness knowingly and maliciously tells untruths in the witness box, and as a result an innocent person is imprisoned, nevertheless no action lies against that witness. . . . The reason lies in public policy. Witnesses must be able to give their evidence without fear of the consequences. They might be deterred from doing so if they were at risk of being sued for what they said. So the law gives a witness the cloak of absolute immunity from suit. This applies not only to statements made by a witness in the box, but also to statements made whilst he is giving his proof to his solicitor beforehand. The reason is because the protection given to the witness in the box would be useless to him if it could be got round by an action against him in respect of his proof . . . .

354. Donoghue (or M'Alister) *v.* Stevenson, [1932] A.C. 562

The appellant's friend purchased a bottle of ginger beer from a retailer in Paisley and gave it to her. The respondents were the manufacturers of the ginger beer. The appellant consumed some of the ginger beer and her friend was replenishing the glass, when, according to the appellant, the decomposed remains of a snail came out of the bottle. The bottle was made of dark glass so that the snail could not be seen until most of the contents had been consumed. The appellant became ill and served a writ on the manufacturers claiming damages. The question before the House of Lords was whether the facts outlined above constituted a cause of action in negligence. The House of Lords *held* by a majority of three to two that they did. It was stated that a manufacturer of products, which are sold in such a form that they are likely to reach the ultimate consumer in the form in which they left the manufacturer with no possibility of intermediate examination, owes a duty to the consumer to take reasonable care to prevent injury. This rule has been broadened in subsequent cases so that the manufacturer is liable more often where defective chattels cause injury. The following important points also arise out of the case.

    (i) It was in this case that the House of Lords formulated the test that the duty of care in negligence is based on the foresight of the reasonable man.

    (ii) Lord Macmillan's remark that the categories of negligence are never closed suggests that the tort of negligence is capable of further expansion.

    (iii) The duty of care with regard to chattels as laid down in the case relates to chattels not dangerous in themselves. The duty of care in respect of chattels dangerous in themselves, e.g. explosives, is much higher.

(iv) The appellant had no cause of action against the retailer in contract because her friend bought the bottle, so that there was no privity of contract between the retailer and the appellant. Therefore terms relating to fitness for purpose and merchantable quality, implied into such contracts by the Sale of Goods Act, 1893, did not apply here.

355. Best v. Samuel Fox & Co. Ltd., [1952] 2 All E.R. 394

Best was a workman at the defendants' factory and because of an accident caused by the defendants' negligence he was emasculated. Best's claim for damages was successful but his wife also claimed damages for loss of her husband's *consortium* through the defendants' negligence. The House of Lords *held* that her claim failed because the *damnum* was not of a kind recognised by law. "It is true that a husband is entitled to recover damages for loss of *consortium* against a person who negligently injures his wife, but this exceptional right is an anomaly at the present day. A wife . . . was never regarded as having any proprietary right in her husband . . ." *per* Lord Morton of Henryton. *N.B.* Some American jurisdictions allow such a claim.

356. Electrochrome Ltd. v. Welsh Plastics Ltd., [1968] 2 All E.R. 205

A lorry driver employed by the defendants drove the defendants' vehicle into a fire hydrant near to the plaintiffs' factory. Water escaped from the damaged hydrant and the supply had to be cut off while repairs were carried out. The plaintiffs lost a day's work at their factory and sued for this loss. However, since they were not the owners of the hydrant it was *held* that no action lay. They had suffered loss but there had been no infringement of their legal rights.

N.B. Presumably such a loss as that suffered by the plaintiffs could have been covered by insurance.

357. The Mayor of Bradford v. Pickles, [1895] A.C. 587

The corporation had statutory power to take water from certain springs. Water reached the springs by percolating (but not in a defined channel) through neighbouring land belonging to Pickles. In order to induce the corporation to buy his land at a high price, Pickles sank a shaft on it, with the result that the water reaching the corporation's reservoir was discoloured and its flow diminished. The corporation asked for an injunction to restrain Pickles from collecting the subterranean water. *Held*—An injunction could not be granted. Pickles had a right to drain from his land subterranean water not running in a defined channel. (This right of a landowner was established by the House of Lords in *Chasemore* v. *Richards* (1859), 7 H.L. Cas. 349.) Any malice which he might have had in doing it did not affect that right, since English law knows no doctrine of abuse of rights. No use of property which would be legal if due to a proper motive can become illegal because it is prompted by an improper or malicious motive.

357a. Langbrook Properties v. Surrey County Council, [1969] 3 All E.R. 1424

The plaintiffs claimed that buildings on their land had suffered from subsidence caused by the defendants' conduct in pumping out excavations for the construction of a motorway near Sunbury-on-Thames. They claimed damages for nuisance and negligence. *Held*—by Plowman, J.—the claim disclosed no course of action, a landowner being entitled to abstract underground percolating water as much as he wished regardless of resulting damage to his neighbour. (*Bradford Corporation* v. *Pickles*, 1895, *applied*.)

358. Wilkinson v. Downton, [1897] 2 Q.B. 57

The defendant, "as a practical joke," called on Mrs. Wilkinson and told her that her husband had been seriously injured in an accident and had had both his legs broken. Mrs. Wilkinson travelled to see her husband at Leytonstone, and believing the message to be true, sustained nervous shock and in consequence was seriously ill. This action was brought for damages for false and malicious representation. Damages were awarded. The court *held* that intentional physical harm is a tort even though it does not consist of a trespass to the person. Further, whether the act is malicious or by way of a joke is irrelevant.

359. Dulieu v. White, [1901] 2 K.B. 669

The defendant, who was driving a van negligently, ran into a public house. The plaintiff, who was pregnant, was in the public house and because of the shock became ill and gave birth to a premature and mentally deficient child. It was *held* that she could recover damages.

360. Jennings v. Rundall (1799), 8 Term. Rep. 335

An infant hired a horse to take a ride. He injured it by excessive riding. It was *held* that the injury was essentially a breach of the contract of hiring. Therefore the infant was not liable in tort.

361. Ballett v. Mingay, [1943] K.B. 281

The appellant was an infant and he borrowed from the respondent an amplifier and a microphone. When the respondent demanded the return of the articles, the appellant failed to do so having lent them to another. The infant was sued in detinue. It was suggested that in this action the respondent was seeking to make the appellant liable in tort for an act which was really a breach of contract and for which, as an infant, he could not be liable. *Held*—The infant was properly sued in tort because his action in parting with possession of the articles was not allowed by the contract of bailment and was therefore outside the terms of the contract.

362. Donaldson v. McNiven, [1952] 1 All E.R. 1213

The defendant lived in a densely populated area of Liverpool and allowed his thirteen-year-old son to have an air rifle on condition that he did not use it outside the house. The defendant's house had a large cellar and the boy was told to use the rifle there. Without the defendant's knowledge the boy fired the air rifle at some children playing near to the house, injuring the plaintiff, a child of five. *Held*—In the circumstances the precautions taken by the defendant were reasonable and would have been adequate but for the son's disobedience, which could not have been foreseen because the boy was usually obedient. The defendant was not guilty of negligence.

363. Bebee v. Sales (1916), 32 T.L.R. 413

A father allowed his fifteen-year-old son to retain a shot gun with which he knew he had already caused damage. The father was *held* liable for an injury to another boy's eye.

N.B. Cases 362 and 363 were decided on the ordinary principles of negligence at common law. However, since the Air Guns and Shot Guns Act, 1962, an action may lie against the parent for breach of statutory duty. The Act makes it a criminal offence to give an air weapon to a person under fourteen years, and restricts the use or possession of air weapons by young persons in public places except under supervision. Certain additional statutory duties arise under the Firearms Act, 1965. In any case breaches of these statutory duties could be relied upon as evidence of negligence. Furthermore a person injured might now claim compensation from the Criminal Injuries Compensation Board. The age of the child causing the injury is not a bar to a claim against the Board because payments will be made even though the child inflicting the injury is below the age of criminal responsibility. In *Gorely* v. *Codd*, [1966] 3 All E.R. 891, the plaintiff was injured by a pellet from Codd's air rifle when they were larking about in a field in open country. Codd was sixteen-and-a-half years of age and when the plaintiff sued Codd's father the Court found that he had given proper instruction to his son and was not liable at common law. Since the shooting did not occur in a public place there was no breach of the Air Guns and Shot Guns Act, 1962.

364. Carmarthenshire County Council *v.* Lewis, [1955] 1 All E.R. 565

A boy aged four years was a pupil at a nursery school run by the appellants who were the local education authority. The boy and another were made ready to go out for a walk with the mistress in charge who left them for a moment in order to get ready herself. She did not return for ten minutes, having treated another child who had cut himself. During her absence the boy got out of the classroom and made his way through an unlocked gate, down a lane, and into a busy highway. He caused the driver of a lorry to swerve into a telegraph pole, as a result of which the driver was killed. His widow brought an action for damages for negligence. *Held*—In the circumstances of the case the mistress was not negligent so the liability of the local authority was not vicarious. However, they were negligent themselves because they had not taken reasonable precautions to keep the young children who used the premises from getting out into the highway.

364a. Butt v. *Cambridgeshire and Isle of Ely County Council* (1969), *The Times*, November 27th, 1969.

The plaintiff was a pupil in a class of 37 girls of nine and ten years of age. She lost an eye when another girl in her class waved pointed scissors which the the children were using to cut out illustrations. The teacher was giving individual attention to another child. *Held*—by the Court of Appeal—that her claim for damages failed. The teacher was not under a duty to require all work to stop while she was giving individual attention to members of the class. She was not negligent so that there was no vicarious liability in the local authority. The local authority was not liable for its own negligence in that evidence of experienced teachers showed that there was no fault in the system of using pointed scissors.

365. Morriss *v.* Marsden, [1952] All 1 E.R. 925

The defendant took a room at an hotel in Brighton, and whilst there he violently attacked the plaintiff who was the manager of the hotel. Evidence showed that at the time of the attack the defendant was suffering from a disease of the mind. He knew the nature and quality of his act, but did not know that what he was doing was wrong. The plaintiff sued for damages for assault and battery. *Held*—Since the defendant knew the nature and quality of his tortious act, it did not matter that he did not know that what he was doing was wrong, and he was liable in tort.

366. Law *v.* Llewellyn, [1906] 1 K.B. 487

Law appeared at Bridgend magistrates' court to prosecute two persons for obtaining money by false pretences. He was advised by counsel that, in the absence of certain witnesses, it would not be possible to secure a conviction. Law agreed to withdraw the charges and, after he had done so, Llewellyn, who was a presiding magistrate, said words which meant that the plaintiff was a blackmailer and had brought unfounded criminal charges. He also added that a term of imprisonment would do the plaintiff good. Law brought this action against Llewellyn for defamation, and it was *held* that judicial immunity extended to Llewellyn and therefore Law's claim showed no reasonable cause of action.

367. Dickinson *v.* Del Solar, [1930] 1 K.B. 376

The plaintiff had been knocked down by a car driven by the defendant's servant. The defendant was the First Secretary of the Peruvian Legation in London. The Head of the Legation directed the defendant not to plead diplomatic privilege, and the defendant entered an appearance in the action. The plaintiff succeeded and the defendant's insurance company refused to indemnify their client, saying, in effect, that his diplomatic immunity was immunity from liability. *Held*—The insurers were liable to indemnify the defendant. Diplomatic agents are not immune from liability for wrongful acts, but are merely immune from suit. This immunity can be waived with the sanction of the sovereign of the state in question, or an official superior of the person concerned. The defendant's act in entering an appearance operated as a waiver of diplomatic privilege, and judgment was properly entered against him.

368. D. & L. Caterers Ltd. and Jackson *v.* D'Anjou, [1945] 1 All E.R. 563

The plaintiffs owned a West-End restaurant called the "Bagatelle." The defendant made certain statements alleging that the restaurant was operated illegally and obtained its supplies on the Black Market. *Held*—The statements were defamatory and a limited liability company could sue for slander without proof of special damage. Where the slander related to its trade or business, the law implied the existence of damage to found the action.

369. Poulton *v.* London and South Western Railway Co. (1867), L.R. 2 Q.B. 534

The plaintiff was arrested by a station-master for non-payment of carriage in respect of his horse. The defendants, who were the employers of the station-master, had power to detain passengers for non-payment of their own fare, but for no other reason. *Held*—Since there was no express authorisation of the arrest by the defendants, the station-master was acting outside the scope of his employment and the defendants were not liable.

370. Campbell *v.* Paddington Borough Council, [1911] 1 K.B. 869

The defendants, in accordance with a resolution duly passed, erected a stand in Burwood Place in order that members of the council might view the funeral procession of King Edward the Seventh passing along the Edgware Road. The plaintiff, who occupied certain premises in Burwood Place, often let the premises for the purpose of viewing public processions passing along the Edgware Road. The stand obstructed the view of the funeral procession from the plaintiff's house and she was unable to let the premises for that purpose. *Held*—As the stand constituted a public nuisance, the plaintiff could maintain an action for the special damage which she had sustained through the loss of view. The corporation were properly sued, and the fact that the erection of the stand was probably *ultra vires* did not matter.

371. **Garrard** *v.* **Southey (A. E.) and Co. and Standard Telephones and Cables Ltd.,** [1952] 2 Q.B. 174

Two persons employed by electrical contractors were sent to work in a factory on electrical installations. The electrical contractors continued to employ the men, paying their wages, stamping their insurance cards, and retaining the sole right to dismiss them. The electricians worked exclusively at the factory and used the factory canteen. The occupiers of the factory supplied them with all materials, tools and plant, except for certain special tools belonging to the electricians themselves. They were supervised by a foreman employed by the occupiers and they followed the system laid down in the factory. One of the electricians was injured when he fell from a defective trestle owned by some building contractors who were also working in the factory. *Held*—The occupiers of the factory, and not the electrical contractors, owed the injured electrician the common law duty of a master to his servant (to provide proper plant and equipment) and they were liable to him for breach of that duty.

372. **Mersey Docks and Harbour Board** *v.* **Coggins and Griffiths (Liverpool) Ltd. and McFarlane,** [1947] A.C. 1.

A firm of stevedores had hired from the Harbour Board the use of a crane together with its driver to assist in loading a ship lying in the Liverpool docks. The contract of hire was subject to the Board's regulations, one of which contained the clause: "The driver provided shall be the servant of the applicants." The driver of the crane was a skilled man appointed and paid by the Board, and the Board alone had power to dismiss him. The stevedores told the driver what they wanted the crane to lift but had no authority to tell him how to work the crane. McFarlane, who was a checker employed by the forwarding agents, was noting the number and marks on a case which the crane had picked up when he was trapped because of the negligence of the crane driver in failing to keep the crane still.

The question to be determined was whether in applying the doctrine of vicarious liability the general employers of the crane driver or the hirers were liable for his negligence. The Board contended that, under the terms of the contract between the Board and the stevedores, the stevedores were liable. *Held*—by the House of Lords—

(i) The question of liability was not to be determined by any agreement between the general employers and the hirers, but depended on the circumstances of the case. The test to apply was that of control.

(ii) The Board, as the general employers of the crane driver, had not established that the hirers had such control of the crane driver at the time of the accident as to become liable as employers for his negligence. Although the hirers could tell the crane driver where to go and what to carry, they had no authority to tell him how to operate the crane. The Board were, therefore, liable for his negligence.

373. Wright v. Tyne Improvement Commissioners (Osbeck & Co. Ltd., Third Party), [1968] 1 All E.R. 807

Tyne Improvement Commissioners hired a crane to Osbeck & Co. Ltd., under a written contract whereby the hirers agreed "to bear the risk of and be responsible for all damage, injury or loss whatsoever, howsoever and whensoever caused arising directly or indirectly out of or in connection with the hiring or use of the said crane." The plaintiff, who was a docker employed by Osbeck & Co., was injured when a wagon, in which he was standing to receive timber, was negligently moved forward by the capstan driver causing the plaintiff to collide with timber being lowered into the wagon by the crane. The plaintiff and the crane driver did all they could to avoid the accident but failed to do so and it was accepted that the capstan driver, who was employed by the Commissioners, was wholly to blame. Under the doctrine of vicarious liability the Commissioners were also to blame. When the action was tried at Newcastle upon Tyne Assizes Waller, J., awarded the plaintiff damages of £2,985 10s. 10d. against the Commissioners but dismissed a claim by the Commissioners against Osbeck & Co., as hirers of the crane, for an indemnity against the plaintiff's claim by virtue of the clause quoted above. The Commissioners now appealed against the dismissal of the claim for indemnity. *Held*—by the Court of Appeal—that as the accident arose directly or at least indirectly, out of or in connection with the use of the crane, the indemnity clause entitled the Commissioners to an indemnity against Osbeck & Co. even though the use to which the crane was being put was not a blameworthy cause of the accident.

374. Cassidy v. Ministry of Health, [1951] 2 K.B. 343

The plaintiff's left hand was operated on at the defendants' hospital by a whole-time assistant medical officer of the hospital. After the operation the plaintiff's hand and forearm were put in a splint for fourteen days. During this time the plaintiff complained of pain but was merely given sedatives by the doctors who attended him. When the splint was removed, it was found that all four fingers of the plaintiff's hand were stiff, and that his hand was virtually useless. The plaintiff sued the defendants for negligence. *Held*—The defendants were liable in spite of their absence of real control over the type of work done by the doctors employed by them. Denning, L.J., stated that only where the patient himself selects and employs the doctor will the hospital authorities escape liability for that doctor's negligence. If the person causing the harm is part of the organisation, the employer is liable.

375. Lee (Catherine) v. Lee's Air Farming Ltd., [1960] 3 All E.R. 420

In 1954 the appellant's husband formed the respondent company which carried on the business of crop spraying from the air. In March, 1956, Mr. Lee was killed while piloting an aircraft during the course of top soil dressing, and Mrs. Lee claimed compensation from the company, as the employer of her husband, under the New Zealand Workers' Compensation Act, 1922. Since Mr. Lee owned 2,999 of the company's 3,000 £1 shares and since he was its governing director, the question arose as to whether the relationship of master and servant could exist between the company and him. He was employed as the company's chief pilot under a provision in the articles at a salary to be arranged by himself. *Held*—Mrs. Lee was entitled to compensation because her husband was employed by the company in the sense required by the Act of 1922, and the decision in *Salomon* v. *Salomon & Co.*[31] was applied.

376. Century Insurance Co. Ltd. *v.* Northern Ireland Road Transport Board, [1942] A.C. 509

A tanker belonging to the respondents, and driven by one of their employees, was delivering petrol to a garage in Belfast. While the tanker was discharging petrol at the garage, the driver lit a cigarette and threw away the lighted match. The resulting explosion caused considerable damage. The contract under which the petrol was being delivered said that the respondents' employees were to take their orders from a petrol company to which the tankers were hired, a firm named Holmes, Mullin and Dunn, though they were not by virtue of this to be deemed the hirers' employees. The appellants had insured the defendants against liability to third parties, and pleaded that no claim could be made on them because, although the driver was admittedly negligent, he was at the time the servant of the hirers. *Held*—The appellants must pay the third party claim because the terms of the contract as a whole did not involve a transfer of the employees to Holmes, Mullin and Dunn; therefore, the respondents were liable for the negligence of the driver and were entitled to claim under their insurance.

377. Limpus *v.* London General Omnibus Co. (1862), 1 H. & C. 526

The plaintiff's omnibus was overturned when the driver of the defendants' omnibus drove across it so as to be first at a bus stop to take all the passengers who were waiting. The defendants' driver admitted that the act was intentional, and arose out of bad feeling between the two drivers. The defendants had issued strict instructions to their drivers that they were not to obstruct other omnibuses. *Held*—The defendants were liable. Their driver was acting within the scope of his employment at the time of the collision, and it did not matter that the defendants had expressly forbidden him to act as he did.

378. Vandyke *v.* Fender, [1970] 2 All E.R. 335

Mr. Vandyke and Mr. Fender were employed by the same firm and lived thirty miles from the business premises. The employer agreed to supply a car to Mr. Fender and to pay him 50p a day for petrol for the journey. The journey could have been made by train but was more convenient by car. Two other employees who lived in the same area were also carried. On one occasion the car loaned to Mr. Fender was not available and he was allowed to use a car belonging to the company secretary. While driving this car an accident occurred resulting in an injury to Mr. Vandyke who claimed damages from the company. It was *held* that the company was liable because Mr. Fender, though not a paid driver, was driving the car as the company's agent and they were liable for his negligence. The question then arose as to which of the insurance companies involved should indemnify the company. If the risk was to be borne by the employers' liability insurance it was necessary to show that the accident occurred during and in the course of Mr. Vandyke's employment, otherwise the risk would be borne by a road traffic insurance policy of Mr. Fender's which covered him while driving someone else's car. It was *held*—by the Court of Appeal— that a man going to or from work as a passenger in a vehicle provided by his employers for that purpose is not in the course of employment unless he is obliged by the terms of his employment to travel in that vehicle. If not then, as here, the liability must be borne by the road traffic insurers and not by the employers' liability insurers.

378a. *Nottingham* v. *Aldridge; Prudential Assurance Co.* (1971), *The Times*, February 23rd, 1971

In this case a Post Office trainee was returning to his normal work in his father's van after spending the week-end at his home having attended a training course the previous week. He was carrying another trainee, Nottingham, as a passenger and was entitled to a mileage allowance from the Post Office for himself and his passenger. Nottingham was injured as a result of an accident caused by the defendant's negligent driving. *Held*—by Eveleigh, J.— that the Post Office was not liable because the two trainees were not in the course of employment while travelling to work; nor was Aldridge the agent of the Post Office for the purposes of the journey. The vehicle did not belong to the Post Office nor was it provided by them. They had not prescribed the method of travel; admittedly a mileage allowance was payable but travelling expenses of any other kind would have been paid, e.g. bus or train fare. The question of agency was one of fact and on the facts of this case Aldridge was not an agent. The company which had insured the van was therefore liable to indemnify Aldridge in respect of his own liability to Nottingham.

379. Britt *v.* Galmoye and Nevill (1928), 44 T.L.R. 294

The first defendant, who had the second defendant in his employment as a van-driver, lent him his private motor car, after the day's work was finished, to take a friend to a theatre. The second defendant by his negligence injured the plaintiff. *Held*—that as the journey was not on the master's business and the master was not in control, he was not liable for his servant's act.

380. Armstrong *v.* Strain, [1952] 1 K.B. 232

The plaintiffs purchased a bungalow from Strain and during the negotiations Strain's agent made certain statements about the property and in particular that it was in nice condition. The property was subject to subsidence of the clay foundations, and had been underpinned several times, but the agent was aware of one underpinning only. After the plaintiffs had purchased the bungalow, large cracks appeared in the walls and the plaintiffs sued Strain and the agent for fraudulent misrepresentation. *Held*—They were unable to prove fraud because the ingredients of deceit were split, Strain having knowledge of the defects but not having made the statement, and the agent having made the statement without full knowledge of the defects. Devlin, J., at first instance suggested that Strain might have been liable if the evidence had shown that he deliberately kept his agents in ignorance of the defects in the expectation and hope that they would mislead the plaintiff, but the evidence did not establish this. Regarding an action for breach of warranty, Devlin, J., held that no warranty could arise out of the rather casual conversations which preceded the sale. Regarding liability of the agent in negligence, there was no duty of care in respect of careless misstatements of this sort, following *Candler* v. *Crane, Christmas*, 1951.[504]

N.B. In *Hedley Byrne* v. *Heller and Partners*, 1963,[194] the House of Lords decided that there was a duty of care in respect of careless misstatements of this kind, and this decision may provide a remedy in negligence in a situation like that in *Armstrong* v. *Strain*. Furthermore, a principal is presumably liable for the negligent misstatements of his agent under the Misrepresentation Act, 1967. (See now *Gosling* v. *Anderson*, 1972.)[650]

381. Morris *v.* C. W. Martin & Sons Ltd., [1965] 2 All E.R. 725

The plaintiff sent a mink stole to a furrier for the purpose of cleaning. The furrier later told the plaintiff by telephone that he did not clean furs himself but intended to send the stole to the defendants, one of the biggest cleaners of fur in the country. The plaintiff knew of Martin & Sons and agreed that the stole be sent to them. Martin & Sons did work only for the fur trade and had issued to the furrier printed conditions which provided that goods belonging to customers were at customer's risk when on the premises of Martin & Sons, and that they should not be responsible for loss or damage however caused, though they would compensate for loss or damage to the goods during the cleaning process by reason of their negligence, but not by reason of any other cause. The furrier knew of these conditions when he handed the stole to the defendants and the defendants knew that it belonged to a customer of the furrier but they did not know that it was Morris. While in the possession of Martin & Sons the fur was stolen by a youth named Morrisey who had been employed by them for a few weeks only, though they had no grounds to suspect that he was dishonest. The plaintiff sued the defendants for conversion or negligence but the County Court Judge felt bound by *Cheshire* v. *Bailey*, 1905,[609] and held that the act of Morrisey, who had removed the stole by wrapping it round his body, was beyond the scope of his employment. In the Court of Appeal it was *held* that *Cheshire* v. *Bailey*, 1905,[609] had been impliedly overruled by *Lloyd* v. *Grace, Smith & Co.*, [1921] A.C. 716 (where it was held that a solicitor was liable for the criminal frauds of his managing clerk so long as the clerk was acting in the apparent scope of his authority). The defendants, as sub-bailees, were liable to the plaintiff, and on the matter of the exemption clause the Court of Appeal said that the terms of such a clause must be strictly construed, and since they referred only to goods "belonging to customers" this could be taken to mean goods belonging to the furrier and not to the furrier's customer, and because of this ambiguity the clause was inapplicable.

N.B. The above decision applies only to bailees for reward and only in circumstances where the servant is entrusted with, or put in charge of, the bailor's goods by his master. The mere fact that the servant's employment gave him the opportunity to steal the bailor's goods is not enough.

382. Ormrod *v.* Crossville Motor Services Ltd., [1953] 2 All E.R. 753

By an arrangement between the owner of a motor car and his friend, the friend was to drive the car from Birkenhead to Monte Carlo in order that the owner, the friend and the friend's wife, might use the car during their holiday in Monte Carlo. The owner of the car was travelling to Monte Carlo in another car as a competitor in the Monte Carlo Rally. Owing to the friend's negligent driving, the car was involved in a collision in which a motor bus was damaged. The question of the liability of the owner of the car for the damage arose. *Held*— The friend was acting as the owner's agent in the matter. The owner had an interest in the arrival of the car at Monte Carlo, and the driving was done for his benefit. Accordingly the owner was vicariously liable for his friend's negligence.

382a. *Launchbury* v. *Morgans*, [1971] 1 All E.R. 642

In this case the family car was registered in the name of the wife though it was used mainly by the husband who worked seven miles from home. The wife had asked her husband not to drive the car home himself if he had been drinking. On one occasion the husband had been drinking heavily and asked a friend, C, to drive him home together with three other passengers. There was an accident caused by the negligent driving of C and the husband and he were killed. The three passengers were injured and sued the wife claiming that she was liable vicariously for the negligence of C. *Held*—by the Court of Appeal—that the wife was liable. If the husband had been driving he would have done so as the wife's agent. On appeal to the House of Lords ([1972] 2 All E.R. 606) it was held that the wife was not liable. The concept of agency required more than mere permission to use. Use must be at the owner's request or on his instructions.

382b. *Rambarran* v. *Gurrucharren*, [1970] 1 All E.R. 749

In this case Rambarran, a chicken farmer in Guyana, owned a car which was used by several of his sons, Rambarran himself being unable to drive. One of his sons, Leslie, damaged Gurrucharren's car by negligently driving the family car. The Privy Council found that Rambarran was not liable for Leslie's negligence because he did not know that Leslie had taken the car since he was away from home at his chicken farm at the time in question. Furthermore, there was no evidence to show what the purpose of Leslie's journey was, but it was clearly not for any business or family purpose. Ownership of the vehicle was not enough in itself to establish liability.

383. **Klein** *v.* **Calnori** (1971), *The Times*, February 19th, 1971

The defendant, Calnori, was the manager of a public house at Sunbury-on-Thames. While he was busy at the bar a Mr. Freshwater, who knew Calnori, took his car and drove it away without his permission. Later Freshwater telephoned Calnori and told him he had taken his car. Calnori told him to bring it back. On the way back to Sunbury Freshwater collided with Klein's stationary car severely damaging it. Klein alleged that Calnori was liable for this damage because Freshwater was his agent. By asking Freshwater to bring the car back Freshwater was driving it partly for Calnori's purposes. *Held*—by Lyell, J.—Calnori was not liable. If Freshwater had borrowed the car with Calnori's consent then the loan to Freshwater, for his own purposes, would have involved returning it. In these circumstances Calnori would not have been liable for an accident on the return journey. Therefore Calnori's liability could not be greater in circumstances in which the car had been taken without his consent and had been used solely for the taker's purpose.

384. **Bower** *v.* **Peate** (1876), 1 Q.B.D. 321

The plaintiff and defendant were respective owners of two adjoining houses, the plaintiff being entitled to the support for his house of the defendant's land. The defendant employed a contractor to pull down his house and to rebuild it after excavating the foundations. The contractor undertook the risk of supporting the plaintiff's house during the work and to make good any damage caused. The plaintiff's house was damaged in the progress of the work because the contractor did not take appropriate steps to support it. *Held*—that the defendant was liable. The fact that the injury would have been prevented if the contractor had provided proper support did not take away the defendant's liability. A person employing a contractor to perform a duty cast upon himself is responsible for the contractor's negligence in performing it.

385. Salsbury *v.* Woodland, [1969] 3 All E.R. 863

The defendant employed, as an independent contractor, an experienced tree-feller to fell a large tree in his front garden. The contractor was negligent and the tree fell towards the highway bringing down telephone wires on to the highway and causing the plaintiff injury. *Held*—by the Court of Appeal—the defendant was not liable though the contractor was. There was no special liability in the defendant merely because the contractor was employed to work near, as distinct from on, the highway.

386. Padbury *v.* Holliday and Greenwood Ltd. and Another (1912), 28 T.L.R. 494

The defendants were employed to erect certain premises in Fenchurch Street, and the contract involved the employment by the defendants of sub-contractors to carry out the special work of putting metallic casements into the windows. While this work was being carried out an iron tool was placed by a servant of the sub-contractors on the window sill. The casement was blown by the wind and the tool fell and struck the plaintiff who was walking in the street below. The placing of the tool on the window sill was not the normal practice adopted in the work involved. *Held*—that the injuries were caused to the plaintiff by an act of collateral negligence on the part of a workman who was a servant of the sub-contractors and not of the defendants and that the latter were not, therefore, liable for the consequences of that negligence.

387. Murray *v.* Harringay Arena Ltd., [1951] 2 K.B. 529

David Charles Murray, aged six, was taken by his parents to the defendants' ice rink to watch a hockey match. They occupied front seats at the rink, and during the game the boy was hit in the eye by the puck. This action was brought against the defendants for negligence. *Held*—The risk was voluntarily undertaken by the plaintiffs. The defendants had provided protection by means of netting and a wooden barrier which, in the circumstances, was adequate, since further protection would have seriously interfered with the view of the spectators.

388. Hall *v.* Brooklands Auto-Racing Club, [1933] 1 K.B. 205

The plaintiff paid for admission to the defendants' premises to watch motor-car races. During one of the races a car left the track, as a result of a collision with another car, and crashed through the railings injuring the plaintiff. It was the first time that a car had gone through the railings, and in view of that the precautions taken by the defendants were adequate. In this action by the plaintiff for personal injuries, it was *held* that the danger was not one which the defendants ought to have anticipated, and that the plaintiff must be taken to have agreed to assume the risk of such an accident.

389. Bennett *v.* Tugwell, [1971] 2 W.L.R. 847

In this case it was *held*—by Ackner, J.—that Bennett, who was injured while travelling in Tugwell's father's car, could not recover damages although

Tugwell was insured under a comprehensive policy. This was because Tugwell proved that Bennett voluntarily assented to be carried at his own risk. He had seen and appreciated the effect of a dashboard notice which read—"Passengers travelling in this vehicle do so at their own risk."

390. Geier *v.* Kujawa, [1970] 1 Lloyd's Rep. 364

The plaintiff was a German girl who spoke little English. She was injured while travelling as a passenger in a car driven by the defendant and sued him for negligence. The defence was—

(i) that the defendant had not been negligent;

(ii) the plaintiff was contributively negligent in that she was not wearing the seat belt provided;

(iii) that the plaintiff was *volens* because of a notice on the dashboard which read—"Warning. Passengers ride at their own risk and on condition that no claim shall be made against the driver or owner in the event of loss or injury."

Held—by Brabin, J.—

(i) that on the facts the defendant had driven negligently;

(ii) that the plaintiff was not contributively negligent because the accident took place in 1964 before the Government had publicised fully the advantages of using safety belts, the plaintiff had never seen one before and did not know how to use it nor did the defendant instruct her;

(iii) that the plaintiff was not *volens* because she had not read or even seen the notice on the dashboard.

N.B.

(i) Although the plaintiff was a minor at the time of the accident this was not put in issue and did not form part of the decision.

(ii) These problems have been solved by compulsory passenger insurance, Motor Vehicles (Passenger Insurance) Act, 1971.

391. Baker *v.* James Bros., [1921] 2 K.B. 674

The defendants were wholesale grocers and they employed the plaintiff as a traveller. He was supplied by the defendants with a motor car, the starting gear of which was defective. The plaintiff repeatedly complained about this to the defendants, but nothing was done to remedy the defect. While the plaintiff was on his rounds, the car stopped, and he was injured whilst trying to re-start it. *Held*—Notwithstanding the plaintiff's knowledge of the defect, he had never consented to take upon himself the risk of injury from the continued use of the car. He was not guilty of any contributory negligence and was entitled to recover damages.

392. Dann *v.* Hamilton, [1939] 1 K.B. 509

The plaintiff had been with a party to see the coronation decorations in London. They made the journey in the defendant's car. During the day and evening the defendant had consumed a quantity of intoxicating liquor, but he drove the party back to Staines where they all got out. The plaintiff was at this point a 2d. bus ride from her home but she accepted the defendant's invitation to take her there. During this part of the journey there was an accident caused by the defendant's negligence, and the plaintiff was injured. She now sued in respect of these injuries and the defendant pleaded *volenti non fit injuria. Held*—That the defence did not apply and the plaintiff succeeded. She had knowledge of a potential danger, but that did not mean that she assented to it.

N.B. The court left open the question where the driver was "dead drunk" or "very drunk." In such a case the maxim might have applied.

393. Smith v. Baker and Sons, [1891] A.C. 325

Smith was employed by Baker and Sons to drill holes in some rock in a railway cutting. A crane, operated by fellow employees, often swung heavy stones over Smith's head while he was working on the rock face. Both Smith and his employers realised that there was a risk the stones might fall, but the crane was nevertheless operated without any warning being given at the moment of jibbing or swinging. Smith was injured by a stone which fell from the crane because of negligent strapping of the load. The House of Lords *held* that Smith had not voluntarily undertaken the risk of his employers' negligence, and that his knowledge of the danger did not prevent his recovering damages.

394. Imperial Chemical Industries Ltd. v. Shatwell, [1964] 2 All E.R. 999

George and James Shatwell were certificated and experienced shotfirers employed by I.C.I. Statutory rules imposed an obligation on them personally (not on their employers) to ensure that certain operations connected with shotfiring should not be done unless all persons in the vicinity had taken cover. They knew of the risks of premature explosion which had been explained to them; they knew of the prohibition; but on one occasion because a cable they had was too short to reach the shelter, they decided to test without taking cover rather than wait ten minutes for their companion Beswick who had gone to fetch a longer cable. James gave George two wires, and George applied them to the galvanometer terminals. An explosion occurred and both men were injured. At the trial it was found that James was guilty of negligence and breach of statutory duty for which the employers were held vicariously liable, damages being assessed at £1,500 on a basis of 50 per cent contributory negligence. The Court of Appeal affirmed, but the House of Lords *reversed*, the decision and *held* that, although James's acts were a contributory cause of the accident to George, the employers were not liable.

(*a*) They were not themselves in breach of a statutory duty.

(*b*) They could plead *volenti non fit injuria* to a claim of vicarious liability.

(*c*) They had shown no negligence. They had instilled the need for caution, made proper provision, and even arranged a scale of remuneration in a way which removed a temptation to take short cuts.

(*d*) The Shatwell brothers were trained men well aware of the risk involved so the principle of *volenti non fit injuria* applied. Lord Pearce said: "The defence (of *volenti non fit injuria*) should be available where the employer was not in himself in breach of a statutory duty and was not vicariously in breach of a statutory duty through the neglect of some person of superior rank to the plaintiff and whose commands the plaintiff was bound to obey or who has some special and different duty of care."

N.B. If the employers had been compelled to rely on the defence of contributory negligence, they might have escaped liability if only one man were involved and treated as solely responsible, but where two men were involved, as here, they would have been vicariously liable for James's contribution to George's injury and for George's contribution to James's injury so they would have been compelled to partially compensate each man.

395. Haynes v. Harwood and Son, [1935] 1 K.B. 146

The defendants' servant left his van unattended in a street and the horses bolted with it. The plaintiff was a police constable on duty in a police station and seeing the horses bolting into a crowded street, and realising that, unless the horses were stopped, people in the street, including many children, would be likely to be injured, he darted out of the police station and, at great risk to himself, seized one of the horses and managed to bring them to a standstill. He was injured in doing so. It was *held* by the Court of Appeal that the defendants had been negligent, that the plaintiff was not guilty of contributory negligence, and that the damage was not too remote. The defendants also alleged assumption of risk by the plaintiff, but the court decided that the plaintiff's knowledge of the risk was not a bar to his claim.

396. Baker v. T. E. Hopkins and Son Ltd., [1959] 1 W.L.R. 966

The defendants were building contractors and were engaged to clean out a well. Various methods had been used in order to pump out the water, including hand-operated pumps, but eventually a petrol-driven pump was employed. The exhaust from the engine on the pump resulted in a lethal concentration of carbon monoxide forming inside the well. Two of the defendants' employees went down the well to carry on the work of cleaning it and were overcome by the fumes. Baker was a local doctor and, on being told what had happened, he went along to give what assistance he could. He was lowered down the well on a rope, and on reaching the two men, he realised that they were beyond help. He then gave a pre-arranged signal to those at the top of the well and started his journey to the surface. Unfortunately the rope became caught on a projection and Dr. Baker was himself overcome by fumes and died. His executors claimed damages in respect of Dr. Baker's death. *Held*—The defendants were negligent towards their employees in using the petrol-driven pump and the maxim *volenti non fit injuria* did not bar the claim of Dr. Baker's executors. Although Dr. Baker may have had knowledge of the risk he was running, he did not freely and voluntarily undertake it, but acted under the compulsion of his instincts as a brave man and a doctor.

397. Cutler v. United Dairies (London) Ltd., [1933] 2 K.B. 297

The defendants' carman left the defendants' horse and van, two wheels being properly chained, while he delivered milk The horse, being startled by the noise coming from a river steamer, bolted down the road and into a meadow. It stopped in the meadow and was followed there by the carman who, being in an excited state, began to shout for help. The plaintiff, a spectator, went to the carman's assistance and tried to hold the horse's head. The horse lunged and the plaintiff was injured. In this action by the plaintiff against the defendants for negligence it was *held* that in the circumstances the plaintiff voluntarily and freely assumed the risk. This was not an attempt to stop a runaway horse so that there was no sense of urgency to impel the plaintiff. He therefore knew of the risk and had had time to consider it, and by implication must have agreed to incur it.

398. Hyett v. Great Western Railway Co., [1948] 1 K.B. 345

The plaintiff was employed by a firm of wagon repairers and he was on the defendants' premises with their authority to carry out his duties. While repairing a wagon he saw smoke rising from one of the defendants' wagons in the same siding and went to investigate. The floor of the wagon, which contained paraffin oil, was in flames. The plaintiff was trying to get the drums of paraffin oil out, when one of them exploded and injured him. Evidence showed that the defendants knew that there was a paraffin leakage in the wagon, but had nevertheless allowed it to remain in the siding. *Held*—The plaintiff was entitled to recover damages from the defendants, and the maxim *volenti non fit injuria* did not apply. A man may take reasonable risks in trying to preserve property put in danger by another's negligence.

399. **Videan** *v.* **British Transport Commission**, [1963] 2 All E.R. 860

A child managed to get on to a railway line and was injured by a trolley. The Court of Appeal *held* that the child's presence was not in the circumstances foreseeable and the defendants did not owe him a duty of care. However, a duty was owed to his father who tried to rescue him.

400. **Wooldridge** *v.* **Sumner**, [1962] 2 All E.R. 978

A competitor of great skill and experience was riding a horse at a horse show when it ran wide at a corner and injured a cameraman who was unfamiliar with horses and who had ignored a steward's request to move outside the competition area. The rider was thrown, but later rode the horse again and it was adjudged supreme champion of its class. The cameraman brought an action for damages, and at the trial was awarded damages on the ground of negligence. *Held*, on appeal, that no negligence had been established because (i) any excessive speed at the corner was not the cause of the accident, and was not negligence but merely an error of judgment; and (ii) the judge's finding that the horse would have gone on to a cinder track without harm to the plaintiff if the rider had allowed it to, was an inference from primary facts and unjustified, and in any event an attempt to control the horse did not amount to negligence.

> Per Diplock, L.J., "If, in the course of a game or competition, at a moment when he has not time to think, a participant by mistake takes a wrong measure, he is not to be held guilty of any negligence. . . . A person attending a game or competition takes the risk of any damage caused to him by any act of a participant done in the course of and for the purposes of the game or competition, notwithstanding that such act may involve an error of judgment or a lapse of skill, unless the participant's conduct is such as to evince a reckless disregard of the spectator's safety. The spectator takes the risk because such an act involves *no breach of the duty of care* owed by the participant to him. He does not take the risk by virtue of the doctrine expressed or obscured by the maxim *volenti non fit injuria*. . . . The maxim in English law *pre-supposes a tortious act* by the defendant. The consent that is relevant is not consent to the risk of injury but consent to the lack of reasonable care that may produce that risk."

400a. *Wilks* v. *Cheltenham Home Guard Motor Cycle and Light Car Club*, *The Times*, March 25th, 1971.

The plaintiffs were father and daughter and they sued in negligence for injuries received as spectators at a motor cycle scramble at Withybridge on 21st September, 1966. They were in an enclosure fenced off with stakes and ropes designed to keep spectators in. Some ten feet away from this fence was another rope designed to keep any motor cycle from intruding into the enclosure. A competitor, Mr. Ward, left the course, crashed through the safety rope and struck the plaintiffs. It was *held*—by the Court of Appeal—that Mr. Ward was not negligent. He was going at about ten miles per hour when he left the track and although he lost control this could be expected in a scramble of this kind. A competitor in a race must use reasonable care. But that meant reasonable care having regard to the fact that he was a competitor in a race in which he was expected to go "all out" to win. A batsman was expected to hit a six if he could, even if it landed among the spectators. So in a race a competitor was expected to go as fast as he could, as long as he was not foolhardy. In a race a reasonable man should do all that he could do to win, but he should not be foolhardy.

401. Stanley v. Powell, [1891] 1 Q.B. 86

The defendant was a member of a shooting party, and the plaintiff was employed to carry cartridges and also any game which was shot. The defendant fired at a pheasant, but a shot glanced off an oak tree and injured the plaintiff. *Held*—The plaintiff's claim failed. The defendant's action was neither intentional nor was it negligent.

402. Nichols v. Marsland (1876), 2 Ex.D. 1   Act of God ✗

For many years there had existed certain artificial ornamental lakes on the defendant's land, formed by damming up of a natural stream the source of which was at a point higher up. An extraordinary rainfall "greater and more violent than any within the memory of witnesses" caused the stream and the lakes to swell to such an extent that the artificial banks burst, and the escaping water carried away four bridges belonging to the county council. Nichols, the county surveyor, sued under the rule in *Rylands* v. *Fletcher*. *Held*—The defendant was not liable for this extraordinary act of nature which she could not reasonably have anticipated. The escape of water was owing to the act of God, and while one is bound to provide against the ordinary operations of nature, one is not bound to provide against miracles.

403. Cresswell v. Sirl, [1948] 1 K.B. 241

The defendant, a farmer's son, was awakened during the night by dogs barking, and on going out found certain ewe sheep in lamb, penned up by the dogs in a corner of a field. The dogs seemed about to attack the sheep and had been chasing them for an hour. A light was turned on the dogs, who then left the sheep and started for the defendant. When they were about 40 yards away, the defendant fired and killed one of the dogs. The owner of the dog sued the defendant for damages. In the county court, judgment was given for the owner of the dog on the ground that such a killing could be justified only if it took place while the dog was actually attacking the sheep. In the view of the Court of Appeal, however, the defendant could justify his act by showing that it was necessary to avert immediate danger to property. It was not necessary that the dog should actually be attacking the sheep. This decision is affirmed by Sect. 9 of the Animals Act, 1971 which now covers the situation.

404. Cope v. Sharpe (No. 2), [1912] 1 K.B. 496

The plaintiff was a landowner and he let the shooting rights over part of his land to a tenant. A heath fire broke out on part of the plaintiff's land and the defendant, who was the head gamekeeper of the tenant, set fire to patches of heather between the main fire and a covert in which his master's pheasants were sitting. His object was to prevent the fire spreading. In fact the fire was extinguished independently of what the defendant had done, and the plaintiff now sued the defendant for damages for trespass. *Held*—The defendant was not liable because when he carried out the act it seemed reasonably necessary, and it did not matter that in the event it turned out to be unnecessary.

405. Beckwith *v.* Philby (1827), 6 B. & C. 635

In this case it was *held* that the mistaken arrest of an innocent man on suspicion of felony by an ordinary citizen is not actionable as false imprisonment, if the felony has been committed, and if there are reasonable grounds for believing that the person arrested is guilty of it.

406. National Coal Board *v.* Evans (J. E.) & Co. (Cardiff) Ltd. and Another, [1951] 2 K.B. 861

Evans & Co. were employed by Glamorgan County Council to carry out certain work on land belonging to the council It was necessary to excavate a trench across the land, and Evans & Co. sub-contracted with the second defendants to do this work. An electric cable passed under the land, but the council, Evans & Co., and the sub-contractors had no knowledge of this and it was not marked on any available map. During the course of the excavation a mechanical digger damaged the cable so that water seeped into it causing an explosion. The electricity supply to the plaintiff's colliery was cut off, and they sued the defendants in trespass and negligence. Donovan, J., at first instance, found that the defendants were not negligent, but were liable in trespass. The Court of Appeal *held* the defendants were entirely free from fault and there was no trespass by them.

407. Buron *v.* Denman (1848), 2 Exch. 167

The captain of a British warship was *held* not liable for trespass when he set fire to the barracoon of a Spaniard slave trader on the West Coast of Africa and released the slaves. The captain had general instructions to suppress the slave trade, and in any case his conduct in this matter was afterwards approved by the Admiralty and the Foreign and Colonial Secretaries. It seems, therefore, that neither the official responsible nor the Crown can be sued for injuries inflicted upon others outside the territorial jurisdiction of the Crown, if these are authorised or subsequently ratified by the Crown.

408. Nissan *v.* Attorney-General, [1967] 2 All E.R. 1238

The plaintiff, a British subject, was the tenant of an hotel in Cyprus. In December, 1963, the Government of Cyprus accepted an offer that British Forces stationed in Cyprus should give assistance in restoring peace to the island. The British troops occupied the plaintiff's hotel for some months and the plaintiff now sued the Crown for compensation. It was *held inter alia* that the Crown was obliged to pay compensation and that a plea by the Crown of "act of state" was no defence as against a British subject.

409. Johnstone *v.* Pedlar, [1921] 2 A.C. 262

Johnstone was the Chief Commissioner of the Dublin Metropolitan Police. He was the defendant in an action in which Pedlar sued for the detention of £124 in cash and a cheque for £4 15s. 6d. Pedlar was convicted of being engaged in the illegal drilling of troops in Ireland, and the above property was found on him at the time of his arrest. Pedlar, who was a naturalised citizen of the United States of America, sued for the return of his property, and the defence was "Act of State." A certificate given by the Chief Secretary for Ireland was put in at the trial, certifying that the detention of the property was formally ratified as an act of state. *Held*—Pedlar was entitled to claim his property, because the defence of "Act of State" cannot be raised against an alien who is a subject of a friendly nation.

410. Vaughan *v.* Taff Vale Railway (1860), 5 H. & N. 679

The defendants were *held* not liable for fires caused by sparks from engines run under statutory authority and constructed with proper care.

N.B. By the Railway Fires Acts, 1905 and 1923, British Rail is under a liability of up to £200 for damage to crops caused by fire resulting from sparks from engines run under statutory authority, though the advent of diesel and electric trains makes the statute somewhat out of date.

411. Penny *v.* Wimbledon Urban Council, [1899] 2 Q.B. 72

The defendants, acting under powers conferred upon them by Sect. 150 of the Public Health Act, 1875, employed a contractor to make up a road in their district. The contractor removed the surface soil and placed it in heaps on the road. The plaintiff, while passing along the road in the dark, fell over one of the heaps, which had been left unlighted and unguarded, and was injured. She now sued for damages. *Held*—She succeeded. Although the council were operating under statutory powers they must, if they do acts likely to cause danger to the public, see that the work is properly carried out, and take reasonable measures to guard against danger. The council did not discharge this duty by delegating it to a contractor, and the local authority were liable for negligence.

412. Marriage *v.* East Norfolk Rivers Catchment Board, [1950] 1 K.B. 284

In pursuance of their powers under Sect. 34 of the Land Drainage Act, 1930, the Catchment Board deposited dredgings taken from the river on the south bank of that river, so raising its height by one to two feet. When the river next flooded, the flood waters instead of escaping over the south bank, as they had always done, ran over the north bank and swept away a bridge leading to a mill owned by the plaintiff. Sect. 34(3) of the Land Drainage Act, 1930, provided that, in the event of injury to any person by reason of the exercise by a drainage board of any of its powers, the board concerned should make full compensation, disputes being settled by a system of arbitration. The plaintiff had issued a writ for nuisance against the board. *Held*—No action in nuisance lay; the plaintiff's only remedy was to claim compensation under Sect. 34(3).

413. Parry *v.* Cleaver, [1969] 1 All E.R. 555

The plaintiff was injured by the defendant's motor car and had to retire from the police force. He was entitled to a pension of £3 18s. 6d. per week for life. The defendant had admitted liability and the court was asked to decide whether the pension should be ignored in arriving at an assessment of damages. *Held*— by the House of Lords—the pension was similar to private insurance arrangements an should be ignored in assessing damages. The principle of *British Transport Commission* v. *Gourley*, [1955] 3 All E.R. 796, was inapplicable.

414. Hewson v. Downes, [1969] 3 All E.R. 193

The plaintiff, aged 66, suffered injuries when the defendant, by negligent driving, pinned him against the wall of a shop. The plaintiff was still employed at the time of the accident but retired as a result of it. *Held*—by Park, J.—that the State retirement pension which he was receiving should not be taken into account in assessing damages. (*Parry* v. *Cleaver*, 1969,[413] *applied*.

415. Smith v. London and South Western Railway Co. (1870), L.R. 6 C.P. 14

During a hot and dry summer the defendants' employees cut certain hedges and trimmed grass. They left the resultant clippings by the side of the railway track for a fortnight and the sparks from a passing engine set fire to them. This fire ran two hundred yards, crossed the roadway, and eventually damaged the plaintiff's cottage. *Held*—Although a reasonable man would have foreseen the possibility of fire, he would not have foreseen the danger to the cottage. Nevertheless, the defendants were liable because, although the damage was a freak, they were liable for all direct consequences of their act, foreseeable or not.

416. Re Polemis and Furness Withy and Co., [1921] 3 K.B. 560

Stevedores were unloading the hold of a vessel which contained drums of petrol. There was some leakage from certain of the drums and the hold was filled with highly inflammable vapour. Through the negligence of a stevedore a plank was knocked into the hold, where, in its fall, it struck a spark, setting the vapour alight. The ensuing fire destroyed the ship. It was *held* that the employers of the stevedores were liable for the total loss, even though the negligent stevedore could not have reasonably foreseen that his act would destroy the ship, though he might have foreseen some damage. The destruction of the ship was a direct consequence of the negligent act, and damages were recoverable.

417. Liesbosch, Dredger v. S.S. Edison, [1933] A.C. 449

The dredger *Liesbosch* was lost after being dragged into open sea from her mooring in Patras harbour. This was the result of the negligence of the navigator of the S.S. *Edison*. The *Liesbosch* was engaged in dredging Patras harbour, and the contract provided for heavy penalties for delay. The dredger could have been replaced by the purchase of a new one, but the owners of the *Liesbosch* were poorly placed financially and could not afford to do so immediately. They had, therefore, to hire a dredger (the *Adria*) in the meantime at great expense. The plaintiffs included this additional hiring in their claim for damages for the loss of the *Liesbosch*. *Held*—Damages in respect of the hiring were not recoverable under the rule in *Re Polemis*. This damage was not caused by the defendants' negligence but by the plaintiffs' poverty. However, the plaintiffs were entitled to the value of the *Liesbosch* as a going concern, not simply her value as a rather old dredger, on the basis that you take your victim as you find him.

418. Overseas Tankship (U.K.) Ltd. v. Morts Dock and Engineering Co. Ltd. (the Wagon Mound), [1961] A.C. 388

The appellants were the charterers of a ship called the *Wagon Mound*. While the ship was taking on furnace oil in Sydney harbour, the appellants' servants negligently allowed oil to spill into the water. The action of the wind and tide carried this oil over to the respondents' wharf where the business of shipbuilding and repairing was carried on. The servants of the respondents were at this time engaged in repairing a vessel, which was moored alongside the wharf, and for this purpose they were using welding equipment. The manager of the respondents, seeing the oil on the water, suspended welding operations and consulted the wharf manager who told him it was safe to continue work—a decision which was justified, because previous knowledge showed that sparks were not likely to set fire to oil floating on water. Work, therefore, proceeded with safety precautions being taken. However, a piece of molten metal fell from the wharf and set on fire a piece of cotton waste which was floating on the oil. This set the oil alight and the respondents' wharf was badly damaged. The Supreme Court of New South Wales held the appellants liable for the extensive damage by fire, and in doing so followed *Re Polemis*.[416] The case now came before the Judicial Committee of the Privy Council on appeal. *Held*—the appellants were successful in their appeal, the Judicial Committee holding that *Re Polemis*[416] should no longer be considered good law, and that foreseeability of the actual harm resulting was the proper test. On this principle, they held that the damage caused by the fire was too remote, though they would have awarded damages for the fouling of the respondents' slipways by oil, if such a claim had been made, since this was foreseeable.

N.B. In *Overseas Tankship (U.K.) Ltd.* v. *Miller Steamship Property Ltd. (The Wagon Mound (No. 2))*, [1966] 2 All E.R. 709, the same blaze had caused damage to the respondent's ships. However, it was found as a fact that the risk of some damage by fire was foreseeable and the respondents recovered in negligence and also nuisance. The Privy Council *held* that in the case of nuisance, as of negligence, it is not enough that the damage was a direct result of the nuisance if the injury was not foreseeable.

419. Hughes v. Lord Advocate, [1963] 1 All E.R. 705

Workmen opened a manhole in the street and later left it unattended having placed a tent above it and warning paraffin lamps around it. The plaintiff and another boy, who were aged 8 and 10 respectively, took one of the lamps and went down the manhole. As they came out the lamp was knocked into the hole and an explosion took place injuring the plaintiff. The explosion was caused in a unique fashion because the paraffin had vapourised (which was unusual) and been ignited by the naked flame of the wick. The defendants argued that although some injury by burning was foreseeable, burning by explosion was not. *Held*—by the House of Lords—that the defendants were liable. "The cause of this accident was a known source of danger, the lamp, but it behaved in an unpredictable way . . . This accident was caused by a known source of danger but caused in a way which could not have been foreseen and in my judgment that affords no defence." (*Per* Lord Reid.)

419a. Bradford v. Robinson Rentals, [1967] 1 All E.R. 267

In January, 1963, the plaintiff, a television engineer aged 57, was told by his employer to drive an old van from Exeter to Bedford, exchange it there for a new one and drive back to Exeter, a round journey of some 500 miles involving about 20 hours' driving.

The plaintiff protested because the weather was severe but he undertook the journey. The radiator of the old van had to be refilled frequently and neither of the vans had a heater so that the windscreen had to be kept open to prevent the formation of ice. The plaintiff took all reasonable precautions to protect himself from the cold but even so he sustained permanent injury to his hands and feet from frostbite. *Held*—that the defendant had been negligent and judgment was given for the plaintiff. Liability in negligence does not depend upon the precise nature of the injury being foreseeable. It is enough if the injury was of a kind that was foreseeable even though the form that it took was unusual. *Some* injury from cold was foreseeable.

419*b* *Weiland* v. *Cyril Lord Carpets*, [1969] 3 All E.R. 1006

The plaintiff was injured when the bus on which she was travelling had to brake suddenly as a result of the negligent driving of the defendant's vehicle by one of their employees. As part of her treatment she had to have a collar fitted to her neck and in consequence was unable to use her bi-focal spectacles with her usual skill. At a later stage this caused her to fall down some stairs sustaining further injuries. *Held*—by Eveleigh, J.—that the second injury was attributable to the original negligence of the defendants and they were liable in damages. If an injury affects a person's ability to cope with the vicissitudes of life and thereby is the cause of another injury, the latter injury is a foreseeable consequence of the former within the terms of *The Wagon Mound*, 1961,[418] and *Hughes* v. *Lord Advocate*, 1963.[419]

420. Doughty *v.* Turner Manufacturing Co., [1964] 1 All E.R. 98

Doughty, a workman, was injured in a factory where he worked. A workman accidentally knocked an asbestos cement cover into a cauldron of sodium cyanide which was rendered molten by being raised to 800°C., eight times the heat of boiling water. The cover fell some four to six inches, and one or two minutes afterwards the heat caused a chemical change in the asbestos cement whereby it released water, which turned into steam and caused an explosion of the hot liquid which injured Doughty. Such an eruption was not expected, and indeed its cause was only discovered by subsequent experiments carried out by Imperial Chemical Industries Ltd., which revealed that the immersion of such a cover, or indeed any other object containing actual moisture, and its subjection to a temperature of 500°C., would cause such an eruption. Such a phenomenon could not have been known to the defendants beforehand. The Court of Appeal allowed an appeal by the Turner Manufacturing Co. against an award by the lower court of £150 damages to Doughty. It was *held* that a splash, such as was caused by the falling cover, would be a foreseeable danger and should be guarded against, but this was not the cause of the accident, and in any case the lid fell only a few inches and the heavy liquid would not travel far. Although the eruption had the same effect as a splash, it was quite unrealistic to regard it as a variant of the perils of splashing. The cause was quite different. it would be wrong to make such an inroad into the doctrine of foreseeability.

N.B. It might be thought that the plaintiff should have recovered damages in this case on the principles laid down in *Hughes* v. *Lord Advocate*, 1963.[419] It was a negligent act to fail to take reasonable care to prevent the cover from being knocked into the liquid. This being so it should not have mattered whether the cover caused a splash or an eruption. Injury caused by either event should have resulted in an award of damages.

421. Tremain *v.* Pike, [1969] 3 All E.R. 1303

The plaintiff, who was a herdsman, contracted Weil's disease through handling hay and washing his hands in a water trough both of which were contaminated by the urine of rats with which the farm was badly infected. Weil's disease is rarely contracted by human beings, but when it is, it results from the skin coming into contact with the urine of rats. *Held*—by Payne, J.—that the plaintiff's employer was not liable. Although the defendant was negligent in that a prudent farmer would have called in a rodent officer to deal with the infestation, the resulting injury to the plaintiff was not foreseeable, though an injury arising from a rat-bite or food poisoning by consumption of food or drink contaminated by rats might have been.

N.B. This decision seems to be out of line with *Hughes* v. *Lord Advocate*, 1963,[419] and *Bradford* v. *Robinson Rentals*, 1967.[419a] An infestation of rats is a known source of danger to man. The fact that they attacked in an unusual and unpredictable way should not have affected the right of the plaintiff to damages.

422. Smith *v.* Leech Braine & Co. Ltd., [1962] 2 W.L.R. 148

The plaintiff was the widow of a person employed by the defendants. Mr. Smith's work consisted in lowering articles into a galvanising tank containing molten zinc. On one occasion he was struck on the lip by a piece of molten metal which caused a burn. This resulted in a cancer from which he died three years later. Mr. Smith's work had given him a pre-disposition to cancer and the question arose whether, since the *Wagon Mound*, the so-called "thin skull rule" had disappeared, so that the plaintiff had to show that the cancer was foreseeable. The Lord Chief Justice, Lord Parker, finding for the plaintiff, said in the course of his judgment: "I am satisfied that the Judicial Committee of the Privy Council did not have what are called 'thin skull' cases in mind. It has always been the common law that a tortfeasor must take his victim as he finds him."

423. Scott *v.* Shepherd (1773), 2 Wm. Bl. 892

On the evening of a fair-day at Milborne Port, Shepherd threw a lighted squib on to the market stall of one Yates who sold gingerbread. Then one Willis, in order to protect the wares of Yates, threw it away and it landed on the stall of one Ryal. He threw it to another part of the market house where it struck the plaintiff in the face, exploded and put out his eye. *Held*—Shepherd was liable for the injuries to Scott because there was no break in the chain of causation. Shepherd should have anticipated that Willis and Ryal would act as they did.

424. Davies *v.* Liverpool Corporation, [1949] 2 All E.R. 175

The plaintiff was trying to board a tramcar belonging to the defendants at a request stopping place. An unauthorised person (a passenger) rang the bell, whereupon the car started, throwing the plaintiff off the platform and causing her injury. The conductor was on the upper deck collecting fares. Evidence showed that the car had been standing at the request stop for an appreciable time, and that the conductor had been upstairs for the whole of that time, though it was not a particularly busy period. In this action for negligence brought by the plaintiff, it was *held* that the defendants were liable for the negligent act of the conductor. He should have foreseen that if he was absent from the platform of the car for an appreciable time, some passenger might ring the bell. The act of the passenger did not, therefore, break the chain of causation because it was just that sort of act which the conductor was employed to prevent.

425. Cobb v. Great Western Railway, [1894] A.C. 419

The railway company allowed a railway carriage to become overcrowded, and because of this the plaintiff was hustled and robbed of £89 1s. He now sued the company in respect of his loss. *Held*—This was too remote a consequence of the defendant's negligence. The robbery was a *novus actus interveniens* breaking the chain of causation.

426. Sayers v. Harlow U.D.C., [1958] 2 All E.R. 342

The defendants owned and operated a public lavatory. The plaintiff having paid for admission entered a cubicle. Finding that there was no handle on the inside of the door, and no means of opening the cubicle, the plaintiff had tried for some ten to fifteen minutes to attract attention. Having failed to do so, and wishing to catch a bus to London in the next few minutes, she tried to see if there was a way of climbing out. She placed one foot on the seat of the lavatory and rested her other foot on the toilet roll and fixture, holding the pipe from the cistern with one hand and resting the other hand on the top of the door. She then realised it would be impossible to climb out, and she proceeded to come down, but, as she was doing so, the toilet roll rotated owing to her weight on it and she slipped and injured herself. She sued the defendants for negligence. In the county court the defendants were found negligent, but, as the plaintiff was in no danger on that account, and as she chose to embark on a dangerous act, she must bear the consequences. It was *held* by the Court of Appeal that her act was not a *novus actus interveniens*, and the damage was not too remote a consequence of the defendants' negligence. She was thirty-six years of age, and in her predicament her act was not unreasonable, though if she had been an old lady it might have been. However, the damages recoverable by the plaintiff would be reduced by one quarter in respect of her share of the responsibility for the damage.

426a. McKew v. Holland and Hannen and Cubitts (Scotland) Ltd., [1969] 2 All E.R. 1621

McKew sustained an injury during the course of his employment for which his employers were liable. The injury caused him occasionally and unexpectedly to lose the use of his left leg. On one occasion he left a flat and started to descend some stairs which had no handrail. His leg gave way and he sustained further injury. *Held*—by the House of Lords—that his conduct in trying to descend the stairs was unreasonable and thus broke the chain of causation. The subsequent injury was therefore too remote and the employers were not liable.

427. Philco Radio Corporation v. Spurling, [1949] 2 All E.R. 882

Certain packing cases containing inflammable film scrap were delivered in error by the defendants to the plaintiffs' premises. No warning as to their contents was given on the cases. The cases were opened by the plaintiffs' servants, and a foreman recognised the contents as inflammable, and gave instructions that the scrap was to be replaced, and that there was to be no smoking in the vicinity. He telephoned the defendants and arranged to have the cases delivered to their proper destination, 150 yards away. Before the cases had been moved, a typist employed by the plaintiffs negligently set light to the scrap with a cigarette, and it exploded causing damage. The defendants pleaded that the proximate cause of the damage was the typist's act and that the chain of causation was broken. *Held*—The defendants were negligent in not ensuring that such dangerous material was properly delivered. The act of the typist did not break the chain of causation; she did not intend to injure her employer, and when she approached the scrap with a cigarette she did so as a joke. Her act was not such a conscious act of violation as to relieve the defendants from liability.

428. Hambrook v. Stokes, [1925] 1 K.B. 141

The defendant left his lorry unattended on a sloping street and because of his negligence in failing to brake the vehicle properly, it began to run away. The plaintiff's wife had just left her children further down the street though they were in fact round a bend and not within her view. However, she saw the lorry moving and suffered shock, which resulted in her death, because she feared for the safety of her children. Her husband brought this action for loss of her services and was *held* entitled to recover damages provided that the shock was brought about by his wife's own experience and not by the account of bystanders.

429. Owens v. Liverpool Corporation, [1939] 2 K.B. 394

A funeral procession was making its way to the cemetery when a negligently driven tram owned by the defendants collided with the hearse and overturned the coffin. Several mourners who were following in a carriage suffered shock and it was *held* by the Court of Appeal that they were entitled to damages.

429a. Hinz v. Berry, [1970] 1 All E.R. 1074

Mrs. Hinz witnessed a car accident in which her husband was killed and her children injured. The accident was caused by the negligent driving of the defendant. As a result of seeing the accident Mrs. Hinz, who had been a vigorous and lively woman, became morbid and depressed for years afterwards. *Held*—by the Court of Appeal—she was entitled to damages of £4,000 for nervous shock.

Somehow or other the court has to draw a line between sorrow and grief for which damages are not recoverable; and nervous shock and psychiatric illness for which damages are recoverable. The way to do this is to estimate how much the plaintiff would have suffered if, for instance, her husband had been killed in an accident when she was fifty miles away; and compare it with what she is now, having suffered all the shock due to being present at the accident. The evidence shows that she suffered much more by being present.

(*Per* Lord Denning, M.R.)

430. Chadwick v. British Railways Board, [1967] 1 W.L.R. 912

A serious railway accident was caused by negligence for which the Board was liable. A volunteer rescue worker suffered nervous shock and became psychoneurotic as a result. The plaintiff, as administratrix of his estate, claimed damages for nervous shock. It was *held* that—

    (i) damages were recoverable for nervous shock even though the shock was not caused by fear for one's own safety or that of one's children;

    (ii) in the circumstances injury by shock was foreseeable;

    (iii) the defendants ought to have foreseen that volunteers might attempt rescue and accordingly owed a duty of care to those who did.

431. Hay (or Bourhill) v. Young, [1943] A.C. 92

The plaintiff, a pregnant Edinburgh fishwife, alighted from a tramcar. While she was removing her fish-basket from the tram, Young, a motor cyclist, driving carelessly but unseen by her, passed the tram and collided with a motor car some fifteen yards away. Young was killed. The plaintiff heard the collision, and after Young's body had been removed, she approached the scene of the accident and saw a pool of blood on the road. She suffered a nervous shock and later gave birth to a stillborn child. The House of Lords *held* that her action against Young's personal representative failed, because Young owed no duty of care to persons whom he could not reasonably anticipate would suffer injuries as a result of his conduct on the highway.

432. Baker v. Willoughby, [1968] New L.J. 1197

In September, 1964, the plaintiff was involved in an accident on the highway caused by the negligent driving of the defendant, but attributable as to one quarter to the plaintiff's contributory negligence. The plaintiff received serious injuries to his left leg, but after long hospital treatment he took up employment with a scrap metal merchant. On 29th November, 1967, while in the course of his employment, the plaintiff was the innocent victim of an armed robbery receiving gunshot wounds necessitating the immediate amputation of his left leg which was already defective because of the previous accident. The question of the amount of damages for the plaintiff's injuries in the road accident of September, 1964, came before the Court for assessment in February, 1968. *Held*—by the Court of Appeal—that no consequence of the accident of September 1964 survived the amputation of the plaintiff's left leg and the defendant was liable only for loss suffered by the plaintiff up to November 29th, 1967. Damages are compensation for loss arising from a tortious act and cease when by reason of recovery, supervening disease, or further injury there is no continuing loss attributable to that act.

N.B. The House of Lords, [1969] 3 All E.R. 1528, reversed the Court of Appeal decision holding that damages are not merely compensation for physical injury but for the loss which the injured person suffers. This loss was not diminished by the supervening event and the second injury was irrelevant.

433. Performance Cars Ltd. v. Abraham, [1961] 3 All E.R. 413

The plaintiffs owned a motor-car which was damaged in a collision with a car driven by the defendant. The damage to the plaintiffs' car was such that it would necessitate respraying the whole of the lower body. Two weeks before the accident the plaintiffs' car had been involved in another collision which had also made respraying of the lower body of the car necessary. The plaintiffs obtained judgment against the driver responsible for the first collision but that judgment was not satisfied and the car had not been resprayed at the time when the second collision took place. The Court was asked to decide whether the plaintiffs were entitled to recover as damages from the defendant the cost of respraying the lower body of their car. *Held*—by the Court of Appeal—that the plaintiffs were not entitled to recover the cost of respraying from the defendant because that damage was not the result of his wrongful act.

433a. Cutler v. Vauxhall Motors Ltd., [1970] 2 All E.R. 56

In 1965 the plaintiff grazed his right ankle as a result of an accident at work for which the defendants were responsible. In 1966 the plaintiff had an operation for varicose veins in both legs. He would have had to have the operation a few years later had the grazeing not occurred. The trial judge awarded £10 for the graze and nothing for the operation. *Held*—by the Court of Appeal—the sum awarded was adequate. The defendant's liability for the operation had not been established.

434. United Australia Ltd. *v.* Barclays Bank Ltd., [1941] A.C.1.

In November, 1934, certain debtors of United Australia sent to them a crossed cheque for £1,900 payable to their order. On 12th November that cheque, purporting to have been indorsed in the name of United Australia by one A. H. Emons, their Secretary, in favour of M.F.G. Trust, was presented at a branch of the respondent bank for payment into the account of M.F.G. at that branch, and the amount was shortly collected, received and paid by the bank. On 13th May, 1935, the appellants, who alleged that Emons had no authority to indorse the cheque, issued a writ against M.F.G. claiming £1,900 as money lent to M.F.G. or as money had and received to the appellant's use (i.e. an action in quasi-contract). This action never came to final trial and M.F.G. afterwards went into liquidation. On 8th November, 1937, the appellants brought this action against the respondents for conversion of the cheque. *Held*—by the House of Lords—that the appellants by merely initiating proceedings against M.E.G. in quasi-contract had not thereby elected to waive the tort of conversion by the bank and were not precluded from bringing the present action. It is judgment and satisfaction in the first action which constitutes a bar to a second action.

435. Verschures Creameries Ltd. *v.* Hull and Netherlands Steamship Co. Ltd., [1921] 2 K.B. 608

Certain boxes of margarine were delivered by the plaintiffs to the defendants, who were carriers and forwarding agents, to be carried by sea to Hull and thence forwarded to two customers in Liverpool and Manchester, S. Beilin and R. Beilin respectively. When the goods arrived at Hull the plaintiffs instructed the defendants not to deliver to the Beilins but to deliver to a Mr. Schneiderman of Manchester, but in the event the goods were delivered to R. Beilin. The plaintiffs, having heard of the misdelivery, nevertheless invoiced the goods to R. Beilin and sued him and recovered judgment for the price of goods sold and delivered. Failing to get satisfaction from Beilin, the plaintiffs took proceedings in bankruptcy against him. *Held* they could not afterwards sue the forwarding agents for negligence and breach of duty.

436. Letang *v.* Cooper, [1964] 2 All E.R. 929

In July, 1957, the plaintiff was run over by a motor car negligently driven by the defendant. She issued a writ on 2nd February, 1961 (that is after the three years' period of limitation provided by Sect. 2 (1) of the Law Reform (Limitation of Actions, etc.) Act, 1954, had expired), claiming damages for personal injuries in negligence and in the alternative trespass to the person. Since the claim in negligence was statute-barred, she hoped to succeed in trespass to the person, believing the six-year limitation period to apply in this case. The action failed. It was *held* by the Court of Appeal that where the injury was not intentional, the only action is negligence not trespass. In the course of his judgment Lord Denning, M.R., said: "The truth is that *the distinction between trespass and case is obsolete*. We have a different sub-division altogether. Instead of dividing actions for personal injuries into *trespass* (direct damage) or *case* (consequential damage), we divide the causes of action according as the defendant did the injury intentionally or unintentionally. . . . If intentional, it is the tort of assault and battery (or trespass to the person). If negligent and causing damage, it is the tort of negligence."

Elsewhere Lord Denning made a point of interpretation: "It is legitimate to look at a report of the committee that preceded legislation in order to see what was the mischief at which the statute, when enacted, was directed, but not in order to interpret the words of the statute according to the recommendations of the committee."

437. Brook *v.* Hoar, [1967] 1 W.L.R. 1336

The plaintiff, Martin Brook, was born on 6th October, 1944, and throughout his childhood he had lived with his parents. From the age of seventeen he had had a key to the front door, had worked and given his mother money for his keep and had lived an independent life. He bought a motor cycle without his father's consent and was sometimes described by his father as a "young lodger."

On 19th November, 1962, when aged eighteen, he was driving his motorcycle along Highgate Road, N.W.5. when he was involved in a collision with a motor car driven by the defendant, Richard Hoar, and he received personal injuries. On 6th October, 1965, he attained his majority. By a writ issued on 25th February, 1966, he claimed damages for personal injuries and loss of his motor cycle caused by the negligent driving of the defendant. The defendant denied negligence and contended that the plaintiff's action was barred. The plaintiff contended that at the time when the action accured he was an infant and therefore under a disability and was not in the custody of a parent within the meaning of Sect. 22 of the Limitation Act, 1939. Therefore time did not start to run against him until he reached his majority. *Held*—by Melford Stevenson, J.—that as the plaintiff had enjoyed complete economic freedom and independence from his parents he was not at the time the action accrued in the custody of a parent and being under a disability until he attained his majority in October, 1965, the action was not statute barred.

437a. Hewer *v.* Bryant, [1969] 3 All E.R. 578

Paull, J. *held* that "custody" meant legal custody in the technical sense so that a fifteen year old boy who was earning his keep away from home as a farm trainee and financially independent of his father was regarded as in the custody of his father at the time when he was seriously injured while a passenger in a negligently driven farm vehicle. Since the father had not brought an action in the three years which followed, the boy's claim was statute barred.

437b. Todd *v.* Davison (1970), 115 Sol. Jnl. 223

The minor sued by his mother and next friend for injuries received in a street accident when he was six years old. The action was brought after the normal three year period had run out, and the boy's action was statute barred unless he could show that he was not in the custody of his parents when the cause of action accrued. The House of Lords *held* that custody meant factual control and not mere legal custody. However, the boy was in fact in the custody of his parents at the relevant time and his action was statute barred. The inadequacy of his parents was irrelevant.

438. Beaman *v.* A.R.T.S. Ltd., [1949] 1 All E.R. 465

In November, 1935, Mrs. Beaman, before leaving for Istanbul, deposited with the defendants several packages to be sent to her as soon as she gave notice requesting it. In May, 1936, the defendants at her request dispatched one of the packages but afterwards regulations made by the Turkish authorities prevented the dispatching of the other packages and Mrs. Beaman asked the defendants to keep them in store pending further instructions. Three years later the defendants, who had not received instructions, wrote and asked the plaintiff to insure the contents of the packages. She did not do so but replied saying that she was hoping to return to England. However, the outbreak of war while she was still in Turkey prevented this.

On the entry of Italy into the war in 1940 the defendants, being a company controlled by Italian nationals, had their business taken over by the Custodian of Enemy Property. Wishing to wind up the business as soon as possible, the manager of A.R.T.S. Ltd. examined the packages, reported that they were of no value and gave them to the Salvation Army. No steps were taken to obtain the plaintiff's consent. The plaintiff returned to England in 1946 and commenced proceedings more than six years after the packages were disposed of, claiming damages for conversion. The defendants set up the defence that the action was barred by Sect. 3 of the Limitation Act, 1939. The plaintiff relied on Sect. 26 which provides that where "(*a*) the action is based on fraud of the defendant . . . or (*b*) the right of action is concealed by the fraud of any such person . . . the period of limitation shall not begin to run until the plaintiff has discovered the fraud . . . ."
Held—

(i) That the action for conversion was not "based on fraud" so that Sect. 26 (*a*) had no application.

(ii) The conduct of the defendants constituted a reckless "concealment by fraud" of the right of action within Sect. 26 (*b*). Therefore the plaintiff's action was not barred.

N.B. It appears that it is not necessary to prove a degree of moral turpitude to establish fraud for the purposes of Sect. 26 (*b*). Thus in *Kitchen* v. *Royal Air Force Association*, [1958] 1 W.L.R. 563, solicitors negligently concealed a payment of money on behalf of the plaintiff and this conduct was held to amount to "fraud" for the purposes of Sect. 26 (*b*) even though the court accepted that the solicitors were not dishonest.

438a. *Eddis* v. *Chichester Constable*, [1969] 2 All E.R. 912

The plaintiffs were trustees of a settlement. The trust property included, among other heirlooms, a valuable painting. In 1951 the tenant for life under the settlement sold the painting to a consortium who resold it to an art gallery in America. The tenant for life had no authority or power to sell the painting and concealed the sale from the trustees. The tenant for life died on 26th May, 1963, and on 7th March, 1966, the trustees, having discovered that the painting had been sold, commenced an action for conversion against members of the consortium. The defence was that the claim was statute barred. *Held*— by the Court of Appeal—that it was not. The fact that the trustees had an action in 1951 had been concealed by the fraud of the tenant for life and the period of limitation of six years did not begin to run until the fraud was discovered by the trustees in 1963.

438b. *Archer* v. *Moss* (1970) 114 S.J. 971

In 1951 the plaintiff bought houses from the defendant who was an estate developer. In 1965 it was discovered that the foundations were inadequate and not according to specification and that the houses would have to be pulled down. The plaintiffs sued for damages and the defendant pleaded that the claims were statute-barred. *Held*—by the Court of Appeal—that the plaintiffs' right of action had been concealed by the builder who had not followed the specification. The builder was the agent of the estate developer for this purpose. It followed that the plaintiffs' claim was not statute barred since they had only discovered that they had a cause of action in 1965.

439. **Turbervell** *v.* **Savage** (1669), 2 Keb. 545

In this old case a man laid his hand menacingly on his sword, but at the same time said, "If it were not assize time I would not take such language from you." *Held*—This was not an assault because it was assize time, and there was no reason to fear violence.

440. **Fagan** *v.* **Metropolitan Police Commissioner,** [1968] 3 All E.R. 442

Fagan was driving his car when he was told by a constable to draw into the kerb. He stopped his car with one wheel on the constable's foot and was slow in restarting the engine and moving the vehicle off. He was convicted of assault on the constable and Quarter Sessions dismissed his appeal. He then appealed to the Queen's Bench Divisional Court where it was *held*—dismissing his appeal—that whether or not the mounting of the wheel on the constable's foot had been intentional the defendant had deliberately allowed it to remain there when asked to move it and that constituted an assault. The decision seems to extend the law because there was no act but merely an omission. Furthermore, there was no intentional application of force but only a failure to withdraw it. A more appropriate charge might have been false imprisonment because the constable could not presumably have moved while the wheel remained on his foot.

441. **Fowler** *v.* **Lanning,** [1959] 1 All E.R. 290

By a writ the plaintiff claimed damages for trespass to the person. In his statement of claim he alleged that on 19th November, 1957, at Vineyard Farm, Corfe Castle, in the County of Dorset, the defendant shot the plaintiff. By reason of the premises, the plaintiff sustained personal injuries and suffered loss and damage; particulars of the plaintiff's injuries were then set out. The defendant denied the allegations of fact and objected that the statement of claim disclosed no cause of action, because the plaintiff had not alleged that the shooting was either intentional or negligent. *Held*—In an action for trespass to the person, onus of proof of the defendant's intention or negligence lay on the plaintiff and the plaintiff must allege that the shooting was intentional or that the defendant was negligent, stating the facts alleged to constitute the negligence. The plaintiff's statement of claim, therefore, disclosed no cause of action.

442. **Bird** *v.* **Jones** (1845), 7 Q.B. 742

A bridge company enclosed part of the public footway on Hammersmith Bridge, put seats on it for the use of spectators at a regatta on the river, and charged admission. The plaintiff insisted on passing along this part of the footpath, and climbed over the fence without paying the charge. The defendant, who was the clerk of the Bridge Company, stationed two policemen to prevent, and they did prevent, the plaintiff from proceeding forwards along the footway in the direction he wished to go. The plaintiff was at the same time told that he might go back into the carriage way and proceed to the other side of the bridge if he wished. He declined to do so and remained in the enclosure for about half an hour. *Held*—There was no false imprisonment, for the plaintiff was free to go off another way.

443. Herd *v.* Weardale Steel, Coal and Coke Co. Ltd., [1915] A.C. 67

The plaintiff was an employee of the defendant company and at 9.30 a.m. on 30th May, 1911, he descended the defendants' mine. In the ordinary way he would have been entitled to be raised at the end of his shift at 4 p.m. The plaintiff and two other men were given certain work to do which they believed to be unsafe, and they refused to do it. At about 11 a.m. they, and twenty-nine men acting in sympathy with them, asked the foreman to allow them to ascend the shaft. The foreman, acting on instructions from the management, refused this request. At about 1 p.m. the cage came down carrying men, and emptied at the bottom of the shaft. The twenty-nine men were refused permission to enter, but some got in and refused to leave the cage, which was left stationary for some twenty minutes. At 1.30 p.m. permission was given for the men to leave and the plaintiff was brought to the top. He now sued for false imprisonment. *Held*—There was no false imprisonment. There was a collective agreement regarding the use of the cage, and the plaintiff's right to be taken to the surface did not arise under the agreement until 4 p.m. The defendants were perfectly willing to let the plaintiff ascend, but were not required in the absence of any emergency to provide him with the means of doing so except in accordance with the agreement.

444. Meering *v.* Grahame White Aviation Co. Ltd. (1919), 122 L.T. 44

The plaintiff, being suspected of stealing a keg of varnish from the defendants, his employers, was asked by two works policemen to accompany them to the Works Office to answer questions. The plaintiff, not realising that he was suspected, assented to the suggestion and even suggested a short cut. He remained in the office for some time during which the works policemen stayed outside the room without his knowledge. The plaintiff later sued for false imprisonment and the question arose as to whether the plaintiff must know that the defendant is restraining his freedom. *Held*—The plaintiff was imprisoned and his knowledge was irrelevant, though knowledge of imprisonment might increase the damages.

445. Christie *v.* Leachinsky, [1947] A.C. 573

The appellants, without the necessary warrant, arrested the respondent for unlawful possession of a number of bales of cloth. They had reasonable grounds for thinking that the bales were stolen but did not disclose this until later. *Held*— by the House of Lords—that the arrest was unlawful.

445a. R. v. *Kulynycz*, [1970] 3 W.L.R. 1029

The defendant was convicted of possessing drugs contrary to the Drugs (Prevention of Misuse) Act, 1964. He resided in Cambridge and was suspected of supplying drugs to persons who "pushed" them in King's Lynn. He was arrested in Cambridge by a police officer who told him that a warrant for his arrest had been issued at King's Lynn on suspicion of offences committed there. The offences were not specified and in fact no warrant had been issued. At the police station in Cambridge the full nature of the charge was made clear to the defendant. He was committed for trial to Norfolk Quarter Sessions on an indictment charging possession of drugs in Cambridge. Under Sect. 11(1) of the Criminal Justice Act, 1925, Norfolk Quarter Sessions had jurisdiction to try the case only if the defendant was "in custody on a charge for the offence" in Norfolk. On that basis the question for decision was whether the defendant was in lawful custody when he appeared before Norfolk Quarter Sessions. It was *held* by the Court of Appeal (Criminal Division) that he was because although the original arrest was unlawful in that there was no specification of the offences (*Christie* v. *Leachinsky*, 1947),[445] the defendant was informed of these in sufficient detail at Cambridge police station. It was not necessary that he should be released and re-arrested. It did not matter that the police officer was wrong in saying that a warrant had been issued. An arrested person is not bound to know whether he is arrested on warrant or on reasonable suspicion.

445b. *Wheatley* v. *Lodge* (1970), 114 S.J. 907

The defendant's car collided with a parked vehicle. A constable saw him about an hour later and smelling alcohol on his breath, cautioned him and said that he was arrested for driving under the influence of drink contrary to Sect. 1(c) of the Road Safety Act, 1967. The defendant was deaf and could not lip read though the constable did not know this. Nevertheless the defendant got into a police car which the constable pointed to and was taken to the police station where he indicated his deafness. From then on the charge and all relevant matters were made clear to him by written and printed matter. On the question of the lawfulness of his arrest it was *held* by the Queen's Bench Divisional Court that the original arrest was valid. A police officer arresting a deaf person had to do what a reasonable person would do in the circumstances and the magistrates were clearly of the opinion that the constable had done so.

446. **Alderson** *v.* **Booth**, [1969] 2 All E.R. 271

The defendant's car was involved in an accident and he was asked by a constable to take a breath test. This proved positive and the constable then said to the defendant, "I shall have to ask you to come to the police station for further tests." The defendant went with the constable to the police station and after a further test was charged with driving contrary to Sect. 1(1) of the Road Safety Act, 1967 in that the proportion of alcohol in his blood was beyond the permitted limit. The magistrates were not satisfied that the defendant knew he was under compulsion when he went to the police station with the constable and decided that he had not been arrested. Arrest being a necessary part of the procedure under the 1967 Act, the information laid against the defendant was dismissed. The prosecution appealed to the Queen's Bench Divisional Court where it was *held* that:

(*a*) it was no longer the law that there could be no lawful arrest without an actual seizing or touching;

(*b*) there might be an arrest by mere words provided the defendant submitted and realised he was under compulsion—however, constables should use very clear words; the best thing to say was "I arrest you."

The prosecution's appeal was dismissed because although the magistrates decision was surprising in the circumstances they had felt as a matter of fact that the defendant did not know he was under compulsion.

447. Southport Corporation *v.* Esso Petroleum Co., [1954] 2 Q.B. 182

The Esso company's tanker became stranded in the estuary of the River Ribble. The master of the tanker discharged oil in order to re-float the ship. The action of the wind and tide took the oil on to the corporation's foreshore and caused damage. The corporation sued in trespass and negligence. Devlin, J., at first instance, thought that trespass would lie, but on appeal to the Court of Appeal, Denning, L.J., contended that there could be no trespass because the injury was not direct, but was caused by the tides and prevailing winds; in trespass the injury must be direct and not consequential. In the House of Lords, [1956] A.C. 218, Lord Tucker agreed with Denning, L.J., though in the House of Lords trespass was not pursued. The appeal was based on negligence and the defendants were *held* not liable.

N.B. This case illustrates the difficulties of trying to recover for oil pollution damage in negligence or trespass. The action for nuisance has similar difficulties. *Rylands* v. *Fletcher* does not apply because, among other things, the oil does not escape from the land but from the sea and the sea is the equivalent of a public highway. Oil pollution is now dealt with by the Merchant Shipping (Oil Pollution) Act, 1971, which provides a more straightforward method of making claims.

448. Kelson *v.* Imperial Tobacco Co., [1957] 2 All E.R. 343

The plaintiff was the lessee of a one-storey tobacconist's shop and brought this action against the defendants, seeking an injunction requiring them to remove from the wall above the shop a large advertising sign showing the words "Players Please." The sign projected into the air space above the plaintiff's shop by a distance of some eight inches. The plaintiff claimed that the defendants, by fixing the sign in that position, had trespassed on his air space. *Held*—The invasion of an air space by a sign of this nature constituted a trespass and, although the plaintiff's injury was small, it was an appropriate case in which to grant an injunction for the removal of the sign.

N.B. The plaintiff seemed prepared for the sign to remain until he became involved in a dispute with the defendants regarding the quota of cigarettes supplied to him. It was after the dispute that he brought this action, but the court found that the plaintiff's claim was not affected by his acts.

448a. Woollerton and Wilson v. *Richard Costain (Midlands) Ltd.* (1969), 119 N.L.J. 1093

In this case the Court granted to the owners of a factory and warehouse in Leicester an injunction restraining the defendants from trespassing on and invading air space over their premises by means of a swinging crane. The injunction was suspended for twelve months to enable the defendants to finish their work, the defendants having offered to pay for the right to continue to trespass and to provide insurance cover for neighbouring properties. It was also *held* that it was no answer to a claim for an injunction for trespass that the trespass did no harm to the plaintiff.

449. The Six Carpenters' case (1610), 8 Co. Rep. 146a

Six carpenters went into an inn in Cripplegate and, having consumed a meal of wine and bread, refused to pay for it. Their right to enter was conferred by law, the place being an inn. *Held*—They were not liable because their act was a non-feasance, not a misfeasance. The complaint related to something they had not done, i.e. they had not paid, and trespass *ab initio* depends upon misfeasance.

450. Elias and Others *v.* Pasmore and Others, [1934] 2 K.B. 164

The plaintiffs were officials of the National Unemployed Workers' Movement, and certain of them were tenants of premises occupied by the movement. These premises were entered by the defendants who were inspectors of the Metropolitan Police. One of the plaintiffs was arrested on a warrant on a charge of sedition, but the police also seized at the same time a number of books and papers. Some of these were returned to the plaintiffs, though others were later used at the trial of one of them, a trial which resulted in his conviction. The police still retained certain of the documents after the trial. *Held*— The defendants were trespassers *ab initio* in respect of the documents which were not used and which were unlawfully seized, but this did not make them trespassers *ab initio* in respect of their entry on the premises, for there was justification for that. The plaintiffs were entitled to damages for the detention of certain documents after the trial, and for the seizure of the documents which were returned.

451. Chic Fashions (West Wales) *v.* Jones, [1968] 1 All E.R. 229

Police had reasonable grounds for believing that certain garments in the plaintiff company's shop had been stolen. They obtained a search warrant in respect only of clothing made by "Jan Peters" of Leicester. They did not find any garments of "Jan Peters" make, but they found and seized sixty-five garments of other makes which they reasonably believed to be stolen property. The plaintiff company gave an explanation as to the possession of these garments which the police accepted and the garments were returned. The plaintiff company then alleged trespass against the police, saying that although their entry was lawful it was for the restricted purpose of seizing "Jan Peters" garments and by taking others they had committed trespass *ab initio*. *Held*— by the Court of Appeal—that the police were not liable. Lord Denning said that when a constable entered premises by virtue of a search warrant for stolen goods he could seize not only the goods which he reasonably believed to be covered by the warrant but also any other goods which he honestly believed on reasonable grounds to have been stolen and to be material evidence on a charge of stealing or receiving. The lawfulness of his conduct must be judged at the time and not by what happened afterwards. At one time a man could be made a trespasser *ab initio* by the doctrine of relation back but that was no longer true.

Diplock, L.J., said that the common law was not static. It comprised those rules which governed men's conduct in contemporary society on matters not expressly regulated by legislation. Today stealing was more widespread than it had ever been since statistics of crime were available. In 1967 the question at issue should be answered by allowing the appeal. The decision in *The Six Carpenters' Case*, 1610[449] was doubted.

452. Wood *v.* Leadbitter (1845), 13 M. & W. 838

Wood purchased a ticket for one guinea which entitled him to come into the stand, and the enclosure surrounding it, at Doncaster race course. The ticket was valid for the period of the race meeting. Lord Eglington was the steward of the Doncaster races and, while the races were going on, the defendant, who was Lord Eglington's servant, asked the plaintiff to leave. Wood refused to go and the defendant ejected him using no more than reasonable force. *Held*— It was lawful for Lord Eglington, without returning the guinea or giving any reason for his action, to order any holder of a ticket to leave the stand and enclosure, even though such holder had not misconducted himself. The plaintiff's licence to remain could, therefore, be revoked, so making him a trespasser. From then on he could be removed by the use of reasonable force.

453. Hurst *v.* Picture Theatres Ltd., [1915] 1 K.B. 1

Hurst paid sixpence for an unreserved seat at the defendants' theatre. He was given a metal check, which he gave up at the door, and was then shown to a seat. Some time later he was asked if he had paid for admission and replied that he had. He was then asked to go and see the manager, but he refused to do so. Eventually the manager sent the doorkeeper to eject the plaintiff, the police having refused to do so. The doorkeeper lifted the plaintiff out of his seat, whereupon the plaintiff walked out quietly. He now sued for damages for assault and false imprisonment. The defendants contended that they were entitled, without giving reasons, to ask the plaintiff to leave, and if he did not do so, to remove him, using no more than reasonable force. *Held*—The plaintiff's claim succeeded. The defendants could not revoke the plaintiff's right in that way so as to make him a trespasser.

454. Winter Garden Theatre (London) Ltd. *v.* Millenium Productions Ltd., [1948] A.C. 173

The respondents were permitted by a contractual licence to use the Winter Garden Theatre, Drury Lane, which belonged to the appellants, for the purpose of producing plays, concerts or ballets in return for a weekly payment of £300 a week. There was no express term in the licence providing that the appellants could revoke it. However, the appellants did revoke it, giving the respondents one month in which to quit the premises, but stating that they were prepared to give fresh notice for a later date if the respondents required further time in which to make other arrangements. The respondents contended that the licence could not be revoked so long as the weekly payments were continued. The appellants claimed that it was revocable on giving reasonable notice. *Held*—On a proper construction of the contract the licence was not intended to be perpetual, but nevertheless could only be determined by reasonable notice. What was reasonable notice depended on the commitments of the licensees and the circumstances of the parties. In this case the notice given by the appellants was reasonable and valid to determine the licence.

454a. *Hounslow London Borough Council* v. *Twickenham Garden Developments* [1970] 3 W.L.R. 538

A building owner granted a licence under a building contract to a builder to enter on his land and do work there. The procedure for terminating the the building contract involved an architect giving notice that the work was not being carried out properly. Such a notice was given but the building contractor refused to leave the land and carried on his work. The owner claimed an injunction and damages for trespass. *Held*—by Megarry, J.—in view of the fact that it was not certain whether the architect's notice had been given as a result of following proper procedures the contract had not necessarily been terminated and the builder was not, unless and until that was done, a trespasser. The owner's action failed.

455. Hemmings *v.* Stoke Poges Golf Club, [1920] 1 K.B. 720

The plaintiff was employed by the defendants and occupied a cottage belonging to them. Later he left the defendants' service and was called upon to give up possession. On refusal, he and his property were ejected with no more force than was necessary. *Held*—The defendants were not liable for assault or trespass.

456. The Tubantia, [1924] P. 78

The plaintiff, who was a marine salver, was trying to salvage the cargo of the S.S. *Tubantia* which had been sunk in the North Sea. He had discovered the wreck and marked it with a marker buoy, and his divers were already working in the hold, when the defendant, a rival salver, appeared on the scene and started to send divers down to salvage cargo from the wreck. *Held*—Whoever was the owner of the property salvaged, the plaintiff was sufficiently in possession of the wreck to found an action in trespass.

457. Bridges *v.* Hawkesworth (1851), 21 L.J. Q.B. 75

The plaintiff was a traveller for a large firm with which the defendant, who was a shopkeeper, had dealings. One day when the plaintiff called at the defendant's shop on business, he noticed and picked up a parcel, which was lying on the floor of the shop and which contained bank notes to the value of £55. The plaintiff handed the notes to the defendant, asking him to give them to the owner. Three years later, the owner not having been found in spite of advertisements, the plaintiff asked for the notes and the defendant refused to deliver them up. The plaintiff sued in conversion. *Held*—The property in the notes belonged to the finder, except as against the true owner, and not to the owner of the shop.

458. Elwes *v.* Brigg Gas Co. (1886), 33 Ch.D. 562

The plaintiff leased land to the defendants for ninety-nine years. The lessees were carrying out excavations for the erection of a gasometer when they discovered an ancient boat cut out of an oak. The boat was in a good state of preservation. The question of title to the boat arose. *Held*—The boat did not pass to the lessees by virtue of the lease and belonged to the plaintiff as lessor.

459. South Staffordshire Water Co. *v.* Sharman, [1896] 2 Q.B. 44

The plaintiffs sued the defendant in detinue, claiming possession of two gold rings found by the defendant in the Minster Pool at Lichfield. The plaintiffs were owners of the pool and the defendant was a labourer employed by them to clean it. It was in the course of cleaning the pool that the defendant came across the rings. He refused to hand them to his employers, but gave them to the police for enquiries to be made to find the true owners. No owner was found and the police returned the rings to the defendant who retained them. *Held*—The rings must be given over to the plaintiffs. The plaintiffs were freeholders of the pool, and had the right to forbid anyone coming on the land; they had a right to clean the pool out in any way they chose. They possessed and exercised a practical control over the pool and they had a right to its contents.

460. Corporation of London and Others *v.* Appleyard and Another, [1963] 2 All E.R. 834

Two workmen, in the course of their employment on a building site, found an old wall safe in the cellar of a demolished building. The safe contained banknotes to the value of £5,728 and the owner of the notes was never found. The Corporation of London owned the freehold of the site which was subject to a building lease in favour of Yorkwin Investments. Clause 15 of the lease provided that every relic or article of antiquity or value which might be found in or under any part of the site belonged to the Corporation, and should be carefully and without avoidable damage removed and delivered to the Corporation. *Held*—The Corporation was entitled to the notes as against anyone except the true owner because—

(i) the wall safe formed part of the leased premises and its contents were *de facto* in the possession of Yorkwin who had a better title than the workmen; but

(ii) the Corporation was entitled to the notes under Clause 15 of the lease.

461. Hannah *v.* Peel, [1945] K.B. 509

The defendant owned a house in Shropshire which he had never actually occupied. During the second world war the house was requisitioned for Army purposes. The plaintiff was stationed in the house and found, in an upstairs room which he was occupying, a brooch whose condition indicated that it must have been lost for some considerable time. The plaintiff, thinking the brooch might be valuable, handed it to the police. The real owner was never traced, and the police handed the brooch to agents of the defendant, the chief constable being given an indemnity against any claim to the brooch. The defendant later sold the brooch for £66. The plaintiff now claimed the brooch as finder, and the defendant claimed it as the freeholder of the property. *Held*—The plaintiff was entitled to the brooch or its value because the defendant had never been in actual possession of the house, and had no knowledge of the brooch until the plaintiff found it.

462. Armory *v.* Delamirie (1722), 1 Stra. 505

A chimney sweep's boy found a jewel and handed it for valuation to a goldsmith, who took the jewel from its setting and gave the setting back to the boy, offering him 1½d. for the jewel. The boy turned down the offer and the goldsmith refused to return the jewel. The boy sued the goldsmith in trover (now conversion). *Held*—The boy succeeded since, as the finder, he had a good title except as against the true owner.

463. Jarvis *v.* Williams, [1955] 1 All E.R. 108

Jarvis agreed to sell some bathroom fittings to Peterson and at Peterson's request delivered them to Williams. Peterson refused to pay the price and Jarvis agreed to take them back if Peterson would pay for collection. Peterson accepted this offer and Jarvis sent his lorryman, with a letter of authority, to collect the fittings but he was told that he could not take them, so he returned empty-handed. Jarvis claimed against Williams in detinue for the return of the goods. *Held*—On the delivery to Williams the property in the goods passed to Peterson, and the arrangement for recollection did not re-vest the property in Jarvis. It follows that at the time of collection, Jarvis had no right of property in the goods to sustain an action in detinue.

464. Leake *v.* Loveday and Brooks (1842), 4 Man & G. 972

In 1837 A bought goods from B and allowed B to remain in possession of them until 1839. B became bankrupt but neither A nor his assigneees made any claim on the goods which B retained until 1841 when the sheriff seized and sold them. After the sale B's assignees notified the sheriff of their claim who, on receiving an indemnity, handed over the proceeds of the sale to them. It was *held* that since A was not in possession of the goods, the sheriff could set up the title of the assignees of B.

465. Fouldes *v.* Willoughby (1841), 8 M. & W. 540

The plaintiff had put his horses on the defendant's ferry boat and, a dispute having arisen, the defendant asked the plaintiff to take them off. The plaintiff refused so the defendant did so, and since the plaintiff refused to leave the boat, the defendant ferried him across the river. The plaintiff sued in conversion. Maule, J., directed the jury that the putting of the horses ashore was a conversion, but on appeal, the Court of Exchequer *reversed* the decision and found there was no conversion. Lord Abinger, C.B., said: "In order to constitute a conversion it is necessary either that the party taking the goods should intend some use to be made of them by himself or by those for whom he acts, or that owing to his act, the goods are destroyed or consumed to the prejudice of the lawful owner. The removal of the horses involved not the least denial of the right of the plaintiff to enjoyment or possession of them and was thus no conversion."

466. Oakley *v.* Lyster, [1931] 1 K.B. 148

Oakley, a demolition contractor, agreed to pull down an aerodrome on Salisbury Plain and reinstate the land, a process which involved disposing of 8,000 tons of hard core and tar macadam. He thereupon rented three and a half acres of a farm on the opposite side of the road on which to dump it. He sold 4,000 tons, but in January, 1929, there was still 4,000 tons undisposed of when Lyster bought the freehold of the farm. Shortly afterwards Oakley found that some of the hardcore was being removed on Lyster's instructions, and Oakley saw him and was told that Lyster had bought the land and all that was on it, and on 9th July, 1929, his solicitors wrote to Oakley to this effect and forbade Oakley to remove the hard core otherwise he would become a trespasser on Lyster's land. Correspondence followed but at the trial it was admitted that Oakley was a lawful tenant and owner of the hard core. While the correspondence was continuing, Oakley agreed to sell the 4,000 tons to Mr. Edney, but in view of Lyster's claim, Edney withdrew and the stuff was undisposed of. The conversion alleged was the removal by Lyster of some of the hard core and the denial of title in the correspondence. *Held*—The defendant was liable in damages for conversion. In the correspondence Lyster was asserting and exercising dominion over the goods inconsistent with the rights of the true owner, Oakley. Nor was it sufficient to allow Oakley to resumë dominion over the hard core and remove it. He was entitled to damages of £300 for the loss of the sale to Edney.

467. Elvin and Powell Ltd. *v.* Plummer Roddis Ltd. (1933), 50 T.L.R. 158

A fraudulent person ordered a consignment of goods from the plaintiffs in the name of the defendants. He then telephoned the defendants in the plaintiff's name, saying that the goods had been dispatched to them in error and that they would be collected. The fraudulent person then himself collected the goods from the defendants and absconded with them. The plaintiffs now sued the defendants for conversion. *Held*—As involuntary bailees of goods, the defendants had acted reasonably in returning them, as they believed, to the plaintiffs, by a trustworthy messenger. They had not committed conversion.

468. Munro *v.* Willmott, [1949] 1 K.B. 295

The owner of a motor car parked it in the yard of an inn. The tenant of the inn gave his permission and charged a rent of 5s. The owner of the car was moved away from the district on business, and was unable to take the car because it was not in good running order. Three years later the tenant found that the car was causing an obstruction because he had by then let a garage on the premises to the St. John Ambulance Corps, and it was difficult for them to get ambulances in and out of the yard. Being unable to trace the owner, the tenant had certain repairs carried out on the car at a cost of £85, and later sold it by auction for £105, less commission of £5. The value of the car at the date of judgment was £120. The plaintiff later returned to the inn and, on finding that the car had been disposed of, brought this action for detinue and conversion. *Held*—The tenant was not an agent of necessity and was liable to the plaintiff for detinue and conversion of the car. The measure of damages was the value of the car at the date of judgment, less any increase in value resulting from the money spent on it by the defendant. Judgment was therefore given for the plaintiff for £35.

469. The Winkfield, [1902] P. 42

This was an Admiralty action arising because a ship called the *Mexican* was negligently struck and sunk by a ship called the *Winkfield*. The *Mexican* was carrying mail from South Africa to England during the Boer War. The Postmaster General made, among other things, a claim for damages in respect of the estimated value of parcels and letters for which no claim had been made or instructions received from the senders. The Postmaster General undertook to distribute the amount recovered when the senders were found. An objection was made that the Postmaster General represented the Crown and was not liable to the senders (see now Crown Proceedings Act, 1947). *Held*—As a bailee in possession the Postmaster General could recover damages for the loss of the goods irrespective of whether or not he was liable to the bailors.

470. Wickham Holdings Ltd. *v.* Brooke House Motors Ltd., [1967] 1 All E.R. 117

Brooke House Motors bought a car from a person who was not the owner but had a hire purchase agreement with Wickham Holdings. Brooke House Motors asked Wickham Holdings what the "settlement figure" was and were told that it was £274 10s.— but that they would accept £270 if paid within seven days. Brooke House Motors failed to pay this sum and Wickham Holdings sued them in conversion recovering the value of the car, i.e. £365. On appeal by Brooke House Motors to the Court of Appeal it was *held* that Wickham Holdings could only recover £274 10s.— which was the value of their interest in the vehicle.

471. Castle *v.* St. Augustine's Links Ltd. and Another (1922), 38 T.L.R. 615

On 18th August, 1919, the plaintiff was driving a taxicab from Deal to Ramsgate when a ball played by the second defendant, a Mr. Chapman, from the thirteenth tee on the golf course, which was parallel with the Sandwich Road, struck the windscreen of the taxicab. In consequence a piece of glass from the screen injured the plaintiff's eye and a few days later he had to have it removed. He then brought this action. *Held*—the plaintiff succeeded. Judgment for £450 damages was given by Sankey, J. The proximity of the hole to the road constituted a public nuisance. *c/f Bolton v. Stone*, [1951] A.C. 650, where cricket balls had been hit out of the ground and into the highway six to ten times in thirty-five years but had injured nobody. *Held*—no nuisance.

472. Terry *v.* Ashton (1876), 1 Q.B.D. 314

A lamp projected from the defendant's premises over the highway. It fell and injured the plaintiff who then sued the defendant in respect of his injuries.

The defendant had previously employed an independent contractor, who was not alleged to be incompetent, to repair the lamp and it was because of the negligence of that contractor that the lamp fell. Even so the defendant was *held* liable and the decision suggests that there is strict liability in respect of injuries caused by artificial projections over the highway.

473. Bliss *v.* Hall (1838), L.J. C.P. 122

The defendant carried on the trade of a candle-maker in certain premises near to the dwelling house of the plaintiff and his family. Certain "noxious and foul smells" issued from the defendant's premises and the plaintiff sued him for nuisance. The defence was that, for three years before the plaintiff occupied the dwelling house in question, the defendant had exercised the trade complained of in this present establishment. *Held*—This was no answer to the complaint and judgment was given for the plaintiff.

474. Adams *v.* Ursell, [1913] 1 Ch. 269

The plaintiff was a veterinary surgeon and he purchased a house in 1907 for £2,370. In November, 1912, the defendant opened a fried fish shop at premises adjoining the plaintiff's house. Very soon after the commencement of the business, the plaintiff's house was permeated with the odour of fried fish, and the vapour from the stoves filled the rooms "like fog or steam." The plaintiff sued the defendant for nuisance, seeking an injunction. *Held*—An injunction would be granted because the defendant's activities materially interfered with the ordinary comfort of the plaintiff and his family; and it did not matter that the shop was in a large working-class district and therefore supplied a public need.

475. Christie *v.* Davey, [1893] 1 Ch. 316

The plaintiff was the occupier of a semi-detached house, and she and her daughter gave pianoforte, violin and singing lessons in the house, four days a week for seventeen hours in all. There was also practice of music and singing at other times, and occasional musical evenings. The defendant was a wood-carver who occupied the contiguous portion of the house, and he found the musical activities of the plaintiff and her family somewhat annoying. In addition to writing abusive letters, he retaliated by playing concertinas, horns, flutes, pianos and other musical instruments, blowing whistles, knocking on trays or boards, hammering, shrieking or shouting, so as to annoy the plaintiffs and injure their activities. *Held*—What the plaintiff and her family were doing was not an unreasonable use of the house, and could not be restrained by the adjoining tenant. However, the adjoining tenant was himself restrained from making noises to annoy the plaintiff, the court being satisfied that such noises had been made wilfully for the purpose of annoyance.

476. British Celanese Ltd. *v.* A. H. Hunt (Capacitors) Ltd., [1969] 2 All E.R. 1252

The defendants allowed metal foil to escape from their land and foul the bus bars of overhead electric cables. The plaintiffs lost power and their machines were clogged up and time and material wasted. *Held*—by Lawton, J. that—

(*a*) the defendants were not liable under *Rylands* v. *Fletcher*, because there was no non-natural use of land;

(*b*) the defendants owed a duty of care to the plaintiffs and could be liable in negligence, the plaintiffs had a proprietory interest in the machines which were damaged and could recover loss flowing from that, pure economic loss was not involved;

(*c*) the defendants were liable in nuisance, an isolated happening such as this could create an actionable nuisance and the plaintiffs were directly and foreseeably affected.

477. Hollywood Silver Fox Farm Ltd. *v.* Emmett, [1936] 2 K.B. 468

The plaintiffs were breeders of silver foxes, and erected a notice board on their land inscribed: "Hollywood Silver Fox Farm." The defendant owned a neighbouring field, which he was about to develop as a building estate, and he regarded the notice board as detrimental to such development. He asked the plaintiffs to remove it, and when this request was refused, he sent his son to discharge a 12-bore gun close to the plaintiff's land, with the object of frightening the vixens during breeding. The result of this activity was that certain of the vixens did not mate at all, and others, having whelped, devoured their young. The plaintiff brought this action alleging nuisance, and the defence was that Emmett had a right to shoot as he pleased on his own land. *Held*—An injunction would be granted to restrain Emmett. His evil motive made an otherwise innocent use of land a nuisance.

N.B. It seems at first sight difficult to reconcile the above case with *Mayor of Bradford* v. *Pickles* (1895).[357] The difference probably is in the fact that *Hollywood Silver Fox Farm* v. *Emmett* was an action for nuisance by noise, so that the defendant's motive was relevant in establishing the tort. In *Mayor of Bradford* v. *Pickles*, the action was really one for interference with a servitude or right over land, and motive was not relevant in establishing the rights of the parties.

478. Malone *v.* Laskey, [1907] 2 K.B. 141

The defendants owned a house which they leased to a firm named Witherby & Co., who sub-let it to the Script Shorthand Company. The plaintiff's husband was employed by the latter company, and was allowed to occupy the house as an emolument of his employment. A flush cistern in the lavatory of the house was unsafe, the wall brackets having been loosened by the vibration of the defendants' electric generator next door. The plaintiff told Witherby &

Co. of the situation, and they communicated with the defendants who sent two of their plumbers to repair the cistern gratuitously. The work was carried out in an improper and negligent manner, and four months later the plaintiff was injured when the cistern came loose. The plaintiff sued the defendants (i) in nuisance, and (ii) in negligence. *Held*—There was no claim in nuisance against the defendants. The plaintiff was not their tenant, and in nuisance the tenant is the person to sue, not other persons present on the premises, though such persons may have a claim where the nuisance is a public nuisance. Further, there was no claim in negligence, because the defendants owed no duty of care: firstly, because there was no contractual relationship; secondly, because the defendants did not undertake any duty towards the plaintiff. They were under no obligation to carry out repairs but sent their plumbers merely as a matter of grace. This was a voluntary act and was not in any sense the discharge of a duty. The defendants were not in occupation of the premises and had not invited the plaintiff to occupy them.

N.B. The case still represents the law regarding nuisance. Regarding the claim for negligence it was overruled in *Billings* v. *Riden*, [1958] A.C. 240, where it was held that there may be liability in negligence, where premises are left in a dangerous condition by workmen so that injury results, even though the injured person is not the occupier but is a visitor to the premises.

479. Wilchick *v.* Marks and Silverstone, [1934] 2 K.B. 56

Landlords who had let premises with a defective shutter, and had expressly reserved the right to enter the premises to do repairs, were *held* liable along with their tenant, to a passer-by injured by the shutter.

480. Mint *v.* Good, [1951] 1 K.B. 517

Landlords were *held* liable to the infant plaintiff, who was injured when a wall on the premises, which they had let, collapsed on to the highway. They had not reserved the right to enter to do repairs, but the Court of Appeal stated that such a right must be implied, because the premises were let on weekly tenancies and it was usual to imply a right to enter to do repairs in such tenancies.

481. Harris *v.* James (1876), 45 L.J.Q.B. 545

A landlord was *held* liable for the nuisance created by his tenant's blasting operations at a quarry because he had let the property for that purpose. The tenant, therefore, inevitably created a nuisance.

482. Brew Brothers *v.* Snax (Ross), [1969] 3 W.L.R. 657

In June, 1965, the freehold owners of premises leased to them for a term of 14 years. The lease contained covenants by the tenants regarding repairs, payment of maintenance expenses and viewing by the landlords. In November, 1966, one of the walls of the premises tilted towards the neighbouring premises which belong to the plaintiff. It was shored up but caused an obstruction for 18 months. It appeared that the reason why the wall had tilted was the seeping of water from certain drains and the removal of a tree by the tenants. The plaintiffs sued the landlords and the tenants, and the landlords contended that the responsibility fell entirely on the tenants under the lease. *Held*—by the Court of Appeal—

(*a*) the tenants were responsible for repairing defects pointed out by the landlords but that the work required on the wall was not within the terms of the lease;

(*b*) the landlords must be presumed to know the state of the premises and were liable for nuisance in that they allowed the state of affairs to continue;

(*c*) the tenants were jointly liable in nuisance in that they failed to put the matter right, this liability was quite independent of their duties under the lease.

483. Sedleigh-Denfield *v.* O'Callagan and others, [1940] A.C. 880

One of the respondents (a college for training foreign missioners) was the owner of property adjoining the appellant's premises in Mill Hill. On the boundary of the property owned by the College there was a ditch and it was admitted that the ditch also belonged to the college. About 1934, when a block of flats was erected on the western side of the appellant's premises, the county council had laid a pipe and grating in the ditch but no permission was obtained and no steps were taken to inform the college authorities of the laying of the pipe. However, the presence of the pipe became known to a member of the college who was responsible for cleaning out the ditch twice a year. The council had not put a guard at the entrance to the pipe to prevent its being blocked by debris. The pipe became blocked and the appellant's garden was flooded. He claimed damages from the college on the ground that the pipe was a nuisance. *Held*—by the House of Lords—the college was liable because it appeared that they should have known about the pipe and realised the risk. Furthermore they had adopted the nuisance by using the pipe to drain their land.

484. Sturges *v.* Bridgman (1879), 11 Ch. D. 852

For more than twenty years the defendant, a confectioner, had used large pestles and mortars in his premises in Wigmore Street. Then the plaintiff, a physician in Wimpole Street, built a consulting room in his garden abutting on the confectioner's premises. The noise and vibration made by the confectioner's activities interfered materially with the plaintiff's practice. He sued for an injunction to prevent the offensive activities and the defence was that the defendant had acquired a prescriptive right to commit the nuisance. *Held*— Though it was possible to acquire a right, the defendant had not done so, because the nuisance only arose when the consulting room was built.

485. Earl *v.* Lubbock, [1905] 1 K.B. 253

The plaintiff was employed by a firm of mineral water manufacturers, and the defendant, a wheelwright, had agreed with the plaintiff's employers that he would keep a certain number of their delivery vans in repair. The defendant failed to keep a certain van in repair, the result being that a wheel came off while the plaintiff was driving, and he suffered injuries. The plaintiff sued the defendant for negligence. *Held*—The plaintiff could not maintain an action against the defendant, since any duty the defendant had to repair the van properly was owed to the plaintiff's employer, with whom he had a contract, and not to the plaintiff.

486. East Suffolk Rivers Catchment Board *v.* Kent, [1941] A.C. 74

The respondents were owners of land in Suffolk protected by a wall from inundation by a tidal river. As a result of spring floods and a northerly gale, the wall was breached and the respondents' land was flooded. The appellants, acting under Sect. 34 of the Land Drainage Act, 1930, attempted to repair the breach. However, their approach to the job was rather inefficient and the respondents' land was flooded for much longer than it need have been and they now sued for damages. *Held*—The damage was due to the forces of nature and the appellants, in trying to put the matter right, were acting under a mere power so that they were under no duty to the respondents. Sect. 30 of the Land Drainage Act did not place upon a Catchment Board an imperative duty to repair a breach of this kind, but gave the board permissive power to do so. They had exercised their discretion honestly, and could not be made liable for damage which would have been avoided had they exercised their discretion in a more reasonable way. Furthermore, the appellants were guilty of an omission rather than a positive act because they did not cause the harm but were merely slow in doing good.

487. The World Harmony, [1965] 2 All E.R. 139

A collision occurred in the Bosphorus in December, 1960, between two ships, as a result of which one of the two ships drifted into a third and all three were wrecked. The *Tarsus*, the innocent third ship, was under charter to one of the plaintiffs and he suffered *pecuniary loss* by having to find another ship to carry goods for him. Hewson, J., *held* that the claim in negligence would have to be restricted to the physical loss of actual chattels on board the *Tarsus* at the time of the collision as damages could not be awarded in respect of mere pecuniary loss.

N.B. In *Margarine Union G.M.b.H.* v. *Cambay Prince Steamship Co. Ltd.*, [1967] 3 All E.R. 775, a similar problem arose. The defendants had negligently failed to fumigate their ship so that a cargo of copra being carried on the ship was damaged by cockroaches. Part of the the cargo was sold to the plaintiffs but it was agreed that they acquired no title to their part of the cargo until it was unloaded and separated from the bulk. Thus, the plaintiffs had no legal title to the goods at the time of the defendants' negligent act. Therefore, the plaintiffs were suing for economic loss arising from having to obtain other copra, and their action failed. Roskill, J., felt that this conclusion had not been affected by the *Hedley, Byrne*[194] case.

488. Weller & Co. *v.* Foot and Mouth Disease Research Institute, [1965] 3 All E.R. 560

The defendants carried out experiments on their land concerning foot and mouth disease. They imported an African virus which escaped and infected cattle in the vicinity. As a consequence two cattle markets in the area had to be closed and the plaintiffs, who were auctioneers, sued for damages for loss of business. *Held*—by Widgery, J.—that so far as negligence was concerned the defendants owed no duty of care to the plaintiffs who were not cattle owners, and had no proprietary interest in anything which could be damaged by the virus. Furthermore, the defendants owed no absolute duty to the plaintiffs under *Rylands* v. *Fletcher*, 1868, because the plaintiffs had no interest in any land to which the virus could have escaped.

489. S.C.M. (United Kingdom) Ltd. *v.* W. J. Whittall & Son Ltd., [1970] 3 All E.R. 245

A workman employed by the defendants who were carrying out construction work near the plaintiffs' factory, cut into an underground electric cable so that the power to the plaintiffs' factory failed. The plaintiffs made typewriters and the lack of power caused molten materials to solidify in their machines which were *physically* damaged. The machines had to be stripped down and reassembled and production was brought to a halt for seven and a half hours. In the Court of Appeal the plaintiffs limited their claim to damages in respect of the physical damage to the machines and the financial loss *directly* resulting from that damage. This enabled the court to decide that the plaintiffs' property had foreseeably been damaged by the defendants' act so that the plaintiffs could recover for damage to the machines and the consequential financial loss flowing from it. Nevertheless the Court went on to consider economic loss in the context of negligence and dealt in effect with the position as it might have been if the power cut had stopped production without damaging the machines. The following aspects of the judgments are important: *Per* Lord Denning, M.R.—

> In actions of negligence, when the plaintiff has suffered no damage to his person or property, but has only sustained economic loss, the law does not usually permit him to recover that loss. Although the defendants owed the plaintiffs a duty of care, that did not mean that additional economic loss which was not consequent on the material damage suffered by the plaintiffs would also be recoverable; in cases such as *Weller & Co.* v. *Foot and Mouth Disease Research Institute,* 1965,[488] and *Electrochrome Ltd.* v. *Welsh Plastics Ltd.,* 1968,[356] the plaintiffs did not recover for economic loss because it was too remote to be a head of damage, not because there was no duty owed to the plaintiffs or because the loss suffered in each case was not caused by the negligence of the defendants.

Per Winn L.J.

> Apart from the special case of imposition of liability for negligently uttered false statements, there is no liability for unintentional negligent infliction of any form of economic loss which is not itself consequential on foreseeable physical injury or damage to property.

490. Clay *v.* A. J. Crump & Sons Ltd. and Others, [1963] 3 All E.R. 687

Garage owners employed demolition contractors to demolish an old building, and building contractors to erect an extension to a garage in Dudley. They also employed an architect to prepare plans and supervise both operations. The old building and the gable wall at the end of the existing garage were to be demolished to allow for an extension which would lengthen the existing building. Having demolished the old building, the demolition contractors were told to leave the gable wall for the time being. Before the demolition contractors left the site, two walls supporting the gable wall had been knocked down and the earth had been dug out from the foundations of the gable wall, thus exposing unsafe foundations. The architect inspected the site just before the demolition contractors left and could, if he had carried out a proper inspection, have seen that the wall was unsafe. However, he did advise the building owners that it was safe. The foreman of the demolition company also declared the wall safe. The building contractors did not examine the wall in any detail because they relied, as the architect and demolition contractors should have assumed they would, on the wall being left safe. The plaintiff was a labourer employed by the building contractors, and while he was on the site, the gable wall collapsed and injured him. He now sued the demolition contractors, the architect and the building contractors. *Held*—All three were liable being in breach of a duty of care owed to the plaintiff—the damages being apportioned 42% against the architect; 38% against the demolition contractors; and 20% against the building contractor. Regarding the architect's liability the Court of Appeal said that he owed a duty of care to the plaintiff because he gave an assurance of the safety of the wall. It was also argued for the architect that *Candler* v. *Crane, Christmas & Co.*, 1951,[504] provided him with a defence because his contract was with the building owner only and he could not owe a duty of care to the plaintiff. Here the Court of Appeal said that *Hedley Byrne & Co. Ltd.* v. *Heller & Partners Ltd.*, 1963,[194] had thrown doubt on the rule in *Candler's* case and the architect could not derive assistance from it. The building contractors were liable because they owed a duty to the plaintiff to see that the place where he had to work was safe. It should be noted that the architect was in effect liable for an omission because he should have foreseen the danger and carried out a proper inspection of the wall.

491. Home Office v. Dorset Yacht Co. Ltd., [1970] 2 All E.R. 294

The respondents' yacht was damaged by a number of Borstal boys who had escaped at night from an island when they were left uncontrolled by their guards. The respondents sued the Home Office for the amount of damage. *Held*—by the House of Lords—

(i) The officers guarding the boys owed a duty of care to the respondents. The fact that the boys might take nearby yachts was foreseeable. The Home Office was therefore liable vicariously for the negligence of the officers.

(ii) The fact that the Borstal was conducted under statutory authority did not warrant unreasonable acts or justify negligent conduct.

(iii) There was no ground in public policy for granting *complete* immunity from liability in negligence to the Home Office or its officers in respect of the acts of prisoners or other detainees.

492. Daniels v. R. White and Sons Ltd., [1938] 4 All E.R. 258

The plaintiffs, who were husband and wife, sued the first defendants, who were manufacturers of mineral waters, in negligence. The plaintiffs had been injured because a bottle of the first defendants' lemonade, which they had purchased from a public house in Battersea, contained carbolic acid. Evidence showed that the manufacturer took all possible care to see that no injurious matter got into the lemonade. It was *held* that the manufacturers were not liable in negligence because the duty was not one to ensure that the goods were in perfect condition but only to take reasonable care to see that no injury was caused to the eventual consumer. This duty had been fulfilled.

493. Paris v. Stepney Borough Council, [1951] A.C. 367

The plaintiff was employed by the defendants on vehicle maintenance. He had the use of only one eye and the defendants were aware of this. The plaintiff was endeavouring to remove a bolt from the chassis of a vehicle, and was using a hammer for the purpose, when a chip of metal flew into his good eye so that he became totally blind. The plaintiff claimed damages from his employers for negligence in that he had not been supplied with goggles. The defendants showed in evidence that it was not the usual practice in trades of this nature to supply goggles, at least where the employees were men with two good eyes. The trial judge found for the plaintiff, but the Court of Appeal reversed the decision on the grounds that the plaintiff's disability could be relevant only if it increased the risk, i.e. if a one-eyed man was more likely to get a splinter in his eye than a two-eyed man. Having found that the risk was not increased they allowed the appeal. The House of Lords reversed the judgment of the

Court of Appeal, holding that the gravity of the harm likely to be caused would influence a reasonable employer, so that the duty of care to a one-eyed employee required the supply of goggles, and Paris therefore succeeded.

494. Haley *v.* London Electricity Board, [1964] 3 All E.R. 185

The appellant, Haley, a blind man who was on his way to his work as a telephonist, tripped over an obstacle placed by servants of the London Electricity Board near the end of a trench excavated in the pavement of a street in Woolwich. He fell and suffered an injury which rendered him deaf, and brought about his premature retirement from his employment. The guard was sufficient warning for sighted people but was by its nature inadequate to protect or warn the blind. It consisted of a hammer hooked in the railings and resting on the pavement at an angle of thirty degrees, and Haley's white stick, which he was properly using as a guide, did not encounter the obstacle with the result that instead of warning him he fell over it. Evidence was given that about one in five hundred people were blind and there were 258 registered blind people in Woolwich, many of whom were capable of walking in the streets alone, taking the normal precautions such blind persons were accustomed to take. The House of Lords *held*, reversing the decision of the Court of Appeal, that the London Electricity Board were liable in negligence. Those engaged in operations on the pavement of a highway must act reasonably to prevent danger to passers-by including blind people who must, however, also take reasonable care of themselves. The Board had not fulfilled this duty and were liable in damages for negligence which were assessed at £3,000 general damages, and £2,250 special damages, Haley's retirement being accelerated by four years.

495. Watt *v.* Hertfordshire County Council, [1954] 2 All E.R. 3681

A fireman was injured by a heavy jack which slipped while being carried in a lorry which was going to the scene of an accident. The lorry was not equipped to carry such a heavy jack but it was required to free a woman who had been trapped in the wreckage. No proper vehicle was available and it was *held* that the fire authority was not liable.

496. Latimer *v.* A.E.C. Ltd., [1953] 2 All E.R. 449

A heavy rainstorm flooded a factory and made the floor slippery. The occupiers of the factory did all they could to get rid of the water and make the factory safe, but the plaintiff fell and was injured. He alleged negligence in that the occupiers did not close down the factory. *Held*—the occupiers of the factory were not liable. The risk of injury did not justify the closing down of the factory.

497. Byrne *v.* Boadle (1863), 2 H. & C. 722

The plaintiff brought an action in negligence alleging that, as he was walking past the defendant's shop, a barrel of flour fell from a window above the shop and injured him. The defendant was a dealer in flour, but there was no evidence that the defendant or any of his servants were engaged in lowering the barrel of flour at the time. The defendant submitted that there was no evidence of negligence to go to the jury, but it was *held* that the occurrence was of itself evidence of negligence sufficient to entitle the jury to find for the plaintiff, in the absence of an explanation by the defendant.

498. Roe *v.* Minister of Health, [1954] 2 Q.B. 66

Two patients in a hospital had operations on the same day. Both operations were of a minor character and in each case nupercaine, a spinal anaesthetic, was injected by means of a lumbar puncture. The injections were given by a specialist anaesthetist, assisted by the theatre staff of the hospital. The nupercaine had been contained in sealed glass ampoules, stored in a solution of phenol. After the operations both patients developed symptoms of spastic pariplegia caused by the phenol, which had contaminated the nupercaine by penetrating almost invisible cracks in the ampoules. In the event, both patients became permanently paralysed from the waist down, and they now sued the defendants for negligence. *Held*—The defendants were vicariously liable for the negligence (if any) of those concerned with the operations, but on the standard of medical knowledge in 1947, when the operations took place, those concerned were not negligent. The cracks in the ampoules were not visible on ordinary examination, and could not be reproduced even by deliberate experiment. It was true that in 1954, when the case was brought, phenol used for disinfectant purposes was tinted so that it might be seen on examination, but the case must be decided on medical knowledge at the time when the operations were carried out. It was also suggested that once the accident has been explained, there is no question of *res ipsa loquitur* applying. Nor does the maxim apply when many persons might have been negligent. Denning, L.J., suggested that every surgical operation is attended by risks, and one cannot take the benefits of surgery without accepting the risks. Doctors, like the rest of us, have to learn by experience. Further, one must not condemn as negligence that which is only misadventure.

499. Pearson *v.* North-Western Gas Board, [1968] 2 All E.R. 669

The plaintiff's husband was killed by an explosion of gas which also destroyed her house. It appeared from the evidence that a gas main had fractured due to a movement of earth caused by a severe frost. When the weather was very cold the defendants had men standing by ready to deal with reports of gas leaks, but unless they received reports there was no way of predicting or preventing a leak which might lead to an explosion. *Held*—by Rees, J.—that assuming the principle of *res ipsa loquitur* applied, the defendants had rebutted the presumption of negligence and the plaintiff's ease failed.

500. Jones *v.* Lawrence, [1969] 3 All E.R. 267

A boy aged seven years and three months ran out from behind a parked van across a road apparently without looking in order to get to a fun fair. He was knocked down by Lawrence who was travelling on his motor cycle at fifty miles per hour in a built-up area. The boy's injuries adversely affected his school work and he subsequently failed his eleven-plus examination. In action on his behalf for damages it was *held* by Cumming-Bruce, J.—that

(*a*) his conduct was only that to be expected of a seven-year-old child and could not amount to contributory negligence;

(*b*) the failure to obtain a grammar-school place and the permanent impairment of his powers of concentration affected his job attainment potential and were factors to be taken into account in assessing damages.

501. Oliver *v.* Birmingham Bus Co., [1932] 1 K.B. 35

A grandfather was walking with his grandchild aged four, when a bus approached quickly and without warning. The grandfather, being startled, let go the child's hand and the bus struck the child. It was *held* that the damages awarded to the child should not be reduced to take account of the grandfather's negligence.

502. Atkinson *v.* Newcastle and Gateshead Waterworks Co. (1877), L.R.2 Ex. D. 441

The plaintiff's timber yard caught fire and was destroyed, there being insufficient water in the mains to put it out. The defendants were required by the Waterworks Clauses Act, 1874, to maintain a certain pressure of water in their water pipes, and the Act provided a penalty of £10 for failure to keep the required pressure and 40s. for each day during which the neglect continued, the sums being payable to aggrieved ratepayers. The plaintiff sued the defendants for loss caused by the fire on the ground that they were in breach of a statutory duty regarding the pressure in the pipes. *Held*—The defendants were not liable. The statute did not disclose a cause of action by individuals for damage of this kind. It was most improbable that the legislature intended the company to be gratuitous insurers against fire of all the buildings in Newcastle.

503. Gorris *v.* Scott (1874), L.R. 9 Exch. 125

A statutory order placed a duty on the defendant to supply pens of a specified size in those parts of a ship's deck occupied by animals. The defendant did not supply the pens, and sheep belonging to the plaintiff were swept overboard. The plaintiff claimed damages from the defendant for breach of statutory duty. *Held*—The plaintiff could not recover for his loss under breach of statutory duty, because the object of the statutory order was to prevent the spread of disease, not to prevent animals from being drowned.

504. Candler *v.* Crane, Christmas & Co., [1951] 2 K.B. 164

The defendants, a firm of accountants and auditors, prepared the accounts and balance sheet of a limited company at the request of its managing director, knowing that they were required to induce the plaintiff to invest money in the company. The plaintiff, relying on the accounts, invested £2,000 in the company. The accounts were negligently prepared and failed to give an accurate picture of the company's financial state. The company was wound up within a year and the plaintiff lost his money. He now sued the accountants in negligence. The Court of Appeal *held* that, in the absence of a contractual or fiduciary relationship between the parties, the defendants owed no duty of care to the plaintiff in preparing the accounts. Denning, L.J., thought that the defendants might be held liable because they knew that the accounts were to be shown to the plaintiff, though he would not have found them liable to complete strangers.

505. Clayton *v.* Woodman & Son (Builders) Ltd., and Others, [1961] 3 All E.R. 249

The plaintiff was a bricklayer employed by the first defendants, Woodman & Son, a firm of builders. The builders had entered into a contract with the second defendants, a regional hospital board, to install a lift at a hospital. The work was carried out in accordance with the instructions given by a firm of architects who were made third defendants. An architect employed by the third defendants allowed the plaintiff to cut a chase or wide groove in an unsupported gable. This had the effect of weakening the gable and the architect should have known that it would fall if not supported. The plaintiff cut the chase, and the gable collapsed and injured him. The question of the liability of each of the defendants arose. At first instance Salmon, J., *held*—(*a*) The first defendants (the builders) were liable for negligence at common law because they had failed to provide a safe system of work. They were also liable for breach of their statutory duty under the Building (Safety, Health and Welfare) Regulations, 1948. (*b*) The second defendants (the hospital authorities) were not liable. They were not in breach of their duty under the Occupiers' Liability Act, 1957. Further, they were not vicariously liable for the negligence of the architect since he was an independent contractor. (*c*) The architects were liable. The decision in *Candler* v. *Crane, Christmas & Co.* (1951)[504] did not apply, because the architect was not making careless misstatements, but was giving careless orders or instructions, and in any case the injury here was physical not financial.

N.B. In *Clayton* v. *Woodman & Sons (Builders) Ltd. and Others*, [1962] 2 All E.R. 33, the Court of Appeal reversed the part of the above decision which found the architect liable, saying that the question of his liability did not arise for decision because (*a*) The architect had not given orders to the bricklayer. All he had done was to refuse to allow the gable to be demolished, and he was bound to do this because he had instructions to preserve certain features of the building of which the gable was one. The cutting of the chase followed from that refusal. (*b*) From then on it was the duty of the plaintiff's employers to provide a safe system of doing the job, and they were solely responsible.

506. Mutual Life Assurance *v.* Evatt, [1971] 1 All E.R. 152

Evatt had made certain investments in P. Ltd. and wished to know whether he should retain these investments or expand them. P. Ltd. and the assurance company were both subsidiaries of the same holding company, the only relationship between Evatt and the assurance company being that Evatt was one of their policy holders. On the basis of that and the assurance company's personal knowledge of P. Ltd's affairs Evatt sought the assurance company's advice as to P. Ltd.'s financial prospects. The advice was given, without any disclaimer, and Evatt invested accordingly. Soon afterwards the investments fell in value and Evatt claimed that the advice was given negligently. It was *held*—by the Judicial Committee of the Privy Council (Lords Reid and Morris dissenting) that there was no cause of action. The liability in the *Hedley Byrne* case was limited to persons who held themselves out as being skilled in the subject matter of the inquiry and, since it was no part of the business of an insurance company to give advice on the financial position of other companies the appeal was allowed.

It would not in their Lordships' view be consonant with the principles hereto accepted in the common law that the duty to comply with that objective standard should be extended to an advisor who, at the time which his advice is sought, has not let it be known to the advisee that he claims to possess the standard of skill and competence and is prepared to exercise diligence which is generally shown by persons who carry on the business of giving advice of the kind sought. He has given the advisee no reason to suppose that he is acquainted with the standard or capable of complying with it, or that he has such appreciation of the nature and magnitude of the loss which the advisee may sustain by reason of any failure by that advisor to attain that standard as a reasonable man would require before assuming a liability to answer for the loss.

Per Diplock, L.J.

507. Anderson (W.B.) and Sons *v.* Rhodes (Liverpool), [1967] 2 All E.R. 850

The plaintiff and the first defendant were wholesalers in the Liverpool fruit and vegetable market. In April, 1965, the manager of a newly-formed company bought some potatoes for cash from Rhodes & Co. and later purchased potatoes from them on credit. The manager of Rhodes & Co. made no credit inquiries about the new company. The market rule was that payment should be made within seven days of invoice but at all material times substantial amounts were overdue as between Rhodes & Co. and the new company, but the salesman and buyer of Rhodes & Co. were not informed of this fact. Rhodes & Co. also acted from time to time as commission agents and their buyer, a man called Reid, later arranged sales on a commission basis between the new company and the plaintiffs. Reid represented orally to the plaintiffs that the new company was credit-worthy and he acted throughout in good faith. The plaintiffs supplied goods in credit to the new company which then became insolvent and could not pay its debts. The plaintiffs sued Rhodes & Co. for negligence in representing that the new company was credit-worthy. *Held*—by Cairns, J.—that the plaintiffs were entitled to recover damages against Rhodes & Co. because—

(i) Rhodes & Co. owed a duty of care to the plaintiffs in respect of Reid's representations acting as their servant or agent;

(ii) Rhodes & Co. were vicariously liable for the negligence of their manager who knew that the new company was not credit-worthy even though Reid and not the manager made the representation;

(iii) Sect. 6 of the Statute of Frauds Amendment Act (Lord Tenterden's Act), was not a defence to a claim based on negligence as distinct from fraud.

508. Wheat *v.* E. Lacon & Co. Ltd., [1966] 1 All E.R. 582

The manager of a public house was permitted by the owners, Lacon & Co., to take paying visitors who were accommodated in a part of the premises labelled "Private." The plaintiff's husband, while a paying visitor, was killed by a fall from a staircase in the private part of the premises. Lacon & Co. denied liability on the ground that they were not occupiers of the private part of the premises. *Held*—by the House of Lords—

(i) that the defendants retained occupation and control together with the manager;

(ii) the deceased was a visitor to whom the defendants owed a common duty of care;

(iii) on the facts the staircase, though not lit, was not dangerous if used with proper care.

Wheat's claim therefore failed because there was no breach of the duty of care.

509. Cook *v.* Broderip, *The Times*, 27th February, 1968

The owner of a flat employed an apparently competent contractor to put in a new socket. Mrs. Cook, who was a cleaner, received an electric shock caused because the socket was faulty. It appeared that the contractor had negligently failed to test the socket for reversed polarity. *Held*—by O'Connor, J.—that Major Broderip, the owner of the flat, was not vicariously liable for the contractor's negligence and was not in breach of duty under the Occupiers' Liability Act, 1957. Damages of £3,081 were awarded against the contractor who was the second defendant.

510. Bunker *v.* Charles Brand & Son, [1969] 2 All E.R. 59

The plaintiff's employers were engaged as sub-contractors by the defendants who were the main contractors for tunnelling in connection with the Victoria Line. The plaintiff was required to carry out modifications to a digging machine. He had seen the machine *in situ* and was taken to have appreciated the danger in crossing its rollers when in operation. He was injured while attempting to cross the rollers in the course of his work and sued for damages. *Held*—by O'Connor, J.—that the defendants having retained control of the tunnel and the machine were the occupiers. They were not absolved from liability under the Act of 1957 merely because of the plaintiff's knowledge of the danger. Knowledge was not assent. However, the plaintiff's damages were reduced by 50 per cent on the ground of his contributory negligence.

511. Yachuk *v.* Oliver Blais & Co. Ltd., [1949] A.C. 386

In this appeal from the Supreme Court of Canada to the Judicial Committee of the Privy Council the facts were as follows: a servant of Oliver Blais & Co. Ltd. had supplied five cents' worth of gasoline in an open lard pail to certain boys, aged nine and seven, who told him that they needed it for their mother's car, which had run out of petrol down the road. In fact they wanted it for a game of Red Indians. The boys dipped a bullrush into the pail and lit it. This set fire to the petrol in the pail and the boy Yachuck was seriously injured. The Judicial Committee *held* that the company was liable for the negligence of its servant in allowing the boys to take away the gasoline. The question of contributory negligence did not arise, because there was no evidence that the infants appreciated the dangerous quality of gasoline. The company was fully responsible even though the boys had resorted to deceit to overcome the supplier's scruples.

512. Gough *v.* National Coal Board, [1954] 1 Q.B. 191

The defendants were owners of a colliery which included a small railway which was constantly in use. The railway lines were not fenced or guarded, although there were houses on both sides. The public had for a long time been permitted to cross the lines, and children often played on the wagons, although the defendants' servants had been told to keep children off. The plaintiff, a boy aged six and a half, was seriously injured when he jumped off a wagon on which he had been riding. At the trial the boy admitted that he knew he was not supposed to ride on the wagons, and that his father had threatened to punish him if he did. Nevertheless it was *held* that the defendants were liable. The fact that children had for many years played near the railway made them licensees, and although the boy was strictly speaking a trespasser as regards the wagon, he was allured by the slow-moving wagons which the defendants knew were an attraction to children.

512*a*. *Herrington* v. *British Railways Board*, [1971] 2 W.L.R. 477

In this case the Court of Appeal *held* that by allowing the fence bounding a live electrified railway line to fall into disrepair, the Board had shown a reckless disregard towards a child trespasser who got on to the line and was injured. There was evidence to show that the master at a local station knew that children had been seen on the line but had not inspected the fence. Reckless disregard for a trespasser's safety remains the test of an occupier's liability to a trespasser. (See also case No. 653.)

513. Mourton *v.* Poulter, [1930] 2 K.B. 183

The owner of certain land wished to carry out building operations on it, but before he could so do, it was necessary to fell a large elm tree. The land was unfenced, and children of the locality were in the habit of using it as a playground. During the process of felling, a large number of children gathered near the tree, and Poulter, who had been employed to fell the tree, warned the children of the danger likely to arise when the tree came down. He failed to repeat the warning when the tree was about to fall, and the plaintiff, a boy of ten, was crushed by the falling tree. *Held*—The defendant was liable. Even though the children were trespassers, he owed them a duty to give adequate warning.

514. Griffiths *v.* Liverpool Corporation, [1966] 2 All E.R. 1015

The plaintiff tripped and fell on a flagstone which rocked on its centre. In this action against the highway authority for breach of Sect. 1(1) of the Highways (Miscellaneous Provisions) Act, 1961, it appeared that a regular system of inspection was desirable but was not carried out because the authority could not get tradesmen to put right faults discovered. The present fault could, however, have been put right by a labourer and no shortage of labourers was alleged. *Held*—by The Court of Appeal—the authority had not brought itself within the statutory defence in Sect. 1(2) and damages should be awarded.

515. Daily Mirror Newspapers *v.* Gardner, [1968] 2 All E.R. 163

The executive committee of the retailers' federation recommended their members to boycott the *Daily Mirror* for one week after that newspaper had announced that the retailers' discount rate was to be reduced when the price of the newspaper was increased. The newspaper asked for interlocutory injunctions requiring the committee to communicate with their members and withdraw the recommendation on the grounds—

(i) that it was an unlawful interference with the newspaper's contracts with the wholesalers because the wholesalers would not want to take copies of the *Daily Mirror* if the retailers would not take it; and

(ii) that it was equivalent to an agreement contrary to the public interest within Sect. 21 (1) of the Restrictive Trades Practices Act, 1956.

Held—by the Court of Appeal—that a sufficient *prima facie* case had been made out on both grounds and the injunctions would be granted.

516. Emerald Construction Co. Ltd. *v.* Lowthian, [1966] 1 All E.R. 1013

Trade Union officials took action to hamper the work of a building firm, contending that the firm should employ its labour direct and not on a "labour only" sub-contracting system. The union objection to this method of contracting for labour is that the men are not servants of the contractor and the contractor has therefore the advantage of employing without the corresponding obligations, e.g. redundancy payments, which would arise in respect of a servant.

The union did not know until the action had been commenced that the subcontract gave the men a right to end it if the building firm did not make reasonable progress with the job. The builders asked for an interlocutory injunction to restrain union officials from attempting to terminate the subcontract. *Held*—by the Court of Appeal—that a case had been made out for an interlocutory injunction. An action for inducement to commit a breach of contract will lie even if the defendant is not aware of its precise terms if the facts show that he intended to have the contract terminated by breach or otherwise. The case also decided that a "labour only" subcontract was not a "contract of employment" within the Trade Disputes Acts, 1906 and 1965.

517. Lumley v. Gye (1853), 2 E. & Bl. 216

The plaintiff, who was the manager of an opera house, made a contract with a *prima donna* Johanna Wagner for her exclusive services for a period of time. Gye induced Johanna Wagner to break her operatic engagement with the plaintiff and sing for him. It was *held* that whatever might have been the origin of the right to sue in such cases as this, it was not now confined to actions by masters for the enticement of their servants but extended to wrongful interference with any contract of personal service.

518. J. T. Stratford and Son v. Lindley, [1964] 3 All E.R. 102

The plaintiff company sued the officers or a watermen's union who, in order to obtain union recognition in a subsidiary company of the plaintiffs, had put an embargo on work connected with the plaintiff company but not in regard to the subsidiary. The object of the officers of the union was to use their power to the best advantage and so they directed the embargo at the main company rather than the subsidiary in which they wanted recognition. The terms and conditions of employment of the company's employers were not in dispute. The intended and natural result of the embargo was to induce breaches of the contracts of persons hiring barges from the plaintiff company (although no direct approach was made to such persons), because no one would work the plaintiff company's barges. Furthermore the action of the union officials necessarily involved inducing breaches of contract between their members and the company. On an application for an injunction it was *held*—by the House of Lords—

(i) that there was a *prima facie* case of wrongful interference with the main company's business;

(ii) that there was no "trade dispute" within the meaning of the Trade Disputes Act, 1906, this was merely an inter-union dispute about recognition;

(iii) the contracts interfered with, i.e. barge-hiring contracts, were not contracts of employment so that Sects. 1 and 3 of the Trade Disputes Act, 1906, did not apply (*per* Lord Pearce).

519. Torquay Hotel Co. Ltd. v. Cousins, [1969] 2 W.L.R. 289

The plaintiffs were the owners of the Imperial Hotel, Torquay and the defendants were Mr. Frank Cousins, the General Secretary of the Transport and General Workers' Union together with certain other officials of that union and the union itself.

Hotel workers in Torquay had not in the past been very keen on joining trade unions but those who wished to join a union had become members of the National Union of General and Municipal Workers. This union held the field in Torquay until 1967 but at that time the Transport Union started to recruit members in the hotels at Torquay and by December, 1967, they had recruited 400 members. A local branch of the Transport Union was formed on 1st January, 1968. During the week beginning 23rd January, 1968, the district secretary of the Transport Union tried to achieve recognition of that union at the Torbay Hotel but the managing director refused because he said he was in active negotiation with the Municipal Workers' Union.

A strike was then called at the Torbay Hotel which was picketed by members of the Transport Union. Fuel oil supplies to the hotel were cut off because the oil tanker drivers, most of whom were members of the defendant union, would not pass the pickets. These events were publicised in the Press, as also were some remarks about the need to make a stand made by Mr. Chapman, the manager of the plaintiff's hotel, the Imperial, none of whose employees were members of the Transport Union.

Members of the Transport Union then picketed the Imperial Hotel and the officials of that union caused tanker drivers to refuse to deliver fuel to the hotel and warned Esso, the hotel's regular suppliers, and Alternative Fuels Ltd., who had made one delivery after dark when the pickets had gone home, that there would be trouble if supplies were delivered. As a result Esso did not fulfil their contractual obligation to deliver and Alternative Fuels Ltd. could not make further deliveries. The contract with Esso had a *force majeure* clause which provided that Esso should not be liable for non-delivery if an emergency arose. The defendant union refused to comply with a demand for an undertaking to withdraw the "blacking" of the Imperial Hotel and so the plaintiffs issued a writ claiming, *inter alia*, injunctions against the defendant union and damages and injunctions against individual union officials for conspiracy, intimidation, wrongful procurement of a breach of contract and for actionable interferance with subsisting trade or contractual relations. The defendants relied, *inter alia*, on Sects. 3 and 4(1) of the Trade Disputes Act 1906. At first instance Stamp, J. granted the plaintiffs interlocutory injunctions against the defendants, one of the grounds being that the defendants had violated the plaintiff's contractual rights with Esso and were threatening those with Alternative Fuels, and that, even though no breach of contract was involved with Esso in view of the *force majeure* clause, such interference was tortious. *Held*—by the Court of Appeal (in dismissing the defendants' appeal, save in respect of the injunctions against the defendant union)—

(a) As the plaintiffs employed no members of the defendant union and the defendants' acts were directed against the manager of the Imperial Hotel, such acts were not in furtherance of a trade dispute within the meaning of the Trade Disputes Act 1906.

In my opinion, there was at the material times a trade dispute between the union and the Torbay Hotel: none between the union and the Imperial Hotel proprietors. Nor do I think that the "blacking" of the Imperial is properly to be regarded as an act done in furtherance of the Torbay dispute. Any dispute between the union and Mr. Chapman, or his company, was a personal dispute: a union may have a dispute with an individual whose view about the merits of a trade dispute or an issue in that dispute the union wishes to controvert or cause to be disclaimed. Yet there may be in such a case between the same parties no trade dispute as defined in Section 3, which stresses primarily the characteristic of a dispute with an employer;

neither Chapman nor the Hotel employed T.G.W.U. members. In the present case I reserve my opinion upon the question whether there can ever be a trade dispute within the section with any person who is not an employer of a member or members of the union claiming to be in dispute with him: as at present advised I think not."

(*Per* Winn L.J.)

(*b*) The *force majeure* clause did not mean that Esso's failure to deliver was not a breach of contract, but simply that no liability arose upon that breach. In consequence the defendants were liable for their direct interference when they contracted the oil companies. (*Per* Russell and Winn, L.JJ.)

(*c*) The defendants had directly interfered with the plaintiffs' rights under the contracts with the oil companies and it did not matter whether or not a breach of contract actually resulted. Interference causing a breach was to be equated with interference which did not. In both cases *direct* interference was actionable, unless justified, while *indirect* interference was actionable only if the means used were unlawful. "The principle of *Lumley* v. *Gye*, 1853,[517] is that each of the parties to a contract has a 'right to performance' of it: and it is wrong for another to procure one of the parties to break it or not to perform it. The principle was extended a step further by Lord Macnaghten in *Quinn* v. *Leathem*, [1901], A.C. 495, so that each of the parties has a right to have his 'contractual relations' with the other duly observed. 'It is,' he said at p. 510, 'a violation of legal right to interfere with contractual relations recognised by law if there be no sufficient justification for the interference.' That statement was adopted and applied by a strong board of the Privy Council in *Jasperson* v. *Dominion Tobacco Co.*, [1923] A.C. 709. It included Viscount Haldane and Lord Sumner. The time has come when the principle should be further extended to cover 'deliberate and direct interference with the execution of a contract without that causing any breach.' That was a point left open by Lord Reid in *Stratford (J.T.) & Sons Ltd.* v. *Lindley*, 1965.[518] But the common law would be seriously deficient if it did not condemn such interference. It is this very case. The principle can be subdivided into three elements:

First, there must be *interference* in the execution of a contract. The interference is not confined to the procurement of a *breach* of contract. It extends to a case where a third person *prevents* or *hinders* one party from performing his contract, even though it be not a breach.

Second, the interference must be deliberate. The person must know of the contract or, at any rate, turn a blind eye to it and intend to interfere with it: see *Emerald Construction Co.* v. *Lowthian*, 1966.[516]

Third, the interference must be *direct*. Indirect interference will not do. Thus a man who "corners the market" in a commodity may well know that it may prevent others from performing their contracts, but he is not liable to an action for so doing. A trade union official, who calls a strike on proper notice, may well know that it will prevent the employers from performing their contracts to deliver goods, but he is not liable in damages for calling it. *Indirect* interference is only unlawful if unlawful means are used. . . . A trade union official is only in the wrong when he procures a contracting party *directly* to break his contract, or when he does it indirectly *by unlawful means*. . . . This point about unlawful means is of particular importance when a place is declared "black". At common law it often involves the use of unlawful means. Take the Imperial Hotel. When it was declared "black", it meant that the drivers of the tankers would not take oil to the hotel. The drivers would thus be induced to break their contracts of employment. That would be unlawful at common law. The only case in which "blacking" of such a kind is lawful is when it is done "in contemplation or furtherance of a trade dispute", . . . for, in that event, the act of inducing a breach of a contract of employment is a lawful act which is not actionable at the suit of any one; . . . Seeing that the act is lawful, it must, I think, be lawful for the trade union officials to tell the employers and their customers about it. And this is so, even though it does mean that those people are compelled to break their commercial contracts. The interference with the commercial contracts is only indirect, and not direct: . . . So, if there had been a "trade dispute" in this case, I think it would have protected the trade union officials when they informed Esso that the dispute with Imperial was an "official dispute" and said that the hotel was "blacked". (*Per* Lord Denning, MR.)

(*d*) Since Sect. 4(1) of the Trade Disputes Act 1906 prohibited both an action for damages and an injunction in respect of torts by or on behalf of a trade union, the injunction against the defendant union must be discharged.

520. Rookes *v.* Barnard, [1964] 1 All E.R. 367

Rookes, who was employed in the design office of B.O.A.C., resigned from membership of his trade union. Under an agreement made in 1949 between B.O.A.C. and its employees it was provided that no lockout or strike should take place and any disputes should be referred to arbitration. This agreement formed part of each contract of employment. Rookes' office was subject to a "closed-shop" agreement and when he refused to re-join the union certain officials of the union served notice on B.O.A.C. that unless Rookes was removed they would withdraw the labour of their members, and would not go to arbitration. They were thus in breach of their contract. As a result B.O.A.C. lawfully terminated Rookes' contract of service after giving a much longer period of notice than the contract required. Rookes brought an action for damages against the defendants for using unlawful means to induce B.O.A.C. to terminate the contract of service with him and/or conspiring to have him dismissed by threatening B.O.A.C. with strike action if he were retained. A jury awarded Rookes £7,500 damages on the basis of a direction in the summing up that any deliberate illegality might be punished by exemplary damages. The Court of Appeal reversed the decision holding that, although the tort of intimidation existed, it did not cover threat to break a contract. Rookes appealed to the House of Lords and the defendants cross-appealed on the question of damages. The House of Lords allowed the appeal and the cross-appeal and ordered a new trial on the question of damages, making the following decisions—

(i) That on the facts the defendants had committed the tort of intimidation.

(ii) That Sect. 1 of the Trade Disputes Act, 1906, afforded no defence, because the tort could have been committed by one person and if it had been it would have been actionable. *N.B.* Sect. 1 of the Act of 1906 provided—

. . . that an act done in pursuance of an agreement or combination of two or more persons shall, if done in furtherance or in contemplation of a trade dispute, not be actionable unless the act, if done without any such agreement or combination, would be actionable.

(iii) That Sect. 3 of the Trades Disputes Act, 1906, did not protect the defendants because their interference with Rookes' employment was brought about by unlawful intimidation. (Lord Evershed, *dubutante.*) *N.B.* Sect. 3 of the Act of 1906 provided—

An act done in contemplation or furtherance of a trade dispute shall not be actionable on the ground only that it induces some other person to break a contract of employment, or that there is interference with the trade, business, or employment of some other person, or with the right of some other person to dispose of his capital and his labour as he wills.

(iv) That there is nothing to differentiate a threat of a breach of contract from a threat of physical violence or any other illegal threat. The nature of the threat is not material in an action for intimidation. (Lord Devlin.)

(v) Exemplary damages can be awarded only in cases of (*a*) oppressive, arbitrary or unconstitutional acts by government servants; (*b*) where the defendants' conduct had been calculated by him to make a profit for himself which might exceed the compensation payable to the plaintiff; (*c*) where expressly authorised by statute.

521. Allen *v.* Flood, [1898] A.C. 1

The plaintiffs were shipwrights engaged by the day by a concern called the Glengall Iron Company. The defendants, who were officials of a trade union, advised the manager of the company to discharge them, threatening to give proper notice of a strike if he did not. There was, however, no evidence of conspiracy, intimidation, coercion or breach of contract, though the defendants acted with malice. The plaintiffs were not engaged by the company and sued the defendants for damages. The House of Lords *held* that the plaintiffs' action failed, because the defendants had not been guilty of any wrong.

522. Crofter Hand Woven Harris Tweed Co. Ltd., *v.* Veitch, [1942] A.C. 435

Veitch and the other defendants were officials of the Transport and General Workers Union. The dockers at Stornaway on the island of Lewis were all members of the union and so were most of the employees in the spinning mills on the island. The yarn when spun in the mills was woven into tweed cloth by crofters working at home, the woven cloth being finished in the mills. The tweed thus produced was sold by the owners of the mill as Harris Tweed. The Crofter Company also produced tweed cloth but their yarn was not spun on the island but was obtained more cheaply on the mainland. This cloth was sold as Harris Tweed but did not bear the trade mark in the form of a special stamp. The mill owners making the genuine Harris Tweed were being pressed by the union to increase wages but they said that they could not accede to union requests because of the damaging competition of the Crofter Company. Consequently Veitch and others acting in combination placed an embargo on the Crofter Company's imported yarn and exported tweed by instructing dockers at Stornaway to refuse to handle these goods The dockers obeyed these instructions but were not on strike or in breach of contract. The Crofter Company sought an interdict (or injunction) against the embargo. The House of Lords *held* that the union officials were not liable in conspiracy because their purpose was to benefit the members of the union and the means employed were not unlawful.

523. Byrne *v.* Deane, [1937] 1 K.B. 818

The plaintiff was a member of a golf club in which there had been some gaming machines. The defendants, Mr. and Mrs. Deane, were proprietors of the club. As a result of a complaint being made to the police the machines were removed. Shortly afterwards, the following typewritten lampoon was placed on the wall of the club house near to the place where the machines had stood—

For many years upon this spot
You heard the sound of the merry bell
Those who were rash and those who were not,
Lost and made a spot of cash
But he who gave the game away,
May he Byrne in hell and rue the day.   Diddleramus.

The plaintiff brought this action for libel alleging that the defendants were responsible for exhibiting the lampoon, and that the lampoon was defamatory in that it suggested that he was disloyal to his fellow club members. *Held*—The words were not defamatory because the standard was the view which would be taken by right-thinking members of society, and, in the view of the court, right-thinking persons would not think less of a person who put the law into motion against wrongdoers.

524. Youssoupoff v. Metro-Goldwyn-Mayer Pictures Ltd. (1934), 50 T.L.R. 571

The plaintiff was a member of the Russian Royal House. The defendants produced in England a film dealing with the life of Rasputin who had been the adviser of the Tsarina of Russia. The film also dealt with the murder of Rasputin. In the course of the film, a lady (Princess Natasha), who was affectionate towards the murderer of Rasputin, was also represented as having been raped by Rasputin, a man of the worst possible character. The plaintiff was married to a man who was undoubtedly one of the persons concerned in the killing of Rasputin. The plaintiff alleged that because of her marriage reasonable people would think that she was the person who was so raped. The action was for libel. *Held*—The action was properly framed in libel and the plaintiff succeeded.

N.B. This case is generally accepted as authority for the view that a defamatory talking film is always libel. However the rape of Princess Natasha was in the pictorial part of the film and not on the sound track. It is also uncertain whether a plaintiff can sue for a slanderous imputation of rape without proving special damage. The Slander of Women Act, 1891, provides that the "words spoken and published . . . which impute unchastity or adultery to any woman or girl shall not require special damage to render them actionable." However lack of consent, which is essential in rape, may mean that there is no imputation of unchastity.

525. Cassidy v. Daily Mirror Newspapers Ltd., [1929] 2 K.B. 331

A man named Cassidy or Corrigan who was well known for his indiscriminate relations with women, allowed a racing photographer to take a photograph of himself and a lady, and said that she was his fiancée and that the photographer might announce his engagement. The photograph was published in the *Daily Mirror* with the following caption: "Mr. M. Corrigan, the race-horse owner, and Miss X whose engagement has been announced." The plaintiff, Cassidy's lawful wife, who was also known as Mrs. Corrigan, sued the newspaper for libel alleging as an innuendo that, if Mr. Corrigan was unmarried and able to become engaged, she must have been co-habiting with him in circumstances of immorality. *Held*—Since there was evidence that certain of her friends thought this to be so, she was entitled to damages.

526. Morgan v. Odhams Press, [1971] 2 All E.R. 1156

In 1965 *The Sun* reported that a kennel girl had been kidnapped by a dog-doping gang. In or about the relevant period various witnesses had seen her in the company of Mr. Morgan whose friend she was. The newspaper article made no mention of Mr. Morgan's name. Nevertheless he began an action against the newspaper pleading that he had been libelled by innuendo in that persons would think he was involved either in the kidnapping or the dog-doping, or both. *Held*—by the House of Lords—that—

(a) the newspaper article was not, by itself, capable of being so understood;

(b) an article to be defamatory of a person need not contain a " key or pointer " showing it refers to him. Evidence is admissible to import a defamatory meaning to otherwise innocent words.

527. Tolley v. J. S. Fry & Sons Ltd., [1931] A.C. 333

The plaintiff was a well-known amateur golfer. The defendants published an advertisement without the plaintiff's consent containing his picture and underneath the following words—

> The caddy to Tolley said, "Oh Sir,
> Good shot, Sir! That ball, see it go, Sir.
> My word, how it flies,
> Like a cartet of Fry's,
> They're handy, they're good, and priced low, Sir."

The plaintiff brought an action for libel, alleging an innuendo. It was said that a person reading the advertisement would assume that the plaintiff had been paid for allowing the use of his name in it, and that in consequence he had prostituted his amateur status as a golfer. *Held*—The evidence showed that the advertisement was capable of this construction and the plaintiff was awarded damages.

528. Sim v. Stretch (1936), 52 T.L.R. 669

The defendant had encouraged the plaintiff's housemaid to leave the plaintiff's employ and re-enter the defendant's. The defendant later sent the following telegram to the plaintiff: "Edith has resumed her services with us to-day. Please send her possessions and the money you borrowed, also her wages." The telegram was said to impute that the plaintiff was in financial difficulties and had in consequence borrowed from his housemaid, and that he had been unable to pay her wages, and was a person of no credit. The plaintiff succeeded at first instance and in the Court of Appeal, but the House of Lords reversed the judgment, *holding* that the telegram was incapable of bearing a defamatory meaning. In the words of Lord Atkin: "It seems to me unreasonable that, when there are a number of good interpretations, the only bad one should be seized upon to give a defamatory sense to the statement." It was also in this case that Lord Atkin suggested the following test of a "defamatory" statement: "Would the words tend to lower the plaintiff in the estimation of right-thinking members of society generally?"

529. E. Hulton & Co. v. Jones, [1910] A.C. 20

A newspaper published an article descriptive of life in Dieppe in which one Artemus Jones, described as a churchwarden at Peckham, was accused of living with a mistress in France. All persons concerned contended that they were ignorant of the existence of any person of that name, and the writer of the article said that he had invented it. Unfortunately the name so chosen was that of an English barrister and journalist, and the evidence showed that those who knew him thought that the article referred to him. *Held*—The newspaper was responsible for the libel and the plaintiff was awarded damages.

N.B. In cases of this kind the defence of offer of amends may be available under Sect. 4 of the Defamation Act, 1952. However, it is by no means certain that it would have been available on the actual facts of this case, because Sect. 4 applies only where the defendant can show that he and his servants or agents have taken all reasonable care with regard to the publication. On the facts of *Hulton* v. *Jones* it seems that the publication was attended by some carelessness.

530. Knupffer v. London Express Newspaper Ltd., [1944] A.C. 116

The plaintiff was head in the United Kingdom of a Russian Refugee organisation, active in France and the United States of America, but having only twenty-four members in England. An article in the newspaper ascribed Fascism to this "minute body established in France and the United States of America," but without mentioning the English branch. *Held*—The article was not defamatory of the plaintiff since he was not marked out by it, even assuming that it was defamatory to call someone a Fascist.

531. Alexander v. The North Eastern Railway Co. (1865), 6 B. & S. 340

The defendants published the following notice—

> North Eastern Railway. Caution. J. Alexander, manufacturer and general merchant, Trafalgar Street, Leeds, was charged before the magistrates of Darlington on 28th September, for riding on a train from Leeds, for which his ticket was not available, and refusing to pay the proper fare. He was convicted in the penalty of £9 1s., including costs, or three weeks' imprisonment.

In this action for libel, the plaintiff contended that the defence of justification could not lie because, although he had been convicted as stated, the alternative prison sentence was fourteen days not three weeks. *Held*—The substitution of three weeks for a fortnight did not make the statement libellous. It could be justified, since the rest of it was true.

532. Goody v. Odhams Press Ltd., [1966] 3 All E.R. 369

The plaintiff had been convicted of taking part in the "Great Train Robbery" and brought a libel action against the defendants for an article in their newspaper after the trial describing his alleged part in that crime. *Held*—the defence of justification failed because the fact that one court had been satisfied as to the guilt of the plaintiff in a criminal matter was not admissible as evidence of his guilt in another trial, and the defendants would have to prove his guilt in order to justify the statements in the article. It was not enough to prove the conviction. (*Hollington* v. *Hewthorn*, [1943] K.B. 587, followed but disapproved.) However, the plaintiff's previous convictions within the previous sixteen years were cogent evidence of his bad reputation and were admissible in mitigation of damages. Nominal damages were awarded.

533. London Artists v. Littler, [1969] 2 All E.R. 193

In 1965 four of the principal actors and actresses in a play called *The Right Honourable Gentleman* simultaneously wrote to the defendant, who was the producer of the play, terminating their engagements by four weeks' formal notice. This was, of course, highly unusual and the defendant wrote to the actors and actresses concerned wrongly accusing the plaintiffs, who were their agents, of conspiracy to close down the play. The defendant also communicated the letter to the press. The defendant was now sued for libel. It was *held*—by the Court of Appeal—that he had libelled the plaintiffs because although the subject matter of the allegations was of public interest, i.e. the fate of the play, the defence of fair comment did not apply to the allegation of a plot which was an allegation of fact. The allegation of a plot was defamatory and had not been justified. In fact it seemed that all the actors and actresses involved had their own good and different reasons for leaving the play. There was no evidence of combination.

534. London Association for the Protection of Trade *v.* Greenlands, [1916] 2 A.C. 15

The respondents were a limited company carrying on business as drapers and general furnishers at Hereford. The appellants were an unincorporated association consisting of about 6,300 traders and had, as one of their objects, the making of private inquiries as to the means, respectability and trustworthiness of individuals and firms. A member of the association was about to sell goods to the respondents and he asked the association to report on them, and particularly to say whether the respondents were a good risk for credit of between £20 and £30. In the report submitted, the association declared that the respondents were a fair trade risk for the sum mentioned, but said that they had heavy mortgages charged on their assets, and that the assets barely covered the loans. In fact the mortgages were secured by a charge upon the real and leasehold property only, and all other assets were entirely free from any mortgage whatever, and constituted a large and valuable fund. The respondents were originally the plaintiffs in an action for libel contained in the statement about the mortgages, and the statement that they were only good for credit of between £20 and £30. *Held*—The occasion was privileged and thus the respondents had no claim in the absence of malice, which they had not proved. Judgment was therefore given for the appellants.

535. Osborn *v.* Thomas Boulter & Son, [1930] 2 K.B. 226

The plaintiff, a publican, wrote a letter to the defendants, his brewers, complaining of the quality of the beer. The defendants sent one of their employèes to investigate and report. After receiving the report, Mr. Boulter dictated a letter to his typist in which he suggested that the plaintiff had been adding water to the beer, and pointing out the penalties attaching to this if the plaintiff was caught. The plaintiff sued, alleging publication to the typist and certain clerks. *Held*—The occasion was privileged, and since the plaintiff could not prove malice in the defendants, his action failed.

536. Beach *v.* Freeson, [1971] 2 W.L.R. 805

A member of Parliament wrote to the Law Society complaining of the conduct of a firm of solicitors reported to him by his constituents. He also sent a copy of the letter to the Lord Chancellor. *Held*—by Geoffrey Lane, J.—that both publications were protected by qualified privilege. The privilege arose out of a Member of Parliament's duty to his constituents and the responsibilities of the Law Society and the Lord Chancellor.

537. Egger *v.* Viscount Chelmsford, [1964] 3 All E.R. 406

Mrs. Egger, a judge of Alsatian dogs, was on the list of judges of the Kennel Club, and Miss Ross, the secretary of a dog club in Northern Ireland, wrote to the Kennel Club asking them to approve of Mrs. Egger as a judge of Alsatians at a show. The assistant secretary of the Kennel Club, C. A. Burney, wrote to

Miss Ross to say that the committee could not approve the appointment. Mrs. Egger brought an action for libel against the ten members of the committee and the assistant secretary on the grounds that the letter reflected on her competence and integrity. There were two long trials at both of which the judge ruled that the occasion was privileged. The jury disagreed the first time, but at the second trial the jury found that the letter was defamatory and that five members of the committee were actuated by malice but three were not. The other two had meanwhile died. The judge gave judgment against all the defendants including the assistant secretary. *Held*—on appeal—The defence of qualified privilege is a defence for the individual who is sued, and not a defence for the publication. It is quite erroneous to say that it is attached to the publication. The three committee members innocent of·malice were entitled to protection and were not liable. The assistant secretary also had an independent and individual privilege, and was not responsible or liable for the tort of those members of the committee who had acted with malice. Even in a joint tort, the tort is the separate act of each individual; each is severally answerable for it; and each is severally entitled to his own defence.

538. Chapman *v.* Lord Ellesmere and Others, [1932] 2 K.B. 431

The plaintiff was a trainer and one of his horses, after winning a race, was found to be doped. An inquiry was held by the Stewards of the Jockey Club, as a result of which they decided to disqualify the horse for future racing, and to warn the plaintiff off Newmarket Heath. The decision was published in the *Racing Calendar*. The plaintiff contended that the words were defamatory because they implied that he had doped the horse. The defendants, who were the proprietors of the *Racing Calendar*, contended that the words were not defamatory, and meant simply that the plaintiff had been warned off for not protecting the horse against doping. Evidence showed that it was a condition of a trainer's licence that the withdrawal of that licence should appear in the *Racing Calendar*, which was also to be the recognised vehicle of communication for all matters concerning infringement of rules. *Held*—The plaintiff being bound by the terms of his licence, the doctrine of *volenti non fit injuria* applied as regards publication in the *Racing Calendar*, so that the plaintiff had no cause of action.

539. Davis *v.* Rubin, [1967] 112 S.J. 51

The plaintiffs were chartered accountants of good reputation and they wished to buy the lease of business premises. The defendants, who were the landlords, wrote to the holder of the lease saying that they would not accept the plaintiffs if the lease was assigned and referred in a defamatory fashion to the plaintiffs' business and references. The plaintiffs claimed damages in respect of the libel published in the letter, and were awarded £4,000 each. The Court of Appeal, allowing the defendants' appeal, said that the damages were "excessive, extravagant and exorbitant." There had been publication to one person only and there was no evidence that the plaintiffs' reputation had been diminished in the minds of other persons. A reasonable sum would not have exceeded £1,000 each and a new trial was ordered.

540. Emanuel *v.* Greater London Council (1970), 114 S.J. 653

A contractor employed by the Ministry of Public Building and Works removed prefabricated bungalows from the Council's land. The contractor lit a fire and negligently allowed sparks to spread to the plaintiff's land where buildings and goods were damaged. The plaintiff claimed against the G.L.C. and it was *held*—by James, J.—that—

(*a*) on the facts the Council remained in occupation of the site;

(*b*) the contractor was not a "stranger" to the Council since they retained a power of control over his activities; and

(*c*) although the Council had not been negligent and were not vicariously liable for the contractors' negligence since they did not employ him, they were strictly liable under *Rylands* v. *Fletcher* for the escape of fire.

541. Read *v.* J. Lyons & Co. Ltd., [1947] A.C. 156

The appellant was employed by the Ministry of Supply as an Inspector of Munitions in the respondent's munitions factory. In the course of her employment there she was injured by the explosion of a shell which was in course of manufacture. She did not allege negligence on the part of the defendants, but based her claim on *Rylands* v. *Fletcher*. The trial judge found that there was liability under the rule, but the Court of Appeal and the House of Lords reversed this decision, *holding* that the rule did not apply since there had been no escape of the thing that inflicted the injury. In the words of Viscount Simon, L.C., "Escape for the purpose of applying the proposition in *Rylands* v. *Fletcher* means escape from a place which the defendant has occupation of, or control over, to a place which is outside his occupation or control." It was also suggested in this case that the rule in *Rylands* v. *Fletcher* does not extend to personal injuries, but only to injury to property.

542. Charing Cross Electricity Supply Co. *v.* Hydraulic Power Co., [1914] 3 K.B. 772

The defendants' water mains under a public street burst and damaged the plaintiffs' cables which were also laid under the street. *Held*—The defendants were liable under the rule in *Rylands* v. *Fletcher*, because the rule was not confined to wrongs between owners of adjacent land and does not depend on ownership of land. Here it could be applied to owners of adjacent chattels.

543. Attorney-General *v.* Corke, [1933] Ch. 89

The defendant was the owner of disused brickfields, and he permitted a number of gypsies to occupy them and live in caravans and tents. The gypsies threw slop water about in the neighbourhood of the fields and accumulated all sorts of filth thereabouts. The court *held* that *Rylands* v. *Fletcher* applied, and an injunction was granted against the defendant. While it was not unlawful to license caravan dwellers, it was abnormal use of land, since such persons often have habits of life which are offensive to those persons with fixed homes.

544. Perry *v.* Kendricks Transport, [1956] 1 W.L.R. 85

The defendants had placed on their parking ground a disused coach, having drained off the petrol and screwed a cap over the entrance pipe. The plaintiff, a boy of ten, was injured as he approached the parking ground by an explosion of petrol fumes from the coach. The trial judge found that the cap had been removed by some unknown person, and that a lighted match had been thrown in the tank, probably by one of two boys who hurried away as the plaintiff approached. The Court of Appeal *held* that the facts were within the rule in

Rylands v. *Fletcher*, but the defendants were not liable because the escape was caused by the act of a stranger.

545. Giles *v.* Walker (1890), 24 Q.B.D. 656

The defendant wished to redeem certain forest land and ploughed it up. Thistles grew up on the land and thistle-seed was blown in large quantities by the wind from the defendant's land to that of the plaintiff. *Held*—There was no duty as between adjoining occupiers to cut things such as thistles which are the natural growth of the soil; therefore the defendant was not liable. Presumably if a person deliberately set thistles on his land he would be liable under the rule in *Rylands* v. *Fletcher*, for it is not usual to cultivate weeds on one's land.

N.B. An action for nuisance would probably have succeeded here, because a person is liable for a nuisance on his land (even if he has not caused it) if he lets it continue.

546. Davey *v.* Harrow Corporation, [1957] 2 All E.R. 305

The roots of the defendants' elm trees spread to the plaintiff's land and caused damage to the plaintiff's property. *Held*—The defendants were liable in nuisance, whether the trees were self-sown or not. It was no defence to an action for nuisance that the thing causing the nuisance was naturally on the defendants' land, though it might be a defence to liability under the rule in *Rylands* v. *Fletcher*.

547. Greenock Corporation *v.* Caledonian Railway Co., [1917] A.C. 556

The corporation, in laying out a park, constructed a concrete paddling pool for children in the bed of a stream, thereby altering its course and natural flow. Owing to rainfall of extraordinary violence, the stream overflowed and poured down the street, flooding the railway company's premises. The House of Lords *held* that this was not an act of God and the corporation was liable. The House of Lords indicated the restricted range of the defence of act of God and of the decision in *Nichols* v. *Marsland* (1876),[402] distinguishing that case on the grounds that whereas in *Nichols* v. *Marsland* the point at issue was the liability for storing water in artificial lakes, the point here was interference with the natural course of a stream, and anyone so interfering must provide even against exceptional rainfall.

548. Rickards *v.* Lothian, [1913] A.C. 263

The defendant was the occupier of business premises and leased part of the second floor to the plaintiff. On the fourth floor was a men's cloakroom with a wash basin. The cloakroom was provided for the use of tenants and persons in their employ. The plaintiff's stock in trade was found one morning seriously damaged by water which had seeped through the ceiling from the wash basin on the fourth floor. Examination showed that the waste pipe had been plugged with various articles such as nails, penholders, string and soap, and the water tap had been turned full on. The defendant's caretaker found the cloakroom in proper order at 10.20 p.m. the previous evening. *Held*—The defendant was not liable under the rule in *Rylands* v. *Fletcher* because the damage had been caused by the act of a stranger.

549. Peters *v.* Prince of Wales Theatre (Birmingham) Ltd., [1943] K.B. 73

The defendants leased to the plaintiff a shop in a building which contained a theatre. In the latter there was, to the plaintiff's knowledge, a sprinkler system installed as a precaution against fire and the system extended to the plaintiff's shop. In a thaw, following a severe frost, water poured from the sprinklers in the defendants' rehearsal room into the plaintiff's shop and damaged his stock. The plaintiff claimed damages for negligence, and under *Rylands* v. *Fletcher*. *Held*—There was no negligence on the part of the defendants and there was no liability under *Rylands* v. *Fletcher*, because the sprinkler had been installed for the common benefit of the plaintiff and defendants.

THE LAW OF PROPERTY

550. Re Draper's Conveyance, [1967] 3 All E.R. 853

In 1951 a house was conveyed to a husband and wife in fee simple as joint tenants at law *and* of the proceeds of the trust for sale. In November, 1965, the wife was granted a decree nisi of divorce and this was made absolute in March, 1966. In February, 1966, she applied by summons under Sect. 17 of the Married Women's Property Act, 1882, for an order that the house be sold and in her affidavit asked that the proceeds of sale be distributed equally between her husband and herself. The court made such an order in May, 1966, and in August, 1966, a further order was made under the Act of 1882 that the former husband give up possession of the house. In spite of the order the former husband remained in possession until January, 1967, when a writ of possession was executed. Four days later he died without having made a will. The former wife now applied to the court to determine whether she held the proceeds of any sale absolutely (which would have been the case if she and her former husband had been joint tenants at his death) or for herself and the deceased's estate as tenants in common in equal shares (which would have been the case if there had been severance.) *Held*—Severance of a joint tenancy in a matrimonial home may be effected by the wife's issue of a summons under Sect. 17 of the Married Women's Property Act, 1882, and her affidavit in support. The affidavit had stated the former wife's wish for severance and had operated accordingly. Therefore she held any proceeds of sale as trustee for herself and the estate of her former husband as tenants in common in equal shares.

551. Shell-Mex and B.P. Ltd. *v.* Manchester Garages Ltd., [1971] 1 All E.R. 841

The plaintiffs, by an agreement contained in a document called a licence, let the defendants into occupation of a petrol filling station for one year. The parties had some disagreements during this time and at the end of the year the plaintiffs asked the defendants to leave. The defendants refused claiming that the agreement gave them a business tenancy protected by the Landlord and Tenant Act, 1954, Part II, which deals with the method of terminating business tenancies. This method had not been followed by the plaintiffs. *Held*—by the Court of Appeal—it was open to parties to an agreement to decide whether that agreement should constitute a lease or a licence but the fact that it was called a licence was not conclusive. However, in this case it was a licence because the plaintiffs retained, under the agreement, the right to visit the premises whenever they liked and to exercise general control over the layout, decoration and equipment of the filling station. These rights were inconsistent with the grant of a tenancy.

552. Walsh *v*. Lonsdale (1882), 21 Ch.D. 9

The defendant agreed in writing to grant a seven years' lease of a mill to the plaintiff at a rent payable one year in advance. The plaintiff entered into possession without any formal lease having been granted, and he paid his rent quarterly and not in advance. Subsequently the defendant demanded a year's rent in advance, and as the plaintiff refused to pay, the defendant distrained on his property. At common law the plaintiff was a tenant from year to year because no formal lease had been granted, and as such his rent was not payable in advance. The plaintiff argued that the legal remedy of distress was not available to the defendant. *Held*—As the agreement was one of which the court could grant specific performance, and as equity regarded as done that which ought to be done, the plaintiff held on the same terms as if a lease had been granted. Therefore the distress was valid.

553. Hill *v*. Tupper (1863), 2 H. & C. 121

Hill was the lessee of land on the bank of a canal. The land and the canal were owned by the lessor, and Hill was granted the sole and exclusive right of putting pleasure boats on the canal. Later Tupper, without authority, put rival pleasure boats on the canal. Hill now sued Tupper for the breach of a so-called easement granted by the owner of the canal. *Held*—The right to put pleasure boats on the canal was not an interest in property which the law could recognise as attaching to land. It was in the nature of a contractual licence which could not be enforced against the whole world. Tupper could have been sued by the owner of the canal, or by Hill, as lessee, if he had also been granted a lease of the canal.

554. Bass *v*. Gregory (1890), 25 Q.B.D. 481

The plaintiffs were the owners of a public house in Nottingham, and the defendant was the owner of some cottages and a yard adjoining the plaintiffs' premises. The plaintiffs claimed to be entitled, by user as of right, to have the cellar of their public house ventilated by means of a hole or shaft cut from the cellar to an old well situated in the yard occupied by the defendant. The plaintiffs claimed an injunction to prevent the defendant from continuing to block the passage of air from the well. *Held*—The right having been established, an injunction would be granted because the access of air to the premises came through a strictly defined channel, and it was possible to establish it as an easement.

N.B. In *Bryant* v. *Lefever* (1879), 4 C.P.D. 172 the plaintiff and defendant occupied adjoining premises, and the plaintiff's complaint was that the defendant, in rebuilding his house, carried up the building beyond its former height and so checked the access of the draught of air to the plaintiff's chimneys. The Court of Appeal held that the right claimed could not exist at law, because it was an attempt to claim special rights over the general current of air which is common to all mankind.

555. Crow *v*. Wood, [1970] 3 All E.R. 425

This case arose out of damage done on a farm in Yorkshire by sheep which strayed on to it from an adjoining moor. The owner of the sheep, who was the owner of another farm adjoining the moor, raised, as a defence against an action for trespass, an obligation on the plaintiff to fence her own property to keep the sheep out. It was *held*—by the Court of Appeal—that a duty to fence existed as an easement and that it had passed under Sect. 62 of the Law of Property Act, 1925, when the defendant purchased his farm, even though his conveyance and previous ones had made no reference to the obligation of other farmers to keep up their fences. However, the right was appurtenant to the land sold and therefore became an easement in favour of the purchaser and his successors in title.

556. Re Ellenborough Park, [1956] Ch. 131

Ellenborough Park was a piece of open land near the seafront at Weston-Super-Mare. The park and the surrounding land was jointly owned by two persons. The surrounding land was sold for building purposes, and the conveyances granted an easement over the park in favour of the owners of the houses. The owners of the houses undertook to be responsible for some of the maintenance, and the owners of the park agreed not to erect dwelling houses or buildings, other than ornamental buildings, on the park. The park was later sold, and the question of the rights of the owners or occupiers of the houses fronting on to the park to enforce their rights over the park arose. It was contended that the rights created by the conveyances were not enforceable, because they did not conform to the essential qualities of an easement, and that they gave a right of perambulation which was not a right legally capable of creation. *Held*—The rights granted to the owners of the houses were enforceable as a legal easement.

557. Phipps v. Pears, [1964] 2 All E.R. 35

A Mr. Field owned two houses, Nos. 14 and 16 Market Street, Warwick, and in 1930 he demolished No. 16 and built a new house with a wall adjacent to the existing wall of No. 14. In 1962 No. 14 was demolished under an order of Warwick Corporation, leaving exposed the wall of No. 16. This wall had never been pointed; indeed it could not have been because it was built hard up against the wall of No. 14. It was not, therefore, weatherproof, the rain got in and froze during the winter causing cracks in the wall. The plaintiff claimed for damage done, claiming an *easement of protection*. It was *held* by the Court of Appeal that there is no such easement. There is a right of support in appropriate cases, but No. 16 did not depend on No. 14 for support; the walls, though adjoining, were independent. Lord Denning, M.R., said in the course of his judgment: "A right to protection from the weather (if it exists) is entirely negative. It is a right to stop your neighbour pulling down his house. Seeing that it is a negative easement, it must be looked at with caution because the law has been very chary of creating any new negative easements. . . . If we were to stop a man pulling down his house, we would put a brake on desirable improvement. If it exposes your house to the weather, that is your misfortune. It is no wrong on his part. . . . The only way for an owner to protect himself is by getting a covenant from his neighbour that he will not pull down his house. . . . Such a covenant would be binding in contract; and it would be enforceable on any successor who took with notice of it, but it would not be binding on one who took without notice."

558. Ward v. Kirkland, [1966] 1 All E.R. 609

The wall of a cottage could only be repaired from the yard of the adjoining farm. Before 1928 both properties belonged to a rector and the tenant of the cottage repaired the wall without seeking the permission of the tenant of the farm. In that year the cottage was conveyed to a predecessor in the title of Ward and in 1942 Mrs. Kirkland became the tenant of the farm. From 1942 to 1954 work to the wall was done with her permission as tenant and in 1958 she bought the farm. In October, 1958, Ward did not make entry on to the farmyard to maintain the wall because Mrs. Kirkland would not let him enter as of right. In this action, which was brought to determine, amongst other things, whether Ward was entitled to enter the farmyard to maintain the wall and for an injunction to prevent interference with drains running from the cottage through the farmyard, it was *held* by Ungoed—Thomas, J.—

(i) assuming such a right could exist as an easement it would not be defeated on the ground that it would amount to possession or joint possession of the defendant's property;

(ii) that although such a right was not created by implication because it was not "continuous and apparent" yet the advantage having in fact been enjoyed it was transformed into an easement by Sect. 62 of the Law of Property Act, 1925;

(iii) no easement had arisen by prescription because permission had been given between 1942 and 1958;

(iv) permission having been granted by the rector to Ward to lay drains from the cottage through the farmyard and Ward having incurred expense in so doing it was assumed that the permission was of indefinite duration and an injunction would be granted to prevent interference with the drains by Mrs. Kirkland.

559. Tehidy Minerals *v.* Norman, [1971] 2 W.L.R. 711

The owner of a number of farms adjoining a down claimed to be entitled to grazing rights over it. The facts of the case were as follows—

(*a*) the farms and the down had been owned by one person until 19th January, 1920;

(*b*) the down had been requisitioned by the Government on 6th October, 1941;

(*c*) during the period of requisition the owners of surrounding farms had grazed cattle on the down by arrangement with the Ministry concerned;

(*d*) on 31st December, 1960, the down was derequisitioned and the association of farms which had made the arrangements with the Ministry entered into a further arrangement with the owner of the down for the maintenance of certain fences erected by the Ministry and grazing continued but under the control of the association of farmers.

On appeal from a decision of the County Court judge that the farmers were entitled to grazing rights over the down it was *held* by the Court of Appeal—that

(*a*) as there had been no enjoyment of the grazing rights between 6th October, 1941, and 31st December, 1960, except by permission of the Ministry, the farmers could not claim thirty years prescription which the Act of 1832 required for a profit to be established by user as of right;

(*b*) despite the extreme unreality of such a presumption it must be presumed that a modern grant, since lost, had been made of grazing rights at some time between 19th January, 1920, and 6th October, 1921, i.e. twenty years before the requisition, this presumption could not be rebutted by evidence that no such grant had been made but only by evidence—of which there was none—that it could not have been made;

(c) the period of twenty years applied to profits as well as to easements for the purposes of the law of lost modern grant although the Act of 1832 provided for different periods in the two cases;

(d) only the demonstration of a fixed intention never at any time to assert the right or to attempt to transmit it to anyone else could amount to an abandonment of an easement or profit, thus the acquiescence by the farmers in the arrangement under which the association controlled the grazing for a period of time did not amount to abandonment.

560. Kelly v. Barrett, [1924] 2 Ch. 379

The owner of an estate in Hampstead developed it for building purposes. He made a new road through it, and sold plots of land along the road to a building firm who erected dwelling houses on the land. The purchasers undertook that the houses built should be used as private dwelling houses only. The owner of the estate did not retain any land except the road, which was afterwards taken over and vested in the local authority. A subsequent purchaser of two adjoining houses carried on a nursing and maternity home in them. The tenant for life under the former estate owner's will and one of the original purchasers claimed an injunction to restrain the defendant's activities. *Held*—No injunction could be granted because the agreement was not a valid building scheme, and the vendor's successor did not retain any interest capable of being affected by the restrictions.

561. Arab Bank Ltd. v. Ross, [1952] 2 Q.B. 216

The plaintiffs claimed to be holders in due course of two promissory notes made by Ross and payable to "Fathi and Faysal Nabulsy Company," a firm of which the two men named were the only partners. Ross alleged that he had been induced to make the notes by the fraud of the payees, and attempted unsuccessfully to show that the plaintiffs had knowledge of this fraud and had not taken the notes in good faith. The plaintiffs claimed to be holders in due course, but the point was taken that the indorsement on the notes was simply "Fathi and Faysal Nabulsy" with the omission of the word "Company." *Held*—By the Court of Appeal, that an indorsement could be valid to pass the property without being regular on the face of it. Regularity is different from validity. The Arab Bank were not holders in due course, because the indorsement was not regular, but were holders for value. Although the indorsers were in fact the only two partners, the word Company did not imply this, and therefore the indorsement was not manifestly regular by reference only to the instrument. The circumstances under which an indorsement gives rise to doubt is a practical matter and is best answered by the practice of bankers. This practice insists that the indorsement shall correspond exactly with the payee as named.

562. Diamond v. Graham, [1968] 2 All E.R. 909

A Mr. Herman was anxious to borrow the sum of £1,650 for immediate commitments and he asked a Mr. Diamond whether he would lend him that sum. Mr. Diamond agreed provided Mr. Herman could repay by the following Monday the sum of £1,665. Mr. Herman said that he would have a cheque from a Mr. Graham by that time which he would ask to be made payable to Mr. Diamond. Mr. Diamond then drew a cheque for £1,650 in favour of

Mr. Herman. Mr. Herman could not get a cheque from Mr. Graham on the following Monday because he was not available on that day. However Mr. Herman presented the cheque for payment but Mr. Diamond countermanded payment and told the bank manager not to pay it until authorised by Mr. Diamond. Some days later Mr. Herman obtained a cheque from Mr. Graham in favour of Mr. Diamond. Mr. Graham asked who was providing Mr. Herman with temporary relief and was told it was the plaintiff. Mr. Herman gave the cheque to Mr. Diamond who paid it into his bank and authorised payment of his cheque to Mr. Herman. However, the cheque drawn by Mr. Graham was dishonoured. Mr. Herman had also drawn a cheque in favour of Mr. Graham and this was also dishonoured, Mr. Diamond's cheque being the only one paid. Mr. Diamond now sued Mr. Graham on his unpaid cheque. The defendant argued that the plaintiff was not a holder for value within Sect. 27 (2) of the Bills of Exchange Act, 1882, because no value had passed between him and Mr. Graham. It was *held* by Danckwerts, L.J., that there was nothing in Sect. 27 (2) which required value to be given by the holder of a cheque so long as value had been given by someone. Here value had been given as follows—

(i) by Mr. Herman who gave his own cheque to Mr. Graham in return for Mr. Graham drawing a cheque in favour of Mr. Diamond; and

(ii) by Mr. Diamond when he released his cheque to Mr. Herman.

Thus, Mr. Diamond was a holder for value of the cheque and was entitled to judgment and the appeal must be dismissed. Diplock and Sachs, L.JJ., also dismissed the appeal.

563. Childs *v.* Monins and Bowles (1821), 2 Brod. and B. 460

The defendants were the executors of Thomas Taylor, and as such executors made a promissory note as follows: "Ringwould, December 28th, 1816, as executors to the late Thomas Taylor, of Ringwould, we severally and jointly promise to pay to Mr. Nathaniel Childs the sum of £200 on demand, together with lawful interest for the same. J. Monins, Phineas Bowles, executors." *Held*—The executors were personally liable. The words "on demand" implied that the executors had assets to satisfy the note. If they had meant to limit their liability, they should have added the words "out of the estate of Thomas Taylor." Burrough, J., said, "The insertion of the words 'as executors' cannot alter the case if, on the whole instrument, the parties appear liable."

564. Greenwood *v.* Martins Bank Ltd., [1933] A.C. 51

The appellant, who was a dairy man in Blackpool, opened with the respondents a joint account in the name of himself and his wife. Cheques drawn on this account were to bear the signatures of them both. Later on the appellant opened a further account with the respondents in his own name, though the wife kept the pass books and cheque books in respect of both accounts. In October, 1929, Greenwood asked his wife to give him a cheque, saying he wanted to draw £20 from his own account. His wife then told him that there was no money in the bank, and that she had used it to help her sister who was involved in legal proceedings over property. He asked her who had forged his signature but she would not say. However, she did ask him not to inform the respondents of the forgeries until her sister's case was over. Greenwood complied with this request until 5th June, 1930, when he discovered that there were no legal proceedings instituted by his wife's sister and that his wife had been deceiving him. He told his wife that he intended to go to the bank and reveal her forgeries, but before he actually made the visit she shot herself. Greenwood now claimed £410 6s. od. from the Bank on the grounds that this sum had been paid out of his own account and the joint account by means of forged cheques. The Bank pleaded ratification, adoption or estoppel. *Held*—There could be no ratification or adoption in this sort of case, but the essential elements of estoppel were present. The appellant's failure to inform the Bank was a representation that the cheques were good. The Bank had suffered a detriment because, if Greenwood had told the Bank when his wife first confessed to forgery, they might have brought an action against her. Under the law *existing at that time* they could not bring such an action after her death. The Bank had, therefore, a legal right to debit Greenwood's account with the amount of the forged cheques.

565. Bank of England *v.* Vagliano Bros., [1891] A.C. 107

Glyka, a clerk of Vagliano Bros., forged the signatures of Vucina and Petriai and Co. as drawer and payees of bills drawn on Vagliano Bros. The bills were accepted by Vagliano, since he knew the parties concerned and had done business with them. Glyka got possession of the bills and then forged indorsements in favour of fictitious persons whereby he was able to cash them with the Bank of England. Glyka was arrested and acknowledged the forgeries but the Bank had debited Vagliano Bros. account with the sums paid out. Vagliano now sued the Bank for repayment. *Held*—by the House of Lords on appeal— Fictitious does not mean "imaginary" but "feigned" or "counterfeit." The bills were fictitious from beginning to end and all the persons were feigned or counterfeit persons put forward as real persons, and were not less fictitious because real persons did correspond to the names used. Since bills drawn payable to a fictitious payee can be treated as payable to bearer, the Bank of England was in order in paying them and Vagliano Bros. failed in their action.

566. Baxendale *v.* Bennett (1878), 3 Q.B.D. 525 C.A.

As a result of transactions between the defendant and a Mr. Holmes, the latter drew a bill on the defendant which the defendant accepted, returning it to Holmes. In the event Holmes did not need the bill and returned it to the defendant. The bill was blank as to the drawer's name. The defendant placed the bill in an unlocked drawer in his chambers at the Temple from which it was taken by a person or persons unknown. When the bill came into the hands of the plaintiff, who was admitted to be a *bona fide* holder for value, the document had been completed by the insertion of the name of "W. Cartwright" as drawer. No such man as Cartwright was known to the defendant and the name was inserted without his knowledge and consent. The plaintiff, as indorsee, sued the defendant as acceptor. *Held*—The defendant was not liable: (i) *Per* Bramwell, L.J., because the negligence of the defendant, if any, was not the proximate or effective cause of the loss, and therefore the defendant was not estopped from denying the validity of the bill; (ii) *Per* Brett, L.J., because the bill was drawn without the authority of the defendant and the defendant had not been guilty of negligence.

567. Gardner *v.* Walsh (1855), 5 E. & B. 83

This was an action against the defendant and Elizabeth Burton and Alice Clarke on a promissory note now overdue. The defendant agreed to be jointly and severally liable to pay to the plaintiff or his order the sum of £500. Evidence showed that Elizabeth Burton was indebted to the plaintiff and she agreed to get two sureties, the defendant and Alice Clarke, to join her in a joint and several promissory note to the plaintiff. Burton and Walsh signed the note together and gave it to the plaintiff. The plaintiff got Alice Clarke to sign it although the defendant did not know there was to be another party. In this action on the note Walsh alleged that the note was avoided by virtue of a material alteration after issue, namely the addition of another party without Walsh's knowledge. *Held*—The addition of Clarke's name was a material alteration and if made after the note was issued would avoid it.

568. Burnett v. Westminster Bank, [1965] 3 All E.R. 81

P had for a number of years had accounts at the X branch and the Y branch of the defendant bank. The bank then began to issue him with cheque books with a notice on the cover to this effect "the cheques in this book will be applied to the account for which they have been prepared." In the course of a transaction P used an X branch cheque but altered it as payable at Y branch and later stopped payment by giving notice to Y branch. The cheque was electronically sorted by a computer which was not equipped to read the alteration and the cheque went to X branch, which paid it. P sued the bank for the amount of the cheque. *Held*—The bank should not have debited P's account with the cheque and he succeeded.

N.B. P seems to have succeeded largely because he was an *existing* customer and the notice was on the cover. The court did say that if such a cheque book was in fact issued to a customer on opening an account, he might be bound by it, and any customer would have been bound by a notice printed on each cheque.

569. Tournier v. National Provincial and Union Bank of England, [1924] 1 K.B. 461

Tournier banked with the defendants and, being overdrawn by £9 6s. 8d., signed an agreement to pay this off at the rate of £1 a week, disclosing the name and address of his employers, Kenyon & Co., with whom he had a three months' contract as a traveller. The agreement to repay was not observed and the bank also discovered, through another banker, that Tournier had indorsed a cheque for £45 over to a bookmaker. The manager of the bank thereupon telephoned Kenyon & Co. to find out Tournier's private address and told them that Tournier was betting heavily. Keynon & Co., as a result of this conversation, refused to renew Tournier's contract of employment. Tournier sued the bank for slander and for breach of an implied contract not to disclose the state of his account or his transactions. Judgment was entered for the defendants but the Court of Appeal allowed Tournier's appeal and ordered a new trial. Bankes, L.J., laid down four qualifications to the duty of non-disclosure: (*a*) Where the disclosure is under compulsion of law; (*b*) where there is a duty to the public to disclose; (*c*) Where the interests of the bank require disclosure; (*d*) where the disclosure is made by the express or implied consent of the customer. Atkin, L.J., said: "I do not desire to express a final opinion on the practice of bankers to give one another information as to the affairs of their respective customers, except to say it appears to me that if it is justified it must be upon the basis of an implied consent of the customer."

570. Sunderland v. Barclays Bank Ltd. (1938), *The Times*, November 25th

Mrs. Sunderland had drawn a cheque in favour of her dressmaker on an account containing insufficient funds. The cheque was returned because the bank knew she indulged in gambling and thought it unwise to grant her an overdraft. Mrs. Sunderland complained to her husband and the manager of the bank informed him, over the 'phone, of the wife's transactions with bookmakers. Mrs. Sunderland regarded this as a breach of the bank's duty of secrecy, but in fact the husband's telephone conversation was a continuation of one of her own in which she requested the bank to give an explanation to the husband concerning the return of the cheque. The bank pleaded implied authority to disclose. du Parcq, L.J., gave judgment for the defendants and affirmed the criteria relating to disclosure laid down in *Tournier v. National Provincial and Union Bank of England*, 1924.[569] However, each case must depend on its own facts. The relationship of husband and wife was a special one. The demand by Dr. Sunderland for an explanation required an account of why the bank had done what it had done. It might be said that the disclosure was with the implied consent of the customer and the interests of the bank required disclosure. Since the husband had taken over conduct of the matter, the manager was justified in thinking that the wife did not object to the offer of an explanation. If judgment had been for the plaintiff, the damages were assessed at forty shillings—nominal damages.

571. London Joint Stock Bank Ltd. v. Macmillan and Arthur, [1918] A.C. 777

Macmillan and Arthur were customers of the bank and entrusted their clerk with the duty of filling in cheques for signature. The clerk presented a cheque to a partner for signature, drawn in favour of the firm or bearer, and made out for £2 0s. 0d. in figures but with no sum written in words. The clerk then easily altered the figures to £120 0s. 0d. and wrote "one hundred and twenty pounds" in words, presenting the cheque to the bank and obtaining £120 in cash. The firm contended that the bank could only debit them with £2; the bank alleged negligence on the part of the firm. *Held*—by the House of Lords—that the relationship of banker and customer imposes a special duty of care on the customer in drawing cheques. A cheque is a mandate to the banker to pay according to the tenor. The customer must exercise reasonable care to prevent the banker being misled. If he draws a cheque in a manner which facilitates fraud, he is guilty of a breach of duty as between himself and the banker, and he will be responsible to the banker for any loss sustained by the banker as a natural and direct consequence of this breach of duty. If the cheque is drawn in such a way as to facilitate or almost to invite an increase in the amount by forgery if the cheque should get into the hands of a dishonest person, forgery is not a remote but a very natural consequence of such negligence. The bank could, therefore, debit Macmillan and Arthur with the full £120 0s. 0d.

Cf. *Scholfield* v. *Earl of Londesborough*, [1896] A.C. 514 where it was held that the drawer of a bill of exchange owed no such duty to other parties.

572. Slingsby v. District Bank, [1931] All E.R. Rep. 147

The executors of an estate drew a cheque payable to John Prust & Co. but left a space between the payee's name and the printed words "or order." A fraudulent solicitor named Cumberbirch wrote "per Cumberbirch and

Potts" after the payee's name. He then indorsed the cheque and received payment. *Held*—There was no negligence on the part of the executors; it was not a usual precaution to draw lines before or after the name of the payee and the executors were entitled to recover the amount of the cheque from the bank.

N.B. If the precaution of filling in the gap after the payees' name is more usual now than in 1931, then a present-day court may not follow Slingsby because the question of what is usual is purely one of evidence.

573. Gibbons *v.* Westminster Bank Ltd., [1939] 2 K.B. 882

The plaintiff drew a cheque for rent which she gave to her landlords and which was dishonoured in error. The bank had credited to another account funds paid in by the plaintiff sufficient to meet the cheque. The bank offered her £1 1s. od. in full satisfaction of her complaint, but the jury found that she did not accept this. As a result of the bank's action the plaintiff's landlords insisted thereafter that she pay her rent in cash. However, she did not claim special damage and was not allowed to amend her statement of claim during the trial. *Held*—The plaintiff was entitled to nominal damages of forty shillings. A trader is entitled to recover substantial damages for wrongful dishonour without pleading or proving actual damage, but a person who is not a trader is not entitled to recover substantial damages for the wrongful dishonour of a cheque, unless the damage he has suffered is alleged and proved as special damage.

574. Davidson *v.* Barclays Bank Ltd., [1940] 1 All E.R. 316

Davidson was both a cash and credit bookmaker who drew a cheque for £2 15s. 8d. on his account. The bank had previously paid a cheque for £7 15s. 9d. which Davidson had stopped by letter, and this wrongful payment made it appear that Davidson had not funds to meet the cheque for £2 15s. 8d. which was therefore returned marked "Not sufficient" across its face. The plaintiff alleged libel in that the bank held him out to be a person who had drawn a cheque on an account without sufficient funds to meet it, and gave the impression that the plaintiff and his firm were unsafe to do business with or to deal with on credit. The bank pleaded that the words were published only to the payee to whom they owed an explanation as to why the cheque had not been met; that the words were published in the honest though mistaken belief that they were true; and that the occasion was privileged. *Held*—The bank had no duty to publish. There was no common interest requiring such a communication. The bank made a mistake in returning the cheque and this was the reason for the need for explanation. It was self-created. The case is essentially different from one where the bank might make an error in replying to a specific request for a reference, since then the occasion of privilege is already constituted. Judgment was given for the plaintiff for £250.

575. Jayson *v.* Midland Bank Ltd., [1968] 1 Lloyd's Rep. 409

The plaintiff claimed damages for breach of contract and libel against the bank who had returned two cheques drawn by her marked "refer to drawer." She alleged that the bank had agreed to pay the cheques if she paid £100 into her account the following week (which she in fact did). The bank's contention was that they had agreed to pay the cheques only if the plaintiff's overdraft limit of £500 was not exceeded (which it would have been if the cheques concerned had been paid.) The action was tried before Blain, J. and a jury and the jury *found* as follows—

   (i) the bank's contention was proved;

   (ii) the effect of the words "refer to drawer" was to lower the plaintiff's reputation in the eyes of right-thinking people and was defamatory—however, this did not avail the plaintiff because the bank was quite justified in its action; and

   (iii) the plaintiff would have exceeded the overdraft if the cheques had been met.

An appeal to the Court of Appeal against judgment for the bank was dismissed.

N.B. This case goes some way towards removing the doubts which had previously existed regarding the defamatory nature of the words "refer to drawer." This decision supports the view that they are defamatory and unless the bank can plead justification, it would seem to be liable.

576. Curtice *v.* London, City & Midland Bank Ltd., [1908] 1 K.B. 293

The plaintiff drew a cheque for £63 in favour of a Mr. Jones to pay for some horses. When the horses were not delivered he stopped the cheque by a telegram to the bank which was delivered into the bank's letter box at 6.15 p.m. The telegram was not noticed on the next day and the bank paid the cheque. only to find on the following day both the telegram which had been overlooked and a written confirmation of countermand which had been posted. The plaintiff was notified that the countermand was received too late to be effective, and he retorted by drawing a cheque on the bank for the whole of his funds, including the £63, which the bank naturally enough dishonoured. The plaintiff brought an action for money had and received. The county court gave judgment for the plaintiff; the Divisional Court dismissed the bank's appeal; but it was *held* by the Court of Appeal that there had been no effective countermand of payment and the bank were not liable for money had and received. They might have been held liable in negligence, but the damages would not then have been the same. Cozens-Hardy, M.R., said: "There is no such thing as a constructive countermand in a commercial transaction of this kind."

577. Brewer *v.* Westminster Bank, [1952] 2 All E.R. 650

Cheques drawn on an estate account required the signature of each of the two executors. One executor drew over £3,000 by forging the signature of his co-executor. The latter brought an action for a declaratory judgment to the effect that the account should not have been debited. The declaration was refused by the court on the grounds that a joint contractor could not sue on a joint contract unless the other joint contractor could sue also, which in this case he could not. The decision has been criticised and in fact settlement was made, the bank paying the plaintiff the full amount claimed, and costs.
(See now *Jackson* v. *White and Midland Bank Ltd.*, [1967] 2 Lloyd's Rep. 68.)

578. Woods *v.* Martins Bank Ltd., [1958] 3 All E.R. 166

The plaintiff claimed, amongst other things, damages against the defendant bank and Mr. Joseph Johnson, the manager of the defendants' Quayside branch at Newcastle upon Tyne, and the case is reported only on the liability of the bank. The bank had advertised investment advice, saying "the very best advice is available through our managers," and as a result of a request for financial advice by the plaintiff, who was a customer, the manager arranged for the plaintiff to invest £14,800 in a private company called Brocks Refrigeration, although, to the manager's knowledge, the company had a considerable overdraft and was in need of funds. The whole of this sum was eventually lost. The bank's defence was that the giving of financial advice was not part of a banker's business, relying on earlier decisions that had suggested this, and that they were not therefore vicariously liable for the negligence of their manager, since he was not acting within the scope of his employment. *Held*—By Salmon, J., (i) The limits of a banker's business could not be laid down as a matter of law. In this case the advertisement showed that the giving of financial advice was part of the business and therefore the bank was vicariously liable for the act of its servant, the manager. (ii) The duty to give proper and not negligent advice extended to potential customers as well as existing customers.

579. Schioler *v.* Westminster Bank Ltd., [1970] 3 All E.R. 177

Mrs. Schioler was Danish, residing in England but domiciled in Denmark. She opened an account in 1962 with a bank in Guernsey. Dividends were forwarded in sterling to the Guernsey branch by a Malaysian company and Mrs. Schioler's account was credited without deduction of U.K. income tax to which she was not liable unless the dividends were sent to a branch in the United Kingdom. In 1969 the Malaysian company converted its shares from sterling units into Malaysian dollars. They also sent the 1967 dividend voucher and warrant to the Guernsey branch expressed in Malaysian dollars. The Guernsey branch lacked the facilities to realise the warrant so it was sent to the bank's stock officer in England for realisation. The dividends thus became liable to U.K. income tax. In this action by the plaintiff for breach of contractual duty by the bank it was *held*—by Mocatta, J.—that in the absence of special arrangements bankers could not in discharge of their contractual duties in crediting an account with a dividend be obliged to consider the tax implications to the customer or consult him before acting in accordance with their ordinary practice.

580. Lloyds Bank Ltd. *v.* E. B. Savory & Co., [1933] A.C. 201

Two clerks, Perkins and Smith, stole bearer cheques from Savory & Co., their employers, who were stockbrokers, and paid them into branches of Lloyds Bank—Perkins into an account at Wallington, and Smith into his wife's account at Redhill and subsequently at Weybridge. The clerks paid in the cheques at other branches, using the "branch credit" system, with the result that the branches in which the accounts were kept did not receive particulars of the cheques. Neither bank made inquiries concerning the employers of Smith and Perkins. The frauds were discovered and Savory & Co. brought an action against the bank for conversion. The bank pleaded Sect. 82 of the Bills of Exchange Act, and denied negligence, since the "branch credit" system was in common use by bankers. At first instance judgment was given for the bank, but this was reversed on appeal and the bank then appealed to the House of Lords. *Held*—The appeal should be dismissed as the bank had not been able to rebut the charge of negligence. With regard to the defence under Sect. 82, the court held that, although the branch credit system had been in use for forty years, it had "an inherent and obvious defect which no reasonable banker could fail to observe." Lord Wright said: "Where a new customer is employed in some position which involves his handling, and having the opportunity of stealing, his employer's cheques, the bankers fail in taking adequate precautions if they do not ask the name of his employers. . . . Otherwise they cannot guard against the danger known to them of his paying in cheques stolen from his employers." This is not the ordinary practice of bankers but that does not acquit them of negligence. Such inquiries should be made on the opening of an account even though they could turn out to be useless if the customer changed his employment immediately afterwards.

581. Orbit Mining and Trading Co. Ltd. *v.* Westminster Bank, [1962] 3 All E.R. 565

The plaintiff company had an account with the Midland Bank, and cheques drawn on this account had to be signed by two directors. One of these directors, A, was often abroad and had been in the habit of signing cheque forms in blank before going abroad, assuming that the other director authorised to sign, B, would use the cheques only for trading purposes.

B added his signature to three cheque forms and inserted the word "cash" between the printed words "Pay" and "or order" and passed the cheques for collection to the Westminster Bank Ltd., where he had a private account. The Westminster Bank collected the sums due on the cheques and B used the money for his private purposes. The Westminster Bank did not know that B was connected with the plaintiff company and his signature on the cheques was, in any case, illegible. Each cheque form was crossed generally and was stamped "for and on behalf of" the company under which appeared the signatures of A and B. *Held*—The three instruments in this case were not cheques, but were documents issued by a customer of a banker intended to enable a person to obtain payment from the banker within Sect. 4 (2) of the Cheques Act, 1957, and since the bank had acted without negligence it was entitled to the protection of the Act in respect of the collection of an instrument to which the customer had no title.

582. Marfani & Co. *v.* Midland Bank, [1967] 3 All E.R. 967

The managing director of the plaintiff company signed a cheque for £3,000 drawn by the office manager Kureshy payable to Eliaszade and gave it to Kureshy for despatch. However, Kureshy opened an account with the cheque at the Midland Bank by falsely representing that he was Eliaszade and that he was about to set up a restaurant business. The bank asked for references and Kureshy gave the names of two satisfactory customers of the bank, and one of these references indicated, while on a visit to the bank, that Kureshy, whom he knew as Eliaszade. would be a satisfactory customer. The second referee did not reply to the bank's inquiry. Kureshy then drew a cheque for £2,950 on the account and absconded. It appeared that the bank did not ask to see Kureshy's passport and his spelling of Eliaszade was inconsistent with the spelling on the cheque. Further the bank officials did not notice the similarity in handwriting between the cheque and the indorsement. The plaintiff company sued the bank for conversion and it was held that the bank had not fallen short of the standard of ordinary practice of careful bankers and was protected by Sect. 4 of the Cheques Act, 1957.

583. Westminster Bank Ltd. *v.* Zang, [1965] 1 All E.R. 1023

Mr. Zang, having lost heavily at seven-card rummy, drew a cheque for £1,000 payable to "J. Tilley or order," receiving from Mr. Tilley £1,000 in cash to pay part of his gambling debts. The £1,000 cash belonged to Tilley's Autos Ltd., a company of which Mr. Tilley was managing director. Tilley took Zang's cheque to his bank, asking them to credit the account of the company, which was overdrawn. Tilley did not indorse the cheque before paying it in. The cheque was dishonoured and the bank returned it to Tilley so that he could sue Zang. The action was commenced but discontinued and the cheque was returned to the bank who sued Zang as holder in due course or holder for value of the cheque. The bank failed in its claim. The reasons given in the Court of Appeal were—

(i) as the payee (Tilley) had asked the bank to credit the cheque to the account of a third party (Tilley's Autos), the cheque had not been received for collection within the meaning of the Cheques Act, 1957, Sect. 2, and as the cheque was not indorsed the bank were not "holders" (*per* Denning, M.R.);

(ii) the cheque had been received for collection but the bank had not given value, so that Sect. 2 did not apply (*per* Salmon, L.J.);

(iii) the cheque had been received for collection but the bank in returning the cheque to Tilley lost their lien and consequently the protection of Sect. 2 (*per* Danckwerts, L.J.).

In the House of Lords their Lordships unanimously held that the cheque had been received for collection, but the bank had not given value.

The company's account was overdrawn, but it was hard to see how, by crediting the cheque to the account and reducing the overdraft, the bank gave value for it, because in fact interest had been charged on the original amount of the overdraft unreduced by the cheque. There was no agreement express or implied to honour the cheques of Tilley's Autos before they had been cleared, and consideration could not, therefore, be established in this way.

584. Barclays Bank Ltd. *v.* Astley Industrial Trust, Ltd., [1970] 1 All E.R. 719

Mabons Garage Ltd. were motor dealers who banked with the plaintiffs and arranged hire-purchase transactions with the defendants. In November, 1964, the plaintiffs gave Mabons a temporary overdraft up to £2,000 and on 18th November, when the account was £1,910 overdrawn, cheques for £2,673 drawn by Mabons were presented for payment. The bank manager agreed to pay them only after receiving an assurance from the directors of Mabons that cheques for £2,850 in favour of Mabons and drawn by the defendants would be paid into the account the next day. On 19th November, when Mabons overdraft stood at £4,673, two further cheques for £345 drawn by Mabons were presented for payment and the bank manager refused to pay these until he had received the defendants' cheques for £2,850. On 20th November the defendants stopped their cheques which it appeared they had been induced to draw by the fraud of Mabons' directors. In an action by the bank claiming to be holders in due course of the cheques, the defendants alleged that the bank had not taken them for value. *Held*—by Milmo, J.—that the bank was holder in due cause since—

(*a*) a banker who takes a cheque as agent for collection can also be a holder in due course under Sect. 2 of the Cheques Act, 1957;

(*b*) the bank was a holder in due cause. They were holders because they had a lien on the cheques and were entitled to hold them pending payment of the overdraft. The value was the overdraft of £4,673. An antecedent debt would support a bill of exchange.

The bank was entitled to recover the amount of the cheques from the defendants.

585. Robins & Co. *v.* Gray, [1895] 2 Q.B. 501

The plaintiffs dealt in sewing machines and employed a traveller to sell the machines on commission. The plaintiffs' traveller put up at the defendant's inn in April, 1894, and stayed there until the end of July, 1894. During this time the plaintiffs sent the traveller machines to sell in the neighbourhood. At the end of July, the traveller owed the defendant £4 for board and lodging, and he failed to pay. The defendant detained certain of the goods sent by the plaintiffs to their traveller, claiming he had a lien on them for the amount of the debt due to him although the defendant knew that the goods were the property of the plaintiffs. *Held*—The defendant was entitled to a lien on the plaintiffs' property for the traveller's debt.

586. Larner *v.* Fawcett, [1950] 2 All E.R. 727

The defendant owned a racehorse and made an agreement with a Mr. Davis under which it was agreed that Davis would train and race the filly and receive half of any prize money she might win. Davis, unknown to the defendant, agreed to let Larner have the animal to train. Larner did so, and when his charges had reached £125, he discovered that Fawcett was the true owner. Larner, being unable to recover the cost of training and feeding the filly from Davis, who had no funds, now applied to the court for an order for sale. Fawcett was brought in as defendant. *Held*, by the Court of Appeal, that Larner had a common law lien for his charges, and although such a lien does not carry with it a power of sale, the power given in the Rules of the Supreme Court to make an order for sale was appropriate here, particularly since the filly was eating her head off. Fawcett had not made any attempt to get his property back but had clothed Davis with all the indicia of ownership. An order for sale would therefore be made unless Fawcett paid into court the amount of Larner's charges by a given date.

587. Knightsbridge Estates Trust Ltd. *v.* Byrne, [1939] Ch. 441

The plaintiffs were the owners of a large freehold estate close to Knightsbridge. This estate was mortgaged to a friendly society for a sum of money, which, together with interest, was to be repaid over a period of forty years in eighty half-yearly instalments. The company wished to redeem the mortgage before the expiration of the term, because it was possible for them to borrow elsewhere at a lower rate of interest. *Held*—The company was not entitled to redeem the mortgage before the end of the forty years because, in the circumstances, the postponement of the right was not unreasonable, since the parties were men of business and equal in bargaining power. A postponement of the right of redemption is not by itself a clog on the equity of redemption; much depends upon the circumstances. Further, the postponement did not offend the rule against perpetuities, which did not apply to mortgages.

588. Noakes *v.* Rice, [1902] A.C. 24

The appellants were a brewery company and the respondent wished to become the purchaser of a public house owned by the company. The respondent borrowed money from the company in order to effect the purchase, and agreed that the company should have the exclusive right to supply the premises with malt liquors during the period of the mortgage and afterwards, whether any money was or was not owed. The respondent subsequently gave notice to the company that he was prepared to pay off the money secured by the mortgage, if the company would release him from the above-mentioned contract. This was refused and the respondent asked the court for relief. *Held*—The covenant was invalid as a clog on the equity of redemption in so far as it purported to tie the public house after payment of the principal money and interest due on the security.

589. Kreglinger *v.* New Patagonia Meat and Cold Storage Co., [1914] A.C. 25

The appellants were a firm of merchants and wool brokers. The respondents carried on the business of preserving and canning meat, and of boiling down carcasses of sheep and other animals. The appellants advanced money to the respondents, the loan being secured by a charge over all the respondents' property. The appellants agreed not to demand repayment for five years, but the respondents could repay the debt at an earlier period on giving notice. The agreement also contained a provision that the respondents should not sell sheepskins to anyone but the appellants for five years from the date of the agreement, so long as the appellants were willing to purchase the same at an agreed price. The loan was paid off before the expiration of the five years. *Held*—The option of purchasing the sheepskins was not terminated on repayment, but continued for the period of five years. The option was a collateral contract which was not a mortgage and in no way affected the right to redeem the property.

590. Cityland and Property (Holdings) Ltd. *v.* Dabrah, [1967] 2 All E.R. 639

A first mortgage of £2,900 was granted by the seller of property to a purchaser and was expressed to be repayable in the sum of £4,553 for which the property was charged. The £4,553 was to be repaid over six years by equal monthly instalments and there was no mention in the mortgage of any interest. The whole of the balance of the £4,553 became payable if the borrower defaulted and for this reason Goff, J., *held* that the premium amounting to £1,653 was an unreasonable collateral advantage and therefore void under the principle in *Kreglinger's Case*, 1914.[589] The Judge having disallowed the premium was prepared to allow interest at seven per cent on a day-to-day basis which he thought to be somewhat more than market rates, but in fact it was far below market rates. The premium was an interest computation of nine-and-a-half per cent, non-reducing over six years and if it had been expressed as such in the mortgage it would appear that the court could not have set it aside since the court can only set aside unreasonable collateral advantages. However, in regard to interest rates, it appears that "equity does not reform mortgage transactions because they are unreasonable," Greene, M.R., in *Knightsbridge Estates Trust Ltd.* v. *Byrne*, 1939.[589] But this case was not cited to Goff, J. It would seem that for the future interest in mortgages should be expressed as such and not disguised as premium.

591. White v. City of London Brewery Co. (1889), 42 Ch.D. 237

The plaintiff had a lease of a public house in Canning Town, and he mort-gaged it to the defendants to secure a loan of £900 with interest. One year later, no interest having been paid since the date of the mortgage, the defendants entered into possession of the public house. They later let the premises on a tenancy determinable at three months' notice under which the tenant was to take all his beer from the defendants. Eventually the lease was sold by the defendants, and the plaintiff asked the defendants to account and pay him what should be found due. *Held*—The defendants must account to the plaintiff for the increased rent they might have received if they had let the public-house without the restrictive condition regarding the sale of the defendants' beer, since a "free house" would produce more rent than a "tied house."

592. Moffat v. Kazana, [1968] 3 All E.R. 271

The plaintiff hid banknotes in a biscuit tin in the roof of his house. He sold the house to the defendant, one of whose workmen discovered the money. In this action by the plaintiff to recover the money it was *held*—by Wrangham, J.— that the plaintiff succeeded. He had never evinced any intention to pass the title in the money to anyone. Therefore his title was good, not only against the finder, but also against the new owner of the house.

593. Hayward v. Challoner, [1967] 3 All E.R. 122

The predecessors in title of the plaintiff landowner let land to the rector of a parish at a rent of 10s. a year. The rent was not collected after 1942 and the plaintiff now sued for possession. *Held*—by the Court of Appeal—that a right of action in respect of rent or possession must be held to have accrued when the rent due was first unpaid, and therefore was barred by the Limitation Act, 1939. The rector as a corporation sole had acquired a good squatter's title.

594. Littledale v. Liverpool College, [1900] 1 Ch. 19

The plaintiffs had a right of way for agricultural purposes over a strip of grass land belonging to the defendants. The plaintiffs put up gates which they kept locked at each end of the strip, and used the grass for grazing, keeping the hedges of the strip clipped. They now claimed ownership of the land by virtue of adverse possession. *Held*—The plaintiffs' acts could be construed as protect-ing the right of way, rather than excluding the owner, and were insufficient to establish the plaintiffs' title to the land.

595. Ashby v. Tolhurst, [1937] 2 All E.R. 837

The plaintiff drove his car on to a piece of land at Southend owned by the defendants. He paid 1s. to an attendant who was the defendants' servant and was given a ticket. He left the car with the doors locked. When he returned his car had gone, the attendant having allowed a thief, who said he was a friend of the plaintiff, to drive it away. The ticket was called a "car-park ticket" and contained the words "The proprietors do not take any responsibility for the safe custody of any cars or articles therein, nor for any damage to the cars or articles however caused nor for any injuries to any persons, all cars being left in all respects entirely at their owner's risk. Owners are requested to show ticket when required." *Held*—

(i) The relationship between the parties was that of licensor and licensee, not that of bailor and bailee because there was in no sense a transfer of possession. There was, therefore, no obligation upon the defendants towards the plaintiff in respect of the car.

(ii) If there was a contract of bailment, the servant delivered possession of the car quite honestly under a mistake and the conditions on the tickets were wide enough to protect the defendants.

(iii) There could not be implied into the contract a term that the car should not be handed over without production of the ticket.

N.B. Where the plaintiff hands over the key, the court may find a transfer of possession and a bailment, but the delivery of the key is not conclusive.

596. Ultzen *v.* Nicols, [1894] 1 Q.B. 92

A waiter took a customer's overcoat, without being asked to do so, and hung it on a peg behind the customer. The coat was stolen and it was *held* that the restaurant keeper was a bailee of the coat and that there was negligence in supervision on the part of the bailee.

N.B. In this case the servant seems to have been regarded as taking possession, but it is unlikely that a bailment will arise if a customer merely hangs his coat on a stand or other device provided by the establishment.

597. Deyong *v.* Shenburn, [1946] 1 All E.R. 226

An allegation that an actor who left his clothes in a dressing room had constituted the theatre owners bailees of the clothes was not sustained.

598. Newman *v.* Bourne & Hollingsworth (1915), 31 T.L.R. 209

The plaintiff went into the defendant's shop on a Saturday in order to buy a coat. While trying on coats she took off a diamond brooch and put it on a show case. She left the shop having forgotten the brooch; an assistant found it and handed it to the shopwalker who put it in his desk. By the firm's rules the brooch ought to have been taken to their lost property office. The brooch could not be found on the following Monday. *Held*—There was evidence to support the trial judge's finding that the firm had become bailees and had not exercised proper care.

599. Neuwirth *v.* Over Darwen Industrial Co-operative Society (1894) 70 T.L.R. 374

A concert hall was hired for an evening performance. No mention was made of rehearsal but the orchestra rehearsed in the hall during the afternoon without opposition from the proprietors or the keeper of the hall. After the rehearsal Neuwirth left his double-bass fiddle in an ante-room in such a position that when the hall keeper came to turn on the gas in the ante-room he could not do so without first moving the instrument. The fiddle fell and was badly damaged. *Held*—There was no contract of bailment between the parties. The care of musical instruments was outside the scope of the hall keeper's authority and there was no evidence that he had been guilty of negligence in the course of his employment.

600. Hyman *v.* Nye (1881), 6 Q.B.D. 685

The plaintiff hired a landau with a pair of horses and a driver for a drive from Brighton to Shoreham and back. The plaintiff was involved in an accident owing to a broken bolt which caused the carriage to upset so that the plaintiff was thrown out of it. *Held*—The trial judge's direction to the jury that the plaintiff must prove negligence was wrong. There was an implied warranty that the carriage was as fit for the purpose for which it was hired as skill and care could make it.

601. Reed *v.* Dean, [1949] 1 K.B. 188

The plaintiffs hired a motor launch called the *Golden Age* from the defendant for a family holiday on the Thames. The plaintiffs set sail at about 7 p.m. on 22nd June, 1946, and at about 9 p.m., when they were near Sonning, they discovered that a liquid in the bilge by the engine was on fire. They attempted to extinguish the fire but were unable to do so, the fire-fighting equipment with which the launch was supplied being out of order. The plaintiffs had to abandon the launch and suffered personal injuries and loss of belongings. The plaintiffs admitted to a fireman after the accident that they might have spilt some petrol when the tank was refilled. *Held*—The plaintiffs succeeded because there was an implied undertaking by the defendant that the launch was as fit for the purpose for which it was hired as reasonable care and skill could make it. Further, as the launch had caught fire due to an unexplained cause, there was a presumption that it was not fit for this purpose. The defendant's failure to provide proper fire-fighting equipment was a breach of the implied warranty of fitness.

602. Houghland *v.* R. Low (**Luxury Coaches**) Ltd., [1962] 2 All E.R. 159

The defendants supplied a coach for the purposes of an old people's outing to Southampton. On returning the passengers put their luggage into the boot of the coach. During a stop for tea the coach was found to be defective and another one was sent for and the luggage was transferred from the first coach to the relief coach. The removal of the luggage from the first coach was not supervised, but the restacking of the luggage into the new coach was supervised by one of the defendants' employees. When the passengers arrived home a suitcase belonging to the plaintiff was missing and he brought an action against the defendants for its loss. It was *held*, by the Court of Appeal, that whether the action was for negligence or in detinue, the defendants were liable unless they could show that they had not been negligent. On the facts they had failed to prove this and were therefore liable. It was in this case that Ormerod, L.J., made some observations on bailments in general. The County Court Judge had found that the bailment was gratuitous and that the defendants were liable only for gross negligence. Dealing with this question, Ormerod, L.J., said "For my part I have always found some difficulty in understanding just what was gross negligence, because it appears to me that the standard of care required in a case of bailment or any other type of case is the standard demanded by the circumstances of the particular case. It seems to me to try and put bailment, for instance, into a water-tight compartment, such as gratuitous bailment on the one hand and bailment for reward on the other, is to overlook the fact that there might well be an infinite variety of cases which might come into one or other category."

603. Global Dress Co. *v.* W. H. Boase & Co., [1966] 2 Ll. Rep. 72

B & Co. were master porters and had custody of thirty cases of goods belonging to G & Co. at a Liverpool dock shed. One case was stolen and G & Co. brought an action for damages against B & Co. B & Co. offered evidence of their system of safeguarding the goods and the County Court Judge at first instance found the system to be as good as any other in the Liverpool Docks, but notwithstanding this he found B & Co. liable. On appeal to the Court of Appeal it was *held* that if B & Co. could not affirmatively prove that their watchman was not negligent it was of no avail to show that they had an impeccable system, and the appeal should be dismissed. Thus the onus of proving that their servant was not negligent lay upon B & Co.

604. Doorman *v.* Jenkins (1834), 2 Ad. & El. 256

The plaintiff left the sum of £32 10s. with the defendant, who was a coffee-house keeper, for safe custody and without any reward. The defendant put the money in with his own in a cash box which he kept in the taproom. The taproom was open to the public on a Sunday but the rest of the house was not and the cash was, in fact, stolen on a Sunday. Lord Denman *held* that the loss of the defendant's own money was not enough to prove reasonable care and the court found for the plaintiff.

605. Brabant *v.* King, [1895] A.C. 632

This action was brought against the government of Queensland for damage to certain explosives belonging to the plaintiff which the government as bailees for reward had stored in sheds situated near the water's edge on Brisbane River. The water rose to an exceptional height and the store was flooded. The question of inevitable accident was raised and also the degree of negligence required. The Privy Council *held* that because of the nature of the site the bailees were required to place the goods at such a level as would in all probability ensure their absolute immunity from flood water, and the defendants were held liable. The Privy Council went on to say that in a case of a deposit for reward the bailees were "under a legal obligation to exercise the same degree of care, towards the preservation of the goods entrusted to them from injury, which might reasonably be expected from a skilled storekeeper, acquainted with the risks to be apprehended from the character either of the storehouse or of its locality; and the obligations included, not only the duty of taking all reasonable precautions to obviate these risks but the duty of taking all proper measures for the protection of the goods when such risks were imminent or had actually occurred." Counsel for the government suggested that a bailee was not liable for damage caused by the defects in his warehouse where these defects were known to the bailor, in this case the proximity of the warehouse to the Brisbane River. The Privy Council dismissed this argument on the grounds that it was a dangerous one, not supported by any authority. They said that the bailor could rely on the skill of the bailee in this matter. It will be seen from this decision that a bailee for reward is liable even in the case of uncommon or unexpected danger, unless he uses efforts which are in proportion to the emergency to ward off that danger.

606. Wilson *v.* Brett (1843), 11 M. & W. 113

Wilson was in process of selling his horse and Brett volunteered to ride the horse in order to show it off to a likely purchaser. Brett rode the horse on to wet and slippery turf and the horse fell and was injured. Brett pleaded that he was not negligent but the court *held* that he had not used the skill he professed to possess when he volunteered to ride the horse and that he was liable.

607. Saunders (Mayfair) Furs v. Davies (1965), 109 S.J. 922

The plaintiffs delivered a valuable fur coat to a shop belonging to the defendants, on sale-or-return terms. The defendants displayed it in their shop window and at 2.30 a.m. one morning the coat was stolen in a smash-and-grab raid. *Held*—That in all the circumstances and because of the valuable nature of the property, the defendants had taken an unreasonable risk and were negligent in leaving the coat on display in the window all night.

608. Coldman v. Hill, [1919] 1 K.B. 443

The defendant was a bailee of cows belonging to the plaintiff. Two of these cows were stolen through no fault of the defendant, though he failed to notify the plaintiff and did not inform the police or take any steps to find the cows. The plaintiff now sued him for negligence and it was *held* by the Court of Appeal that it was up to the defendant to prove that, even if notice had been given, the cows would not have been recovered. In the circumstances of this case that burden had not been discharged and the defendant was liable.

609. Cheshire v. Bailey, [1905] 1 K.B. 237

In this case jewellery had been deposited in a carriage by the hirer and was stolen by thieves. It transpired that the coachman, who was the servant of the person who let out the carriage, was in league with the thieves, but it was *held* that the owner of the carriage was not liable for the loss because the dishonesty of his servant was beyond the scope of employment.

610. Davies v. Collins, [1945] 1 All E.R. 247

An American Army officer sent his uniform to the defendants to be cleaned. It was accepted on the following conditions—"Whilst every care is exercised in cleaning and dyeing garments, all orders are accepted at owner's risk entirely and we are unable to hold ourselves responsible for damage." The defendants did not clean the uniform but sub-contracted the work to another firm of cleaners. In the event the uniform was lost and the defendants were *held* liable in damages. The Court of Appeal took the view that the limitation clause operated to exclude the right to sub-contract because it used the words "every care is exercised," which postulated personal service.

611. Edwards v. Newland, [1950] 2 All E.R. 1072

The defendant agreed to store the plaintiff's furniture for reward. Later, without the plaintiff's knowledge, the defendant made arrangements with another company to store the plaintiff's furniture. The third party's warehouse was damaged by a bomb and they asked the defendant to remove the furniture but this was not done immediately because there was a dispute about charges. Eventually the plaintiff removed his furniture but some pieces were missing. *Held*—The plaintiff could recover from the defendant because he had departed from the terms of the contract of bailment by sub-contracting. However, the defendant was not entitled to damages against the third party because the latter, though a bailee, had not, in the circumstances, been negligent.

612. Learoyd Bros. & Co. v. Pope & Sons, [1966] 2 Ll. Rep. 142

The plaintiffs entered into an agreement with a carrier for the transport of their goods. The carrier sub-contracted the work to the defendants, who were also a firm of carriers, though the plaintiffs had no notice of this arrangement.

The lorry was stolen while the defendants' driver was in the wharf office upon arrival at London Docks, and the carrier with whom the plaintiffs had contracted paid some of the plaintiffs' loss and the plaintiffs now sued the defendants for the balance. *Held*—That the defendants were bailees to the plaintiffs, notwithstanding the absence of any contract between them, and that the defendants' driver was negligent in leaving the lorry unattended and therefore the defendants were liable for the plaintiffs' loss.

613. Rogers Sons & Co. *v.* Lambert & Co., [1891] 1 Q.B.318

The plaintiffs had purchased copper from the defendants but did not take delivery of it and left it with the defendants as warehousemen. The plaintiffs then resold the copper to a third person. Sometime later the plaintiffs asked for delivery of the copper from the defendants but the defendants refused to deliver on the grounds that the plaintiffs no longer had a title to it. *Held*— This was no defence to an action of detinue. The defendants must show that they were defending the action on behalf, and with the authority, of the true owner.

THE LAW OF TRUSTS

614. Re Remnant's Trusts, Hooper *v.* Wenhasten, [1970] 2 All E.R. 554

Remnant left property to his daughters Dawn and Merriel and to their children in remainder. The will contained forfeiture provisions which stated that if at the death of either daughter a child of hers was a member of the Roman Catholic faith, attended a Roman Catholic Church, or was married to or living with a Roman Catholic, he or she should forfeit all rights under the will. Merriel's husband was a Roman Catholic, two of her daughters attended a Roman Catholic Church and a third was baptised a Roman Catholic. Dawn and Merriel asked the Court's approval of an arrangement under the Variation of Trusts Act, 1958, whereby the forfeiture provisions might be deleted and £10,000 set aside out of the shares of Dawn and Merriel on trusts for their respective children. *Held*—by Pennycuick, J.—that the arrangement was obviously for the benefit of Merriel's children, and Dawn's children obtained a certain and accelerated interest of £10,000. Furthermore although a forfeiture provision was not in itself undesirable, the deletion of this one would be for the benefit of the children of both Dawn and Merriel. If left it would operate as a deterrent on Dawn's children in regard to the selection of a spouse and could cause serious dissension between the two families. The arrangement was approved.

615. Re Weston's Settlements (1968), 112 S.J. 641

The Court of Appeal, exercising its statutory discretion under Sect. 1 of the Variation of Trusts Act, 1958, on behalf of infant and unborn beneficiaries, refused to appoint new trustees resident in Jersey or to approve a scheme by which the trusts of two English settlements of English shares with a value of £800,000 would be transferred bodily to Jersey and operated under Jersey law, where the sole object was to avoid United Kingdom taxation, in particular Capital Gains tax. Lord Denning, M.R., said in the course of his judgment that two propositions were clear (i) in exercising its discretion the Court must do what was truly for the benefit of those who could not protect themselves; (ii) it could consent to a scheme to avoid taxes which was not necessarily contrary to public policy; *but* (iii) the court should consider not merely the financial benefit to infants or unborn children but also their eductional and social benefit. Many things were more worth while than money and one was to be brought up in England which was still "the envy of less happier lands."

N.B. In *Re Windeatt's Will Trusts*, [1969] 2 All E.R. 324, the Court made an order under Sect. 1 of the Variation of Trusts Act, 1958, for the approval of an arrangement whereby two trustees resident in Jersey should be appointed and the fund transferred to them under new trusts which corresponded in every way with those set out by Mr. Windeatt in his will. *Re Weston's Settlements* was distinguished because Jersey was the permanent home of the beneficiaries, i.e. the testator's daughter and her family, she having lived there for 19 years.

616. Re Gibbard's Will Trusts, [1966] 1 All E.R. 273

A testator by his will created a testamentary power, which was not coupled with a trust to appoint his residuary estate "amongst . . . any of my old friends" with a gift over in default of appointment. *Held*—the description was precise enough for there to be claimants who should be able to identify themselves as "old friends" and the power was valid.

617. McPhail v. Doulton, [1970] 2 All E.R. 228

By deed dated 18th July, 1941, a fund was established by a Mr. Baden for the benefit of officers and employees of Matthew Hall and Co. Ltd. Clause 9(*a*) of the deed provided as follows—

"The trustees shall apply the net income of the fund in making at their absolute discretion grants to or for the benefit of any officers and employees or ex-officers or ex-employees of the company or to any relatives or dependents of any such persons in such amounts at such times and on such conditions (if any) as they think fit."

The issue before the House of Lords was whether on its true construction the provisions of Clause 9(*a*) constituted a trust binding the trustees to distribute income in accordance with its provisions or was a mere power not imposing such a duty. If it was a trust the personal representatives of Mr. Baden claimed that it was void for uncertainty and that they were entitled to the capital sum as part of the estate and did not have to make payments to the staff of the company. *Held*—(*a*) Clause 9(*a*) was mandatory and constituted a trust; (*b*) (Lord Hodson and Lord Guest dissenting) the trust was not void for uncertainty. "The conclusion which I would reach, implicit in the previous discussion, is that the wide distinction between the validity test for powers and that for trust powers, is unfortunate and wrong, . . . and that the test for the validity of trust powers ought to be similar to that accepted by this House in *Re Gulbenkian's Settlement Trusts*, [1968] 3 All E.R. 785, for powers, namely that the trust is valid if it can be said with certainty that any given individual is or is not a member of the class." (*Per* Lord Wilberforce).

618. Keech v. Sandford (1726), Sel. Cas. t. King 61

A person had a lease of the profits of Romford Market and he devised his estate in trust for his infant. Before the lease expired the trustee applied to the lessor for a renewal for the benefit of the infant. The lessor refused to grant such a renewal, fearing that the infant's incapacity in law might prevent the exercise of certain remedies by the lessor if the need arose. He agreed to renew it in favour of the trustee personally. The trustee had a lease made out to himself.

Held—The trustee held the new lease on a constructive trust for the benefit of the infant.

N.B. The rule propounded in *Keech* v. *Sandford* has now developed into two branches—

1. The original rule relating to leases. For example, a partner who renews a partnership lease for himself renews it for the partnership, and a mortgagor who renews a lease which secures his mortgage holds the new lease subject to the same security.

2. The general concept of constructive trusts. This has nothing to do with leases and really means that a trustee cannot make a profit out of the trust. So a trustee profiting from the use of trust property must account for profit made, and must also make up any losses.

618a. *Protheroe* v. *Protheroe*, [1968] 1 All E.R. 1111

In this case a husband and wife were jointly interested in a leasehold property, the wife having paid the deposit and the husband the mortgage repayments though the property was in the husband's name. After ten years of marriage the wife filed a petition for divorce and the husband, with the aid of a mortgage, purchased the freehold of the property. It was held that the husband and wife were jointly entitled to the freehold (which was, of course, more valuable than the leasehold), though the husband was entitled to be reimbursed the expenses of purchasing the freehold and his mortgage repayments in respect of the freehold. (*Keech* v. *Sandford* applied.)

619. Barclays Bank *v.* Quistclose Investments, [1968] 3 All E.R. 651

In the spring of 1964 Rolls Razor Ltd., was in financial difficulties having an overdraft of £484,000 with the bank against a permitted limit of £250,000. The bank informed the company that it would cease to do business unless the position improved. Rolls Razor then obtained a loan of £209,719 from Quistclose on condition that it was used to pay an ordinary share dividend declared by Rolls Razor on 2nd July, 1964. The bank was aware of this condition and the money was paid into a separate account.

On 27th August, 1964, Rolls Razor went into voluntary liquidation and the dividend had not been paid. Quistclose brought an action against Rolls Razor and the bank claiming—

(i) that the money which they had lent had been held on trust to pay the dividend;

(ii) that the trust having failed the money was held on a resulting trust for Quistclose;

(iii) that the bank having had notice of the trust could not retain the loan by way of set-off of Rolls Razor's indebtedness to the bank in respect of the overdraft.

Plowman, J., at first instance upheld the bank's claim to set-off but the Court of Appeal reversed his decision. On a further appeal to the House of Lords it was *held*—

(1) that not only was the Rolls Razor company under a contractual duty to repay Quistclose the money lent but since the particular and only purpose of the loan had failed the money was subject to a resulting trust for Quistclose; and

(2) that it was plain that the bank knew of the purpose of the loan and was therefore a trustee of the money for Quistclose.

The bank was therefore ordered to pay back the sum of £209,719 to Quistclose.

620. Re West Sussex Constabulary's Widows, Children and Benevolent (1930) Fund Trusts, [1970] 1 All E.R. 544

In 1930 a benevolent fund was set up to provide for the widows and orphans of former members of the West Sussex Constabulary. In January, 1968, the West Sussex force was amalgamated with other police forces in Sussex. At the time of amalgamation the fund stood at £35,000. The question of the distribution of the fund arose and it was held by Goff, J. that it should be dealt with as follows—

(*a*) the part representing contributions from former members and surviving members went to the Crown as *bona vacantia*, though there might be a right to recover in contract on the ground of frustration;

(*b*) the part raised by raffles, collecting boxes and sweep-stakes was *bona vacantia* and went to the Crown, there being an intention on the part of each donor to part with his money outright to a non-charitable fund;

(*c*) that part which arose out of legacies and donations should be held on resulting trusts for the donors and their estates, the gifts having been made for a particular purpose which had failed.

621. Re Shaw Deceased, [1957] 1 W.L.R. 729

The will of George Bernard Shaw set up a trust to apply income for a period of twenty-one years from his death towards inquiry into the substitution of a new English alphabet for the present one, and towards the persuasion of the government and public to adopt the new alphabet. *Held*—The trusts were not charitable because they involved no element of teaching and so were not for the advancement of education. The trusts, being private, failed because of lack of someone to enforce them, the object being an inanimate thing, i.e. an alphabet.

622. Bannister *v.* Bannister, [1948] 2 All E.R. 133

Two cottages at Mountnessing, Essex, worth £400, were sold for £250 under an oral contract, one of the terms of the contract being that the vendor be allowed to reside rent free in one of the cottages for as long as she lived. The conveyance made no mention of this undertaking. Subsequently the purchaser brought an action to recover possession of the cottage in which the vendor was living. *Held*—The cottage was conveyed on trust for the defendant, and the grantee was a trustee for the defendant. Although a trust over land normally requires written evidence, this was a case in which it would have been a fraud on the defendant to insist on it. Therefore she was allowed to prove the trust by oral evidence.

623. Re Pugh's Will Trusts, [1967] 3 All E.R. 337

By a will dated 31st January, 1962, Mr. Pugh appointed a Mr. Morton, who was a solicitor, to be his executor and trustee. In clause 6 of the will Mr. Pugh gave all his residuary estate "unto my trustee absolutely" and the clause continued "and I direct him to dispose of the same in accordance with any letters or memoranda which I may leave with this my will and otherwise in such manner as he may in his absolute discretion think fit." No letters or memoranda were left and Mr. Morton asked the court to determine whether he took the residuary estate upon trust or beneficially. *Held*—he took upon trust and since that trust was void for uncertainty of objects, Mr. Morton held the residue of the estate upon trust for Mr. Pugh's next-of-kin. In considering the effect of the direction added to the gift, Pennycuick, J., said: "At first sight the second line of the direction looks like a general power, but there is a long train of authorities which is I think, conclusive to the contrary. The effect of the authorities . . . is that where one finds a gift on trust to apply the subject matter in such manner and for such purposes, or whatever the words may be, as the donee may think fit, then that represents a trust for undefined objects such as the court cannot execute, and the trust is void, always, of course, in the absence of any further indication of intention."

624. Re Bateman's Will Trusts, [1970] 3 All E.R. 817

In 1924 John Bateman made a will directing his trustees to pay the income from two sums of £20,000 to his two daughters for life with remainders over to their children. He also told his trustees to set aside a sum of £24,000 to pay the income "to such persons as shall be stated by me in a sealed letter in my own handwriting and addressed to my trustees and on the death of each person so named and in the case of females on marriage I direct the share of income so given shall be divided between my said daughters." The testator died in 1931 and the trustees paid income of the £24,000 fund in accordance with a letter left by the testator. On the death of one of the daughters in 1968 issues relating to the validity of the dispositions in the letter were raised. *Held*—by Pennycuick, V.C.—that the direction concerning the sealed letter was invalid as it referred to a future non-testamentary instrument.

625. Re Adams and Kensington Vestry (1884), 27 Ch.D. 394

A testator gave all his estate, real and personal, to his wife absolutely "in full confidence that she will do whatever is right as to the disposal thereof between my children." *Held*—The wife took the property free from any trust.

626. Sale v. Moore (1827), 1 Sim 534

Edward Moore, a clerk, made a will which provided for a legacy and annuity, and then left the residue to his wife, Mary Moore, on these terms—"The remainder of what I die possessed of . . . I leave to my dear wife aforesaid, recommending to her and not doubting, as she has no relations of her own family, but that she will consider my near relations, should she survive me, as I should consider them myself in case I should survive her." Edward Moore died in 1812; Mary Moore, the testator's widow, made a will in 1822 giving legacies to the testator's brother, John Moore, and to several other persons and annuities to the testator's sisters, Mary Moore and Fanny Moore. These last two not only claimed their annuities, but also claimed, along with John Moore, the whole of the property possessed by the testatrix and formerly belonging to the testator, contending that she had only a life interest and that they were entitled by virtue of a trust. It was *held* by the Vice-Chancellor that there was no ground on which to imply a trust. To construe words of recommendation as a command is to make a will for the testator. In any case, if the words could be construed as creating a trust, the words were coupled with a degree of uncertainty. Did the testator mean his relations at his own death or at his wife's death? Moreover to ask his wife to "consider" his near relations as he would have done is much too indefinite and *uncertain*.

627. Re Rose, [1952] Ch. 449

Eric Hamilton Rose was registered owner of shares in the Leweston Estates Company. On 30th March, 1943, he executed two transfers in respect of the shares, one in favour of his wife, and the other in favour of his wife and another person, to be held by them upon certain trusts. The transfers were not registered until 30th June, 1943. Mr. Rose died more than five years after executing the transfers, but less than five years after they were registered, and the question of liability for estate duty arose. *Held*—The gift was effective in equity from 30th March, 1943, because Mr. Rose had done everything it was necessary for him to do to make the transfer effective and binding on him. Therefore, the shares were not assessable for estate duty. Although the gift was not effective at law until registration, Mr. Rose was in the meantime a trustee for the transferees.

628. Antrobus v. Smith (1805), 12 Ves. 39

The owner of shares in a company assigned the shares to his daughter by a written memorandum to this effect on the back of the share certificate. The company's articles required a transfer of shares to be in writing and under seal. *Held*—Since the owner's interest was a legal one, he must comply with the legal requirements, and the memorandum was not effective either to assign the shares to his daughter or to constitute a trust.

629. Kekewich v. Manning (1851), 1 De G.M. & G. 176

Trustees held certain shares upon a trust for A for life with the remainder to B. B, by deed, assigned her equitable interest in the remainder to the trustees of her marriage settlement to be held on trust for C. *Held*—A perfect trust in favour of C had been created. Since the interest was equitable, B could not comply with the method of transferring the shares at law, but this was not necessary. Actually although a deed had been used to assign the shares, writing alone would have been enough whether the property had been real or personal.

630. Jones v. Lock (1865), 1 Ch. App. 25

Robert Jones had a son aged nine months, and one day, on his return from a trip to Birmingham, the child's nurse said, "You have not brought baby anything." Jones thereupon produced a cheque for £900 made payable to himself, placed it in the child's hand for a moment, and said it was for the baby. He later visited his solicitor to make an appointment to alter his will so that he might provide for his son. He died the same day, and the cheque was found in his safe by the solicitor who was one of the executors. Payment was obtained in favour of the estate. In the Court of Chancery it was held that there had been a declaration of trust in favour of the child. The legatees under the will of Robert Jones appealed. *Held*—There was no trust. The cheque required endorsement and did not pass to the child by delivery. Further, the acts of Robert Jones were not sufficient to convert him into a trustee in respect of the cheque. His subsequent actions revealed that he still considered himself the unfettered owner of the instrument. Loose conversations of this kind should not be allowed to operate as declarations of trust.

631. Oppenheim v. Tobacco Securities Trust Co. Ltd., [1951] A.C. 297

The respondents held certain investments on trust to apply the income in providing for the education of employees, or former employees, of British

American Tobacco Co. Ltd., or any of the subsidiary or allied companies without any limit of time. It was necessary to establish the trust as charitable, otherwise it was void for perpetuity. The House of Lords *held* that it was not a charitable trust. The question of public benefit is vital to such a trust, and the beneficiaries under this trust were to be ascertained by reference to a contract of service between the company and either of their parents. It would be dangerous to establish such a test as relevant in deciding public benefit because although this concern had many employees and ex-employees, the test might be applied to a firm with only ten employees and this would clearly not be for the public benefit in any sense.

N.B. In *Re Compton*, [1945] Ch. 123 an educational trust confined to the lawful descendants of three named persons was held not to be a charitable trust. These rules to not cover trusts for relief of poverty. In *Dingle* v. *Turner*, [1972] 1 All E.R. 878 a trust for "poor employees" was held valid.

632. Re Koettgen's Will Trusts, [1954] 1 Ch. 252

A trust was created to further the commercial education of British-born persons, with a direction that preference should be given to the employees of a particular firm, but that not more than seventy-five per cent of the available income in any year should be applied for the benefit of the preferred beneficiaries. *Held*—The trust was a valid charitable trust and not void for perpetuity. Upjohn, J., thought that the trust was of a sufficiently public nature. The decision has been criticised on the grounds that it allows a non-charitable trust to be valid in perpetuity merely because a small proportion of the fund is to be used for the public benefit.

633. Gilmour v. Coates, [1949] A.C. 426

A trust had been created in favour of a Carmelite convent, and the question arose as to whether the trust was charitable. The convent was comprised of cloistered and purely contemplative nuns who did not do public work outside the convent. In the view of the Roman Catholic Church the prayers offered by the nuns were for the benefit of the public, and their life of self-denial provided an example which was beneficial to the public. *Held*—Although intercessory prayers might well be answered, it was impossible to prove this in the way in which a court demands proof. It was a question of faith not susceptible of proof in the legal sense. The trust was not therefore a charitable trust.

634. Re Gwyon, [1930] 1 Ch. 225

The Reverend John Gwyon had set up a trust to establish a foundation to be known as "Gwyon's Foundation for Clothing Boys." The income was to be applied to providing knickers for boys of a specified age, being the sons of parents resident in Farnham, the balance (if any) to be applied for the benefit of boys resident in Windlesham, Chobham, Egham and Woking. No boy was to be eligible if supported by another charity or whose parents were in receipt of parish relief or who was a black boy. The court had to decide whether this was a trust for the relief of poverty. *Held*—None of the conditions imported poverty; in fact a millionaire's son might have qualified. Therefore the trust was not a charitable trust.

635. Inland Revenue Commissioners v. Baddeley, [1955] A.C. 572

The question was whether a conveyance of land to trustees should be stamped at a reduced rate on the ground that the trust was a charitable one. The object of the trust was to be achieved by providing moral, social and physical training, together with recreational facilities, for Methodists resident in West Ham and Leyton. *Held*—The trust was not wholly for religious purposes, therefore it failed under the test of religion, and it could not be held to be for the benefit of the public since it was confined to the adherents of a particular religion.

636. Re Scarisbrick, [1951] Ch. 622

A testatrix directed her trustees to hold her residuary estate "upon trust for such relations of my son and daughters as in the opinion of the survivor of my said son and daughters shall be in needy circumstances . . . and for such charitable objects, either in Germany or Great Britain, as the survivor of my said son and daughters shall by will or deed appoint." The power of appointment was not exercised. The residue would therefore go to the heir at law if the above clause failed for perpetuity. The residuary gift was therefore divided into two parts: (i) A gift to a class of relations and (ii) a gift in favour of charitable objects in Germany or Great Britain. At first instance it was held that the first part failed as a trust for the relief of poverty, though the second part was good as a charity. The Court of Appeal *held* that both parts were good since, as the law now stands, a trust for the relief of poverty is not disqualified as ranking as a charitable trust merely because its application is confined to a class of relations so that its potential beneficiaries do not comprise the public or a section thereof. (See also *Dingle* v. *Turner*, (1972), p. 599.)

637. Chichester Diocesan Fund & Board of Finance (Inc.) v. Simpson, [1944] A.C. 341

A testator, Mr. Diplock, left the residue of his estate on trust "for such charitable institution or institutions or other charitable or benevolent object or objects as his executors might in their absolute discretion select." After the executors had wound up the estate, they distributed the residue among several charities. Diplock's next-of-kin claimed that the residue was void for uncertainty. At first instance the residuary bequest was held valid, but the Court of Appeal reversed the decision, and the charities concerned appealed to the House of Lords. *Held*—Since the residue might be solely applied to benevolent purposes, the trust was not a charitable trust.

637a. Re Wootton's Will Trusts, Trotter v. Duffin, [1968] 2 All E.R. 618

It was *held* by Pennycuick, J., that the words "an organisation or body not being registered as a charity but in the opinion of my trustees . . . having charitable objects" set out in a will did not create a charitable object (*a*) because the qualification was not the intrinsic character of the organisation or body, but the opinion of the trustees who might make a mistake; and (*b*) because the organisation chosen by the trustees need not have exclusively charitable objects.

638. Re Coxen, [1948] Ch. 747

A testator entrusted to the Court of Aldermen of the City of London the management of a large fund for the benefit of orthopaedic hospitals, allowing an annual sum of £100 for a dinner for the Court of Aldermen, on the occasion of their annual meeting for the purposes of the trust. *Held*—Although the provision for an annual dinner was not charitable, it was valid as conducive to the attainment of the charitable purposes.

THE LAW OF SUCCESSION

639. Re Groffman, Groffmen v. Groffman, [1969] 2 All E.R. 108

The testator said to two of his four guests in the lounge of his house "I should like you now to witness my will". It appeared that at the same time he gestured to his coat pocket which contained a folded document which he did not take out. The court accepted that he had already signed the document. He then took one of the proposed witnesses into the dining room and took the document from his pocket, unfolded it and revealed his signature without saying any more. The guest, having signed the document as a witness, went back to the lounge where he remained while the other witness went to the dining room and added his signature. *Held*—by Sir Jocelyn Simon, P.—

(*a*) that the gesture towards a document which the proposed witnesses could neither see nor have the opportunity of seeing was not an acknowledgement within the meaning of Sect. 9 of the Wills Act, 1837; and

(*b*) that there was not otherwise any such acknowledgement and therefore the will was not valid.

640. Re Wingham, [1949] P. 187

The deceased was in the Royal Air Force and in October, 1942, he was sent to Canada for training. In March, 1943, he wrote a document, which he described as his will and which was signed but not attested. He later became a pilot instructor and in August, 1943, he died as a result of an aircraft accident whilst still in Canada. The court had to determine whether the deceased was "in actual military service" when the document of March, 1943, was made. If so his will was valid, since he would be entitled to make a privileged will. *Held*—The words "actual military service" in the Wills Act, 1837, meant "active military service," and any soldier, sailor or airman was entitled to make a privileged will, if he was actually serving with the armed forces in connection with operations which were or had been taking place, or were believed to be imminent. Therefore, the document was a valid will.

641. Re Newland, [1952] P. 71

On 25th July, 1944, the deceased, who was an apprentice employed by a steamship company, made a will while on shore leave in England. Within a week he returned to his ship which sailed on 1st August, 1944. When he made the will, the deceased was an infant and the will was invalid, unless the deceased was a seaman at sea within the meaning of Sect. 11 of the Wills Act, 1837, and Sect. 1 of the Wills (Soldiers and Sailors) Act, 1918. On some unknown date the will had been altered by the striking out of a bequest. The alteration had been initialled by the deceased, but there was no evidence to show whether it had been done before or after execution of the will. This application was for a grant of probate omitting the bequest. *Held*—The deceased, being employed by a steamship company when he made the will, and being then about to sail on a voyage, was a seaman at sea at the material time and the will was valid. There was also a presumption that the alteration was made while the deceased was "at sea" and no formalities were required for its alteration. The bequest was, therefore, validly revoked.

642. Cheese v. Lovejoy, [1877] 2 P.D. 251

A testator drew a line through part of his will leaving the words legible, and wrote upon it, "This is revoked." A housemaid gave evidence that the testator had kicked the paper into a corner of the sitting room amongst some other papers, and that she had picked it up and kept it in the kitchen for about seven or eight years until the testator's death. In an action for probate of the will, next-of-kin contended that the will had been revoked. *Held*—The will could be admitted to probate. The testator had not destroyed it, and the words of revocation were not signed and attested. A mere intention to revoke was not sufficient.

643. Gill *v.* Gill, [1909] P. 157

The plaintiffs propounded, as executors, the will of John Hinchcliffe Gill. The defendants were next-of-kin wishing to dispute the will. The defendants claimed that the will had been revoked, having been torn up by the deceased or his wife, who was one of the plaintiffs, in his presence and by his direction, with intent to revoke. Evidence showed that the wife had torn the will in front of her husband alter he had made offensive remarks to her. It seemed that the testator had always treated this as a joke, and had told people what his wife had done in her temper and that he laughed at it. A few months before his death he had said that he had left everything to his wife if she survived him. *Held*—The will was not revoked and could be admitted to probate.

644. Sugden *v.* Lord St. Leonards (1876), 1 P.D. 154

The testator was a distinguished Lord Chancellor and was formerly an Equity lawyer. He had made a most complicated will in which he had a great interest, and had on many occasions asked his daughter, Miss Sugden, to read it over to him. The will could not be found after his death. The court admitted the will to probate on Miss Sugden's testimony as to its contents, being satisfied that there was sufficient evidence to rebut the otherwise natural presumption that the will had been revoked.

645. In the Estate of Bridgewater, [1965] 1 All E.R. 717

The testator made three wills on 26th May, 1954, 27th March, 1960, and on 29th March, 1960. The second and third wills differed only in the directions the testator gave to the executor, Mr. Ensor, his solicitor, as to the disposal of his body after death. The testator wrote to Mr. Ensor on 29th August, 1960 as follows: "Thank you for your note with enclosure; you will find the old will has been deposited at the Municipal Bank, the new one having been destroyed." The reference to the old will was the one of 27th March, 1960, and not the one made in 1954. The testator died on 29th November, 1962, and only the first will was found in the safe, i.e. the one made in 1954. However, Mr. Ensor had a copy of the third will and a draft of the second one in his files. Mr. Ensor, the applicant, moved for a grant of probate of the will of 29th March, 1960. *Held*—The construction of the testator's letter was that the earlier will had been deposited and the later will destroyed believing that this would set up again the revoked will of 27th March. This it could not do, since the will of March 29th contained a clause revoking all former wills. However, the doctrine of *dependent relative revocation* (or conditional revocation) applied, and since the testator's intention was to revoke the third will conditional on validating the second, which condition was not fulfilled, the will of 29th March, 1960, remained unrevoked and would be admitted to probate.

646. Sallis *v.* Jones, [1936] P. 43

A will dated 27th June, 1927, ended with the words, "I hereby declare that this will is made in contemplation of marriage." On 7th November, 1927, the testator married the defendant; he died on 17th November, 1934. *Held*—Before Sect. 177 of the Law of Property Act, 1925, could operate to prevent the testator's marriage from revoking his will, there must be express reference in the will to a particular marriage, followed by solemnisation of that marriage. Here there was merely a general declaration of contemplation of marriage, and accordingly the will was revoked by the testator's marriage.

647. In the Estate of Langston, [1953] 1 All E.R. 928

On 4th November, 1935, the testator made a will leaving everything "unto my fiancée, M.E.B." and appointing her sole executrix. On 7th January, 1936, the testator married M.E.B., and on 28th December, 1952, he died. This was an application for probate by the executrix. *Held*—The testator was expressing the fact that he was contemplating marriage with a named person M.E.B., and so the will was not revoked by the testator's subsequent marriage to her.

RECENT CASES

THE LAW OF CONTRACT

648. Barrington *v.* **Lee,** [1971] 3 All E.R. 1231

In August 1964 Mr. Lee instructed various estate agents including a Mr. Adams and F. J. Elliott (Estate Agent) Ltd. to sell his house. Mr. Adams was approached by a Mr. Bohener, who agreed to purchase the house for £2,400 subject to contract and paid a deposit of £100. At a later stage Mr. Bohener also paid £140 to the other agents F. J. Elliott. The sale fell through and Mr. Bohener asked for the return of his deposits. Mr. Adams returned the £100 but Elliotts did not return the £140. Mr. Bohener sued Elliotts and obtained a judgment but the company then went into liquidation and the judgment debt was not paid. Mr. Bohener then died and his executrix, Mrs. Barrington, sued Mr. Lee for the money. Chapman, J., at first instance *held* that Mr. Lee had no defence because of the decision of the Court of Appeal in *Burt* v. *Claude Cousins & Co. Ltd.*, 1971.[47a] Mr. Lee appealed to the Court of Appeal, where it was *held*—

(i) the court ought not to follow *Burt's* Case. The case could not be brought within the exceptions stated in *Young* v. *Bristol Aeroplane Co. Ltd.*, [1949] K.B. 718, but this was no longer necessary. Where a deposit is paid to an estate agent in the course of negotiations and before any contract there is an implied promise by the agent to repay the money if negotiations break down and he alone can be sued for it. (Re Lord Denning, M.R.);

(ii) in view of the fact that Elliotts had expressly received the £140 as stakeholders, both Elliotts and Mr. Lee were liable to return it on the basis of money had and received. But in such a case a judgment against the agent is, so long as it subsists, a bar to any proceedings against the principal. Since Mr. Bohener had obtained a judgment against Elliotts for the money, he (or his executrix Mrs. Barrington) could not successfully sue Mr. Lee. (per Edward Davis and Stephenson, L.JJ.)

649. Lewis *v.* **Averay,** [1971] 3 All E.R. 907

Mr. Lewis agreed to sell his car to a rogue who called on him after seeing an advertisement. Before the sale took place the rogue talked knowledgeably about the film world, giving the impression that he was the actor Richard Green in the "Robin Hood" serial. He signed a dud cheque for £450 in the name of "R. A. Green" and was allowed to have the log-book and drive the car away late the same night when he produced a film studio pass in the name of "Green." It was *held*—by the Court of Appeal—that Mr. Lewis had effectively contracted to sell the car to the rogue and could not recover it or damages from Mr. Averay, a student, who had bought it from the rogue for £200. The contract between Mr. Lewis and the rogue was voidable for fraud but not void for unilateral mistake.

N.B. The distinctions drawn in some of these cases are fine ones. It is difficult to distinguish *Ingram*[166] from *Phillips*[165] and *Lewis*. The question for the court to answer in these cases is whether or not the offeror at the time of making the offer regarded the identity of the offeree as a matter of vital importance.

The general rule seems to be that where the parties are face to face when the contract is made identity will not be vital and the contract voidable only. *Ingram* would appear to be the exceptional case.

650. Gosling v. Anderson, *The Times*, 6th February, 1972

Miss Gosling, a retired schoolmistress, entered into negotiations for the purchase of one of three flats in a house at Minehead owned by Mrs. Anderson. Mr. Tidbury, who was Mrs. Anderson's agent in the negotiations, represented to Miss Gosling by letter that planning permission for a garage to go with the flat had been given. Mrs. Anderson knew that this was not so. The purchase of the flat went through on the basis of a contract and a conveyance showing a parking area but not referring to planning permission which was later refused. Miss Gosling now sought damages for misrepresentation under Sect. 2 (1) of the Misrepresentation Act, 1967. *Held*—the facts revealed an innocent misrepresentation by Mr. Tidbury made without reasonable grounds for believing it to be true. Mrs. Anderson was liable for the acts of her agent and must pay damages under the Act of 1967. The Court ordered an inquiry as to damages before the local county court judge.

(Note the effect of this case and the Misrepresentation Act 1967, on *Armstrong* v. *Strain*, 1952.[380] Before the 1967 Act, where both agent and principal were innocent of actual fraud there was no cause of action in damages. Now there need not be any question of fraud. Where the statement is made negligently the agent may be made liable for his own negligence and the principal is liable also under the doctrine of vicarious liability.)

651. Kenyon, Son and Craven Ltd. v. Baxter Hoare & Co. Ltd., [1971] 2 All E.R. 708

The defendants stored nuts for the plaintiffs. The contract included an exception clause under which the defendants were not liable for loss or damage unless due to their "wilful neglect." The nuts were seriously damaged by rats. The defendants' servant had made some effort to control the rats but had not, through ignorance, used appropriate measures. The plaintiffs sued for breach of the contract of bailment. *Held*—the defendants neglect could not be said to be "wilful." They were not, therefore, guilty of a fundamental breach and could rely on the exception clause (*Suisse Case* applied).[226] The plaintiffs' claim failed.

652. Hill v. C. A. Parsons & Co. Ltd., [1971] 3 All E.R. 1318

The defendants capitulated to demands from a trade union (DATA) that certain of their employees should be required to join that union. The plaintiff, a chartered engineer aged 63 with 35 years' service, was accordingly told to join and when he refused was given one month's notice. He then started proceedings for, *inter alia*, an injunction to prevent the company from terminating his employment. The Court of Appeal (Stamp, L.J. dissenting) felt that six months, would have been a proper period of notice and granted an injunction which in effect resulted in specific performance of the contract of service for that period of time.

(*Note:* The Court was obviously influenced by the fact that by the time six months had elapsed the Industrial Relations Act 1971, would be in force and give greater rights of compensation to the plaintiff. Nevertheless, Lord Denning, M.R., treated the decision as based on the principle *ubi jus ibi remedium* (where there is a right there is a remedy) and regarded Mr. Hill's right to damages as inadequate, thus allowing the Court to grant an injunction.

THE LAW OF TORTS

653. O'Connell v. Jackson, [1971] 2 All E.R. 129

The defendant, who was driving a car, came out of a minor road on to a major road and collided with the plaintiff who was riding a moped. The plaintiff was thrown on to the road and suffered severe head injuries. Medical evidence showed that if the plaintiff had been wearing a crash helmet his injuries would have been much reduced. *Held*—the plaintiff's damages would be reduced by 15 per cent. Although it was accepted and admitted that the defendant was solely responsible for the accident, one must always take into account the possibility of others being careless, and by not wearing a crash helmet the plaintiff had contributed to the harm suffered.

654. Dutton v. Bognor Regis Urban District Council, [1972] 1 All E.R. 462

In 1958 a builder, Mr. Holroyd, bought some land for development. One of the plots was on the site of a rubbish tip which had been filled in. A building inspector employed by the council inspected the foundations of a house to be built on the plot and passed them. The house in question was completed and sold to a purchaser in 1958 who resold to the plaintiff, Mrs. Dutton, in 1960. In 1963 the house was examined by a surveyor after cracks had appeared in the walls and a staircase had slipped. The surveyor informed Mrs. Dutton that the house had been built on a rubbish tip which was not a stable foundation. Mrs. Dutton sued the local authority for damages. *Held*—by the Court of Appeal—

(i) a local authority had extensive legislative control over building operations and must exercise that control with reasonable care;

(ii) as a result of the decision in *Hedley Byrne*[194] a professional man who gave guidance to others owed a duty of care not merely to his client but also to others who might in the ordinary course of events rely on his skill;

(iii) a professional man who have advice as to the safety of buildings, machinery or materials owed a duty to all those who might suffer injury as a result of their subsequent use;

(iv) the inspector should have realised that once the foundations were covered the defect would not be discovered until damage actually emerged;

(v) thus the inspector should have had later purchasers in mind when carrying out his inspection (Lord Atkin's "neighbour" test in *Donoghue* v. *Stevenson*, 1932[354] applied);

(vi) the defendants were therefore vicariously liable for their servant's negligence.

655. British Railways Board v. Herrington, [1972] 1 All E.R. 749

In this case, the House of Lords affirmed the decision of the Court of Appeal (see case **512a**) and held the Board liable, but on the following grounds—

(i) where an occupier knows that there are trespassers on his land or knows of circumstances which make it likely that trespassers might come on to his land and also knows of physical facts in relation to the state of his land or some activity carried out on the land which would constitute a serious danger to persons on the land who were unaware of these facts, the occupier is under a duty to take reasonable steps to enable the trespasser to avoid the danger;

(ii) the duty will only arise where the likelihood of the trespasser being exposed to the danger is such that by the standards of common sense and common humanity the occupier could be said to be culpable in failing to take reasonable care to avoid the danger.

INDEX TO STATUTES

INDEX TO CASES

Note. The number of the case in the Appendix is printed in **bold type;** the page on which the case is cited is printed in ordinary type.

GENERAL INDEX

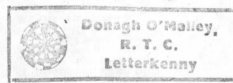